From Cape Charles to Cape Fear

Fire Ant Books

From Cape

THE NORTH ATLANTI

Robert M. Browning Jr.

THE UNIVERSITY OF ALABAMA PRESS

TUSCALOOSA AND LONDON

harles to Cape Fear

OCKADING SQUADRON DURING THE CIVIL WAR

Copyright © 1993
The University of Alabama Press
Tuscaloosa, Alabama 35487– 0380
All rights reserved
Manufactured in the United States of America

designed by Paula C. Dennis

∞

The paper on which this book is printed meets the minimum
requirements of American National Standard for Information
Science-Permanence of Paper for Printed Library Materials,
ANSI Z39.48-1984.

Library of Congress Cataloging-in-Publication Data

Browning, Robert M., 1955–
From Cape Charles to Cape Fear : the North Atlantic
Blockading
Squadron during the Civil War / Robert M. Browning, Jr.
p.   cm.
Includes bibliographical references and index.
ISBN 0-8373-5019-5 (pbk: alk. paper)
1. United States.   Navy.   Atlantic Blockading Squadron
(1861–1865)
2. United States—History—Civil War, 1861–1865—Blockades.
3. United States—History—Civil War, 1861–1865—Naval
operations.
I. Title
E600.B86   1993
973.7'5—dc20   92-38697

British Library Cataloguing-in-Publication Data available

Contents

Illustrations

Tables

Preface

At 4:30 A.M. on 12 April 1861, the report of a gun boomed across Charleston Harbor. The gunshot began a forty-hour bombardment of Fort Sumter, South Carolina, signaling the start of the Civil War. A naval expedition consisting of three steam gunboats under the command of Captain Gustavas Vasa Fox was sent by President Abraham Lincoln to relieve the fort. Arriving off the harbor, Fox found that he was powerless to support the fort's garrison. Therefore, during the next day, the crews watched the bombardment. After a formal surrender, the naval force carried off the fort's garrison, participating in this momentous event essentially as a witness.

Following the fall of Fort Sumter, the nation's attention focused on other events. Wild excitement increased as Lincoln publicly declared that an insurrection existed and called for 75,000 militia from the Northern states. On 19 April, soldiers and civilians clashed in Baltimore. The Baltimore riot caused a flurry of rumors and created concerns that Washington might be isolated from the North. Within hours of the riots, the United States Navy was formally given its first wartime task when President Lincoln proclaimed his intention to blockade seven of the Southern states. All the national excitement created by the riots and Fort Sumter's surrender caused few people to give much attention to the announcement. Consequently, the navy was launched into the conflict amidst a sea of national crises and hardly received any notice.

Civil War naval history has been treated in much the same manner. Although American historians have devoted more attention to the Civil War than almost any other subject, they have generally treated the United States Navy as a minor player. Frequently the presence of the gunboats has been ignored or omitted from the narratives. The few monographs that detail naval activity during the war fail to show the encompassing role that the naval forces played. Most of these narrate the story in the typical shot-and-shell or the great-leader approaches. Furthermore, no one has scrutinized the Union navy by studying a single squadron. This lack of scholarship is surprising since, during the war, the navy performed numerous roles and missions that were crucial to Union victory.

The North Atlantic Blockading Squadron, created in September 1861, was one of the coastal blockading squadrons. The squadron is worthy of study because it played a major role in the outcome of the war. The operational area of the squadron included the coast and inland waters of North Carolina and Virginia. In writing this book, I sought to place the squadron's role into the proper military perspective in the eastern theater. This was accomplished by analyzing the various factors that hampered or aided the squadron's performance.

Maintenance of the blockade is the most recognized task of the United States Navy during the Civil War, but the navy performed many other important duties crucial to the war effort. Numerous Union successes in the East were made possible only by the presence of the naval forces. They provided logistical protection and security as well as fire support to the Union armies.

Geography, logistics, politics, and bureaucracy all affected the overall implementation and maintenance of the blockade and other naval activities. The navy virtually had to be redeveloped along an entirely different precept. Before the war, the United States had built warships that were more capable of commerce raiding and coastal defense. In 1861, the Union needed warships capable of blockade and invasion. To fight a conflict of this type, the navy found it had to build and purchase a tremendous number of gunboats. With the increased number of vessels, and their maintenance at a distance, new logistical consider- ations had to be met. Difficulties associated with these issues had a great impact on the squadron's effectiveness and activities.

The study of a single squadron gave me the opportunity to reexamine many of the long-standing views of naval activity. I certainly have not provided all the answers. There are entire studies that should be under- taken on naval logistics, Confederate strategy, and the Union war bu- reaucracy. The other squadrons also deserve further and more detailed study by historians. Nevertheless, I hope his book will add to the understanding of just how important the navy was during the Civil War.

Every author knows that books are made possible only by the help of others. While preparing this work, I received a great deal of assistance and encouragement from teachers, colleagues, friends, institutions, and family. I would like to thank Robert E. Johnson of The University of Alabama for his encouragement and help. I also wish to express grati- tude to William N. Still, Jr., who helped with the conception of this project. I wish to thank Richard Von Doenhoff of the National Ar- chives, who guided me through the old naval records, and William Sherman, who helped me find some obscure Treasury Department records. Thanks go to the staffs of the Library of Congress Manuscript Division, the Duke University Manuscript Collection, the University of North Carolina Southern Historical Collection, Princeton University, the College of William and Mary, East Carolina University, and the New-York Historical Society. I am grateful for the help from the staff at the U.S. Naval Historical Center, Washington, D.C., particularly Chuck Haberlein and Ed Finney. I would also like to extend my grati- tude to the interlibrary loan staffs at the Prince William County Library and The University of Alabama, especially Catherine T. Jones. Special thanks to Dave Cipra, who helped with the graphics and kept my computer running. I would also like to thank Don Canney and Kevin Foster, who used a critical eye with parts of the manuscript.

Most importantly, I would like to thank my family and especially my wife, Susan. She spent endless hours typing and proofreading the manu- script and has suffered through years of sharing her time with my work.

From Cape Charles to Cape Fear

ONE

Had failure been possible

The Navy's Response to War

In April 1861, Abraham Lincoln did not fully comprehend the role that the United States Navy would play during the Civil War. Winfield Scott, the general in chief of the United States Army, likewise did not project a role other than blockade for the navy. Scott proposed to defeat the South by a combination of a naval blockade and pressure applied by the army from all points, in the fashion of a snake that kills its victim by constriction. Scott's farsighted scheme was aptly called the Anaconda Plan, and the Union eventually followed Scott's basic premise. The navy began the war with the vision of providing only the coils of an anaconda. But as the war developed, it would also offer the striking power of a venomous snake. Lincoln's call for a blockade, which created the need for a large navy, may have been his wisest wartime decision.[1]

The United States Navy was far from strong in April 1861 and was incapable of blockading the entire coast. A list of naval vessels compiled in that month contained only ninety names. Fifty were sailing vessels, of which the larger were useful mainly as receiving and training ships. Of the forty steam vessels listed, two were unfinished, three were relegated to duty as receiving ships, and three were stationed on the Great Lakes. Eight others, including five steam frigates, were in ordinary. These five steam frigates constituted the main element of American naval strength. Although formidable warships, they could not effectively perform as blockaders in the South's shallow waters because of their deep drafts. The navy had only three armed vessels ready for service on the Atlantic Coast at the outbreak of war. The remaining vessels were in the Gulf of Mexico or on foreign stations, from which some did not return for six months.[2]

Events during the first weeks of April rushed headlong before Lincoln could formulate his plans for a blockade. During this time, the nation's largest naval facility at Norfolk, Virginia, had been abandoned and destroyed. When Lincoln called for mobilization of the United States militia on 15 April, the people of Virginia reacted with indignation and began moving quickly toward secession.[3] Lincoln and the navy did not prepare for such a rapid turn of events and found themselves powerless to stop the crisis as it developed. The loss of the nation's largest navy yard left the service in a much weaker position to carry out the president's plans of a blockade.

The responsibility for the safety of Norfolk rested on the shoulders of the commandant of the yard, Captain Charles S. McCauley. McCauley, an old, inept product of the navy's seniority system, showed no real leadership during the first weeks of April and only slowly reacted to the events that threatened the yard. McCauley's defense of the facility was hampered because disloyal officers fled to join the Confederacy, leaving only himself and one other officer to supervise the defenses. He also had no line of communication with Washington, an insufficient number of men, and an active enemy opposing him. Captain McCauley, unaware of the Navy Department's intentions and particularly of Lincoln's and Winfield Scott's decision to hold Fort Monroe at the expense of Norfolk if necessary, made few provisions for abandonment or defense. As the commandant vacillated, the Virginians sank obstructions in the Elizabeth River and gathered in Norfolk to attack. Conspicuously absent from the scene was Captain Hiram Paulding, who commanded all the naval force in Virginia. Secretary of the Navy Gideon Welles had assigned Paulding responsibility for the yard and gave specific instructions to prevent Norfolk's capture.[4]

On the 20th, a day after the blockade was announced, McCauley received information that convinced him that he could not defend the yard. The Virginians had led him to believe that rebel reinforcements were arriving by rail to attack the facility and, perhaps more damaging, that they were erecting batteries across the river that would prevent the removal of the ships and supplies. Afraid the yard would be captured intact, McCauley quickly made the decision to destroy it and its contents. At 8:00 P.M. on the 20th, several hours after the first torches were applied to government property, Paulding finally arrived with reinforcements of 370 men and the screw sloop *Pawnee*. McCauley immediately made preparations for defense, but Paulding realized that the yard could not be defended and ordered everything destroyed.[5]

The destruction was done hurriedly, haphazardly, and incompletely by the Union forces, leaving in enemy hands over 3,000 pieces of ordnance, including some 300 Dahlgren guns of the most modern type, a fine dry dock, several well-equipped workshops, and an immense amount of other materials and small arms. Paulding towed the sloop of war *Cumberland* out of the yard with *Pawnee*, leaving eleven other warships behind, the most important being the steam frigate *Merrimack*. The monetary cost of this destruction to the country was $1,980,000 for the ships and close to $8,000,000 for the property in the yard. Admiral David Dixon Porter later observed about this loss that "great as was . . . the loss of our ships, it was much less than the loss of our guns."[6] The property left behind enabled the beleaguered Confederacy to arm coastal fortifications when the South had virtually no facilities for producing ordnance. It also denied the use of the facility to the United States, which would create a logistical hardship once the blockade had been implemented.

McCauley received the blame for the loss of Norfolk, yet because of its importance, responsibility must also be shared by Lincoln, Welles, Paulding, and Flag Officer Garrett J. Pendergrast, the last of whom commanded the vessels on the Atlantic Coast. Lincoln had sent most of the readily available vessels to relieve Fort Sumter and Fort Pickens. His prompt call for troops and his proclamation of a blockade led to Virginia's secession and found the United States with virtually no force to defend Norfolk. Lincoln had failed to grasp the volatile situation and did not prepare for the consequences. Welles had urged Lincoln to

reinforce the yard but had issued confusing orders to his officers concerning their responsibilities. Pendergrast and Paulding both showed
poor judgment during the crisis and failed to reinforce the navy yard.
Paulding, in fact, seemed to have never planned to save Norfolk, having
come prepared to destroy the yard by bringing with him a large quantity
of powder and spirits of turpentine. McCauley acted indecisively because he had been kept ignorant of the Navy Department's wishes and
merely reflected the great confusion in Washington during the first few
weeks of the war. Lincoln had adopted a policy of defending federal
property and staunchly tried to hold Fort Sumter and did successfully
hold Fort Pickens, but he made little attempt to hold Norfolk.[7] The loss
of Norfolk weakened a navy that was far from strong, leaving an even
smaller number of ships to patrol the vast coast of the South.

Lincoln's proclamation of his intent to blockade the South met with
some disagreement in his own cabinet. A number of heated discussions
ensued over the diametrically different plans to stop the South's trade.
The first assumed that the rebellion was an internal struggle and that the
government could simply close its Southern ports. Under United States
law, the Union could order a closure of its ports, but this was an
ineffective measure because an offender against the ordinance of closure
could only be dealt with in American territorial waters. On the other
hand, an offender of a blockade could be chased into the open sea.
Closure of the Southern ports had been continually discussed as Lincoln
pushed forward the implementation of the blockade. Lincoln's secretary
of the navy, Gideon Welles, was one of the major proponents of this
method of trade interdiction. Welles, whose long beard had earned him
the nickname "King Neptune," led the fight for closing the ports in the
cabinet meetings.

Closing the ports appeared simple, requiring only an executive order,
but there were legal loopholes. Any vessel that challenged this order by
attempting to run into a closed port would only have violated a United
States revenue law. The offender thus could only be tried in a federal
court in the state and district where the infraction occurred, which was
impossible because these were under Confederate control. Some also
feared that foreign countries might consider this an attempt at a "paper
blockade." Closing the ports, likewise, would not force European nations to acknowledge this action, because international law did not
recognize this form of trade interdiction.

Secretary of State William Henry Seward persuaded Lincoln to adopt a blockade. Seward knew that blockades were recognized by most of the nations of the world, which might help avoid international complications. By issuing a notification of a blockade, the Union implicitly gave the Confederacy belligerent status, because a blockade is usually a belligerent right and implies that there is fighting with an external enemy.[8]

Ignoring the fact that he did not have a large navy, Lincoln declared what was for many months, in effect, a paper blockade and announced his intention to stop Southern trade. Some believed that a comprehensive blockade would require as few as thirty vessels and that as few as six ships could effectively blockade the ports of both North Carolina and Virginia.[9]

The British government announced its neutrality on 13 May 1861. The British did not protest Lincoln's intentions to blockade the South, because their long-term naval interests lay in expanding and maintaining the blockade practice. Although the American blockade annoyed them, created animosities, and was at times inconvenient, Britain, as the world's foremost maritime power, knew it would establish convenient precedents for them in the future. The London *Times* summed up this feeling by stating that "the normal state of this country in time of war is that of a belligerent, and, . . . blockade is by far the most formidable weapon we possess. Surely we ought not to be overready to blunt its edge or injure its temper?" France confirmed its acceptance of the blockade three days after the British on 16 May.[10] With French support, it became clear that Europe would recognize the United States blockade if it were executed according to international law. This apparently resolved one of the Union's earliest and gravest problems.

Lincoln, having at least one method of interdicting Southern trade, left the question of closing the ports to the discretion of Congress. The Treasury Department recommended that Congress close the Southern ports and empower the president to collect customs duties on shipboard, without a formal blockade. Penalties for violation included forfeiture of both ship and cargo. Congress responded favorably to the recommendation and within a week had the bill on the president's desk, whereupon he signed it into law on 13 July. The Ports Act gave the United States two means of interdicting the South's trade, greatly satisfying Welles and alarming Europe. The Ports Act, however, did not direct the president to close the ports; it merely authorized him to do so. Lincoln realized the ineffectiveness of his newly acquired powers and used only section five. On 16 August, he issued a proclamation that forbade intercourse with the insurgent states.[11]

European reactions to this were as some feared. The English foreign secretary, Lord John Russell, commented: "It is impossible for Her Majesty's government to admit that the President or Congress of the United States can at one and the same time exercise the belligerent right of blockade, and the municipal right of closing the ports of the South." He added that the government would not dispute the United States rights of blockade but that "an assumed right to close any ports in the hands of insurgents would imply a right to stop vessels on the high seas without instituting an effective blockade."[12]

Despite the British reaction, the United States held firm on its right to close the ports. Seward, however, feared foreign intervention and, noting increasing pressure from Europe, persuaded Lincoln not to use this power. As matters developed, the president did not close a single port until 11 April 1865, long after the threat of intervention.[13]

In mid-April, Garrett J. Pendergrast, flag officer of the Home Squadron, immediately attempted to set up an efficient blockade with the few gunboats available. Most of his naval force consisted of deep-draft vessels, which were of little use for blockading on the shallow Southern coast. Despite the small number of vessels and the large number of ports to be covered, Pendergrast still believed he could blockade the principal ports, and on 30 April 1861, he stated that he had "sufficient naval force" to carry out the president's proclamation. This judgment by Pendergrast proved to be incorrect; he did not have enough force for Virginia alone. The navy did not legally blockade many ports for months, as the early method of blockade resembled sentry duty for the vessels—passing from port to port until they ran out of supplies or coal. Many vessels that might have been on the blockade at this early date were assigned other functions, were returning from foreign stations, or were receiving repairs to enable them to serve.[14]

On 1 May, Flag Officer Silas Horton Stringham took command of the squadron blockading the Atlantic Coast from Alexandria, Virginia, to Key West, Florida. Stringham had entered the navy in 1809 and had served as captain for nearly twenty years. He was a veteran of the

Mexican War and had commanded the Brooklyn, Norfolk, and Boston navy yards and the Brazil and Mediterranean squadrons during his long career.[15]

Stringham's newly formed command, the Coast Blockading Squadron encompassed nearly 1,000 miles of coastline. In less than three weeks, it became known as the Atlantic Blockading Squadron, a command consisting of fourteen gunboats and the Potomac Flotilla. Stringham believed that twelve or fifteen more vessels would be all he would require for a "strict blockade." Welles, on the other hand, believed that the coast could be blockaded by placing one large ship and two of lighter draft at the principal ports. He wrote Stringham in June that "it is possible that some of the lighter craft may in thick weather and at night run the blockade, but your great effort will be to prevent it."[16]

The lack of blockaders made it impossible for an adequate number to watch each port, and the coast of North Carolina early in the war did not receive as high a priority as other coastal areas. Merchant vessels going to Charleston were early warned of the blockade and then proceeded to Wilmington, which had rail connections to Charleston and Virginia. A substantial foreign trade continued to pass in and out of North Carolina ports. During the early months, English merchantmen loaded naval stores at Beaufort and Wilmington, cleared for Nassau and New Providence, and then sailed for New York.[17]

The British viewed the blockade of the North Carolina coast as "totally ineffective," a charge that figures show was well founded. Wilmington, later to become the Confederacy's most important port, continued to be ignored for some time, as were Beaufort, Ocracoke, and other inlets. During the period from 1 May 1861 to 25 July 1861, Wilmington's traffic alone amounted to over ninety-three vessels entering and seventy-seven clearing this port. Charleston during a similar period had only eighteen vessels that cleared. Most of the trade was carried in and out by schooners coming and going to other Southern ports. Welles became frustrated by the early difficulties with the blockade and wrote to Stringham: "Can not Wilmington or Beaufort be formally blockaded and coast guard duty performed by such force as you have?"[18]

The sounds and inlets on the coast of North Carolina became a haven for blockade runners and for privateers, who sortied out and returned before blockaders could react. The shallow water and small forts at the inlets prevented warships from chasing them into the sounds. Privateers captured scores of prizes at the Hatteras rendezvous by using the lighthouse as a lookout for merchantmen and to signal the presence of blockaders and merchant ships. Privateers dashed out to capture vessels, which they brought back to the safety of the sounds. The brisk business of the privateers prompted a committee of the New York Board of Underwriters to demand that something be done about this problem. Blockaders found it difficult to capture privateers because the dangerous coast and rough weather at Hatteras compelled them to stay far at sea. While stationed off Hatteras, the screw steamer *Stars and Stripes* used two anchors and her engine to hold position because of the rough weather.[19]

The Confederate naval force in the sounds also threatened the blockaders off the North Carolina coast. The state purchased a heterogeneous force of merchantmen and canal boats and converted them into gunboats, which became known as the "mosquito fleet." As Union vessels patrolled off the coast more frequently, the Confederate navy gradually incorporated the privateers into its service, and all of the state's vessels later joined the Confederacy.[20]

Leaders in Washington became increasingly concerned over the privateers at Hatteras and the inlet's value as a back door to Virginia. The first step in negating this was the conception of a combined army and navy force to attempt the capture of the forts that controlled the inlet. The Union navy's role concerning combined operations was not clearly defined early in the war. Secretary of War Edwin M. Stanton insisted that he could "order naval assistance" and that the navy was "secondary and subject to the control and direction of the military branch of the Government."[21] Welles, however, had other thoughts.

In an attempt to devise an overall strategy and to solve naval problems, Gideon Welles created a Commission of Conference, also called the Blockade Strategy Board. Before this board met, the Navy Department had no strategic plan and addressed every problem as it arose. The idea for the creation of this board originated with Professor Alexander Dallas Bache, the superintendent of the United States Coast Survey. Organized on 27 June 1861, the board consisted of Bache; chief engineer of the Army Department of Washington, John G. Barnard; and two naval officers, Captain Charles H. Davis, who acted as recorder and secretary, and Captain Samuel Francis Du Pont, who served as chairman.[22]

The Blockade Strategy Board met frequently at the Smithsonian Institution from July to September, preparing six major reports and four supplementary ones. Collecting hydrographic, topographic, and geographic information, its members developed strategies and devised methods to render the blockade more effective. The board accumulated the information necessary to establish logistical bases on the Atlantic Coast and recommended points in South Carolina, Georgia, and Florida to be seized as coaling stations and naval bases. The board also prepared a general guide for all blockading operations, which the Navy Department followed closely throughout the war.[23]

Strategy and organizational changes were hammered out after thorough discussion and debate among the board members. Their recommendations were discussed and modified by the president, the cabinet, and Winfield Scott.[24]

Although the board's proceedings were confidential and not intended for the public, accounts of the meetings began to appear in Northern newspapers in July, negating the effectiveness of its strategical deliberations.[25]

The board considered Charleston and Savannah the major ports to watch on the Atlantic Coast but believed that, in North Carolina, Wilmington's commercial significance and Beaufort's deep channel warranted their attention. Both ports had excellent rail connections north and south, giving them added importance to the Confederacy.[26]

The board believed the quickest method of blockade along the coast of North Carolina would be to obstruct the channels with hulks filled with stone. Its members realized that the channels would be blocked only temporarily but that during that time the United States could build and fit out more vessels. The board suggested that Oregon, New, Hatteras, Ocracoke, New River, New Topsail, Bogue, Lockwood's Folly, and Tubbs inlets be obstructed.[27]

The idea of sunken hulks had been brought up as early as April 1861, but the thought of blockade by this method brought protests from Europe. The British Foreign Office called this method of blockade a "measure of revenge, and irremediable injury against an enemy."[28] The

French press called it "an act of inhuman and barbarous revenge" and "an act of vandalism . . . only worthy of the dark ages." Seward defended this action by calling it a temporary measure to aid the blockade without permanently injuring the harbors and inlets. The secretary of state also claimed that the United States never planned to sink vessels in the main channels, wishing to obstruct only the lesser ones.[29]

Some officers declared that the obstructions would be of temporary and slight service, owing to the constant shifting of the channel entrances.[30] These objections proved to be well founded. Although the navy attempted to close several Southern ports and inlets by sinking stone-laden vessels, in no case were they effective.

In July, the board discussed the occupation of coastal positions and the capture of inland North Carolina towns on the Pasquetank, Chowan, Roanoke, Pamlico, and Neuse rivers. The members firmly believed that the sparsely occupied coast would prevent any interference with their operations and later considered the capture of Beaufort and Fort Macon, which they believed would take a short siege and only 4,000 men.[31]

The Union navy faced many obstacles in its attempt to blockade the Southern ports. One of the greatest impediments (and one that would not change during the war) was the geography of the Southern coast. Extremely shallow over its entire length, the coast contained 189 harbors, inlets, and rivers. Each of these offered refuge, and an efficient blockade would require that all be watched. Many of the Southern waterways, however, were too shallow for large vessels, which restricted their use. Moreover, only four in North Carolina and Virginia had railroad connections, which limited the value of those not connected by rail.[32]

Both North Carolina's and Virginia's shorelines had large bodies of water within their boundaries. The ocean front of Virginia included the eastern shore and beach extending south of Cape Henry forty miles to the North Carolina boundary. Along this stretch of coastline were several bays and small inlets.[33] Norfolk and Richmond were considered the best ports in Virginia; although both had good rail connections to the interior, the shallow depth of the James River restricted some of the trade into Richmond, the political and industrial capital of the Confederacy. These ports, however, were closed from the beginning of the war to outside trade by the Union navy's control of Chesapeake Bay.

North Carolina's coast, more rugged and extensive than that of Virginia, consisted of a long series of barrier islands that protruded into the ocean in three places: Cape Hatteras, Cape Lookout, and Cape Fear. The barrier islands were broken by shallow inlets that led to two large sounds, on which small vessels could travel great distances without being in the open sea. The sounds and inlets of North Carolina, however, were too shallow to be of use by large vessels. North Carolina's major port cities of Wilmington and New Bern were also commercially limited because larger vessels could not use their facilities. The two states were linked by the Dismal Swamp Canal, which allowed greater access between the state's two vast inland waterways.[34]

The naval forces blockading Virginia and North Carolina would have more shoreline to cover than any other squadron during the Civil War. On the other hand, this great expanse of coastline became a liability to the Confederacy, as the sounds of North Carolina and the Chesapeake Bay became inland seas open for invasion. The plenitude of inlets, creeks, and rivers gave the Union forces an immense advantage by threatening the flanks of Confederate land forces.[35]

The Confederacy's earliest hopes of security to these open and accessible bodies of water lay in a coastal defense system, begun after the War of 1812 under President James Monroe. These coastal forts were built to deny vessels access to the coast and to prevent amphibious landings. In actuality, there could never be enough forts on the long coastline to prevent these completely. By 1861, the seaboard forts in the United States numbered fifty-seven and were inadequately armed. The army's chief engineer, Brigadier General Joseph Totten, considered the four forts in North Carolina and Virginia in relatively good repair.[36]

In the South, Virginia was the state most open to invasion early in the war due to its proximity to the Northern states; thus Virginia's coastal fortifications were strengthened and new ones constructed in the summer of 1861. Receiving the help of the other Southern states, Virginia strengthened its defenses on the main rivers.[37] The capture of the Norfolk Navy Yard with its large cache of ordnance enabled Virginians to strengthen the works around the Chesapeake and at the mouths of the rivers. Likewise, troops from other Southern states poured into the Old Dominion to check any movement by Union forces.

North Carolina, the last state to leave the Union, began its defensive preparations late. The absence of a central ordnance pool, adequate numbers of engineers, and a strong central government also hampered these efforts. Because of a misunderstanding between the state and the Confederate government, North Carolina was unable to implement any large-scale defensive preparations. As the war developed, the Old North State pleaded for ordnance, but it never acquired a sufficient amount to arm its coastal defenses adequately.[38]

Hatteras was among the weakest of the Confederate coastal defensive positions. The Confederates, realizing the importance of the inlet, seized the area early in the war and by the fall of 1861 had built forts at Oregon, Ocracoke, and Hatteras inlets. Fort Hatteras, just over 200 yards from the inlet, was an almost square earthen fort mounting only twelve short-range smooth-bore guns; five other guns, including a ten-inch Columbiad, had not been mounted. Fort Clark, a smaller earthen fort about 500 yards east of Fort Hatteras and nearer the ocean, mounted only five thirty-two-pound smooth bores and two smaller guns. At Ocracoke Island, the earthen defense Fort Ocracoke (Fort Morgan) mounted eight guns, with a capacity to mount fifty. The last, Fort Oregon, a strong work mounting numerous guns, lay on the south side of Oregon Inlet.[39]

The defenses were hastily constructed and poorly manned. More importantly, however, they were isolated from the mainland by the same sounds they protected. Without support from the Confederate government, the state of North Carolina did not have the capacity to defend the Outer Banks. In August 1861, only six regiments defended North Carolina's 400-mile coast, in part because many of the state's troops were in Virginia and because many Confederate conscripts had to be turned away for lack of arms.[40] The feeble defense consisted of small units dispersed along the whole coast. The state should have defended the Outer Banks more completely or withdrawn and concentrated along the mainland.

Realizing this weakness, the Union leaders decided to strike a blow on the South by capturing Hatteras Inlet. This would end some of the privateering activity and perhaps give the navy a secure base along the coast. Union General John Wool, the commander of the Department of Southeastern Virginia, requested 25,000 men for coastal operations but received only 886 for an attack on the forts at Hatteras Inlet.[41] A combined army and navy expedition commanded by Flag Officer Silas

Stringham and Major General Benjamin F. Butler assembled off Hatteras on 27 August 1861, with seven warships, the screw frigates *Minnesota* and *Wabash*, the paddle frigate *Susquehanna*, the screw sloop *Pawnee*, the converted merchant steamer *Monticello*, the ex-revenue cutter *Harriet Lane*, the sloop of war *Cumberland*, and two transports and several small steamers.

Before dawn, the infantry prepared for the landing, and the sailors readied their guns. Just before 9:00 A.M., *Wabash,* towing *Cumberland*, stood toward the outer bar, with *Minnesota* following, flying Stringham's flag. At 10:00 A.M., the warships began attacking Fort Clark while moving in a circle—an innovative tactic for American warships. Meanwhile, the troops began disembarking into wooden fishing boats and metal surfboats. The steamers *Pawnee, Monticello*, and *Harriet Lane* covered the landing without interference from the fort because of the latter's short-range artillery. In the breakers, the wooden boats broke apart, while the iron surfboats sank, which left the soldiers on the beach with no provisions and no means to escape. By 11:30, Butler had managed to land only 320 troops about two miles north of Fort Clark. Outgunned by the naval vessels and with troops in a position to storm the fort, the rebels thought it best to withdraw southward to Fort Hatteras shortly after noon.[42]

Once the Confederates had struck their flag, the Union infantry advanced, covered by *Monticello* and *Harriet Lane*. As a result of some mistake on the part of the Confederates, they had failed to put up a flag on Fort Hatteras. Thinking both forts had surrendered, Stringham ordered *Monticello* and *Harriet Lane* into the channel to take possession of Fort Hatteras. *Harriet Lane* grounded on the way in, while *Monticello* steamed within range of the fort. The Confederate gunners showed that their short-range guns could hit a target in the channel—five shots struck the vessel before she could feel her way back to the sea.[43]

The weather became increasingly harsh and later prohibited the landing of more Union troops. Those on the beach remained there with only the support of several gunboats, which lay close to shore until morning. The situation looked grim for the Union troops ashore, while Confederate morale was boosted by the arrival of Commodore Samuel Barron with 230 officers and men, raising the Confederate number to approximately 650 men on the island. Barron conceived a counterattack on Fort Clark, but additional troops did not arrive, and he discarded the idea in favor of strengthening the works at Fort Hatteras.[44]

At 5:30 A.M. on 29 August, the fleet weighed anchor and prepared to engage Fort Hatteras. *Susquehanna*, *Wabash*, and *Minnesota* opened fire at 8:00, and *Cumberland* and *Harriet Lane* joined the action later. When the fire became heavy, Barron and his staff held a council to consider surrender. The fort's defenders faced an impossible situation; their artillery could not reply to the long-range naval guns, the fort was low on ammunition, the occupants had no way to escape, and reinforcements were not likely to come. A shell dropped down the ventilator shaft of the fort's magazine while Barron and his staff were in council, which hastened their decision for surrender, and shortly after 11:00 a white flag rose over the fort.[45]

The victory came at a good time for the North. Northern morale had been shattered by the defeat at Bull Run in July, and now the Union had its first victory. Furthermore, this victory cost no Union lives and had secured between 600 and 700 prisoners.[46]

Strategically, the battle was significant because it gave the Union forces a potential base on the rugged coastline and deprived the privateers of a rendezvous. The victory probably also changed a few thoughts on the invulnerability of coastal defenses and the assumption that shore batteries were superior to gunboats.[47] Even though these two fortifications were extremely small and weakly armed, later actions would show that much stronger forts could not stand against a naval attack assisted by a coordinated amphibious assault.

When the forts at Hatteras fell, one North Carolinian expressed his and other Tar Heel sentiments when he wrote, "The vandals are on our coast—our soil is invaded."[48] Union leaders, however, misjudged the Confederates' strength and did not prepare to follow up this success, which they could have done with relative ease. Light-draft Union vessels might have advanced into the sounds, since only two gunboats each armed with a single gun were there to prevent it. Two considerations influenced Stringham's and Butler's decision. The draft of the vessels would not allow them to go over the bar, and Butler could not garrison additional captured positions. A critic of the expedition, Lieutenant John Sanford Barnes on board *Wabash*, stated: "the enemy never had more faithful allies than they had in the brutal folly, supreme ignorance and want of ordinary military and naval perception of Como.

Stringham and Gen. Butler, whom I am ashamed to call our leaders! Had failure been possible, we should have encountered it."[49]

Immediately after the capture of the inlet, Commander Stephen C. Rowan suggested that Hatteras be held as a base for later operations. The Blockade Strategy Board concurred and suggested that Ocracoke Inlet also be captured and held. The board still intended to sink obstructions in Oregon and Loggerhead inlets. Upon reaching Fort Ocracoke, the Union forces found the fort abandoned and its contents destroyed, thus giving the Union navy undisputable control of both inlets.[50]

After the Hatteras expedition, both Stringham and Butler quickly returned north. Butler, a political appointee, looked to further his military career and took all the captured Confederate colors "he could lay his hands on."[51] Many saw this as an attempt by both Butler and Stringham to grab the greatest laurels, and Lieutenant John Bankhead wrote Assistant Secretary of the Navy Gustavus Fox that other officers joked about the situation: "That after the fight they had a foot race North to see who should get there first and get the most credit. Butler beat Stringham— Had they both remained, we might have had the whole coast in our possession."[52]

After Commodore Stringham returned north, he came under immediate attack. Rather than congratulating him on his victory, both the press and the Navy Department criticized his actions. The department questioned his maintenance of the blockade, while the press wondered why he did not follow up his victory. Butler on the other hand received almost no censure and obtained most of the credit, when in fact it was a naval victory with the army playing only a secondary role.[53]

Disgusted with the department's criticism of his conduct of the blockade and the public's castigation of the Hatteras expedition, and sensing that he had fallen from the department's favor, Stringham offered his resignation on 16 September 1861. It came at an opportune time, for the department, acting under the advice of the Blockade Strategy Board, had considered a division of the Atlantic Blockading Squadron. The board realized that the extent of the coast, the augmented forces, and the complicated nature of the geography of the Southern coast would require more than one man's supervision. A reduction in Stringham's command likely would have injured his dignity and compelled him to resign.[54]

During the early months of the war, the navy had certainly failed to do the main job that the department had tasked it with—to set up an efficient blockade. The blockade, though, was recognized by European nations, which drove all legal commerce away from the Southern ports. The inefficiency of the blockade in this case was less crucial than its legal establishment and foreign recognition. On the other hand, the navy's participation at Hatteras was necessary for victory. Even though the attack was uncoordinated and weak, this early cooperative effort between the Union armed forces was a sample of the part the navy would play in the eastern theater.

The navy had not met the expectations of some, and failure seemed to follow the department. But compared with the army, the navy had made a good showing and would be an important factor in the war.

TWO

Glory again to our arms

The Capture of Eastern North Carolina

Near mid-morning 23 September 1861, several officers climbed into a boat lying beside the frigate *Congress*. The last man on board was Captain Louis Malesherbes Goldsborough, a rather large man with a temper to match. The captain's gig made its way across Hampton Roads toward the frigate *Minnesota*. As the boatswain piped Goldsborough on board, the ship's crew, in full uniform, stood at attention on the port side of the frigate. The officers and men uncovered their heads, while the guard presented arms and the drums played a ruffle. After a brief ceremony, the gunners on *Minnesota* fired a thirteen-gun salute. This signaled not only the change of command in the Atlantic Blockading Squadron but also the birth of the North Atlantic Blockading Squadron.[1]

Born in Washington, D.C., on 18 February 1805, Goldsborough had been warranted a midshipman at the extremely early age of seven and entered service four years later. Before the war, he had a distinguished career; he commanded the ship of the line *Ohio* during the Mexican War, served as superintendent of the Naval Academy for four years, and commanded the Brazil Squadron, a naval career of nearly fifty years.[2]

Goldsborough took command of the naval forces

on the Atlantic Coast at a time of great change. Since July, the Blockade Strategy Board had urged that the Gulf and Atlantic Coast blockading squadrons be divided. Since April, the navy had grown immensely, and the inherent responsibilities spawned the creation of four squadrons from two. After Stringham's resignation, a division of forces was not as sensitive an issue, and Welles appointed two younger and more energetic men to command the newly divided Atlantic Coast squadron. Louis Goldsborough would assume command of the North Atlantic Blockading Squadron, and Samuel Francis Du Pont would command the South Atlantic Blockading Squadron. The dividing line between these two squadrons was the boundary between North and South Carolina. However, Goldsborough directed all naval forces on the Atlantic Coast for five weeks, since the two squadrons did not officially form until Du Pont left Hampton Roads for South Carolina on 29 October. This early responsibility led Goldsborough to remark to his wife: "I am excessively busy. I have a heavy load on my shoulders, my command now consists of some thirty odd vessels."[3]

Goldsborough was considered a conscientious, veracious, and capable officer by some of his peers. Others, particularly those who served under him, did not generally respect him. For example, Paymaster William Keeler stationed on board *Monitor* felt that "the Commodore is not the man for the position he occupies—real merit never placed him there. He is coarse, rough, vulgar & profane in his speech, fawning & obsequious to his superiors—supercilious, tyrannical, & brutal to his inferiors." Keeler added: "He hasn't the first qualification of an officer or a gentleman & I don't know of any officer under him who respects him in the least. He is monstrous in size, a huge mass of inert animal matter & is known throughout his whole fleet by the very significant appellation of 'Old Guts.'"[4]

Two days after taking command, Secretary of the Navy Welles ordered Goldsborough to obstruct some of the major inlets along the North Carolina coast. Welles felt that by closing the inlets Confederate privateers and rebel gunboats would be less of a threat to Union shipping. He ordered Oregon, Loggerhead, and Ocracoke inlets be blocked with sunken hulks but Hatteras be left open. Goldsborough in turn instructed Commander Henry S. Stellwagen to close the inlets, but the small force of rebel gunboats within the sounds, bad weather, and a lack of pilots with knowledge of the inlets made it difficult for him to do his assigned task.[5]

Stellwagen failed to sink a single hulk, and Lieutenant Commander Reed Werden replaced him. Werden and the other officers on the blockade believed these inlets were impossible to obstruct because of their unstable nature. They felt that the shifting sands would form new channels around the hulks, but they nevertheless attempted to complete their assignment. Werden faired no better, being plagued by the same problems that Stellwagen had encountered. A combination of rotten and leaking hulks, harassing Confederate gunboats, and rough weather made the job impossible to carry through.[6]

The Confederates, with their light-draft vessels armed with rifled guns, continued to use the open inlets to threaten Union shipping. Their gunboats had the capability of passing out of the shallow inlets and capturing prizes before the Union warships could react. This threat became real on 1 October, when the Confederates captured the Union steamer *Fanny* bound to Loggerhead Inlet with quartermaster stores for the army.[7]

This event embarrassed the navy and reinforced the need to obstruct the inlets. But by the first week of November, not a single hulk had been sunk. Goldsborough, who became weary of the excuses of his subordinates, told Werden that "what the Department wishes is to have its orders executed, if possible, and nothing more." By 14 November, Werden had obstructed Ocracoke Inlet with three hulks.[8]

The Navy Department meant these measures to close the inlets to be a temporary solution to the threat of privateers. The Blockade Strategy Board had already formulated elaborate plans to capture bases on the coast for logistical and strategical purposes. The board visualized the creation of a force to land and to establish lodgments on the entire Southern coast. In October, Brigadier General Ambrose E. Burnside began promoting the idea of a Coast Division to attack coastal areas. He believed that a special division created from Northern seacoast towns could be easily trained and would be accustomed to disembarking from ships.

Burnside was able to convince the War Department that his plan was sound. Burnside received command of an amphibious division consisting of three brigades whose sole purpose was to threaten the coastline, to land, to penetrate, and to hold positions along the seaboard.[9]

The Coast Division initially prepared to operate in the Chesapeake Bay area, but instead North Carolina became the choice for an attack. The assumption that a substantial number of North Carolinians remained loyal to the United States may have precipitated the abandonment of a Chesapeake operation. If so, a move by the federal forces into this area might bring the state back into the Union with little or no fighting. This assumption, based partly on the fact that North Carolina had been the last state to secede, could not have been more incorrect. Some officers reported a lack of loyalty and related that many loyal men had fled. But Unionist and some Northern papers exaggerated loyal sentiment in eastern North Carolina. Army and navy officers both wrongly claimed that thousands of loyal men would flock to the Union standard and that they would meet little resistance from the rest. The capture of Hatteras had already greatly alarmed the people of North Carolina. The Wilmington *Daily Journal* reflected this fear by lamenting that the state would now have to guard its shores "against the roost-robbing, house-burning and negro thieving forays" of the Union navy.[10]

The Union leaders, from the beginning of the war, misjudged the attitudes of the inhabitants and destroyed the few ties that they may have made early in the war. The vandalism perpetrated by federal soldiers on the Outer Banks did little to convince other inhabitants of the state that the Union troops meant them no harm. Lieutenant Francis U. Farquher complained, "All the inhabitants that I conversed with unite in complaining of vandalism of our troops, some houses being completely rifled. Such conduct on the part of our soldiers is but little calculated to conciliate those who may be most useful to us." Commander Steven C. Rowan suggested that the Union forces should attempt to cultivate Union sentiment in eastern North Carolina.[11]

During the first months of the war, the rugged coast of North Carolina and its shallow inlets had offered protection as a barrier against the Union navy. However, the capture of the Hatteras forts now provided a firm and secure position from which the Union could advance into the state's interior. Within the Outer Banks lay two large sounds, Pamlico and Albemarle, and four smaller ones, Croatan, Currituck, Core, and

Bogue. These large bodies of water became a liability to the Confederacy, because it had no navy to stop the federal forces from entering the sounds. Some of the state's major cities lay directly on the sounds or were connected to them by navigable rivers.

The first priority for the expedition was Roanoke Island, which lay between Albemarle and Pamlico sounds. The capture would give the Union forces a base from which to operate inside the sounds and then a staging area from which to recapture Norfolk. The capture of Roanoke Island would further allow the armed forces to strike virtually anywhere along the inland waters of the state, and the navy could use the sounds as a convenient anchorage for vessels of shallow draft.

As the Union forces prepared for an expedition to Roanoke Island, Union leaders also projected the eventual capture of other strategic points, including New Bern, Beaufort, Fort Macon, and the Albemarle and Chesapeake canal. In mid-January 1862, a force of about 100 vessels rendezvoused in Hampton Roads and on 12 January sailed for Hatteras Inlet with "colors flying and bands playing."[12]

The Burnside Expedition, as it was called, was mismanaged from the start because the army and navy retained control of their own ships. Goldsborough called this heterogeneous force his "paste-board fleet." The problems began to multiply as the gunboats and transports arrived at Hatteras Inlet. Cape Hatteras was, and still is, one of the most dangerous points on the coast. The inlet had only six feet of water in places, and many of the army's vessels drew eighteen feet. Furthermore, the local pilots refused to guide them in. To get the vessels over the bars, some had to be lightened, some were tugged, some were towed stern foremost while their propellers gouged out channels, and others were kedged over the bar. No one anticipated the delays, and before many of the army transports could be brought in, they ran out of water, making the already seasick troops more miserable. It was fortunate that the gunboats were able to supply the troops water with their condensers.[13]

The situation worsened when a gale swept the area and endangered the whole expedition. Anchor cables snapped, and collisions threatened the transports. During the gale the captains kept their vessels "running backwards + forwards all night to avoid collission [sic] with the loose vessels."[14] The storm so scattered, wrecked, or drove many of the expedition ashore that they did not reassemble for about two weeks. The

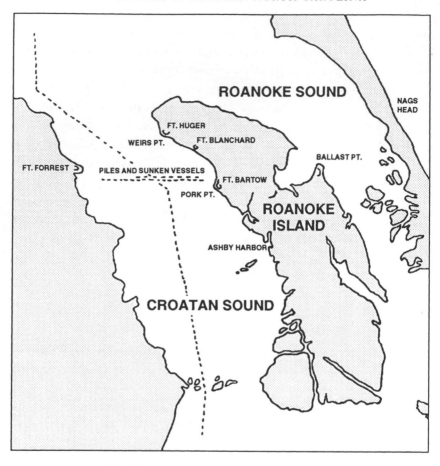

DEFENSES OF ROANOKE ISLAND

army lost three major vessels in the storm, *City of New York* with supplies and ordnance, *Pocahontas* with more than 100 horses, and the army gunboat *Zouave*.[15]

Goldsborough had worried constantly about getting the fleet through the shallow channel and wrote to Welles on 29 January, "My patience is well-nigh exhausted." Many of the army commanders kept their men busy while waiting for the fleet to reassemble. To prepare them for the future operations, they exercised the men at small-boat drills. By 31 January, nineteen naval vessels lay in the sounds, and all the army vessels necessary for the attack had come over the bar. Goldsborough wrote to Fox that he had been "hanging by the eyelids" due to the difficulties of getting the army into the sounds. He suggested that "in case of another joint expedition, everything concerning all the vessels should be arranged exclusively by the Navy, & kept under Naval control. *Duality*, I assure you, will not answer."[16]

The rebels had watched as the Union ships steamed over the bar and began sending calls for reinforcements. The pleas of the state's leaders seemed to fall on deaf ears. For months, local authorities had tried to mobilize troops for the defenses of the state. Shortly after the capture of Hatteras, the governor of North Carolina, Henry T. Clark, wrote to Secretary of War Judah P. Benjamin and complained about the lack of troops to defend the state. He reminded Benjamin that North Carolina had sent Virginia some 13,500 stand of arms and now had none. He also pleaded with Benjamin to send some of the state's armed regiments back because "we have disarmed ourselves to arm you."[17]

Major General Robert E. Lee, who supervised the defenses on the Southern coast, indicated the Confederate government's view of the crisis. When asked for reinforcements by Brigadier General Joseph R. Anderson, commander of the District of Cape Fear, he declined. He told Anderson, "I should be pleased to be able to send you my whole force if required, but I beg that you will not rely upon it, but endeavor to organize a sufficient force for your purpose independent of any re-inforcement from this department." The largest body of troops within distance to support the sounds of North Carolina were at Norfolk under the command of Major General Benjamin Huger, whose department included Roanoke Island. As the Union ships crossed into the sound, Confederate president Jefferson Davis asked and later ordered Huger to send all the force he could spare.[18]

In addition to a lack of troops, the state was in other ways wholly unprepared to resist the Union expedition. Indeed, the federal army could have landed virtually unopposed in any port on the state's inland waters. Brigadier General Daniel Harvey Hill, while in charge of the state's defenses, pleaded for more long-range guns, ammunition, carriages, and powder. Hyde County, one of the state's richest counties, had ten places the Union forces could land but only one English nine-pounder "of great age and venerable appearance." When the federal ships arrived off the coast, Brigadier General Henry A. Wise, in command of Roanoke Island, had only two undermanned North Carolina regiments and part of a third—a total of 1,435 men with which to oppose 13,000. Only seventeen companies, 800 men, were stationed at Nags Head in reserve.[19]

The Confederate high command could only hope that the small number of defenders might turn back a Union attack. The troops, though, were poorly equipped. Hill later complained that the Confederates fought at Roanoke Island with "antiquated smooth-bore cannon, mounted on the front wheels of ordinary farm wagons, drawn by mules with plow harness on." Hill further lamented that one regiment went into battle armed with "squirrel rifles and fowling-pieces; and carving knives in place of bayonets."[20]

Roanoke Island was defended by five forts. A lack of implements had retarded the building of adequate defenses, and a scarcity of ordnance had prevented the state from arming them properly. Fort Huger on Weir's Point mounted twelve guns; Fort Blanchard, 1,200 yards south of Fort Huger, mounted four guns; and Fort Bartow, two and one-half miles farther south on Pork Point, mounted nine guns. A masked battery of three guns in the center of the island guarded these three forts from an assault from the rear. A two-gun battery on the eastern side of the island also guarded the water approaches. A seven-gun battery named Fort Forrest lay on the mainland across the sound from Pork Point, which provided a cross fire on the channel running through Croatan Sound. In addition to these forts, the Confederates had driven a double row of piles across the sound to compel the Union vessels to attack the forts from a distance. The piles, placed ten feet apart, allowed some of the smaller Confederate vessels to pass through them. Sunken hulks, added to the pilings as the Union expedition came over the bar, bolstered the defenses.[21]

While the Confederates attempted to mobilize troops and improve their defenses, the expeditionary force successfully gathered in the sounds. On 5 February, the Union forces formed into three divisions and began their movement toward Roanoke Island. Heavy fog and "furious gusts of wind and rain" on the 6th postponed the attack until the following day.[22] The thick fog cleared on the morning of the 7th, and the gunboats prepared for action. As the gunboats got under way, Goldsborough shifted his flag from the steamer *Philadelphia* to the ferryboat *Southfield*. Goldsborough tried to infuse spirit in his men by

hoisting the signal on board his new flagship: "Our country expects
every man to do his duty."[23] At about 11:00, the combined fleet, led by
the steamers *Ceres*, *Putnam*, and *Underwriter*, approached the island in
two divisions, the rear division towing the troop transports. The attacking division subdivided again—one portion to engage the Confederate
gunboats and the other to fire on the forts. Only seven enemy vessels
mounting a total of eight guns opposed Goldsborough's fleet, comprising nineteen gunboats that mounted fifty-seven guns.[24]

At 11:25, the engagement began when the side-wheel steamer *Underwriter* fired inland at Ashby Harbor. After determining that the enemy
had not placed a battery at the intended landing site of the army, the
landing forces were readied. By 12:00, the remaining Union gunboats
had begun firing on Fort Bartow and the enemy vessels. The Confederate forts that lay north of the obstructions did not participate in the fight,
because the federal fleet remained beyond the reach of their guns and
Fort Bartow could only bring four of its nine guns to bear on the
gunboats. These four guns fired so accurately that the gunboats within
range withdrew southward, which masked one of the four guns that
could be brought to bear on the fleet.[25]

During the battle, the Confederate vessels did their best to reply to
the fire of the Union warships. The Union warships, being better armed
and with guns of greater range, held the advantage. The Confederate
warships were thus compelled to move closer to the Union squadron for
their shots to be effective. The Confederate vessels' only hope of success
lay in luring the enemy's gunboats beyond the obstructions, so that the
upper forts could take part in the fray.

During the day, the Union gunboats were struck several times by
Confederate batteries, but none were seriously damaged. Lieutenant
Charles Flusser, commanding *Commodore Perry*, boldly steamed within
800 yards of the rebel batteries. The ex-ferryboat grounded, and before
Flusser could get her off, she received seven hits, none of which did any
real harm. Potentially, the most critical situation developed on board
Valley City. A Confederate shell passed through the magazine and
exploded in a locker, beyond which contained the pyrotechnics of the
ship. John Davis, a gunner, acting quickly and bravely, sat on an open
barrel of powder and remained there "as the only means to keep the fire
out" and thus likely saving the ship.[26]

The rebel steamers did not fare well during the day's fight. The superior firepower of the Union gunboats drove them north of the piles, eliminating the threat they posed to the transports. *Curlew* received a shot at her waterline, which forced her crew to run her ashore, and *Forrest* became disabled and retired to Elizabeth City. The remaining Confederate gunboats withdrew in the afternoon when they exhausted their supplies of ammunition.[27]

At 4:30 P.M., while the navy engaged the island's fortifications, the army transports, with the aid of the navy and Butler's armed steamers and floating batteries, landed 10,000 men just north of Ashby Harbor. Midshipman Benjamin H. Porter also brought ashore six howitzers with naval gun crews to help with the Union advance.[28] The army did not move far inland and bivouacked by midnight.

The Union gunboats ceased their fire at 6:00 P.M. on the 8th. Six hours of bombardment had failed to put Fort Bartow out of action. The naval bombardment had substantially damaged the fort, but during the night, the Confederates repaired the damage.[29] The next day, shortly after 7:00 P.M., the Union infantrymen began to move inland. Porter brought up his six guns on the "double quick," and they reached the middle of the island, where they came upon the rebel battery, which guarded a road and the rear of the forts to the north. While the infantry moved into position to assail the works, Porter employed his six howitzers to drive the enemy from their guns. For three and a half hours, the naval gunners fired on the enemy, while advancing the guns after each firing. They did this with "great coolness and determination," which enabled the army to storm and capture the enemy battery.[30]

While the Union troops advanced to the northern end of the island, nine Union vessels began removing the obstructions. The Confederate vessels had not been able to harass the Union gunboats and thus were not a factor in the fight on the second day. Just minutes after the first Union vessel steamed through the pilings, the Confederate steamer *Curlew* was set on fire and destroyed, and an American flag rose over Fort Bartow, signaling a Union victory.[31]

The Union had won a great victory and at a small cost. The navy suffered casualties of six killed, seventeen wounded, and two missing. The army suffered just over 250 casualties. The Union forces captured five forts, defended by about 2,000 of the enemy—reinforcements amounting to 500 having arrived in time for the surrender.[32]

Gustavus Vasa Fox, the newly appointed assistant secretary of the navy, wrote to Goldsborough: "Glory again to our arms through your skill and judgment." The capture of Roanoke Island provided the Union forces many strategic options and advantages, while making the Confederate positions more vulnerable to future attacks. The Union army could now threaten Norfolk from the rear. The navy could provide the army with the mobility to strike virtually anywhere in the eastern portion of the state and could strengthen all of the future Union positions by water in a few hours. The threat of a mobile force would keep a large number of Confederate soldiers committed to the sounds to defend against any movement by Union forces. The Union leaders immediately had thoughts of exploiting the victory. Fox considered North Carolina "a fine base to push any number of troops into the interior, so that with North Carolina and Tennessee in our possession, or nearly so, we divide them."[33]

The Confederates realized the importance of this loss. A lack of men and weapons, inadequate planning, and a poorly organized and divided command structure helped provide an easy Union victory.[34] Brigadier General Wise stated that "such is the importance and value, in a military view, of Roanoke Island, that it ought to have been defended by all the means in the power of the Government. It was the key to all the rear defenses of Norfolk." It gave the Union forces access to two sounds, eight rivers, four canals, two railroads, and four-fifths of Norfolk's corn, pork, and forage supplies. Wise added that it "lodges the enemy in a safe harbor from the storms of Hatteras, gives them a rendezvous, and large, rich range of supplies, and the command of the seaboard from Oregon Inlet to Cape Henry. It should have been defended at the expense of 20,000 men and of many millions of dollars."[35]

After the debacle at Roanoke Island, Confederate Flag Officer William F. Lynch moved what remained of his naval force twelve miles up the Pasquotank River to Elizabeth City. Elizabeth City was strategically important because of its connections with Portsmouth and Norfolk via the Dismal Swamp Canal. If the Union forces captured the town, they would control the remaining water routes connecting the two states.

Lynch realized that his small, poorly armed gunboats were no match for the Union squadron and could have escaped up the canal with most of his force. Instead, he chose to stay because he believed that abandoning Elizabeth City "would have been unseemly and discouraging . . . as I had urged the inhabitants to defend it to the last extremity."[36]

On 9 February, Goldsborough learned that the Confederate gunboats had withdrawn to Elizabeth City and ordered Commander Stephen Clegg Rowan in pursuit. Fourteen vessels carrying thirty-seven guns under Rowan's command steamed up the sound with intentions of also destroying the canal above the city if possible. That day, Rowan saw the smoke of two steamers and chased the rebel gunboats *Sea Bird* and *Appomattox* into the Pasquotank River. Approaching darkness prevented further pursuit, and the Union fleet anchored ten miles below Elizabeth City. That night, Rowan called the commissioned officers on board *Delaware*, where he informed them that the ships suffered a shortage of ammunition. He told them that the vessels had an average of about twenty rounds for each gun and that any move against the enemy would be a "reconnaissance in force, to be converted into an attack [if Rowan] . . . deemed it prudent." He instructed his officers not to fire a single shot until he gave the order and then they should fight "hand to hand" to "economize ammunition."[37]

Flag Officer Lynch faced overwhelming odds but did what he could to defend the town. The defenses of Elizabeth City were poor at best. Only one battery, mounting four thirty-two pounders situated on Cobb's Point above the town, guarded the river approaches. William Harwar Parker, the captain of the CSS *Beaufort*, described the battery as a "wretchedly constructed affair" that "resembled an African ant-hill." Lynch expected the Union gunboats to reduce the work before they moved upriver. Therefore, on the morning of the attack, he placed ammunition and men from his fleet ashore. The flag officer also came ashore to direct personally the fire from the battery at Cobb's Point. The Confederate gunboats *Appomattox*, *Beaufort*, *Ellis*, *Fanny*, and *Sea Bird* remained upstream lined across the river, near the town. The armed schooner *Black Warrior* lay moored on the opposite side of the river near the fort. One of Lynch's final instructions to his officers was to escape with their vessels or to destroy them.[38]

At dawn on the 10th, the Union vessels steamed up the river in three columns. Rowan realized he could not waste ammunition on the Cobb's Point fort. His main goal was the destruction of the enemy fleet. When Rowan's flotilla advanced to within three-quarters of a mile of the shore battery, he hoisted the signal "Dash at the enemy."[39]

For Lynch, the Union vessels did the unexpected. They ran past the battery on Cobb's Point and then bore down on his fleet. Lynch's preparations to engage the Union vessels from shore were for nothing, and the Confederate gunboats were no match for the superior firepower of the Union warships.

The battle was fierce but brief. As the Union gunboats advanced up the river, the rebel gunboats got under way and a melee ensued. The rebel gunboat *Fanny* stood toward the approaching Union gunboats. As she passed *Commodore Perry*, her crew attempted to board the Union gunboat, but small-arms fire drove them back. The vessels on both sides rapidly fired their big guns, but the Union gunboats held the advantage. The crew of *Black Warrior* abandoned her and set her afire. Meanwhile *Delaware*'s crew managed to board and capture *Fanny*. At about the same time, the Union side-wheel steam tug *Ceres* captured the abandoned Confederate steamer *Ellis*. For the Confederates, the battle was lost as quickly as it had begun. The remaining three Confederate steamers tried to escape to the Dismal Swamp Canal. Lieutenant Charles Flusser, commanding *Commodore Perry*, observed the withdrawing side-wheel steamer *Sea Bird* and ordered the pilot to run her down. At a distance of 200 yards, Flusser's vessel put a shot through *Sea Bird* amidships. Flusser prepared his men to board the Confederate gunboat, but *Sea Bird* struck her colors at a distance of fifty yards. Flusser immediately ordered the helm to be put over, but his "men were so crazy with excitement and made so much noise that the helmsman could not hear." Thus *Commodore Perry* bore down on *Sea Bird* and, instead of capturing her, smashed her port bow and sank her.[40]

The steamers *Beaufort* and *Appomattox* successfully managed to escape the battle. *Appomattox* withdrew, firing a howitzer from her stern while in retreat. *Appomattox*, however, was too wide by just two inches to get through the canal and had to be destroyed, and only the screw steamer *Beaufort* escaped. The destruction of the Confederate fleet, however, had cost Lynch only four killed and six wounded.[41] This engagement ended the threat of the "mosquito fleet" and left the Union navy in complete control of the interior waters in the sounds of North Carolina. Union control of the sounds strategically altered the war in eastern North Carolina. The Union forces now had the capability to land anywhere that shallow-draft vessels could operate.

The naval vessels made use of their freedom of movement and actively began probing Confederate defenses after the Elizabeth City battle. The shortage of ammunition, however, limited the squadron's offensive movements. Nevertheless, on the 12th, four Union gunboats visited Edenton and destroyed eight cannons and a vessel on the stocks and captured two schooners. On the 14th, three federal vessels visited the Albemarle and Chesapeake canal at the North River. They towed the two schooners that they captured at Edenton and planned to obstruct the canal to keep the rebels from using it for naval sorties from Norfolk. When the gunboats reached the canal, they found it obstructed but made the obstructions more complete by sinking the two schooners and a dredging machine the Confederates had left behind.[42]

Now that the federal forces controlled Albemarle Sound, Union leaders entertained thoughts on securing bases from which to push farther inland. Rowan had heard that a strong Unionist sentiment existed in Winton, located about thirty miles from the mouth of the Chowan River. To ascertain the truth of this news, he sent eight gunboats carrying the 9th Regiment New York volunteers and elements of the 4th Rhode Island Infantry. If the force met no resistance, the expedition might have attempted to destroy the bridges of the Seaboard and Roanoke Railroad, about twenty miles above Winton.

On the morning of the 19th, the gunboats entered the mouth of the river and proceeded slowly upstream. Winton, a fishing village, lay on a high bluff screened with oak trees. The ships had became separated while coming up the river, and *Delaware*, all alone, prepared to anchor as she came within sight of the town. At a landing at the foot of the bluff a Negro woman stood waving, as if to beckon the gunboats there. In *Delaware*'s crosstrees, Colonel Rush Hawkins, the commander of the army portion of the expedition, acted as a lookout. Just as *Delaware* moved to the wharf and prepared to anchor, Hawkins spied troops and artillery high on the bank of the river. The colonel shouted, "Ring on, sheer off, rebels on shore." Hawkins repeated himself several times before the pilot understood him and finally changed *Delaware*'s course, missing the wharf by ten feet. Instantaneously a terrific fire of musketry and artillery opened up from the high banks, which riddled the wheel-house and upper joiner work of the steamer and knocked Hawkins out of the rigging. Not able to elevate her guns sufficiently to return the fire, *Delaware* steamed up the river past the village. *Commodore Perry*, the gunboat next in line, steamed quickly up the river. Lieutenant Com-mander Flusser immediately brought *Commodore Perry* into a position to throw shrapnel into the town. The combined firepower of *Commo-dore Perry* and *Delaware* drove the Confederate gunners from their positions, and *Delaware* ran back downstream out of danger.[43]

The following day, the gunboats returned and found no Confeder-ates to deny them access to the town. The gunboats landed three boat howitzers and the 9th New York and the 4th Rhode Island regiments below Winton. Flusser placed the guns in a position to command all the approaches to the town. Finding only evidence of the Confederate troops' presence but no guns or soldiers, Hawkins ordered the town burned. He gave two reasons for his actions: he believed that the ambush the day before gave him an ample reason to burn the town and that the buildings there had been used by the Confederates for storage and quarters. The Union soldiers torched and ransacked Winton and "came flocking back to the boats loaded down with household goods, books, articles of food, and anything they found that suited their fancy."[44]

The Union soldiers thoroughly destroyed the town, leaving nothing but a "collection of houseless chimneys." Hawkins immodestly stated that the destruction of Winton was "the first instance during the war on our side where fire has accompanied the sword."[45] The burning of Winton, however, did not help the Union cause. Only two days before the incident, Goldsborough and Burnside had issued a proclamation to the residents of North Carolina stating, "We shall inflict no injury unless forced to."[46] Feelings of loyalty to the Union in this area disap-peared, and it consolidated and strengthened anti-Union feelings in the state.

At the beginning of March, the Union forces prepared to attack New Bern, while the Confederate forces had reinforced the city and strength-ened the defenses. On 8 March, Gustavus Fox recalled Goldsborough to Hampton Roads because the ironclad *Virginia* had attacked the Union fleet and threatened the entire naval force there. With Goldsborough absent, command of the naval arm of the expedition passed to Commander Stephen Rowan.[47]

On 11 March, transports carrying approximately 11,000 men rendezvoused with fourteen navy gunboats at Hatteras Inlet. Leaving the next day, the fleet steamed up the Neuse River and just after 6:00 P.M., with a storm approaching, anchored at the mouth of Slocum's Creek.[48]

The Confederate defenses at New Bern were extensive. General Richard C. Gatlin, commander of the Department of North Carolina, stripped troops from other points in the state to defend the city. Guarding the land approaches to the town were 4,000 troops under the command of General Lawrence O'Bryan Branch. Branch had also suffered the same shortages as the officers preparing defenses for Roanoke Island: implements, ordnance, and labor. Seven defensive works guarded the town; the most heavily armed, Fort Thompson, mounted thirteen guns. The gunboats and the transports had to pass obstructions in the river, which consisted of iron-capped pilings and sunken vessels arranged to present a formidable barrier. While ascending the Neuse River, the navy would also find thirty torpedoes, each containing 200 pounds of powder.[49]

On the morning of 13 March, the gunboats prepared for action. Rowan changed flagships and hoisted his pennant on *Delaware* in a heavy fog and steady rain. Rowan placed the screw steamers *Stars and Stripes* and *Louisiana* on the west side of the river and *Valley City* and *Hetzel* on the east side. The gunboats began the attack by shelling the woods on the west bank of the Neuse River to drive the rebels from the intended landing site of the army.

At 8:00, with no enemy in sight, three brigades disembarked and were covered by the navy. They landed in what one man described as a "mud hole," and the troops advanced while the gunboats shelled the woods before them, in one of the first uses of a creeping barrage. To coordinate the gunfire between ship and shore, the army utilized rockets to guide the naval gunners' aim and range. Three gunboats moved ahead of the infantry to unmask a Confederate battery and, once finished, allowed the army to proceed. The shells from the gunboats fell near the Union troops, "splintering and cutting off trees, and ploughing great furrows in the ground," but a torrential rain slowed the infantry's advance.[50]

Early on the morning of the 14th, the Union troops again began to move toward the town. Rain, fog, and smoke from the guns "completely shut out the light of day," but the gunboats steamed ahead of the Union army and supported it with their large guns. The navy added more firepower to the Union assault by landing a battery of six howitzers. Lieutenant Roderick Sheldon McCook commanded the battery, and he and his men advanced with the army, dragging the guns through the mud until they could go no farther, suffering two killed and eleven wounded.[51]

Branch's defenses included six miles of the river, which he found impossible to defend with his small force, and he abandoned some of his strongest works. As the Confederates withdrew into the works closer to the city, they became a more cohesive force and their positions became more defensible. The gunboats steaming ahead of the troops enfiladed the rebel defenses, which gave the Union troops a tremendous advantage. The firepower of the naval vessels became a key element for Union victory. In an effort to support the army as closely as possible, Rowan instructed his ships to fire just ahead of the Union lines. He explained to Goldsborough, "I commenced throwing 5, 10, 15 second shells inshore and notwithstanding the risk, I determined to continue till the general sent me word. I know the persuasive effect of a 9-inch [shell], and thought it better to kill a Union man or two than to lose the effect of my moral suasion."[52]

The overwhelming naval firepower allowed the Union infantry to continue advancing near the works of the enemy, where they were halted. The gunboats maintained their fire at the defenses on the river, while the outnumbered Confederates held their flanks against Union attacks. As the Union troops moved along an interior road, the naval shells fell in advance of the troops and dropped inside the rebel parapets, forcing them to retreat. Finally, in danger of being overwhelmed by Union troops, the rebel lines collapsed, and the Confederate soldiers fled to avoid capture.[53]

Rowan hoisted the signal "Follow my motions," and the Union gunboats steamed past the obstructions and up the river toward New Bern. Both *Commodore Perry* and *Stars and Stripes* became impaled while attempting to pass through the iron-capped piles. As the gunboats moved upriver, many of the townspeople fled in the "greatest haste, leaving everything behind them." Arriving at the edge of town, the Union warships found that the retreating rebels had set New Bern on fire in several places. Lieutenant Charles Flusser impressed a few locals, both white and black, and put the fire out before much damage was done. Flusser's efforts to salvage the town only saved it for the federal soldiers. When they arrived, they began to pillage the houses and shops and were stopped only when General Burnside came into the town and posted guards about the city.[54]

As usual, the army took the lion's share of the laurels. Rowan wrote to Samuel Du Pont that "the affair at New Bern was well managed, but, as usual, the Army with its corps of reporters monopolized the credit." The victory cost the army 90 killed and 380 wounded, while the navy had suffered only a few casualties. The Union forces inflicted casualties of 64 killed, 101 wounded, 200 captured, and over 200 missing. During the campaign, Rowan's forces captured and destroyed dozens of vessels and also captured thousands of barrels of rosin, turpentine, and pitch, which would net the officers and men of the expedition thousands of dollars in prize money.[55]

After the victory at New Bern, the squadron continued to probe Confederate positions. On 21 March, Lieutenant Alexander Murray took *Louisiana*, *Delaware*, and *Commodore Perry* to Washington, North Carolina. Expecting opposition, an army transport carrying eight companies of Massachusetts volunteers accompanied the gunboats. Meeting no resistance except for obstructions in the river, the soldiers landed with a regimental band and marched to the courthouse and raised the American flag. The navy's main purpose for visiting the city was to recover the lenses of the Hatteras lighthouse, which the rebels reportedly took to Tarboro. The Union forces nevertheless profited, because the retreating rebels destroyed a gunboat building there. After looking at the town, Lieutenant Murray suggested to Rowan that possession of Washington might be advantageous to the Union. He recommended the town be fortified and held, and Washington later became one of the Union posts in the sounds.[56]

Thus far, the combined Union forces had met only weak resistance, for Confederate leaders in Richmond had done virtually nothing to stop the Burnside expedition. Now Robert E. Lee wrote to President Davis that another "disaster" in North Carolina would be "ruinous," and he immediately sent reinforcements to the state after the fall of New Bern.[57] Burnside, though, had already planned to capture Beaufort, which had one of the state's finest harbors. The loss of this city would not only deny the port to the Confederacy, but in the hands of the Union, it would also become a key logistical base for the maintenance of the blockade.

Fort Macon, guarding the inlet into the harbor, was an important element in the defense of Beaufort. The fort, finished in 1833, was built specifically to guard the city against a naval attack, but it remained ungarrisoned until 1842 and had, since that time, decayed from twenty years of neglect. The Confederates, led by Captain Josiah Pender, captured the fort in April 1861 but found only four guns mounted and a solitary ordnance sergeant stationed there as a custodian. The Confederates made immediate improvements to the fort and eventually mounted forty-three guns, but only three volunteer companies garrisoned it as late as June 1861.[58]

On 23 March, before moving his men into a position to put Fort Macon under siege, Brigadier General John Parke asked for the fort's surrender in order to "save the unnecessary effusion of blood." The commander of the fort, Colonel Moses J. White, declined the Union offer, confident that his undermanned and undergunned fort could withstand a siege and hoping that reinforcements would arrive. Parke began moving his men into position, and on 29 March, they established a beachhead on Bogue Banks. With the beachhead in place, "every available hour of night and day was spent in transporting men, siege train, and supplies" to the eastern end of the island. With the investment of Fort Macon under way, the army, unopposed by the Confederates, captured Beaufort, Carolina City, and Morehead City, thereby cutting off any means of escape for the garrison.[59]

Parke spent three weeks preparing for a bombardment and began firing on Fort Macon at 6:00 A.M. on the morning of 25 April. High winds and rough seas prevented the army from communicating with the gunboats, and consequently the navy learned about the attack only after hearing the first shots. At 8:00, the steamers *Daylight, State of Georgia*, and *Chippewa* and the bark *Gemsbok* got under way and prepared for action. The three steamers moved in a circle, firing as they came within range of the fort at a distance of just over a mile. *Gemsbok* remained at anchor while firing at the fort. The fort immediately replied to the gunboats' fire, cutting rigging and sending an eight-inch shot through *Daylight* but doing little damage otherwise. Rough weather prevented accurate firing by the gunboats, and they withdrew after seventy-five minutes.[60]

Parke had a great deal more success. At close range, they threw 1,150 shells into the fort and dismounted or disabled nearly half of the fort's guns in ten hours of firing. At 4:30 P.M., a flag of truce appeared over Fort Macon, and the following morning, Colonel White and the garrison surrendered.[61]

The capture of the fort was the last major action of the Union expedition and had been accomplished with a minimum number of casualties; the navy had only one wounded and the army one killed and two wounded.[62] The Union forces now had possession and control of all the major strategic points along the interior coastline of the state.

Before the investment of Fort Macon could be completed, Burnside became concerned that gunboats being built at Norfolk might still come through the canals into North Carolina. To prevent this, Burnside sent an expedition to destroy the locks of the Dismal Swamp Canal at South Mills and to block further the Albemarle and Chesapeake Canal by blowing in its banks. On 16 April, Lieutenant Charles Flusser, commanding the screw steamer *Whitehead* and the side-wheel tug *General Putnam*, steamed up the Pasquotank River to within three miles of the locks at South Mills. The river became "so crooked that he considered it very hazardous to go further," and he turned back. The next day 3,000 men under Brigadier General Jesse Reno, escorted by naval vessels, landed below Elizabeth City. Reno met an inferior but resolute Confederate force of less than 1,000 and withdrew hastily, leaving his dead and wounded on the field. He returned to Elizabeth City to be taken off by the navy. Rowan termed this the "South Mills stampede," and Reno claimed he would never "do any more fighting for the Navy."[63]

Since Reno's expedition had failed to destroy the locks at South Mills, Rowan felt compelled to keep a strong force off Elizabeth City in case gunboats from Norfolk attempted to pass through the canal. Hearing a rumor that the Confederates had plated their new gunboats, Rowan requested the double-ender *Miami* be sent to him to "run down the coats of mail" that might come through the canals. On 23 April, *Lockwood*,

Whitehead, *Shawsheen*, and *Putnam* further blocked the Albemarle and Chesapeake Canal by sinking a schooner at its mouth. They added stumps, brush, rails, and tree trunks to complete the obstruction, leaving the naval vessels to watch only the Dismal Swamp Canal.[64]

The capture of Norfolk on 10 May greatly relieved the naval officers in the sounds and ended the threat of gunboats moving into North Carolina via the canals. With this threat abated, the navy began to probe Confederate defenses in the eastern portion of the state by moving into the rivers. The loss of Norfolk also made Confederate positions in northeastern North Carolina more tenuous, because Union troops could now attack this portion of the state by using Norfolk as a base. With control of the sounds, the army, with the aid of the navy, could strike at any point. The mobility of the Union army was a potent threat to the Confederates and forced them to garrison extra troops in the eastern portion of the state to protect the areas that remained under Confederate control. It likewise caused the rebels to withdraw into areas less accessible to the Union navy, thereby losing a total of two and a half million acres of fertile land that annually produced a great deal of pork and fish and over five million bushels of corn.[65]

The Union forces successfully exploited a weak point in the Confederate defenses. The Confederate government had not provided enough men to defeat the Union forces and could not defend the eastern portion of North Carolina, which proved to be too extensive. This problem was compounded by the fact that the navy had given the Union forces a great edge by providing mobility that the Confederates could not match. Divided commands, confusion, and the failure to assign this area a high priority all made the Union offensive efforts successful. By the spring of 1862, General George B. McClellan was committed to his campaign on the peninsula, which forced Burnside to be cautious because he could not expect reinforcements. This caution consumed much of the ardor of Burnside's campaign. After Robert E. Lee drove McClellan's army from Richmond in the Seven Days' Battles, McClellan ordered Burnside to send men from the sounds. Burnside dispatched nearly 8,000 men from New Bern on 6 July, ending the major offensive operations in North Carolina and a proposed move on Goldsboro and its rail connections.[66]

Once these men had left the state, the Union army was placed in a defensive posture. Burnside's successors were linked directly to the presence of the naval forces, and army movements were contingent upon naval support. Lieutenant Charles Flusser summed up the relationship between the army and navy for the remainder of the war in eastern North Carolina when he wrote a letter to his mother: "The fact is these fellows here [the army] are as in the most much afraid to get beyond the gunboats fire. They always whip the enemy when we are with them, and get whipped in our absence."[67]

THREE

The Peninsular Campaign

An anonymous Southern composer managed to capture the essence of the war in the East with a satirical song entitled "Richmond Is a Hard Road to Travel." One of the verses recounts the "half a dozen trips and the half a dozen slips" of the Union forces attempting to capture Richmond.[1] The capture of Richmond, the Confederate capital from 1861 until the war's end, was the main goal of the Union commanders in the East. The Union navy played an important and decisive role in the theater by giving the United States Army advantages of mobility, greater firepower, and solid lines of communications against the Confederate land forces. The navy there became an indispensable component in the war for Union victory but an element that the army commanders normally failed to understand and exploit.

The blockade of the coast developed slowly as a result of constant and increasing demands for gunboats in the Chesapeake Bay. Both Union and Confederate forces secured as many strategic points as they could because both capitals were accessible by this bay. The Union navy blockaded the Chesapeake, which sealed off Norfolk and Richmond from the sea, and trapped a number of Southern vessels within the

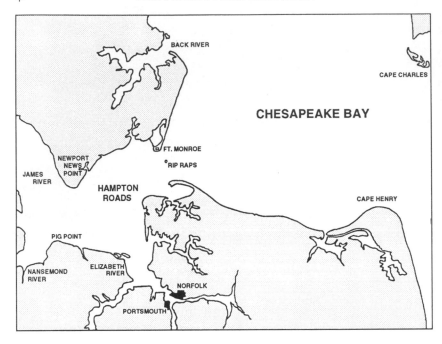

HAMPTON ROADS AND APPROACHES

bay. Early operations in the bay also included reconnaissance missions, and in May 1861, *Monticello* attacked a Confederate battery building at Sewell's Point.[2]

Without a navy to speak of, the Confederates defended the rivers by building earthen batteries at their mouths and sinking obstructions in them to keep Union vessels out or at least to slow their progress. A few merchantmen were armed as well. The Union navy attempted to keep the rebels from building batteries by firing on working parties, but by early June 1861, the Southern defenses in the Chesapeake area mounted no less than 181 guns.[3]

An area important to both the Northern and Southern forces was Hampton Roads. Here was the confluence of three major rivers: the James, Nansemond, and Elizabeth, the latter two with canal connections to North Carolina and the former directly to Richmond. Furthermore, the forts in the area were extremely valuable to the Union. The most important, Fort Monroe, guarded the channel into the Chesapeake and became a bastion for the army and a convenient logistical base for the navy. The Rip Raps, a small island built by the government before the war, provided a cross fire on the channel in Hampton Roads. Fort Calhoun, on the island, lay unfinished at the war's start. In March 1862 the government renamed it Fort Wool in honor of Major General John Wool.[4] Other forts were also quickly constructed by both sides to defend this strategically important area.

The North and its navy, however, controlled the water from the beginning of the war. Confederate Secretary of the Navy Stephen Mallory realized that the South could not match the Union's naval construction program and attempted to negate this advantage with an ironclad building project. Mallory decided it better to build a small number of vessels not vulnerable to enemy fire. The Confederacy was not completely lacking facilities for building warships and marine machinery, but it had major problems to overcome. President Davis's nominal interest in naval matters, an inadequate transportation system, undeveloped natural resources, a small labor pool, and dispersed manufacturing facilities all hampered any large building program that Mallory may have initiated.[5]

The Union vessels retained control of Chesapeake Bay and Hampton Roads until 8 March 1862, the day the Confederate ironclad *Virginia* attacked the Union fleet. This event changed the complexion of the war in the East.

Designed by John M. Brooke and John L. Porter, with the help of Confederate Chief Engineer William P. Williamson and Mallory, *Virginia* became the pride of the Confederate navy and a terror to the Union. Built from the hull of the United States frigate *Merrimack*, she was a formidable weapon of war with her two layers of two-inch ironplate and ten guns. From bow to stern, *Virginia* measured 262 feet and had a casemate 170 feet long, which sloped at a 36-degree angle. Her greatest limitations were her power plant and draft. Her engines had been under repair at the Norfolk Navy Yard when she lay there as a frigate, and her subsequent scuttling had not improved their condition. The ironclad's speed was reputed to be as high as seven knots, but she rarely reached this speed and probably could make no more than about five knots. Her twenty-two-foot draft and her low freeboard limited her to a small area of the bay and its tributaries.[6]

Learning of the Confederacy's plans for an ironclad, Welles created a three-member board to consider design proposals for an Union ironclad. Of the seventeen designs submitted, the board picked three. The three warships built, *Monitor*, *Galena*, and *New Ironsides*, all varied in design and principle, and all later served in the North Atlantic Blockading Squadron. *Monitor*, the first to be completed, was the prototype of more than fifty similar vessels. She was 172 feet long, her beam 41½ feet; she had a draft of 10½ feet; and she carried a battery of two eleven-inch Dahlgrens. *Virginia*'s conversion from a frigate was quick; therefore, *Monitor* had to be completed as soon as possible. By working around the clock, the builders managed to launch the vessel in 100 days.[7]

Even though her construction was hurried, *Monitor* did not reach the Chesapeake before *Virginia*, and five smaller gunboats, *Beaufort*, *Raleigh*, *Patrick Henry*, *Teaser*, and *Jamestown*, sortied to meet the blockading fleet. *Virginia*'s attack on the Union's naval forces could not have been better timed. When the ironclad appeared, Goldsborough and a large number of his warships were preparing to attack New Bern, North Carolina.

On 8 March 1862, the *Virginia*, with her sides "fully greased," steamed into Hampton Roads under the command of Captain Franklin Buchanan. Buchanan had served in the United States Navy for forty-five years before offering his resignation to join the Confederacy. He brought a great deal of experience to the Confederate navy, and his seniority enabled him to command *Virginia*. Guiding the armorclad down the Elizabeth River, Buchanan could see that the frigates *Minnesota*, *Roanoke*, and *St. Lawrence* lay off Fort Monroe at anchor, and *Congress* and *Cumberland* lay off Newport News. Lookouts on board *Minnesota* spotted *Virginia* just before 1:00 P.M., but the ironclad's slow speed allowed the Union vessels an hour to clear for action. During this hour, the crews made what preparations they could but still met the ironclad with laundry hanging from the rigging, and boats remained on board both *Cumberland* and *Congress*.[8]

Shortly after 2:00 P.M., *Virginia* and *Congress* exchanged shots as the Confederate ironclad passed at 1,500 yards. After passing *Congress*, she began to fire on the sloop of war *Cumberland*, and the shots immediately took effect, one shot killing an entire gun crew. *Cumberland*, anchored athwart the river, could not be swung to meet the enemy and thus could not bring her guns to bear. The ponderous ironclad, after raking the hapless *Cumberland*, then rammed her, striking her at almost a right

angle just below the berth deck. Next the ironclad fired one of her bow
rifles into the helpless frigate, killing an additional ten men. The ensuing moments were tense aboard *Virginia*, because her ram remained in
the Union warship as the latter lay sinking. Fortunately for the ironclad,
the ram broke off in her victim like the stinger of a bee. *Virginia*
continued to rake *Cumberland* for about an hour, until the latter listed to
port and sank with her colors flying.[9]

After destroying *Cumberland*, the Confederate ironclad and two of
her consorts, the screw steamers *Beaufort* and *Raleigh*, steamed toward
the frigate *Congress*, which lay aground in shallow water. At 3:30,
Virginia hove to off her stern and began to rake the vessel with hot shot
and incendiary shell. Although only two of her guns could bear on the
ironclad, *Congress*'s crew, which suffered over 100 casualties in the first
minutes of the fight, continued firing for an hour before surrendering.
When the Union vessel struck her colors, Buchanan ordered *Raleigh*
and *Beaufort* to take off the prisoners. Observing the surrender of the
frigate, Union forces ashore directed fire at both vessels, which
wounded Confederate and Union seamen alike. Buchanan ordered the
destruction of *Congress* and was shortly thereafter shot in the leg. Command of the *Virginia* passed to Lieutenant Catesby Jones.[10]

While *Virginia* methodically destroyed the Union warships, the
smaller Confederate gunboats played a minor role in the battle. The
side-wheel steamers *Jamestown* and *Patrick Henry* and the tug *Teaser*
stayed at a distance and attacked the batteries at Newport News and
later fired on the grounded vessels. *Raleigh* and *Beaufort* likewise fired at
the Union ships and acted as tenders to the ironclad. The larger Union
vessels failed to get into the fight because they grounded while coming
to the aid of *Cumberland* and *Congress*.[11]

In three hours, *Virginia* had destroyed two of the Union navy's most
powerful weapons. Jones next planned to attack *Minnesota*, but he
changed his mind. He turned the ironclad back to the Elizabeth River,
because only two hours of daylight remained and low tide was approaching.[12]

Virginia had withstood an incredible pounding, the fire of the Union
vessels had swept away everything on the outside of her casemate—
anchor, smokestack, boat davits, and flagstaff. Furthermore, two guns
were disabled by shells that had struck their muzzles. Confederate

casualties, though, were less than 60, while the Union suffered heavy casualties of 300 dead and 100 wounded.[13]

At dusk, the situation looked extremely grim for the Union navy in Hampton Roads. But at 2:00 A.M., the Union ironclad *Monitor* arrived, having been hurried from New York. She immediately steamed next to *Minnesota* and lay there during the night, should the rebel warship return the next day.[14]

Catesby Jones had every intention to finish what had been started the day before. At 6:00 A.M., after readying his ship and getting up steam, *Virginia* got under way and stood toward *Minnesota*. Almost three hours lapsed before the unwieldy ironclad could steam within range of the frigate. In clear view, lying beside *Minnesota*, was a strange-looking craft that some thought might be a water tank. As *Virginia* approached, the craft got under way and steamed between *Virginia* and her prey. As the two antagonists neared one another, the contrast of their size was that of "pigmy to a giant." The Confederate ironclad steamed toward the Union "cheesebox on a raft" and at 8:45 A.M. exchanged fire. *Monitor* fired about every seven or eight minutes, while *Virginia* returned whole broadsides. Both ironclads pounded each other for four hours at short range, which convinced many of the importance of building armored vessels. During the battle, both vessels tried to ram the other, while inflicting little damage to the other's armor with their guns. More damage may have been inflicted, but *Monitor*'s gunners used smaller charges of powder to prevent an accidental explosion of their guns. Likewise, *Virginia* had carried only shells into battle, expecting to fight wooden ships.[15]

Monitor protected the frigate *Minnesota*, keeping between her and *Virginia*, until she had to withdraw for about thirty minutes to replenish the ammunition in her turret. *Virginia* did not follow *Monitor* but instead turned toward the frigate. As *Virginia* approached, the frigate fired a broadside that "would have blown out of the water any timber-built ship in the world." The ironclad continued to approach but stopped about a mile from the Union vessel because of shallow water. *Virginia* fired a shot from her rifled bow gun, which tore through the Union warship. The tugboat *Dragon*, attempting to free *Minnesota* from the bottom, received the second shot, which passed through her boiler, causing it to explode.[16]

Monitor returned to the fight, and in one of the exchanges, a shot struck her pilothouse, temporarily blinding Captain John Worden. For a second time, the Union vessel withdrew, and at least half an hour elapsed before she was under the direction of Executive Officer Samuel D. Greene. *Monitor* stood down toward Fort Monroe in water too shallow for *Virginia* to follow, and the tide was ebbing, so the Confederate ironclad steamed back toward the Elizabeth River, believing *Monitor* had given up the fight. When *Monitor* turned, her crew observed the Confederate vessel steaming in the opposite direction, and like the crew of *Virginia*, they believed that they had won the day.[17]

Monitor had seemingly done the impossible. She had stopped a vessel many times her size and armament and had successfully prevented the destruction of the Union fleet. This fact did not calm many leaders of the North, who felt that the ironclad might escape from the Chesapeake. Mayors, army and naval officials, and private citizens made various plans to prevent the ironclad's escape, including sinking obstructions in the harbors of the major cities on the East Coast, building large timber rafts, and removing buoys to confuse enemy pilots. Goldsborough and Welles were more pragmatic and discussed obstructing the Elizabeth River. Goldsborough knew it was not necessary to do anything beyond this because *Virginia*'s low freeboard would not allow her to go to sea.[18]

Both the North and the South claimed victory after the battle. *Monitor* won a tactical victory because she accomplished her major goal of protecting *Minnesota*, and *Virginia* failed in her objective of destroying the frigate on the second day. The Confederate ironclad, however, won a strategic victory; her presence denied the Union navy use of Hampton Roads and the James River, and she protected both Norfolk and Richmond. The battle also altered Union naval strategy. During the rest of the war the United States Navy became overly conservative when approaching areas controlled by Confederate ironclads. The rebels later built more ironclads and retained control of the upper James River until the end of the war, thwarting Lincoln's hopes of a quick victory.[19]

Even before the appearance of *Virginia*, Goldsborough had shown fear of Confederate attacks upon his squadron.[20] Still in North Carolina when *Virginia* made her attack, he hurried back to the Chesapeake. Convinced that the Union navy lay in a precarious position, he urged the completion of more ironclads, even if they had to work on them "day and night" with an "increased force."[21] Gideon Welles sensed Goldsborough's fears and commented, "I have never been satisfied with the conduct of the flag-officer in those days, who was absent in the waters of North Carolina,—purposely and unnecessarily absent, in my apprehension, through fear of the Merrimac, which he knew was completed, and ready to come out."[22]

To keep the ironclad confined to the Elizabeth and James rivers, Welles sent Goldsborough several vessels to watch her, and a period of stalemate began. By day, each side observed the other, and by night, the Union navy sent tugboats toward Sewell's Point to watch the ironclad's movements. Union leaders realized that *Monitor* was the only vessel capable of stopping *Virginia*, and Lincoln had directed Welles not to risk her. Union inactivity caused one of her officer's to remark that the government regarded *Monitor* "as an over careful house wife regards her ancient china set—too valuable to use, too useful to keep as a relic, yet anxious that all should know what she owns & that she can use it when the occasion demands."[23]

The Union navy formulated a plan to strike at the Confederate ironclad if the right situation occurred. Goldsborough requested a half-dozen fast steamers so that he could ram her. The flag officer had no problem acquiring vessels for this task and by the end of March had seven. Shipping magnate Cornelius Vanderbilt even loaned one of his own vessels. Manning these vessels was another matter; several crews refused to serve.[24]

Other schemes to destroy the Confederate ironclad also circulated. Quartermaster General Montgomery Meigs suggested boarding *Virginia* and throwing grenades or shells down the smokestack, so that an overwhelming force of men using ladders and grapples could capture her. John Dahlgren, the commandant of the Washington Navy Yard, suggested dropping shells down the funnel by lowering the yards of *Minnesota*. Private interests likewise planned to destroy the vessel for a commission of $500,000. They proposed to use "submarine armors," which were to contain 1,500 to 2,000 pounds of government powder.[25]

The Confederates had similar plans to capture *Monitor*. The main idea hinged on the weak spots of the vessel: the smokestack, the ventilators, the pilothouse, and the gap between the deck and the turret. Four vessels were to run *Monitor* down, so that three special boarding parties with prescribed duties could neutralize her. One group using hammers and wedges would prevent the turret from turning by hammering wedges in the gap between the turret and the deck. A second group planned to throw grenades and combustible material into the ventilators and smokestack. A third would put a wet sail over the pilothouse to obscure the view of the helmsman. The remaining men with pistols and cutlasses were to keep *Monitor*'s crew from escaping, so that she could be towed back to Norfolk.[26] Since both navies had virtually identical plans, each waiting for the other to make the first move, neither vessel ever met again in battle.

On 11 April, *Virginia* and a couple of gunboats entered Hampton Roads to entice *Monitor* into the roadstead. The Union vessels remained at a distance, but *Naugatuck*, a former revenue steamer, exchanged a few shots with the rebel ironclad. Captain Josiah Tattnall, who replaced Buchanan as commander of *Virginia*, realized the Union vessels planned to ram the ironclad, and he refused to commit his vessel too far into the channel.[27]

The rams of the Union navy all drew less water than *Virginia* and might have attempted to run her down. The Union steamers, however, waited with hopes that the ironclad might venture into the roadstead, where they could maneuver more easily. This inactivity was noted by an officer of *Monitor* who wrote that the Union and Confederate gunboats "steamed back and forth . . . each waiting for the other to knock the chip off his shoulder."[28]

While the ironclads remained at their respective distances, General George Brinton McClellan, who replaced the aged Winfield Scott as commander in chief of the Union armies, moved twelve divisions to Fort Monroe. He planned to march up the peninsula between the York and James rivers and to end the war in a quick stroke by capturing the Confederate capital. *Virginia*'s control of the James River forced McClellan to land his army in a place where she could not destroy his transports, but the general's approach on Richmond from this direction gave him several advantages. The Union navy's control of the Chesapeake Bay and later the York River enabled McClellan to supply his army, to protect his flanks, and to withdraw quickly if necessary. The Confederate forces, however, gained an advantage because their defensive lines were now decreased to the width of the peninsula.

McClellan began his advance on 4 April, but his army ran into General John Bankhead Magruder's 11,000 men, who had thrown defensive fortifications across the peninsula to slow the Union army. The Confederate leaders had not planned to act completely on the defensive. In February, Flag Officer Buchanan envisioned an attack on Newport News with *Virginia* and Magruder's forces. "Prince John" Magruder agreed to an assault initially but doubted that the ironclad could intimidate the Union forces enough to make them evacuate the town. He therefore decided to strengthen his second line of defenses instead. The ironclad had a more influential effect than the Confederate leaders thought. Two weeks later, on 9 March, McClellan gave Major General John Wool the authorization to evacuate Newport News if the Confederates obtained complete control of Hampton Roads.[29]

Secretary of War Stanton hinted to Welles that McClellan's movement into the Chesapeake might include a move on Norfolk, an action that Goldsborough favored. The capture of Norfolk would open the James River and would make Confederate positions on the peninsula less defensible. Stanton probably suggested this to secure more naval aid for the campaign. McClellan had asked for all the available naval force that could be spared from the East Coast. The success of the whole campaign depended on control of the water, and the army did not hesitate to ask for assistance, although it kept the navy unaware of its plans. McClellan, extremely reticent, had not consulted the navy on the movement of troops to the peninsula, and he rarely consulted with Goldsborough during the whole campaign.[30] Welles, too, realized the importance of this expedition and the capture of Norfolk, but a fine balance had to be struck between serving the army's wishes and carrying out the other duties of the squadron—particularly the blockade.

Goldsborough maintained his naive belief that *Virginia* would steam into Hampton Roads so that his whole force could run her down. He did, however, keep the protection of McClellan's troops as his first priority. The army likewise remained cautious. John G. Barnard, the chief engineer of the Army of the Potomac, told Fox that "the possibility of the *Merrimack* appearing again paralyzes the movements of this army." Goldsborough commented about this situation, "The salvation of McClellan's army . . . greatly depends upon my holding the Merrimac steadily and securely in check. . . . My game therefore is to remain firmly on the defensive unless I can fight on my own terms."[31]

McClellan's slow advance allowed the Confederate troops to move and easily to oppose the "Young Napoleon." General Joseph Johnston's army faced nearly twice as many men, with water flanking both sides. The ironclad *Virginia* kept the Union vessels out of the James River, but only batteries at Gloucester Point and Yorktown guarded the York River. If these batteries could be reduced, the York River would be open to Union naval vessels and army transports, which would allow a flanking movement.

Asked to cooperate with the army in the reduction of the batteries, Goldsborough sent seven vessels under the command of Commander John S. Missroon to McClellan. Four of the gunboats were to cover the landing of troops at the tip of the peninsula, and three were to cover troops landing up the Severn River; both movements were designed to take the batteries in reverse. Missroon immediately reported "formidable" works, which in his opinion could destroy his vessels "or three or four times their numbers and class."[32] Goldsborough, though, would not give Missroon more force because he understood that the army would reduce the batteries and because he still had a consuming fear of *Virginia*. Missroon requested that the army reduce a masked battery of four guns southeast of Yorktown, but McClellan did nothing. Missroon reluctantly stated that he could advance and remarked to McClellan: "If you want me to take the boats under fire say so, and it shall be done at once, no matter at what cost."[33]

McClellan, Lincoln, and Welles began to urge that Missroon run by the batteries with hopes of relieving pressure on the army, but Missroon became more apprehensive. He became convinced that the batteries were extensive, and balloon observations seemed to support him. McClellan meanwhile remained extremely cautious and slowly moved his forces into a position to place the Confederate positions under siege.[34] Goldsborough would not order Missroon to run by the batteries, because once the vessels had steamed past the batteries, they could no longer be supplied. Furthermore, Missroon's vessels might be needed if *Virginia* sortied from the Elizabeth River and tried to cut McClellan's communications.

Periodically the gunboats at the mouth of the York River threw shells into the works, but the Confederate guns outranged those of the navy. To alleviate this problem, Missroon received the side-wheel steamer *Sebago* in mid-April. Armed with a 100-pound Parrott rifle, she could reach the Confederate batteries and suspend the work there. Missroon remarked to Fox, "I could do more with three 100 pr. Parrott guns than with 12 gunboats of the present armament."[35] Missroon eventually reported that fifty guns bore upon his vessels and asked to be relieved because of the criticism he received.[36]

Missroon failed to show any initiative at Yorktown. He could have run by the batteries at night, for once his gunboats had gone beyond them, they would have been safe because the guns pointed downstream. Shortly after the Confederates abandoned the fortifications, Fox called them "insignificant." The batteries, however, were not as insignificant as Fox claimed. At Yorktown, at least twenty-nine guns could be turned on the water, while at Gloucester Point, the Confederates had mounted eight. The river was likewise extremely narrow; at one point, only 1,000 yards separated the batteries on both sides. Nine- and ten-inch Dahlgrens and eight-inch Columbiads made up the majority of the guns mounted at Yorktown.[37]

Goldsborough and McClellan had "fully discussed" the navy's role at Yorktown. Goldsborough had only agreed to cover the army's movements, and McClellan had been satisfied with the original number of vessels committed by the navy. Two years later, during a congressional investigation, Gustavus Fox defended the navy's actions at Yorktown, but he showed inconsistency with earlier observations. Fox stated that McClellan never "required that [the navy] . . . should attack Yorktown, or that it was ever expected." He further claimed that the Confederate batteries were situated too high and beyond the reach of the naval guns. Fox also recalled during the investigation that "wooden vessels could not have attacked the batteries at Yorktown and Gloucester with any degree of success."[38]

Had the vessels ascended the York River to the Richmond and York Railroad bridge, they might have cut Confederate communications to the east. This move would have caused a great concern for the Confederate army on the peninsula and endangered its left flank. Had Missroon run by the batteries, however, there was no guarantee that McClellan would have attacked and reduced them. Thus Missroon's vessels would have had eventually to run past them again.

Missroon must have realized that without army assistance a naval attack would accomplish little. His small force could merely annoy the

Confederates, and it would require a sizable number of men to attack, capture, and garrison the works. Missroon can merely be faulted for a lack of initiative, and the real blame must be placed on McClellan, who failed to move his forces quickly to reduce and capture the works. After Missroon balked at running past the batteries, McClellan delayed a month before beginning a siege. The Confederates eventually withdrew from Yorktown, abandoning works mounting fifty-six guns (three burst), with emplacements for a total of ninety-four guns.[39]

After the Confederates abandoned Yorktown on 3 May, Commander William Smith, Missroon's replacement, immediately pushed up the York River. General Johnston withdrew toward Richmond with McClellan in pursuit, which allowed Commander Smith with the steamer sloop *Wachusett*, the screw steamer *Chocura*, and the side-wheel steamer *Sebago* to go as far as West Point on 6 May. Here they covered the landing of General William B. Franklin's division, which threatened Johnston's flank. The next day, the Union vessels helped support Franklin by firing and driving away Confederate artillery, and on the 11th, they advanced as far as White House on the Pamunkey River.[40]

While the navy neutralized the threat of the Confederate ironclad, McClellan began to inch up the peninsula. The gunboats in the Chesapeake essentially had nothing to do. One officer complained: "The supineness & want of energy exhibited in keeping the two hundred guns that are afloat here, silent & useless when they could render effective service, is disgraceful & shameful. . . . Day after day we remain torpid and inactive."[41]

This inactivity led to a presidential visit at the beginning of May. Late in the evening of 6 May, John Rodgers, the senior officer in the James River, talked with Lincoln about the possibility of a naval movement up the James River to cut off Confederate supplies and communications. Convinced of the soundness of the plan, Lincoln ordered the ironclad *Galena* and two gunboats up the river without Goldsborough's endorsement. William Keeler aboard *Monitor* remarked that the presidential visit "seems to have infused new life into everything, even the superannuated old fogies begin to shew some signs of life & animation." John Rodgers, commanding *Galena*, led his ironclad and the wooden gunboats *Aroostook* and *Port Royal* up the James River on 8 May, shelled two batteries, and then halted because *Galena* ran aground off Hog Island.[42]

While the former three vessels crept up the James River, *Naugatuck*, *Monitor*, the screw sloops *Seminole*, *Dacotah*, and *San Jacinto*, and the paddle-wheel sloop *Susquehanna* fired at the batteries on Sewell's Point. *Virginia* got under way and steamed out toward the federal fleet, causing the Union vessels to flee to a position under the guns of Fort Monroe. Goldsborough had instructed *Monitor* to engage *Virginia* only if the rams could be used. Again the navy may have missed an opportunity to utilize the shallow-draft gunboats to run down *Virginia*.[43]

As McClellan continued his slow advance up the peninsula, Johnston gradually fell back toward Richmond. Stretching his defensive lines to the breaking point, General Johnston began to withdraw troops from points now difficult to hold. On 10 May, he abandoned many of the batteries around the Elizabeth River and withdrew troops from Norfolk. Goldsborough, who had urged an attack on Norfolk even before *Virginia*'s sortie, was pleased when, on 11 May, 6,000 troops arrived off Ocean View, Virginia. This motley collection of ferries, barges, and steam tugs managed to land the troops without mishap. They marched on Norfolk and arrived outside the city late that afternoon.[44]

Flag Officer Josiah Tattnall knew it would not be long before Union forces occupied the town and had made plans to get *Virginia* into the James River. Pilots told him that she could be lightened to eighteen feet—enough to get her to within forty miles of Richmond. The pilots failed to tell the flag officer that this would be possible only under the most favorable conditions of wind and tide. Tattnall later learned these facts, but only after he had lightened *Virginia*, exposing her hull, which left her in no condition to fight. He therefore had no choice but to destroy her. On 11 May, he ran the ironclad ashore off Craney Island and set her on fire. Just as the troops were landing at Ocean View, the flames reached her magazine, and she exploded with a terrific pyrotechnic show. Perhaps more important than the loss of the ironclad to the Confederacy was the loss of Norfolk and the navy yard.[45]

The Northern public rejoiced over the destruction of *Virginia*. The ironclad had been the major threat to both the army and the navy. Her destruction allowed the Union navy to move freely into Norfolk and up the James River. The ironclad's destruction also gave McClellan control of the water surrounding the peninsula, increasing his offensive options and enhancing his chances of success.

The vessels in the Chesapeake became an offensive force, now that Goldsborough had virtually nothing to oppose him. The James River became a liability for the Confederacy because it acted as a thoroughfare into the heart of the Confederate capital. Goldsborough, taking advantage of the situation, sent *Monitor* and *Naugatuck* to join the double-ender *Port Royal*, the screw steamer *Aroostook*, and *Galena* up the James. Goldsborough instructed the officers to reduce all the rebel works along the river, to steam to Richmond, and to shell the city until it surrendered. The gunboats could not destroy the Confederate batteries as they advanced because their guns could not be elevated sufficiently, so they bypassed them and continued toward Richmond.[46]

Only fortifications and obstructions at Drewry's Bluff lay between the Union navy and the Confederate capital. The bluff, about 100 feet above the water, overlooked a bend on the river eight miles below Richmond. In addition to formidable batteries, rifle pits lined the riverbanks. The Confederates had also placed piles and sunken vessels filled with stones across the river to keep Union vessels from passing. Above the obstructions lay the remnants of the Confederate navy.[47]

On the overcast morning of 15 May, Commander John Rodgers on board *Galena* approached the bluff, followed by *Monitor*, *Naugatuck*, *Aroostook*, and *Port Royal* in single line ahead. The ex–revenue cutter *Naugatuck* took the lead at Harrison's Bar to sound the channel and warn of obstructions and torpedoes. Sighting the batteries at 7:35 that morning, *Galena* steamed to a distance of 600 yards from the Confederate guns and dropped anchor. *Monitor* anchored just below *Galena*, and the wooden gunboats anchored at a safer distance of 1,300 yards.[48]

At 7:45, the Union gunboats began to attack the batteries. The rebel gunners replied and struck *Galena* with their first shot. Within minutes *Naugatuck* was out of action, when her Parrott rifle exploded, leaving her with only her howitzers, which she used against rebel sharpshooters on shore. Before 9:00, Lieutenant William Jeffers, commanding *Monitor*, observed that his vessel was not drawing much fire and moved her between *Galena* and the rebel batteries. After moving to the new position, *Monitor* could not elevate her guns to provide effective fire, and she dropped back to her first anchorage.[49]

Fort Drewry, commanded by Captain Augustus H. Drewry led the Confederate artillerymen, mostly men from Chesterfield County. The

naval contingents from *Patrick Henry* and *Virginia* did not take part in
the fight. Heavy rains had destroyed the casemate manned by *Patrick
Henry*'s crew under the command of Captain John R. Tucker. Lieutenant Catesby Jones's nine-inch Dahlgren failed to take part in the action
because it was positioned around a curve in the river. The local farmers-
turned-soldiers who manned the other guns showed good marksman-
ship by striking *Galena* frequently. The gunners also forced *Aroostook*
and *Port Royal* to change their anchorage, while they were driven from
their guns many times by the fire from the Union vessels. At 11:00, an
eight-inch shell ignited a cartridge being carried by a powder boy on
Galena causing a great deal of smoke. Since *Galena*'s ammunition was
nearly exhausted, Rodgers signaled to break off the action.[50]

Galena had received most of the attention of the Confederate batteries
and was described after the battle as a "slaughter house."[51] In an engagement of a little over three hours, the Confederates had struck the
flagship forty-three times. *Galena* had casualties of twelve men killed
and twenty-one wounded, one mortally. Only three men were wounded
in the other vessels. The Confederates had suffered only seven killed
and eight wounded. Writing to Goldsborough shortly after the battle,
Rodgers stated: "We demonstrated that she is not shoot-proof." Years
later, while talking of this incident, he remarked: "The *Galena* was a
mistake. The monitor was the right principle. We could not afford
mistakes, fighting in such a war. . . . I had to prove the *Galena* a mistake.
The poor fellows who died on board her that day did not die in vain."[52]
Rodgers was only partially right, *Galena* could not effectively fight
enemy batteries at close range because of her thin armor, but she did
have a greater firepower than vessels of the monitor class. Had *Monitor*
been able to bring her guns to bear at a short range at Drewry's Bluff, she
would have made little difference in the outcome because of her slow
rate of fire.

This movement by the navy to within eight miles of Richmond gave
it control of nearly all the waters surrounding the peninsula. Consequently, the Confederates evacuated batteries at Hardin's Bluff and
Day's Point. The Union gunboats controlled the James River as far as
City Point and controlled the York River as far as White House. To
maintain this control, Welles ordered Goldsborough to withdraw vessels from the sounds of North Carolina. He also transferred gunboats

from other theaters so that the James and York rivers and their tributaries could be kept open. Welles realized that the shallow and narrow James River, guarded by the formidable rebel batteries at Drewry's Bluff, would require a combined effort by both the army and navy to reach Richmond.[53]

Goldsborough, meanwhile, approached McClellan on the evening of 20 May to arrange a joint movement. The general preferred not to operate together until he crossed the Chickahominy River. McClellan, though, operated north of the Chickahominy for about a month, waiting for reinforcements. Furthermore, as the general moved his army closer toward Richmond, he advanced beyond his naval support on the James—to a point that the gunboats could be of no help. By 4 June 1862, the navy's only point of safe communication with the army was at Jamestown Island, well in McClellan's rear.[54]

To assist the army, the navy began using light draft vessels to extend its operations into the tributaries of the James. They were sent up the Chickahominy thirty-five to forty miles above its mouth and into the Appomattox River with intentions of destroying the railroad bridge at Petersburg. The gunboats also protected McClellan's transports at White House on the Pamunkey River.[55]

Goldsborough remained interested in advancing up the James but relied on McClellan to reduce Drewry's Bluff. Goldsborough assumed that McClellan could not detach a force to carry out the reduction of the batteries because of the overwhelming numbers of the enemy. McClellan insisted that the army was in a desperate situation and was "hanging by the eye-lids."[56] Had McClellan reduced the works below Richmond, there would have been little to stop the naval vessels from steaming to the Confederate capital.

Lincoln, chafing at McClellan's deliberate advance, suggested that the railroad bridge at Petersburg be destroyed in order to cut Confederate communications. The government offered a sum of $50,000 to individuals willing to do so. A "submarine propeller" called *Alligator* was sent up to Commander Rodgers, the senior officer in the James River, to help destroy the bridge and possibly to operate against Drewry's Bluff. Invented by a Frenchman, this semi-submersible vessel was offered to the United States government. Forty-seven feet long and propelled by hand, she could operate in eight feet of water while only partially exposed to sight. In tests Rogers found her steering to be defective, and she could not stay under water for any length of time, so Rodgers sent her back to Fort Monroe.[57]

On 26 June, a flotilla of nine vessels led by Rodgers steamed up the Appomattox to destroy the railroad bridge. The gunboats advanced under Confederate musket fire, while *Galena* shelled City Point to mislead the enemy. When the flagship *Port Royal* went aground, the lighter draft vessels continued toward the bridge until the tug *Island Belle* grounded. Local contrabands reported that Confederate artillery was being sent toward the river, so the seamen stripped and burned her to keep her from falling into rebel hands. The remaining gunboats retired downstream without destroying the bridge.[58]

One of the most important duties of the navy during the campaign was to convoy and protect army supply vessels on the York River bound to and from the army's base at White House. Without naval support, this base would have been impossible to hold. At Gaines Mill on 27 June, General Robert E. Lee, the new commander of the Army of Northern Virginia, nearly cut the Army of the Potomac's communications at White House. Using as many as 400 transports, McClellan began changing his base from the York River to the James River on the night of the 27th. To cover his strategic withdrawal, he asked naval vessels to go as far as possible up the Chickahominy. To cover his left flank, he asked that the gunboats on the James River go as far as New Market. The side-wheel steamers *Delaware* and *Satellite* were sent into the Chickahominy, and *Galena*, *Aroostook*, and the side-wheeler *Mahaska* moved into Turkey Creek to protect the army's left flank.[59]

What began as an orderly withdrawal soon turned into a fast-paced retreat. Lee relentlessly pursued the Northern army, and McClellan began eagerly to seek the sanctuary of the James River and the protection of the gunboats. McClellan set up his new base at Harrison's Landing, as Lee pushed the Northern army farther each successive day during the Seven Days' Campaign. On 1 July, the Seven Days' Campaign ended east of Richmond when McClellan's retreating army made a defensive stand at Malvern Hill.

With the Union forces pressed against the river, the Confederates attempted to drive them into the water. Brigade after brigade advanced across an open field, half a mile wide. Numerous Union batteries defended the Yankee position, and the gunboats likewise participated in the battle. Guided by signals from shore, the large naval guns helped to decimate the Confederates as they emerged from the woods. The Southerners made several attempts to reach the Union lines, but each of the attacks was successfully repulsed. The rebels could not respond to the naval fire, prompting one Confederate general, Daniel Harvey Hill, to comment: "It was not war—it was murder."[60]

Although the navy had helped to frustrate Lee's attempt to destroy McClellan's army, the Army of the Potomac remained captive in its fortifications at Harrison's Landing, protected by the navy. Goldsborough instructed John Rodgers not to send vessels to Hampton Roads, because McClellan had pleaded for the navy to keep as many as possible near the landing to protect the army's camps and communications.[61] Rodgers realized the plight of the army and told Goldsborough that "the gunboats may save them, but the points to be guarded are too many for the force at my disposal. . . . To save the army, as far as we can, demands immediately all our disposable force. . . . Now, if ever, is a chance for the Navy to render most signal service." General Lee, however, had no intention of attacking McClellan at Harrison's Landing, because he was "too secure under cover of his boats to be driven from his position."[62]

Rodgers, who had selected Harrison's Landing as McClellan's base, oversaw the protection of the transports. The landing extended forty miles on the north bank of the James River, it served as an excellent anchorage for supply vessels, and it could be defended quite easily by placing artillery on a ridge overlooking the river. Both flanks of the landing were accessible to gunboats by two creeks, which enabled the navy to provide fire support. The gunfire was made more accurate by cutting strips of bark off trees near the river as range markers for the naval gunners.[63]

On 4 July, Rodgers ordered *Monitor* and the double-ender *Maratanza* on a reconnaissance mission up the James. At Haxall's, below Turkey Bend, the gunboats discovered the Confederate vessel *Teaser*. As soon as *Teaser* sighted the double-ender, she opened fire. *Maratanza* responded, and her third shot passed through the boiler of the Confederate gunboat, whose crew "precipitately abandoned her." On board were papers concerning torpedo defenses in the James, some personal effects, and a Confederate observation balloon.[64]

The strained relationship between Goldsborough and McClellan became worse after the general's forces had been pinned against the river. Poor communication, McClellan's reserved manner, the shortage of naval vessels, and the undefined roles of both branches had driven a wedge between Goldsborough and McClellan. For these reasons, on 6 July, the gunboats in the James River were organized as the James River Flotilla and placed under the independent command of Commodore Charles Wilkes. Wilkes, though, would cause more problems than he solved. He was a stern disciplinarian and had a persecution complex. Lincoln and Seward picked Wilkes to command, not Welles, who had a low regard for the new flag officer. Welles wrote in his diary: "He is very exacting towards others, but is not himself as obedient as he should be. Interposes his own authority to interrupt the execution of orders of the Department." Welles then correctly predicted "that he will be likely to cause trouble to the Department. He has abilities but not good judgment in all respects."[65]

Wilkes superseded Rodgers, who had commanded the James River vessels. Rodgers also had a low opinion of Wilkes. He commented: "My own private opinion is that he is but little removed from an absolute fool."[66]

The decision to give Wilkes an independent command infuriated Flag Officer Goldsborough. Welles gave Wilkes an independent command within the squadron, which Goldsborough commanded technically but could not control. Goldsborough wrote that this "wounds my sensibilities as an officer most sorely, and places me in a most humiliating attitude before the public and Navy."[67]

Wilkes had twenty-three vessels under his command at a time when the army lay inactive. He helped convoy supply vessels along the river, protected the army's position at Harrison's Landing, and exchanged fire along the banks with rebel troops. The most important action the James River Flotilla participated in was the withdrawal of the Army of the Potomac from the peninsula beginning 15 August. The army crossed the Chickahominy and marched back to the tip of the peninsula, where McClellan had landed four months earlier. On 29 August, after the army's withdrawal, Welles instructed Wilkes to turn his short-lived command back to Goldsborough. Goldsborough, however, received only twelve of the twenty-three vessels.[68]

Goldsborough became the second flag officer to become a casualty of politics. Wilkes's independent command had subjected Goldsborough to "scurrilous and unmerited attacks" by the newspapers. Goldsborough believed these "vile and vulgar" writings had a "prejudicial effect" on his character, and he asked to be relieved.[69] Goldsborough had never had a good rapport with the press, having declared the previous December, "I dread reporters more than I do the Devil himself!"[70] Another factor that weighed on Goldsborough was his commitment as a family man and his absence from home for three years. Wilkes's independent command convinced Goldsborough that the Navy Department was displeased with his performance. Goldsborough was correct. Welles wrote in his diary, "he was proving himself inefficient,—had done nothing effective since the frigates were sunk by Merrimac, nor of himself much before."[71] Welles therefore did not hesitate to accept his resignation.

The role of the Union navy in the peninsular campaign has often been portrayed as insignificant. But the navy's role should not be diminished. The navy supported the army by its presence in the James, York, Pamunkey, Chickahominy, and lesser rivers and creeks. The Union navy cooperated in skirmishes, provided important fire support at Malvern Hill, kept communications open, protected the army when it was backed against the river, and facilitated its retreat. The navy consequently made the whole campaign possible and prevented the Confederate army from delivering what may have been a death blow to the Union forces at Harrison's Landing. McClellan's slow-developing campaign never utilized the navy as an offensive force and so allowed the Confederate forces to block his every move. Furthermore, Goldsborough never knew McClellan's plans in advance, which destroyed the unity of the operations. McClellan's failure to understand the advantages that the navy provided him probably contributed as much to his unsuccessful attempt to capture Richmond as any single cause.

FOUR

We have no use for the river

The Navy in the Eastern Theater

Following the Peninsular campaign, the navy's role in the eastern theater was characterized by idleness. During the next two years, the Union army failed to utilize the gunboats in the Chesapeake. The successive Union commanders attempted to outmaneuver the Confederate army to capture Richmond. They failed to use the navy and the advantages that control of the water could give them. They likewise failed repeatedly to capture the rebel capital. While the opposing armies struggled to win the war, the Confederate navy actively built ironclads to challenge the Union navy's control of the James River. Once completed, the ironclads would complicate Union strategy until the end of the war.

With Goldsborough's resignation, Gideon Welles once again had to choose a flag officer for the squadron. Welles surprised some officers by choosing Samuel Phillips Lee, whom he promoted to acting rear admiral. Lee, born in Virginia on 13 February 1812, had less experience than his predecessor. He married the daughter of the influential Montgomery Blair, the postmaster general, and thus was also related by marriage to Gustavus Fox. Lee had had a long but relatively normal naval career. He became a midshipman in 1825, fought in the Mexican War, commanded the blockading vessel *Vandalia* off Charleston, and did serve with distinction under David Glasgow Farragut at New Orleans on the screw sloop *Oneida*. He was perhaps one of the most conscientious and efficient officers in the navy but was considered timid by some.[1]

Many questioned Lee's promotion, feeling that his influence had secured him the command. John Rodgers wrote his wife: "I should quite as leave have him as any other—he is sensible—and as far as I see modest. He is efficient—he is above me on the register, and whether he is admiral commodore or senior officer amounts in fact to the same right to command." He further commented that "Lee has deserved the promotion as much as anyone—and has had the influence to get it—other people who have had equal merit have not had the influence."[2]

Lee's fleet captain, John Sanford Barnes, described Lee as being about average in height and possessing a "sparse" frame. He claimed that Lee "was too modest and retiring, careful and conservative in his views of duty, never expressing himself, or giving his opinions, impulsively or emphatically." He also observed that Lee was sensitive to criticism, was conscientious, and that his personal courage was "undoubted."[3]

Lee hoisted his pennant on *Minnesota* on 4 September 1862, taking command of the squadron at its lowest point of activity. The Navy Department had turned its attention to projects farther south, and for two years, Lee would merely keep the status quo in the Chesapeake. With the army unwilling to cooperate in a joint move, the navy could advance no farther. John Rodgers summed up the navy's potential in Virginia. "We have no use for the river if the army does not approach Richmond along the river. . . . When the city falls, the batteries lying between Norfolk and Richmond will fall of themselves. When the main [Confederate] army has been defeated, no fragment of it can hold earthworks which can be attacked at once by land and water."[4]

Lee's initial concern in the James River was the ironclad *Richmond*. Launched in May before the fall of Norfolk, the Confederates towed her to Richmond and rapidly finished her. Lee asked Rodgers to submit his views on the situation in the James River. Rodgers assessed Confederate strategy well; he knew the best place for the ironclad to fight would be in a narrow channel. Here she could not be outgunned by a large number of Union vessels, she would not expose her armor, and she would

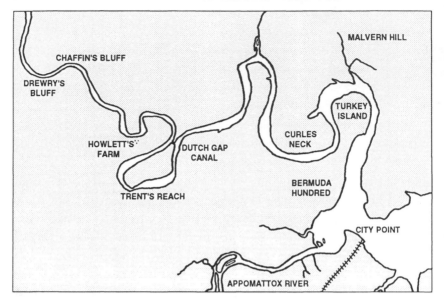

THE JAMES RIVER

eliminate the chances of being a target for ramming. For the Union gunboats, the river was the least favorable place to fight, because only one or two vessels could attack *Richmond* at one time. Obstructions at Drewry's Bluff prevented the Union gunboats from steaming to Richmond and the fort's elevation made it impossible for warships to reduce the works. Rodgers pointed out that if the ironclad could be lured to Newport News, the navy could maneuver to defeat her, because the channel was over a mile wide.[5]

Heeding Rodgers's advice, Lee kept his vessels in a defensive posture at Newport News. Lee feared that the gunboats in his command were insufficient to contend with the ram, which he believed had good speed, light draft, and "extraordinary thickness of woodensides + of plating." He claimed that even *Minnesota* with her large number of guns could not deliver a broadside to an ironclad at close range and that her draft limited her to a small area of the channel at Newport News. Lee also felt that *Galena* was weak and vulnerable and that *Monitor* was too slow and was liable to be rammed by the ironclad or one of her consorts. Lee requested that *New Ironsides*, the most formidable of the ironclads, be sent to Newport News to reinforce his command. He also asked for a fast steamer that carried two rifled guns capable of penetrating iron and with a bow and stern strengthened for ramming.[6] By 1 October, *New Ironsides* lay off Newport News.

Lee established Newport News as the navy's most advanced station on the James River. Here he stationed tugs with their steam up, three miles above the fleet. Lee instructed the tugs to keep responsible officers on watch and to be ready to slip their cables.[7] During the winter of 1862–63, Lee remained content to let his vessels lie idle but did participate in minor operations.

In the spring, the Confederates began coordinated offensive movements in eastern North Carolina and southeastern Virginia. Given an independent command, General James Longstreet began to press federal forces, which brought the Union navy back into activity. South of the James River and into North Carolina, Longstreet's interest centered on the vast wealth of stores in the region. Longstreet's head of commissary informed him that, east of the Chowan River, he could collect tons of bacon and vast amounts of salted fish if he could hold the Union forces in Suffolk. By doing so, his supply wagons would be free to gather stores without exposure to raids. Longstreet acted on this advice and made plans to reduce Suffolk if a "fair opportunity" arose.[8]

In April, Longstreet moved two divisions to contain the Union forces in the Suffolk area, with hopes of driving them to Norfolk. Suffolk, about fifteen miles southwest of Norfolk, lay on the Nansemond River, five miles south of Western Branch. The upper part of the Nansemond was crooked, narrow, and difficult to navigate. Lee called it a "mere creek."[9] General John J. Peck, commanding the Union forces in the area, feared that if the rebel troops crossed the river, they would cut his communications, and he immediately requested naval aid to prevent this. Lee responded and sent Lieutenant Roswell H. Lamson in *Stepping Stones*, an ex-ferryboat that had retained her prewar name. Five other vessels steamed into the upper Nansemond, while Lieutenant William Barker Cushing and four gunboats left to patrol the lower reaches of the river.[10]

This coordinated Confederate attack stretched the resources of the Union navy. Lee remained concerned about the Confederate ironclad in the James, and thus he could not lend further assistance to Peck. Besides the Confederate movements in southeastern Virginia, Lee had to respond to requests for reinforcements in the sounds of North Carolina and at Williamsburg, which were also under attack. Lee became critical of the army and declared that it "should cease the impolicy of occupying so many detached and weak positions, and relying upon what were called ferryboats in New York and gunboats here to make such positions tenable." His resources strained, Lee asked the Navy Department for reinforcements. The best Welles could do was to tell Lee that "efforts are being made to place at your disposal an adequate force to enable you to respond to the frequent calls on the part of the army for assistance."[11]

Longstreet's men dug in on the western bank of the Nansemond and with muskets and artillery continually harassed the Union vessels. Peck employed his forces so that Lieutenant Roswell H. Lamson's gunboats guarded his rear—a distinction that Lee abhorred. In a letter to Cushing, Lee wrote: "It is very flattering to have the Army rely upon the Navy, but where so great a result is at stake it is proper that the general should not make the mistake of foregoing those judicious auxiliary measures to secure so important a point as the protection of his rear."[12]

Gunboats on the Nansemond engaged Confederate batteries on 12 April and all the next day. On 14 April, *Stepping Stones*, *Mount Washington*, and the army steamer *West End*, moving toward Suffolk, observed a freshly constructed fortification, which appeared to have nothing but riflemen inside. After shelling the work for a short time, Lieutenant Lamson, on board *Mount Washington*, gave a signal for the gunboats to run past the fortification. At 400 yards, the enemy opened fire from seven pieces of artillery, which they had rolled from the woods. A shot went through the boilers of *Mount Washington*, which caused her to lose power and to drift onto the riverbank. *West End* also ran aground, and both vessels had to be towed out of danger by *Stepping Stones*. Farther down the river, the side-wheel steamer *Mount Washington* grounded once more, and, again, the Confederate gunners attacked her. With ten pieces of artillery, six on Hill's Point (Fort Huger), and four to the right of the gunboats, the rebel gunners created a murderous cross fire. Lieutenant Cushing brought *Commodore Barney* out of Western Branch to join the fight and forced the rebels to shift their batteries, saving *Mount Washington* from certain destruction. The latter, however, was unable to move until high tide and had to be withdrawn by warping her down the river under fire from the rebels. Union casualties for the two days were five killed, fourteen wounded, and one missing.[13]

Lieutenant Cushing, whose crew had fought well, came out of the fight optimistically. He wrote Lee: "I can assure you that the *Barney* and her crew are still in good fighting trim, and we will beat the enemy or sink at our posts."[14] Shortly after this action, Brigadier General George Getty, who commanded the 3rd Division 9th Army Corps north of Suffolk, requested that a gunboat be sent to Suffolk to add to his "security." He then asked if one of Lamson's ships would steam up the river to draw the fire of the enemy, so that he could ascertain the positions of the batteries. Lamson replied to Peck that he did not think Lee would approve of "exposing the boats to artillery merely to find their position and without other object in view."[15] Instead, on 18 April, Lee withdrew his vessels from the upper Nansemond to a position above Western Branch. The removal of naval support upset Peck, who believed seven miles of river too great a distance to guard and to prevent Longstreet's divisions from crossing.[16]

The most dangerous point on the Nansemond River for the navy was at Hill's Point, just above where the Western Branch flowed into the Nansemond. To pass this spot, the gunboats came within fifty yards of a rebel battery. To make future movements up the river less hazardous, Lamson made plans to take the Hill's Point battery. He arranged with the army to embark 500 men and land them near the guns, but the troops arrived late. Lamson was infuriated. He wrote to Lee, "We have fought the rebels every day since last Sunday, except to-day, with a heavy loss . . . and the army have lain on their bank or in their earthworks without a man hurt, and have utterly failed to render me the assistance and support they ought to have given."[17]

On 19 April, Lamson on board *Stepping Stones*, accompanied by the ferryboat *Commodore Barney* and the small tug *Primrose*, embarked 270 men to capture the Confederate battery at Hill's Point. On *Stepping Stones*, a canvas screen circled the deck, concealing the infantry on board. To further deceive the enemy, the gunboats steamed as if they intended to pass the batteries, but *Stepping Stones* instead turned into the bank. The infantry quickly disembarked from both ends of the ferryboat. The Union troops charged the Confederate position, while seamen dragged four boat howitzers to the crest of a ravine, where they commanded the rear of the battery. The rebels were completely surrounded and surrendered, losing over 150 prisoners and five pieces of artillery.[18]

The engagement, styled the "Capture of Stribling's Battery," allowed the navy some freedom in patrolling the upper Nansemond, but Lee thought it "impracticable" to keep the enemy from eventually crossing this "crooked creek." Some army officers agreed with Lee and believed that naval support was unnecessary in the river because of its narrowness. The enemy with artillery and musketry could throw pontoons across the river with relative ease. Only a land force positioned on the opposite bank in a fortified position could stop such a movement. Cushing stated: "It is too small a stream for many boats to maneuver at once and about all they can do is to give confidence to the army."[19]

Realizing that his gunboats could not prevent the enemy from crossing, Lee had them withdraw into the lower Nansemond. The army evidently needed the confidence that the navy provided and requested that Lee return the gunboats. The presence of the navy had allowed the army to keep fewer men in defensive positions, and without the navy, Major General John Dix placed armed quartermaster boats in the upper Nansemond. General Peck, who had placed a "great reliance" on the gunboats, abandoned the fortified position on Hill's Point, placing the navy once again under the threat of fire from the enemy. The gunboats were thus impelled to remain in the lower reaches of the river, and the Northern papers censured Lee rather than Peck.[20]

On 21 April, a boat's crew of five men was lured ashore and captured by the rebels. The following day, Cushing took ninety men and a howitzer in search of them. Cushing's small force advanced to Chuckatuck, a small town on Chuckatuck Creek, and they drove off a small number of cavalry and captured the town. Inflicting two deaths on the enemy and suffering one casualty, Cushing returned to the vessel having shown that the enemy was no longer "in strong force near Suffolk."[21]

The Suffolk campaign cost the navy a large number of casualties and disabled several vessels. The crews spent many sleepless nights on the river due to the rebel sharpshooters, while the vessels received much abuse from enemy gunfire. *Stepping Stones*, for example, was constantly harassed by rebel sharpshooters and artillery during the campaign and also relied on army provisions because a shot had rendered her galley stove useless. She lost her bulwarks; the boats were shot to pieces; the anchor, which had been shot away during one fight, had been replaced by a heavy iron kettle; and the smokestack looked like a "nutmeg grater" and her planking like an "old target."[22]

By 10 May, most of the fighting had ceased, except for a few rebel cavalry reconnaissance missions. At Lee's request, the army destroyed Confederate earthworks in the area and began to cut down trees on the west bank of the river. The army also strengthened and erected new works on the east side, which made the presence of the navy no longer necessary.[23]

Admiral Lee preferred that the army consolidate its defensive positions rather than construct these fortifications. The army had developed an offensive pattern, which placed the navy in a subordinate role. The Union army drove Confederate forces out of an area, then usually held its position, expecting the navy to cover its flanks and keep open the communications. Lee wrote to Welles that the army could abandon works in the Yorktown and Norfolk area and free 20,000 to 30,000 troops. These men, according to Lee, were "scattered and holding . . . a frontier line, liable to attack in detail." Lee believed that if these men were "concentrated for the effectual prosecution of a campaign; . . . it would leave the gunboats free to move about and preserve a strict blockade instead of occupying positions rendered necessary only by the positions of the Army."[24]

Thus the navy in the eastern theater served to protect weak posts threatened by the enemy. The gunboats could be quickly shifted from one point to another. As long as the army positioned itself near water, it could be immediately supported with firepower and additional troops if it came under assault. This relationship allowed the army to keep fewer men at each post and complicated any Confederate attack—all at the expense of the navy. Illustrative of this policy was General Dix's movement of troops in September 1862 from Yorktown to protect Washington. Because of Robert E. Lee's move into Maryland, Halleck requested gunboats, and Welles ordered Rear Admiral Lee to protect Yorktown in the army's absence.[25]

The navy did give the Union army greater mobility, as is evident by the successful attack on Stribling's Battery. On 4 June, the navy took 400 infantry up to Walkerton, twenty miles from West Point on the Mattapony River. After disembarking, the infantry destroyed a foundry, machinery, mills, and grain and captured horses, mules, and cattle. The

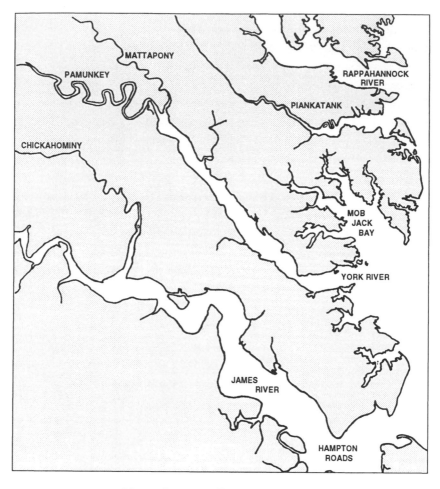

MAJOR RIVERS IN EASTERN VIRGINIA

navy kept the river clear and dispersed rebels by firing on them from the river.[26]

An even more potent threat was mobile cavalry. Some naval vessels, particularly the former ferryboats, could carry large numbers of cavalry, which made it possible to threaten enemy positions and destroy huge amounts of material. The side-wheel steamer *Mahaska* could carry as many as 200 horses and riders, while *Western World*, originally a Hudson River cattle boat, could carry nearly 300 horses and riders.[27] With this added offensive capability, the Union armed forces accomplished many things that otherwise would have been impossible.

This mobility produced results on 25 June, when the Union gunboats landed cavalry at White House on the Pamunkey. Four naval gunboats accompanied by two army vessels brought up over 1,000 mounted troops, who rode nearly thirty miles to the Virginia Central Railroad bridge over the South Anna River. The cavalry destroyed the bridge and captured over 300 mules, nearly 60 horses, and over 100 officers and enlisted men, with a loss of only three killed and five wounded. The greatest single prize captured during the raid was Robert E. Lee's son, Brigadier General William H. F. "Rooney" Lee, who was recuperating from a wound received at Brandy Station in June.[28]

With control of the York River and its tributaries, the Union navy prevented the rebels from building earthworks. The navy actively patrolled the river and destroyed works under construction. By 20 July 1863, no enemy earthwork remained along the river south of West Point, but the Confederates intensified their efforts of placing torpedoes in the water in hope of driving the gunboats out of the river. Progressively the Confederate strategy worked, because by May 1864, the navy did not venture any farther up the river than West Point.[29]

The James River was strategically important to the Confederates, and they tried to retain some control over it. In addition to their ironclad building program, the rebels began building an earthwork, Fort Powhatan, at a bend in the river between City Point and the mouth of the Chickahominy River. In May, Rear Admiral Lee suggested a joint effort to take the work before the Confederates could make it fully operational. A delay by the Union forces might allow the Confederates to complete it, and once the enemy finished the battery, any effort to capture it would require a larger force. The fort never presented any danger to army movements, and thus General Dix refused to help destroy it. He claimed that his movable force was "comparatively small" and inadequate to capture the fort.[30]

The relationship between the army and navy had developed little since the beginning of the war. In May, Dix forwarded Lee a list of the places he felt required gunboats for defense. These points included Fort Monroe, Norfolk, Suffolk, Yorktown, Williamsburg, and West Point. In essence, Dix was defining what he believed were the navy's key responsibilities. Dix could hardly have expected Lee to take him seriously when the army continued to be irresolute about its own actions.

The navy transported the army to West Point in early May, only to have it abandoned by the army in less than a month.[31] Lee had viewed this as just another impulsive move by the army, and a prime example of its policy of occupying detached posts with expectations of naval support to make them safe.

Army officers, however, continued to view the role of the navy as a subordinate one. They made impetuous demands for attacks, did not give Lee any details, and expected the navy to respond quickly. Daylight, tides, river conditions, and vessel dispositions affected the navy's abilities to respond when called. At times Lee was unable to cooperate because of inadequate notice.

The lack of cooperation was perhaps one of the major problems of the war in the eastern theater. The possibility of taking Fort Powhatan was discussed once again in the fall of 1863, but Lee expressed concerns about a lack of vessels and the necessity to defend other areas. Furthermore, without army support, a naval move would be useless. Fox advised Lee: "The question of occupying Fort Powhatan is a military one. In reference to military operations, should the War Department decide to make such occupation, the naval force under your command will be increased."[32]

Cooperation between the army and navy could have yielded many positive results. The navy was capable of clearing the James and York rivers of enemy batteries if the army chose to advance on Richmond from the southeast. Alone, the navy could not make any prolonged movement up the rivers, because of its dependency upon the army to garrison captured and destroyed strategic points. Any movement up the James without army support would have been no more effective than a raid. Without a cooperative spirit, the navy's position increasingly became weaker as a result of the building of Confederate ironclads.

Confederate ironclads became Lee's major concern in Virginia as the war progressed. The Confederacy's success with *Virginia* had convinced Mallory that armored vessels could defend inland waters. By 1864, the Confederacy had completed three ironclads, and the James River Squadron became a fleet in being, requiring an increasing number of Union gunboats to check them. Because of the substantial obstruction at Drewry's Bluff, both the Union forces and the Confederates could only watch the others' movements. The Confederate ironclads and a half-dozen wooden gunboats remained above the obstructions at Drewry's Bluff, while the Union vessels through 1863 continued to remain off Newport News and send picket boats up the James to watch for the enemy.[33]

Union naval confidence was further weakened by a Confederate attack on the flagship of the North Atlantic Blockading Squadron. At 2:00 A.M. on 9 April 1864, Lieutenant Hunter Davidson, commanding a small screw steamer twenty-five feet in length and fitted with a spar torpedo, attacked the frigate *Minnesota*. Striking her below the water-line, abaft the port main chains, the torpedo dismounted several guns and inflicted considerable damage to the warship, with only fifty-three pounds of powder in the charge. All the special precautions taken to ensure the safety of the warships at night had failed. The tug *Poppy* lay astern of *Minnesota* as protection but failed to keep her steam up and could not pursue the enemy. Concerned that the torpedo boat came 100 miles beyond Confederate lines, made a successful attack, and escaped without harm, a number of army and navy expeditions searched for her. Landing numerous boat crews in and around the small creeks in the immediate vicinity of Hampton Roads, the navy made an extensive search but found nothing.[34]

The situation in the eastern theater changed drastically during the spring of 1864. In March, President Lincoln, in the presence of his cabinet, commissioned Ulysses S. Grant a lieutenant general. Having achieved success in the western theater, he took command of all the Union forces and quickly directed the Army of the Potomac to move toward Richmond.

Rear Admiral Lee requested that the department send him light-draft monitors so that he could cooperate in this move against the Confederate capital. The two ironclads in the squadron, *Roanoke* and *Atlanta*, were not suitable to ascend the James. The former drew too much water to go out of sight of Newport News, and the latter was not able to go "within sight of City Point." The remaining gunboats would also be limited in their movement because of their deep drafts.[35]

In early April, Major General Benjamin Butler conferred with Grant about participating in the upcoming campaign. Butler, by 1864, had become the most controversial of all the Union generals during the war. He served as military governor of Louisiana and in 1863 was given command of two corps, called the Army of the James, and used Fort Monroe as his headquarters. Everywhere the general went, he seemed only to complicate matters rather than to improve them.

Phillips Lee, like many of Butler's contemporaries, found him pompous and egotistical. The general also had made Lee's job more difficult by his being tied to speculating schemes in North Carolina. The relationship was strained further in January, when Butler accused Lieutenant Commander John H. Upshur of *Minnesota* of spreading word of a proposed combined army and navy operation. Butler wrote Lee that the "officers in the navy are more leaky than their own vessels" and demanded an investigation. A court of inquiry found Upshur innocent, but nevertheless the strain between the two men increased. Lee became somewhat paranoid of Butler's political connections and believed that the general sought to "get rid" of him. Lee handled Butler with courtesy and respect in his official correspondence, but in letters to his wife, he referred to Butler as a "gas bag" and called him "fatty of Lowell."[36]

Butler, the highest-ranking volunteer general, proposed to land troops at Bermuda Hundred, fortify the peninsula formed by the James and Appomattox rivers, and use this position as a base to attack Richmond from the south. A successful campaign by Butler from this direction would tie up General Robert E. Lee's forces and prevent reinforcements from reaching him. Phillips Lee realized that a movement up the James of this magnitude would require a sizable naval force to cover a landing, to protect the army's position, and to keep open communications. Lee believed he would need at least four ironclads, ten or twelve double-enders, and tugs and other vessels to support the army.[37]

On 4 May, General Grant moved the Army of the Potomac across the Rapidan River, ending its inactivity since Gettysburg. The Army of Northern Virginia blocked this movement with several bloody encounters in the wilderness near Fredericksburg. Meanwhile, Grant had approved Butler's plan, and on 5 May, seven wooden gunboats steamed up the James dragging for torpedoes. Five ironclads (four monitors and *Atlanta*), each towed by two vessels, followed the gunboats to Harrison's Bar, and the army transports and supply vessels brought up the rear. One of the participants wrote that this "motley array of . . . coasters and river steamers, ferry-boats and tugs, screw and side-wheel steamers, sloops, schooners, barges and canal-boats raced or crawled up the stream . . . in what seemed to be some grand national pageant." Butler eventually landed 39,000 troops and planned to drive toward Richmond, cut the Richmond to Petersburg railroad, and perhaps take Drewry's Bluff.[38]

The Confederate riverine forces remained in a defensive posture as the Union vessels neared Richmond. The main element of Confederate defense in the James River below the obstructions at Drewry's Bluff was the torpedo. Lee had proceeded cautiously, aware of the destructive potential of torpedoes. The damage that the ferryboat *Commodore Barney* had suffered when a 1,000-pound torpedo exploded near her bow in August 1863 was still fresh in his mind. The day following the army's debarkation at City Point, the ferryboat *Commodore Jones*, followed by the ex-ferryboat *Commodore Morris* and the double-ender *Mackinaw*, began dragging for torpedoes near Four Mile Creek. As they advanced up the river, a large electrically detonated torpedo exploded under *Commodore Jones*. The concussion lifted the gunboat out of the water, her wheels "revolving in mid air," completely destroying her, and killing forty men.[39]

On 7 May, while looking for more torpedoes, *Shawsheen* unknowingly approached six pieces of artillery and four companies of Confederate soldiers on a cliff at Turkey Bend. Effective artillery and musket fire from the shore quickly disabled the gunboat and drove the gun crews from their guns. The ship surrendered and was set afire and destroyed by the Confederates, with the loss of twenty-seven captured and an unknown number killed and missing in action.[40]

These successive losses only made Lee more cautious. On 14 May, the admiral transferred his flag to the more shallow drafted side-wheel steamer *Agawam* in order to personally oversee the removal of torpedoes. The Confederacy might have stopped the approaching Union vessels by using both the ironclads and torpedoes. The Confederate navy had recently added two more ironclads to the force in the James River, *Virginia II* and *Fredericksburg*, which made it a powerful force to reckon with. The Confederate ironclads could have prevented Lee from sending wooden vessels to drag for torpedoes. By doing so, the Union monitors might have taken the van to contend with the Confederate ironclads. The rebels would have then had a chance to sink the Union ironclads with torpedoes, the weapon to which they were most vulnerable. Phillips Lee realized the potential for this type of action and instructed the senior naval officer in the James, Captain Melancton Smith, that he should attack the enemy when they appeared without waiting for signals.[41]

The Union gunboats, though, continued clearing the James of torpedoes without any major harassment. Operating with Union troops, they dragged the river and put pickets ashore at night to warn against sudden attacks. Lee created a "torpedo and picket division" to prevent any further loss and assigned the three side-wheel steamers *Stepping Stones*, *Delaware*, and *Tritonia* to this division. As the gunboats moved up the river, they removed scores of torpedoes of various descriptions until they came under fire from Confederate batteries at Chaffin's Bluff.[42]

The Confederate navy meanwhile laid behind the obstructions at Drewry's Bluff in the upper James, which continued to limit their offensive capabilities. Mallory had requested that an opening be made as early as 2 January, but he could not persuade Secretary of War James A. Seddon to use the ironclads offensively. According to a clerk in the War Department, "Mr. Mallory's usual red face turned purple. He has not yet got out the ironclad Richmond, etc. which might have sunk Gen. Butler's transports."[43] On 23 May, the Confederates blasted a hole in the obstructions. This allowed the ironclads to move down the river to end mine-sweeping operations and compelled the Union ironclads to take the van. Flag Officer John K. Mitchell, who commanded the James River Squadron, immediately ordered his ships sent below the obstructions. The ironclad *Fredericksburg* passed through on the 23rd and *Virginia II* and *Richmond* on the following day.[44]

With the Confederate ironclads free, Mitchell and General Pierre Gustave Toutant Beauregard met to consider a joint movement against the Union forces. Mitchell prepared to attack at night using torpedoes, fire vessels, and his gunboats. After several delays, Beauregard withdrew his support for a combined attack, believing that Grant would move his army south of the James, which he eventually did.[45]

Meanwhile, Butler's troops moved beyond their landing site at Bermuda Hundred, and the squadron continued to convoy troops and protect them by engaging the enemy. Butler chose a good defensive position with water on three sides, which allowed the naval vessels to participate when needed. Butler was generally uncommunicative with

Lee and made a move toward Petersburg without discussing naval assistance. He extended his attack toward Drewry's Bluff on 16 May, but the rebels drove him back. Butler told Lee that this was merely a "feint" and never asked for cooperation. The press, however, blamed Lee and the navy for not cooperating.[46] Both of Butler's corps marched back to Bermuda Hundred, "the historic bottle, which was at once carefully corked by a Confederate earth work."[47]

While Butler remained captive behind his fortifications, the Confederates continued preparing defenses in an attempt to stop the advance of the Union navy. They built a battery at Howlett's Farm on the south bank of the James River to attack the Union ironclads if they advanced up the river. Battery Dantzler commanded the length of Trent's Reach and, by 25 June, mounted four guns with a fifth ready for mounting.[48]

The James remained relatively quiet while Grant's and Lee's armies fought in the Wilderness and at Cold Harbor. Grant's staggering losses undermined his determination to fight north of Richmond, so on 12 June, he boldly began moving his army south of the James over a pontoon bridge protected by the ironclad *Atlanta* and the little screw steamer *Pequot*.[49]

When Grant moved south of the river, he became dependent on City Point for supplies, and it became vital to his campaign that the Confederate ironclads not be given the chance to descend the river and destroy his base. Part of Butler's original plan included the use of obstructions to contain the Confederate vessels, torpedoes, and fire rafts in the upper James River. Although critical for the army, the obstructions, as Butler wrote to Lee, "would add to the security of his fleet." Before moving his army, Grant ordered the obstruction of the James River. Butler secured several hulks for sinking, and Lee offered to help with the obstructions with the understanding that it be an army operation. On 15 June, the army engineers sank the first hulks on the Trent's Reach Bar. Phillips Lee, from the beginning, was reluctant to sink obstructions and had written to Welles: "The Navy is not accustomed to putting down obstructions before it, and the act might be construed as implying an admission of superiority of resources on the part of the enemy." Lee also wanted a chance to fight the enemy ironclads, commenting that "myself and [my] officers desire the opportunity of encountering the enemy, and feel reluctant to discourage his approach."[50]

Lee's hunch was correct. On 23 June, the New York *Herald* contained a scathing attack on Lee. It called Lee "unfit for the important position he now occupies" and blamed the navy for sitting idle and having a "shamefully easy time" while the army took heavy losses. The *Herald* stated that the navy should steam to the wharves of Richmond and said about the obstructions: "if mere idleness were not enough, Admiral Lee has just performed an act that, we doubt not, has called an honorable blush to the cheek of every officer in his fleet. He has sunk boats in the river . . . to prevent the rebel rams from getting out at his ships." Finally the paper pointed out that if the ironclads were not invincible, then they were a failure and the government had wasted money in their construction.[51]

Any criticism of the navy was unfair. Tactically the balance of naval power in the James River was relatively equal. The Union had four monitors and *Atlanta* to counter the Confederates' three ironclads, but the narrowness of the river prohibited the Union navy from deploying its superior numbers. With obstructions in the river, Welles felt secure enough to order the monitor *Tecumseh* to be sent south. Her replacements, unarmed steam tugs, were to be fitted with 150-pound torpedoes. Lee planned to use the tugs to attack the Confederate ironclads, but instead of light-draft, low-pressure steam tugs, the department sent him deep-draft and noisy high-pressure vessels. Grant remained concerned about his City Point depot. He believed that two ironclads should always be in the river and thought it "imprudent to withdraw" ironclads, because their presence prevented the enemy from "taking the offensive."[52]

On 19 June, Flag Officer Mitchell allowed his ironclads to drop down the James to Trent's Reach, about 3,000 yards from the Union monitors, and anchor out of sight of the Union vessels. Within a few minutes, five shells, fired from a fifteen-inch gun, dropped within yards of the Confederate ironclads and slightly wounded two men. One Confederate officer claimed that this was "the most remarkable shooting I had ever seen or heard of."[53] The rebel officers believed that a signal tower that lay between them and the monitors directed the fire. Unable to respond, the Confederate vessels moved back up the river. In reality, the fire had not been so remarkable. The signal tower merely signaled the presence of the Confederate ironclads, while the guns had been fired to show some prominent individuals how they worked. By chance, the shots struck near the rebel ironclads.[54]

Two days later, the Union monitors discovered a new line of works with six embrasures but few mounted guns. *Tecumseh*, still in the James, began to fire into the works at 10:30 A.M. The monitors *Canonicus*, *Onondaga*, and *Saugus* later joined the action. Mitchell moved his squadron in position to open a cross fire on the Union vessels at 12:30. *Saugus* suffered some damage in the engagement—a few dented and fractured armor plates, and some broken and loosened bolts. The action demonstrated that the combined firepower of the Confederate batteries and ironclads would prevent wooden vessels from advancing as far as Trent's Reach.[55]

On 22 June, Gustavus Fox and General Grant made arrangements to add to the obstructions at Trent's Reach, so that two of the four James River monitors could be withdrawn to other theaters. The department purchased twelve canal boats and sank five in the reach in July. By September, the obstructions included torpedoes, five schooners, one bark, and eight canal boats, all connected by a series of booms, hawsers, and nets, the latter to keep floating torpedoes from drifting downstream. Lee had boxes built around the hatches of the hulks and kept a steam pump and a dredging vessel nearby. With these he could clear the channel in a matter of a few hours, should the monitors be ordered up the river. Also in July, the navy obstructed Turkey Creek and Four Mile Creek at their mouths by cutting down trees and planting stakes with logs in between them as a precaution against floating torpedoes.[56] While the obstructions were being placed in the river, Butler's stalled advance allowed the Confederates to position themselves between Grant and Petersburg, Virginia. Robert E. Lee's men entrenched themselves outside the city, and a long siege began.

During the first week of July, General Robert E. Lee sent Lieutenant General Jubal Early toward Washington, D.C., to threaten the capital. Lincoln, anxious to destroy Early's force, asked Grant to send reinforcements. Welles telegraphed Lee to send *Atlanta* and three or four gunboats to Washington. Lee perceived Early's movement as a major threat to Washington and personally took his flagship, *Malvern*, to the capital. Welles had ordered Lee to stay in Hampton Roads and sent Lee telegrams to keep him at his station, but Lee failed to receive any of these until he had arrived at the Navy Department with *Malvern*.[57] Five days later, Welles censured Lee for leaving his station and for "yielding to the panic that was created." Welles felt that Lee had "compromised the action and efficiency of the squadron."[58] Welles ended his diatribe by ordering Lee to visit Wilmington and the other points of his command.

Early's raid was the most action that either side had experienced for some time. During the summer of 1864, Grant had tried unsuccessfully to breech General Lee's defensive lines, while Butler remained "corked" in at Bermuda Hundred. Neither the Confederate nor Union vessels had done much as well, because neither could advance because of the obstructions. In July, Butler conceived the idea of excavating a channel through Farrar's Island at Dutch Gap. It seemed a simple proposition; the channel would only be 174 yards long, and he estimated that 4,000 men could complete it in ten days. Begun on 10 August, the gap was to be built to allow the Union ironclads to get above the powerful rebel batteries that commanded Trent's Reach. In Butler's words, "the dog could get at the fox and destroy him." Many observers in the Navy Department believed the whole idea was ridiculous. Butler never finished the canal during the war, and it served only to keep the Union soldiers occupied, while allowing the Confederate ironclads to practice their gunnery skills on the laborers.[59]

As the Union and Confederate forces maneuvered at Petersburg, the Navy Department began to plan an attack on Wilmington, North Carolina. These plans forced a change in squadron commanders. Rear Admiral David Dixon Porter came east from the Mississippi Squadron and replaced Lee in October 1864.

Porter immediately began to make changes for more effective river operations. He ordered the gunboat officers to put up splinter netting and had them place chains on their sides to protect them from shot. In addition, he ordered locomotive lanterns for the James River monitors to enable the lookouts to spot torpedoes. Porter also gave carte blanche to his commanders for gunnery practice. Porter thought they had a "great aversion" to firing their guns. He told his officers to "go ahead + try to kill somebody the Rebs are in easy range."[60]

Porter likewise made a significant personnel change by replacing Senior Officer Melancton Smith with Commander William A. Parker, who "never had the ram fever." Porter described Parker as "a sturdy old chap who looked as if he had been cut out of a big timber-head and was apparently bull dog all over."⁶¹ Porter, who was offensive-minded, apparently believed Parker would act aggressively without his guidance as he prepared for the capture of Fort Fisher, North Carolina.⁶²

The Confederates combined their offensive and defensive strategies by remaining above the obstructions, looking for an opportunity that might change the fortunes of the war. In January, this opportunity arose. Heavy rains in January caused a freshet that carried away part of the obstructions on the James River. In addition, Porter had taken most of the monitors to attack Fort Fisher, leaving only *Onondaga* on the James River. Mallory seized this occasion to order the ironclads down the James. Mallory hoped to defeat or to drive the Union vessels downstream, so that the ironclads could then cripple Grant's army by destroying his supply base at City Point. The loss of City Point might force Grant to abandon the siege of Petersburg. Mallory ordered Flag Officer Mitchell downstream on 16 January, but being overcautious, Mitchell stalled for a week. Just after dark on 23 January, a Confederate squadron consisting of the flagships *Virginia II*, *Richmond*, *Fredericksburg*, the gunboat *Drewry*, the torpedo boat *Torpedo,* and the torpedo launches *Scorpion*, *Hornet*, and *Wasp* finally moved toward the obstructions. *Fredericksburg*, having the lightest draft, got over the obstructions, but *Virginia* and *Richmond* grounded, causing a delay of the attack.⁶³

As soon as Mitchell's squadron came in sight, Parker took *Onondaga* downstream. He explained his actions later: "I moved the *Onondaga* below the pontoon bridge because I thought there would be more room to maneuver the vessel, and to avoid the batteries bearing on Dutch Gap. . . . I thought my chances of capturing the whole fleet would be increased by allowing them to come down the river to the bridge, where I intended to attack them."⁶⁴

This movement by the Confederate ironclads and the retreat by the Union monitor alarmed General Grant, who realized that if the Confederates could remove the obstructions at their leisure they could attack City Point. Grant, with Welles's consent, took matters into his own hands and began ordering gunboats up the James River, "the orders of any naval commander to the contrary notwithstanding."⁶⁵

In the darkness, with an ebbing tide, *Drewry* and *Scorpion* also grounded. The Union forts at Trent's Reach fired on the rebel gunboats during the night but did little or no damage. As daylight approached, Mitchell sent *Scorpion* downriver to recall *Fredericksburg* so that she

REAR ADMIRAL DAVID D. PORTER
(Courtesy the U.S. Naval Historical Center)

REAR ADMIRAL SAMUEL P. LEE
(Courtesy the U.S. Naval Historical Center)

REAR ADMIRAL LOUIS M. GOLDSBOROUGH
(Courtesy the U.S. Naval Historical Center)

could protect the grounded vessels. At 7:10, a shell exploded in *Drewry*'s magazine, "blowing her to pieces" and damaging *Scorpion*.[66]

The monitor *Onondaga* appeared on the scene at 10:30, just as the ironclads got free of the bottom. *Virginia II*, which up to this time had been struck seventy times by the guns of the forts with little effect, was struck twice by the fire from *Onondaga*. One of the solid shots fired by the monitor's fifteen-inch guns shattered the six-inch armor plate and damaged her inner woodwork, killing one and wounding two.[67]

After this confrontation, Mitchell recalled his squadron back up the James. The gunboat *Drewry* had been blown up, the torpedo launch *Scorpion* abandoned, and *Wasp* damaged. Mitchell now realized his ironclads could not withstand the fire of a fifteen-inch gun.[68]

At 9:00 that night, the Confederate squadron again moved down the James to make another attempt while the tide was still high. *Virginia II* led the others, but steam escaping from her damaged exhaust pipe and smokestack interfered with the pilot's vision and prevented him from steering the vessel. Mitchell called a council of war, and he called off the attack because of the damage done to *Virginia II* and the loss of the other two vessels.[69] At this point, the Union warships had not been reinforced, and had the Confederates attacked, they might have destroyed Grant's supply base at City Point.

Parker's move downstream could be partially justified. Had the ironclads and the torpedo vessels sunk *Onondaga*, there would have been little to prevent them from steaming on to City Point. Parker's major error was his delay in attacking the stranded ironclads on the morning of the 24th, when his fifteen-inch guns could have damaged the Confederate squadron irreparably.

Later that day, Welles removed Parker from command. The latter hoped that Porter would intercede and begged for forgiveness. "Only allow me one more chance to retrieve my reputation and your good opinion . . . one unfortunate mistake ought not to ruin the hopes of a lifetime."[70] Porter was livid and wrote Fox, "I don't care if they hang him." Porter answered Parker, "No man ever had a better chance than you had to make yourself known to the world. . . . The Department could pursue but one course in your case . . . and it must have been as mortifying to them as it was to me . . . to say nothing of the odium brought upon the navy."[71]

Mallory was also displeased with Mitchell's actions and ordered him relieved by Raphael Semmes. Semmes was promoted to rear admiral and confirmed by the Confederate Senate on 15 February 1865, the day he was given command of the James River Squadron.[72]

Caution was the watchword of Parker's replacement, William Radford, the new commander of the James River Division. Porter immediately strengthened the division by sending *Atlanta*, *New Ironsides*, and *Saugus* to join *Onondaga* in the James. Radford relied heavily on picket boats and spar torpedoes as his first line of defense near the obstructions. He instructed his tugs to run down the enemy, should they appear below the obstructions, and sent torpedo boats and cutters above the obstructions after dark to warn of an enemy advance.[73]

The Confederate ironclads never again tested the Union obstructions. Grant continued to stretch Lee's defensive lines, and on 2 April, General Robert E. Lee ordered the evacuation of Petersburg. The loss of Petersburg forced the abandonment of Richmond and sealed the fate of the ironclads. Semmes ordered the destruction of his squadron when he heard of Lee's orders, ending the existence of the major adversary of the United States Navy in the eastern theater.[74]

The Union navy had played an extremely important role in eastern Virginia and had been indispensable to the operations of the army. The navy kept communications open between the army and its supply bases, made the safe movement of troops possible, and, more importantly, made their weak positions strong. It also allowed the army to move with fewer restraints. Union control of the James River negated the Confederacy's advantage of interior lines. Without control of the James River, the Confederacy found it difficult to defend Richmond and Petersburg simultaneously, because the James River virtually ran between the two. The defense of Richmond would have been easier had the South controlled the river. Grant's entire campaign, once he shifted south of the James, depended on the navy, which protected his base at City Point. Without this base, Grant would have been forced to fight General Lee along entirely different lines. Both Grant and McClellan were able to advance on Richmond but never far beyond the support of the navy. Grant, however, used the navy and the river to his advantage and was ultimately successful in the capture of the Confederate capital.

FIVE

The enemy are . . . within the ring

Stalemate in North Carolina

By mid-1862, the strategic situation in North Carolina seemed a stark contrast to that of Virginia. Combined operations had allowed the Union forces to capture all the major towns that lay near the inland waters of the state. They faced no naval threat and only small numbers of the enemy. The army garrisoned the major towns, while the navy maintained control of the waters. On 10 May, the situation improved for the Union forces with the capture of Norfolk, Virginia, which relieved any possibility that a Confederate attack might be launched from this point to recapture any of the state.[1]

The Union positions in North Carolina were not as secure as one might imagine because of the geographic characteristics of the state. The Confederates not only had the advantage of interior lines, but each Union garrison also lay isolated from the others by water, poor roads, thick woods, and swampy, impassable terrain, which gave the Confederates ample opportunity to strike at each post without fear of quick support from one of the others. The role of the navy therefore was to act as the link between the towns and to give the army the support necessary to maintain

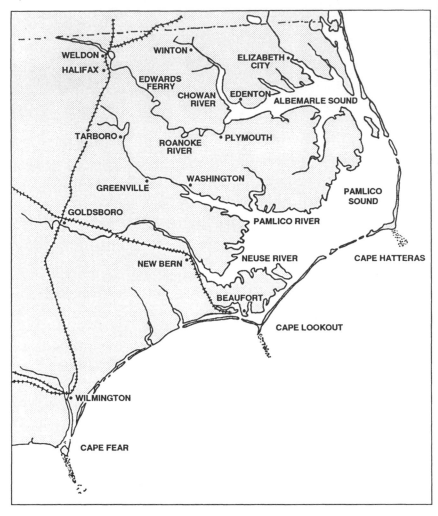

EASTERN NORTH CAROLINA

control of the area—a relationship that greatly increased the options of the army but limited those of the navy.

With the Peninsular campaign in motion, Goldsborough reduced the number of vessels in the sounds to support McClellan in Virginia. General Burnside complained of this reduction and claimed that if the gunboats remained absent, he would be forced to evacuate captured positions in the sounds. The gunboats were gradually reduced, leaving only seventeen vessels in the sounds at the end of May and a week later only thirteen.[2]

The War Department showed little concern by later withdrawing two divisions and then complaining that the navy had not done enough to protect the garrisons. Gustavus Fox, reacting to these complaints, wrote to Goldsborough, "I would not trouble myself much about what the other branch wishes in the sounds, providing you leave enough to protect them. Precious little thanks we ever get for saving them."[3]

Union leaders focused more on the Virginia theater and promoted Burnside to major general. Departing for Virginia in July to join the Army of the Potomac, he left Brigadier General John Foster in command at New Bern. Foster realized the army could only function in a defensive position and concentrated on strengthening his works. One of the soldiers commented that, with the troops, fortifications, and the gunboats, he felt safe, and that if "anybody comes here with any hostile intent, hell will begin to fill up pretty soon."[4]

While Foster strengthened his works, the navy began to probe existing Confederate defenses. On 9 July, Lieutenant Charles Flusser, commanding *Commodore Perry*, *Shawsheen*, and *Ceres* with a small number of infantry, advanced up the Roanoke River. The Confederates found that they could fire from the river's high bank because the Union vessels could not elevate their large guns to return the fire. The vessels arrived at Hamilton, a small town on the south bank of the river, about forty miles from its mouth. Here at Hamilton, Flusser had landed 100 soldiers and sailors with a field piece. The Confederates, having no strong force there, hastily deserted the town and left behind *Wilson*, a small steamer. Having no intention of holding Hamilton, the Union vessels, with *Wilson* in tow, returned to Plymouth without further harassment from the enemy.[5]

After a six weeks lull in the fighting and further withdrawals of Union troops, the Confederates became bold enough to attack. They first planned to attack Plymouth in early September but assailed Washington instead. Concealed by fog on the morning of 6 September, the rebels surprised the federal pickets and raced into the town, "giving vent to their exuberance of spirits in loud, continuous cheers and demonic yells."[6] The gunboats could not take any action early in the fight because their fire might hit friend and foe alike. As soon as the fog lifted, the screw steamer *Louisiana* and the army gunboat *Picket* opened fire, but shortly after their first shots, the magazine of *Picket* accidentally exploded, "tearing the boat to pieces" and killing the captain and nine-teen men.[7] *Louisiana* maintained her fire and "did excellent service" in driving the rebels from the streets. Union reinforcements later arrived and drove the rebels out of the town. The naval presence thus played an important role in stopping the Confederate's first bid to recapture one of the Union posts.[8]

Later that month, Major General John Dix, commander of the 7th Army Corps, sent a dispatch to Lieutenant Commander Flusser re-questing cooperation in an attack on Franklin, Virginia, just across the border of North Carolina. Dix planned to move toward Franklin with 12,000 men to cut off the retreat of 7,000 rebels and to destroy a pontoon bridge over the river. On 2 October, the two ferryboats *Commodore Perry* and *Hunchback* and the steamer *Whitehead* steamed up the Chowan and then into the Blackwater River, anchoring about three miles below Franklin.[9]

At 5:45 the next morning, the vessels got under way, shelling the banks as they went. The twisting channels of the narrow river slowed their progress. High banks concealed Confederate troops. Lieutenant Commander Charles Flusser led the way in *Commodore Perry*, followed at some distance by *Hunchback* and *Whitehead*. At 7:00, as *Commodore Perry*'s men ran a line out to swing around a bend, less than a mile from Franklin, the enemy attacked. The Confederate infantry was too close and too high on the banks for the naval guns to be effective, and the crewmen were ordered to take cover below. Attempting to escape Con-federate fire by running up the river, *Commodore Perry* first ran onto the bank and then, after getting off, rounded the bend, only to find the river barricaded by felled trees.[10]

Thwarted, the vessels remained three hours, waiting for the Union forces to arrive. In a stream of bullets, Lieutenant William Barker Cushing, just a month short of his twentieth birthday, ran a field piece out on the deck of *Commodore Perry* in an attempt to drive off the Confederate sharpshooters. Lieutenant Commander Flusser said that "Cushing behaved like a gallant boy. I had frequently to oblige him to seek shelter from the enemy's fire." At 10:30, the gunboats retired downstream, and for four more hours, the enemy poured volley after volley on their decks. Farther down the river, the gunboats came upon another barricade of fallen trees placed across the river to trap them, but they managed to force their way through to safety.[11]

The army did not arrive until 1:00 P.M. General Dix had changed his plans, but the steamer that was to have notified the navy was a day late with the message. Dix later wrote to Lee that his men had heard the firing from fifteen miles' distance, meaning that they had not even come close to Franklin. Dix claimed the "greatly superior numbers" of the enemy kept his men "at bay during the entire day, waiting for the gunboats." Yet the army's light casualties—two men killed, five wounded, and one missing—indicate that it actually did little fighting. By contrast, the gunboats suffered casualties of four killed and fifteen wounded before being able to retire downstream.[12]

The senior officer in the sounds, Commander Henry K. Davenport, opposed these expeditions. Rear Admiral Lee agreed that the gunboats were unfit for service "in these narrow and crooked rivers" without the support of the army. Lee maintained that in places where the gunboats could not defend themselves, they could not assist the army.[13]

Despite Davenport's objections, the navy forces remained active throughout November. On the 9th, his forces made a reconnaissance up the Tar River to determine the depth of the water and the character of the area around Greenville. The mission, led by Second Assistant Engineer John L. Lay, consisted of the army transport steamer *North State*, a flatboat, and a launch. At 9:00 that morning, *North State* ran aground on a sandbar a mile from Greenville. Continuing in the flatboat and the launch, the Union tars were guided to the edge of town by Union sympathizers, or "buffaloes," who were verbally chastised as they entered the town. The seamen then entered Greenville under a flag of truce and received its surrender from the mayor. Soon afterward, however, shooting broke out, and in response, Lay had a howitzer brought up and fired several stands of grapeshot. Returning to the boats, Lay learned that the enemy had killed one of his men, and in retaliation, he burned the bridge over the Tar River because the rebels "had disregarded a flag of truce."[14]

Two weeks later, in another river operation under Davenport's command, William Cushing steamed up the New River in the captured Confederate gunboat *Ellis*. His objective was "to sweep the river, capture any vessels there, capture the town of Jacksonville, or Onslow Court House, take the Wilmington mail, and destroy any salt works." After running five miles up the river, Cushing came upon a vessel loaded with cotton and turpentine, which the rebels had burned to

prevent its being captured. At 1:00 that afternoon, he reached Jacksonville and seized the public buildings, a large cache of mail, and the slaves
of the postmaster. After about an hour and a half, he steamed back down
the river with two schooners and shelled a rebel camp. Farther down, a
group of Confederate soldiers fired muskets at *Ellis*, but Cushing soon
drove them away with his guns. Darkness prevented further movement,
and *Ellis* remained that night in the river with the enemy's signal fires in
sight.[15]

At daylight, *Ellis* got under way and passed a battery of two guns on
a bluff. After an hour of firing, the Union gunboat forced the enemy
battery to withdraw and continued downstream. Farther downstream,
the pilot ran *Ellis* aground, and all attempts to lighten her failed. That
night, Cushing and his crew removed all they could from the ship. His
men took one of the schooners to safety, while Cushing remained
behind with six volunteers to fight the pivot gun. Early in the morning,
the rebels returned with more guns and began firing on the steamer
from four points, cutting it to pieces. No longer able to resist effectively,
Cushing and his men fired the vessel and climbed into a small boat.
Rowing down the river, Cushing and his men managed to keep ahead of
their Confederate pursuers; they reached the captured schooner and
sailed to Beaufort. The whole mission had not cost the Union a single
casualty.[16]

The episode, though, did demonstrate the vulnerability of the gunboats in the rivers and sounds of North Carolina, which became a matter
of increasing concern. Musketry and artillery fire effectively limited the
navy's performance and capabilities. Goldsborough had begun protecting naval vessels in the James River with boiler iron as a measure against
snipers.[17] Iron protection for gunboats in the sounds became mandatory,
because none of the ironclads then under construction could operate in
the sounds as a result of their deep draft, and specially designed shallow-
draft monitors were not due to be completed for some time.

Early protection for most of the vessels consisted of sandbags and
cotton bales, but these did not protect some of the vulnerable portions of
the ship nor the men well. While on the Mississippi, Rear Admiral
David Dixon Porter claimed that shells had easily deflected off his
tinclads. Rear Admiral Phillips Lee decided, shortly after taking command of the squadron, to plate his vessels in the sounds with three-

eighths-inch boiler iron and one-half-inch bar iron, but on a more extensive scale than Goldsborough had done.[18]

Lee was particularly interested in protecting the pilothouses, steam drums, machinery, and batteries of his vessels. It was difficult to protect all parts of the ships because of their construction, particularly those whose machinery lay above the decks.[19] Placing the boiler iron on the vessels compromised other qualities. The added weight increased their draft, caused a drop in speed, affected their compasses, and made the vessels less stable.

Lee instructed the chief of the Bureau of Construction and Repair, John Lenthall, to attempt placing iron plates on certain vessels without increasing their drafts—an almost impossible request. The steamer *Valley City* was to have her batteries, pilothouse, and engine room protected, along with part of the gun deck—a total of four and a half tons of iron. This weight was too much for some ships, but one alternative was to enlarge the existing vessel. The side-wheel tug *General Putnam*, slated to receive iron plates, was analyzed by the department to determine the effects of the added weight. Before the addition of any iron, the vessel's guards were not more than eighteen inches from the water, and it was estimated that the additional weight would make the vessel unsafe in a seaway. Engineers suggested the addition of eight to ten feet to the vessel's midsection to accommodate the weight of the iron. The department, however, did not consider the vessel worth the cost of the alterations, and it reduced the plating, leaving the crew and machinery less protected.[20]

The process of protecting the vessels was lengthy. Some went north to be fitted with the iron, while others received their protection in the sounds. The boiler iron brought to the sounds came in coal vessels in small amounts over a long period of time. The delays were caused by problems of purchasing and shipping the iron and the fact that the mills that rolled the "ordinary light or thin" iron had broken down trying to roll heavier plates for the monitors. But before the war's end, over 100,000 pounds of boiler iron arrived there.[21]

With the iron-plating program well under way, Rear Admiral Lee maintained that control of the sounds depended on having shallow-draft ironclads there, and it became more critical after the Confederates began building their own. Lee appealed to Fox to remedy this situation, but no shallow-draft ironclad was ever completed in time to be used in the sounds.[22]

The condition of the vessels also affected the performance of the navy in this region. Many had not been to a repair facility since they had come to the sounds for the Roanoke Island expedition, and constant use and abuse made them "lame ducks." Davenport used the worst of these gunboats as floating batteries and distributed them to different parts of the sounds in order not to weaken any one place. Lee wanted to increase the numbers of vessels there by taking some from Hampton Roads, but he hesitated, "lest Washington and Baltimore should be left open to a rebel raid by sea."[23]

During the winter of 1862, the Union and Confederate forces both became active again. In November, General Foster decided to advance on Hamilton with a small force supported by the navy. Working their way up the narrow, twisting river, *Valley City*, *Hunchback*, *Hetzel*, *Seymour*, and *Commodore Perry* and the army gunboat *Vidette* visited Hamilton in search of rebel gunboats. They found no gunboats being built but found evidence of an ironclad being built farther upriver. Foster sent an expedition toward Tarboro, accompanied by four naval howitzers and their crews. Meanwhile, *Valley City* and *Commodore Perry* steamed up the river to divert the enemy. Foster's expedition failed to reach Tarboro and returned to Hamilton to the safety of the gunboats.[24]

In December, the Confederates countered with an offensive move of their own. On the 10th, *Commodore Perry*, one of the two naval vessels stationed at Plymouth, left to operate on the Chowan River. The Confederate land forces took advantage of the gunboat's absence to strike the town. Shortly before 5:00 A.M., the rebels attacked in force, surprised the Union sentinels, and drove the Union soldiers back into the town. Acting Volunteer Lieutenant Charles F. Behm had his men beat to quarters and trained *Southfield*'s port guns on the town. The Union forces, meanwhile, withdrew to a defensive position near the custom house. The seamen could not fire without hitting the Union infantry, so Behm had the anchor hove up, and the double-ender ferryboat stood up the river and returned the fire of the enemy howitzers. The enemy battery began firing on *Southfield*, and the third shot went through the steam chest of the side-wheel ferryboat. This shot not only disabled the engine but also made it impossible to get to the magazine because of escaping steam. Behm ordered the boats lowered so that the vessel could be towed downstream. On the way down the river, *Southfield* met *Commodore Perry*, which had returned after hearing the gunfire. *Commodore Perry* towed *Southfield* back to Plymouth, where they found army headquarters and half of the town burned and no enemy in sight.[25]

The next day, General Foster marched out of New Bern with 10,000 infantry, 640 cavalry, and 40 guns. His objective was to destroy the railroad bridge over the Neuse River at Goldsboro, a movement planned to coincide with General Burnside's advance on Fredericksburg. If he was successful, a move on Wilmington would be possible (see chapter thirteen). The navy played a large role in the expedition by sending four vessels with Foster and supplying the officers and crews for five army transports.[26]

Low water in the Neuse River prevented the vessels from proceeding up the river as far as planned. They were, however, important in supporting the army and taking off the wounded during the campaign. Foster fought at Kinston on the 14th and at Whitehall on the 16th, where his men damaged the ironclad gunboat *Neuse* with artillery fire. On the 17th, the army fought its way to the Wilmington and Weldon Railroad bridge over the Neuse River near Goldsboro and burned it. The damage was slight, and the Confederates built a temporary structure over the Neuse in a couple of days. But it did interrupt major rail traffic for three weeks.[27]

The raid into the interior of the state accomplished little. The Union troops had moved with relatively little resistance through the state, which led many to believe that nothing could go wrong. Shortly after the expedition, Alexander Murray, the senior officer in the sounds, remarked: "Everything appears to be secure now in the sounds."[28]

After Robert E. Lee's victory at Fredericksburg, he sent Lieutenant General James Longstreet and two divisions south of the James River. Longstreet was to prevent federal forces from moving toward Richmond from the south. In February, Longstreet replaced Major General Gustavus W. Smith as commander of the Department of Virginia and North Carolina, and Major General Daniel Harvey Hill took command of the troops in North Carolina. Longstreet had no intentions of being idle and planned to press the federal troops rather than "lying still to await the enemy . . . before he moves upon us."[29]

The situation in the state changed drastically for the Union after the

Goldsboro expedition. The Navy and Army departments planned a joint move on Wilmington, which was canceled. The army had sent about 12,000 men to North Carolina to operate with Major General Foster, but they had hardly disembarked when orders arrived sending two divisions and a brigade of artillery to Port Royal, South Carolina, to operate against Charleston.[30]

The transfer of these troops played into the hands of the Confederate leaders. They were concerned about the fertile eastern counties of North Carolina and particularly those east of the Chowan River, which were important in providing much of the sustenance of Lee's army. To protect lines of supply and to gather the produce that lay within Union military lines, the Confederate army planned to make advances on Union garrisons and push their lines inward while the supplies were removed and transported north. The Confederates planned diversionary attacks on New Bern and Washington, North Carolina, and on Suffolk, Virginia.[31]

The operation in North Carolina began late on 13 March 1863, almost a year to the day after the fall of New Bern. The rebels gathered on the outskirts of the city and drove in the Union pickets. Early the next morning, rebel batteries began firing on Fort Anderson, an unfinished earthwork fortification on the north bank of the Neuse River across from New Bern. The 518-ton ferryboat *Hunchback*, which lay aground at the time, and an armed schooner immediately returned the fire. After a heavy cannonade, Brigadier General John Pettigrew asked for the surrender of the Union fort. The fort's commander, Lieutenant Colonel Hiram Anderson, delayed his answer, which provided an opportunity for the gunboats to get into position to support the fort. Before receiving a reply, the side-wheel steamer *Hetzel* and the tug *Shawsheen* arrived, both being towed into battle because they needed repairs. The revenue cutter *Agassiz* and the side-wheel steam tug *Ceres* also arrived shortly thereafter. When all the naval vessels had assembled, they gave the fort's defenders the firepower advantage and outranged Pettigrew's artillery, making his positions tenuous. Therefore, the Confederate forces had to withdraw without storming the fort. Pettigrew's failure to take the fort without delay was a tactical blunder that cost him the fort and possibly the town.[32]

The presence of the gunboats had saved Fort Anderson from surrender. Colonel Johnathan S. Belknap, who sent men to relieve the fort, wrote to Davenport: "Your well-directed fire drove the enemy from the field; covered the landing of the Eighty-fifth New York, sent to the relief of the garrison, and the repulse of the rebel army was complete." He followed with an accolade the navy rarely received from the army: "Allow me, Commodore, in the name of the officers and men of my command, to express my admiration of the promptitude and skill displayed by your command on that occasion. The Army is proud of the Navy."[33]

This praise only concealed the real relationship between the services. Four days before New Bern was attacked, General Foster had drawn away the gunboats by requesting naval assistance in the Pamlico Sound at Hyde County, over sixty miles from New Bern. Before the attack, Foster told Senior Officer Alexander Murray that his reconnaissance showed no enemy in the New Bern area. Writing shortly afterward to Lieutenant Commander Charles Flusser, Murray commented: "Genl. Foster is really ignorant about GunBoat matters, that I must request you to give only respectful consideration to his suggestions, but by no means to permit them to conflict with your judgment." Murray added: "He is a very good fellow for land engineering, but I regret he should carry his ambition so far as to aspire to Naval renown." Davenport had the following comment: "Murray is right. The Navy is perfectly disgusted with the Army movement. . . . Foster has neither discretion or judgment. Don't allow him to influence you. I would not give you plain, practical, *common* sense for all the major Genl's in the Army."[34]

After the Confederates failed to take New Bern, Hill turned his attention to the small town of Washington. The rebels did not undertake this without considering the advantages that the Union gunboats gave to the town's defenders. Even though Union forces on the peninsula formed by the Roanoke and Pamlico rivers were weak, the gunboats could land reinforcements and cut off supply trains, and thus a sufficient force would have to be committed for this operation. Robert E. Lee realized that Union positions in the state were mainly defensive in nature and that "if driven from them they easily escape to their gunboats." Lee then added: "Unless therefore they will come out into the country I do not know how you can advantageously get at them."[35]

General Hill moved his force of 9,000 men on the north and south banks of the Pamlico River, cutting off any prospect of reinforcement by land from New Bern and on 30 March laid the town under a siege that would last over two weeks. Major General Foster, learning of the impending Confederate attack, boarded a steamer and hurried from New Bern to direct the Union defense and joined the garrison of 1,200 men one day before the siege commenced. Supporting the troops and defending the town were the naval vessels *Louisiana* and *Commodore Hull*. To prevent further reinforcements from reaching the town, Hill placed artillery on Rodman's and Hill's points on the southern bank and at Swan Point on the northern bank of the Tar. The guns at Hill's Point, fifty to seventy feet above the water, overlooked obstructions and guarded a very narrow passage. Reinforcements or supplies had to run the gauntlet of the batteries and obstructions, which virtually cut off Union communication.[36]

The vessels above the batteries, *Louisiana* and *Commodore Hull*, played an important role; they protected the bridge crossing the Tar River and exchanged fire with the Confederate positions on 30 and 31 March. Davenport rushed other vessels from Plymouth and New Bern to Washington, but they remained below the obstructions and batteries, about five miles below the town. A critical situation developed on the third day of the siege when a strong wind lowered the water in the river. Acting Master William G. Saltonstall ran *Commodore Hull* aground while changing her position, and both vessels had nearly exhausted their ammunition after the previous two days' fight. The men were piped below to protect them from enemy fire, to which they responded only occasionally, while maintaining a reserve to keep the enemy from crossing the bridge. The only thing that prevented the Confederates from destroying the gunboats was that they were out of ammunition on the first day of the siege and received further supplies in "driblets."[37]

The Union vessels protecting the town lay in the river at the mercy of the Confederate guns and used small boats to run the blockade for ammunition, which enabled them to continue the fight. On 3 April, a new battery opened up on the vessels protecting Washington, and after firing only five shots, the gunboats "knocked . . . [the enemy's] batery [*sic*] into a cocked hat and they left on the double quick."[38]

The situation began to look less hopeless the next day, when *Ceres* ran the blockade, bringing ammunition and extra firepower for the two gunboats in Washington. The navy continued to protect the town and to harass the Confederate batteries, while the naval force below continued to lie in the river and shell Hill's Point. One of the Union vessels even had a calliope, which added a certain flair to their presence. One Confederate remarked: "Every day after dinner they would play it for a while and then shell our position for an hour or two. They never did any real harm; it was almost as if it were done for an evening's entertainment."[39]

Meanwhile, the Union army made several efforts to relieve the town and garrison. The first, under the command of Brigadier General Henry Prince, arrived off Hill's Point with 2,500 men, but Prince decided it too risky to take the batteries. A second expedition under Brigadier General Francis B. Spinola also failed to break through the attackers. The Union garrison began to feel the effects of the siege by being put on short rations. One soldier commented, "We have come down to very small rations . . . of pork and bread, and no beef; and limited to half a dipper of coffee at a meal."[40] Pettigrew became concerned that the gunboats might pass up the river and asked Hill for "all the movable rifle artillery or rather 'anti-gunboat,' that I can get." On 13 April, however, the side-wheel steamer *Escort* virtually nullified the siege by running past the batteries on Hill's Point with supplies and reinforcements. The steamer's second trip through on the 14th convinced Hill of the uselessness of the attack, and he withdrew.[41]

The investment of Washington was a mild success for the Confederacy and a victory for the North. While both sides continued their artillery duel, Hill accomplished his goals of removing large amounts of commissary supplies. But Hill had shown little resourcefulness and made no strong effort to take the town. The resources of Foster's command had been stretched to the limit, and he had considered the evacuation of Plymouth in order to reinforce and hold Washington. The outnumbered Union forces had prevented the town's capture, again with crucial help from the navy. Davenport commented to Gustavus Fox shortly after the siege that "if the Army is managed every where as it is here I do not anticipate great results."[42]

In addition to the problems that arose from the relationship with the army, one of the constant sources of difficulty for the senior officer in the sounds was the quality of the vessels he commanded. In the scheme of the squadron organization, the sounds command retained vessels of the

lowest quality. There were several reasons for this. Many of the gunboats were ex-merchantmen converted for naval use and stationed in the
sounds because of their shallow draft. Furthermore, the gunboats in the
sounds did not go for repairs as often as those on the blockade and could
remain anchored at their stations. They usually remained out of the
range of the enemy's guns, they were not threatened as much by the
weather, and they could be towed into action or out of danger by a
consort. For example, both the *Hetzel* and *Shawsheen* had to be towed
into action at New Bern. Increasingly these vessels became more unsuitable for military use because of a lack of repairs.[43]

Before the attacks on New Bern and Washington, eight of fourteen
gunboats in the sounds needed repairs. Many were almost useless but
could not be sent north because of the repeated Confederate attacks.
Makeshift repairs kept them serviceable and enabled them to stay at
their stations, which kept the naval force as strong as possible under the
circumstances. The double-ender *Miami* serves as a good example. She
had a good battery, but her draft kept her from serving as needed. Her
engines were completely worn out, and she could hardly move. Her
commanding officer, Acting Lieutenant Robert Townsend, complained
that she was constructed with unseasoned wood and leaked badly because her timbers were "shrunk by the southern sun, shaken by the
frequent discharges of her heavy guns, and strained by repeated contact
with the bottom or the shore."[44]

The army's policy of occupying a great number of posts further
complicated the navy's task of protecting the towns. Phillips Lee was
seriously concerned about the army's dependence on naval aid, and
shortly after taking command of the squadron, he questioned the army's
policy of holding so many posts in the sounds of North Carolina. After
the raid on New Bern and the siege of Washington, Lee again brought
up this matter. He believed that the Union forces held too many points
with too few men. He recommended the abandonment of the towns of
questionable importance and the leveling of existing defenses. He
pointed out several towns that the army did not occupy and that held no
advantage to the enemy.[45]

The navy first occupied Washington and Plymouth and guarded the
towns by lying in the rivers. Later the army posted a company in each
town to act as a picket guard for the gunboats. Eventually the army
increased the guards until the towns became permanent army posts.

Foster defended the army's strategic policy. He felt that he could not abandon any of the posts, arguing that his troops kept the enemy from using the towns as arsenals and shipyards and that his possession gave the gunboats control of the river. He added that the towns provided excellent landing places for offensive operations and enabled the army to retain control of fertile areas, which otherwise the Confederates could use to their advantage.[46] Gunboats with a picket guard, however, could have accomplished similar goals. A policy of fewer and smaller garrisons would have freed a large number of Foster's men and relieved the navy from protecting them. Control of the water allowed the army to land virtually anywhere in the sounds or rivers to destroy anything the rebels might use to their advantage. The War Department was determined to hold its positions, the cohesiveness of which was made possible only with naval support. After the initial capture of the coastal towns, the army remained virtually inert and confined naval activity. Some of Lee's contemporaries interpreted this as inactivity and blamed him for merely keeping the status quo in the sounds.

After Hill's two military operations, his forces withdrew to participate in the Gettysburg campaign, crippling any plans of further attacks on the Union-held towns. The Union forces likewise made no important military moves until 1864, except for several raids on the Wilmington and Weldon Railroad. In late July 1863, three gunboats accompanied an army expedition to put the railroad out of operation. While the Union cavalry made an unsuccessful attempt to destroy the Wilmington and Weldon Railroad bridge over the Roanoke River at Weldon, Flusser burned a bridge over the Meherrin River to prevent the enemy from bringing troops from Franklin, Virginia.[47]

With a pause in the fighting, Flag Officer Lee saw his chance to withdraw some of his squadron for much-needed repairs. To do so, he requested that the towns be better fortified, so that naval protection would be less essential. Foster complied, and in August, Lee withdrew five vessels (about one third); once these were repaired and returned to their stations, he withdrew six more.[48]

After Robert E. Lee's Gettysburg campaign, both the Union and Confederate armies settled down into winter quarters, but in North Carolina, plans were under way to strike at New Bern. General Lee wrote to Jefferson Davis, "The time is at hand when, if an attempt can be made to capture the enemy's forces at Newbern, it should be done. I can now spare troops for the purpose, which will not be the case as spring approaches." General Lee felt that the Union garrisons would not be ready for an attack and that a "bold party" could capture Union gunboats and surprise the town. Davis approved the plan and even suggested that Lee command the expedition.[49]

The New Bern operation called for boldness. General Lee declined to lead the attack, so the Confederate high command chose Major General George E. Pickett for the task. Pickett, the commander of the Department of Virginia and North Carolina, prepared to strike and capture New Bern with 13,000 men in a three-pronged assault. The most daring part of the operation was assigned to the Confederate naval force, led by Commander John Taylor Wood. A fellow officer described Wood as a "fine-appearing man, with a commanding presence, every inch a sailor, and an accomplished officer. . . . His hair and eyes were dark, complexion swarthy, with a muscular frame, possessing, in fact, a physique far above the average allotted to man."[50] He planned to capture a Union gunboat, to get the vessel under way, and then to cruise after another on the night before the Confederate infantry attack. He could then operate with them against the city on the following day. Bringing boats from as far away as the James River by rail, Wood assembled his motley group of fourteen cutters, surfboats, and launches above New Bern on 31 January 1864.[51]

Wood and his men made their preparations on the night of 1 February, but darkness and fog prevented them from locating a Union vessel. During the next day, the 300 Confederate officers and men hid in Bachelor's Creek and located the ship they planned to capture: *Underwriter*, a 341-ton side-wheel steamer with two eight-inch shell guns and a twelve-pound howitzer.[52]

The next night, *Underwriter* lay moored at a wharf in the Neuse River, under the guns of a shore battery and of forts Anderson and Stevenson, with her steam low and her fires banked. The Confederate boats stealthily approached, and the watch on the ship did not see them until they were within 100 yards of the steamer. *Underwriter*'s men did not immediately challenge the rebel boats because several of the ship's boats had not returned from an expedition and they mistook them for Union tars. As Wood and his men converged on the gunboat, the men on watch challenged the boats, and when no answer followed, they sprang the alarm rattle. The watch detail directed small-arms fire toward the approaching rebels as Wood shouted, "Give way, boys." All the Confederates echoed Wood's cry and pulled quickly toward *Underwriter*. They boarded her without much difficulty because the boarding netting was down, and the ship's larger guns could not be depressed enough to fire on the approaching enemy. Lieutenant Benjamin P. Loyall reached the deck first, with Wood right behind him.[53]

A short bloody struggle with cutlasses and pistols ensued, but the Confederates quickly subdued the outnumbered crew of the steam gunboat. The noise of the battle aroused the garrison in Fort Stevenson, which began to fire on the Union vessel. Other batteries nearby also fired on the gunboat as Wood attempted to get steam up. The banked fires prevented him from turning the engine over, and the heavy fire from shore made it necessary for him to set fire to his prize. Wood and his men captured nearly half *Underwriter*'s crew, but lost a number of them on the way back up the river.[54]

Had Wood been successful, Pickett's attack on New Bern might have succeeded. Davenport, the senior officer in the sounds, sent all the force he could spare to New Bern to protect the town. *Miami*, *Southfield*, and *Whitehead* arrived on 4 February. Pickett's coordinated attack on New Bern never developed. Commander Wood's unsuccessful mission alerted the army and failed to neutralize the naval force, so Pickett abandoned the operation because he believed that control of the water was essential for success.[55] Although the navy had been embarrassed, the safety and defense of the Union positions had depended on the advantages a strong navy gave to the defenders of the town.

While the Confederate army periodically attempted to reconquer lost territory, the Confederate Navy Department remained active, building ironclad gunboats to contest the waterways of the state. During the fall of 1862, the government made contracts with two firms to build armored vessels for the sounds. The firm of Howard and Ellis of New Bern built one at Whitehall on the Neuse River, and the firm of Martin and Elliott began building two—one at Edward's Ferry on the Roanoke and a second one on the Tar River at Tarboro. The vessel being built at Tarboro had to be destroyed before completion, but two ironclads were still under construction when Pickett advanced on New Bern. General Robert E. Lee was anxious for their completion and maintained an interest in their progress because he contemplated coordinated movements on both New Bern and Plymouth.[56]

In the spring of 1863, the Confederates laid down the keel of the ironclad *Albemarle* at Edward's Ferry on the Roanoke River above Plymouth. Constructed in a cornfield, her iron plates were shipped from Richmond, and the shafting for the machinery came from the naval foundry at Charlotte, North Carolina. Once completed, *Albemarle* measured 152 feet long and 45 feet at her extreme width, had a draft of 8 feet, and had two engines, each with 200 horsepower. Her builders laid two layers of iron plating perpendicular to one another and fastened them over a backing of sixteen inches of wood. Her offensive weapons included an eighteen-foot iron-sheathed prow and two rifled Brooke guns, each gun pivoted through three ports to make her a formidable vessel of war. In November 1862, the Confederates laid down the ironclad *Neuse* eighteen miles southeast of Goldsboro, at Whitehall on the Neuse River. Designed by John L. Porter, *Neuse* was of the same class and similar dimensions.[57]

Aware of the threat posed by these ironclads, the Union Navy Department signed contracts for twenty light-draft monitors. Lee saw the need for the monitors shortly after taking command of the squadron and wrote to Fox that "our supremacy in the sounds of N.C. can, I apprehend, only be maintained by ironclads adapted to the navigation there."[58] As the war progressed and the Confederate ironclads neared completion, the ex-merchantmen, with their thin iron plating and machinery and boilers above the waterline, quickly became obsolete.

The navy signed contracts for light-draft monitors in the spring of 1863 and planned for them to be completed that fall. The builders projected their draft to be six feet, four inches to enable them to go into the sounds. They were designed to have single turrets and armor eight inches thick and to mount two eleven-inch guns. The Navy Department placed Chief Engineer Alban C. Stimers in charge of the building program, and he altered the plans, which caused numerous problems. *Chimo*, the first vessel launched, instead of having fifteen inches of freeboard, had only three, and this without a turret or stores.

The Union commanders in the sounds knew that the Confederates would soon have their armorclads ready and, with good reconnaissance and excellent intelligence, knew their specifications.[59] Completion of an ironclad would give the Confederates a good opportunity to attack one of the river towns, because an ironclad could flank Union positions along the rivers, which could jeopardize Union possession of all the towns in the region. Welles, Lee, and the Navy Department were aware of this problem, but their options were few because of the delays in the Union ironclad building program. Furthermore, the army did not take the threat seriously and refused to help destroy the ironclads as they were being built.

Lee wrote to Fox only six weeks after taking command, "can't we have some ironclads built quickly to suit the sounds?"[60] An inadequate military force, unsuitable naval vessels, noncooperation between the army and navy, and lack of a coordinated comprehensive strategy all combined to nullify any advantages the Union had in destroying the rebel armorclads before they were finished. Without shallow-draft ironclads, the navy went on the defensive.

Crippled vessels and much improvisation were mustered to neutralize the threat of *Neuse* and *Albemarle*. As an example, the army mounted a 200-pound Parrott rifle at Plymouth to stop the ironclad, hardly enough firepower to do the job. Butler wrote to Major General Peck that he believed that Plymouth was as "safe as Fortress Monroe, provided you keep from being surprised," and concluded that he would "be very much surprised" if the 200-pound Parrott gun could not keep the ironclad at bay. Obstructions became the main naval defense against the ironclads. The navy obstructed the Roanoke River with sunken hulks filled with stone and added iron-capped piles that slanted upstream to secure the hulks to the bottom. As *Albemarle* neared completion, the naval forces feverishly laid down more pilings and hulks with torpedoes attached to them. The Neuse River likewise became filled with hulks and piles placed there by both Union and Confederate engineers, each fearing the other's vessels.[61]

All this naval activity did not convince the army of the seriousness of the threat of ironclads, particularly the commander of the Department of Virginia and North Carolina, Major General Benjamin Butler. Since assuming command of the department in November 1863, he had done virtually nothing to neutralize the threat of the ironclads. Foster had the manpower to carry out an expedition to destroy either of the rams, as evidenced by the raids on the Wilmington and Weldon Railroad. S. P. Lee and the Navy Department urged the War Department numerous times to destroy the ironclads. The army in North Carolina, though, normally only advanced inland with an escort of gunboats. The rams' construction sites lay far enough upstream in shallow water, which made it too dangerous for naval support, so the army would not budge. Butler believed that hulks were not necessary in the rivers and that pilings would do the job. He even commented to Lee, "I do not much believe in the ram, either in the Roanoke or the Neuse." Thus no army cooperation to attack the vessels was forthcoming, and Butler in fact withdrew troops from the area.[62]

While the Union leadership responded with inactivity, the Confederates began planning a joint attack on New Bern and Plymouth using the two rams in an effort to rid the eastern part of the state of Union forces. Both the local Union naval and army officers knew of the Confederate intentions, but they could not convince the War Department to arrange for a major expedition. Also, none of the local Union commanders showed any desire or initiative to plan an expedition, even though Butler had suggested that General Peck consider this option. Delays in construction of *Neuse* pushed the Confederate operation further back, and *Neuse* could not be made ready for a combined attack with the *Albemarle* until April 1864.[63]

With a reorganized command structure, four brigades, and some artillery and cavalry, the Confederate War Department gave Brigadier General Robert F. Hoke orders to move on Plymouth. Hoke met with Commander James W. Cooke of the ironclad *Albemarle*, to get his assurance that she could participate with the ground forces. Cooke had a reputation for fearlessness—Gilbert Elliott, the builder of the ironclad, claimed that Cooke "would fight a powder magazine with a coal of fire."[64]

Hoke deployed his men around Plymouth on 17 April, and skirmishes began late that afternoon. Hoke reorganized his men into three brigades numbering about 7,000 men, while Union Brigadier General Henry W. Wessels had nearly 3,000 men stationed among his numerous earthworks and forts.[65] Commander Charles W. Flusser with a flotilla of four vessels—*Miami*, *Southfield*, *Ceres*, and *Whitehead*—positioned his gunboats in the river to aid in the defense of the town.

On the morning of 18 April, Cooke left Hamilton to cooperate with Hoke. A recent freshet made it necessary for *Albemarle* to proceed down the river, stern foremost with chains dragging from her bow, because the swift current made it impractical to steer her bow-first. Delayed several times by breakdowns, she anchored three miles above Plymouth on the evening of the 18th. Cooke's major concern was getting his ironclad over the obstructions placed in the channel. A party of men led by Gilbert Elliott examined the obstructions and found that the freshet had raised the water level enough to allow the ironclad to pass over them. On the morning of the 19th, *Albemarle* steamed past the obstructions and Fort Gray, which overlooked the river. The 200-pound Parrott rifle placed there to stop the ironclad fired a few shots, striking her several times with as much effect as "pebbles thrown against an empty barrel," and she continued downstream.[66]

The man responsible for stopping the ironclad, Charles Flusser, was the senior officer at Plymouth. Flusser, "a little below medium height, sparsely built, of light complexion, bronzed from exposure, . . . [had] a long tawny moustache, the ends of which he sometimes unconsciously pulled while talking."[67] Flusser's contemporaries considered him "courageous to a degree of foolhardiness." Anticipating a fight with the ironclad, Flusser had declined command of the frigate *Minnesota* or a vessel off Wilmington "while there existed a chance of a rebel iron-clad coming down the Roanoke."[68] He was about to get his chance.

Having learned of *Albemarle*'s approach, Flusser communicated to Lee, "I need no reinforcements, am confident of success." Flusser sent the lightly armored screw steamer *Whitehead* up the river to locate the ironclad, while he busied himself with repulsing the attacking Confederates in the town and readying the vessels for the armored enemy. Flusser fastened his two most powerfully armored vessels, the double-enders *Miami* and *Southfield*, together with chains and spars so that they could be handled as a single ship, in hopes of maneuvering *Albemarle* between them, where he could destroy her by pounding her plates in with his guns. He likewise planned to suspend a large torpedo on chains between these gunboats so that it could "crush in the deck, or stun all those below it—probably both." Flusser found that once he had lashed his gunboats together they could not effectively protect the Union positions ashore from Confederate infantry, so he separated them. But just before the ram appeared, he changed his mind and quickly refastened them with hawsers.[69]

The rebel ironclad, accompanied by the vessel *Cotton Plant* carrying

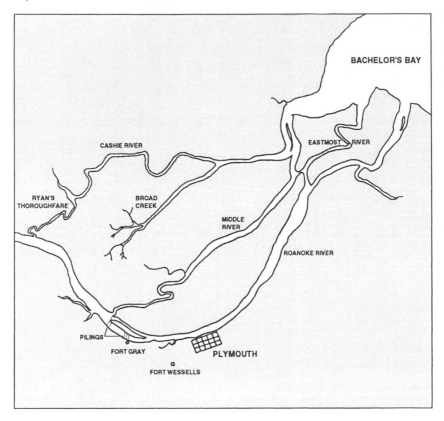

THE MOUTHS OF THE ROANOKE RIVER

sharpshooters, advanced toward the Union vessels along the southern shore of the 300-yard-wide river. Then the ram suddenly turned toward the middle of the stream with its throttle wide open. The Union vessels lashed together, being less maneuverable, became a target for the unwieldy Confederate ram, which struck *Miami* a glancing blow and then plowed into *Southfield*, parting the forward hawsers "like so much yarn."[70]

At contact, the two Union vessels opened fire on *Albemarle*, and the ram replied with her bow gun. Some of the Union guns had been used to shell Confederate positions earlier that day and not all had changed to solid shot to fight the ironclad. Flusser, who fired the first two shots, began to aim a third gun when the division officer warned him that a shell remained in that particular nine-inch Dahlgren gun. Flusser replied, "Never mind my lad we will give them this first and solid shot after." Having pulled the lanyard, he became an early casualty when the shell from his gun broke up on the ram's armor and ricocheted, killing him instantly. The Union vessels continued to fire at *Albemarle* with solid shot but with no effect as *Southfield* slowly sank. The sinking vessel momentarily trapped the ram of *Albemarle*, but when the gunboat settled on the bottom, she rolled away from the ironclad.[71]

The ineffectiveness of the Union guns and the sinking of *Southfield* gave the ironclad an overwhelming advantage. Acting Volunteer Lieutenant Charles A. French, the commander of *Southfield*, had the remaining hawsers cut. French took command of *Miami* after some of his officers and crew had escaped on board. He then withdrew *Miami*, lest she might also become a victim.[72]

By the end of the day, the Confederates had invested all the Union works around Plymouth, and *Albemarle* and *Cotton Plant* controlled the river and besieged the town. The rebel ironclad "added materially to the discomfort and danger of the Union troops with enfilading fire from its guns." On the 20th, the Confederates advanced against the Union left and penetrated the town. The remaining federal soldiers retreated into Fort Williams. General Hoke asked for its surrender to prevent the further loss that a protracted siege would invoke, but Brigadier General Henry Wessels refused. Within an hour, Hoke began firing into the Union positions from four directions, and at 10:00 A.M., a white flag rose over the works.[73]

The Union forces had had the tables turned on them by losing control of the river. The rivers of the state gave an advantage to the combatant that could control them. Until the attack on Plymouth, the Union navy had complete control of the water. The ironclad, once gaining control of the Roanoke River, placed the garrison at Plymouth in a vulnerable position. Furthermore, Confederate control of the water made it impossible for the Union gunboats to flank the rebel forces or to disrupt their interior lines of communication. The day Plymouth surrendered, an acquaintance of Flusser wrote that "the enemy are making good use of the advantage which they have always had of us in this struggle, that of being within the ring."[74]

The Navy Department, alarmed at the success of *Albemarle*, could do little about neutralizing its threat with the ironclads at hand. Gustavus Fox wanted to try to take *Tecumseh* into the sounds by lifting her over the shallow bars with camels. He asked John Ericsson if it could be done, but the next day he realized that by the time the camels could be made ready, the ram would have done all the damage she could do.[75]

The ram's appearance had been predicted three weeks before the town surrendered, and the Union leaders had done nothing. They had been aware of the weaknesses of their defenses but felt secure with naval support. The fortifications there, however, depended on naval superiority and were not built to withstand an attack without control of the water approaches. Butler had presumed that the navy could hold the river and blamed the navy for the loss of the town. Lee pointed out that the navy had nothing to do with the building of the fortifications and that Butler had shown no concern about the ram and had believed the fortifications and garrisons there to be sufficient. Upon receiving Butler's charges, Lee reminded Welles that he had suggested the abandonment of some of the army's posts in the sounds a year earlier, almost to the day.[76]

After the loss of Plymouth, the Union felt compelled to abandon Washington, North Carolina. On 24 April, General Grant wired Butler, "It will be much better to hold Newberne strongly, than to have little posts picked up in detail." Hoke laid siege to the town on 27 April, but the Union army had already made a decision to withdraw, and Hoke did not assail the works. The navy, of course, played an important role in the withdrawal by evacuating troops and stores and covering the departure.[77]

While Hoke patiently waited for the Union troops to withdraw, the federal soldiers and some sailors sacked the town. They broke in houses, shops, and sutlers' establishments and burned one-third of the town. "Gangs . . . patrolled the city, breaking into the houses and wantonly destroying such goods as they could not carry away." One Union officer claimed that the men were "guilty of an outrage against humanity, which brings the blush of shame to the cheek of every true man and soldier."[78]

Commander Henry Davenport, the senior naval officer in the sounds, anticipated Hoke's next move—an attack on New Bern. Hoke planned to offset the Union army's advantage of naval support by using *Albemarle* to help with the attack. The ram *Neuse*, also intended to participate in the attack, grounded on a sandbar in the Neuse River on

27 April, and after several attempts to free her, it became obvious that *Albemarle* would have to attack the town alone. General Pierre Gustave Toutant Beauregard, who just several days before had received command of the Department of North Carolina and Southern Virginia, thought that an attack using *Albemarle* "should meet with complete success."[79]

While the Confederates readied *Albemarle* for a move against New Bern, Lee replaced Henry Davenport with Captain Melancton Smith, who received instructions to keep the ram in the Roanoke River. Described by one of his fellow officers as a "spunky old gentleman," Smith had instructions to ram the ironclad in order to drive in her knuckle or to drive her ashore. Swift shallow-draft double-enders sent to Albemarle Sound were assigned this task. Lee also suggested that the gunboats try to get alongside the ram and pound in her armor with their heavy guns, hoping that the nuts and bolts on the inside would fly off like canister. The Navy Department, however, seemed to prefer ramming. Even Benjamin Butler became concerned enough to send three shallow-draft army gunboats to help run the ironclad down.[80]

The ironclad's appearance temporarily caused the officers watching her to forget their instructions. On the afternoon of 29 April, the Confederate ironclad steamed out of the Roanoke River into Albemarle Sound. The alarmed Union commanders withdrew to Roanoke Island, leaving the whereabouts of the ram unknown. *Albemarle* did not sortie far into the sound but threatened all communication with Norfolk via the canal system.[81]

While the Confederate attack on New Bern materialized, the Union forces prepared to land at Bermuda Hundred in Virginia for a strike toward Richmond. This development made it imperative that the Confederate forces attack and capture New Bern, so that the forces could move into southern Virginia to protect Richmond. Jefferson Davis wrote to Beauregard that the town must be taken by a "*coup de main* [or] the attempt must be abandoned."[82]

At 2:00 P.M. on 5 May, Captain Cooke in *Albemarle*, with the troop-laden *Cotton Plant* on one side and the captured steamer *Bombshell* on the other side, steamed into the sound to attempt a passage to New Bern. The Union vessels reacted quickly and stood up the sound in two columns, with the double-ender *Mattabesett* at the van of the lead column and another double-ender, *Miami*, at the head of the other. Captain Melancton Smith's force consisted of four double-enders and four smaller wooden steamers. Melancton Smith had instructed the commanders of the double-enders to attack the ironclad while the small steamers engaged the troop-laden launches expected to accompany the Confederate flotilla.[83]

At 4:40 P.M., as the two forces converged, *Albemarle* opened fire with her bow pivot on *Mattabesett*. The first shot destroyed a launch and wounded several men, and her second shot damaged the ship's rigging. *Albemarle* then attempted to ram the lead vessel but missed, while the Union gunboats following *Mattabesett* surrounded the ironclad and began pouring broadside after broadside onto her armor. *Bombshell*, hulled by several shots, surrendered after only five minutes, and *Cotton Plant* withdrew up the river.[84]

A melee ensued as the larger Union vessels maneuvered for a good position to ram the ironclad, while the smaller steamers fired at such a rapid rate that the larger ships could not approach her. While the Union gunboats continued to hammer the ironclad's armor, *Miami* attempted to explode a torpedo under her knuckle, and *Commodore Hull* made an attempt to foul *Albemarle*'s propeller with a seine.[85]

Twenty-five minutes after the exchange of the first shots, Lieutenant Commander Francis A. Roe, commanding the double-ender *Sassacus*, saw an opportunity to ram *Albemarle*. Roe ordered his engineer to throw waste and oil in the fires to build up steam and backed his vessel slowly to a distance of 400 yards from the enemy ram. The Union gunboat shot ahead, and before contact Roe ordered the crew to lie down. The 974-ton *Sassacus*, steaming approximately ten knots, struck *Albemarle* just abaft her beam. Edgar Holden, the assistant surgeon on board *Sassacus*, recalled that the collision "shook the ship like an earth quake, we struck full and square on the iron hull, careening it over and tearing away our own bows, ripping and straining our timbers at the waterline." *Sassacus* continued to push against *Albemarle* while water poured over the Confederate vessel's deck. The two antagonists began firing at each other almost muzzle to muzzle, but the shells of *Sassacus* "flew into the air like a pea." The shots aimed at *Sassacus* took effect. One shell crashed through the ship, while a second shot hit the boiler and scalded a number of men. Water pouring from the boiler caused the double-ender to list to port. Confederate tars, thinking they might capture the Union gunboat, attempted to board her. Well-directed fire from *Sassacus*, however, drove them below. As the *Sassacus*'s damaged boiler emptied, the ship lost momentum, and the two ships drifted apart.[86]

For all practical purposes, the battle was over, but both sides continued heavy firing until 7:30 P.M., when *Albemarle* steamed back into the Roanoke River.[87] The engagement was a tactical draw but a strategic defeat for the Confederates, since the ironclad could not aid Hoke in his attack on New Bern. The ironclad continued to be a threat to the Union navy, protected Plymouth, and required a large number of vessels to keep it out of the sounds. The action was an important one for the squadron, because it showed that the naval forces in the sounds could hold their own against the ram. It further relieved Phillip Lee's fears that Smith would require additional support, which would require the transfer of the gunboats engaged in the Bermuda Hundred campaign.

During the battle, the fire from the Union guns had struck the ram over 280 times. This greatly massed firepower only killed one man on board the ironclad. The muzzle of the stern gun was struck off by a solid shot, iron plates had been torn away and loosened, her steering mechanism was damaged, and her stack damaged so badly that butter, lard, and bacon had to be thrown in the fires to enable the severely damaged ironclad to get back upriver.[88]

The Union navy suffered heavier casualties. The *Sassacus* had five men killed and fifteen wounded, *Mattabesett* had two killed and six wounded, and *Wyalusing* had one killed—a total of eight killed and twenty-one wounded.[89]

Once *Albemarle* had passed back up the river, the navy began a policy of containment. Immediately after the battle, Smith tried to place torpedoes in the Roanoke River two and one-half miles from its mouth. In the middle of May, the containment policy was altered in favor of trying to entice the ironclad out of the river, with hopes of ramming her in the more expansive waters of the sound. Smith sent vessels about ten miles from the mouth of the Roanoke River, to make the blockade appear weak in hopes of deceiving the enemy. The ram did make an appearance on 24 May but did not come out of the river and later steamed back up the Roanoke.[90]

In June, Smith continued to lay torpedoes at the mouth of the

A Sawyer class Gunboat. These 974 ton double enders performed well off Wilmington and in the sounds of North Carolina.

Miami, a Double-ender in the Sounds of North Carolina. *Miami* was one of the most unreliable vessels during the war. A couple of sailing vessels lay on her other side. (*Courtesy the U.S. Naval Historical Center*)

Roanoke and acquired vessels with torpedoes. The navy also proposed to mount heavier eleven-inch guns on the warships assigned to watch the ram. Lee believed that the reason that *Albemarle* had not been severely damaged in the previous fight was due to the light charges in the guns.[91]

The War Department meanwhile became interested in recapturing Plymouth, a move that would require naval cooperation. The Union naval force in the sounds, while looking strong on paper, could hardly be called a strong force. Nearly all the vessels needed repairs, some were completely broken down, and others were barely able to function. Captain Smith, willing to cooperate, wrote Brigadier General Innis Palmer, commanding the district of North Carolina, "If in your judgment it is deemed important to recapture Plymouth, I am ready with my diseased gunboats to cooperate with you."[92]

After the loss of Plymouth, the leadership in the sounds changed several times. In June, Lee had detached Henry Davenport from *Hetzel* as the senior officer in the sounds. Captain Melancton Smith held this post for about one month. In July, Rear Admiral Lee reorganized the squadron's divisions. Under the new organization, Smith was detached to command the James River Division, and Commander William Macomb became the officer for the 3rd Division in the North Carolina sounds. On 1 September, Welles gave Commodore Stephen C. Rowan independent command of the vessels in the sounds. After Admiral Porter was selected to replace Lee, Rowan's orders were revoked, and Macomb, who had not officially turned over the vessels, continued to command the sounds flotilla.[93]

While the Union forces contemplated the recapture of Plymouth, Commander John N. Maffitt, a famous blockade runner, replaced Cooke as commander of *Albemarle*. Maffitt, a fearless individual, wanted to use the ironclad as an offensive weapon and made plans to attack the Union naval forces. Brigadier General Laurence S. Baker, commander of the 2nd District of North Carolina and Southern Virginia, protested, believing it would risk not only the ironclad but also the town of Plymouth. Confederate Secretary of the Navy Mallory did not interfere and let Maffitt captain his own ship. Maffitt did advance to the mouth of the Roanoke on the morning of 6 August and again on the 7th but never ventured any farther. In September, he returned to running the blockade and turned over his command to Alexander F. Warley.[94]

It became obvious that the Confederates planned to use *Albemarle* solely as a defensive weapon and that the Union ships would not be able to draw her from the safety of the river. Thus Phillips Lee began making plans to destroy her at her moorings and even authorized William Cushing to take 100 men to capture her. Reconnaissance showed that she could still fight, and Plymouth's recapture depended on the ironclad's destruction. On 25 May, five men from *Wyalusing* volunteered to try to destroy the ram. They ascended the Middle River in a dinghy with two torpedoes, each containing 100 pounds of powder, to destroy the ironclad. Landing in a swamp parallel to *Albemarle*, they transported the torpedoes on a stretcher, and two of the five men slid into the water to place the torpedoes across the ram's bow. As they approached the ironclad, lines connecting the two torpedoes fouled a schooner, and they had to abandon the mission only yards from their objective.[95]

After this failure, Lee again approached the one man he thought had the audacity to lead a mission to destroy *Albemarle*—the legendary William Cushing. Lee suggested that Cushing attack *Albemarle* with an india rubber boat or a steam barge fitted with a torpedo. Cushing agreed and immediately began to organize an expedition. He went to New York to supervise the fitting out of two torpedo launches. Each launch measured over forty feet long and had a draft of only three and a half feet. Each carried a twelve-pound howitzer and a torpedo projecting on the end of a fourteen-foot boom. One of the launches broke down and was captured while en route to the North Carolina sounds, but this loss did not deter Cushing, who decided to continue with his mission.[96]

On the night of 27 October, Cushing and thirteen officers and men entered the Roanoke River in the launch. They had to ascend the river for eight miles. In the darkness, they crept up the river and came upon the wreck of *Southfield* one mile below Plymouth. A picket guard stationed on the former Union gunboat failed to detect the small steamer as it glided by. Cushing and his men continued up the river and managed to get near the wharf where *Albemarle* was moored without being discovered. Steaming closer, the Union launch was finally seen by the Confederates, who sprang the alarm and began firing at the boat. Cushing steered the launch close to *Albemarle* and observed a log barrier ten feet wide, which lay around the side of the ironclad to prevent torpedoes and boats from striking it. Cushing, guiding his launch alongside the ram, sheered off so that he could strike *Albemarle* at a right angle. The men on board the ironclad and ashore maintained a murderous fire on the launch but could not stop Cushing and his men. After steaming a short distance, Cushing turned the launch around. He opened the throttle, steamed toward the ram, ran over the log barrier, and fired his howitzer into the ironclad. Cushing then lowered the boom onto the ram, and the torpedo exploded, opening a hole in *Albemarle* "big enough to drive a wagon in." As Cushing pulled the lanyard on the torpedo, *Albemarle*'s gun crew fired 100 pounds of grapeshot into the launch, which shattered it. Cushing ordered the men to save themselves, but only he and one other man escaped; the rest were killed, captured, or drowned.[97]

Cushing became an immediate hero, and for this daring exploit, Congress advanced him one grade to the rank of lieutenant commander. David Porter, who had had "no great confidence in his success," likewise received a great deal of credit, even though Lee had instigated and planned the project. Reporters used *Albemarle*'s destruction to "illustrate the change in squadron commanders" and to show that Porter was more active than Lee.[98]

Porter later praised Cushing's efforts and remarked that Cushing "was always ready to undertake any duty, no matter how desperate, and he generally succeeded in his enterprises, from the fact that the enemy supposed that no man would be foolhardy enough to embark in such hazardous affairs where there seemed so little chance of success."[99]

On 29 October, with the threat of *Albemarle* ended, Commander Macomb ordered six vessels up the Roanoke. A seventh gunboat steamed up the Middle River to cut off vessels or stores that the enemy might try to remove. At noon, the flotilla came within range of the batteries protecting Plymouth and exchanged shots. The Union vessels advanced to within a mile of the batteries but discovered obstructions blocking the river and then withdrew. On the following dry, six gunboats ascended the Middle River and by late that afternoon lay in the Roanoke River above Plymouth. On 31 October, Macomb lashed four vessels in pairs so that those nearest the batteries could stay in motion if their machinery became damaged by gunfire. For further protection, the double-enders blew off the steam in their starboard boilers to prevent the engine room gangs from being scalded. Shortly after 9:30 A.M., Macomb hoisted the signal to get under way, and they approached the batteries in line ahead.[100]

As the vessels advanced, the Confederate batteries opened fire and directed it principally toward *Commodore Hull* and *Shamrock*. When the gunboats neared the enemy batteries, Macomb gave the order "Go ahead fast," and they quickly assembled directly opposite the rebel guns and began to drive the gun crews away with grapeshot and canister. A shot from *Shamrock* exploded in a Confederate magazine, which panicked the town's defenders and enabled the navy to land and take the batteries without any further struggle. Macomb's "distinguished conduct" in the recapture of Plymouth earned him an advancement in grade of ten numbers.[101]

Plymouth was once again in Union hands, but Macomb did not have instructions from Porter and was unsure whether he should hold or evacuate the town. Porter later instructed him to hold the town but to send all the guns to Hampton Roads—a precaution ensuring superior naval firepower should the Confederates return.[102]

After the evacuation of Plymouth, the rebels moved thirty miles upstream to the fortifications at Rainbow Bluff (Fort Branch) on the Roanoke River. The navy made immediate plans to capture the fort and then move to destroy a rebel ram thought to be under construction farther up the river. Porter suggested that Butler take 1,500 men from New Bern for the expedition and instructed Macomb to cooperate with Brigadier General Palmer, who was to lead the army portion of the attack.[103] The War Department planned, in conjunction with the attacks on Fort Fisher, to move up the Roanoke to prevent supplies and reinforcements from reaching Wilmington over the Wilmington and Weldon Railroad.

Macomb, with five vessels and a picket boat, started up the river on 9 December and stopped at Jamesville to communicate with the army. The steamer *Otsego* stopped her engines and prepared to anchor when a torpedo exploded under her port side, and within seconds, another torpedo exploded under her port pivot gun, sinking her in minutes. The following day, Macomb sent the tug *Bazely* to take men and an officer from *Otsego* before going to Plymouth with dispatches. When the tug steamed to within a few yards of the sunken *Otsego*, another torpedo exploded, sinking *Bazely* and killing two men.[104]

As a precaution against further losses, the navy had to drag for torpedoes and work its way slowly up the river, while the Confederates harassed the gunboats with musket fire from the banks. The Roanoke became extremely narrow and crooked farther upstream, and as the gunboats advanced, they frequently fouled their rigging on trees and lost rails and torpedo catchers as they swept close to shore. In most cases, steam power could not be used in the upper reaches of the river, so the gunboats used hawsers made fast to trees to warp themselves ahead.[105]

As the Union warships advanced up the river, Confederate Brigadier General Gabriel Rains, one of the earliest proponents of torpedo warfare, planted over 100 torpedoes in the Roanoke River between Jamesville and Poplar Point. The gunboats succeeded in picking up eighty of these infernal machines. When the vessels had advanced as far as Poplar Point, about five miles from Fort Branch, the enemy began to fire on them with muskets and quickly brought up five or six pieces of artillery. Before the Confederate guns could be driven away, they killed three seamen and wounded three more.[106]

The army part of the expedition never materialized because of poor planning and overestimation of the enemy's strength, so the gunboats discontinued their maneuver. Lacking proper support, the navy could not advance without suffering further casualties and certainly could not take the fort without Palmer's assistance. So on 22 December, the vessels withdrew to Plymouth, arriving on the 25th.[107]

After this episode, the Navy Department's attentions turned to the capture of Wilmington, and the sounds became an insignificant theater of the war. The navy discontinued offensive operations and remained in a defensive posture. Macomb placed spar torpedoes on movable vessels, continued attaching more torpedoes to obstructions, and linked chains across the Roanoke to discourage the enemy from surprising the Union gunboats. Only two potential threats remained in this region, the grounded *Neuse* and the ironclad being built farther up the Roanoke. Porter believed that he had never had "ram fever" but showed a touch of it when he commanded Macomb to use all his vessels as torpedo boats. He instructed that each gunboat have a spar fitted to the bow and that the large rowboats be fitted with torpedoes to destroy any ironclad that ventured out of the river. As matters developed, the Union vessels in the sounds never faced another threat, because the Confederates destroyed their warships to prevent their capture in March and April 1865.[108]

The role of the navy in the sounds of North Carolina cannot be underestimated. The mere presence of the vessels gave a psychological lift to the detached Union garrisons. Each time the Confederate forces attacked, the Union garrisons knew that the navy was not far away, and nearly every challenge to Union control was turned back as a result of naval fire support. In fact, it can be argued that the Union posts in eastern North Carolina were made possible by the navy.

A major strategic failure of the Union forces was to allow the Confederates any chance to complete the ironclads. The combined strength of the army and navy could have overwhelmed anything that the Confederates could have put into the field to stop them. The indifference of the army commanders, who seemed content to lie behind their fortifications, eventually cost them the towns of Plymouth and Washington.

Secondly, the federal forces failed to disrupt the interior lines of communication of the Confederacy, in particular, to destroy the Wilmington and Weldon Railroad, which was early recognized as important to the Confederate war effort.[109] The Union forces made only five mediocre attempts to destroy portions of the tracks. The use of this line allowed the Confederates to maintain their interior lines during the entire war and to ship goods north and south with few interruptions. Using the rivers and naval support, the Union forces might have truly hurt the Confederacy by striking deep within the state to destroy bridges, railroads, factories, and other production sites.

Union control of portions of North Carolina aided the Union directly, and it disrupted the Confederate war effort. Control of the eastern portion of the state allowed the Union to recruit and remove valuable raw products. The Confederates lost the benefit of some of the fertile eastern counties of the state, which produced bountiful supplies of corn, fish, and pork. The Confederate high command realized this importance, but to wrest the towns from the grasp of the federal troops, they also had to confront the navy.

While the Union did benefit to some degree, one might question the overall value of the Union army's decision to maintain control of all the major towns in the eastern part of the state. For three years, the troops stationed there accomplished little, and by 1864, they were needed to press the rebels in other areas. The presence of the Union garrisons required the Confederate leaders to expend men to counter any Union movement, but the extensive fortifications required to protect the towns necessitated a large body of Northern troops and gunboats as well.

When the Union remained inactive, the Confederates benefited, even though they had to keep troops nearby to counter any federal movement. One might argue that the Union's failure to exploit the victories in 1862 increasingly favored the South.

The greatest strategic shortcoming of the Union army was its failure to utilize fully the navy to project its superior power. In contrast, the Confederacy used its limited naval power extremely well in the sounds. Confederate naval strategy prescribed that the ironclad was best utilized as a defensive weapon.[110] But during the last year of the war, the Confederates attempted to use their rams as offensive weapons in North Carolina in an endeavor to drive the Union forces out of the eastern portion of the state. This plan had great merit and might have changed the course of the war in the state, had it succeeded.

SIX

Uncle Sam's web feet

Operations in the Interior Waters

In August 1863, Abraham Lincoln wrote to his friend James Conkling, "Nor must Uncle Sam's web feet be forgotten. At all the watery margins they have been present. Not only on the deep sea, the broad bay, and the rapid river, but . . . wherever the ground was a little damp, they have been, and made their tracks."[1] Nowhere else during the war was this statement more true than in the sounds, rivers, and inland waterways of North Carolina and Virginia. In these waters, the Union gunboats not only supported army positions but also attempted to stop an enormous network of contraband trafficking, regulated fishing activities and legal trade, removed torpedoes, and fought with guerrillas. The gunboats performed these duties in areas that the Union forces usually only marginally controlled, making their work extremely dangerous.[2]

The vessels that patrolled these interior areas were usually small light-draft low-pressure steamers armed with rifled guns and howitzers. The senior officers never had a sufficient number of these gunboats and constantly asked for additional support. Tugs and ferryboats both made serviceable warships in these areas. Tugs were usually fast, maneuverable, and strongly built, standing up well to the rigors of military service. Ferryboats also adapted well to river service. Built strong to carry the heaviest horse-drawn vehicles, they could carry heavy ordnance and had power enough to push away ice in the rivers. They also drew little water, enabling them to run close to the shore and far up into the rivers. An added advantage of the double-enders was their ability to proceed in either direction.[3]

Ferryboats could perform remarkably in swift currents and twisting rivers. *Stepping Stones* could "pass through such a narrow place that the water could not be seen by looking over the guards on either side, and both wheels would be digging in the mud."[4] Operations in the rivers frequently caused accidental damage. The gunboats sustained injury to their hulls and rudders as a result of frequent contact with the bottom. They also lost boats, foremasts, smokestacks, spars, and anything else that might come in contact with overhanging trees.[5]

Operations in the upper reaches of the rivers were always dangerous. The enemy could suddenly appear almost anywhere and might bring horse-drawn artillery. Many of the gunboats, being converted merchantmen, had exposed boilers and machinery, which made them more vulnerable to enemy fire. The gunboats found movement difficult and commonly had to run up the river for some distance before being able to turn around. At other times, the warships relied on hawsers made fast to trees on either side of the river so that they could be turned or warped ahead. In many places, the banks of the rivers were extremely high. In terrain such as this, the warships could not effectively use their large guns, and if attacked, they normally withdrew. The enemy with artillery sometimes followed and harassed the vessels and often blocked their retreat with felled trees. If aground, the crews of the steamers might empty the boilers and throw their coal overboard to get afloat, which left them helpless.[6] For these reasons, the gunboats rarely traveled alone.

For the safety of the warships, the crews took certain precautions. They triced up boarding nettings nearly six feet high, made of rope or wire, when the ships anchored during the night and in fog. As an added precaution, it was suggested that trees be cut down in areas most likely to conceal rebel sharpshooters. In April 1864, Admiral Lee issued instructions for all the vessels inside Cape Henry. He ordered gunboats to stay under way at night and to remain in position by using leads and

Commodore Morris above and *Commodore Perry* below. These two vessels were both converted ferryboats and performed well in shallow waters of both North Carolina and Virginia. Note the boiler-iron protection on each vessel. *(Courtesy the U.S. Naval Historical Center)*

bearings except in fog. He instructed them to keep a good head of steam and to be ready to move quickly and to leave their guns cast loose during the night and in fog. To prevent the warships from reacting slowly during a surprise attack, Lee required commanding, executive, and watch officers to keep their clothes on at night. Porter continued these measures and, as an added precaution, later prohibited boats from leaving the gunboats after sunset, requiring that every boat be hoisted and the vessels prepared for night action.[7]

The men were always to be ready to answer a call to repel boarders, and some even slept with revolvers and cutlasses strapped to their sides. A well-armed vessel kept an assortment of muskets, hand grenades, boarding pikes, and cutlasses all stored in a prominent place for ready use. Not all the gunboats, however, were fortunate enough, particularly early in the war, to have all the weapons needed on this service.[8]

Besides the iron plating that gradually protected the bulwarks and pilothouses of the vessels, chains and bales of cotton and hay were also used. Crews normally secured hammocks so that they could stop musket balls and splinters, and aboard *Young Rover*, the tars used them to protect the boilers. Lacking adequate protection, the crew of *Hunchback* rigged up a breastwork of sails to conceal themselves from snipers.[9]

During most of the war, small boats, launches, and cutters managed a great deal of the blockade and reconnaissance work in the rivers. This duty was not only arduous but also dangerous, and a large number of seamen were killed and captured while so engaged. Launches carried light Dahlgren howitzers, which allowed the crews of the launches to defend themselves. One of the men described this duty, "There is no great degree of comfort cramped in a boat all night . . . watching noiselessly at the mouth of a creek, not too far inland and yet near enough to keep good guard . . . but such was our work, night after night."[10]

The gunboats were obligated to so many tasks that manpower problems plagued the officers. The men were continually on reconnaissance missions, boat expeditions, or picket duty in the rivers. Shortages of men frequently occurred, particularly when seamen went ashore for picket duty. Shortages prevented the commanders from maintaining the proper watches, and working the guns became problematical. Men from the army, and extra marines, were sometimes assigned to gunboats for landing parties. Even with the critical shortages in manpower, the large numbers of blacks stationed on board the vessels were not utilized well. Shortly after receiving command in the James River, Commander William Parker instructed his officers, "You will not employ Negroes as lookouts, as they are not fit to be entrusted with such important duties."[11]

Reconnaissance missions were among the most important duties of the gunboats. The collection of information concerning all aspects of the enemy undermined the Confederate war effort. The officers gathered information from local whites, free blacks, and contrabands, but they did this with caution. Charles Flusser expressed his reservations when he wrote, "I fear the 'reliable contraband' was sent in by Messieurs les Secesh. I do not think anyone can outlie a North Carolina white, unless he be a North Carolina negro."[12]

River work became more hazardous when the rebels began to employ torpedoes. The use of torpedoes by the Confederacy forced the Union naval forces to modify their patrolling efforts and kept the gunboats out of certain areas, particularly at night. This allowed the rebels to continue their small-scale blockade running activities on the interior waterways. Matthew Fontaine Maury demonstrated a floating torpedo with a percussion trigger in June 1861, and within a month, Union vessels began picking them up in the waters of Virginia. Maury later went to Europe as a Confederate naval agent, and Lieutenant Hunter Davidson took his place and continued Maury's work until the war's end. The Confederates used many different types of torpedoes ranging from wax-sealed barrels to metal tanks holding 2,000 pounds of powder. Those most often used in the eastern theater were made of copper, tin, or iron and held between 100 and 150 pounds of powder. The most destructive, of course, were the largest.[13]

The discovery, removal, and disposal of torpedoes grew to be one of the major tasks of the naval riverine forces. To find the devices, boats towed pairs of canoes with anchors and grapnels connected between them to snag the torpedoes. The boat crew kept this device at a great enough distance for a torpedo to explode without harming them. When vessels moved up the rivers, skirmishers went ashore to search for wires leading to galvanic batteries, which the rebels used to set off the torpedoes. In the James River, this became such an important task that Lee created a Picket and Torpedo Division. Gunboats that operated in the rivers sported "torpedo catchers"—structures of booms and nettings rigged out in front of the vessels to push the torpedoes past or to detonate them harmlessly.[14]

Despite the precautions, six of the North Atlantic Blockading Squadron's gunboats were sunk or damaged by torpedoes during the war. Four vessels not belonging to the squadron but in its jurisdiction were also sunk. After mid-April 1864, with larger and more advanced mechanisms in use, the Confederates became more successful in sinking Union ships.[15]

The interruption of enemy trade developed into one of the most important duties of the riverine forces. Contraband goods seeping into eastern Virginia came from two areas—from the eastern counties of North Carolina and from Maryland and the eastern shore of Virginia. Union sorties and raids, along with constant surveillance, retarded this trade but never stopped it completely. The major goal of the Union expeditions was to destroy the means by which this commerce was carried out. They destroyed boats, bridges, carts, Confederate storage facilities, and production sites. During the war, the squadron also captured and destroyed thousands of head of livestock and hundreds of thousands of bushels of corn and grain. This policy injured the Confederate war effort and devastated the local populace. Some of the more humane Union officers, however, chose to redistribute the food rather than to destroy it.[16]

The northeastern counties of North Carolina were extremely valuable to the Confederate war effort. Six counties in this area annually produced 10,000,000 pounds of pork and bacon and 40,000 bushels of corn. Farther south, in Onslow County, the average annual crop amounted to 300,000 bushels of corn. Vast stores of fish, oysters, and other goods were also produced. To get these goods into Virginia, small vessels used the Chowan River. Sometimes as many as 100 boats passed Edenton at night, coming across the Albemarle Sound to and from Washington, Tyrell, and Hyde counties. This route was called "one of the great thoroughfares to the army of General Lee." North Carolinians sent corn, grain, cotton, tobacco, tallow, and meat through the eastern counties from as far south as Beaufort.[17]

The majority of the products coming south into Virginia originated in Maryland and the eastern shore of Virginia. Many of these goods traveled into Maryland via Baltimore, Philadelphia, and New York. Smuggled goods often landed at the tip of the peninsula formed by the Rappahannock and York rivers. From the peninsula, the contraband made its way to Richmond and sometimes south into North Carolina. Secessionists in Worcester County on the Atlantic Ocean traded with New York and sent goods through Chincoteague Bay to the eastern shore counties of Virginia, where they sent them across the Chesapeake Bay. Contraband items coming south included millinery goods, clothing, coffee, sugar, salt, and small arms. To prevent smuggling, gunboats searched vessels on the Chesapeake, and boat crews kept close watches on the small rivers and creeks at night.[18]

To cripple this trade, the squadron destroyed hundreds of small boats and canoes. Phillips Lee did his utmost to incapacitate these small operations. In a five-month period between November 1862 and March 1863, the squadron destroyed more than 250 boats and small vessels in the inland waters. Lee initiated night reconnaissance to stop the communication and during the day sent patrols to destroy the small vessels. The Union missions were so effective that the Confederates began taking their boats out of the water and placing them on wagons to carry them a safe distance away. The Confederates also sank their canoes and boats in creeks, whence they could be floated at night to run the blockade. Those individuals not using their vessels to run the blockade but wishing to prevent their seizure had to keep them well beyond the range of the gunboats. After seizing one North Carolinian's schooner, the Union officer asked him why she lay so far up the creek, and he responded, "To keep the damned Yankees from stealing her."[19]

Patrolling the tidewater area with its plenitude of rivers, creeks, and landing sites stretched the resources of the squadron. In September 1863, five gunboats operated in the York River and Mobjack Bay vicinity. This allowed one vessel for every five miles. The necessity of patrolling these areas was costly to the overall efficiency of the squadron, considering at that time only twelve gunboats watched Wilmington and the numerous inlets north and south.[20]

The naval force was augmented by small shallow-draft lightly armed army gunboats and revenue cutters. The army had dozens of small vessels of various sizes that worked the interior waters, as an added force and sometimes under the direction of naval officers. The revenue cutters under the Treasury Department also patrolled the interior waters, examining passing vessels and seizing many ships and large quantities of illegal goods.[21]

The small guerrilla bands in the tidewater areas posed a constant threat to the Union naval operations, with vessels spread so thin. These bands generally operated in the same areas that most of the inland blockade running occurred. Many of the inhabitants in the coastal areas were neutral and simply took the side of the most powerful. Guerrillas were successful because there was no incentive for the loyal people outside of Union control to act in a loyal manner. Furthermore, the army and navy could offer no security or protection from the bands who operated in the outlying areas. The navy set an early policy in the towns by asking for the "neutrality and good conduct" of the people but would "promise nothing in the way of protection to any . . . residing on shore."[22] Inhabitants may have been affected because the officers and men of boat expeditions did "not generally carry with them evidence of the authority under which they were acting nor [did they] . . . always wear the uniform distinctive of their grade and position."[23]

Loyalties were further divided when crews of Union gunboats went ashore and returned with livestock and foraged goods. In February 1863, sailors from *Commodore Morris* stole 400 or 500 pounds of bacon, a calf, and over two dozen fowls. On a second trip, they brought off two hogs, more poultry, and some other articles, while *Stepping Stones* in the same area stole and killed seven or eight hogs. Private citizens claimed that the sailors had also taken the keys to the meat houses so that they could steal food during the day and night and contended that the sailors threatened them if they did not cooperate. The seamen on *Commodore Morris* denied the charges, stating that they had only destroyed items destined for the rebel army. After these incidents, Lee instructed his officers not to "meddle with private property." He wrote to Lieutenant Commander John P. Gillis: "You are reminded that private property is not to be seized . . . unless you have satisfactory evidence that it is intended or has been transferred for public use of the rebels."[24]

These actions only served to stir the populace against the Union forces. In Virginia, various bands of guerrillas operated along the seaboard, bands organized in Gloucester and Mathews counties and in the

Suffolk area—the areas in which smuggling took place. Union vessels often came under fire and sometimes landed parties that burned houses, barns, and other buildings in retribution.[25] As the war progressed, guerrilla bands became bolder and better organized. In Mathews County, Virginia, they had boats on wheels that could move rapidly to and from the water. One of the groups operating around Mathews County was led by John Taylor Wood, whose band captured the steamers *Reliance* and *Satellite* by surprise attack on 23 August 1863.[26]

Another bold move was the capture of four schooners by an organization in Mathews County called the Marine Coast Guard. Led by John Yates Beall, this small band had previously cut the telegraph cable that ran between Cherrystone and Old Point Comfort and had destroyed the machinery and lens in the Cape Charles lighthouse. In September 1863, they crossed Chesapeake Bay and captured four schooners on the Atlantic side of the eastern shore of Virginia. They then set three of the vessels adrift and took the last to Milford Haven, where they landed as many of the goods as possible and then burned the prize. A punitive strike, utilizing a combination of army and navy gunboats and cavalry, captured a number of these men, but most fled into the countryside upon the approach of the Union forces. This Union sortie did cripple the organization's striking capacity and hurt local blockade running by destroying 150 boats and schooners in the immediate area. Some concluded that it was impossible for the small number of gunboats stationed between Fort Monroe and the Piankatank River to keep these men from repeating their actions.[27]

North Carolina was not without its bands of guerrillas. Governor Zebulon Vance encouraged Home Guard units and armed them well with accoutrements that the state privately ran through the blockade. They operated out of the Chowan River and the Pungo River areas. Irregulars in the New Bern vicinity, called the Whitford Gang, captured and burned the coal collier *Sea Bird* in May 1863. Groups of men also ranged the northeastern counties of the state. A "nest of rebels" located in Hyde County made it dangerous for small vessels to blockade Ocracoke Inlet only fifteen miles distant. Guerrilla bands also caused major problems along the canals between Suffolk, Virginia, and South Mills, North Carolina.[28]

One of the bolder escapades was the capture of the mail steamers

Arrow and *Emily* on 15 May 1863. Thirty members of the Pasquotank guerillas jumped on board the sixty-ton *Arrow* as she steamed by a drawbridge at Coinjock. Proceeding down the canal, they also managed to surprise the crew of the ninety-four-ton side-wheel steamer *Emily*. They boldly steamed into Albemarle Sound and into the Chowan River and ascended the Blackwater River as far as Franklin, Virginia, far out of the reach of the larger Union gunboats.[29]

Repeated attacks in this area compelled the army to send an expedition there in December 1863. The expedition, led by Brigadier General Edward A. Wild, marched from Norfolk on 5 December. Wild, a zealous abolitionist, had raised regiments of black troops in the New Bern area, called Wild's African Brigade. Wild's force on the expedition included four regiments of black troops and portions of a couple of others, totaling over 1,800 men. The main purpose of the trip was to flush out guerrillas and to bring out blacks for the Union army. The expedition, though, served only to tweak the emotions of the local populace. Wild's men lived off the land, taking food and livestock and burning houses and barns as they went. They seized hostages and hanged one man accused of being a guerrilla. Wild returned to Norfolk after twenty days, having freed about 2,500 negroes. But he managed only to recruit between 70 and 100 blacks and had completely stirred the populace against the Union. Butler claimed that Wild had done his job with "great thoroughness, but perhaps with too much stringency."[30]

Wild's expedition produced the opposite of the anticipated results; the rebels' guerrilla organization remained strong and active. Governor Zebulon Vance continued to encourage this type of activity. Equally determined, Butler threatened more "visitations from the colored troops" if these groups did not disband. Butler's threat did not carry much weight, because in September 1864, the mailboat *Fawn* was burned by rebels in the Chesapeake and Albemarle canal. Commander William Macomb dispatched marines from ships in the area to arrest prominent citizens and held them as "hostages" in order to determine who had destroyed the mailboat.[31]

The small guerilla bands created a nuisance and caused the navy an inordinate amount of trouble. The squadron had a great deal of responsibility, and the lack of cooperation between the service branches only diminished its effectiveness to deal with these groups. The wedge between the army and navy grew steadily, beginning in the spring of 1862. By that fall, a controversy began over the trade of Norfolk, Virginia, which created a conflict that raged between the Navy, War, and Treasury departments.

In May, the Confederates abandoned Norfolk, and the federal army took possession and immediately prohibited civilian trade with the Confederacy. A month later, Major General John A. Dix took command of the military department and quickly reversed this policy. With the backing of Secretary of War Stanton and Secretary of the Treasury Salmon P. Chase, Norfolk was opened for limited trade. This policy directly confronted Lincoln's proclaimed blockade of the port and produced complications for the navy, which intended to carry out this proclamation. Neutral nations also found this policy unfair and were not permitted to participate in this trade.

Dix justified the trade into Norfolk to end the suffering and allow for the "necessaries and comforts of life" to which he thought the inhabitants were entitled. He argued that the navy's presence in the harbor was not to enforce the blockade but to enforce the military occupation.[32]

Initially the clearances were allowed for vessels that had entered Norfolk by virtue of "military necessity." Flag Officer Goldsborough allowed vessels with army passes to proceed with few questions. That September, Goldsborough was replaced by Rear Admiral Phillips Lee, who within two weeks of his appointment began to question the issuance of these permits. Lee discovered that Brigadier General Egbert L. Viele, the military governor of Virginia, had issued passes for private speculators to export shingles and other merchandise. Not wanting to transgress his authority, Lee consulted Welles. Welles reminded Lee that Norfolk remained under a blockade because, according to the president's proclamation of May 1862, Norfolk did not have the same status that opened the ports of New Orleans, Port Royal, and Beaufort. Only army supplies, authorized by Major General John A. Dix, were admitted into Norfolk, and no return cargoes were allowed. Furthermore, only permits signed or authorized by the secretaries of War, Treasury, or Navy could be honored, and other vessels connected with illegal traffic should be seized.[33]

Vessels coming into occupied areas were to stop and allow naval guard vessels to examine their cargoes; the only exceptions were mail boats and transports with troops. Certificates for passage into the interior areas were necessary, or detention was required. Only supplies to the army, sutlers' goods, wood, and fishing, oyster, and market boats with supplies for the army could pass after examination. Army transports that traveled beyond Hampton Roads or from the James River to the Nansemond River had to stop again and allow the senior naval officer at Newport News to examine their passes.[34]

Welles, Dix, and Chase each had differing opinions on how trade in the interior waters should be conducted. Dix, the commander of the military department, argued that trade should be regulated by permits, which he issued through his provost marshals.[35] Welles knew that men close to Dix were selling licenses to trade and felt that the blockade should remain strict. The secretary of the Treasury, Salmon P. Chase, wanted the blockade to be relaxed to allow citizens to trade local products for things necessary for their survival. Welles wanted the trade either restricted to the terms of the blockade or open to all that wished to trade, not a policy in between. Welles, though, had a clear view of the situation. In his diary he wrote, "There is, I can see, a scheme for permits, special favors, . . . and improper management in all this; not that Chase is to receive any pecuniary benefit himself, but in his political aspirations he is courting, and will give authority to General Dix, who has, he thinks political influence." Welles added that Dix "has on his staff and around him, a set of bloodsuckers who propose to make use of the blockade as a machine to enrich themselves."[36]

The policies of the Navy and Treasury departments were not even close in conception. Thus there could never really be any compromise. Dix realized that Lee must act on instructions from the Navy Department, while Dix had adopted the loose instructions of the Treasury Department whenever they seemed beneficial. Dix felt that neither he nor Lee was responsible for the disagreement and saw it as a "conflict between two Departments of the Government."[37] Stanton complicated this issue by falsely telling Dix that the cabinet had resolved the issue of Norfolk's trade by putting it under his personal direction. Dix sent Lee a note asking if he would allow "the passage of vessels from the Nansemond and Yorktown, with exports under my permit?" Lee, however, stood his ground, stating that he was still bound by the president's original proclamation, which had not been officially modified.[38]

On 11 November, Lincoln issued an executive order regulating trade in Norfolk. It stated that vessels that were issued clearances by the Treasury Department and that had been certified by Dix could legally go to Norfolk. The cargoes could only be for the military necessities of the department and could return with "domestic produce" by permits also issued by Dix.[39] The orders eventually were extended to include Suffolk and the Nansemond River.

With Dix and his staff handling the permits, those wishing to use their political influence to obtain passes could do so and make large profits on contraband trade. Reports claimed that tens of thousands of dollars of supplies entered Norfolk and went to General Lee's army. Supplies also went south into North Carolina, ending in the hands of rebel agents at the southern end of the Dismal Swamp Canal. Welles wrote, "As I anticipated, continued and increasing abuses and much illicit traffic are going on under the army permits issued by General Dix to pass the blockade. It will be difficult to stop the abuse, now that it has commenced."[40] Both Lee and Dix realized that the system was imperfect and that there were abuses. For a short while, Dix stopped all permits for goods going into Norfolk and claimed he would confine some of the "commercial transactions . . . to retail dealers."[41] Northern speculators with high connections clamored for special considerations and began shipping vast quantities of goods under the guise of military necessity. With a virtual monopoly on trade, great sums of money were made to the detriment of the war effort. It has been estimated that as many as 8,000,000 pounds of bacon went through Confederate lines by this route.[42]

With this arrangement, the squadron still maintained a guard vessel at Fort Monroe and Norfolk to regulate traffic. The guard vessel hoisted a flag during the day and lights during the night to identify herself to merchantmen. Vessels going to either place were to stop, and if they failed to do so, they risked being fired upon. Those with passes could proceed, whereas others were searched for contraband goods. The army maintained a list of steamers that it employed. Those on the list could pass the guard vessel freely during the day but were required to stop at night. Dix failed to keep the list current, which caused delays when the guard vessel stopped steamers on the inward passage. The general became increasingly perturbed that army vessels had to stop at the guard ship at Fort Monroe. He maintained that the revenue cutter at the fort was there for the purpose of examining his vessels. He also complained that stopping at the guard vessel caused inconvenience and delays. He wrote to the president that "Admiral Lee is blockading one of our forts by one of our gunboats, a novelty in war which is without precedent."[43]

General Butler created quite a stir during his tenure while commanding the Department of Virginia and North Carolina. Based on the president's order of 11 November 1862, he also had the authority to regulate trade and to issue passes for merchandise. He likewise collected money on many activities within his department. He charged a one-percent fee on all merchandise entering his department in Virginia and North Carolina. He rented booths in Norfolk to merchants and hucksters. He charged a freight tariff between Fort Monroe and Norfolk and required money for vessels clearing at Fort Monroe. Many abuses only accentuated the graft of his subordinates and resentment by many different groups. The navy did not have authority to stop illegal trade once the cargoes were landed. The Treasury Department had its own problems with "looseness of business habits" and did not have the manpower to handle the great volume of trade and eventually conceded to Butler and his cronies. Phillip Lee's chief of staff, John Sanford Barnes, commented about Butler, "His bombastic style, petty fogging ways and extreme care of his own private person made of him a most repulsive character."[44]

Lee, aware of the illegal trade, continued his insistence upon tight security measures. He wrote Butler in May 1864 that the navy tried to "keep the blockade in good faith—and this cannot be properly done if army transports are not to answer the hail and communicate when directed to do so." The admiral, however, could not stop the sale of army supplies and sutlers' goods, which still bypassed the blockade into Confederate lines by the routes mentioned earlier.[45]

During the latter part of the war, under new trade store provisions, individuals were able to buy large quantities of goods and use carts to carry them away. They could then transfer the goods to a convenient hiding place and carry them across the rivers at night. Two of the most often used points of departure were Queen's and King's creeks above Yorktown. Army officials did not believe that blockade running fell under the scope of army affairs. Neither did they concern themselves with illegal trade because of the "long standing ill-feeling between portions of the army and navy, and a jealous feeling in regard to control of the waters."[46]

When Porter took command of the squadron, he enforced the stringent rules that Lee had initiated and maintained. On 19 November 1864, Lincoln issued a proclamation that opened the ports of Norfolk, Fernandina, and Pensacola to trade, beginning on 1 December, under the same provisions as the earlier ports—ending many of the navy's worries.[47]

The problems the squadron encountered in North Carolina were just as severe as those encountered in Virginia. On 12 May, with much of the eastern portion of the state under the control of the Union forces, Lincoln proclaimed the opening of Beaufort to trade. One week later, the president appointed Edward Stanly as the military governor of the state with wide and sweeping authority.[48] The combination of army, civilian, and naval officials in this area led to conflict between the former two and the navy.

Before the war, Stanly had been one of the state's most prominent Whig leaders; he had a strong devotion to the Union and hated secession. Stanly's short stature, his small face, and large forehead did not reveal his fiery temper. Stanly's duties as military governor were to attempt to bring eastern North Carolina back into the fold of the Union and maintain "peace and Security." Congress hampered his efforts from the start, and his exaggeration of Union sentiment in the state only aggravated it. Furthermore, armies of occupation are rarely given warm receptions, and the Union troops had vandalized, robbed, and mistreated the local inhabitants, which had not endeared them to the citizens of the state.[49]

One month after taking office, Stanly attempted in the eastern counties to relieve the suffering brought about by the war. He also hoped to solidify a small base of support in the state. To do so, he opened trade to New Bern and Washington and allowed the inhabitants to take cargoes of pine lumber to the West Indies. Stanly also permitted Northern merchants to trade within Union lines and to purchase local products.[50]

Stanly had exceeded his authority by issuing passes, according to Lincoln's proclamation of May 1862, which had only opened Beaufort. Stanly's permits allowed vessels to trade in virtually all the navigable waters of the state with "loyal citizens" who had permits. The vessels sailed to New Bern, Washington, Plymouth, and other towns. They then traveled back to Beaufort with cargoes of cotton, turpentine, tar, and other products and cleared from that point.[51]

Complicating matters further, Brigadier General Viele did not confine his activities to Virginia. In July 1862, Viele sent three schooners to Plymouth to sell goods. Stephen C. Rowan, the senior officer in the sounds, sent these "adventurers" back to Virginia.[52]

In the ensuing months, Stanly continued to issue permits that directly contradicted Lincoln's proclamation and contravened naval authority, and a crisis became inevitable. In December 1862, Stanly embroiled himself in a dispute involving trade to loyal citizens. The naval officers in the sounds knew that this trade did relieve some of the suffering of the people in the eastern counties, but at the expense of helping the enemy, who could buy these products from disloyal citizens. On 2 December, after checking with Welles, Lee ordered that only cargoes destined for the army, with permits signed by the War, Treasury, or Navy Department could enter the blockaded region. Vessels carrying return cargoes must have permits from the general commanding the department that certified they were carrying army or other government property. To be sure that the vessels had their proper papers, he placed guard ships at Hatteras and Ocracoke inlets. Stanly was informed of the Navy Department's decision but interpreted these instructions to mean that internal trade could continue within the state, and he continued to issue many permits to this effect.[53]

Stanly authorized the schooner *Mary Jane Kennedy*, carrying salt, to trade in the sounds "in any of the navigable waters of North Carolina." Commander Henry Davenport of *Hetzel* would not let the schooner clear from New Bern to Plymouth because this was contrary to his instructions from Lee. The governor modified his permit to allow the schooner to go to Plymouth without breaking its cargo. Stanly added, "This permission I hope you will respect . . . I think your instructions from the admiral have no reference to such cases . . . I shall be compelled to regard your further interference in this case as a disregard of my order, which it will be my duty to sustain."[54] Davenport let the schooner proceed.

Davenport decided he needed to have a "frank and friendly conversation" with the governor concerning this topic and pointed to the "latitude of the first permit." Stanly understood Davenport's point of view but insisted that the people needed salt sold under the supervision of the military, and that any naval officer disobeying his orders and seizing a vessel "would lay himself liable to arrest." Davenport writing to Lee reported that the subject was a "delicate one to touch" and asked for instructions.[55]

The senior officer in the sounds, Commander Alexander Murray, "in consideration of the respect due to the high position of Governor Stanly," gave orders to honor the passes. This concession by Murray did not please Lee, who reminded Murray of his instructions of 2 December, which did not authorize Stanly's permits. Lee sternly reminded Murray that "your instructions come from the Navy Department through me, and it is not competent for Governor Stanly to give you orders or instructions in regard to the blockade or any portion of your naval duties."[56]

Stanly appealed to Secretary of War Stanton and threatened to resign over this issue. He was perturbed because he believed that the navy was infringing on his authority as the military governor. The War Department did nothing to help Stanly in his struggle with the navy and told him that naval authority overrode his in the navigable waters. Stanly refused to accept this as a final ruling and continued to issue permits.[57]

Despite his instructions, Commander Alexander Murray, the senior officer, allowed vessels with Stanly's permits to proceed, notwithstanding commands by Welles and Lee that they not be recognized. In February, Lee wrote to Murray and complained of "irregular and defective" boarding returns. Murray ostensibly began to follow Lee's instructions. But on 25 March, Lee named six instances between 1 February and 25 February 1863 in which Murray had allowed the blockade to be violated. Lee ordered Murray relieved a few days later.[58]

The problem resolved itself when Stanly resigned in January 1863, but the navy continued to be annoyed by army officials and sutlers who worked together to send stores into the state with unauthorized passes. The sutlers risked little by shipping goods into North Carolina, because their property could not be condemned as prize of war if it were transported in violation of "the conditions of their permit or without due authority."[59] Their goods could only be condemned if they were captured in violation of the blockade.

There was little regulation of legally shipped sutlers stores, and large amounts of supplies made their way into Confederate lines. Sutlers shipped goods to Roanoke Island, and contraband went from there up the Chowan River. An even greater thoroughfare was the railroad that connected Beaufort and New Bern. Goods could be legally shipped into Beaufort because it was an open port. But the railroad was "used without limit for transporting sutlers and other goods," which in effect made New Bern an open port also. In May 1863, the Revenue Marine Service stopped this practice, thus upholding the spirit of the blockade once again.[60]

The Treasury Department had an ever-expanding role in North Carolina as the war progressed. At times, this was beneficial to the navy, and at other times, aggravating. The revenue cutters acted as an adjunct force to enforce the laws concerning the blockade. They had likewise seized a number of schooners trading under Governor Stanly's orders. They made cruises within the interior waters and boarded and inspected vessels and boats. Generally, they did this within the ports themselves and confined their activity to seizing illegal goods. It was not possible to properly examine all the vessels as they came into port, so the officers often examined the cargo as it was discharged.[61]

In March 1863, Congress passed an act that provided for the collection of abandoned property and prevention of fraudulent trade. Secretary of Treasury Salmon P. Chase appointed David Heaton as special agent for the Third Special Agency, which comprised the state of North Carolina. Heaton arrived in Beaufort in May and immediately met with officers of the armed forces, the Revenue Marine Service, the provost marshal, sutlers, citizens, and traders.[62]

To decrease the suffering of the local people within the military lines, certain goods were allowed to be imported for sale to the public. The Treasury agents regulated the flow of goods by keeping local special agents and agency aids at all of the major posts in the sounds. All goods came through Beaufort and were transported to entities called trade districts.[63]

The trade districts were a growing irritation to Phillips Lee. On the west side of each trade district was a strip of territory five to eight miles in width, called a supply district. All parties in these supply districts were permitted to keep "trade stores" or to sell merchandise after taking an oath of loyalty, filing a bond, and obtaining a permit. The Treasury

Department originally permitted the trade stores to obtain only $2,000 worth of goods a month, but by August 1863, this amount had doubled. Sutlers in these areas could trade with parties outside the regiments, their only limitation being to sell goods from a prescribed list.[64]

The Treasury Department did not have the manpower nor the organization to regulate the volume of merchandise coming and going in North Carolina. While the navy was tasked with the job of the blockade, the officers could do nothing to stop the enormous volume of goods from coming into the state. Both the Army and Treasury departments accused the other of allowing abuses. Heaton accused Butler of bringing large cargoes through Hatteras "under the plea of 'military necessity,' when no necessity existed, and . . . brought in exclusively for speculative purposes."[65] A year later, Butler accused Heaton of overestimating the amount of goods necessary for the sustenance of the people. He pointed out that over seventy dollars a month was being imported for every man, woman, and child within the jurisdiction of the Treasury Department.[66]

There is no doubt that agents and disloyal merchants sold goods at huge profits that benefited the Confederacy. General Benjamin Butler even became personally tied to illicit trade by issuing a permit for the vessels to trade in areas not open for that purpose. Gideon Welles called one of these trips "a little, dirty, speculating intrigue."[67] A clause in the Treasury regulations allowed anyone buying local goods and exporting them from the Southern states to bring in supplies and merchandise of one-third of that value. A trade store located at South Mills above Elizabeth City contained $30,000 worth of goods and had sold double or triple that amount in two months.[68]

Large sums of money flowed into the Treasury's coffers and to those who could curry favor to obtain permits. The motive of profit outweighed all the efforts of the navy to stop it. During the war, the Treasury Department granted thousands of permits for "legal" trade, which netted the department tens of thousands of dollars. By February 1864, the goods coming into Beaufort averaged over $100,000 a month. Meanwhile, exported items such as naval stores, beeswax, wood, hides, cotton, shingles, flax, potatoes, and tobacco rose from under $10,000 in April 1864 to over $100,000 by that September.[69]

The Union navy later benefited by the occupation of eastern North Carolina. Before the war, North Carolina had been a center of the country's naval stores production and in 1860 produced about seventy-five percent of all the South's naval stores products. By 1863, the Union navy needed large quantities of naval stores, and the Navy Department coordinated the removal of these products from the state. In July 1863, Welles instructed Lee to find a reliable person to determine whether these products could be produced and at what cost, as the navy was paying prices nearly ten times higher than when the war began.[70]

Fleet Paymaster Charles C. Upham traveled to the sounds to work with the Treasury Department on this project. Special Treasury Agent David Heaton, who helped to supervise the purchases, published a notice on 18 August that the government was interested in buying naval stores. To prevent speculation, the government advertised that it would not buy products that had changed hands after 25 July. To provide relief to the local inhabitants, each family was allowed to sell one barrel of turpentine or its equivalent in tar every two weeks.[71] There were no large lots of naval stores, therefore Upham had to go into the "country" for them. By mid-October, he had 1,250 barrels at Morehead City and New Bern, and before the end of the month, shipments were going north.[72]

The purchase of these products led to a great savings for the navy. The department paid only one-third the amount that it had paid before the purchasing program began. To save additional money, the department began to distill the products in the sounds at a further savings of twice the amount, had they been distilled in New York. After 1 November, the department planned to have two distilleries in operation, which would give it the capacity to distill fifty barrels of naval stores a day. By mid-February, the navy was overseeing five distilleries, which produced over 700 barrels of pitch, rosin, and spirits of turpentine each week.[73] By 1 September 1864, Upham had shipped nearly 25,000 barrels of naval stores to northern ports. There was on hand in the sounds at this date enough crude product to make nearly 7,000 more barrels of pitch and turpentine, and the department planned to purchase nearly three times this amount.[74]

The state was also rich in timber resources, and in January 1864, the navy tried to arrange to buy 350,000 cubic feet of yellow pine timber for the Bureau of Construction and Repair. Bureau Chief John Lenthall wanted to procure this lumber in the same manner that the navy had

purchased the naval stores. Benjamin Butler, as usual, became involved
with the affair. Lee could not arrange the purchase because the army
had monopolized all the labor in the region. A month later, Benjamin
Butler wrote Lee that he believed that by May he could supply the navy's
timber and that he had purchased the necessary sawmills "as a means of
revenue in carrying on negro affairs."[75]

In addition to the duties of the blockade and the regulation of trade,
the navy also performed the thankless job of regulating fishing vessels.
The allowance of fishing created a situation that complicated enforcement of the blockade. In the Chesapeake Bay and the sounds of North
Carolina, hundreds of men relied on fishing for their livelihood, and
prohibition of this activity would have created a great amount of hardship on the coastal inhabitants. The Navy Department placed no restrictions upon fishing and oystering and left this matter to the squadron
commanders' discretions.[76] Before Lee took command, few problems
apparently existed, and the fishermen were allowed to continue their
avocations much as they had before the war began. In Virginia, Admiral
Lee's early policy was to allow oystering and fishing in open boats for
consumption by the armed forces and the inhabitants of each region.
Oystermen could not violate the blockade and had to remain in areas of
the "outer blockade." They could fish in the Chesapeake Bay and in the
mouths of the rivers and were examined if they passed above the guard
vessels.[77]

As in the trade imbroglio, Lee did not have control of all the fishing
vessels because both Army and Treasury officials issued permits. None
of the branches could coordinate the issuance of permits, nor could they
agree on boundaries. One morning, a whole fleet appeared at the mouth
of the Nansemond in an area not open for oystering. These boats were
"quite large, and all suited to smuggling supplies up creeks."[78] Lee had
evidence that oyster boats with army permits carried on a substantial
trade with the enemy in the creeks in the Norfolk area, and boats were
continually caught beyond the prescribed limits.[79]

The fishing boundaries constantly changed as a result of the persis-
tent attempts to smuggle goods. The gunboats found the blockade hard
to enforce because of the large number of fishing boats and Lee's lack of
light-draft vessels to watch them. In January 1863, Lee prohibited the
use of the Back and Nansemond rivers, the James above Newport News,

the Western Branch of the Elizabeth River, and all creeks. There were exceptions. Lee issued some permits for the Nansemond, but kept these boats under strict surveillance and allowed no "market boats" in the river. In the York vicinity alone, about 700 men, mostly contrabands, engaged in the oyster trade. In the Hampton Roads area on a given day, 29 schooners, 141 sloops, and 117 boats lay there oystering. One particular problem that arose over the changing boundaries was that oystermen had planted oysters in areas that no longer were open to their boats. In these cases, Lee allowed the boats to go above the guard vessels a couple at a time, which prevented financial ruin for the oystermen.[80]

In December 1863, after continued complications, Lee revoked all the oystering permits that he had issued and transferred the responsibility to the army under the direction of Butler. He did this so that all trade would conform with Lincoln's proclamation of 11 November 1862, and he instructed that all the guard vessels respect the permits issued by the general. When Porter took command, he began to reissue fishing permits and allowed commanding officers in the sounds and James River likewise to grant them.[81]

Fewer problems relating to fishing occurred in North Carolina, and it appears that the navy allowed the fishermen to pursue their activity with few restrictions. The inhabitants of the state did little oystering and mainly fished with seine nets. Roanoke Island had a large black population that existed primarily on fishing. Several large fisheries also operated on the Chowan River, and great quantities of fish were sent north to feed Robert E. Lee's troops. In an effort to prevent the movement of the fish, the navy placed restrictions upon the amounts that could be stored at certain points. Citizens could not have more than 10 barrels per person and could not keep an amount greater than 100 barrels in any place. The large storage areas could be no closer than seven miles from each other and had to be at least one mile from navigable waters.[82]

The role of the navy in the rivers and tidal areas was truely diversified. The lack of cooperation among the Treasury, War, and Navy departments intensified the rivalries and only made the work of the navy more difficult. The navy dealt with the other branches of the government in a firm manner but also with caution and discretion. The responsibilities of the war and of the blockade were overwhelming, and these duties engaged a great number of gunboats and personnel. These obligations had a great impact on the operations of the squadron and certainly decreased its effectiveness to carry out some of its more important tasks.

SEVEN

Results go far different from those desired

Acquiring and Maintaining the Fleet

When President Lincoln announced his intention to blockade the coasts of the Southern states, he probably did not grasp the unprecedented scope of this undertaking. The coastline from the Potomac to the Rio Grande stretched 3,500 miles and contained nearly 200 harbors, inlets, and rivers.[1] To carry out the impossible task of sealing these entrances, the United States Navy had neither the vessels, the personnel, nor the facilities to maintain such a blockade. Wartime logistics is characterized by the nation's ability to produce and the consumption by the armed forces of that which is produced. The North Atlantic Blockading Squadron functioned within a government bureaucracy in a rapidly induced wartime situation in which industry played a large role. But inadequacies of the government, the slowness with which northern industry responded to the tremendous demands of the war, and the ebb and flow of the war all affected the squadron. These factors prevented the quick implementation and enforcement of the blockade, restrained the efforts of the squadron during the entire war, and touched on nearly every aspect of its performance.

The government had the immediate need of a large

number of ships to implement the blockade. Since large building pro-
grams take years, the navy immediately embarked on a widespread
project of purchasing and chartering vessels. Gideon Welles selected
several prominent individuals, mostly shipping merchants in New
York, and consulted with them as an informal board of advisors on
matters of acquisition. Several months into the war, some officials still
believed that if the navy purchased as few as fifty ships, mostly sailing
vessels, they could maintain a blockade. The navy's need for ships,
though, never waned, and by 1865, the service had acquired over 500
vessels—the majority powered by steam.[2]

Chartering vessels partially solved the navy's lack of warships and
seemed economical because many believed the war would be short. The
navy signed short-term charter parties after an examination showed
that the vessel could run at least six months. Contracts reflected the
varied but specific needs of the service, being made by the hour, by the
day, by the month, by the trip, and by the ton. In most instances, the
owners of the vessel had everything to gain and little to lose. Some
owners earned as much as $1,500 a day, and sometimes the government
paid for the fuel, navigators, pilots, and insurance. The owners in turn
usually paid for all repairs and maintenance.[3]

Many of the charters gave the government an option of purchasing
the merchantmen after a specified length of time, an agreeable arrangement for both parties.[4] If the war ended quickly, the government would
not lose money in the resale of the vessel. If the vessel proved unsuitable
to the government, a second contract would not be drawn. Some of the
leased ships, however, were found to be invaluable to the navy, and they
were purchased before the end of the charter period. In 1861, a seller's
market existed, and as a result of the demand for vessels, the owners
often made handsome profits on their rates.

While charters temporarily solved the problem of acquiring vessels, it
was by no means perfect. Many of the chartered vessels were old and
worthless to their owners, but because of high demand, the navy renewed the leases or purchased them. Good examples in the squadron
were *Monticello*, *Mount Vernon*, *Dawn*, and *Cambridge*. Naval officers
examining *Mount Vernon* and *Dawn* claimed they were "unfit for
recharter." *Monticello* was in bad repair, and her commanders repeatedly complained about her during the war. At the beginning of the war,

she leaked excessively, she was not coppered, she rolled badly, her boilers leaked, and she had numerous other problems. The machinery of *Cambridge* was so exposed that she was labeled "valueless for war purposes."[5] Yet the navy eventually purchased all of them, and they served during the entire war.

The sudden demand for vessels worked counter to the interest of the United States. Owners successfully bargained for exorbitant rates for their property at amounts as high as five times what they should have been. The navy chartered the two steamers *Monticello* and *Mount Vernon* for $8,000 a month and eventually bought them for $75,000 each. In contrast, *Dawn*, a smaller vessel, cost $7,000 a month to lease and sold for only $35,000.[6] At these rates, the owners of the former two would have earned the total cost of their vessels within ten months, while the owners of *Dawn* could have done so in five months.

While chartering vessels solved immediate needs, when the Navy Department realized the war would not be short, it began to purchase many vessels. Boards of officers made the majority of the acquisitions. These boards usually consisted of commandants of navy yards, naval constructors, ordnance officers, and usually an engineer if a steamer was being examined. With assistance from naval agents, these men would advertise for bids, inspect the vessels, and bargain for a charter or for a purchase.[7]

Problems immediately arose from this particular system because of the large scale of operations. Welles stated that boards of officers acting in a "mercantile capacity . . . for which they had neither been practically trained, nor professionally commissioned, would be subjected to great embarrassment and disadvantage in their dealings with sellers of ships and professional ship brokers, in a market suddenly pressed by a heavy and preemptory demand."[8] The owners of a vessel for sale, having learned that their vessel had been surveyed, would set a price well above its true worth and could receive twice its value. Naval officers not only bought obsolete ships but also ones that had had their gear removed prior to the sale. As a guide, Gustavus Fox later advised purchasers to offer thirty-five dollars a ton for sailing vessels and seventy-five dollars a ton for steamers with machinery in good order.[9]

The system of purchase proved to be so inefficient in its methods and organization that George D. Morgan, the brother-in-law of Gideon

Welles, recommended an investigation. Welles also found the system inadequate and extremely fraudulent. In April, Welles hired Morgan to act as a proxy or commercial agent in New York for purchasing and chartering vessels. Welles knew that hiring Morgan would provoke cries of nepotism, but Morgan was the only New York merchant he knew. Instead of inviting proposals, receiving sealed bids, and awarding contracts to the lowest bidder, the navy used Morgan, who bargained more effectively. Morgan worked with naval officers but acted as the navy's sole agent, which eliminated the possibility of competition between agents. By 1 December, Morgan had purchased nearly 200 ships for the United States at a substantial savings to the government.[10]

The employment of Morgan served to create more criticism of Welles and the department. During the first few months of the war, Welles came under attack from newspapers and from Senator John P. Hale, the chairman of the Senate Committee on Naval Affairs. Hale was particularly critical of the loss of the Norfolk Navy Yard and of the methods used in purchasing vessels. Welles was required to go through hearings at a time when his efforts were needed to oversee the implementation of the blockade. Hale in particular was vehement in his attack, but for a selfish reason—he, like many others, wanted special favors in the form of contracts for his constituents, which Welles refused to grant. Welles successfully defended his policies and had the support of the chairman of the House Committee on Naval Affairs, Charles Sedgwick, who pointed out that Welles had purchased a navy out of necessity, not by law. Immense profits could still be made, and midway through the war, Welles wrote in his diary that he still received offers from "interested patriots who had old steamers to sell which no one would buy."[11]

Even with the feverish haste with which the navy purchased vessels, the blockade suffered during the early months of the war. The acquisition of vessels greatly strengthened the navy but did not bring it to the size requisite to blockade the South. These inadequacies can be seen on the coasts of North Carolina and Virginia. During the war's first months, ships steamed up and down the coast with no fixed stations.[12] It took the department three months to acquire sufficient force to release just one gunboat for the blockade of Wilmington.

Welles realized that a naval building program would take time and acquired virtually every merchant steamer in the Northern ports that could be advantageously converted to a naval vessel. This policy was necessary, but many of the vessels proved unsuited for the blockade. The first twenty steamers that the navy purchased and chartered could mount naval guns and could be used to transfer troops and supplies. These vessels varied from screw-propeller steamers to ferryboats. The largest of these ships displaced about 2,000 tons, but the majority only displaced between 100 and 800 tons. By December 1861, the department had purchased 79 steamers and 58 sailing vessels, and before the end of the war, it purchased a total of 418 vessels, of which 313 were steamers.[13] The numbers purchased thus eventually made up approximately two-thirds of the entire navy.

The rapid rate of acquisition, though, did not ensure quick placement in service. The yards remained crowded with merchantmen being converted to gunboats. These vessels normally required strengthening to carry their heavy batteries. The merchant steamers also usually needed at least two more pumps, because in battle they might take on water rapidly. The Navy Department sometimes repaired machinery and often replaced the boilers before commissioning them.[14] The hasty methods of purchase and conversion would later impair the blockade, because these gunboats would require the most care while in service.

Prizes in large numbers also joined the navy. Sailing vessels were often used by the squadron as coal and supply hulks, while steamers served on the blockade. Captured blockade runners were in constant demand in the North Atlantic Blockading Squadron. Condemnation and refitting, though, took a long time. Some steamers had to have few alterations, but normally they had to be strengthened and had to be altered to house the officers and men. To speed up condemnation and refitting, Rear Admiral Lee sent his ablest men north, but his initiative was not successful. These prizes, he wrote, "could have been discharged condemned turned over to the Navy and fitted, amply fitted, all in a week or ten days."[15] Many did not arrive on station for a year after their capture. In some instances, the conversions cost the government a sum greater than the original value of the vessel. The long delays and high costs became so critical that Welles instructed that the prizes be "fitted in the cheapest manner and without the fixtures of a regular man-of-war which are unnecessarily expensive."[16]

Converted merchantmen provided ships to the navy at a time when nothing else could be made ready for service. While these vessels played an important role in the blockade, it was the specially built naval vessels that made the greatest contribution. The monitor class, the double-enders, and the screw sloops played significant parts in the war—all made possible by the North's superior industrial capacity. The United States, however, did have numerous problems in shifting its production and meeting the logistical needs of the expanding navy. Before the outbreak of the conflict, the government had authorized the navy yards to build seven steam sloops of war. This number was later increased to eight to allow each navy yard to build two sloops. Later the Navy Department authorized the construction of six more warships along the same lines but slightly larger. The yards, though, could not handle all the necessary construction, and most of the gunboats had to be built under contract by private firms. Private contractors eventually built 124 vessels, while the navy yards built only 55.[17]

The private contractors realized early that they would handle much of the naval construction. In the war's first months, contractors, lobbyists, and speculators "hurried to the assault on the treasury like a cloud of locusts alighting down upon the capital to devour the substance of the country." The contractors, "strangers to every patriotic impulse, saw in war only an extraordinary opportunity of making a fortune."[18] The navy advertised in newspapers for bids for gunboats, and the firm with the lowest bid received the contract. The government often provided drafts for the builders and at other times solicited models, specifications, materials, and plans. There were so many plans, propositions, and inventions presented to the Navy Department at the beginning of the war that Welles created an Examining Board to look them over.[19]

In an attempt to regulate the contractors, the government inserted clauses into the agreements to keep production on schedule. The government usually placed some sort of an incentive in the contract for the firm to finish early. This performance bond usually stipulated that the contractor would gain or lose a specified sum of money for each day or month that the completion was delayed. Contracts likewise normally guaranteed that government inspectors could reject unsatisfactory materials and workmanship.[20]

Even with the checks and inspections, many of the contractors still managed to cheat the government. Contract overruns and overcharges were extremely common and totaled as much as 200 percent per vessel. Owners of private firms made large sums of money by using cheap materials and by allowing poor workmanship. Some of the contract-built vessels were "carelessly finished," and breakdowns were frequent. Contractors who cheated the government by using production shortcuts and who performed fraudulent work were usually discovered too late. But it was the gunboats' efficiency and ultimately the war effort that suffered until the problem could be remedied. The operational ability of the squadron was the major victim of fraud and careless workmanship, because the vessels were less capable of long-term and problem-free service. They often had to be sent to repair facilities to be rebuilt, they were slower, they handled poorly, and they did not perform satisfactorily at sea. The vessels built by private firms did not perform as well as those built by the navy yards and had a reputation of being weak and poorly constructed. One seaman in the squadron wrote home expressing his observations: "These contract built boats 'aint worth a cuss' a very little firing + they are all to pieces."[21]

Shallow-draft steamers were particularly needed by the squadron to patrol off Cape Fear and in the inland waters. The navy had immediately contracted with private shipyards to build twenty-three heavily armed screw gunboats that drew only ten feet of water. These vessels were called the "ninety-day gunboats" because the builders completed some within three months of the signing of the contracts. In 1861, the navy began building the Octorara class—twelve fast, double-ended, light-draft paddle-wheel steamers—to operate along the coast and rivers. These proved so successful that the department decided to build twenty-seven similar but slightly larger gunboats of the Sassacus class in the fall of 1862. Contractors built seventeen of the twenty-seven and were to complete the gunboats within six months but completed none within a year's time and some not until the end of the war. Furthermore, the builders did not meet the needs of the government. When the contractors drafted plans, they frequently could not meet all of the government's specifications in regard to draft, speed, and capacity of coal, but they built the ships nevertheless.[22]

There were various reasons for delays. Many of the contractors building hulls could not finish the vessels because the private firms building the engines were not able to complete their work on time.

Changes made by the government also created problems. Between the signing of the contracts and the ships' completion, the prices of construction had sometimes tripled. Many private firms complained that they lost money on the construction of the gunboats and asked Congress for relief. They argued that they had not been given drawings at the time that they made the bids and claimed that government inspectors had driven up the prices by requesting standards above those specified. They also asserted that the availability of materials had changed after the contracts had been signed, that labor costs had risen immensely, and that strikes had impeded construction.[23]

The government-built gunboats were likewise flawed, particularly the shallow-draft double-enders for inland use. Those built at the Portsmouth and Boston navy yards all exceeded their designed draft by about three feet. Welles wrote that, "if as a general thing, results go far different from those desired and expected are obtained, the Department could not but doubt the professional ability of those to whom the construction of vessels is confided."[24] The navy had had similar problems with the shallow-draft ironclads. Chief Engineer Alban Stimers changed the specifications and caused the vessels to be unusable for the purpose for which they were designed. The absence of the light-draft monitors and double-enders particularly limited the squadron's strategic options in the sounds of North Carolina. The absence of a shallow-draft ironclad weakened the federal forces, causing them to be overwhelmed by *Albemarle*.

Ironclads presented special problems to the government during the war, because not one of the navy yards was capable of building them. Even most of the private yards did not have the equipment to build them and found it difficult to employ men with sufficient knowledge and experience. Assistant Secretary of the Navy Gustavus Fox placed John Ericsson in charge of their construction, which allowed him to choose the firms that built the vessels. As a result of the lack of facilities and the special needs of the monitor class, the government eventually established its own yard, workshop, and docks for them at League Island, Pennsylvania.[25]

From the beginning of the conflict, Welles realized that the classes of warships then under construction would not be suitable to operate along the Southern coast. The Navy Department, however, failed to develop and produce a single warship that was capable of catching the fastest blockade runners or one that could efficiently blockade the coast. This is because the department could never totally break away from sail propulsion. The department was aware of the problems of ships with both sails and steam machinery ten years before the war began. The department did reduce sail rigs to a great degree during the war. Unreliable engines and high fuel consumption had compelled the department to keep sails as an alternative method of propulsion. The need for steam vessels on the blockade became more essential as the blockade runners began to increase their speeds. But Gideon Welles pursued a building policy that dictated that all screw vessels of war intended as permanent warships of the navy be built with spars and sails to "render them efficient as sailing vessels." Yet the chief of the Bureau of Construction and Repair, John Lenthall, knew that it was "not practical to combine in one vessel steam power lying wholly below the water line and sufficient to give great speed and such distribution of sail as to make the steamer as efficient under sail alone as though it was a purely sailing vessel."[26]

Building engines for the warships delayed the placement of ships into service more than any other factor. The navy yards had no facilities to produce engines on a large scale, and few shipbuilders had this capability either. In May 1861, a survey showed that only thirty-eight engines could be built in four months' time, six of these by firms with financial problems. Contractors who built engines increased during the war but could not meet the demand. The government found it difficult to hold the contractors to a specified time, and by 1863, the navy took the builders' terms at any cost because they could not obtain any better.[27]

Labor and material problems seemed to be the greatest reasons for delays. During the winter of 1863, the failure of firms building engines to meet their contractual obligations prompted Welles to instruct the commandants of some of the yards to begin to lay off fifteen percent of their carpenters. Since the machinery for the warships could not be supplied as fast as the hulls, the new ships had begun to lay in the yards waiting for their machinery to arrive. The engine contractors responded by rushing to complete their work, using inferior materials, unskilled workmen, and cutting corners on production methods. Many gunboats subsequently suffered breakdowns while at their stations. This later compelled the government to buy English engines through its London agents, Baring Brothers and Company.[28]

The nature of the blockade showed that only steam vessels could maintain a strict blockade. During the war, the United States Navy thus only built or entered contracts to build steam vessels. This tremendous growth of the navy presented problems to the department that it had never before faced. The nature of naval service, and particularly the blockade, subjected steam machinery to stress not encountered in normal movement. Warships remained at their stations for long periods of time, which introduced hardships on the engines. The machinery usually remained under steam at all times to propel the warships to catch blockade violators, or to get them out of the range of the enemy's guns.

The necessity for frequent repairs to the warships handicapped the North Atlantic Blockading Squadron, since a constant procession of vessels were withdrawn from their stations periodically for repairs or refitting. Weeks or months might intervene before repairs could be made to steamers that had received serious damage or needed extensive repairs. Because of the crowded conditions of the repair facilities, gunboats that needed repairs normally remained at their stations, by necessity, for long periods of time. The flag officers usually insisted that the gunboats remain at their stations if their absence would weaken the blockade.[29] Thus in the sounds of North Carolina and to a lesser extent at Cape Fear, the gunboats lay at their stations in a crippled condition because their presence was essential.

The policy of keeping unrepaired gunboats at their stations usually worked to the detriment of the machinery. Spare parts were often unavailable, and in some instances, every day that the engines remained in operation, the need for repairs became more acute and threatened the complete breakdown of the engines. Engineers normally used every expedient to keep their machinery running, but the engines of the blockaders, particularly later in the war, usually remained in constant motion, which made some incidental repairs difficult or impossible.[30] Service during the winter months compounded the problems with machinery and caused the loss of nearly one-third of all the vessels for repairs or refueling.

The tremendous increase in the navy's steam fleet also created a dearth of qualified personnel to handle the steam machinery. Volunteers flocked to the Navy Department because the pay was so much greater than in other branches of the service, but they could not be trained effectively since no school existed. Regular engineer officers had to pass a rigorous examination, but acting appointments and volunteers might encounter little or no scrutiny and learned mainly from experience. Welles realized that technologically the United States lagged behind some European countries in steam engineering and sent a chief engineer to Europe for information. Fox, meanwhile, suggested establishing of a professorship of steam engineering at the Naval Academy.[31]

The breakdown of machinery, especially the boilers, was by far the most common source of complaint from officers. Converted merchantmen generally posed more problems, because they had older engines, and they often lay exposed, subjected to both the weather and the enemy's gunfire. In many cases, the ships' officers became confused when their machinery broke down because of the lack of knowledge of steam mechanics. Early in the conflict, officers frequently worried more about their boilers exploding than they did about the enemy.[32]

Many of the warships in the squadron had their boilers above the waterline and occasionally in full view. When an enemy projectile hit the boilers, it sent hot water over the deck, scalding and killing crew members. Many ships protected their steam drums and boilers with sandbags, cotton, iron plating, and coal. Exposed boilers made some ships less seaworthy because the weight of the water in the boilers above the waterline affected the vessel's center of gravity.[33]

The most prevalent derangement of boilers was leaks. Repairs at sea could be dangerous and time consuming. Sometimes the coal used to protect the boilers had to be hoisted from the hold to the deck in order to get to the boiler to make repairs. Repairing leaks also required that the fires be drawn, which might cause some careful consideration before repairs were undertaken if in a river or in the sounds. These ships normally withdrew for repairs to avoid surprise by an unexpected enemy. Patches and plugged or replaced tubes solved the leaks and for some ships made up part of the daily routine.[34]

Some gunboats remained at their stations with no means of making these simple repairs. For others, these repairs were impossible because of the wretched condition of the boilers, with iron so thin that the patches would not hold. Vessels in this condition usually broke down every few days. Department policy, and the lack of warships, normally meant that the crews of the gunboats made what repairs they could.

Most ships waited until they could be spared to go to a repair facility or until a boiler could be made, which sometimes took months. Gunboats in this condition were inefficient, and they required constant attention by the engineers. The crews on board these vessels often manned the pumps many times a day to rid the bilges of water lost from the boilers.[35]

The exigencies of the war created some of these problems. In several instances, the gunboats left the contractors without an inspection or a trial, and once on station the engineers discovered the defects. A lack of tools was also a common complaint. Without the proper tools, even some of the most minor repairs could not be made. In February 1864, Lee issued a circular that required the steamers of the squadron to carry a prescribed set of tools and materials to ensure that they could make a minimum of necessary repairs.[36]

Abuses by the ships' engineers also caused an inordinate amount of trouble with the boilers and machinery. Engineers and firemen of blockading vessels frequently threw grease, tar, pork, or anything that would burn quickly into their furnaces in order to raise the steam pressure in a chase. Raising steam quickly put a strain on the metal and often caused the seams to break apart.[37] Likewise, these burned items left a residue in the tubes. The engineers blew their boilers down regularly to avoid buildups of salt and scale. But these residues accumulated to such an extent that it caused an uneven heat transference, thereby causing the metal in the tubes to weaken and leak.

Neglect of the boilers and machinery of the squadron's vessels resulting from the inexperience and ignorance of most of the engineers caused a number of problems. *State of Georgia* reportedly had her "oil holes and channels in the brasses clogged up with dirt—the condenser nearly filled with tallow—and a thickness of five inches of tallow and dirt was found in the air pump." Welles warned against this negligence and began dismissing engineers who allowed such abuses.[38]

For a more "rigid and systematic administration of the Engineers Department," Welles had Lee attach the senior engineer of the squadron to the flagship as fleet engineer. The fleet engineer and a boilermaker examined the vessels in the squadron with the purpose of increasing their efficiency.[39] The fleet engineer, however, could not maintain a watchful eye over all the machinery in the squadron.

When the boilers became too defective to repair, they had to be replaced. Replacing boilers, though, was one of the most time-consuming jobs, because parts of the deck had to be taken up in order to remove the defective boiler. To replace and sometimes even to repair them could take six weeks or longer. When the workmen took up the decks, the navy often made other alterations to make the ship more efficient, more seaworthy, or to make room for larger or a greater number of guns. Testing the engines usually delayed any other work, and thus the warships returned to action, much delayed.[40]

By 1863, the replacement of boilers had become a serious problem. The contractors could not get material, and repair times could not even be estimated. Engineer-in-Chief Benjamin Isherwood wrote Lee that "no one will now accept a contract for a boiler with the understanding that they are to be held rigorously to time." He asked Lee to forward a list and drawings of the boilers that the squadron would need during the next year. With the worsening situation, gunboats needing new boilers remained at their stations if their boilers could be made to last. This policy sacrificed reliability, efficiency, and the speed of the warships.[41]

Replacing a ship's boilers often created problems rather than curing them. *Sebago*, a side-wheel steamer of the Octorara class, received a new boiler only four months after her completion. The new boiler allowed her to make only five knots—about half her previous speed. The replacement boiler built for the steam tug *Cohasset* weighed nearly twice what the old boiler weighed, but to expedite the ship's return to duty, the fleet engineer recommended using it despite the extra weight. A boiler for *Ceres* was too large and caused her to draw so much water that she later had to return for a replacement.[42]

Worthless gunboats needing expensive repairs often served in the sounds of North Carolina or in the Chesapeake Bay. This policy concerned the senior officers in these areas. In many cases, the mere operation of these gunboats endangered the ship and the crew. *Miami*, a side-wheel double-ender, may have been the worst vessel in the squadron. Her engines constantly needed repairs, she almost daily patched boilers, and she could hardly move. She had steamed to Hampton Roads in April 1863 for a survey by the fleet engineer, who suggested that she be repaired. Before this could happen, the Confederates attacked Washington, North Carolina, and she went back with the understanding she would receive repairs in three months. After returning to the sounds, *Miami* remained there until the summer of 1864 and never operated other than as a "block-ship," lying at anchor at all times. Her boilers remained in such a wretched condition that she could not carry steam for more than an hour and then only to pump water out of the bilges.[43]

The commanders off Cape Fear also had their problems. The gunboats there had to be in good mechanical order to chase blockade runners and to avoid running aground or coming within range of enemy guns. Senior officer Captain A. Ludlow Case complained that he was "tired with broken down and worn out vessels, and constant complaints of injuries to boilers and engines." He further noted that this situation is understandable "when the character of the vessels is considered, together with the fact of their being kept so constantly under steam without other facilities than the means within themselves, and a suitable time for making repairs."[44]

The squadron extensively used commercial vessels refitted for war, which continually posed problems for their commanders. Most of them, being lightly framed, could not carry heavy naval ordnance. Firing the guns on the ex-merchantmen caused many of their timbers to pull away from the frames and created severe leaks. These gaps had to be constantly recaulked, because leaks not only lowered their efficiency and speed but endangered the vessels. Flag Officer Goldsborough commented that these frail ships had "to be handled almost as carefully as though they represented a basket of eggs."[45] After adding guns, some of them became unseaworthy, and even in mild weather, they rolled excessively. This type of movement made it impossible to use the ship's guns. Sometimes heavy ordnance placed in the bows of ex-merchantmen caused strain on their engines, because it brought the screws out of the water in mild seas. Early in the war, the Navy Department tried many of the ex-merchantmen along the coast, but their design, frailness, insufficient power, and old machinery prevented many from serving on the coastal blockade, though some eventually served in the inland waters.[46]

Heavy ordnance further damaged the ships by causing hogging and sagging. The ferryboat *Hunchback* carried a battery and ammunition weighing forty-seven tons, most of which lay at her extremities. This weight caused her to hog, and her planks warped and sprang leaks. Lieutenant Commander William McCann believed it caused his vessel to be unsafe in action. The side-wheel steamer *Underwriter* sagged so badly during a three-month period that she settled eight inches amidships. Many of the purchased vessels that served in the North Atlantic Blockading Squadron had beam engines. This machinery was well adapted for long, light-draft, and high-speed vessels.[47] Since beam engines occupied most of the waist of a ship, the ordnance lay at the ends, which aggravated the hogging problem.

The blockade suffered greatly because of the inefficiency of the gunboats that patrolled the coast. Engines that malfunctioned while in pursuit of blockade violators caused many lost prizes. At times, ships, because of the poor condition of their machinery, had to be towed to port by other blockading vessels. Many lay helpless in heavy gales, owing to the condition of their boilers, machinery, and ground tackle. Warships on blockade service needed to be fast, efficient, and in good order to capture the fast blockade runners. Commanders off Cape Fear often complained that most of the ships under their command were "cripples." Due to their importance, the blockaders often had preference over other vessels when repairing.[48]

Natural processes also kept gunboats in want of maintenance. Fouling of the ship's bottom continually concerned the officers. Barnacles and plant growth, the latter sometimes over an inch in length, cut down on a vessel's speed and affected her steerage way. The officers tried every contrivance to keep the growth off their ships. They had scrapers that removed the growth as far as they could reach while afloat. But to clean the bottom thoroughly, the gunboat had to be careened or removed from the water and painted with zinc paint.[49]

The ships that patrolled the sounds and rivers regularly struck the bottom or snagged wrecks and obstructions. Accidents of this nature punched holes in the hull or stripped large amounts of copper off the bottom and strained the timbers, which eventually required time in a dry dock. Divers could examine the damaged hulls and sometimes could repair them. Divers made repairs, worked on propellors, and cleaned the hulls to keep ships out of dry dock. These men became such a necessity to the service that Phillips Lee wanted to create the special rate of diver. Contact with the bottom also regularly damaged rudders, which disabled the gunboats until repaired. Vessels in the sounds normally had to remain for long periods of time needing rudder repairs before being hauled out of the water in the sounds or towed north.[50]

An officer wishing to have his warship repaired had to request a survey. A board consisting of one line officer and at least two engineers examined the gunboats and reported in writing "the nature and extent of the accident or derangement, the cause thereof, the probable time of repair, and whom; if any, blame in connexion therewith is to be attributed."[51] After the survey, the ship usually waited for the return of others from repair facilities. This policy kept the blockade from becoming too weak and the repair facilities from becoming too crowded. Gunboats often had only a specific amount of time to have their repairs made; commanders who stayed longer had to account for their delays. When David Porter took command of the squadron in October 1864, he found twenty-five vessels in Norfolk with some type of repair work being done. He began "kicking them out as fast as possible," sending fifteen immediately back to sea. Porter at this time listed nearly one-third of his gunboats as unfit for the outside blockade. Porter believed the Norfolk yard stayed crowded because the engineers did not do enough of their own repairs. He wrote to Fox that he believed that they merely longed "for the joys of Norfolk as the Peri did for paradise."[52]

The delays in the yards never improved during the war and progressively worsened. Delays permeated the whole system because of the limited facilities of the navy yards and their inability to execute the repair work. Repairs that should have been possible in three months often took a year to complete. The United States Navy thus relied heavily on private industry to make many of the repairs. With the war almost over, Gideon Welles commented in 1865: "Our navy yards are, all of them, of limited area, and wholly insufficient for our present navy. Not one of them presents the full requisite conveniences and facilities for promptly fitting out in rapid and efficient manner more than a single vessel at a time."[53]

No one could have predicted the requirements and logistical needs of the navy when the war began. But there were myriad factors that caused delays and hurt the effectiveness of the gunboats. At the beginning of the war, there were only about thirty machine shops in the Northern states, and only eight of these were large establishments. During the war, the yards grew but at a pace too slow to keep ahead of the vessels needing repairs.[54]

Facilities for docking vessels for repair were likewise inadequate. Only one dry dock had been provided for each navy yard, and three of these were made of wood. At the beginning of 1863, there was no dry dock, floating or excavated, that could admit some of the larger gunboats then being built. If a dry dock building program had been started in 1863, it would have taken until the middle of 1864 before a floating dry dock could have been finished. It would have been 1867 or 1868 before a stone dry dock could have been put into operation. Under the existing conditions, some of the larger side-wheel gunboats had to remove their wheels, along with their guns, stores, coal, and so forth before they could be docked.[55]

Another cause for delays was the insufficient waterfront at the navy yards. This kept gunboats waiting for repairs and doubled the handling and transportation of materials. This practice consumed the time of workers, who passed back and forth and cost the government as much as four times the estimated costs of the repairs.[56]

The yards also stayed crowded with vessels that changed their armament and went for refitting. Unpredictable elements such as bad weather, strikes, and shortages of materials also caused delays and crippled operations. By December 1862, no vessel sent north could be returned in less than a month. Repairs that should have taken weeks took as many months. Gideon Welles informed the chief of the Bureau of Yards and Docks in August 1863: "We have now at the yards and at private establishments a number of vessels waiting and undergoing repairs, equal to an entire squadron."[57]

Shortages of timber also delayed repairs and were common in the first months of the war. So critical were these early shortages that the navy did not hesitate to seize lumber whenever it could. The shortages continued through the conflict, and the Navy Department began to search for new areas from which to procure wood. The eastern counties of North Carolina were found to have the resources the navy needed. By 1863, lumber was coming from Washington and New Bern to repair the vessels. Under the direction of Benjamin Butler and Samuel Chase, the army purchased sawmills and was able to supply the navy with wood.[58]

The timber shortage and the subsequent gathering of lumber in

North Carolina did not solve all the problems. Because of the severe shortage, wood that the navy used in repairs was usually green and sometimes cut at the wrong seasons of the year. Repairs had been made "as rapidly as possible both by contract and in the navy yards, using green and unseasoned materials." There was not enough wood of any kind to allow it to season for a year or eighteen months.[59] The green timber used later shrank, causing many of the vessels to leak and to require more frequent repairs.

Interference by members of Congress also impeded the operation of the navy yards and greatly annoyed Welles. The secretary of the navy wrote in his diary: "In scarcely a single instance is the public good consulted in their interference, but a demoralized, debauched system of personal and party favoritism has grown up which is pernicious." Welles complained that the political appointments were a "detriment to the public's interests" and led to a "defective administration."[60]

Many other abuses evident even before the war started grew during the conflict. In particular, theft, graft, and indolence seemed to increase. The number of navy artisans had grown to the unheard-of number of nearly 17,000. But the tremendous increase of the fleet created more work than could be accomplished.[61]

Labor difficulties caused the commandants of the yards some of their worst concerns. In December 1861 and July 1862, Congress passed legislation to prevent strikes and losses of laborers to private firms. These laws directed that wages and hours of employment conform to the private yards in the immediate vicinity in order to discourage competition for jobs. Wages in the private yards, however, were allowed to be ten percent higher, and workers could make more working overtime. The higher wages paid by the private establishments allowed them to pick the best men and left the navy yards short of both numbers and quality laborers. Furthermore, because of the differences in the pay scales among the different navy yards, it was not uncommon for workers to leave one yard and to begin work at another to make a higher wage.[62]

Strikes and the draft also created shortages of workmen. The draft was indiscriminate, and the government and private yards lost many skilled artisans to the army. Men also left some areas to avoid the draft. With no success, both private establishments and the navy asked that their workers, particularly mechanics, be exempt from the draft. Dissat-isfaction with wages or work hours caused strikes, and a long and well-developed strike not only caused additional delays for repairs but also often forced the department to send vessels to other repair facilities.[63]

At the beginning of the war, the most convenient facilities for the squadron were at Washington and Baltimore and in the Hampton Roads area. Washington and Baltimore could, on the average, be reached in half a day's steaming from the Chesapeake Bay, while facili-ties in New York and Philadelphia only took one day, and Boston and Portsmouth two days' steaming.[64]

After the loss of Norfolk, Old Point Comfort became the nearest place that repairs could be made. A small naval machine shop located there could make minor repairs. The Navy Department made an early gesture to increase its size to benefit the squadron and sent ship carpen-ters but never enlarged it to any extent. The facility consisted of a machine shop, carpenters shop, smithy and foundry, mess house and quarters, storehouse and kitchen, and an office—over 7,000 square feet of floor space.[65]

Although this shop served some of the needs of the squadron, it did not have adequate facilities to allow warships to anchor alongside for repairs. This increased the cost of repairs at least thirty-three percent, because the workers had to go back and forth. In December 1862, the department made plans to move the shop to Norfolk. Within two months, they had transferred the machinery, and the buildings were finished shortly afterward. To further expedite minor repairs, the old frigate *Brandywine*, used as a storeship, also had a complement of car-penters, sailmakers, and spare parts.[66]

The Norfolk Navy Yard, one of the country's principal repair facili-ties before the war, became virtually useless to the Union navy after the Confederates destroyed and abandoned it in May 1862. On May 20, when Captain John W. Livingston took command, he found the yard in a deplorable state. Hulks lay in the channel, the docks and the dry dock needed extensive repairs, and almost all the buildings had been de-stroyed. Only the foundry, boiler shop, machine shop, and a few smaller structures could be put in working order in a short time.[67]

A long time elapsed before major repairs could be handled at the Norfolk yard. While the navy struggled to restore the facilities, the army accommodated minor repairs to gunboats at the U.S. Army Ship Yard at Norfolk. During 1863, one of the major goals of the Navy Department was to make the yard capable of functioning as the major repair facility for the North Atlantic Blockading Squadron. In October 1863, the yard still needed tools, machinery, and shops to make it efficient. Throughout the remainder of the year, only minor or supplemental repairs could be made there.[68]

In 1864, because of the immense numbers in the squadron, the Navy Department increased its efforts to make the yard serviceable. Even when the yard had regained most of its capabilities, it continued to fall short of being able to handle all of the required work. The machine shop that the navy removed from Fort Monroe never met the needs of the squadron, and the dry dock remained unusable. Livingston complained that the "yard is frequently so blocked with vessels that those repairing are delayed." Nevertheless, by 1864, the navy yard at Norfolk made more repairs for the squadron than any other facility.[69]

Acting Rear Admiral Lee seemed to have an unusual problem with the vessels that went for repairs at Norfolk. David Dixon Porter shed some light on Lee's problems. He wrote that Livingston "had made himself very disagreeable to Rear Admiral Lee, and had thrown many obstacles in the way of getting his vessels equipped as he desired them to be." Porter also claimed that Livingston was jealous of his superiors and that the Norfolk yard under Livingston "was a one horse concern, and the driver couldn't manage the horse."[70]

The Washington Navy Yard was also convenient to the gunboats stationed in the Chesapeake area. The Washington yard, though, was relatively small, and its main priority was the manufacture of ordnance, ammunition, anchors, chains, and machinery. For this reason and the lack of docking facilities that could accommodate large vessels, the squadron used it infrequently and usually only when other yards were overcrowded.[71]

Philadelphia also served the North Atlantic squadron but with limitations, particularly in the size of the ships it could repair. Furthermore, the facility lay on only seventeen acres and had a limited waterfront. The navy out of necessity rented space to repair and accommodate vessels there, but even this never met the needs of the navy, and eventually it purchased League Island. Ice in the winter also reduced the number of gunboats that could be repaired. For these reasons, some of the private establishments in the city acquired some work.[72]

The North Atlantic Blockading Squadron infrequently used the navy yards at New York, Boston, and Portsmouth, New Hampshire. When other yards became crowded, the gunboats traveled to these facilities. The New York Navy Yard handled a great percentage of the repairs for the other squadrons and normally worked at capacity during the entire war. Since the government yards stayed full, the vessels relied on private shipyards to expedite their return to service. Rear Admiral Francis Gregory supervised the repairs at these facilities. The North Atlantic Blockading Squadron relied heavily on these private establishments to make its numerous repairs.[73]

The naval station at Baltimore and the private facilities there were the most frequently used by the squadron until Norfolk became operational. The commanders of the squadron had their worst problems at the privately owned yards in Baltimore. The work done by the private yards was often executed without contracts, which gave individuals an opportunity for fraud. During the war, when inflation became a problem and their profits were threatened, the contractors' work deteriorated. The engineer in chief, Benjamin Franklin Isherwood, complained to Gideon Welles that repair bills on machinery could be so "exorbitant" that "the cost of the repairs swelled in some cases beyond the actual total value of the machinery when repaired." The contractors often extended work unnecessarily, charged exorbitant prices, and performed careless and imperfect work, which delayed the return of gunboats to their stations and often precipitated their return for repairs a short time later.[74]

Private establishments that made repairs for government vessels had to meet certain standards to apply to the government for work. The government inspected the shops to make certain that the tools, the facilities, and the employees' mechanical and engineering skills could sufficiently perform the prompt and proper repairs to naval machinery. But despite the vigilance of Gregory, who oversaw all contracts, steam machinery, and repair work outside the navy yards, the repairs at Baltimore continued to be imperfect, slow, and expensive. Flag Officer Goldsborough wrote to Fox, "There is something radically wrong at that place. . . . Somebody wants stirring up with a good long pole, if not a knock on the head with it."[75]

The naval station at Baltimore, so limited in its capacity, forced the government to employ private establishments. The naval station had only one set of ways and one dock for screw vessels—both limited in size. Some large side-wheel vessels had to remove their wheels before going into the dock. Others had to discharge coal, ammunition, and guns before getting into the dock, which consumed time because the yard had no crane. The wharf space was also extremely limited and usually remained crowded with merchantmen, because no other wharf had sufficient water. Gunboats trying to get into the dock or onto the ways had to use this wharf to remove their coal, guns, and stores in preparation for receiving repairs.[76]

The aforementioned ports and facilities were less convenient to the gunboats in the sounds of North Carolina and for the blockaders at Cape Fear. The capture of the eastern portion of North Carolina allowed the gunboats to use the small facilities in the state to make repairs. They often made repairs while recoaling, which allowed them to remain on their stations and saved the time involved in going north. Toward the end of the war, many repairs could be made at Beaufort, New Bern, and Washington, and minor repairs could be made at Roanoke Island.[77]

The facilities in the sounds were primitive at best. Beaufort had a small machine shop. At New Bern, the army made use of a locomotive shop that often did repairs for the navy, but army work always took precedence. The squadron also used a small blacksmith shop at the Sparrow Ship Yard in New Bern. Washington had a foundry, a machine shop, a blacksmith's shop, and facilities for hauling ships out of the water, but they needed much initial work to put them in order. Because of the dearth of facilities available to the navy, Phillips Lee attempted to refurbish these. The army's uncertain commitment to garrison Washington permanently caused the navy to hesitate to put the foundry and machine shop in order, and it never adequately furnished the blacksmith shop.[78]

The facilities in the sounds continued to be too limited for many of the major engine and boiler repairs that the gunboats needed, but with the proper supplies, much of the woodwork could be done there. Work progressed slowly, because the navy could only spare a few laborers, and they paid these men only when they worked. As late as October 1862, only one carpenter supervised all the work in the sounds. These facilities never had an adequate number of competent mechanics, and boiler makers and other laborers traveled from other yards to perform the necessary work. The primitive facilities and small numbers of laborers, compounded by the growing numbers of ships, often meant that a trip north resulted in a faster return to action.[79]

The repair problem for the squadron was severe. A gunboat averaged over twenty percent of the war in a repair facility.[80] This figure does not include the periods that she was absent for coal and stores or the time spent traveling for these items, nor does it reflect the time that she laid at her station needing repairs.

These tables merely reflect the number of vessels repairing or on their way to a repair facility. The tables do not take into consideration that there was a substantial number of other gunboats that were useless, disabled, or waiting for repairs. In November 1862, Lee inspected the vessels in the sounds of North Carolina and at Cape Fear and found all but one needing some degree of repairs.[81] These tables likewise do not indicate the repairs that the gunboats made without leaving their stations, nor do they reflect minor repairs made at sea.

Nearly all of the warships stationed in the sounds were in need of major repairs, but they were usually kept at their posts by making only

Table 1. Percentages of Gunboats Absent for Repairs

Year	Average Percentage Repairing	Average Number of Vessels	Average Number Repairing
1861	17	23.5	4.0
1862	13	45.6	6.0
1863	19	57.1	10.6
1864	19	102.0	19.5
1865	10	120.0	12.0
Average for the war	16	71.0	11.0

Note: Figures do not include supply hulks but do include tugs, guard vessels, and dispatch vessels.

Table 2. Gunboats Absent for Repairs by Month

Month	Percentage
June 1861	27
December 1862	25
October 1863	36
November 1863	34
February 1864	25
September 1864	39
October 1864	30

Note: These figures were computed by taking the dispositions of the vessels listed in the ORN and finding the percentage absent for repairs. Notice that some months show high numbers of gunboats absent from their stations.

Table 3. Percentage of Repairs by Facility and Year

Facility	1861	1862	1863	1864	1865	Total Percentage of Repairs
Norfolk/Hampton Roads	11	28	42	58	91	52
Philadelphia	33	5	14	9	0	8
Baltimore	6	39	29	18	6	22
New York	17	8	2	6	3	6
Washington	33	15	5	2	0	6
Sounds*	0	1	2	1	0	1
Portsmouth, N.H.	0	2	0	0	0	0**
Boston	0	2	6	6	0	5

* Repairs that were made in the sounds were of a minor nature; thus most do not show up in the returns.
** Was much less than one percent.

minor alterations. Repair trips normally could be made in less than a day, which did not show on the returns. Furthermore, since their main duty was to guard the towns, they could lie in the rivers and receive the necessary attention.

These tables likewise do not reflect the repairs made at Beaufort to the blockaders stationed off Cape Fear. Many of the blockaders were repaired while coaling, which does not show up on the monthly returns. Gunboats were not even sent to Hampton Roads if the repairs could be made in two days more time than it took to refuel the ship.[82]

It is evident that the need of repairs kept large numbers of gunboats away from their stations or left them at their stations as crippled and ineffective. The navy never solved its repair problems, because as the facilities improved, the numbers of vessels increased. Along with the old and worn out steamers, the new vessels with their myriad problems caused by constant use and shoddy workmanship kept the repair facilities full. Vessels away for repairs negatively influenced the maintenance of the blockade, the support of army positions, and the navy's ability to cooperate in combined operations. Delays in building and outfitting vessels also critically slowed the navy's ability to blockade the coast and perform its vital missions. These problems, though, are not unusual when rapid expansion occurs during wartime. But the logistical absence of these warships perhaps dealt one of the most severe blows to the squadron's effectiveness during the entire war.

EIGHT

No chance for manavelins

Supplying the
Squadron

To maintain an effective blockade, the Navy Department faced the task of supplying warships along a tremendously long coastline. By early 1862, the North Atlantic Blockading Squadron patrolled approximately 450 miles of this coastline, as well as the Chesapeake and its tributaries and the sounds and rivers of North Carolina. The job of supply became more difficult as the number of ships increased and the responsibilities of the squadron grew. An effective blockade and the protection of army positions and communications required a great number of gunboats, and it was important that these ships remain at their stations. Thus the navy had to maintain a system of supply that provided the proper quantities and regularity to ensure this.

Because of the rapid growth of the navy during the first year of the war, Congress reorganized the Navy Department. This reorganization helped the department to make a transition to its growing logistical needs. The number of bureaus was increased from five to eight, which allowed better control of the affairs of the department. The duties of the former Bureau of Equipment and Repair were divided among three new bureaus: the Bureau of Equipment and Recruiting, the Bureau of Construction and Repair, and the Bureau of Steam Engineering. The former Bureau of Ordnance and Hydrography was divided into the Bureau of Ordnance and the Bureau of Navigation.[1]

To maintain the war effort, the bureaus purchased great amounts of material that the navy could not manufacture itself. Even though the reorganization of the bureaus allowed better management, astute individuals could still take advantage of the confusion during the war to make great profits. The incredibly extensive needs of the government, compounded by an economy that was not adapted to wartime production, created waste, fraud, and abuse. The Navy Department relied on the large contractors not only for vessels but also for a great quantity of weapons and equipment. In the haste to make contracts, competition was reduced and high prices were spawned.[2]

All of the required items that the navy yards could not produce for the gunboats were purchased by navy agents at the different yards and naval stations. The Navy Department advertised for all supplies and awarded contracts to the lowest bidder who could guarantee that it would sign the contract if the bid was accepted. The department divided the articles that it normally required into forty-five classes, which allowed dealers to compete by bidding on a specific class of items. When all the items on a contract were delivered, it was considered closed until a new contract was made. Other materials outside the contracts had to be obtained through a navy agent at the lowest market price.[3]

Contractors tried to cheat the government in many different ways. When purchases were made in open market, contractors often sent items to the yards without bills and later charged higher prices. When this occurred, the commandants had to send the inspector of bills to inquire about prices of at least "two respectable dealers" in order to make a list of market prices. Contractors also sent items that were not requisitioned or sent them in greater quantity than had been requisitioned, hoping that they would be accepted and paid for before the error was discovered. The government had constantly to keep its eyes open for those who tried to cheat it. Contractors showed samples and then put in bids with the hope of substituting inferior articles. Lenthall, in particular, closely watched the purchases and questioned those that he thought were not appropriate. His management saved the navy a great deal of money and helped to keep the contracts in line.[4]

Not all of the contractors perpetrated frauds and abuses, and many lost money. Some firms who were inconvenienced by slow government payments were forced to discontinue their business relationships with the government. Contractors were also hurt by wartime inflation. Between the time the contracts were signed and delivery, prices often rose so high that some firms could no longer deliver the goods at the contracted price. The department sometimes allowed the contractors facing these conditions to abandon the contracts without penalty. Others were able to make substitutions for products that had become scarce as a result of the great demands the war had placed on the market.[5]

Shortages of supplies were not uncommon because of the "particular and novel character of the vessels, and [because] the service on which they were engaged required many things that could not be foreseen in any contract."[6] To avoid shortages, the department attempted to keep a reasonable supply of the items that the ships constantly needed. The bureaus frequently ran short of articles, and when contractors were unable to furnish these, the navy agents purchased them in the open market. Items purchased in this fashion not only cost more but also tempted many navy agents to defraud the government. The navy agents found this easy to do since they worked on a percentage.[7]

Welles investigated the fraud between navy agents and contractors, and several were found guilty of theft, bribery, receiving stolen property, and malfeasance in office. He eventually discontinued the use of navy agents and wrote, "I cannot think well of scarcely one of the navy agents."[8] Supplies had been purchased in two ways: in the open market by navy agents and by contract, the latter being preferred. Welles transferred the jobs of the navy agents to the paymasters in the navy, who received no percentages, held naval commissions, and were subject to court-martial.

The navy's demands for equipment at times greatly exceeded the production capacity of the United States, and the department made purchases abroad. In 1862, the United States consul in London purchased 10,000 fathoms of chain cable for the Navy Department because the existing facilities could not keep up with the navy's needs. The navy also purchased machinery to work metal from abroad and from the cargoes of condemned prizes.[9]

To facilitate the implementation of an efficient blockade, the navy needed to secure logistical bases along the southern coastline for "places of deposit for provisions and coal and secure retreats from distress and for repair."[10] But in 1861, no place like this existed on the Atlantic Coast south of Hampton Roads. Thus the vessels stationed along the coast to maintain the blockade were logistically disabled. If supplies could not be sent to the vessels, they had to leave their stations. This lack of bases prompted the capture of the forts at Hatteras Inlet, which the navy saw as a logistical foothold along the coast.

The loss of the Norfolk Navy Yard crippled the supply system for the Navy Department. The yard had been a first-rate facility before its capture. The loss of the yard not only denied the North the use of the facility but also forced other yards to handle the distribution and to compete with the army for the remaining facilities. Much of the North Atlantic Blockading Squadron's supplies were sent from Philadelphia and Baltimore until Norfolk could be utilized once again.

In 1861, Fort Monroe became one of the distribution points of the squadron. That winter, *Brandywine*, a frigate of 1,708 tons, became the general receiving and supply vessel of the squadron.[11] This ship could accommodate a great deal of stores, but she soon proved to be inadequate because of the squadron's constant growth. Furthermore, as the gunboats began patrolling farther from their points of supply, it became more inconvenient to leave their stations for a trip to Hampton Roads.

The Navy Department secured the anchorage at Hatteras to help prevent this inconvenience, but it was never sufficient to handle the squadron's needs. On 2 May 1862, just one week after the surrender of Fort Macon, Flag Officer Goldsborough ordered coal, provisions, stores, and clothing to be sent to Beaufort for vessels operating in North Carolina. Goldsborough further ordered that no vessel stationed at Beaufort or Wilmington was to come to Hampton Roads unless ordered to or unless stores or coal could not be obtained at Beaufort. He put Commander Samuel Lockwood in charge of finding the most convenient and secure place in Beaufort to deposit the coal and stores, thus avoiding demurrage charges, a payment added to the rental of chartered vessels as they lay loaded. One clerk accompanied the provisions and tended to their delivery, the receipts, and their proper disbursement. After the capture of New Bern, stores, coal, and provisions for vessels in the sounds were sent there. Each depot had a separate paymaster and storekeeper and separate requisitions.[12]

As the squadron grew, the procedures for requisitioning supplies changed. Admiral Goldsborough, who commanded a fraction of the ships that his successors would, found that he was "constantly receiving demands of some sort or their requiring my immediate and earnest attention. At times I can scarcely steal a few hours repose in the 24 hours." Goldsborough instructed his officers to submit their requisitions to him, and if he approved them, he forwarded them to the respective bureaus.[13]

Rear Admiral Phillips Lee attempted to reform the system shortly after taking command in September 1862. Gideon Welles had selected Lee, in part, because of his good business qualities. Normally all the requisitions went to *Brandywine* and then to the proper bureaus. Lee had special procedures for the vessels off Cape Fear and in the sounds. Because of the distance that separated them from the flagship and the main depot, Lee asked the commanding officer of each vessel to submit his requisitions for the ensuing quarter to the senior officer, who forwarded them to the paymasters at Beaufort and New Bern. These paymasters made allowances for what they had on hand and then sent the requisitions to Lee. Lee and the fleet paymaster looked at them and then sent them to the proper bureaus. For a more "systematic administration" of accounts, Lee attached the senior paymaster to the flagship as the fleet paymaster. He supervised all the squadron's paymasters, kept the accounts of the storeships, depots, and vessels, and also examined all the requisitions and made recommendations to improve efficiency and economy.[14]

Lee's system failed to work as he had planned, and he lamented that circumstances beyond his control had interfered. He blamed "the frequent change of vessels, the temporary absence of many of them for various causes, the duties of the blockade, so many new officers, and other deranging circumstances." As an expedient for the vessels inside Cape Henry, Lee later allowed the commanding officers to make their requisitions directly to the commander of *Brandywine*.[15]

Clerical problems also distressed both Lee and the department and

continually caused problems in the supply system. Lee constantly received incomplete and delinquent quarterly returns, which resulted in a
shortage of supplies to the gunboats. The Navy Department and ships
labored under an extremely small clerical force to maintain the vast
paperwork. The senior officers had so many duties that they normally
could not give proper attention to the requisitions and usually relied on
clerks and executive officers to do the work. The senior officer in the
sounds, Henry K. Davenport, apologized to Lee about faulty returns:
"I have an ignorant, illiterate executive officer, a man who is a mono-
syllabian; anything beyond that confuses and confounds him."[16]

Lee attempted to solve some of his management problems by appoint-
ing Lieutenant Commander John Sanford Barnes as his fleet captain. Barnes was quite young for such a responsibility but was chosen
because of his business knowledge and his legal accomplishments.
When Barnes came on board *Minnesota*, he found the business of the
squadron all "piled up in confusion on the desks and in the pigeon
holes." Barnes's duties kept himself and the admiral "scribbling from
morning till night." Much of the work can be blamed on Lee's meticu-
lous nature. The admiral placed his correspondence as a high priority,
and Barnes constantly wrote and rewrote, altered it in "phraseology and
not in meaning, signed and sealed, reopened and reread, criticized and
discussed, repunctuated, sometimes to a wearisome minutiae."[17]

When Rear Admiral David D. Porter took command of the squadron
in October 1864, he altered the supply system, in an attempt to substitute
simplicity for many of the forms and procedures. He allowed senior
officers to send reports directly to the flagship and allowed the officer in
charge at Beaufort to handle requisitions without his approval. He
likewise no longer required monthly returns showing expenditures in
stores and other various departments. Porter permitted each commanding officer to keep them and turn them in at the expiration of the cruise
or to pass them to the next commanding officer.[18]

The work of purchasing and distributing food, supplies, and clothing
for the Navy Department was the responsibility of the Bureau of Provisions and Clothing, headed by Paymaster Horatio Bridge. This immense task grew as the war progressed, but Bridge managed the bureau
efficiently and saved the government large sums of money. Bridge
modified procedures at the beginning of the war and bypassed the navy

agents. To avoid paying commissions, the bureau received proposals for articles and made contracts with reputable firms. Complications in supply constantly arose because of the increases in the numbers of ships and the competitive demands by the army. The bureau frequently found it impossible to furnish many of the gunboats with the articles they required, which had an impact on the squadron.[19]

The squadron's constant growth during the war kept the men responsible for tending logistical matters of the vessels extremely busy. Two paymasters and five clerks filled the requisitions for the squadron. *Brandywine* received all the supplies, and then as needed the paymasters reshipped them by chartered vessels to New Bern and Beaufort. This required two separate freights and two separate stowages. Eventually the large quantities of stores needed by the squadron overburdened *Brandywine*, and in March 1863, Lee began to send supplies directly from the North to Beaufort and New Bern and avoided the two separate freights and stowages.[20]

Vessels bringing stores to the sounds encountered many problems because of the shallowness of Hatteras Inlet. The navy employed some of the local "contrabands" as pilots to carry the supply vessels through the swash channel. The navy later stationed a tug and pilot boat there to help the vessels over the bar. Merchantmen that grounded normally blocked the channel and delayed others until their cargoes could be discharged and they could be towed out of the channel. An insufficient number of naval tugs continually delayed the colliers and merchantmen, and the squadron sometimes had to rely on army tugs to tow the traffic over the bar.[21]

Once the supplies arrived, the clerks issued them directly from the transport, restowed them, or sent them to gunboats at other points in the sounds. The warships in the outermost areas received their supplies by chartered schooners. These schooners were towed to the extremities of the blockade, where the warships could take on supplies as needed. Because of the heterogeneous nature of the squadron, some of the gunboats were not equipped to take provisions from other vessels. The tug *Underwriter*, for example, did not have proper spars and purchases for hoisting heavy weights in and out of her hold. This not only delayed the supply process but forced the crew to work harder.[22]

Towing the schooners to the extremities of the blockade enabled the warships to remain at their posts for longer periods of time. Although this solved many problems, it was by no means perfect. Schooners normally went from post to post, and by the time the supply vessel got to the outermost point, the last vessel would receive leftovers. Lieutenant Commander Charles W. Flusser, stationed at Plymouth, North Carolina, complained, "The provision schooner has not one-half of what we need. You skinned her below; the poor devils here only get the leavings. No chance for manavelins at Plymouth."[23]

The hastily implemented supply system was designed to provide fresh food and the necessary stores without inconvenience. It did not always work and produced hardships for the officers and men. One officer in the sounds complained that he had sent in complete returns and only received one-third of some things and none of others. He had had "no small stores and no clothing. We have not had a yard of flannel on board this vessel in seven months, and my men are beginning to look ragged." The vessels stationed off Cape Fear did not fare any better. Acting Assistant Paymaster William Whittemore complained to Lee in June 1863 that he had received only one-third of the paymaster's stores and none of the other stores he had ordered. The stores for the blockaders at this time were nearly exhausted.[24]

The gunboats in the sounds faced a problem that few other vessels in the squadron encountered. Shallow water handicapped their capability to take on a normal amount of supplies. Henry Davenport, the senior officer in the sounds, kept his gunboats supplied with only two months' provisions, because with more weight they might not be able to operate in the waters of the sounds. The vessels there, however, did have one advantage, they could borrow items from the army.[25]

A number of factors affected the logistics of the squadron. Shortages occurred for a number of reasons. Losses from spoilage, delayed returns, mistakes in requisitions, insufficient storage facilities, delays and damage in shipping, contractors who made short deliveries, theft, and bad weather all contributed to shortages.[26]

As the squadron grew, the needs for logistical accommodations for the gunboats in the sounds also grew. The navy increasingly relied on chartered vessels to carry and store supplies, at a great expense to the government. In the sounds, one schooner lay collecting demurrage for sixty-five days, costing the government over $2,000—a price greater than the original freight bill. Others lay in the sounds while their owners collected on the vessels' charter parties. The schooner *Charles S. Carstairs* lay in the sounds for two and one-half years, earning her owner over $23,000. Other problems arose over the nature of this method of storage. The 200-ton schooner *Albemarle* became the principle storeship for the sounds of North Carolina. But Frank J. Hastings, the paymaster, found her to be "entirely inadequate . . . being much too small, having no suitable storerooms for the stowage of clothing + small stores."[27]

In 1863, the squadron procured a building in New Bern as a storage facility for the paymaster's department. Known as the "factory," it was a three-story building next to the water. After some minor repairs, it was ready for use by the end of the year but could not be filled up because of its "light timbers and dilapidated condition." The building never served adequately, because when it rained, the provisions, rigging, and slops inside risked being ruined. The upper floors flooded when it rained hard, while the rooms below stayed damp from the water dripping through the ceilings.[28]

Supplying some of the fresh provisions for the vessels in the North Carolina sounds was relatively uncomplicated. Throughout the war, the Commissary Department of the army provided fresh beef twice weekly for the vessels in the sounds. They did this because "no other arrangement [had] . . . ever been made for supplying the sound squadron."[29] The army used Roanoke Island as a depot. A 500-foot wharf expedited the landing of potatoes, onions, tomatoes, and as much as 900 pounds of beef each week for the gunboats.[30]

Beaufort served as an excellent logistical base for the vessels stationed off Cape Fear. But Beaufort also had limitations. The local houses lay too far from the water to be used for storage, and shallow water at the wharves prevented some of the gunboats' access. Thus, for the first two years of the war, the supplies of coal, food, and ordnance at Beaufort remained afloat. Morehead City, on the peninsula just across the Newport River, had the only storage facility, a railroad depot, but the army quartermaster used it exclusively. The wharf there had seventeen feet at high water, and a railroad line that ran to New Bern went to the docks. At Morehead City, the navy used a small storehouse near the wharf. Fort Macon, likewise, had a small wharf that the navy utilized. By early 1864, the navy had expanded this dock by over 100 feet and had begun to build a further extension of nearly 200 feet. The department also had plans to build at least three landing docks perpendicular to the main dock to give deep-draft vessels access to the facility.[31]

The lack of facilities forced the navy to keep stores on board store vessels and chartered merchantmen. This policy cost a great deal of money and caused considerable loss. Dampness damaged a large amount of the supplies, and bread often became moldy and full of weevils. *William Badger*, the main storage hulk in the sounds, was "totally unfit for the preservation of government property." She was rotten and leaked and was infested with rats that destroyed the stores.[32] Though unfit for a storage facility, she served from 1862 until the end of the war.

The losses incurred by the use of store vessels, compounded by the tremendous amounts that the department paid for demurrage, prompted the navy to have storehouses built at New York and Boston and shipped to Fort Macon. When assembled, the one at Beaufort measured thirty feet wide by ninety feet long. In use by August 1863, the storehouse was filled with the cargoes of four vessels, which freed government hulks to store ordnance and other articles.[33]

The job of supplying the gunboats in the Chesapeake was easy in contrast to that of the sounds and Wilmington. *Brandywine* lay in Hampton Roads and could conveniently supply any gunboats in the bay. Once the gunboats began to operate in the James and York rivers, schooners that carried large amounts of supplies could be towed to the gunboats, so they could remain at their stations for long periods of time. Small amounts were often shared among vessels or taken to the extremities to prolong their stays at their stations. But the gunboats' proximity to the source of supplies in the Chesapeake Bay did not ensure that they would not run short of provisions and supplies.[34]

The squadron's continuous rapid growth forced the department to lease greater numbers of schooners to store provisions and supplies. In January 1864, the navy moved *Brandywine* to the Gosport Navy Yard under the direction of the commandant of the yard, Commodore John Livingston. On the morning of 3 September 1864, a fire destroyed the frigate and forced the movement of much of the naval stores on shore to the Norfolk victualing house. As the Norfolk yard became more important as a repair facility, it became crowded with vessels needing repairs and detained those needing stores.[35]

The supply schooners and storage facilities could not store the items necessary to maintain the fleet and at the same time hold fresh provisions for the squadron. For this reason and for the benefit of the men's health, the Navy Department, early in the war, made plans to purchase side-wheel steamers with good speed to supply fresh provisions to the ships at their stations. These steamers became an important auxiliary to the blockade because they enabled the warships to obtain fresh food, which helped them to remain longer at their stations. Inaugurated by the Bureau of Provisions and Clothing, this system provided large fast steamers fitted with spacious ice houses, some of which could hold 50,000 pounds of fresh beef and 300 tons or more of ice and could also carry livestock.[36]

The navy's implementation of regularly scheduled supply steamers with chill rooms on board was a new venture. The first step taken to provide the vessels along the East Coast came in mid-July 1861. Welles instructed Bridge to send the steamer *Rhode Island* to New York and load her with fresh beef, vegetables, and other supplies for the gunboats south of Cape Hatteras.[37]

Initially three ships, *Supply*, *Rhode Island*, and *Connecticut*, supplied the Atlantic Coast squadron. In the fall of 1861, the Navy Department experimented with a new method of preserving beef on board one of the new fast steamers, the USS *Connecticut*. The usual method of preservation consisted of alternating a layer of ice and layer of meat. The new method consisted of a "chill room," something in the style of a refrigerator on shore. *Connecticut* carried 400 quarters of beef hung on hooks and stowed together as close as possible. She carried 59,000 pounds of beef with 125 tons of ice, about a four to one ratio of ice to beef.[38]

The supply steamers loaded in New York, Boston, Philadelphia, and Baltimore. Not only did they perform the duties of supplying fresh foods, but they also carried other supplies to the ships and carried out many other important responsibilities as well. At times, they "assisted the blockade in several instances by laying by certain steamers while they scaled their boilers and repaired them, besides keeping open the communication between the flag-officers and the . . . individual vessels composing their commands."[39] The supply steamers became the major links in communication with the home front for the officers and seamen. They brought packages, boxes, trunks, and bundles that contained food, clothes, books, and news from home for the men. *Connecticut* at times would carry as many as 400,000 letters and nearly 2,000 packages.[40]

The supply steamers also carried sutlers, who sold various items that added greatly to the comfort of the officers and seamen. The navy regulated the sutlers so that they could not take advantage of the men. They could only charge a price twenty-five percent above what they paid for foodstuffs and other articles, such as tobacco, cigars, paper collars, and so forth. They could make no more than a forty-five percent profit on all other goods.[41]

The system of supply evolved during the war from a haphazard distribution to that of a fairly systemized one. Early in the war, the Navy Department intended to use *Rhode Island* and *Connecticut* alternately and, as far as practicable, to run regularly between New York and Texas, communicating with every vessel from Cape Hatteras to the Gulf of Mexico. This system worked well until the blockading squadrons increased in size.[42]

By mid-1862, with the vast increase in the number of blockaders, the need for more supply vessels became apparent. Since the large supply steamers carried ordnance, gun crews, and ammunition, ships like *Rhode Island* (1,517 tons) could only carry 1,200 barrels—less than a ship of 350 tons. The navy gradually began using chartered schooners to supplement the supply steamers and eventually ordered *Connecticut* and *Rhode Island* to supply the Gulf Coast squadron only, adding *Massachusetts* as the only regular steamer from Virginia to the Florida Keys.[43]

This policy caused immediate and extremely serious problems for the North Atlantic Blockading Squadron. Rear Admiral Lee complained to Secretary of the Navy Welles: "It appears that there are too many stopping places in the two squadrons in the Atlantic for one vessel to attend all and afford the reasonable relief to the officers and crew of this blockade." Irregularity in this service made it necessary for blockaders going north to bring supplies back to the vessels on station, and provisions had to be shared among the ships to keep them at their stations.[44]

Communication problems also arose because of the lack of supply vessels. With only one steamer to supply the two squadrons, communi-

cations were detained at New Bern and Beaufort until an army transport could be utilized to take them north. Vessels supplying the South
Atlantic Blockading Squadron had instructions to stop at Beaufort and
Wilmington on their way south and pick up mail and passengers on the
trip north. Sometimes they failed to stop at all. With the system as it
existed, fresh provisions and supplies arrived at Wilmington every four
to six weeks by way of the supply steamers. The blockaders also occasionally obtained provisions in Beaufort from the army commissary,
who "sometimes furnishes a ration for a ship's company as an especial
favor."[45]

In January 1863, Bridge asked Rear Admiral Lee if he could spare a
vessel to run between Beaufort and Wilmington and a northern port
with supplies. If a vessel could not be spared, he suggested that Lee
charter one. Unable to spare or charter a vessel for nine months, the
blockaders suffered while Lee pleaded for a supply steamer solely for his
squadron. During this time, because of the uncertain and irregular
transportation arrangements, the Bureau of Equipment and Recruiting
sent its supplies by coal vessels from Philadelphia. Finally, in August
1863, the Navy Department ordered *New Berne* to assume the responsibility of supplying the North Atlantic squadron. The 948-ton screw
steamer could carry 300 tons of stores, fresh meat, and ice. The change
had one officer boasting that they had "ice, fresh beef, vegetables &c
every fortnight instead of once a month."[46]

To keep *New Berne* running on schedule, Lee instructed each commanding officer to give her his immediate attention when obtaining the
supplies and mails. They were to send a sufficient number of boats to
receive the supplies and the proper officer to sign all the receipts. *New
Berne*'s trips between New York and the warships off North Carolina
established regularity in the supply system. *New Berne* supplied these
vessels with scheduled stops twice a month, whereas *Connecticut* had
taken over a month between visits.[47]

Blockaders also obtained supplies when they left their stations for
coal or repairs. In the sounds, the sailors could buy chickens, fruits, and
vegetables from the local inhabitants to supplement their shipboard
diets. Their fare while in port was a welcome change from salty food to
fresh meat, vegetables, and soft bread. The men on board vessels in the
interior waterways often foraged for food, gathering sheep, poultry,

swine, and cattle. Occasionally, a lucky blockader captured a blockade runner that carried fruits such as bananas, pineapples, limes, apples, and preserves, which gave the tars an even more varied regimen. The Sanitary Commission also donated and distributed food to supplement the seamen's diets.[48]

The Navy Department provided ordnance supplies to the squadron in a similar fashion to that of the stores and provisions, and constant shortages abounded. Welles believed that the greatest cause for shortages was the variance of the guns used. He stated that the major problem in arming and supplying ordnance supplies arose from the variety of calibers and the changes of armament ordered by the commanding officers.[49]

Because of the demands placed on the Bureau of Ordnance, the gunboats early in the war received almost any gun that could be procured. They removed guns from receiving ships and those of ancient age from shore. It was not uncommon in the middle of the war to find gunboats with guns dating back to the 1840s. Small arms were likewise hard to secure in the early months of the war. *Monticello* was fitted out with fifty condemned carbines, and *Iroquois* was supplied with cutlasses that were "all worthless old-fashioned Roman swords."[50]

The squadron commander approved requisitions for ordnance and then forwarded them to the Bureau of Ordnance. The naval ordnance officer at Fort Monroe received the shipments and forwarded them as needed to the various storage facilities along the coast. The North Atlantic Blockading Squadron was fortunate to be near the Washington Navy Yard, where much of the ordnance was manufactured and could be quickly sent to Fort Monroe. Normally ordnance arrived in chartered schooners, since they could be taken from place to place and returned after being discharged. This worked conveniently, because many of the ex-merchantmen being used as gunboats could not carry a great amount of ammunition.[51]

The ammunition needs of the squadron were immense and fluctuated during the war. Lee attempted to keep 400 rounds for each gun inside Cape Henry and in the main ordnance depot in the sounds. Lee suggested that 100 rounds for each broadside gun and 200 rounds for each pivot gun be stored at Beaufort for the vessels at Wilmington. In the sounds, they attempted to keep at least 150 rounds for each broadside gun and 300 for all others. Even with long-range planning and times when larger numbers of projectiles were stored in the local depots, the ammunition ran short. These shortages occurred because of delays, bad weather, the demands of the other squadrons, unexpected engagements, and borrowing by the army.[52]

The Bureau of Ordnance suffered the most by the loss of Norfolk in 1861. The Norfolk Navy Yard had an ample bombproof magazine, fireproof buildings, filling rooms, storehouses, a railway to a stone wharf that ran out to deep water, and a crane for hoisting guns. It had been built by and for the navy and had served with great convenience for the navy in the past. For some time after the recapture of Norfolk, Major General John E. Wool refused to return the navy yard to the department without an order from the president or the secretary of war. Admiral Goldsborough wrote to Gustavus Fox that Wool should "have this nonsense knocked out of him." Eventually the yard was returned, with the exception of the ordnance magazine, which continued to create a great inconvenience to the navy. Ordnance stores had to be kept at Fort Monroe, piled outdoors and exposed to the elements or kept on board leaky vessels, which were subject to capture by the enemy and cost great sums of money for demurrage charges.[53]

As the war progressed, the Bureau of Ordnance also used Fort Monroe as a "convenient depot for ordnance stores in 'transition' to ports outside the squadron." In 1863, a massive explosion destroyed an ordnance building in Yorktown. This explosion worried General Butler that a similar mishap might befall the large wooden building used for the stowage of naval ordnance just outside of Fort Monroe. He therefore asked the navy to remove the ammunition stored there. The navy, though, could not move its ordnance until it gained control of its Norfolk facility. In early 1864, the army "nominally" returned the Norfolk facilities, but by this time, they had become insufficient for the navy's needs; thus a large part of the ordnance stores remained afloat for the rest of the conflict.[54]

The squadron thus was burdened with having to use schooners to store ordnance for the entire war. This method certainly had more disadvantages than storage ashore. One of the greatest drawbacks was the demurrage charges, which caused an excessive use of funds. Also, some of the schooners leaked so badly that they could barely be kept afloat. Ordnance stored afloat was less accessible than that stored ashore. It was almost impossible to remove it quickly because of the different charges and shells. It was common to discharge one-third of a schooner's cargo to get the particular ordnance needed. Gunboats in a hurry took ammunition in an "irregular manner," which "deranged" the cargo and complicated later withdrawals of ordnance.[55] The schooners did give the navy advantages of mobility. They could be towed to any point that needed ordnance stores, or they could be towed out of danger if threatened.

The gunboats in the sounds had their own particular ordnance problems. Ordnance schooners going to the sounds had to have a draft of eight feet or less. Those that could not get over the swash at Hatteras Inlet had to be lightened. The navy kept ordnance in schooners at New Bern and Plymouth for the vessels in the sounds and at Beaufort for those at Wilmington. In 1862, Lee ordered all ammunition in the sounds to be kept afloat because of the danger of its being captured. But by May 1863, the navy built a small magazine in a fireproof building on a dock at Washington, North Carolina. Both the army and navy used this magazine. Lee allowed naval ammunition to be kept there only if the ordnance schooners would "carry all they can."[56]

Rising demurrage costs prompted Lee to send William Queen, the fleet ordnance officer, to examine all the ammunition afloat in the sounds. Lee instructed him to determine whether depots and magazines should be located at New Bern and Washington to save the government money. Queen could find no building in New Bern that he deemed suitable for a magazine. A surplus of ammunition in the sounds prompted Lee to instruct warships to carry as much ammunition as they could. Davenport, though, reminded Lee that he could not load his vessels too deep because of the shallow water. The navy never found a suitable building at New Bern, and the ordnance stores of a "combustible nature" remained afloat there for the remainder of the war.[57]

The rapid and constant growth of the navy was perhaps the single greatest hardship to overcome in the department's efforts of supplying the gunboats. The lack of adequate logistical facilities, a deficient chain of command, and a shortage of supply vessels to perform the necessary duties only compounded the problems. The Navy Department did show an understanding of these logistical problems and solved or improved them in such a way that they never caused any critical hardships. There would, however, be other aspects of the logistical system that did not improve as the war progressed.

NINE

Economize fuel all you can

Coaling the Gunboats

Gideon Welles once remarked, "Steam has become such an indispensable element in naval warfare, that vessels propelled by sails only, are considered useless for war purposes."[1] This statement was certainly proved true during the Civil War. The change from sail to steam became one of the most important changes that navies made during the nineteenth century. The use of steam vessels as blockaders by the United States Navy in 1861 was innovative. Steamers, generally faster, could move in all weather but could not remain long at their stations without recoaling. The blockade proved to be a test of the use of steam vessels for war purposes and also tested the theory of blockade by these vessels. An effective blockade, however, could only be performed if the gunboats remained at their stations.

The navy had had little experience with steam vessels and did not possess adequate logistical facilities, nor did it have the organizational means to make an easy transition. The navy had used steam vessels in the war with Mexico but had faced an enemy with a negligible navy and did not realize the importance of steam vessels. In the first months of the Civil War, the chiefs of the bureaus of the Navy Department discussed the need for supply vessels and suggested the purchase of five sailing vessels to keep the two squadrons supplied with all their wants, including coal—two for the Atlantic and three for the Gulf of Mexico. Of course, the long supply line to the gulf concerned them most.[2] The North Atlantic Blocking Squadron operated nearer the sources of coal than any other squadron, but this convenience did not ensure fewer problems in supplying the warships.

Early in the war, it became evident that the gunboats could not be provisioned solely by supply ships and that logistical bases would have to be established. Gideon Welles understood the importance of these bases. He commented in 1861 that "it would be inexpedient and attended with much loss of time, as well as great additional expense, to compel the steamers when short of fuel to leave their stations and proceed to the nearest depot, distant in most cases several hundred miles."[3]

The Navy Department took early steps to ensure that some of the problems in supplying the vessels with coal would be resolved. The department decided to establish a coaling base at Fort Monroe. John Lenthall, the chief of the Bureau of Construction and Repairs, asserted that it was "of the first importance to have a supply of coal at that point as between it and Key West there can be no other depot." Bases, however, were obsolete without coal, and the department had been caught unprepared and lacked sufficient coal reserves. During April and May, the navy seized a number of colliers in the Chesapeake. But even with reserves of coal, Fort Monroe did not have wharves or bins to expedite the coaling process.[4]

When the vessels refueled, many factors affected the time involved in the process. The procedure of delivery depended upon the arrangement of the steamers' coal bunkers. Usually machinery and bulkheads separated the bunkers, which meant the coal had to be passed in baskets to the proper locations by the crew. Coal bunkers were sometimes inaccessible because the builders designed them to protect the ships' boilers and machinery. Coal is a bulky item, and each ton displaces about forty-two cubic feet of space. Coal could be hoisted, shoveled into scuttles, or placed on board in bags. The storage of coal in bags seemed to be preferred since they made the movement of coal easier within the confines of the ship, the bags could be stored almost anywhere, and the bags could be made by the crews.[5]

The Monitor *Canonicus* in the James River Receiving Coal or Other Supplies from a Schooner. In the foreground is the tug *Zeta* (picket boat No. 6), which acted as a tender to the monitors and performed picket duty in the river. (*Courtesy the U.S. Naval*

Each coal depot had somewhat different arrangements for refueling the vessels. Usually a pier or pile wharf ran into the water, where coal could be placed on board. When the facilities became crowded, the vessels often used launches or cutters to bring the coal from the wharf. Most depots used wheelbarrows that could carry about 200 pounds of coal. In smooth water, a steamer could refuel directly from a coal collier. Coal passed from the collier to the steamer in tubs that carried just over 100 pounds of coal. This eventually became the preferred and the fastest method of coaling because of the lack of wharf space. At Beaufort, they used iron buckets that could carry 375 pounds of coal, or about six buckets to the ton. They moved these buckets between the bunker scuttles and the colliers on trucks and saved thirty-three percent of the time in coaling the steamers. As the crews placed the coal in the holds, each tenth bucket would be weighed and a receipt given to the master of the collier.[6]

To ensure that coal arrived at the depots in the right quantities, the proper requisitions had to be sent north. Senior officers handled requisi-tions for coal for the first eighteen months of the war. These requisitions went directly to John S. Chambers, the navy agent at Philadelphia. Chambers, appointed navy agent in Philadelphia in May 1861, found it difficult to make purchases because his predecessor left no money in the account. This problem was aggravated further by the fact that during the second quarter of 1862, his bills were five times greater than the previous quarter. During the war, the fuel costs for the navy grew more than sixfold.[7]

Chambers had the monumental task of shipping coal to all points of the blockade, particularly to the other squadrons. Chambers ordered coal in an amount that would be "abundantly sufficient," taking care to have an ample supply to avoid demurrage. In November 1862, the Navy Department ordered Captain Henry Adams to Philadelphia to coordinate the coal shipments. Requisitions went to Adams, who oversaw the coal shipments for all the squadrons. Instead of sending the North Atlantic Blockading Squadron's requisitions directly to Adams, commanders sent them to Rear Admiral Lee, who forwarded the requests to Philadelphia.[8]

As the war progressed, the requisitions began to pass through more hands. They passed from the commanding officers of the vessels to the

acting paymasters at Beaufort and New Bern, hence to the senior officers and to Lee, who forwarded them to Adams. By mid-1864, Adams
preferred to discontinue Lee's approval of the requisitions and preferred
that they come directly from the senior officers. The system failed to
work properly because of the distance between the coal depots and the
source of coal and because of the irregular communication, which kept
the paymasters waiting for bills of lading and receipts of deliveries
before they could fill the returns.[9]

Many unforeseen problems developed during the war, delaying the
movement of coal between the mines and the warships. A shortage of
colliers to take coal to the outermost point of the blockade crippled the
system of coal supply. The navy chartered vessels for transportation of
coal in the open market, and the rates varied with the demand for the
vessels, the season of the year, and the distance the coal traveled in the
collier. This freight charge did not include demurrage. Carelessness and
mishandling also caused delays and added to the demurrage charge.
The average number of lay days at Beaufort was approximately four
weeks. The brig *Alston* lay at anchor collecting demurrage at Hampton
Roads for eighty-five days and cost the government over $2,000. It was
not uncommon for the colliers to earn in demurrage costs a rate twice as
much as agreed and sometimes greater than the cost of the freight of the
cargo.[10]

Some officers believed it better to buy colliers rather than to charter
them, but the government continued to lease them. Most of the colliers
were schooners, but brigs and barks were also employed. At times there
were scarcities of these vessels, because the army also used them as
transports, and early in the war some masters feared privateers. The
shallow inlet at Hatteras likewise limited the number that could be used
to carry coal to the sounds.[11]

The problem with demurrage became so acute that Rear Admiral
Andrew Hull Foote, chief of the Bureau of Equipment and Recruiting,
asked Rear Admiral Lee to rectify the situation. Lee issued a general
order calling attention to the great expense that the government paid for
demurrage. Foote stated that this expense resulted from "commanding
officers of steamers finding it less troublesome and laborious to coal
from full vessels, leaving others which have been more or less discharged, and drawing an expensive demurrage from the Government."

Foote stated that in the future a single vessel would be discharged before the breaking into the cargo of another, "except in cases of absolute necessity, when several vessels must be coaled at once." Often several vessels coaled at the same time, leaving small amounts in the colliers. Lee instructed the coal inspector for the supplies in the Chesapeake Bay, Acting Ensign William Ottiwell, that demurrage could be saved by loading the coal in one and discharging the rest.[12]

Demurrage could also be avoided by keeping the gunboats' coal bunkers full. This was only possible in the Chesapeake Bay and its tributaries. Lee instructed the gunboats there to fill their bunkers every few days or after they had consumed ten percent of their coal. In the fall of 1864, a circular from Joseph Smith, the chief of the Bureau of Yards and Docks, ordered that the colliers should be discharged at the rate of at least eighty tons a day beginning the day they reported. At Norfolk, they discharged over eighty tons a day and still had a large surplus.[13]

Cash-flow difficulties strained the relationship between the government and the carriers. At various times, the government failed to pay the masters of the colliers, and the owners sought other employment. The freight bills owed at Philadelphia in April 1862 totaled over $90,000. Because of delayed payments, the masters were forced at times to sell their bills of lading to brokers at four-percent discounts in order to continue their businesses.[14]

The Navy Department maintained its coal reserves through contracts with coal companies and purchases in the open market. Contracts made early in the war ensured a regular supply for years. The best coal came from the eastern half of Pennsylvania and came to Philadelphia by rail and barge and then was reshipped to points south by the Office of Coal Shipment, headed by Adams. The average coal season lasted from May to November in the canals. River traffic was sometimes delayed during the winter, when ice obstructed the Delaware River, and there was seldom a winter when navigation remained open at all times.[15]

Most of the firms shipping coal to the markets profited by the enlargement of the steam navy and the war. Some railroads saw slight gains in the coal trade to Philadelphia, while others had phenomenal growth. The Philadelphia and Reading Railroad during the war years doubled its tonnage. In 1861, it carried just under one and a half million tons of coal, and in 1863, it carried over three million. Railroads carrying coal to New York likewise profited.[16]

Some of the canal companies also had boom years, while others remained virtually stationary. The Lehigh Coal and Navigation Company had several good years, while the Delaware and Hudson Canal connecting New York saw profits soar over thirty percent both in 1863 and 1864. Little disturbed this prosperity except acts of nature.[17]

On the night of 4 June 1862, a heavy storm lasting thirty hours swept across the coal region. It was considered the most destructive storm ever known by the owners of the mines. Waters rose twenty-seven feet above the low-water mark. Bridges and hundreds of barges were swept down the canals and rivers, causing millions of dollars of damage. This destructive freshet interrupted coal deliveries between one and three months for most firms.[18]

Strikes also retarded the delivery of coal. In 1863, a striking mob closed all the mines in Schuylkill County, Pennsylvania. Using violence, the mob kept the mines closed for four weeks. They retained the coal colliers and shut the pumps off, which allowed water to run into the mines, destroying sections of the shafts. Other strikes at the collieries and striking locomotive coal heavers also slowed the delivery. Rear Admiral Lee thus often instructed his officers to "observe the utmost economy . . . in the expenditure of fuel."[19]

Another event caused an unexpected lapse in the coal shipments. When the Confederate army invaded Pennsylvania in June and July 1863, it caused so much fear that the coal trade stopped for one month. Naval officers scratched their heads wondering why General Robert E. Lee did not destroy the Reading Railroad, a major spur in the supply of coal. The severing of this logistical artery would have affected every squadron.[20]

The problems obtaining coal seemed minor when compared to those that the navy suffered trying to supply fuel with regularity and convenience to the steamers. Within the Chesapeake Bay, the logistical problems with coal were felt least. In the summer of 1861, the navy purchased the 363-ton hulk *Charles Phelps*. She lay in Hampton Roads to aid in the coaling of vessels and to help ensure that coal was always on hand. Furthermore, the navy anchored colliers in many different locations to make the acquisition of coal easy and convenient. As the navy moved up the rivers, the colliers could be towed to the extremities of the Chesapeake Bay and its tributaries.[21]

By the winter and spring of 1862–63, the vessels coaling from the colliers in the Chesapeake used about 500 tons of coal a week. The navy kept colliers at Hampton Roads, Yorktown, and Newport News. In all, about 1,500 to 2,000 tons of coal were to be kept on hand to avoid shortages. After the army established its base at City Point, the gunboats in the James River, which later used 1,000 tons a week, obtained coal there. The navy with some difficulty attempted to keep as much as 3,000 tons of coal at City Point. The monitors received their coal from schooners at Curles Neck to avoid steaming too far from the front lines.[22]

After the Union forces recaptured Norfolk, the squadron once again began to use the yard to receive coal. The wharf space there, however, was not "commodious," and there was always a lack of labor to facilitate the coaling process. In mid-1864, Lee asked that 15,000 tons of coal be kept at the yard for refueling. At this time, the navy needed 2,000 tons each week in Virginian waters, which only added more ships to the great numbers there for repairs. To interfere less with the repairs, Commodore John Livingston, the commandant of the yard, preferred that the gunboats tow a coal schooner into the wide part of the stream to refuel.[23]

In 1864, Lee established a coaling depot at Craney Island, where blockaders could take in coal and avoid the rough weather that was "prevalent" in Hampton Roads. This was particularly advantageous for Livingston, who wrote to Welles that the Norfolk yard was often "incommoded for want of room, as we are constantly discharging coal from one or more vessels . . . the yard is frequently so blocked with vessels, that those that are repairing are delayed."[24]

The distance between Fort Monroe and the outer points of the blockade was too great for warships on the outside blockade to patrol without an intermediary point of supply. In 1861, it was clear that places along the coast would eventually have to be secured. Welles began to consider the acquisition of some point between Fort Monroe and Key West as a coal depot, and eventually the forts at Hatteras were captured to provide an anchorage for the navy.

The Hatteras anchorage had too many limitations, and it could never have been sufficient for the growing needs of the navy. The inlet was too

shallow, the anchorage was exposed to the sea, and in 1861, the gunboats
did not have complete control of the sounds because of the "mosquito
fleet." As a result of the lack of a serviceable base, Silas Stringham kept
slow steamers and those that consumed great amounts of coal in the
rivers and close to a fuel supply.[25] Vessels on the outside blockade had to
go to Hampton Roads until after the Roanoke Island expedition, when
the department began anchoring colliers in the sounds. The deeper
draft vessels at Wilmington, however, were still forced to go to Hampton Roads.

The vessels in the sounds of North Carolina had their own unique
circumstances with regard to coal. Before the capture of Roanoke Island, the navy shipped small amounts of coal in colliers and anchored
them at Hatteras Inlet. After the capture of Roanoke Island, shallow-
draft vessels passed through the shallow Hatteras Inlet channel and
reported to the island, anchoring north of there at Powell's Point. At the
beginning of May, after all the major towns in the region had been
captured, Goldsborough ordered coal to New Bern for the vessels
there.[26]

All the coal coming into the sounds for the duration of the war passed
through Hatteras Inlet—a major inconvenience because of the shallow
water (eleven feet) on the bar there. After crossing the bar, the colliers
then had to cross the Swash Channel, which had only eight feet of water.
Many not having the shallow draft to proceed could be lightened, and
some drew too much water, even when empty, to allow them to pass over
the bar at the Swash Channel.[27]

When a vessel could not get over the bar, lighters had to be sent from
New Bern. All or part of the cargo was then removed, which often took
days. The navy thus chartered vessels to help the colliers pass into the
sounds. In late 1863, the sloop *Granite* lay at the inlet as a guard vessel,
but her crew was tasked to help lighten the coal colliers. Although
constantly short of men, *Granite* did expedite the movement of coal into
other parts of the sound. To expedite delivery further, officers sent
dispatches to *Granite* so that the colliers could be directed to points in the
sound that needed coal. In some cases, the masters of the coal schooners
showed a reluctance to take their vessels into the upper sounds, suppos-
ing that "when they *have* arrived at New Bern they have fulfilled all that
is required of them."[28]

Delays occurred for several reasons. The shallow-draft schooners that the navy employed to carry coal to Hatteras became "scarce" toward the war's end, because of the increasing amounts of coal needed in the sounds. It became extremely important to discharge the vessels and to send them back as quickly as possible. Sometimes these schooners traveled for twelve days to get to their destinations in the sounds once they had crossed the bar. To speed delivery, Melancton Smith requested a tug to tow them to their destinations, allowing a speedier turnaround and saving on demurrage costs. With a shortage of vessels to carry coal, the senior officers in the North Carolina sounds often had to charter schooners to supply the upper sounds and at least once seized schooners with sutlers' stores on board to do so.[29]

The estimates necessary for ordering coal in the sounds remained largely guesswork. The gunboats varied their routines, and additional vessels and constant transfers made the returns more prone to mistakes. Like those in the Chesapeake, the gunboats in the sound spent little time under way and kept their fires banked. Furthermore, a number of the vessels in the sounds were incapable of moving and therefore used little coal. In 1864, the monthly expenditure of coal for the sounds had grown to approximately 2,000 tons a month. The vessels in the Albemarle Sound alone used fifty tons of coal a day, enough for two vessels to move about and the rest to bank their fires.[30]

The variance of coal use complicated the efforts of those trying to keep adequate amounts in every depot. By June 1864, the Office of Coal Shipment in Philadelphia sent an average of 600 tons a week to the sounds, which it deemed an "ample supply."[31]

The navy kept coal at a number of places in the sounds for the convenience of the gunboats. In Albemarle Sound, colliers anchored at Plymouth, Elizabeth City, and Roanoke Island. At New Bern, coal schooners lay in the river. The headquarters of the army was also in New Bern; thus the Neuse River stayed crowded with army vessels, which caused much "inconvenience and annoyance." In May 1863, all the coal and ordnance schooners moved to the side of the river opposite the town for more room and easier access.[32]

Lee eventually asked Commander Davenport to put as much of the coal on shore as possible to prevent the soaring demurrage costs. New Bern had one wharf and later two to aid in coaling the gunboats. Lee ordered that the coal be landed in safe places in New Bern, Washington, and Plymouth and sent lumber to construct coal bins in the sounds.[33] The squadron's shore facilities never adequately stored the enormous and constantly growing amounts of coal needed by the squadron.

The warships in the sounds had a somewhat unusual logistical problem. The vessels could not keep their bunkers full, because full bunkers increased their drafts and thus hindered their performance. But the department's concerns with demurrage costs dictated that the ships carry as much fuel as possible and that the navy not keep too many colliers on hand. Despite long-range planning and numerous depots, the vessels in the sounds ran out of coal. At times, deficiencies could be temporarily remedied by borrowing from the army. In November 1862, the shortage became so acute that all the vessels had to let their fires go out.[34]

The vessels on blockade duty at Wilmington suffered the greatest logistical problems during the war, particularly in regard to obtaining coal. This situation never improved much during the conflict and contributed as much to the squadron's failure to stop blockade running as any other factor. The weather conditions at Wilmington caused a heavy use of coal, because the gunboats had to contend with the tides, heavy weather, and currents. The gunboats also had to keep their boilers ready to make steam to chase blockade runners. The warships in the sounds and the Chesapeake Bay area normally lay within hours of coal supplies. In contrast, since the water off Wilmington was too rough to anchor colliers, the gunboats had to travel for two days to reach the depot at Hampton Roads. The distance to a coal depot was cut in half in May 1862, when the navy delivered coal to Beaufort, North Carolina, for the vessels off Cape Fear.[35]

During 1861 and early 1862, the gunboats patrolling the coastline remained at anchor for long periods of time and used little fuel. The screw steamer *Mystic*, stationed at Wilmington in August 1862, used only fifty pounds of coal a day. Some of the larger vessels carried great amounts of coal, and the gunboats could extend their cruises by borrowing from other blockaders. *State of Georgia*'s coal capacity was so large that she spent much of her time coaling other gunboats. This was done by filling up boats with coal and shuttling them back and forth.[36]

The facilities for the blockaders at Beaufort were no better than those at New Bern. Some of the coal was stored on shore, but the majority was kept afloat. Midway through the war, Lee considered storing coal on the shore near Fort Macon, but he considered it "unfeasible" without the construction of bins and of a dock and a railway from the bins to the dock. The navy wanted land adjacent to the army wharf at Fort Macon and asked for only a narrow strip of land to construct coal bins and to place ordnance and other supplies. The army, in its usual noncooperative manner, claimed it needed the wharf space for the garrison at Fort Macon and for commissary supplies.[37]

To refuel, the vessels made a one-day cruise to Beaufort and returned as quickly as possible. Tides often played a role in getting into the harbor and also affected the blockaders' timetables during the refueling process. Some of the larger gunboats had to calculate their arrivals and departures at precisely high tide in order to coal at Beaufort. Others could not use Beaufort because of their deep drafts and had to go to Hampton Roads. The depth on the Beaufort bar was eighteen feet, but with a swell, it was reduced to fourteen feet or less. All too frequently, a warship would pass over the bar at high tide, and bad weather prohibited her departure for days or weeks.[38]

As the blockaders came into Beaufort Harbor, they usually anchored beside a collier or had a collier towed alongside. When possible, they utilized alternate sides of the collier to coal the gunboats' port and starboard bunkers. The officers often rejected some of the colliers in an attempt to select coal of the highest quality. Coal that contained impurities such as slate made it impossible to keep up high pressures in the boilers, which might cause the loss of a prize. Of course this policy increased demurrage costs, as some vessels lay with their cargoes broken but not completely discharged. Lee allowed the swiftest vessels to choose their coal, while he instructed the slower gunboats to take coal from the colliers that had laid there the longest. Sometimes the engineers threw the inferior coal overboard and refused to give a receipt for it, which caused a great strain on the relationships between the navy and the masters of the colliers. The masters of the colliers, in order to earn more demurrage money, could "create delays and increase demurrages, give little or no assistance in discharging their vessels and make no efforts to get their vessels underway when necessary to move."[39]

The gunboats off Cape Fear required increasingly large amounts of

coal because of their growing numbers and the nature of their blockading duties. Lee's tactical philosophy required that the steamers remain
constantly in motion so that they would at all times be ready to start a
chase. By November 1862, the average consumption was 1,200 tons a
month, and each vessel took an average of 140 tons each time she went to
Beaufort. By October 1863, 800 tons a week were required at Beaufort,
and six months later, the vessels off Wilmington consumed about 4,000
tons a month. When the department began to use the ex-blockade
runners at Wilmington, the supplies of coal had to be augmented with
bituminous coal. The boilers of the ex-blockade runners were designed
to burn soft coal. They could not obtain high pressures in their boilers
and ran slower when they burned hard coal, which made them less
efficient blockaders. In late 1864, as much as 500 to 1,000 tons of
bituminous coal was sent weekly for these vessels, which even with these
quantities ran short.[40]

The channel into Beaufort Harbor could accommodate large colliers.
Colliers entering Beaufort brought an average of 300 tons of coal.
Because of uncertainties in delivery during most of the war, the navy
attempted to keep at least 1,000 tons of coal at Beaufort. This supply was
important not only to ensure that the gunboats could be coaled and sent
back to their stations but also because Beaufort served as a depot for
public vessels passing up and down the coast.[41]

Even with a working margin of 1,000 tons of coal, the depot at
Beaufort ran short. In May 1864, the blockaders had to go to Hampton
Roads for coal, none being available at Beaufort. Lee became excited
and telegraphed Adams in Philadelphia explaining the problem and
asking "cannot this be remedied."[42]

The paymaster at Beaufort could not borrow coal from the supplies in
the sounds because they kept separate accounts and supplies could not be
exchanged. The army quartermasters in both the Chesapeake and
North Carolina sometimes supplied the naval steamers and at other
times borrowed from the navy, which caused shortages for the depots.
The army also borrowed coal without giving receipts and without the
knowledge of the senior naval officers. The practice of lending coal to
the army inconvenienced the squadron, and Lee put a stop to their
indiscriminate borrowing by requiring their requisitions to pass
through him.[43]

During the war, the blockade of the Cape Fear River was continually weakened by the absence of refueling gunboats. As the war progressed, the blockaders performed more cruising and patrolled farther from the entrances of the river, thereby using more coal. For most of the war, the majority of the vessels could stay at their stations for about three or four weeks. An average steamer consumed over fifteen tons of coal a day, which allowed only about eleven days of full steaming. Some of the gunboats stationed off Wilmington were not well adapted for cruising. Larger ships such as *Dacotah* could only carry enough coal for just over six days of full steaming. Half of that time was spent going to and from Beaufort for coal. In September 1863, Lee warned the commanders to "economize fuel all you can" and suggested that they might "find it expedient not to keep more than one of the little vessels moving about at a time, even at night."[44]

Because of the absence of so many vessels for coaling and repairs, the commanders at Cape Fear continually asked that their numbers be increased. With an insufficient number of gunboats to watch the inlets in the Wilmington area, the commanders by necessity had to allow a couple of vessels to go to Beaufort for fuel and await their return before allowing others to go. At times this procedure virtually crippled the effectiveness of the blockade. The differences in the coal capacities of the gunboats, the different amounts of cruising each vessel performed, the weather, and the condition of the machinery—all determined the amount of coal consumed. Those that burned coal at a high rate might need to refuel every ten days and required a week to go to Beaufort, to coal, and to return. Lee suggested to his senior officers that only one vessel go for coal at a time and that the "large vessels capable of carrying a good deal of coal must do all the necessary moving about . . . or the small vessels must do the running and go oftener for coal."[45]

Those vessels that stayed long periods of time at their stations without coaling borrowed from the other vessels on their station by transferring coal in boats or by passing bags of coal. Lee later placed a 699-ton steamer, *Fahkee*, on the sheltered side of Frying Pan Shoals with bags of coal to prolong the stay of the blockaders. This allowed an extension of their cruises and kept the force stronger than otherwise would have been possible. Warships with empty coal bunkers, particularly ex-merchantmen, became less effective blockaders because they could not stay in trim. On one occasion, the steamer *Monticello* ran so low on coal on her way back to Beaufort that the crew made preparations to burn her gun carriages for fuel. Only the eventual sighting of land prevented the crew from burning them.[46]

The procedure of allowing only one vessel or a small number of vessels to go to Beaufort at any one time was never feasible. One chase could empty the steamer's bunkers and require her to replenish her coal. While the largest vessels could stay at their stations three to six weeks, there were times when as many as twelve gunboats were in Beaufort for coal.[47]

One remedy to this disabling situation was to tow colliers to the Cape Fear River. In March 1863, Lee asked Rear Admiral Foote to send coal directly to Cape Fear. Henry Adams, the superintendent of coal shipments, tried to hire colliers to go to Wilmington. But Adams could not persuade the owners to agree to go to Cape Fear under any terms, because they feared that their vessels would be "knocked to pieces in discharging alongside." Lee wrote to Adams that the masters were "under a misapprehension" and that he had never intended to lay the colliers alongside the steamers but to let them ride astern and discharge the coal using a floating wharf, which the blockaders had "used with success . . . [when] discharging one into the other."[48]

When Lee asked the opinion of his officers at Wilmington, they concurred that this plan would be difficult to implement. Colliers generally carried only light ground tackle and no ballast, and at this rough anchorage, they would be at risk. Captain Charles Boggs stated that, since he had been at Wilmington, there had been no day that a collier could have lain beside a gunboat and only a few days in which coaling could be done by boats. Captain A. Ludlow Case agreed that the times were "few and far between" and that his ship was at all times a "rocking cradle" that "would knock the heaviest boats to pieces."[49]

Lee was determined to try this nonetheless, and in the fall of 1863, he sent a coal schooner from Beaufort to New Inlet to recoal *Minnesota*, but "bad weather made it impractical." A year later, this was done successfully when a bark resupplied the side-wheel steamer *Britannia*. For three months, until the capture of Wilmington, the gunboats stationed there were partially supplied from colliers, which allowed a more effective use of the blockading vessels.[50]

Naval logistics have been an uncalculated aspect of the Civil War, but they played a large part in the successes and failures of the Union blockade. The problem of coal consumption only became worse when the navy employed faster warships with larger engines and patrolled greater distances to capture the equally fast blockade runners. The navy never solved the problems of coaling the gunboats and only slightly improved procedures after the navy established its depots. Stopping the illicit trade was difficult inasmuch as one-third to two-fifths of the vessels were constantly away for repairs and fuel. Thus part of the success of blockade running can be directly attributed to the gunboats' absences because of logistical maintenance.

TEN

To make bricks without straw

Men and the Navy

Manpower is one of the most important factors in the running of a ship. A shortage of officers and men, sickness, poor morale, or a combination of these and other factors can influence not only the operation of the vessel but in a larger context can also affect the squadron. One of the first measures of the president was to direct the enlistment of 18,000 men, in addition to the number allowed by law. Furthermore, he authorized an increase of 1,000 in the Marine Corps. The navy increased from 7,600 men in March 1861 to 22,000 that December. Two years later, in December 1863, the navy had 38,000 enlisted men and at the end of the war over 51,000. The number of officers increased from 1,300 in 1861 to 6,700 in 1865. A total of 118,044 men enlisted in the navy from March 1861 to May 1865.[1] Even with these large numbers, the manpower problems of the squadron remained severe during the Civil War—so severe, in fact, that it made insignificant by comparison the problems of getting the ships constructed and outfitted. The lack of recruits, which plagued the navy from the beginning until the end of the war, meant that ships laid at their berths, unmanned, awaiting crews. This was a logistical problem that became one of the most debilitating factors that weakened the navy during the war.

To enlist men for the service, the navy opened recruiting offices called "rendezvous" in nearly every port, town, or village on the East Coast. As the navy secured the towns in eastern North Carolina, it also opened offices in the captured regions in hopes of enlisting loyal citizens, free blacks, and contrabands. Generally the rendezvous in the occupied areas only supplied small numbers of men to the navy and usually remained opened for short periods. The larger cities in the Northeast, such as Boston and New York, provided many recruits and normally had more than one rendezvous open at one time. New York was perhaps the best place to recruit men, and hundreds of men were sent at a time from this port by steamship and train.[2]

The navy shipped the men and placed them on board receiving ships, which the men called "guardos." Old frigates served in this capacity and could accommodate over 1,000 recruits. Those sent to the North Atlantic Blockading Squadron went on board *Brandywine* before being distributed to the vessels. *Brandywine* lay under the guns of Fort Monroe, and one seaman said that she appeared to have "been built a hundred years or more" and had a "certain air of decay about her." The receiving ships also accommodated crews from vessels under long-term repairs. Here they mixed with the inexperienced men when they reshipped. Welles wrote to Garrett J. Pendergrast, the commandant of the Philadelphia Navy Yard, that "the intention of the department is to use all the available men as fast as a ship is ready without regard to the particular vessel to which they belong."[3]

Naval enlistments lagged behind the needs of the service for most of the war. Even though the average number of enlistments in the navy during 1862 amounted to over 1,500 a month and in 1863 over 2,000 a month, the navy continued to suffer from a lack of men. The slow rate of enlistment was aggravated by the lack of a naval bounty payment, in contrast with the high bounties paid by the army. Also, the states did not push naval enlistments because men who shipped in the navy were not counted toward the states' draft quotas.[4]

Recruitment in the early months of the war included some men from the merchant marine. But these men were often ignorant of guns and gunnery, regulations, and discipline. One officer claimed they were "green as gourds," but they adapted better than men with no experience. Fishermen also made up many of the first recruits, who came in such large quantities that they had to be shipped as landsmen.[5]

As more vessels became ready for crews, the pressure to obtain seamen increased. Some unscrupulous individuals enticed foreign seamen, particularly British sailors, into the Union navy after plying them with drink or by drugging them. The navy paid three dollars a head to a person bringing seamen, ordinary seamen, or firemen to enlist and ten dollars a head for landsmen and coal heavers. One of the most active groups doing this were women who kept sailor boardinghouses.[6]

Because of the great demand for men, many foreigners also illegally enlisted in the navy. A rarely enforced act passed in 1813 prohibited foreigners from serving in the United States Navy. Welles told the House of Representatives that, as a result of the manpower shortage, the law had "not been rigidly observed." When enlisting foreigners, however, they did try to ship those with experience.[7]

As the war progressed, the navy's recruits increasingly became less desirable. The rendezvous in Boston normally recruited only one-third of the men as landsmen. But in 1862, great numbers of inexperienced men offered their services at a time when the navy was having difficulty procuring seamen, and the navy enlisted them. With the draft law in effect, many chose to join the navy rather than the army because they thought it the "easiest and least hazardous." Many of the navy's recruits were landsmen and "professional bounty jumpers" and included "God-forsaken-looking ex-ministers, school masters, and lawyers." Another described them as "men of very little principle."[8]

The huge numbers enlisted by the other military branches forced the naval recruiters to lower their standards to meet quotas. The navy turned down few men for naval service, and at times it waived the regulations that governed age and physical requirements. Overzealous officers at the rendezvous sometimes enlisted undesirable men. The navy later discharged many of these men, some after being condemned as "idiots." Commander Augustus Ludlow Case of the steam sloop of war *Iroquois* had a few men that could not even clean themselves, leaving the crew to care for them "as children." He lamented that "it is a great pity that the demand for men should cause recruiting officers to enlist such."[9]

The navy required that a boy joining the service had to be fourteen years or older and had to have a parent's or guardian's signature until he turned eighteen. The navy also accepted a "limited number" of boys

from the "institution for juvenile offenders and vagrant boys." These
boys had to be recommended by the superintendents of the institutions,
because the navy was not to be "a receptacle for this class of offender,
which if admitted, probably would demoralize, instead of improving
the morals and condition of the ship's crews."[10]

Since many believed that the war would be short, the department had
a difficult time enlisting men for three-year tours during the first
months of the war. Thus many of the early enlistments lasted only one
year, and when these enlistments expired in the middle of 1862, the navy
held the men beyond their enlistment period. In special cases, the needs
of the navy became so critical that it signed men for extremely short
enlistment periods. The lack of seamen for the Roanoke Island expedition was so acute that Goldsborough agreed to ship men for one to three
months to have enough crew members to man the vessels in the expedition.[11]

The enlistment of blacks, probably more than any other factor,
helped to alleviate the shortage of men. At the beginning of the war, the
navy had no plans to use these men. Large numbers escaped to the
gunboats or into Union lines, forcing the Union to formulate some
policy. In July 1861, Stringham asked Welles what he should do with
them and asked if he could use them on board the storeships. Welles
answered, "You will do well to employ them."[12]

In September 1861, the Navy Department authorized their employment. Captains could ship blacks at a rating no higher than "boys" and
could pay them ten dollars a month and one ration a day. The navy went
a step further. In December 1862, it allowed "contrabands" to be enlisted
as landsmen and permitted advancement to the rank of seaman, ordinary seaman, fireman, or coal heaver. The department did not permit
them to transfer from one vessel to another with a rating higher than
landsman, unless their vessel went out of commission.[13]

The navy opened special rendezvous to enlist blacks in the service in
eastern Virginia and North Carolina. The army's presence in the area
allowed it to raise several regiments of black soldiers, which the navy
could not match. Rear Admiral S. P. Lee thought that the navy might
obtain more recruits if the "commissary of subsistence be not too gener-
ous of his rations to the poor and indolent."[14]

Almost half of the blacks the navy enlisted were rated as landsmen, and most enlisted from the seaboard states. Black enlistments peaked in July and August 1863. There is some disagreement on how many blacks served the navy during the war. Various studies claim that blacks constituted between eight and twenty-five percent of all seamen, and it appears that the numbers in the North Atlantic Blockading Squadron fell almost exactly between the two figures. The blacks who did serve in the navy usually had the dirtiest jobs or worked on board the supply hulks of the squadron, where blacks made up as much as ninety percent of the crews. The enlistment of blacks greatly alleviated the navy's often severe manpower shortages. When whites could not be shipped, blacks could be, and deficiencies in crews could sometimes be satisfied by filling the vessels with blacks.[15]

In addition to finding enlisted men, a shortage of officers also plagued the navy. The officer corps was decimated by a loss of nearly fifty percent to the Confederacy. A large number of those remaining had served in the navy for years, because the system of seniority, which lacked a provision for retirement, had filled the ranks with older men. This situation left a deficiency in the junior-grade officers. As a result of this shortage, the upper three classes of the Naval Academy were ordered into active service, which produced nineteen-year-old lieutenants.[16]

Because of the small number of officers available, regular officers had to be promoted, and men had to be taken from the merchant service. The navy established master's mates for acting masters and promoted crew members to master's mates. The department sometimes rushed those promoted from the merchant service to sea without gunnery practice. To enter naval service, these men had to pass an examination on seamanship, navigation, and gunnery. The service only offered five grades of line officers to volunteers: acting master's mates, acting ensigns, acting masters, acting volunteer lieutenants, and acting volunteer lieutenant commanders. Regular officers found the volunteer officers far from adequate for sea duty, lamenting that the men promoted from the ranks acted like "blackguards" and "delinquents."[17]

The shortage of regular officers became so acute that in some vessels all of the officers except the captain were volunteers. By mid-1863, ninety-eight percent of all the naval vessels had volunteer officers on board, and nearly half of the ships had all volunteer officers or only one regular officer. In early 1864, the gunboats blockading Cape Fear had a

total of only about "two or three dozen, old and young" regular officers.[18]

Because of the shortages, the squadron's gunboats usually operated
with fewer than the authorized complement of officers. Deficiencies of
this nature made it difficult to keep the watches, hold courts-martial
and courts of inquiry, and command the guns when in action. Charles
Henry Davis wrote to the commandant of the Philadelphia Navy Yard:
"I have become like the gambler who is reduced to his last stake. The
number of available officers is now so very, very small, that when I am
asked to officer a ship I am somewhat in the condition of the Egyptians
who were required to make bricks without straw."[19]

Desertions further drained the personnel pool. Monotony, danger,
and high army bounties contributed to the desertion rate. Blacks deserted less frequently, while foreign-born seamen deserted more frequently. Vessels in port for supplies or repairs offered the men a prime
time to escape. To catch deserters, the navy offered rewards, and detec-
tives made considerable sums of money finding them.[20]

The expiration of enlistments became the Navy Department's single
greatest worry during the war. As enlistments expired, the men normally went north on prize vessels or gunboats returning for repairs or
were transferred on board vessels traveling north. Many of these men
went to their home states merely to collect the bounties offered there.
Lee wanted to pay their bounties at sea to keep them from the army
recruiters, but he was never able to implement this plan.[21]

In early 1864, a shortage of men became a crisis for the North Atlantic
Blockading Squadron. At this time, nearly one-third of all the sailors in
the navy were entitled to their discharge. The vessels on the Atlantic
Coast had only half of their complements, and thirty-five ships awaited
crews. Gustavus Fox wrote to Lincoln: "All the anxieties and panics of
this war I have passed through without a feeling of trouble until the
present moment." Enlistments had fallen so low that rebel prisoners
from Point Lookout and other prisons began to fill the vacancies. Although an extreme measure, they were to be distributed within the
squadron 1 man to every 6 in large vessels, 1 man to 15 in every vessel
with less than 100 men, and none in tugs or small steamers. Lee placed
at least 100 prisoners on his vessels to fill deficiencies and requested
twice this number.[22]

Enlistment problems continued during the summer of 1864. Grant began his Petersburg campaign several months after the navy's three-year enlistments had ended. To help the navy with recruiting, the War Department allowed any man who could furnish proof that he was a "mariner by vocation, or an able seaman, or ordinary seamen" to transfer to the navy. His term of service could not be less than the unexpired term of his military service or less than one year, and transfer enlistments were not to exceed 10,000 men. In one regiment at Fort Monroe, Butler had 300 seamen willing to transfer to the navy. Many of the army recruits, however, hesitated to go to the navy because they feared that they would not get their bounties, which the army paid in installments. Butler inquired about the transfer and discovered that the Army Department considered the transfer optional. The men's bounties thus would be paid out of their prize money, and therefore nearly all declined to go into naval service.[23]

This program helped the navy, but it did not solve the manpower crisis. In a Cabinet meeting on 25 March, Welles brought up for consideration the scarcity of seamen. He asked the army to transfer 12,000 men immediately. He wrote to Lincoln that at that particular time he had thirty vessels without crews and that unless "some extraordinary measures are adopted, we shall be compelled to withdraw vessels from the squadrons for the want of men to man them."[24] The army transferred a regiment, the 30th U.S. Colored troops, to naval service, half of which went to the North Atlantic Blockading Squadron. On 1 April, Secretary of War Edwin Stanton agreed to transfer 12,000 men. A week after Stanton agreed to the transfer, Fox wrote to Lee: "We are beginning to get a few sailors in New York. The 1,000 potato diggers [Irish] are extra, and taken because we won't refuse any human being physically sound."[25]

Nevertheless, the gunboats in the North Atlantic Blockading Squadron remained shorthanded. In July, at the time when the squadron needed 2,000 men, Congress passed a bill to allow men to transfer to the navy from other branches of the armed services. The bill also permitted towns to count naval enlistments as part of their quotas for service in the war and allowed the payment of bounties to naval recruits. By the end of August, Welles wrote in his diary with some relief that "a desire to enter the Navy to avoid the draft is extensive, . . . so that our recruiting rendezvous are, for the time being, overrun."[26]

Diseases and other physical ailments aggravated the already grave problem of manpower and decreased the efficiency of the squadron during the war. The doctors treated a variety of diseases and ailments that kept the small medical staffs extremely busy. Normally about five percent of the crew reported sick each day, and an extremely small number of seamen went ashore to hospitals for treatment.[27]

The appearance of a contagious disease such as smallpox or yellow fever normally affected the whole crew and the ship. Medical officers limited the movements of gunboats with large numbers of sick. If the sick remained on board, the ship's captain might keep his gunboat near the hospital facilities. The appearance of smallpox required that the ship be washed and aired and that the clothing and bedding be sent along with the sick men to the hospital. The gunboat then had to remain in quarantine for three weeks. Yellow fever cases also required a quarantine, but the ship normally sailed north to clear up the disease.[28]

In emergency situations, doctors used hulks and storeships to house the sick. As early as March 1862, *Ben Morgan*, a 407-ton hulk, became a hospital ship. In most cases, these hulks were converted when outbreaks of communicable diseases occurred, particularly smallpox. In the sounds, doctors turned the schooner *Comet* into a hospital for "skin diseases" in the spring of 1864 for the purpose of isolating the sick.[29]

Men requiring treatment ashore were given a medical survey. Three medical officers performed the survey and filled out "cumbrous" forms. Rear Admiral Lee suggested that if a sailor required only hospital treatment, a "simple hospital ticket is all that is necessary." This procedure seems to have been abused, and Lee again began to require a regular medical survey.[30]

The supply steamers carried the seamen with acute cases north for better treatment. The steamers had schedules to make regular stops as a convenience for the passage of the sick. Irregularity in the system caused the sailors at the Cape Fear station to board the supply steamer on its way south and make a trip to Hilton Head and then north again. The senior officer at the Cape Fear River pleaded for the steamer to stop on its way north to pick up invalids and dispatches. Eventually the supply steamer did this, but at the cost of delivering stale provisions. Until the squadron had a supply steamer solely for its use, the trips north continued to be irregular.[31]

Surgeons regularly visited the vessels and the hospitals to ascertain their sanitary conditions and to report their findings to the Bureau of Medicine and Surgery. The fleet surgeon, William Maxwell Wood, noted that the men stationed in the rivers drank river water, which caused diarrhea and typhoid. Wood thus advised the men to drink only condensed water. Some surgeons prescribed fresh vegetables and particularly canned tomatoes, because they thought that they contained the "very best convenient antiscorbutics." One medical officer suggested that the vessels in the inland waters be interchanged with other vessels to minimize the dangers of health problems with other crews.[32]

The squadron had a large number of potential facilities for invalids, but they stayed crowded and were never adequate to meet the expansion of the navy. There were naval or marine hospitals in Portland, Maine; Portsmouth, New Hampshire; Chelsea, Massachusetts; New York, New York; Philadelphia, Pennsylvania; Washington, D.C.; Fort Norfolk and Portsmouth, Virginia; New Bern, Beaufort, Washington, and Plymouth, North Carolina, and the army hospitals at Old Point Comfort, Beaufort, and Ocracoke, North Carolina.[33]

The facilities farther north were less suitable for the use of the squadron. The hospitals located in North Carolina and Virginia, although small, served the squadron's needs but were wholly inadequate. The army retained the naval hospital after the abandonment of the Norfolk Navy Yard, which caused a great inconvenience to the squadron and crowded other facilities. The building, four stories high and built of brick and stone, would have served the navy well. Although the army recognized that the hospital belonged to the navy, it only admitted seamen there when there was room. The navy did occupy a small vacant building near Fort Norfolk, but because of the large number of invalids, many were transferred to New York.[34]

The hospitals in North Carolina were extremely small. Hammond General Hospital at Beaufort served both army and naval personnel and was used mainly for "acute cases" and not for "chronic cases." An officer on *Florida* described the hospital there as a "large rambling tumble down looking building erected for a hotel for those desirous of experiencing the beauties of nature." A small story-and-a-half cottage served as a hospital in New Bern and could only accommodate twelve men. Excessively dirty, it had no mess for the men and a cellar filled with rubbish, while the grounds there were called a "wilderness." In Plymouth, the navy had a hospital in the "best house in town."[35]

Once the men had enlisted, they often found the navy far different from what they had imagined. Although the navy had not changed much for decades, some had joined for adventure and others for prize money, but most found the service monotonous. A tar on board *Florida* stationed off Cape Fear recorded in his diary that one could "get a fair idea of our 'adventures'" if he would go on the roof of a house on a hot summer day and talk to a "half a dozen hotel hallboys, who are generally far more intelligent and agreeable than the average 'acting officer.'" Then he must "descend to the attic and drink some tepid water, full of iron rust. Then go on the roof again and repeat this 'adventurous process' at intervals," until tired out. Lastly, he would "go to bed, with everything shut down tight, so as not to show a light. Adventure! Bah! The blockade is the wrong place for it."[36]

Life at sea, though, varied depending on the gunboat's station and the vessel itself. Some of the ex-merchantmen were commodious and others were cramped, while those built for the navy were generally less spacious. Officers often had pleasant, comfortable, and well-furnished quarters. Captain Benjamin F. Sands wrote that "some officers luxuriated upon the broad decks and in the comfortable wardrooms of the frigates, whilst others were 'cabin'd, cribbed, confined' on board of some of the 'ballyhoos.'" The "ballyhoos," he wrote, were "uncomfortable in storm as in calm, mere sardine boxes in which a certain complement of men and officers were packed and sent to sea." The wardroom of the side-wheel steamer *Delaware* exemplified this problem, because the compartment had only four feet, eleven inches of space between the overhead and the deck.[37]

The seamen generally had significantly less pleasant quarters than those of the officers. Most ships were damp, particularly the ironclads. One tar commented about *Monitor* that "they might as well send a lot of men to sea in a wash tub," while another claimed, "My feet were not dry once in the whole time I was on board the *Monitor*." The lightly framed merchant vessels often leaked. Deck planks sometimes warped because of heavy ordnance, which caused rain to pour through the decks and run onto the crew in their hammocks.[38]

For centuries prior to the Civil War, fleas, lice, and rats on board had made life more miserable for seamen. Fleas and lice spread diseases, and rats could be extremely destructive. Rodents gnawed their way through bulkheads and destroyed food and equipment. *Crusader* was "completely overrun with rats." The commander of the *Crusader* wrote to Rear Admiral Lee that "when the wind is aft the smell from dead rats in the ceiling is so very offensive it is almost impossible to remain in the cabin and ward room state rooms."[39]

The ships were the least comfortable in the winter and summer. In the winter, most of the ships' compartments remained without heat. During the summer, little could be done to cool the vessels. Most of the gunboats had awnings made from old sails to shade the deck. The men stationed in the engine room were particularly unfortunate during the hot months. One sailor who worked in the fire room wrote home, "I will tell you how it feels in the fire room of a hot day you can immagen [sic] how a crab would feal [sic] in a pot of hot watter [sic]."[40]

The daily routine began at 5:30 or 6:00 A.M. The crews began the day being awakened by the boatswain, who with his whistle ordered hammocks unlashed and stowed. Next the men swept the decks, washed their clothing, and polished brightwork. Meals were served at different times but usually at 8:00 A.M., 12:00 P.M., and 5:00 P.M. Between meals, the seamen kept busy with other cleaning chores, painting, standing four-hour watches, and drills.[41] Several times a week, the ship would be thoroughly cleaned and the decks scrubbed down with holy stones.

Drilling the men was an important and frequent function. Each day after the call to quarters, a rapid roll of the drum signaled the men to their battle stations, where they practiced loading and aiming the large guns. Often they lashed old flour barrels together and fired at them from 1,500 to 2,000 yards to sharpen their gunnery skills. The seamen also performed musket drills and fire drills and practiced repelling boarders.[42]

When the tars had free time, they improvised many types of amusements. They read, fished, wrote home, played dominoes, and mended clothing. Others participated in less mundane activities, such as training cockroaches. The chief source of entertainment aboard *Calypso* for some men was to put "personal ads" in Boston's *Waverly Magazine* and then answer the letters they received. Plays and boat races also helped to break the monotony. After sunset, the men normally spun yarns, sang, or danced "a quadrille" on the fantail. Some ships had bands with brass instruments, while others made do with "plenty of boatswains pipes and some banjos and fiddles."[43]

Many different activities helped meet the spiritual needs of the seamen. The ships held church services every Sunday, and the crewmen of the gunboats stationed in the inland waters sometimes attended services ashore. Periodical literature such as *The Sailor's Magazine* and *The Seaman's Friend* gave moral advice and promoted religion on board the vessels and attempted to guide the men away from the temptations of liquor and tobacco. The American Seaman's Friend Society, which published *The Life Boat*, furthered the welfare of the tars by placing thousands of books on board the vessels during the war.[44]

On the blockade at Wilmington, when the weather was pleasant, the ships anchored together so that the officers and, to a lesser extent, the men could visit. The officers could renew acquaintances, discuss the war, exchange yarns, or just "pass away the time the best way they can."[45]

All the various recreational activities on board could not replace leaves of absence or liberty. When a vessel went north for repairs, the commandant of the navy yard often permitted a leave of absence for the officers and sometimes arranged liberty for the crews. Most of the leaves granted to officers lasted only seven to ten days so that they did not interfere with the "speedy repairs of the vessels." The crews from vessels in the sounds were sometimes granted liberty while in New Bern. Contemporaries described New Bern as a "beautiful town" of brick and frame houses, "compactly built." In New Bern, the men could buy local food products, and at one bakery, they could buy hot pies eight inches in diameter for fifteen cents. For two dollars, the wardroom officers could join the Navy Club, where they could play billiards and drink liquor.[46] The visitations by the Union seamen were, however, not always favorably received.

The crews of blockaders often obtained liberty in Beaufort. Charles Post, an enlisted man from a blockader, described Beaufort as a "string of houses, a number of churches and lots of sand." One restaurant there, the Ocean House, provided elegant eating for those who could afford it. Extremely impressed that one restaurant provided silverware and napkins, Post commented that "the elegance knocked me all in a heap." A news correspondent traveling on board the double-ender *Osceola* wrote of taverns and restaurants in the town, but also of "a naval supply store, a clothing store . . . a bowling-alley, where poor beer is sold to poorer people, . . . a billiard-saloon, a post office—hardly large enough to hold the squadron's mails—two churches, and some other stores."[47]

Commonly the seamen found trouble while in port for two reasons, drink and women. The navy had little control of the sailors while ashore, and the tars frequently, while intoxicated, ran into patrols of the army provost general. These encounters only aggravated the poor relations between the services. Prostitutes could always be engaged on shore but sometimes could be brought illegally on board the gunboats. *Iron Age* while in Boston for repairs had the nickname of the "Charleston whorehouse."[48]

Alcohol on ships became such a vexation that Congress abolished the sailor's spirit ration beginning 1 September 1862. The seamen received five cents in lieu of their grog ration, but the decision of Congress never became popular with the majority of the men during the war. This law failed to stop drunkenness on board the vessels, since seamen had no difficulty purchasing intoxicating drinks from various sources ashore. An officer on board *Release* wrote, "in spite of all orders to the contrary, such as stopping the liquor ration and the forbidding of alcoholic liquors to be brought on board, . . . that as much if not more of such liquor continues to be used as ever by the *large* majority of the officers & seamen." Another anonymous individual claimed that at New Inlet the iniquitous blockader *Iron Age* should be called the "drunkards' asylum."[49]

Mealtimes on board ships changed little during the nineteenth century. The men anxiously awaited their meals, but shortages or poor quality could cool enthusiasm and become a source of complaint. One seaman said, "When breakfast's done, the next thing I look forward to is dinner, and when that's done, I look for supper time." The ship's company was divided up into messes of ten or twelve men. The "head man" of every mess, or "cook" as the men called him, obtained the food for his group. The navy issued the men one ration each, and anyone not drawing a ration could draw twenty cents in lieu of this with the permission of the commanding officer.[50]

The officers likewise ate in messes in the wardroom. One officer served as "caterer" and purchased the "provisions and furnishings of the table . . . for the voyage."[51] Since the officers usually purchased their food before leaving port, they controlled the quality, thus their mess bills normally ran higher than the men's. The officers were assessed equal amounts regardless of their pay. Those of the *Monitor* spent about thirty-five dollars a month, which included not only food but the costs of dishes and "table furniture."[52]

The issued ration was thought to be very liberal and cost the government an average of twenty-five cents a day. When the chairman of the

Table 4. Rations Provided by the Navy

Ration	Sun.	Mon.	Tues.	Wed.	Thur.	Fri.	Sat.	Weekly Quantity
Biscuit	14	14	14	14	14	14	14	98 oz.
Beef			1			1		2 lbs.
Pork		1		1			1	3 lbs.
Processed meat	0.75				0.75			1.5 lbs.
Flour			0.5			0.5		1 lb.
Rice	0.5							0.5 lb.
Dried fruit			2			2		4 oz.
Pickles				4			4	8 oz.
Sugar	2	2	2	2	2	2	2	14 oz.
Tea or	0.25	0.25	0.25	0.25	0.25	0.25	0.25	1.75 oz.
Coffee or cocoa	1	1	1	1	1	1	1	7 oz.
Butter	2				2			4 oz.
Desiccated potato					2			2 oz.
Desiccated mixed vegetables	1							1 oz.
Beans		8		8			8	24 oz.
Molasses					32			32 oz.
Vinegar							8	8 oz.
Spirits	0.25	0.25	0.25	0.25	0.25	0.25	0.25	1.75 oz.

Senate Committee on Naval Affairs inquired about adding to the naval ration, Horatio Bridge, chief of the Bureau of Provisions and Clothing, answered that the navy ration was so plentiful that the ships' messes normally commuted for money about two out of ten rations.[53]

The quality of the food was somewhat irregular throughout the squadron. Gunboats stationed near the points of supply might receive fresh provisions semiweekly, and while in port for repairs they might get them daily. The vessels stationed at Cape Fear could not get fresh food on a regular basis. Their crews ate mostly preserved or canned food, which was sometimes of poor quality. Stephen Blanding wrote after the war of worms in the hardtack, cockroaches in the coffee, cheese "as hard as flint," and flour that even when boiled in bags, "could be thrown across the deck without breaking it." Another seaman wrote home, "I am neer [sic] starved if I get much thinner it will take two of us to make one."[54]

The sailors could vary their regimen by substituting other items. Some of the vessels patrolled fertile fishing grounds. The seamen on board *Mystic* caught 800 fish in one day off Cape Fear. The rivers also contained a source of food. The seamen on board *Valley City* used a seine net and "caught shad and herring by the barrel." Gunboat crews in Virginian waters also fished and caught crabs. They anchored over oyster beds where they could tong for oysters, and sometimes oystermen gave shellfish to the vessels.[55]

Foraging and purchasing food also helped to curtail the monotony of the ship's fare. The tars stationed on board vessels in the interior waters stole chickens, pigs, lambs, and cattle, shot snipe, and gathered eggs, vegetables, and fruits. In areas occupied by the army, they could usually buy chickens, eggs, sweet potatoes, and many types of fruit from the local people. When the blockaders captured runners, the sailors sometimes found fruits on board the captured vessels.[56]

Varied foodstuffs periodically arrived from home, along with clothing, books, pipes, tobacco, and other items. Sutlers likewise furnished the men with food and dry goods that they required and could afford to buy. Sutlers might have taken advantage of seamen, but regulation by the government limited their profits.[57]

While blandness characterized the everyday meals, during holidays the officers and men usually created quite a culinary feast. The officers of *Florida* duly kept the traditions of Christmas in a style befitting royalty on land or sea by having "oyster and tomato soups—boiled & baked fish—boiled ham & tongue—roast turkey, roast beef, chicken pie, broiled chickens, roast ducks, clam pie, quails on toast, giblet stew—beets, sweet and irish potatoes, onions, green corn, & peas, asparagus, cranberry sauce, currant jelly." To drink they had claret, sherry, and Catawba wines and ale. And for dessert they had "plum pudding, corn starch do, blanch mange—apple, cranberry, cherry and raspberry pies—fruit cake—can'd peaches and grapes—apples, raisins, figs, chestnuts, almonds, hickory nuts—coffee and chocolate."[58]

Discipline is a relatively invisible but important component to shipboard morale and to the efficient running of the ships. In July 1862, Congress passed twenty-five articles for a more uniform regulation of the discipline in the navy. Punishment for infractions of these articles nevertheless continued to be in the hands of the commanding officer of each vessel. During the war, punishment was less harsh because the navy no longer allowed flogging. Officers did remain stern and strict and had myriad ways of punishing their men.[59]

Punishments could be somewhat exotic. For some offenses, the tars might be sent into the rigging "to study astronomy" for two or three hours while carrying a musket. A similar punishment used by one officer had the seaman sent up the ratlines on the underside, inboard, and forced to hang on. Spitting on the deck, albeit not a serious offense, might mete the offender the task of carrying a spittoon for the other men to use.[60]

Nothing gave the seamen more pleasure at sea than the chase of a blockade runner and the thoughts of prize money. After the capture, condemnation, and sale of the prize, the seamen never received full compensation until their enlistments expired. They usually received only three to five dollars a month for spending money and seldom could get extra money from the paymaster, even if they begged for it. Many got relief by writing home for what they needed. Others had to purchase clothing and supplies from the paymasters, who charged ten percent over invoice price to protect the government from loss. Sometimes the ships' payrolls ran short, which left the tars without liberty money. In New York, bankers often made loans on bounty money due to the seamen and their wives and widows.[61]

Table 5. Sample of Punishments for Crimes

Crimes	Punishment
Drunkenness	Bread and water for 10 days, then dismissal; confinement to ship for 2–3 months without leave
Fighting	Double irons, sweat box
Breaking liberty	Double irons
Missing muster	Sweat box
Cursing a boatswain's mate	Sweat box
Insolence	Double irons
AWOL	Stoppage of liberty; sometimes dismissal from service
Scandalous conduct	Dismissal from service
Uncleanliness or slovenliness	Grog stopped for 1 week
Disobedience of orders	Sweat box
Shirking duty	Sweat box
Unofficer-like conduct	Dismissal from service
Assaulting and striking a superior officer	Imprisoned for 3 years of hard labor
Assaulting and striking a seaman	Loss of one month's pay; confinement in single irons for 1 month
Desertion	7 years' imprisonment
Sodomy	2 years' imprisonment, with ball and chain

Sources: Welles to Lee, 16 July 1864, Lee Collection, LCM; Lee to Welles, 11 February, 17 November 1863, ibid. Punishments were noted in the ship's logs; those consulted were for *Cambridge, Whitehead, Jamestown, Chippewa,* and *Crusader.* Welles to Lee, 13 February 1863, Lee Collection, LCM; William Keeler to Anna, 21 June 1862, *Monitor,* 159.

Shortages of men plagued the squadron during most of the war. The lack of recruits kept ships in port, which hurt the efficiency of the squadron. This affected not only the blockade but also to some extent the squadron's ability to cooperate with the army. The seamen, and to a lesser extent the officers, could do little to change the system. The men on board the ships continued throughout the war to live with their deprivations, monotony, and restlessness. Most of the men longed for the day that their enlistments expired, so they could go "on a regular tare."[62] One seaman stationed on a blockader off Cape Fear expressed his despair, and probably those of his shipmates, when he wrote in his diary, "What luck some people do have! If one of the shells had only hit us the other day we should be going home to glory, cool drinks, and our best girls."[63]

ELEVEN

*We are all anxious to make the
blockade efficient*

The Coastal Blockade

The crew of the Union blockader *Florida* had just
begun to raise anchor when the lookout at the mast-
head shouted, "Sail ho." The officer showed almost no
emotion as he sent word of the strange ship to the
captain. This formality had been repeated so often
with no results that when the crew was beat to quarters they likewise showed little excitement. As *Florida*
slowly turned to sea, Commander John Bankhead
signaled to the flagship, "A strange sail in sight," and
received the normal reply, "Give chase."

With the anchor up and the engineer increasing
steam, the lookout soon identified the vessel as a
steamer, and black smoke made her more suspicious.
After signaling the flagship, that "the strange sail is an
enemy," a squall completely concealed both the flagship and the chase. Guided by the compass, the captain ordered every sail set and passed word to the
engineer to raise steam to the maximum pressure by
throwing oil, grease, and pitch into the furnaces.

After more than a half-hour of pursuit, the squall
passed, and the vessel could be seen on the horizon as
a black speck with a cloud over her. *Florida* began to
gain on her quarry after more than three hours of
pursuit. Several squalls had prevented a clear view of

the vessel. The officers now stood on deck looking through their glasses, speculating on the cargo and the value of the steamer. When four miles separated the ships, Bankhead ordered his rifled gun to be cast loose, and the first shot splashed astern but in range. The third shot splashed water on the deck, and she hove to and showed a white flag. As *Florida* rapidly approached, the crew of the steamer lowered a boat and began throwing objects overboard. *Florida*'s captain ordered a gun loaded with canister and drew under her stern and hailed, "If I see anything more thrown overboard from you, I will sweep your decks with canister."

A boarding party quickly rowed to the prize, which proved to be *Calypso* out of Nassau. After a quick inspection, they found her sinking and the safety valves tied down. The boarding officer drew his pistol, forced the chief engineer below, and managed to save the vessel, which netted the officers and crew of *Florida* more than $37,000. More importantly, however, it denied the Confederacy a cargo of much-needed supplies.[1]

This scene would be repeated many times off Cape Fear. Though the navy began the blockade of this port with one single vessel in July 1861, the blockade there eventually comprised such a large number of ships during the latter part of the war that one blockade runner captain reportedly stated that "the very waves grew tired of holding up their ships."[2] Indeed, the United States Navy's efforts to blockade the Confederacy's most important port slowly grew, as did Wilmington's value to the South.

The North Atlantic Blockading Squadron did not have an enormous stretch of coastline to blockade, as some areas were secured early. At the outbreak of war, the navy controlled Chesapeake Bay, and in August, after the capture of the forts at Hatteras Inlet, the sounds of North Carolina were less accessible to coastal traffic. Naval leaders in the winter of 1861 felt confident that they could virtually stop the remaining Confederate trade. Silas Stringham had postulated earlier in May that the would need only twelve to fifteen more vessels to complete the blockade—four or five of these would patrol off North Carolina. Because of the scarcity of vessels, however, the navy managed to guard closely only the most important ports of the South. Gunboats patrolled the remaining points and performed a "coast guard service" by cruising up and down the coast with no permanent stations.[3]

When the Navy Department initiated the blockade, it considered only two ports north of Charleston important enough to watch—Beaufort and Wilmington, North Carolina. Both had the potential to become major points of entry for the Confederacy, but the Union forces captured Beaufort in April 1862, before it could develop into an important port for the Confederacy.

Wilmington, on the other hand, saw a meteoric rise in trade and lived up to its potential. North Carolina's principal seaport and largest city, with a population of nearly 10,000, it was the state's most important city before the war. Wilmington boasted the largest naval stores market in the country. Small sailing craft carried most of these goods to and from other American ports, and only a small portion was marketed abroad. The foreign trade centered around the exportation of lumber and naval products. From two to three dozen ships arrived and cleared weekly during the peak trading seasons.[4] But no one realized that this town would become synonymous with the word blockade.

Geography and communications more than any other attributes determined Wilmington's growth and importance to the Confederacy during the war. The town itself lay twenty miles from the mouth of the Cape Fear River and fifteen miles from New Inlet, beyond the reach of direct assault by naval vessels. The river could be navigated as far as Fayetteville, 100 miles upstream, and its tributaries were also navigable for shorter distances. The river had two navigable entrances, and between them lay Smith's Island, which stretched for ten miles into the ocean. Frying Pan Shoals extended fifteen miles farther into the Atlantic, making the distance between the inlets by sea some fifty miles, while the distance directly between them was only six or seven. The double inlets required two separate blockading forces to watch the coast and made it possible for those violating the blockade to choose the inlet that better suited their intentions. This separation compounded the existing problems for the blockaders, especially communications, coherence, and support. Wilmington developed into the Confederacy's principal port after Bermuda and Nassau became the major shipping points for blockade goods. Only 570 miles from Nassau and 674 miles from Bermuda, Wilmington would surpass in importance every city in the South, except Richmond, Virginia.[5]

Besides geographical advantages, Wilmington also had good rail

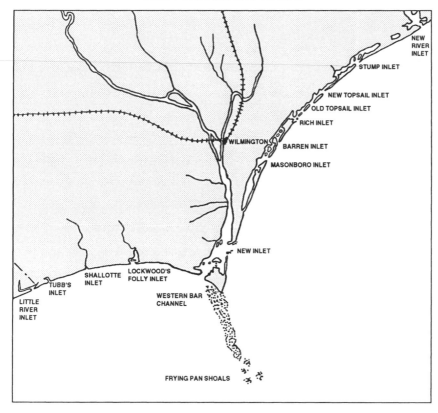

THE APPROACHES TO WILMINGTON, NORTH CAROLINA

connections. The Wilmington and Manchester Railroad ran southwest
to Florence, South Carolina, and had connections with Charleston. The
unfinished Wilmington, Charlotte, and Rutherford Railroad ran west.
The major railroad, the Wilmington and Weldon, ran almost due north
to Weldon, North Carolina, where it connected with the Petersburg
Railroad, giving connections to Richmond. This line lay inland, out of
easy reach of the menacing Union army and thus formed the principal
north-south line east of the Blue Ridge Mountains.[6]

It was the lack of gunboats and seamen to man them that had its
greatest impact on the blockade of Wilmington in the early months of
the war. The navy left Wilmington virtually unwatched for three
months after Lincoln announced his intention to blockade the South.
Welles knew that merchantmen ran in and out of the Cape Fear River
and advised Stringham to station a vessel off Wilmington, "provided it

can be done without weakening other more important points that
should be guarded with unremitting vigilance."[7] Stringham had blockaders cruise along the coast, and some had stopped off Wilmington, but
none had officially declared the port to be under blockade.

International law required that an adequate force be stationed at all
times at the entrance to a port to prevent communication. This concept,
though, could be interpreted widely and remained virtually undefined
by international law. Thus one vessel could qualify as an adequate force.
The blockade was established by notification, and once the navy had
established the blockade of a port, a vessel had to remain on station,
otherwise the blockade would have to be reinstated.[8]

As the blockaders cruised the coast, they stopped vessels and inserted
a notification of the blockade on the register and muster roll and also
noted the time, longitude, and latitude. As the war progressed and an
adequate time had elapsed for knowledge of the blockade, Union naval
officers no longer gave a warning and captured the vessels without
notice.[9]

On 21 July, the screw steamer *Daylight* formally declared the port of
Wilmington blockaded, but she had to abandon her station within a
week because of machinery problems. While off Wilmington, *Daylight*
experienced one of the difficulties related to blockading the dual entrances to Cape Fear. When a small steamer passed out of the Western
Bar Inlet entrance, *Daylight* moved around the shoals to capture her.
After arriving on the southern side of the shoals, she observed several
small vessels passing out of New Inlet. The weakness of the blockade at
this time is illustrated by the fact that during the months of June, July,
and August, at least forty-two vessels entered and cleared from
Wilmington.[10]

The blockade of the port of Wilmington remained weak for several
months, because only one gunboat could be spared to watch both inlets.
This blockader constantly fought the problems of geography by having
to shift her position from inlet to inlet, and it was August before the first
blockade runner was apprehended off Wilmington. The problem of the
divided entrances became even more difficult to overcome when the
Confederates began to signal the whereabouts of the Union ship by
hoisting flags on the Baldhead lighthouse. To confuse the rebels, *Pen-
guin*, the only warship blockading the port, tried to conceal herself in the

daytime and cruised at night, frequently changing her position. By October 1861, three vessels watched Cape Fear entrances, which increased the danger to those trying to evade the blockade.[11]

While maintaining a nominal blockade at Wilmington, the small entrances north of Wilmington remained unwatched. British Commander Algernon Lyons of HMS *Racer*, cruising between Cape Fear and Beaufort in November 1861, noted that not a single gunboat guarded the inlets between Beaufort and Wilmington. He also felt that the navy had not placed Beaufort under a strict enough blockade and wrote, "I am of opinion that one sailing vessel such as the 'Braziliera,' is not sufficient to maintain effectively the blockade of the port of Beaufort."[12]

The early efforts of the navy to blockade Wilmington and other Southern ports was hampered by the lack of shallow-draft vessels to patrol the shoal waters of the Southern coastline. Most of the navy's regular vessels had deep drafts, which made them virtually useless to watch Southern ports because shallow waters forced them to lie so far from the inlets. In 1861, Gideon Welles pointed to the fact that "the principal naval vessels are not, from their great draft of water, adapted to blockade service on our shallow coast."[13] This problem was later solved by acquiring the proper vessels for the blockade.

The lack of suitable blockaders in the first months of the war caused some reflection on the part of the Blockade Strategy Board. The board believed it could close the most important inlets along the coast by sinking hulks laden with stone in them. Recognizing the potential of Wilmington, it considered obstructing New Inlet on 13 July 1861. While discussing this project, the board members pointed out that the Confederacy had made a mistake by not fortifying the inlet. By fortifying New Inlet, the rebels could also have defended the Cape Fear River and Smith's Island, while ensuring that the inlet would remain open to be used by blockade runners. This matter was again studied by the board on 16 July. They had been informed that, strangely enough, the alarmed Confederate leaders, overlooking the potential of this inlet had closed it themselves. Charles Davis wrote in the minutes of the board: "New Inlet is said to have been closed by the people of Wilmington; if not its obstruction can easily be affected [*sic*]."[14]

The Confederates had indeed tried to obstruct the inlet. During the first month of the war, a schooner was towed there and sunk. But the swift currents quickly swept away the obstruction, and vessels passed through the inlet. By the fall of 1861, the strategy board considered obstructing it once more. At a meeting on 2 September 1861, the board recommended a careful reconnaissance of the inlet to determine the extent of the defenses there, the conditions of the channel, and the possibility of closing it with some type of obstruction. Welles approved this recommendation and authorized Flag Officer Stringham to proceed with the reconnaissance.[15]

Before the Union navy could close the channel, it was temporarily and partially obstructed by the Confederates to prevent Union warships from entering. During the middle of December 1861, the tug *Uncle Ben* towed four heavy diamond-shaped wooden cribs, about forty or fifty feet wide and twenty feet deep, to New Inlet. The rebels moored these cribs close together on the shoal and in the channel. They filled three of the cribs with rocks and sunk them in the channel on the northwestern corner of Zeek's Island. The fourth crib was to be sunk at a later date if needed. Before sinking the cribs, the Union blockaders had observed a small steam tug frequently venturing from New Inlet, but after laying down the obstructions, the blockaders had observed the tug coming only from Western Bar Inlet. This furnishes evidence that the Confederates at least temporarily obstructed the channel. Commander Daniel Braine of *Monticello* remarked: "I know that it is an impossibility for her to pass, or any other vessel drawing 9 feet of water."[16] This obstruction lasted only a short time. Within weeks, the cribs were swept away by the swift currents, making it necessary for the Confederate authorities to defend the inlet and for the squadron to blockade it.

The federal Blockade Strategy Board also considered obstructing the channels at Western Bar but dismissed the idea after only a short discussion. In addition to the extreme width of one of the channels and the depth of the water there, the presence of Fort Caswell would have made the placement of obstructions difficult if not impossible.[17]

Union leaders knew that obstructing the channels would only temporarily solve their problems. A strict blockade would require a large number of ships of the right kind. After assuming command of the squadron, Flag Officer Goldsborough wrote Welles that he believed that eight steamers could "effectively" blockade both Wilmington and

Beaufort. A month later, Goldsborough managed to have only two sailing vessels at each of these ports. The flag officer realized that this small number would not be sufficient and continued to stress the need for steam-powered vessels and gunboats that could keep the sea during the winter months.[18]

Keeping a large number of ships off Wilmington proved difficult. During the first year of the war, the warships stationed at Wilmington remained absent a great deal for logistical maintenance and continued to keep semipermanent stations. Sailing vessels could remain for long periods of time, but steamers needed to leave their posts and run to Hampton Roads for coal. A round-trip might take a total of four days if things went well, but delays were common. The steam blockaders continued to ply to and from their stations for supplies until after April 1862, when the Union forces captured Beaufort and began using it as a logistical base for the blockaders. To prolong their stay, the blockaders anchored at their day stations to conserve fuel. During the day, they remained from three to five miles from shore and at night steamed closer to the inlets.[19]

Goldsborough remained preoccupied with the capture of the North Carolina sounds and the squadron's support of McClellan during the Peninsular campaign. The great numbers of vessels needed in these two campaigns strained the squadron's resources. Assigning gunboats for the blockade of the North Carolina coast became difficult and often took a lower priority. During this period, the Confederate secretary of state, Judah P. Benjamin, remarked that he knew of twenty ports not blockaded by the United States and that "it is notorious that there is a large number of ports within the Confederacy and a vast extent of coast absolutely free from any investing force."[20]

The British foreign minister, Earl Russell, also commented on the relaxed state of the blockade and raised a question concerning its legality. On 5 February 1862, Russell wrote about the blockade of Wilmington and Charleston: "It appears from the reports received . . . that although a sufficient force is stationed off those ports, various ships have successfully eluded the blockade; a question might be raised as to whether such a blockade should be considered effective."[21]

Goldsborough gradually increased the force off the Wilmington inlets as more vessels became available. He had considered sailing

The Little Steamer *Eolus*. This steamer was used at Wilmington as a bar blockader because of her good speed, lack of masts and low profile. (*Courtesy the U.S. Naval Historical Center*)

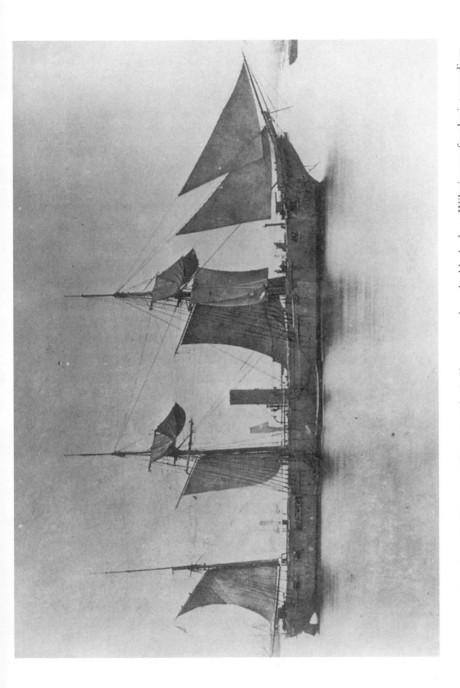

Steam Sloop Thought to Be *Tuscarora* (Wyoming Class). She was used on the blockade at Wilmington for the intermediary stations between the bar and the outer blockade. Designed to be propelled by sail or steam, she was cursed as unsuitable for the blockade as were many others used by the navy. She was slow and consumed much fuel. (*Courtesy the U.S. Naval Historical Center*)

vessels "of poor account—next to good for nothing on such a service."[22] Goldsborough never commanded an adequate number of steam gun-boats to assign sufficient numbers at Wilmington. He thus never formu-lated a complicated tactical plan there. Goldsborough furthermore did not have a sufficient number of ships capable of blockade duty and was compelled to use the vessels at his disposal whether they were efficient or not.

Toward the end of Goldsborough's command, the situation im-proved. He then sometimes had as many as ten steamers stationed at Wilmington (nine screw steamers and one side-wheel steamer).[23] Goldsborough's major contribution to the theory of the blockade was to replace the sailing vessels with faster and more properly armed steam-ers.

While the Union navy built and acquired ships for the blockade, the Confederates built and strengthened their coastal fortifications. The forts and lesser works guarding the approaches to Cape Fear increas-ingly determined the effectiveness of the blockade. In particular, the forts that guarded the seaward approaches became crucial to Confeder-ate successes in blockade running and affected the positioning of the blockaders. As soon as the war started, the Confederate government began placing forts and batteries along the coast, and five became decisive to the defense of Wilmington: Fort Fisher guarded New Inlet and the coast to the north; Fort Anderson lay on the west bank of Cape Fear, north of Fort Fisher; Fort Johnson guarded the anchorages of the blockade runners; Fort Holmes occupied a position on the western corner of Smith's Island; the fifth, Fort Caswell, guarded the Western Bar entrance. Several batteries were later added to guard Smith's Island and the Western Bar more completely. The entire fortification system presented a formidable defense for the port.

The two largest and most important works were Forts Fisher and Caswell. On 16 April 1861, the 30th North Carolina Militia, composed mainly of men from the Wilmington area and led by Colonel John Cantwell, captured Fort Caswell. The old masonry fort initially mounted only two twenty-four-pound guns on decayed carriages. The Confederates rearmed the fort and covered the exposed masonry with sand and iron, which converted the fort into a strong casemated work.[24]

Fort Fisher, the key to all the defenses, had not existed at the war's outset. Soon after the capture of Fort Caswell, the rebels began to build a battery on Federal Point. By July 1862, the fort had grown into a small work about 100 yards long and constructed of sandbags. The fort's armament consisted of seventeen guns but mounted only six large guns, and only two of these, eight-inch Columbiads, were suited for seacoast defense.[25] Fort Fisher grew steadily during the war, developing into the largest earthwork fort in the Confederacy and mounting over forty heavy guns.

These forts proved valuable to blockade runners; they kept the Union warships at a greater distance from the inlets, making the blockade less effective and providing a sanctuary for the violators of the blockade. One blockade-running captain observed that as "long as batteries at the entrance of the port blockaded keep ships at a respectable distance, the blockade will be broken."[26] The Confederate gunners continually reminded the Union ships that they controlled the waters near the forts. One tar stationed on board a warship off Wilmington remarked that "on our right is a rebel fortification from where ever and anon they send a shot over to keep us in good humor."[27]

The senior officer determined the stations of the blockaders in part by the range of the Confederate guns nearby. The Confederates mounted their longest ranged ordnance at Fort Fisher. Until the fall of 1862, vessels at the Western Bar could lie within two and one-half miles of Fort Caswell without being fired upon. That October, the commandant of Fort Fisher, Colonel William Lamb, decided to force the Union vessels to anchor farther from this entrance. He took a detachment of men from Fort Fisher along with two siege guns, which he placed overnight at Fort Caswell. The next day, his men fired on the Union vessels and drove them farther to sea. One shell struck *Maratanza*, killing two and wounding five.[28] To compel the blockaders to lie farther from shore, Lamb began to use imported Whitworth guns, which, when hitched to mules, could be pulled to various points along the beach. The Whitworths could fire their rifled projectiles a distance of five miles. Mobile long-range ordnance and the guns mounted within the forts enabled the Confederates to control a greater portion of the coast, which made the blockade less effective.

Rear Admiral Samuel Phillips Lee eagerly took command of the squadron in the fall of 1862. It was during his command of the squadron that the theory of blockade was advanced to its highest form during the war. Goldsborough, who had completed the conquest of the sounds of North Carolina, left Lee to maintain a blockade from Beaufort to the boundary of North and South Carolina. Within a week of taking command, Lee began considering changes to create a more effective blockade and requested better armed and more "efficient" gunboats. Lee considered strong batteries for the gunboats an essential attribute, yet he lamented that only the steamers *Octorara*, *Monticello*, and *Penobscot* had armaments to suit their duties. Welles had just as much interest in improving the blockade of Wilmington as his flag officer; however, he had no warships to give Lee. Welles sent the admiral a note shortly after Lee took command of the squadron, writing that Wilmington had "never been efficiently blockaded."[29]

Rear Admiral Lee asked the senior officer at Wilmington, Commander Gustavus Scott, about the tactical disposition of the blockaders. To his dismay, he learned that the steamers lay at anchor, day and night, five miles from the inlets and only two miles from each other. Lee instructed Scott to have them shift their berths between evening and morning twilight to a position as close to the bar as possible. He also implemented an innovative plan by instructing that one of the gunboats act as a picket and that the other ships support this vessel, the first instance during the war of using a double line of blockading vessels.[30]

Lee showed his concerns for the affairs of the blockade when he wrote Commander Scott, "I cannot think the positions occupied by the vessels off Wilmington are (as you say) the best in view of the *Kate*'s having twice recently run the blockade and considering the vessels have been lying from five to seven miles off." Scott responded by stressing the needs of the blockade: "Vessels of better speed I hope may be sent here, at New Inlet there are three, one of those at Topsail Inlet and one other absent for coal leaves a single vessel to blockade New Inlet." He added, "We are all anxious to make the blockade efficient and feel sensibly the necessity of additional force."[31]

Lee realized that the small number of warships at Wilmington could not also adequately patrol the coast from the South Carolina boundary to Beaufort. Within this stretch of coastline, twelve inlets lay north of Frying Pan Shoals and four south of the shoals. Most of the inlets could only accommodate shallow-draft vessels, but nevertheless, the Confederates conducted trade through them. The inlets continued to attract trade, and Lee sent gunboats to patrol the inlets regularly. Sorties into these inlets, and the capture and destruction of blockade runners near them, gradually discouraged their use by the Confederates.

The blockaders on the north side of the shoals constantly needed support from the southern side because they watched the vast area between New Inlet and Beaufort. During the fall of 1862, the screw steamer *Daylight* began cruising to New Topsail Inlet every afternoon and then coasted back down to New Inlet in the morning to communicate with the senior officer. A constant shortage of blockaders prevented *Daylight* from cruising the entire distance, and the senior officer only allowed her to go as far as Masonboro Inlet, about half of the previous coverage. In December 1862, Scott wrote to Lee that he still had no "efficient vessels to blockade" and only two for each side of the shoals to watch all the inlets to the north and to the south.[32]

As successful as the squadron was in stopping the trade in the lesser inlets, it failed to stop effectively the runners from going in and out of Wilmington. The gunboats' failure to prevent this trade exasperated the officers. Captain Benjamin F. Sands expressed this frustration shortly after assuming command of the steamer *Dacotah* when he wrote: "It is greatly to our mortification, after all our watchfulness to prevent it, that the enemy succeed in eluding us. None can be more vigilant than we are; the officers of the watch, with a quartermaster always on 'bridge,' lookouts on each bow, gangway and on quarter." He further lamented, "For myself I never pretend to turn in at night, and am frequently on deck during the night inspecting the lookouts in person, taking what sleep I can get in my clothes, ready for a moments call—and I believe it is the same way for all commanding officers." Sands blamed poor visibility on the dark nights, when vessels could not be seen half a mile away; during favorable circumstances, in the absence of the moonlight, one could not see a vessel a mile away.[33]

The Navy Department continually assigned more gunboats to Lee, but the blockade was not becoming any more effective, because the evolving blockade runners were getting faster. It became increasingly evident that the blockade could not be maintained effectively with slow ex–merchant steamers. Blockade runners built specifically to elude the Union vessels had evolved quickly and continuously. This disparity was

abundantly evident at Wilmington, which had predominantly slow
blockading vessels. Lee had only two fast ships stationed there as late as
April 1863, the month the squadron caught its first steamer off the coast.
Isaac Hallock, stationed on board one of the faster ships, the side-wheel
steamer *State of Georgia*, commented that "the Navy Department cannot expect much success in catching blockade runners who steam 15
miles an hour and draw 6 feet of water with blockaders that steam . . . 10
miles an hour and draw 15 feet of water."[34]

Lee and his officers tried to offset the limitations of the gunboats by
changing their tactical dispositions. At New Inlet, the senior officer,
Captain Sands, stationed one vessel on the bar and another slightly
farther west nearer the shore to cut off vessels running up the coast. A
third vessel took its station on a seaward approach. All the gunboats
anchored at their positions after dark and left them before daylight to
avoid being seen by the shore batteries. Sands had stationed a larger
number of blockaders at the Western Bar Inlet, but Lee believed the
force at New Inlet was too weak and ordered Sands to divide the force
more evenly between the two inlets. Between mid-December 1862 and
15 January 1863, Lee increased the number of vessels at Wilmington
from eight to fifteen, but on paper only. Only six or eight vessels
normally remained at the inlets, the others being away for repairs or for
coal, and often only two watched at New Inlet. Several reasons precipitated this high absence rate. Nearly all blockaders were steam vessels,
and under Lee's tactical deployment, they cruised more than they had
previously, which caused a higher consumption of coal and required
more repairs for machinery that constantly stayed in motion.[35]

By February 1863, the Union navy had established a more thorough
coverage of the coast south of Western Bar Inlet. Captain Sands kept a
sailing schooner stationed at Little River Inlet and a steamer at Shallotte
Inlet; the latter also supported the schooner when necessary. The commanders realized that their chief hope of success in preventing the
violation of the blockade would be by using at least two lines of blockaders to find the blockade runners farther away from the inlets.[36] This
could only be accomplished with additional steamers on both sides of the
shoals.

As the coverage of the coast increased, it caused major communication problems. About fifteen vessels were divided between the two sides

of the shoals, and the inlets north and south. When the senior officer's vessel lay on the east side of the shoals it took six or eight hours to communicate with the west side. More rapid communication could be carried out by sending small boats across passages in Frying Pan Shoals, but bad weather made this impossible for as long as a month at a time and reduced the efficiency of the blockade. Lee concluded that the division of the forces caused too many problems and resorted to assigning two senior officers there, one for each inlet: Captain A. Ludlow Case at New Inlet and Captain Sands at Western Bar.[37]

In March, Lee again fine-tuned the blockade. He instructed the steamers to remain as close to the bar as possible during the night, so that if they discovered an escaping blockade runner, they would be ready for a chase. Lee learned that the officers at Wilmington used boats for picket duty at both inlets. Lee stopped this practice and ordered the senior officers to use only steamers. Lee realized the difficulties of not having enough vessels but believed a boat giving signals would either scare away the violator or give a warning too late for the gunboats to make a capture. He thought that the use of picket boats also caused "temptation to a dangerous relaxation of vigilance on board the steamers."[38]

The senior officers sometimes had only large ships to watch the bars. The larger ships could not approach as close to the shore as the smaller gunboats, and experience had shown that larger ships, because of their rigging, could be seen from shore, which made them targets for the long-range guns of the forts. They likewise could be more readily seen by blockade runners, who could then steer to avoid them. To solve this particular problem, Commander Case requested that a tug be sent to New Inlet. He felt that the blockade needed a small fast steamer that could move around at night without being detected. Lee responded by sending the steam tug *Violet* to Wilmington. This ship became the prototype of a class of vessels used as "bar tenders" at Wilmington. *Violet*, a small mastless steamer, had good speed and a light armament. Lee also tried the double-ender ferryboat *Shokokon* off Wilmington because of its speed and maneuverability. The commanding officer, William Cushing, found out that *Shokokon* could not keep the sea, and Lee withdrew her after she nearly foundered in a gale.[39]

The tug *Violet* patrolled in four fathoms of water, about one and a half miles from the beach. She kept her fires banked and twenty-five pounds of steam in her boilers. Lee instructed the bar tenders not to anchor at night but to hold their positions by keeping under way and to maintain a close watch on the bottom to prevent moving ahead or drifting. Gunboats at anchor would be too slow to start a chase and risked losing their anchors. Strong currents and bad weather often made it mandatory to use anchors, thus Lee suggested that the bar tenders might use kedge anchors, even though it would require extra hands at night to handle them quickly. Lee further warned these vessels not to make any noise by blowing off steam, but to let it escape gradually.[40]

Regardless of the positioning of the blockaders, the weather remained one factor that could not be altered and that impaired the effectiveness of the blockade. Thick foggy weather prevailed for long periods of time, which gave blockade runners an edge in escaping the Union ships. Furthermore, the nights were often so dark that only by obtaining bottom soundings with a lead could the gunboats keep their positions. At times, bad weather would last for over a month, with only half a dozen clear days in between. The weather in the spring and winter was particularly harsh and exposed the ships to the most rigorous duty along the whole coast. Gales from the southeast blew on the lee shore and caused blockaders to leave their posts until the wind diminished. The weather particularly favored those trying to escape because they could choose not only the best time to make their escape, but they could also choose the most weakly guarded inlet. Captain Case complained that those running out were never caught. He lamented, "I believe we have yet to learn of the first steamer having been stopped anywhere in so doing."[41]

The geography of the area compounded this problem. Shallow water made the task of the blockaders more difficult. One officer wrote, "Our captains think if they run into six or eight fathoms of water they are very close in, when in fact, we are four or five miles from shore."[42] Blockade runners tried to make the coast fifteen to forty miles above or below the inlets and then run toward the inlet, relying on the shoreline and the pounding surf to conceal them. The Union officers began stationing a blockader close to the shore, held with a kedge anchor, leaving space for a blockade runner to pass by. Blockade runners often got through this space without being detected, but if not, a rocket lit the sky and the blockaders closed around in a prearranged plan. This arrangement was dangerous for the deeper drafted blockaders because they ran the risk of being carried into the breakers by the currents, and once ashore, it was often impossible to get them off.[43] Shoal water was an ever-present hazard, and vigilance did not always ensure the safety of the vessels. During the war, the steamers *Astor*, *Violet*, *Iron Age*, and *Columbia* were all lost along the coast by grounding.

Placing the gunboats in the most advantageous positions while avoiding natural obstacles was difficult. In most cases, the senior officer at each inlet, acting under general instructions from Lee, controlled the immediate disposition of the vessels. In May, Lee moved some of the gunboats farther from the inlets and had the screw steamer *Niphon* cruise on a thirty-mile arc to catch violators farther from the bars. By November, Captain Daniel B. Ridgely, the new senior officer at New Inlet, employed his three fastest vessels from thirty to seventy miles offshore, each vessel cruising a line sixty miles long. Phillips Lee allowed outside operations and long-distance chasing only when the senior officers had a sufficient number of vessels.[44]

By May 1863, the warships at Wilmington had had little success in stopping Confederate trade, and some felt the blockade was impotent. Since Lee had assumed command, the blockaders had captured and destroyed a large number of sailing vessels but only one steamer. One officer wrote: "I am sorry to say that two more steamers ran in last night and had the impudence to blow their whistles—I suppose to give us warning to keep out of the way or else be run down."[45]

Lee made a personal inspection of the tactical deployments in August 1863 and wrote to Welles that Wilmington was "the most difficult port to close on the coast." After the visit, he began writing a flurry of requests for more vessels. Lee believed that he needed twenty-four or thirty good steamers to make the blockade efficient. After observing the squadron, Lee placed the warships at Wilmington into three categories: some fast, some of fair speed, and some "fit to watch, but too slow to catch anything."[46]

On his visit, Lee observed that the vessels lay at anchor and close to shore but did not have any particular station during the day. One officer noted that "the vessels lie in a 'huddle,' the officers visiting from one to

another to pass away time the best way they can." Lee put a stop to this
and ordered the vessels not to lie together, day or night, especially in
thick weather. He prescribed specific day and night anchorages, five off
New Inlet and three off Western Bar Inlet. He also ordered the gunboats to weigh anchor one hour before sunset and to be in their night
positions by dark. A light hoisted on one vessel would guide the blockaders to their night stations.[47]

Despite the changes made by Lee, the inadequate force at Wilmington continued to hamper operations. Neither side of the shoals had
a fixed number of vessels, and the steamers shifted from one side to
the other according to the traffic patterns of the blockade runners.
Sometimes the lack of vessels kept the senior officers from using an
outside cruiser. Two or more vessels cruised offshore during a moonless
night according to Lee's instructions, but when a large number of
blockaders lay at Beaufort coaling, the senior officers had to discontinue
outside cruising. Lee instructed that steamers could only chase if they
retained sight of the violator and only if their absence did not weaken
the blockade. Benjamin Sands directed each vessel, after filling her
bunkers with coal, to leave on the afternoon tide and steam south for
fifty to sixty miles until daylight. The blockader would be in an approxi-
mate position that a blockade runner would be if run out of New Inlet.
This enabled him to have an outside cruiser nearly every day. Sands
arranged the departures of the supply ship *New Berne* in the same
manner.[48]

In December 1863, Lee added another cordon of cruisers to his
blockade. He stationed *Florida* 100 miles southeast of Frying Pan Shoals
to intercept blockade runners, and a week later, he added the 1,600-ton
side-wheel steamer *Quaker City* to the outer line. Lee reconfigured his
tactical positioning by establishing six primary day stations off
Wilmington, three at each inlet. On the northern side of the shoals, the
senior officer stationed his vessel directly off the inlet; a second blockader lay off Masonboro Island, and a third near the tip of Smith's Island.
At the Western Bar, one vessel lay directly off the bar, a second off
Lockwood's Folly Inlet, and a third at the end of Smith's Island. The
remaining vessels were stationed between the primary stations and
divided the space according to the number of gunboats present. At
night, a slower steamer guarded the bar, and a faster one hauled offshore

about five miles past the senior officer, which gave the blockade there three seaward lines of cruisers.[49]

Lee gave specific and extremely detailed instructions to his officers, covering everything from the watches to the ground tackle and prize money. He reminded the commanders that the violators ran the blockade most often between dusk and dawn and usually landed above or below the inlets and ran down the coast near the surf hoping to sneak in without being seen. He ordered the inner line of blockaders to cut off the retreat of the blockade runners but still allowed only the fastest vessels to give chase.[50]

The double-ender *Sassacus* and screw steamer *Pequot* joined the outside blockade in January 1864 to intercept inward-bound blockade runners hovering off Cape Lookout. The commanders stationed their ships at a point where blockade runners would most likely be at dawn, calculating this position by assuming that the blockade runners traveled at a twelve-knot speed. This positioning paid off for *Sassacus*, which destroyed *Wild Dayrell* and *Nutfield* within a four-day period in February.[51]

Maintaining the blockade at Wilmington became increasingly dangerous as a result of threats from Confederate ironclads and commerce raiders. Before 1864, the gunboats had faced virtually no threat from the enemy. The commerce raider *Nashville* had ventured into the operational zone of the squadron in February 1862, when she ran into Beaufort and escaped on 17 March, much to the dismay of the Navy Department. On 24 April, *Nashville* ran into Wilmington carrying a large number of Enfield rifles and ran back out about a week later carrying cotton. Goldsborough wrote to Fox concerning *Nashville*'s escape: "It is a terrible blow to our naval prestige, and will place us all very nearly in the position we were before our victories. . . . You have no idea of the feeling here. It is a Bull Run to the Navy."[52] The Confederate commerce raider *Alabama* never ventured near Cape Fear, but the threat of her so doing had the officers concerned nevertheless. The Navy Department fitted the gunboats with larger ordnance and strengthened their bows for ramming.[53] The success of *Alabama* obliged the Union vessels to remain concentrated off the inlets in fear that they might be lured off and attacked, as in the case of *Hatteras* off Galveston.

The sinking of *Hatteras* by *Alabama* concerned Captain Sands, and he questioned the adequacy of his vessels to deal with commerce raiders. Already faced with an inadequate force, his larger and more heavily armed vessels now would have to protect the smaller and more lightly armed gunboats. The larger warships could keep the seas better, but their slowness made them less desirable as blockaders. Captain Sands complained that the vessels on duty at Wilmington were "not a bit better than was the *Hatteras*, and could not be expected to make a better fight with such a foe."[54]

The Navy Department had overgunned many of the vessels in order to deal with their inadequacies as warships, with the converted merchant ships seemingly the most affected. Gunboats carrying heavy batteries became less efficient blockaders. They frequently were unmaneuverable in heavy seas, to such an extent that the guns could not be worked and the vessel was endangered. Heavy batteries also compromised their speed. There were exceptions. The 1,367-ton steam sloop *Sacramento* at one time carried an insufficient armament. Listed as a second-class warship when the navy fitted her out, she mounted ten guns. But six of her guns were boat howitzers, and four of these were mounted on field carriages. Nothing heavier than a twenty-four-pound gun could be pointed astern. Captain Charles Boggs lamented about the situation, "As well might all her small arms be added in, and she be called a 40 or 50 gun vessel."[55]

Sands found it necessary to instruct his officers that when they sighted a strange vessel, two ships should investigate in order to protect themselves. Lee began to require that weak gunboats not be placed far "beyond reach of prompt support."[56] This is one small way in which the Confederate commerce raiders damaged the blockade. The navy did not have enough vessels at the inlets to operate in this manner and still maintain an effective blockade. Because of the shortage of gunboats at Wilmington, when the senior officers dispatched two vessels on a chase, sometimes only one vessel remained to guard an inlet.

Gideon Welles ignored the commerce raiders for some time, but state governors, insurance companies, ship owners, and corporate magnates all clamored for some protection. Welles's response inadvertently hurt the blockade. He assigned Charles Wilkes an entire squadron to pursue these raiders, and Wilkes's squadron made up the fastest and newest vessels in the navy.[57] Lee also compromised the blockade by periodically sending gunboats in search of the illusive raiders.

Near the end of the war, the port of Wilmington became a base for enemy commerce raiders. The people of Wilmington and the Confederate military leaders feared that this would lead to an increased vigilance on the part of the blockading squadron. General Robert E. Lee even questioned the decision to station them there and thought they should be sent elsewhere to divert the United States Navy's attention.[58] Despite the fears of Confederate leaders, the Navy Department never drastically enlarged the squadron's size to combat or contain the commerce raiders.

The CSS *Tallahassee*, formerly the blockade runner *Atalanta*, was the first serious problem for the Union squadron. On 6 August 1864, under the command of Lieutenant John Taylor Wood, the *Tallahassee*, armed with three guns, escaped through the blockade. She managed to cruise as far north as Halifax, Nova Scotia, and destroyed twenty-six vessels, boarded five others, and released two more. She ran back into Wilmington on 26 August.[59]

At the end of October, *Tallahassee*, now *Olustee*, and *Chickamauga*, the former blockade runner *Edith*, both went to sea under a heavy fire by the blockaders. The latter had been ready to go to sea for some time but drew too much water to get out of Wilmington except on the spring tides. While these Confederate gunboats wreaked havoc on federal shipping, a number of Union ships went in pursuit. As the word spread, vessels began looking for both raiders from Halifax to Wilmington. *Chickamauga* steamed to Long Island Sound and then to Bermuda for repairs and for coal. She destroyed six vessels during her sortie and ran into Wilmington on 19 November again under heavy fire. *Olustee* likewise had a successful trip. Sustaining some damage from shell fire at New Inlet, she cruised off Delaware and destroyed seven vessels. Sighted on 6 November by *Sassacus*, *Olustee* managed to lose her in the darkness. The next day, *Lillian*, *Montgomery*, and *Quaker City* all chased her. *Olustee* opened the engines to full throttle, fired her after gun at *Montgomery*, and escaped into the Cape Fear River.[60]

The Confederate naval vessels in the Cape Fear River also became another threat to the blockaders at Wilmington. Until the spring of 1864, only three Confederate warships guarded Cape Fear—the gunboats *Yadkin* and *Equator* and the floating battery *Arctic*. That spring, the rebels commissioned *Raleigh* and *North Carolina*, two 150-foot ironclads. Both were similar to those in the sounds and mounted four guns. *North Carolina*, though, never became operational because of faulty machinery and eventually sank at her moorings as a result of damage caused by shipworms.[61]

The Confederates built other warships at Wilmington during the war. The rebels began construction of *Wilmington*, a much larger ironclad. Designed as a light-draft ram over 200 feet long, she had to be destroyed in 1865 when the rebels evacuated the town. Auxiliary vessels, such as torpedo boats, were also built. One torpedo boat, *Squib*, operated on the river before the war's end, and two others under construction burned when a fire erupted at the cotton docks in Wilmington.[62]

The fear of Confederate ironclad rams caused much anxiety and had a definite effect on the Union naval officers on the blockade. They began sighting ironclads a year before any were completed. One officer commented, "A terrible disease is prevailing in the fleet here.... It is termed 'ram fever' & is supposed to be brought on by the occasional sights at a rebel ironclad passing up & down the river between Fort Caswell & Wilmington."[63]

The Confederates wisely used the ironclads at Wilmington for harbor defense, not as blockade breakers. The single exception to this policy ended in disaster for the rebels. *Raleigh* sortied from the river on 6 May 1864, with the steamers *Yadkin* and *Equator* as her tenders. *Mount Vernon* observed the movement of these vessels, but her captain did not report the sighting to the senior officer, Captain Sands. At 8:00 P.M., the three ships slipped over the bar, and immediately the side-wheel steamer *Britannia* sighted them, fired a rocket, and opened fire with her thirty-pound Parrott gun. Failing to stop the ironclad, *Britannia* fled to sea. For the next two hours, *Raleigh* steamed about in circles trying to locate another blockading vessel. At 11:45 P.M., *Raleigh* exchanged shots with *Nansemond*, which also escaped in the darkness.[64]

At dawn the next day, the blockaders "had a little confab with the rebble [sic] ram." *Raleigh*, several miles from the bar, followed by her tenders, steamed toward the little screw tug *Howquah*, and put a shot through her stack. *Nansemond*, *Kansas*, and *Mount Vernon* all exchanged shots with *Raleigh*, but not a single shot took effect. At 7:00 A.M., the

Union vessels let *Raleigh* and her two consorts slip back over the bar. This would be *Raleigh*'s last attack. On her way over the bar, she grounded, and the ebbing tide broke her back.[65]

Following *Raleigh*'s attack on the fleet, the officers realized that slow and crippled vessels were not suitable for service at Wilmington. The appearance of the ironclad had frightened the Union officers. Paymaster William Keeler on board *Florida* commented: "It has been 'ram, ram, ram' till as one of the officers remarked the other day, the very atmosphere was impregnated with the smell of mutton." As a defensive measure against another ironclad attack, vessels received heavier armament, and Phillips Lee fitted *Violet* and other warships with spar torpedoes that exploded on impact. The torpedo on *Violet* projected from the vessel on a pole between fifteen and twenty feet long and carried 150 pounds of powder with four fuses that protruded six inches at different angles. The officers of *Violet* found that this arrangement did not work well in rough water—the torpedo becoming more of a danger to the vessel than to the enemy.[66] The extra armament and the torpedoes also compromised the speed and the ability of the warships to capture blockade runners. The Confederate fleet was likewise twice as potent, because the ironclads could steam from either inlet and attack the divided Union forces.

During the first two years of the war, the Confederate government had enjoyed great success in running the blockade of Wilmington in steam vessels. This had been due to geography, weather, the forts, and the presence of its naval vessels. However, the traditional view of blockading had changed a great deal. Rear Admiral S. P. Lee innovated much of this change. Traditionally a navy maintained a blockade by anchoring large vessels outside a port. The quick adoption of steam power by both the blockade runners and the Union warships and the ever-increasing specialization of the vessels running the blockade created the need for change. Sailing vessels, vessels at anchor, and large deep-draft gunboats could not keep a strict blockade along the Southern coast. Lee maintained his blockade by using smaller, faster, and constantly moving vessels. In the last six months of his command, Lee would further improve his tactics.

The tactical dispositions at Wilmington had evolved slowly. In 1863, Lee instructed his officers that the distance the blockaders remained from the bar, the beach, and the enemy must be determined by the light, the state of the weather, and the zeal and good judgment of the commanding officer. Lee instructed the vessels to begin shifting their positions and set stations for the blockaders initiating two lines of gunboats—inshore and outside. In early 1864, the ships began to move about more, and as the number of gunboats increased at Wilmington, Lee added more lines of blockaders.[67] Lee's tactical dispositions only began to become effective by 1864, when he had a sufficient number of vessels stationed off the coast to make it work.

Lee realized that the blockade runners could generally see his vessels long before they could be seen. He therefore instructed the blockading vessels be given a coat of paint a dull lead color like that of the blockade runners. Lee removed the masts and yards of the smaller gunboats guarding the bars and had those vessels work off the high pressure in their boilers by turning in short circles continuously, taking care to avoid collisions. Lookouts wore loose white suits to avoid detection, and officers picked men for their vigilance. Blockaders also kept their guns ready for use on Confederate naval vessels and employed sharpshooters for the enemy's officers, captains, helmsmen, and loaders of guns.[68]

To offset the advantages that steam power had given blockade runners, Lee also gradually developed the most complicated system of blockade used by any squadron during the war. In its most advanced form, it comprised four seaward lines of cruisers. Just off the bars and as close to shore as possible lay the first line, called the bar tenders. These vessels watched the bar and gave a signal if a blockade runner attempted to escape. The bar tenders did not chase. Chasing was the function of a second line of vessels, which supported the bar tenders and moved back and forth like sentries. The divisional officers, in fast gunboats, supported this second line. Beyond these three lines lay the outside blockaders, usually the fastest in the squadron, who cruised on the outside tracks of the blockade runners. Conceding that the blockade runners could normally escape at night, the blockaders kept low steam in their boilers during the dark hours and high steam during the day. Lee determined the placement of the outer line by computing the distance from the inlets that a blockade runner could steam from twilight to dawn.[69] This distance measured at least 160 miles from the inlets. He instructed his senior officers that less than two-fifths of the available force be used as outside cruisers.

Excluding logistical problems, the major adversity Lee faced in implementing his system was having the proper vessels on the blockade. Lee continually requested additional ships, particularly those that could watch the bars, but also those like the 1,725-ton *Connecticut* and the 1,364-ton *Keystone State* because they had an advantage in heavy weather over the blockade runners. Lee constantly improvised and used the vessels assigned to the squadron to their greatest potential. The converted freight steamers, however, did not make the best blockaders, and the vessels he used as bar tenders were often too large. Lee attempted to replace many of these larger vessels with tugs and removed the spars from the larger vessels to cut down their profiles. Lee also made good use of converted blockade runners for outside cruising, but they could not be used for inside work because they were not as maneuverable and were too easily mistaken for blockade runners.[70]

Lee attempted to reorganize the squadron just before Welles relieved him as squadron commander. Lee suggested the establishment of two divisions, one for each side of the shoals. He suggested this to strengthen the authority of the senior officers, thereby giving the divisional officers greater freedom to make decisions. Officers could change orders if necessary but had to defend the changes by a written report. Additionally Lee wanted his divisional officers to have more authority, so that the rear admiral's presence on the blockade would not be necessary.[71]

Lee fell from the grace of the department shortly after this suggestion when Welles censured him for trying to "save the capital" from the raid of Major General Jubal Early. Welles ordered Lee to establish four divisions, one for each inlet of Cape Fear, one for the sounds, and one for the James River. Welles gave command of the James River Division to Melancton Smith and moved the headquarters of the squadron from Hampton Roads to Beaufort. Welles also instructed Lee to visit Hampton Roads only when "public emergency" required it; otherwise, he was to give his "principle attention to the blockade, which has latterly become very inefficient." Lee's censure became common news among the officers and men. One officer remarked, "Rumour has it that he received a severe reprimand from the Department for spending all his

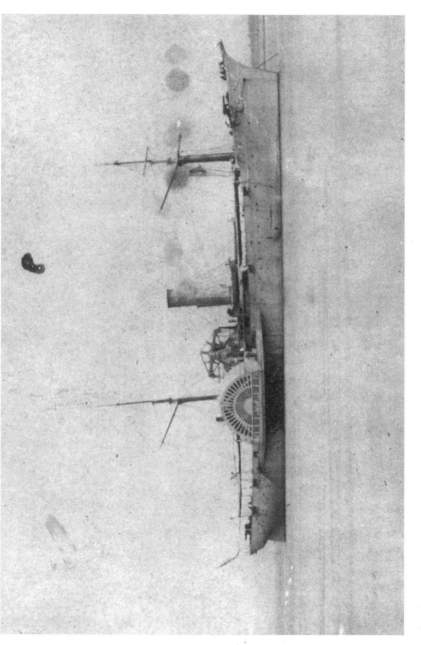

The 1,725-Ton Side-wheel *Connecticut. Connecticut* was valuable as a blockader because her size enabled her to chase and capture blockade runners in heavy seas. *(Courtesy the U.S. Naval Historical Center)*

Fort Donelson, the Ex-blockade Runner *Robert E. Lee*. The ex-blockade runners were sought for use off Wilmington for their speed and, once converted, were often the fastest vessels on the blockade. (*Courtesy the U.S. Naval Historical Center*)

time up the James river where he wasn't needed & neglecting the blockade where they seemed to think his presence was necessary."[72]

Lee's role as squadron commander seemed diminutive because the Union army in the eastern theater had not fought in areas where naval support could be utilized to any great extent. Thus the admiral had not been given many chances to show that he could work with the army, and he likewise had no reputation as a fighter. But naval forces alone could not carry Confederate positions. As fall 1864 approached, an expedition to capture Wilmington was imminent. Grant wanted someone other than Phillips Lee to command the naval portion of a combined expedition, and Welles initiated plans to replace him. Welles hoped to speed things up by reducing Lee's command, in hopes of his resignation. On 1 September, Welles made the Sounds Division a separate and distinct command from the North Atlantic Blockading Squadron, and he placed Stephen C. Rowan in command of the division. This, however, did not seem to ruffle Lee enough for him to offer his resignation, and he had to be replaced by David Dixon Porter at the end of the month.[73]

Porter took command of the squadron only three and one-half months before Fort Fisher fell and did not change Lee's tactical system to any great extent. He did, however, have more influence and was able to secure more vessels and have them repaired more quickly, giving him a greater number and better vessels to work with than Lee had ever hoped to have.

When Porter took command, he made it clear that he wanted his squadron to pay more attention to procedures, rules, regulations, and drills. Porter remained busy planning the capture of Fort Fisher and could not spare a great deal of time to run the blockade. To attend the stationary vessels and to administer the affairs at each inlet, Porter made sure that a regular naval officer remained there as senior officer. He placed two on each side of the shoals in case it became necessary for one officer to be absent to coal or repair his vessel.[74]

The vigilance of the blockade of Wilmington under Porter's direction might be questioned because of the escape and return of the commerce raiders *Olustee* and *Chickamauga*. During this time, over thirty vessels guarded the approaches of Wilmington, but on paper only. At two different times in a three-week period in late October and early

November 1864, only three gunboats remained at New Inlet. Porter seemed more concerned with preparing the squadron for the attack on Fort Fisher; its capture would end the necessity of the blockade.[75]

Porter's disposition of vessels off Wilmington essentially consisted of three half-circles. The arc of one line, comprising twenty vessels, lay close to the bars, with Frying Pan Shoals splitting it in half. Another semicircle of twenty vessels, eight miles apart and twelve or fifteen miles from shore, lay just outside Frying Pan Shoals. The last crescent, 130 miles from land, consisted of vessels 12 miles apart stretching from Beaufort to south of Cape Fear and comprised the fastest vessels of the squadron.[76]

Both Lee and Porter used the same percentages of their vessels as bar blockaders (forty percent) and outside blockaders (sixty percent). Since Porter had greater numbers and swifter vessels, he allowed the fastest bar blockaders to chase the blockade runners, something Lee had been unable to do. Under Lee's command, the gunboats that watched the bars seem to have remained closer to the inlets, while Porter permitted them to patrol farther out, which allowed a greater area of coverage.[77]

Lee found fault with Porter's dispositions and accused him of not closely watching the bars and allowing the blockaders to escape. Lee called this a "profitable blockade . . . where the runners pass out with cotton and the right sort of vessels are provided to chase and capture them." Lee had some grounds for his accusation. Under Lee's command, two-thirds of the steamers captured and destroyed were inward bound, while under Porter's command, only about half of the steamers captured or destroyed were bound to the Confederacy.[78]

The tactical changes made by Lee and Porter did not appreciably change the rates of capture. As the war progressed, the numbers caught each month virtually did not change, while the numbers of blockaders steadily increased. A contributing factor to this relationship is that the Union navy caught slower blockade runners, particularly sailing vessels, in the first years of the war, and the faster vessels specifically built to carry contraband operated during the last two years. Increasingly the gunboats caught the blockade runners farther at sea—and this occurred because a larger number of vessels patrolled off Cape Fear, in turn allowing a more extensive coverage of the coast. Both Lee and Porter believed that they had perfected the best blockade. Porter claimed that Lee "never succeeded in preventing supplies from going in or in stopping cotton from coming out."[79] While this is true, the fact is that neither did Porter.

Despite the numerous tactical changes made during the war and the tremendous increase in the numbers of warships that watched the ports, the blockade was never airtight. Blockade runners evolved to meet the challenge of the blockade. Improvements in engines, hull design, camouflage, and tactics had a great bearing on the success of the blockade runners. The Union navy made great strides to increase the speed of their ships and improved tactical deployments, but weather, darkness, rebel defenses, ruses, and, to some extent, luck offset these advantages and allowed the Confederacy to continue its trade as long as a port remained open.

TWELVE

Ishmaelites upon the broad ocean

The Blockade Runners

The squadron's major function and the reason for its original existence was the blockade of the Confederate coastline. From mid-1862, this meant the blockade of Wilmington and the small inlets directly north and south of the Cape Fear River. The blockade of the port of Wilmington tested not only the tactical positioning of the blockaders but also the stamina of the crews and the durability of the ships. The Cape Fear River accommodated contraband trade before the first Union vessel arrived and continued until the capture of Fort Fisher. Union blockading tactics evolved from a system designed to catch sailing vessels into the elaborate systems of Admirals Lee and Porter, but the blockade was never airtight. The most advanced tactics, together with the most modern ordnance used during the war, could not keep pace with technological progress in other areas. Improvements in steam engineering and vessel construction and design gave the blockade runners an edge in speed, maneuverability, and stealth that could not be overcome by the numerous Union gunboats.

Sailing vessels performed most of the early trade with the Confederacy. But as the Union navy was able to deploy more gunboats to blockade the South, ves-

sels powered by wind alone could not be risked. Sailing vessels were
generally slower than steamers, they could be seen farther at sea, and
they were dependent on the weather and the currents to move. Nevertheless, sailing vessels, particularly fast schooners, continued to run the
blockade for two years into the war.

Stopping the steam blockade runners, though, developed into a major challenge to the squadron as the war unfolded. During 1861, virtually any vessel might be used as a blockade runner, but gradually the
steamships evolved to meet the challenge of the navy. These new,
specially designed steamships constructed expressively for speed usually
displaced between 400 and 600 tons.[1] Most often built of iron or steel,
they sat low in the water, had extremely narrow beams, had rakish
designs, and sometimes had turtleback forward decks to help them
drive through heavy seas. Builders constructed both screw and side-
wheel vessels, each having its advantages. Twin-screw steamers became
common toward the war's end, perhaps because they made little noise,
were more maneuverable, and were less vulnerable to gunfire. The
paddle-wheel steamers, on the other hand, could operate in shallower
water, were easier to extract from shoals, and were slightly faster than
screw-propelled vessels.

Avoiding detection was singularly the most important characteristic
necessary for the success of the blockade runners. In many cases, they
carried only a light pair of lower masts, with no yards. A small crow's
nest on one of the masts often appeared as the only alteration from the
ship's sharp outline. The hull showed little above the water and was
usually painted dull gray to camouflage the vessel. The captain kept the
ship's boats lowered to the gunwales, and some steamers had telescoping
funnels that could be lowered to the deck to maintain a low profile.
English engines became more powerful as the war progressed, and the
boilers normally burned semibituminous English coal, but the blockade
runners used anthracite coal whenever possible because it made little or
no smoke. When approaching the shore, these vessels blew their steam
off under water, showed no lights, and sometimes muffled their paddle
wheels with canvas, all to avoid detection. Some captains even insisted
that their crews wear white clothing, believing that one black figure
could reveal the position of a vessel.[2]

The atmospheric conditions and the weather also hindered the ap-

prehension of sailing vessels and allowed steamers even greater opportunity to remain undetected. The gunboats remained from one-half to
five miles apart, and at times, lookouts could not see fifty yards because
of the fog and the darkness. But even during the day, vessels were hardly
visible, "owing to the peculiar state of the atmosphere." Bad weather
conditions nearly always favored the blockade runners. Southeast
weather forced the blockaders to the north and gave the blockade
runners access to the south inlet, whereas northeast gales drove the
enemy to shelter to the south of Smith Island, which cleared New Inlet.[3]

Under certain stages of the moon and atmosphere, the blockade
runners were almost invisible at even 100 yards and blended so perfectly
with their surroundings that on dark nights only their wakes could be
seen as they steamed by. The famed blockade running captain John
Wilkinson boasted that the ships seemed "almost as invisible as Harle-
quin in the pantomime."[4]

Those running the blockade entered the trade with sound financial
support. The major European nations allowed the Confederates to
establish credit abroad, using letters of credit and foreign bills of exchange and coin to make their purchases. The price of cotton soared
during the spring of 1862 and steadily climbed for the remainder of the
year.[5] The high price of cotton facilitated the Confederate government's
efforts to establish its credit. The sudden demand for goods within the
Confederacy, combined with the high profits to be made in blockade
running, attracted many skilled English mariners to take risks.

High profits likewise lured many foreign businessmen into the trade.
Foreigners not only built and sold ships to run the blockade at huge
profits but also made fortunes by slipping goods through the federal
blockade. A single round-trip might allow profits enough to pay for
both cargoes and the vessel. These high returns ensured that the trade
would continue. A clerk in the Confederate War Office commented,
"About one in every four steamers is captured by the enemy. We can
afford that." James Randall, a clerk at a blockade running firm in
Wilmington, agreed: "Bad luck is expected occasionally, but the percentage of profit is largely in favor of the Confederate steamers. Nearly
every one that had been captured had paid for herself a half dozen
times."[6]

The small carrying capacity of the blockade runners, combined with a high demand for goods, influenced their cargo and the freight rates. The rates quickly increased, and by 1863 the Confederate government fixed them at £60 or $900 in Confederate currency per ton. These high rates influenced the types of goods carried by blockade runners. Guns and accoutrements were economically feasible to transport, yet badly needed items such as railroad rails, marine engines, and locomotives were normally too expensive to carry because of their weight, although a few did come into the South. By 1862, the smaller merchantmen, mostly sailing vessels, rarely carried arms and munitions and usually carried salt and assorted cargoes. Small entrepreneurs owned these ships and could not afford to risk more expensive cargoes in their slow ships. These small entrepreneurs could make potentially large profits on these cargoes but faced greater risks in sailing vessels. By 1864, the Confederate government passed regulations to ensure that at least half of the blockade runners' cargoes be consigned to the Confederacy. The Confederate government provided incentives to those carrying Confederate cotton, and bonds had to be posted by the carriers to ensure that they would comply with the rules.[7] By this time, the small carriers and sailing ships had become largely obsolete in the Atlantic.

Some vessels made their trips into the South in ballast because satisfactory cargoes could not be found. More often it appears that many captains found that the return cargoes were so profitable that they could afford to carry cargo only one way. The odds of being captured on the inward journey were significantly higher, and many carried only ballast to increase their speed and their chances of outrunning the blockaders.[8]

Wilmington's closeness to Nassau and Bermuda, the major points of shipment, helped to establish it as the major port of the Confederacy. Blockade runners clearing for Wilmington stayed at sea for shorter periods of time, which decreased their odds of being seen by blockaders. Furthermore, shorter runs meant fewer machinery breakdowns and more room for cargo instead of coal. Steamers coming from Nassau could make it to Wilmington in as few as forty-eight hours, and those coming from Bermuda could make the trip in seventy-two hours. Nassau and Bermuda both remained busy with the steamers that made the illicit journeys into the South, and as late as 1864, some small sailing vessels from the Gulf of Mexico still sailed to Nassau with cotton.[9]

The inlets north and south of Cape Fear, particularly those to the south, were havens for the illicit trade. The gunboats continually caught small vessels near these inlets. Lockwood's Folly, Shallotte, Tubbs, and Little River inlets had between six and nine feet of water with good entrances and anchorages. At these points, the gunboats lay too far apart, and blockade runners, according to the senior officer off New Inlet, Captain A. Ludlow Case, needed only to make a "bold dash to get in." Blockade running north of Cape Fear was made easier when Lincoln opened Beaufort to trade in May 1862. The squadron caught several vessels cleared for Beaufort from Nassau, Bermuda, or a Northern port trying to sneak into one of the unguarded inlets.[10]

Captains of blockade runners plotted their journeys to give them every added advantage. As a vessel neared Wilmington, the ship's captain would try to cross the Gulf Stream current early in the afternoon to establish the ship's position by chronometer, "so as to escape the influence of that current on his dead reckoning."[11]

While on their journeys to Wilmington or to the inlets north or south of the Cape Fear River, the runners maintained a cautious distance from all vessels so that they would not be discovered. John Maffitt, the captain of several blockade runners, commented: "In fact, nothing in the shape of a steamer was to be trusted, as we entertained the belief that Confederates were Ishmaelites upon the broad ocean—the recipients of no man's courtesy."[12]

The Confederacy aided the blockade runners by several means. Signal flags from shore could guide ships during the day, and saltworks and signal lights guided them in the darkness. By August 1864, the entrances to Wilmington had lighthouses, range lights, and Confederate army signal lights on the coast to guide the vessels in. When a blockade runner arrived at one of the inlets, an effective signal system served to guide her over the bars. On 11 March 1864, the Confederates took an important step to assist navigation. Lieutenant John Wilkinson and seventy Confederate navy men established a system of lights and buoys at the Cape Fear River. This system worked well for a few months until Wilkinson's transfer. Without Wilkinson's capable leadership, the signal system lapsed into obscurity.[13]

The sixty-foot-high mound at the end of Federal Point served not only as an artillery platform but also as a tower for range lights. When a blockade runner made a signal to the beach, the range lights appeared, and when the vessel entered the river, they were extinguished. Each blockade runner carried a Confederate signalman who, by code, could communicate with the shore using flags during the day and a lantern at night.[14]

The blockade runners also had an unintended navigational aid: the blockaders. During the first years of the war, the blockaders remained at anchor and later remained at their positions using their engines when possible to fight wind, current, and tide. Most of the large blockaders had lofty masts and rigging, which betrayed their positions long before their hulls were visible. The officers referred to their vessels as "buoys" and "floating beacons" that could warn the enemy. The larger gunboats could be seen across Frying Pan Shoals, and sailing vessels could be seen two miles farther than steam blockaders on the same station. Because of this unwanted visibility, Lee attempted to have masts and rigging removed from those ships that patrolled close to the bar. Blockade runners also used the senior officer's ship for guidance, because they knew he generally lay about two and a half miles from the river's mouth and showed lights to the cruisers to the left and right. They could use these lights as a guide to the entrance. The Union navy soon discovered this ploy and changed the senior officer's position nightly. Noises also betrayed the blockaders' positions. The Union ships were to be kept in "perfect silence," and the bells were reported to the officers and not struck. But sometimes pumps on the blockaders made a "jerking noise" that could be heard for a mile or more.[15]

A great majority of the blockade runners chose moonless nights to make their trips to Wilmington. This practice led the blockaders to do their refueling on the nights of a full moon when possible and to keep full bunkers on dark nights. The senior officer allowed refueling on the brighter nights because the blockaders could normally see greater distances. At times, this practice virtually crippled the blockade of Wilmington because of the large number of vessels away for coal. In November 1863, eight blockading vessels steamed to Beaufort for coal, leaving the blockade at Wilmington at virtually half strength.[16]

While most of the blockade runners chose moonless nights to make their trips, others made trips on nights that provided some light. Captains and pilots knowledgeable of the Southern coast were at a premium, and the sudden increase in the trade had left some owners with unskilled men. Beginning early in the war, the Union did not parole the captains and pilots of blockade runners, which compounded the problem. Because of a lack of skilled navigators, vessels began to run aground more often. Captains became increasingly cautious as they approached their destinations and had to send boats ashore to ascertain their position. One contemporary commented that he considered it "the lesser of two evils to run the risk of being seen and chased, rather than to take the certain danger of being wrecked, when running in with insufficient light." In fact, contraband cargoes became so valuable that, during the latter part of the war, blockade runners readily took to the beach when sighted by a blockader. Captains would run comparatively worthless vessels aground intentionally and unload them in the surf at a profit to the owners.[17]

Furthermore, some blockade running captains did not fear to steam directly through the fleet. Blockade running captain John Wilkinson remarked: "for although the blockade runner might receive a shot or two, she was rarely disabled; and in proportion to the increase of the fleet, the greater would be the danger of their firing into each other . . . [making them] very apt to miss the cow and kill the calf."[18]

Steaming directly through the fleet became less hazardous by 1864, when the forts at both inlets had been strengthened and expanded. At New Inlet, the shallow water prevented the blockaders from following the runners far. Blockade runners occasionally grounded under the forts' guns and were unloaded by Confederate soldiers. When *Modern Greece* ran aground under the guns of Fort Fisher, two companies of soldiers from the fort saved two-thirds of the cargo. This included 7,000 stands of arms, 2,770 barrels of powder, gray cloth, domestic clothing, medicine, shoes, wines, brandies, spices, and cannon.[19]

Blockade runners often had to lighten their loads on the inward and outward journeys as a means of escape. Outward-bound blockade runners being chased lightened their deck loads by pitching bales of cotton overboard to avoid capture. *Young Republic*, for example, cast 319 bales of cotton overboard, but *Grand Gulf* still overhauled her. A small sandy shoal called the "lump," two or three miles outside the New Inlet bar, also caused many valuable inward- and outward-bound cargoes to be thrown overboard. When *Kate* became stuck on a bar, her crew threw 100 tons of lead overboard before she floated off. The approaches to

Wilmington were said to be "paved as thickly with valuables as a certain place is said to be with good intentions."[20]

The Confederates used long-range Whitworth guns limbered to mules to protect the beached blockade runners. The Confederates kept one gun each at Fort Fisher and at Fort Caswell. At a moment's notice, these guns could be pulled to the site of a beached blockade runner, where they were used to drive off the blockading vessels. Whitworth guns had a range of about five miles, and after each shot, the gun crew changed the position of the gun to keep the Union vessels from replying effectively. When *Hebe* ran aground, Lamb sent two Whitworth guns to protect the wreck. In a terrific gun duel, the two Confederate guns held off five Union warships, including *Minnesota*. With their ammunition exhausted, they were forced to retreat, but the Union sailors captured a Whitworth gun. William H. C. Whiting, commander of the military district at Wilmington, deplored the loss of the gun, which had saved dozens of vessels and millions of dollars for the Confederacy.[21]

Early in the war, as a blockade runner ran past the Union warships, she had little to fear from the enemy's guns. On 13 May 1863, the steamers *Columbia*, *Banshee*, and *Pet* all ran into Wilmington. A soldier stationed at one of the forts in the area commented, "The yankees only fired one gun it don't look like the Blockade is very affective [*sic*] where three can come in at once does it."[22]

By 1864, the navy had made the passage over the bar more dangerous. Lee stationed picket boats on the bar to warn the gunboats of vessels heading to sea. When the Confederates exchanged signals as a blockade runner approached the bar, the blockaders fired randomly in that direction. As the number of blockaders increased, their firepower increased in proportion. When *Florie* ran out of New Inlet on 5 October 1864, the blockaders fired over sixty shots at her. Rear Admiral Porter attempted to make these shots more effective and had the vessels load their guns with grapeshot and canister at short ranges. He stated, "The effect of sinking some three or four will be good, provided they are sunk by our shot or shell while trying to escape."[23]

Once the blockade runners had run past the fleet and lay under the guns of the forts, they were virtually safe, inasmuch as the range of the fort's guns was usually longer than the range of the blockader's guns.

Vessels could anchor under the guns until the tide rose high enough to allow them over the bar. Before 1863, vessels coming into New Inlet crossed the bar immediately, because the fort's guns did not have the range to protect them from the blockading vessels' fire. Once they had anchored in the river, it became time for a celebration of "champagne cocktails; not whiskies and sodas . . . [because] one did not run a blockade every day."[24]

A well-handled steamer could average about one round-trip a month but might make it in as little as eight days. It generally took sixteen days to unload and load another cargo at Wilmington. Local authorities could be a great help, particularly if the captains of vessels made it worth their while. Goods sold to local officials below market price or given as gifts ensured many quick trips. Some of the Confederate vessels ran through the blockade as regularly as packets. But several factors made their trips irregular: the conditions of the blockade, the weather, mechanical conditions, quarantines, cargo availability, the moon, and the tides.[25]

Stevedores loaded the vessels to best utilize their small carrying capacities. These experts packed the cotton so close that a "mouse could hardly find room to hide itself." They placed cargo in every conceivable place, fore and aft, inside and on the weather deck, leaving only openings to the cabins, engine room, and so forth. Captain of the blockade runner *Don*, Captain Augustus Hobart-Hampden, claimed that loaded in this way these vessels looked like a "huge bale of cotton with a stick placed upright at one end of it." Because of their great weight, the steamers often took resin and tobacco as ballast, which allowed them to carry more cotton. The steamer *Advance* attempted to carry so much cotton that she tried eight times to steam past the blockaders and had to turn back each time. Before her ninth attempt, she unloaded 300 bales of cotton and successfully eluded the gunboats.[26]

After loading, the blockade runners dropped down the Cape Fear River and anchored at Smithville to wait for the best opportunity to run out. At Smithville, they could watch the movements of the squadron and could pick the best time to make their escape. Here they could also pick the inlet that would give them a greater chance of success. Rear Admiral Porter observed, "It was very much like a parcel of cats watching a big rat hole: the rat often running in when they are expecting him to run out, and *vice versa*. The advantage was all on the side of the blockade runners. They could always choose their time."[27]

Despite the constant augmentation of Union fleets off Cape Fear, the blockade runners successfully continued to evade the gunboats. On 14 August 1864, one officer counted eight steamers at Smithville waiting to escape. One blue jacket stationed at Wilmington lamented, "We might as well be in Boston for all the good we do in stopping blockade runners, . . . not a night passes that some cotton loaded steamer does not get out and others loaded with guns etc. run in." The problems of stopping vessels from running the blockade of Wilmington is illustrated by the fact that, in the spring and summer of 1863, sailing vessels still eluded the gunboats.[28] Sailing vessels continued to attempt to run the blockade on the North Atlantic station through most of 1864.

The Union navy stressed vigilance as a key component for stopping the Confederate trade. Acting Master Fred Stuart reported to Lee that he stayed at his post so often that in *twenty-five days, I never had my clothes off." Connecticut's* crew even raised a fund of $150 to reward the man who discovered a steamer that the Union ship subsequently captured. Although the captains emphasized vigilance, it did not take long for the men stationed at Wilmington to realize the absurdity of closing the port. Paymaster William Keeler on board *Florida* remarked: "We began to appreciate the difficulties of keeping up a thorough blockade— let no one condemn the occasional running in or out of a vessel." He added, "You may imagine . . . our vessels . . . scattered along from two to four miles apart. What is there to prevent a vessel from running between them in the darkness when it is impossible to see more than three to four hundred feet from the ship?"[29]

The most dangerous moment on blockade duty was the instant a Union vessel sighted a suspicious vessel. Chaos prevailed during the first minutes. Unaware of whether the vessel was a dangerous raider or a blockade runner, the Union ships began the pursuit. They often increased steam and headed into the darkness, not knowing the intentions nor the direction of the enemy. Shots flew in all directions during these uncertain times, and they mistakenly shot at each other and collided with the blockade runners and other blockading vessels. Union lookouts remained ready at all times to remove the tarpaulin hoods that covered the lights, and officers continually peered into the darkness to help avoid collisions. The numerous signals and gunfire that filled the air confused those in command, and "the blockade runner making her fifteen miles an hour would soon pass out of sight."[30]

After sighting a blockade runner, the officers were given instructions to make signals for the rest of the gunboats in the vicinity, so that they might take part in the chase. Inexperience or excitement sometimes caused the officers to fail to make the signals indicating the blockade runner's course. Greed also became a factor. Officers who neglected to make a signal might get a sole share in the prize money for the ship and crew rather than having to share it with other gunboats. Porter became so angry with this practice that he threatened to court-martial officers to "cure them."[31]

An inadequate command structure on board the ships likewise hindered the capture of vessels. The watch officer who had charge of the deck had no power to act, having to report first to the captain and wait for his orders. One officer commented: "The Capt. comes on deck, looks around, satisfies himself as to the correctness of the officer's report & makes up his mind what to do. All this takes time—& when a fast steamer is gliding by us, [we lose] precious time that cannot be recalled or made up for."[32]

The Union ships used rockets, lights, and whistles to signal the courses of the blockade runners, but the captains of blockade runners began using these same objects as ruses to escape. Captain John Wilkinson bought rockets from New York, and a few minutes after his pursuer signaled, he would send up identical rockets at right angles to the course of his vessel. This ploy, which always worked for Wilkinson, became so successful that Porter instructed his officers to use rockets sparingly and that from that time forward the gunboats should show a red light over the stern so they would not be mistaken for a blockade runner and fired upon by their own vessels. If spotted in the daytime, crafty captains raised United States colors, which at a distance often deceived the Union vessels. When chased, they would try to pull out of sight, then at dusk put the helm over hard, changing courses at right angles to the ones they had been steaming.[33]

The chase was the most exciting experience for those on board the blockaders. During a chase lasting hours, a Union warship might fire well over 100 shots at the blockade runner, which kept the crew busy. Hours of pursuit, however, frequently ended with no capture. Crafty blockade-running captains, bad weather, darkness, and engine break-downs all contributed to lost prizes.

Blockading vessels used extraordinary measures to overtake and capture blockade runners. Some gunboats obtained cords of pinewood and some rosin at Beaufort and kept it on board to raise a quick head of steam. In one chase, *Florida* dumped overboard a barricade of 400 sandbags that weighed thirty tons. Warships took down their yards, top masts, and anything else that would offer resistance to the air or threw coal overboard to lighten the ship and to alter the trim. In addition, when the gunboats went to Norfolk, they had their bottoms scraped and painted and then covered with grease or tallow to allow them to slip through the water with ease.[34]

Since speed was a key attribute in catching those violating the block-ade, the outside cruisers were maintained in such a way as to obtain their maximum speeds. To ensure this, Rear Admiral Lee instructed his officers not to overload their ships with supplies and to keep them in the best trim possible. He instructed them to remove extra guns, which required less men, provisions, and ammunition. During a chase, they should not allow officers and men to crowd forward. Despite these measures, as of 1 September 1864, only eight vessels out of the twenty-six stationed at Wilmington could, under the best conditions, obtain a maximum speed of thirteen knots or more. The average for them was slightly over twelve knots—the three fastest being ex–blockade run-ners.[35]

Blockade runners sometimes compromised their natural speed ad-vantage by carrying tremendous amounts of cargo. A quick and fre-quent expedient resorted to was to cast portions of their cargo over-board. The thirteen-knot cruisers had a difficult time catching blockade runners after they had lightened their load. At times, this worked in the favor of the blockaders. A steamer hastily throwing cotton bales or other cargo overboard often altered her trim and slowed down. The seamen casting the cotton overboard usually cut the hoops off the bales so that the cotton would be difficult if not impossible to gather. The slower vessels, which had no real chance of catching the fast blockade runners, are the ones that gathered the cast-off and floating cargoes. Paymaster

William Anderson on *State of Georgia* lamented: "we fellows in the 'three minute class' could afford to stop for and pick up [this cargo]; and what a struggle there was between the boats of the different ships in the rear of the chase, for the possession of this consolatory flotsam!" Lee, however, warned his officers and directed them not to abandon the pursuit until they lost sight of the chase. He feared that some might "neglect their duty . . . to favor pecuniary interests."[36]

After overhauling a blockade runner, the Union captain's main duty was to keep his prize intact. Armed cutters were quickly dispatched to protect the integrity of the prize. The blockade runner crews often tried to destroy their vessels to prevent their capture, and the crews of government-owned steamers were ordered to do so. They kept combustible material placed so that they could quickly set fire to the vessel and escape. They also cut pipes and secured safety valves, which might cause the boilers to explode. Normally the crews of blockade runners threw overboard the important papers, money, and as much cargo and things of value as they could before the cutters arrived. But this practice ceased when they risked being fired upon by the blockader's guns. If the escaping vessel ran aground, the Union seamen had to contend with the rough surf and also the possibility of being fired on from shore. During the war, the squadron lost numerous boat crews in the surf in the act of capturing or destroying blockade runners.[37]

The boarding officer inspected the ship's papers (the bills of lading, the register, the cargo manifest, the invoices, and the charter party). After this examination, the officer determined what to do with the vessel and the cargo. If he considered the vessel innocent of any infractions of the law, she would be released. But if he had any suspicions, the vessel became a lawful prize of war.

Prizes often led to great monetary rewards, and some seamen took great risks to preserve them. In one instance, a boarding party arriving to take charge of a prize found her in a sinking condition. One sailor tied a halyard around his waist, swung himself over the bulwark, and stuck his leg in a shot hole to prevent the prize from sinking before the hole could be plugged from the inside.[38]

The temptation for members of the boarding party to loot the vessel was at times overwhelming. Nothing, however, could be taken from the captured vessel unless its removal could be better justified. Looting was difficult to prevent, but it could mean the forfeiture of the prize. The lack of marine guards was continually felt, particularly in dealing with cargoes containing liquor. The hatches, along with the crews' and officers' quarters, had to be promptly guarded to avoid pillaging. Several vessels that had to be destroyed may have been saved had marines been present to act as sentries. Captains permitted looting, however, if the vessel had no value or if no prize money would be forthcoming. Nevertheless, at times, some of the prizes and their cargoes were of such little value that they were not sent north, and the cargoes were allowed to spoil.[39]

Blockade runners caught off Wilmington went to Beaufort. After being appraised and judged seaworthy, a prize crew went on board and then sailed north for adjudication. Some officers and men were required to stay with the prize as witnesses until condemnation. The squadron experienced a great inconvenience by the detachment and the retention of prize crews in federal courts, which kept valuable men and officers away from their duties at Wilmington. Rear Admiral Lee wanted prize crews to be promptly returned after the prize court proceedings. To expedite matters and to keep his officers with their ships, Lee suggested that six officers be ordered to Wilmington specifically to take charge of prizes.[40]

The court proceedings could be difficult for those trying to condemn the ship. All letters, papers, and documents found on board the vessel accompanied the prize. A prize master took the evidence to the court along with witnesses—the master, mate, supercargo (if there was one), and two or more seamen. Failure to do so could mean the forfeiture of the prize. The prize master made a complete inventory of the cargo and submitted it to the prize court commissioners—if condemned, the ship was sold at auction, and the proceeds were turned over to a treasury or navy agent.[41]

The prize courts generally convened in federal district courts, the principal ones being in New York, Boston, Baltimore, Washington, Philadelphia, Providence, New Orleans, and Key West. Studies show that the expenses of the trials differed, depending on the specific court. A congressional investigation found that Boston costs amounted to 5.83 percent of the value of the prize, at Philadelphia 14.098 percent, and at New York 15.39 percent.[42]

During the trial, the prize court also determined which gunboats should share in the prize money. All vessels within signal distance of the warships making the capture received a share. But the vessels sharing the prize money had to prove they were within signal distance. It was "not enough to place them within a distance at which signals might have been seen." A federal case determined that six miles was the greatest distance that day signals could be read. Some blockaders, in an attempt to get a sole share in the prize money, extended the chase; by doing so, the fastest vessel might leave the slow vessels behind. After steaming beyond signal distance, "they swooped upon their prey, gobbled her up, and shut the rest . . . completely out."[43]

Prize money tended to offset the grueling and monotonous blockade duty. After adjudication costs, one-half of the money went to the navy pension fund and the other half went to the captors in amounts relative to their normal pay. A particularly valuable ship might fetch every member of the vessel several years' pay. When the little tug *Eolus* captured *Hope* off Wilmington in 1864, the acting master won $13,164.85 and the assistant engineers $6,657 each. This amounted to more than four years' pay for all of them. The seamen got over $1,000 apiece, while the cabin boy, whose pay amounted to less than $2.50 a week, received $532.60. Nine days later, *Eolus* captured *Lady Sterling*, which netted one ensign almost $23,000. Not all prizes were this valuable, and sometimes the cost of adjudication exceeded the value of the prize, leaving nothing for distribution to the crew. The system of prize money, though, was particularly good to Rear Admiral Lee, who earned over $125,000 during the war, the highest amount paid to any naval officer.[44]

A drawback to the system was its disproportionate distribution among the officers and men. Slow ships generally caught fewer vessels, and their crews received less prize money. William H. Anderson, on board *State of Georgia*, a fairly slow ship in the latter part of the war, made $80 in prize money during one "season," while officers of corresponding rank in a fast blockader earned as much as $20,000.[45]

For every vessel caught by the squadron, several others successfully eluded their vigilance. It is difficult to determine exactly how many ships ran the blockade *into* Wilmington, because only fragmentary data remain to indicate the volume of the trade. As the war progressed, steamers increasingly became the carriers of the illegal goods, and after 1863, the blockade runners began to run into the Cape Fear River in increasing numbers. In the first year of the war, it is estimated that between 600 and 700 ships of all types ran the blockade from England alone—some estimates are even higher. The most recent scholarship suggests that about 300 different steamers attempted to violate the blockade.[46]

The fragmentary data available show that steamers evaded the blockade virtually at will.[47] It is not necessary to make a complete list to make this point, but a few examples will illustrate their success in running the blockade. The harbormaster at Wilmington estimated that from May 1863 until 31 December 1864, blockade runners made 260 successful trips into Wilmington. This figure is matched by a recent study by Stephen Wise, which lists 261 trips by steamers. Add the sailing craft that also eluded the squadron, and it means that they ran past the blockaders either coming or going on the average of about once every two days. Over 100 different steamers participated in the trade at this port. They came at times five a day and as many as sixteen in fifteen days, so that it had James Randall, a clerk of a blockade running firm, boasting that it "makes a blockade of Wilmington look like a sham."[48]

Marcus Price in his study of blockade running indicated that in 1861 a blockade runner had a one-in-ten chance of being captured; not more than one-in-eight in 1862; one-in-four in 1863; about one-in-three in 1864; and in 1865, after most ports were closed, about a one-in-two chance. The London *Index* noted that, between 1 January 1863 and the middle of April 1864, of the 590 attempted trips into the ports of Wilmington and Charleston, 498 ended with success. These figures indicate that about fifteen percent of the attempts ended in capture. This figure complements the figure of seventy-seven percent of a more recent and comprehensive study by Stephen Wise. Steamers made as many as 1,300 attempts to run through the blockade, 1,000 of which succeeded. Sailing vessels also made several hundred attempts until the blockade became too tight for any hope of success by slow merchantmen.[49]

Evidence shows that large amounts of goods came through the blockade. But since Confederate government records did not survive or were not kept on imported goods, the evidence is incomplete. To balance their foreign trade, the Confederacy exported mostly cotton but did export in small quantities early in the war flour and meal, bacon, hams, lard, linseed oil, corn, rice, tallow, and wheat. The main export staple later was cotton but also large quantities of tobacco, and naval stores.[50]

As the war progressed, Wilmington's importance grew as other Confederate-held ports were closed by Union occupation. In late October 1863, the Confederate government established Wilmington as the principal point of departure for outgoing government freight. The chief of the Confederate army Ordnance Bureau, Josiah Gorgas, had his brother-in-law, Major Thomas L. Bayne of the Confederate army Ordnance Bureau, supervise the government and private vessels carrying Confederate cargoes. Bayne stationed James M. Seixas at Wilmington to oversee the Ordnance Bureau cargoes and the large government-owned steam cotton press, capable of compressing 500 bales of cotton a day.[51]

During the war, about 350,000 bales of cotton ran through the blockade, two-thirds of this from East Coast ports. Wilmington, of course, played a large part in the exportation. The customhouse at Wilmington reported, from 1 January to the end of September 1863, shipping almost 31,000 bales of cotton out of Wilmington. Bayne declared in October 1863 that "five thousand bales of cotton will be sent out this month . . . 15,000 bales of cotton per month will be needed at Wilmington." In the months of January, July, and August 1863, over 6,000,000 pounds of cotton were exported from Wilmington. The cotton shipped from Wilmington annually was worth more than four times all the goods shipped from the entire state of North Carolina in 1858.[52]

During 1862 and 1863, the trade of Bermuda, Nassau, and other ports grew rapidly, which also indicates the success of blockade running. On some of the islands, the growth of foreign trade was phenomenal. The British imported the cotton from the following places in hundred-weights:[53]

	1862	1863
Bermuda	5,024	63,807
Bahamas	43,220	202,009
Barbados	143	16,556
Cuba	27,184	31,920
Puerto Rico	46	1,338

Wilmington's role as the sole port from which the government exported cotton provides the researcher an encapsulated view of the successful trade. James Seixas wrote that the government could not get cotton at times but that the private steamers plying in and out of Wilmington departed "almost daily." In less than six months, from 1 July to December 1864, the Confederate government shipped almost 12,000 bales of cotton and lost about eleven percent. From March to December of the same year, the Confederate government shipped over 27,000 bales of cotton through the blockade.[54]

This trade made many people rich. The *Manchester Guardian* estimated that the English people alone had invested about $66,000,000 in ventures into Wilmington from January 1863 to December 1864. In twenty-two months, from 1 January 1863 until 31 October 1864, the quantity of cotton exported from Wilmington alone was 62,860,463 pounds or 137,937 bales. The paper also estimated that the import and export trade of Wilmington, from the period 1 July 1863 to 30 June 1864, to be $65,185,000. After the first attack on Fort Fisher, a correspondent of the New York *Herald* noted in January 1865: "The utmost activity prevailed in the Anglo-Rebel blockade-running fleet plying between Wilmington and Charleston and Nassau. Cotton valued at $3,500,000 had been landed at Nassau from the above named ports within ten days."[55]

Blockade runners did not enjoy the same success rate on the inward journey, and thus imports lagged behind exports. Nevertheless, tremendous amounts of goods came through the blockade and varied in size from straight pins to marine engines. Most importantly, the Confederacy imported at least 400,000 small arms from Europe and much of this through the port of Wilmington. Frank Owsley estimated that over 300 cargoes of munitions reached the Confederate ports.[56]

With Charleston under Union attack by mid-1863, Wilmington became the major port for imports. Gorgas wrote in his diary, "The only port now left to us is Wilmington." The government, between 1 November 1863 and 25 October 1864, imported vast quantities of supplies, mainly through Wilmington. Blockade runners brought in 1,490,000 pounds of lead, 1,850,000 pounds of saltpeter, 6,200,000 pounds of meat, 408,000 pounds of coffee, 420,000 pairs of shoes, 292,000 blankets, and 136,832 small arms.[57]

The state of North Carolina ran its own ships successfully and imported large quantities of materials. The state brought in lubricating oil, machinery, coffee, medicine, farm implements, leather and shoes equal to 250,000 pairs, 50,000 blankets, gray woolen cloth for 250,000 suits of uniforms, 12,000 overcoats, 2,000 Enfield rifles each with 100 rounds of fixed ammunition, and 100,000 pounds of bacon.[58]

From 1 October 1864 to 1 January 1865, while David Porter commanded the squadron, the Ordnance Bureau imported large quantities of copper and tin, 400,000 pounds of lead, 2,000,000 pounds of saltpeter, 500,000 pairs of shoes, 8,000,000 pounds of bacon, and 50 cannon. Through the ports of Wilmington and Charleston during the same period came large quantities of medicine and coffee, over 50,000 rifles, 316,000 pairs of blankets, and over 1,000,000 pounds of lead. The ease with which the Confederacy imported goods had Gorgas boasting: "We have hitherto had no difficulty in importing arms through the blockaded sea ports."[59]

Later in the war, the Confederate government placed restrictions on blockade runners that prohibited the importation of certain luxury items and required the vessels to reserve half of their cargo space for government cargo. Many believed that this would have an adverse affect and reduce the number of vessels running the blockade. Instead, the numbers increased. The imported cargoes varied for many reasons. It was risky to freight a vessel entirely with valuable or hard-to-obtain supplies, because if the owners lost the vessel, it might be months before new supplies could be found. This also benefited the merchant, who could make a higher profit and could continue to do so. It is also clear that when the Confederacy needed certain items, it found some means to get them past the blockade. Late in 1864, when the Confederate troops needed food, 500,000 rations came into the South, and 2,500,000 more were waiting to be shipped. This was enough food for 100,000 men for two and one-half months.[60]

There is no doubt that a great deal of contraband passed through the blockade. The munitions imports virtually sustained the army during five years of fighting. One may question just how the blockade damaged the Confederate war effort. Porter estimated that, while Lee commanded the squadron, $10,000,000 worth of blockade runners and their cargoes were destroyed. During the war, over 130 vessels were wrecked,

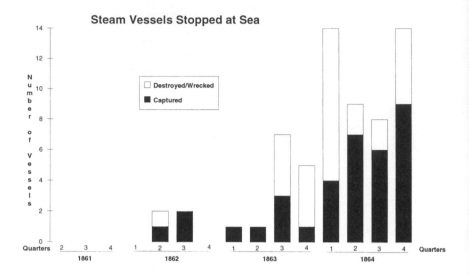

Steam Vessels Stopped at Sea

captured, or destroyed off Wilmington—which amounts to a great loss.
Of these 130, 24 percent were captured steamers, 20 percent were
destroyed steamers; 43 percent were captured sailing vessels, and 13
percent were destroyed sailing vessels. If these vessels averaged somewhat over 200 tons, and an army wagon carried one ton of supplies, then
the blockaders captured and destroyed an equivalent of nearly 30,000
wagon loads of supplies or about 1,000,000 cubic feet of cargo—a sizable
loss.[61] Yet even with heavy losses such as these, the blockade runners
continued to operate profitably. The high profit margin ensured the
continuation of blockade running as long as a vessel had the slightest
chance of getting her cargo through.

　　It is obvious that the blockade did not effectively keep contraband out
of the Confederacy. But it is equally clear that the blockade severely
damaged the Confederate war effort in several ways. Without a blockade, the Confederacy would have been free to import every object
necessary for the continuation of the war and to export freely cotton to
sustain their purchases. This, however, was not the case. Instead, the
South could import only the most important articles, while shipments
containing items such as locomotives, railroad iron, and other equipment and machinery came into the Confederacy in much smaller quantities. The blockade aggravated the monetary system and added to the
tremendous rate of inflation, and financial problems developed abroad.

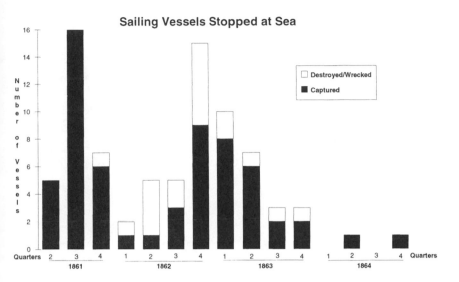

Without an unlimited supply of goods, the government resorted to impressment to fulfill its needs.

The Confederate government remained content during the war to use its open ports to carry their freight. The Confederate government rarely used its resources to reopen captured ports. The Confederacy also had unlimited chances to arm blockade runners and to attempt to break the blockade, but instead, it chose to send out small numbers of commerce raiders and to continue bringing goods into the South in blockade runners that faced small risks. This policy failed when the Union captured and gained control of most of the coastline. Even more damaging was the destruction and the control of Confederate railroads and junctions, which negated the advantages of running the blockade because the goods could not be shipped to the front.

The introduction of steam gradually changed the concept of a blockade. The Union navy, at the outbreak of the war, was not prepared to carry out a blockade and at the same time abide strictly by international law, which had been formulated before the advent of steam blockades. The concept of blockades developed a wider interpretation in international law during the war, which initially only raised European protests rather than actions. The British in 1863 claimed that the blockade was "only nominal." But the blockade became more efficient as the navy employed more vessels and acquired a logistical base at Beaufort. At the war's end, the Union navy controlled the South's shoreline and had probably maintained as strict a blockade as could be expected. In August 1864, Secretary of State William Henry Seward wrote to Lord Lyons, admitting the shortcoming of the blockade maintained against steamers. He believed that "no maritime power" could "maintain so effectual a blockade" as that of the United States. Seward further stated: "I think, therefore, with great deference, that either our blockade must be acknowledged to be sufficient, or it must be held that no lawful blockade can be maintained against contraband traders who enjoy the advantages of steam navigation."[62]

The blockade evolved over four years because of the gradual and better understanding of the circumstances of the service. But even with the large numbers of gunboats off the coast, the Union squadron failed to stop this commerce. One seaman summed up the helpless feelings of his comrades when he wrote his parents, "A steamer came in and the men on her put their finger to their nose . . . so you see that is the way that things go on."[63]

THIRTEEN

We are looking for old Abe's fleet

The Capture of Wilmington

On 2 September 1861, just four days after the surrender of Fort Hatteras, the Blockade Strategy Board discussed the idea of capturing Wilmington. The board deliberated outfitting an expedition in New York, and then landing a few hundred men in surfboats at New Inlet, which the rebels had yet to fortify. Once ashore, the Union force could seize all the depots in the area and destroy the railroad depot at Wilmington. A second idea fostered by the board was a night attack by way of Masonboro or Rich Inlet.[1] The inclination to capture the town or the forts at the entrances to the river became stronger during the war, because the blockaders had an increasingly difficult time trying to stop the contraband trade there. The blockading force gradually increased and tactics continually changed, but Confederate trade increased despite the efforts of the squadron. By 1863, Wilmington had become the Confederacy's major port, and the capture of either of the major forts that guarded the Cape Fear River appeared the only way to check the illicit commerce. Dozens of schemes to capture this port would be discussed at many different levels, but none would bear fruit until the last six months of the war.

The residents of Wilmington knew that the Union forces might attack at almost any time. They frequently became alarmed, and unrestrained rumors circulated every time the Union navy prepared to strike somewhere on the coast. In October 1861, the navy prepared for an attack on Port Royal, South Carolina. One of the prominent ladies of the town, Mrs. Armand J. DeRosset, wrote to a friend that "our town is in a state of excitement expecting the fleet to make an attack at any moment."[2]

The expedition bound for the sounds of North Carolina in early 1862 again started the spread of rumors. David Buie, a soldier at Fort Fisher, commented, "We are looking for the Yankees tomorrow and we are making all the preparations we can to meet them. We are . . . confident of success."[3] Another soldier claimed, "We are looking for *Old Mr. Burnside* to give us a call some of these days. . . . He had better mind how he 'works his quills' about this place or else he may leave with his name slightly changed from Burnside to Burntsides."[4] After the capture of the major points in the sounds, many believed Wilmington would be the next object of Union naval strategy. One man wrote, "We are looking for Burnside soon—hope to be able to keep him out of the Cape Fear."[5]

The Union ships that lay off the coast represented a great deal of manpower and firepower and posed a constant threat to the Confederates. Furthermore, the gunboats continually probed defenses, collected intelligence, and harassed the state's saltworks. The mobility of the navy and the threat of such a force created a great deal of anxiety for the Confederate government. The rebels kept troops close to all the potential landing sites along the coast but could never hope to maintain adequately this defensive posture, because of their continual manpower shortages and growing disparity between the forces under arms.

During the war, the gunboats of the squadron carried out many daring raids, which increased the fears of the local commanders. In December 1861, they burned a Confederate vessel that was being converted for harbor defense at Western Bar. In 1863, they captured the grounded blockade runner *Kate* under the guns of Fort Fisher. South of Western Bar, at Little River and Murrell's Inlet, Union crews landed on numerous occasions, destroying saltworks, vessels, and tremendous amounts of supplies with great success.[6]

While stationed off Wilmington, William Cushing likewise made his presence known by performing some of the war's most daring missions. On 12 August 1863, while in command of *Shokokon*, he made a reconnaissance of New Topsail Inlet. Confederate artillery drove Cushing's party away, but he discovered a schooner, which he determined to destroy. On the night of 22 August, Cushing led two boat crews ashore; they shouldered dinghies across one-half mile of land to avoid the artillery and landed in the enemy's rear. Cushing managed to capture ten men and destroy extensive saltworks and the schooner they had observed. The party returned to *Shokokon* with three prisoners, having released seven, with no casualties.[7]

In February 1864, Lieutenant Cushing and twenty men rowed past Fort Caswell to capture the fort's commanding officer, General Louis Hébert at Smithville. They landed at a hotel in the town and found the general's headquarters. The Union sailors captured the chief engineer of the Smithville defenses but found that Hébert had left for Wilmington. One of Hébert's aides, who escaped "with a great scarcity of clothing," did not give an alarm, thinking the garrison had mutinied. Cushing succeeded in bringing his prisoner off without alarming anyone, and the fort never fired a single shot. Gustavus Fox endorsed these missions and suggested that the "department will not find any fault with any dashing expeditions that give reasonable hope of a result injurious to the enemy, even though they fail occasionally."[8]

On 21 April 1864, the squadron boldly attacked the state saltworks in Masonboro Sound. The navy acquired information about the Masonboro works from six refugees whom they picked up at sea in March. An expedition consisting of six boats carrying a total of 101 officers and men entered Masonboro Inlet and wrecked the works. They claimed to have destroyed fifty or sixty large government wagons, a steam pump, and seven boilers by throwing thirty-pound shells into them. They also destroyed several horse sheds, about 200 salt pans, large vats, reservoirs, and outbuildings. They took some sixty prisoners, without the loss of a single man. This large saltwork had turned out 190 bushels of salt a day for the Confederacy. There is some doubt, however, that the raiding force did the damage it claimed, because salt commissioner David Work avowed, "The greatest damage was to the engines and pumps. . . . If I could pump water, I could run two-thirds of the works today."[9]

Intelligence gathering became an important and often overlooked function of the blockading vessels. Important information came from Union sympathizers who could give sometimes accurate, detailed, and important accounts of fortifications, troop strengths, topographic information, and blockade running activity. Information-gathering expeditions comprised carefully picked men; paymasters, medical officers, and engineers were not allowed on these dangerous missions. During the fall of 1864, Union scouts visited almost the entire area from Fort Fisher to Masonboro Inlet and kept a semiweekly or triweekly communication with the shore. Officers had instructions to examine privately those who volunteered information and to offer them rewards for it.[10]

These raids, while gathering important information and keeping the Confederate's local commander confused, had no effect on the trade at Wilmington. The squadron's blockade of the inlets had likewise been unsuccessful in checking the contraband trade. Only by gaining control of the river could the Union forces close the port. In early 1862, the Navy Department had pushed for the capture of the principal towns in the sounds of North Carolina rather than the capture of Wilmington. In December 1863, Rear Admiral Lee criticized this strategy and believed these captures were "loadstones instead of stepping stones to progress." He asserted that the Union had acquired the eastern portion of the state with relative ease but maintained that these same forces could have taken the whole coast. Lee lamented that "the complete acquisition of the seacoast was abandoned in the favor of the sound towns."[11] Lee might have added that the options of the navy at that time had been limited due to the Peninsular campaign, which took precedent over any movement that may have been made to capture Wilmington.

The squadron actively supported McClellan's campaign on the peninsula, and the Navy Department retained an interest in the capture of Wilmington. The department suggested that Flag Officer Goldsborough prepare to attack Fort Caswell, but only the capture of Richmond would free the necessary troops and gunboats for such an operation. On 12 May, Goldsborough wrote Welles that he would "take the ironclads to Wilmington, N.C., and reduce Fort Caswell." On the same day, he boasted to his wife, "My next job is to take Wilmington, N.C. It is easy in accomplishment comparatively speaking. There all my work as far as my command extends will have been accomplished, I will take *Monitor* and *Galena* there and make short work of it."[12]

On 13 May, the department quickly changed its intentions after the rebels destroyed *Virginia*. The destruction of the ironclad lay the James River again open to Union vessels as far as Drewry's Bluff. For this reason, the department instructed Goldsborough to abandon the plans for the capture of Wilmington. Confident that Richmond would soon be captured, Gustavus Fox told the flag officer that, if he moved quickly after the fall of the Confederate capital, he might attack Wilmington before vessels were ordered to Charleston. Goldsborough, confident that he could capture one of the forts, did not ask for army assistance. He wanted only enough men to garrison Fort Caswell and later claimed that he would use marines for this purpose. Without support from the army, the expedition would never materialize. Yet Goldsborough told Fox that he had instructed Commander Oliver S. Glisson of *Mount Vernon* to take the "small work" at New Inlet, if he could without risking the loss of his vessel. If successful, he could proceed to Fort Caswell, and if it looked weak, he should "make a guarded demonstration against it, & get it if he could." Goldsborough remained confident that *Monitor* and several other vessels could overwhelm the fort. On 2 June 1862, Welles sent Goldsborough the side-wheel steamers *Genesee* and *Tioga* and told him the "operations against Richmond may close favorably at any moment, and, in that case it is believed that a sudden naval demonstration against Fort Caswell will be successful."[13]

The Navy Department's designs for attacking the forts of Cape Fear gradually began to wane. Goldsborough lost the services of *Susquehanna*, a vessel upon which he had largely relied. He had installed two 100-pound Parrott guns on her for shelling the fort. Furthermore, *Monitor* and *Galena* could not possibly be made available for an immediate attack. *Galena* had suffered serious damage in the battle at Drewry's Bluff on 15 May. Goldsborough remained hopeful, but the department ordered that no attack should be made unless he used *Monitor*, otherwise the attacking force would be too weak. By the middle of June, *Galena* was not nearly ready for battle, but *Monitor*, which suffered mechanical difficulties, might possibly be made available.[14]

Officials in Washington also had under consideration an expedition to Charleston, South Carolina. This greatly disappointed Goldsborough, who desperately wanted to regain some of the respect that he had lost during the Peninsular campaign. Due to the failure of McClellan's campaign, the country needed a political victory as well as a

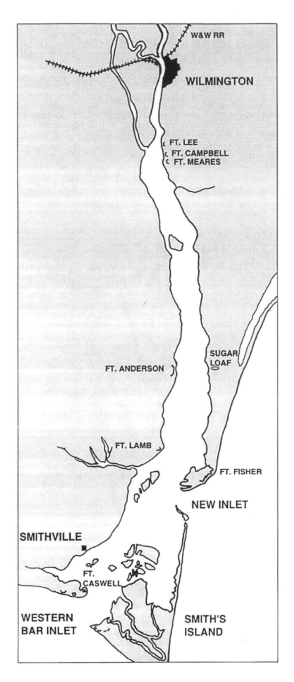

The Cape Fear River

military success, and the navy chose to move against Charleston rather than Wilmington. Assistant Secretary of the Navy Fox commented on this decision, "We should be inclined to skip Fort Caswell . . . for the fall of Charleston is the fall of Satan's kingdom."[15]

Several obstacles prevented anything but a systematically planned capture of Wilmington. By far the greatest was the geography of the coast. The town lay over twenty miles from the mouth of Cape Fear, and the shallow bars at each inlet prohibited large vessels from attacking the forts at close range. One of the soldiers at Fort Caswell remarked, "Our greatest protection is in the 'bar,' a vessel drawing more than fourteen feet cannot cross."[16] The forts guarding the entrances to the river likewise complicated an attack. At the beginning of the war, Fort Caswell lay abandoned and Fort Fisher had yet to be built. Fort Fisher grew from a few batteries in 1861 into a large earthwork fort stretching over a mile. Colonel William Lamb assumed command in July 1862. From that date, construction never stopped until it became the largest seacoast fortification in the country. The weak link in the defense was the fact that neither fort could be defended from a strong attack from land. Brigadier General William H. C. Whiting told Confederate Secretary of War George W. Randolph that the safety of each fort depended on the retention of the other and that the "fall of one, though so far apart, will necessarily result in that of the other."[17] During the spring of 1862, the Confederates also laid down two ironclads at Wilmington, hoping that, when finished, an attack on the city would be even more hazardous.

The change in Union squadron commanders renewed the Union's interest in attacking the forts. The Navy Department no longer had any commitment to defend McClellan's troops on the peninsula. Samuel Phillips Lee immediately began probing the defenses, and his planning, with support from the Navy Department, went far beyond anything Goldsborough had ever conceived.

Realizing that the bars were major obstacles, Lee immediately asked for information concerning the depth of water at each. Because of the extensive fortifications, a survey was a risky venture even by night. Lee placed a great deal of responsibility on Lieutenant Commander Daniel L. Braine, who supervised two surveys of Western Bar in September with good contraband pilots and found ten feet over the bar at low tide.[18]

Lee also tried to find pilots to guide vessels through the inlets. The Union navy had persuaded George Bowen, a captured Wilmington pilot, to help survey the inlet. Earlier, Goldsborough had asked for eight men who were well acquainted with both entrances to Wilmington and tried to get coasting captains out of New York who were considered the best. Not able to find men acquainted with the bars, Welles tried to obtain pilots from the prisoners at Fort Lafayette in New York. He offered them a "large reward" of $5,000 if they would take an ironclad to Wilmington and back. Eventually Lee had three pilots and one "pilot gunner."[19]

By December, all the Union armies began moving in unison to exert a great pressure on the Southern forces. The Navy Department planned an attack on Wilmington to be part of this action. At Fredericksburg, the Confederates badly defeated Burnside's Army of the Potomac, which motivated Washington and the Navy Department to push for an attack at Cape Fear. The Northern leaders viewed this as a possible quick victory to offset the recent debacle. Rear Admiral Samuel Du Pont summed up the navy's plans at Wilmington by claiming that it "was one of those chaotic conceptions, produced by the desire of the President and others 'to strike a blow' somewhere."[20]

In the early stages of planning, the navy considered an attack at either inlet and delayed making a decision to allow Lee to gather information. The department planned to utilize *Monitor* and *Passaic* "to clean out Wilmington and its railroad connections." Major General John Foster, the commander of the Department of North Carolina, proposed to march from New Bern to cut the railroad near Goldsboro, to prevent reinforcements from coming from Virginia, and then to march to Tarboro to destroy the gunboats thought to be under construction there. Foster then planned to attack Wilmington, receiving supplies through New Topsail Inlet by light-draft steamers.[21]

Initially the attack was planned with limited firepower, which would require the simultaneous reduction of one of the forts from the rear and the sea. Fox hoped that the monitors could enter the Cape Fear River at Western Bar while other vessels attacked Fort Fisher from the sea. The monitors could steam up the river, bypass Fort Caswell, and attack Fort Fisher from the rear. Foster and his troops, meanwhile, could march toward Wilmington and with naval cooperation capture the town. Rear

Admiral Lee was apprehensive that the monitors might not be able to pass Fort Caswell, which would divide his force and render an outside attack unsuccessful. Fox remained confident that the monitors could pass up the river and drive the defenders out of the fort. Then the seamen would only have "to land under cover of ships, spike the guns, and all the small gun-boats enter New Inlet, at once and accompany the Iron clads to Wilmington."[22]

Lee had two other alternatives: the monitors could attempt a passage over the shallow bar at New Inlet, or either fort could be reduced from the outside. Those concerned with the project seemed to prefer that the monitors attempt a passage over Western Bar Inlet. They could reduce Fort Caswell first and then attack Fort Fisher and hold New Inlet. Possession of the latter entrance would enable General Foster to come by land or sea. If this were not possible, the ironclads would be "obliged to go to Wilmington, destroy all the vessels, ferry boats, depots, and return; an adventure attended with much risk and wanting in complete success."[23]

The success of this plan depended upon the monitors' reducing and then passing Fort Caswell. But those planning the operation believed that the naval force would be insufficient to reduce the fort. Fox remarked that the monitors' slow rate of fire would not be sufficient to reduce the works. Fox realized that the "popular clamor centers on Charleston," but he considered Wilmington more important militarily and politically. Fox justified this hasty stroke against Wilmington by stating that "we have more force than we shall ever possess again since the ironclads must go south so soon as four are ready."[24] Lee, though, remained dissatisfied with the force put at his disposal and continually asked for additional gunboats and monitors. Welles temporarily transferred nine gunboats and the monitors *Passaic* and *Montauk* to the squadron for the attack.[25]

The military officials and citizens of Wilmington had noted the additional activity of the squadron and suspected an attack. One inhabitant of the town stated in December: "We are looking for old Abe's fleet around here every day. Our Confederate authorities are of the opinion that Wilmington will be the next place of attack . . . though they have been crying wolf wolf. . . . I have no doubt but he will be along some of these days."[26]

The shallow depth of the bar at New Inlet and the unknown nature of the obstructions at Fort Caswell remained the major impediments for an attack. The blockaders continually surveyed the bar but could not find a channel at New Inlet with water sufficient to allow the monitors to cross it. The department believed *Nashville* had run into Cape Fear by way of New Inlet and that she had a draft, when "light," of eleven feet. Fox therefore thought there was a channel deep enough for *Monitor*, which drew only ten and a half feet, while *Montauk* had a draft of eleven and a half. *Passaic* with a draft of twelve feet could reduce her draft to eleven with only seven days' coal. Fox said, "Oh! There is plenty of water. . . . *Nashville* got in there." Captain John P. Bankhead of *Monitor* disagreed. He believed a passage for the monitors was not feasible because the bar was too exposed to the sea and because the winds would make the swells an average of two feet in ordinary weather.[27]

At the Western Bar channel, the passage seemed safe enough, but the officers believed that the rebels had placed obstructions on the "Rip," a shoal spot under the guns of Fort Caswell. They reported that the obstructions on the Rip consisted of two heavy-timber rafts 700 feet long, which stretched across the channel. The rafts were thought to be constructed of timber forty feet long with sharpened ends, connected by chains in mid-channel. It was also believed that at high tide, the whole or parts of it floated. It appears, however, that the only obstructions in the channel consisted of a few sunken vessels, which were far from adequate to block it but enough perhaps to intimidate those planning the attack.[28]

Bankhead suggested that a "sufficient number of ironclads" could engage the different batteries commanding the Rip, but he feared that the supply of ammunition would be exhausted before the works could be reduced. If the navy silenced Fort Caswell's guns, Bankhead thought the obstructions could be leisurely removed. Percival Drayton, the commander of *Passaic*, suggested that the obstructions might be removed by gunfire but feared that only the upper portion near the waterline would be affected. Removal by torpedoes was a possibility, but they were both "uncertain and slow." By 21 December, the department had sent an expert on torpedoes, Julius H. Kroehl, to Wilmington and at least eighty-four torpedoes for possible use on the obstructions.[29]

While the warships surveyed the bars, General Foster was actively attacking the Confederates. He began on 11 December and advanced through Kinston, to Whitehall, then burned the Wilmington and Weldon Railroad bridge over the Neuse River. He destroyed several miles of track to prevent reinforcements from going to Wilmington, should the department maintain its plans for an attack. His forces returned to New Bern on 20 December, claiming his expedition was a "perfect success." Foster then began to make arrangements for the transportation of 12,000 troops from Washington, D.C., to New Bern. The earliest he could leave New Bern with 20,000 men was 5 January. Foster's major concern about this movement was that the Confederates could put troops from either Charleston or Richmond in Wilmington by rail within a day. If the gunboats did not capture at least one fort, then Foster would find it hard to be resupplied.[30]

By mid-December, the attack began to take shape. Lee began calling for two or three more monitors besides *Monitor* and *Passaic*. No conclusion had been made as to the nature of the attack—whether it would be an inside or outside bombardment. Fox mentioned to Du Pont that it looked as if the attack would be attempted with at least two monitors going into the river. On the 15th, the orders went out for the attack. Lee received the *Montauk* and two more gunboats. The department favored an inside attack on Fort Fisher but warned Lee that the plan had been forwarded with the supposition that they could pass Fort Caswell without reducing it. Unsure of the department's preferences for an attack, Lee wrote to Fox, "Let me know just what it is to be. I am willing anyhow."[31]

As December came to a close, the department started to bring the operation into motion. *Montauk*, *Monitor*, and *Passaic* prepared to go to Beaufort, the staging area for the squadron. They would stay there until the plans for the attack became final. Welles told Lee that, if the ironclads could not get over the bars, *Montauk* and *Passaic* would go to Port Royal.[32]

The depth of water over New Inlet Bar continued to be the only obstacle for an inside attack on Fort Fisher. The information gleaned from the night surveys seemed unreliable, because the survey crews collected different data each time. Surveys found twelve feet of water several times but a two-foot swell would have made it hazardous for even the shallow-draft *Monitor* to attempt to run into the channel. With this information, the captains of the ironclads felt that they could not enter New Inlet.[33]

The plan to attack by way of the Western Bar channel did not look promising either. The bar had plenty of water, but the unknown character of the obstructions, the narrow channel, the strong current, and an insufficient number of ironclads to reduce Fort Caswell dampened the prospect of an attack from this inlet. The monitors were hard to steer, and once they had crossed the bar, it would be difficult for them to return for ammunition or coal.[34] The remaining choice was an outside attack.

Lee badly wanted to attack Wilmington. The planning thus far had been disjointed because of his absence from the operations at Cape Fear. In all probability, Lee remained at Hampton Roads to help organize the attack, but his presence only caused confusion and added to the delays. It is puzzling that Lee did not go to Wilmington to supervise the surveys on the bars, since he had a great deal of experience in the Coast Survey and particularly since the whole attack depended on finding a channel for the ironclads.

On 28 December, with insufficient soundings, Lee decided that an inside attack at New Inlet was not possible and wrote Foster to this effect. Lee did not give up on the other possibilities and remained optimistic, telling the general that he could still supply the army through New Topsail Inlet and could attack Fort Fisher from the outside. After the fort fell, the wooden vessels could enter New Inlet and attack the remaining batteries. The squadron could then cooperate with the army to attack Fort Caswell from the north. He wrote Welles that the ironclads would remain in Beaufort until he knew positively that the obstructions at Fort Caswell could be removed. He added that the "Coast Survey charts furnish sufficient data, irrespective of the unreliable night soundings . . . for deciding in the affirmative the question as to the possibility of *Passaic* and *Monitor* entering the Cape Fear River."[35] Welles replied, "As they are founded upon charts and not upon surveys, the Department will give no orders until it is positively known about the bars."[36]

On 29 December, the 1,517-ton side-wheel steamer *Rhode Island*, with *Monitor* in tow, left Hampton Roads for Beaufort in "clear and pleasant" weather. During the night, the swell and the wind increased, and the waves began to break over the ironclad's pilothouse. All during the next day, the weather did not moderate and by the night of the 30th began to worsen. With the waves now washing over the turret, the ship began to pitch and yaw. Striking the water with each swell, the packing around the turret failed to stay in place, water poured down the blower pipes, and seams began to open in the armor. Finally, more water entered the ship than the pumps could handle. At 10:30 P.M., Commander John Bankhead ordered a distress signal be sent to *Rhode Island*. After cutting the towing cable, Bankhead brought *Monitor* up beside *Rhode Island*. All but sixteen men were rescued from the ironclad, and shortly before 1:00 A.M. on 31 December, *Monitor* slipped beneath the waves off Cape Hatteras.[37]

The loss of this vessel ended any prospect for an attack on Wilmington. It is almost certain that the department intended to attack the forts in some manner. Fox commented on the sinking, "We gave him [Lee] the *Passaic* and the old *Monitor*, which unfortunately sunk, breaking up the whole affair." The department might have sent *Monitor* over the bar at New Inlet, since she drew the least water of the three ironclads. An attack at Fort Caswell was likewise now weakened, and Welles wrote in his diary, "It is best, therefore, to push on to Charleston and strengthen Du Pont."[38]

The defects of the ironclads had been substantially demonstrated. They were not really seagoing vessels because of a lack of reserve buoyancy; thus they could not be moved from point to point along the coast without a consort. Their speed and rate of fire were both slow, and they lacked maneuverability.[39] These limitations would affect naval strategy, particularly any move to capture the forts at Cape Fear.

Even after the loss of *Monitor*, Lee remained optimistic that an attack might be made on the forts before the gunboats went south. As he wrote to Welles, he promoted the reduction of Fort Caswell first. Foster traveled to Washington, D.C., to talk to Secretary of War Edwin Stanton. By 5 January, the attack had been canceled. The following day, Welles ordered *New Ironsides* and the monitors *Passaic*, *Montauk*, *Patapsco*, and *Weehawken* to South Carolina.[40]

General Foster had withdrawn support for an attack for a number of reasons. He did not think that a naval attack would be effective, because warships could not pass the bar at New Inlet to attack Fort Fisher from

the river. He also believed that an assault by land would not be successful, because the enemy could detach troops to aid in the defense of the
forts. A march to Wilmington would take seven days, an adequate time
for the enemy to draw men from Richmond, Charleston, and Savannah.
Furthermore, Foster was concerned about logistical support. He worried about landing supplies in a narrow channel with poor landing
facilities that might be defended by batteries. He likewise thought his
supply route would be too long and exposed. Foster's main objection
was the inability to get the ironclads into the river. He believed that
without the cooperation of the ironclads, a force larger than he had
would be necessary.[41]

The concentration of transports in Beaufort and the movement up
and down the coast had alarmed Brigadier General William Whiting.
He believed an attack on the forts was imminent and prepared his
works for such an event. Beauregard sent troops from South Carolina,
and Robert E. Lee moved men farther south to bolster the defenses.
Meanwhile, on 13 January, the gunboats off Cape Fear fired on Fort
Caswell to add to the concern of Whiting and the garrison.[42]

Phillips Lee continued working for an attack on Wilmington. He
retained his pilots and continued the surveys on the bars. For future
operations, Welles promised Lee several light-draft monitors that carried eleven-inch guns. The Navy Department planned for these vessels
to be ready in February and assured Lee their use if he could get them
into the Cape Fear River. Welles asked for a more thorough examination of the inlets, with the possibility of getting the monitors *Sangamon*
and *Lehigh* inside the river, but he did not want to risk the department's
few ironclads on Wilmington. The secretary did tell Lee that a victory at
Charleston, Savannah, or Mobile "would lead the Department to hazard more at Wilmington than would be judicious at the present time."[43]

During February 1863, the Navy Department continued to promise
monitors to Lee. Gustavus Fox told the rear admiral that he could take
the light-draft ironclad *Keokuk* (two eleven-inch guns), the monitor
Catskill, and probably her sister *Nantucket*, because the navy could
"afford to take more risks at Wilmington than would have been advis-
able at first." A week later, Fox promised Lee that the ironclads *Catskill*,
Sangamon, *Lehigh*, *Nantucket*, and *Keokuk* would be provided for any
future expedition against Wilmington.[44]

While Foster and Lee worked out details for another attack, Samuel Francis Du Pont, the flag officer of the South Atlantic Blockading Squadron, became upset that plans to capture Wilmington were still being discussed. Fox had told Du Pont to give Lee the ironclad *Keokuk* and another ironclad, because "Lee is going at Wilmington, which is purely an ironclad-affair." Du Pont pleaded, "I trust in God you are not going to let Foster inveigle you into any Wilmington operation until we are through here." Early in April, Du Pont attacked the Confederate forts in Charleston Harbor with nine ironclads but was repulsed. After this defeat, Lee suggested to Welles that Du Pont's failure did not make an attack on Wilmington any more promising with the ironclads then available to him.[45]

While the Navy and War departments discussed the capture of the forts of Cape Fear, the Confederates wasted no time in strengthening their defenses at both inlets. In addition to bolstering the defenses at the inlets, they also sank more obstructions, built more river batteries, built fortifications in Wilmington, and began a large-scale torpedo system in the river and at the forts. The Confederacy also began to fortify the western end of Smith's Island, the weakest point in the defenses—anticipating the Union's next proposed move.[46]

Admiral Lee began to promote the capture of Smith's Island in April 1863. William Cushing believed that the forts there could be surprised and captured. Lee noted that possession of this weakly defended island might force the Confederacy to abandon stronger positions on the mainland. Lee encouraged Cushing's "dash" and asked Fox if he would "in any manner, even by a 'Go it Ned . . . ' justify the attempt." The capture of the island only met the "approbation" of the department, provided that the army would lend the proper force. Major General Henry Halleck, Lincoln's general in chief, promised to ask General Foster to assist. Foster estimated that he would need 10,000 troops and siege artillery to dislodge the Confederates from the island. He agreed to cooperate, but 8,000 of his men were in South Carolina and many of his men's enlistments would expire shortly. At the beginning of May, this plan faltered when Welles wrote to Lee that Halleck found it impossible to detach troops to reinforce Foster because of all the activity in both the eastern and western theaters. Thus it would be a naval attack if any at all. The inability of the army to cooperate struck down another possible move toward Wilmington. Lee wrote Welles that he did not think a "purely naval attack" could succeed at either entrance of the Cape Fear River. Because of the strength of the defenses and the shoal water, he believed it more difficult to capture Wilmington than Charleston. He added that "the entrances can only be taken by powerful military cooperation."[47]

Proposals for the capture of the inlets continued to materialize but remained on paper only. In June 1864, Colonel James Jourdan, the commander of the subdistrict of Beaufort, made a reconnaissance of the Fort Fisher batteries. He planned to conduct a coup de main on Fort Fisher using 1,200 men and several vessels. Jourdan went on board *Niphon* and steamed down the coast past the batteries, just outside of their range to draw their fire. John C. Howell of *Nereus* commented about the act: "It was a dashing looking affair, altho' tolerably safe, but in a military point of view under the circumstances, I think ill judged."[48]

In June 1864, William Cushing also reconnoitered Cape Fear. His main mission was to determine the whereabouts of the Confederate ironclad *Raleigh*, unaware that she had sunk on 6 May. Cushing and fifteen men rowed past the Western Bar batteries on the night of the 23rd. He noted that *Yadkin*, the 300-ton flagship of Flag Officer William F. Lynch, did not have heavy armament and that the ironclad *North Carolina* would be no match for a monitor. Cushing's men captured a fishing party of twenty-six and a mail carrier with 400 letters and managed to cut the wires between Wilmington and Fort Fisher. On their return, the rebels discovered and pursued them, and only Cushing's ingenuity saved his men from capture.[49]

Lee's desires to capture Wilmington never waned. The capture of the port, however, was never viable until its acquisition became beneficial to the War Department. Welles wrote in his diary, "I have been urging a conjoint attack upon Wilmington for months. . . . But the War Department hangs fire, and the President, whilst agreeing . . . dislikes to press matters when the military leaders are reluctant to move." During the fall of 1864, the capture of Wilmington again was reconsidered. By gaining possession of the railroads, communications could be maintained with General William Tecumseh Sherman, who was then planning a campaign into North Carolina. The War Department now showed a great deal of interest.[50]

After the War Department committed to an attack on Fort Fisher, the Navy Department was confronted with replacing Lee as the squadron commander, one of Grant's conditions when he accepted the expedition. Welles concurred, but to remove Lee would be a delicate matter because he had "discharged his duties intelligently and firmly." Welles judged Lee as being too cautious, and Lee had shown himself as somewhat a pessimist, which limited his foresight. The change of command did not surprise Phillips Lee. He had sensed that he had fallen from the graces of the department as early as March. John Sanford Barnes wrote that, by 1864, Lee looked "quite worn out" and "slept badly."[51] Two years in command of the squadron had finally worn him down. The department had a number of officers to choose from: Louis Goldsborough, Charles Henry Davis, David Glasgow Farragut, David Dixon Porter, John Dahlgren, and Samuel F. Du Pont. The department chose Farragut, who had recently captured the port of Mobile. But Welles was offering the position to a sick man, who would be ordered to get the squadron ready to attack Fort Fisher in less than a month. Farragut turned down the command, and Welles then offered it to David Dixon Porter. Welles wrote in his diary, "Admiral Porter is probably the best man for the service, better in some respects than Farragut."[52]

On 12 October, "Black Dave" Porter hoisted his flag on board *Malvern*. Porter received a squadron of about 100 vessels, which within two weeks grew to over 150. To ensure a successful operation against Wilmington, Welles gave Porter some of the best gunboats from the other squadrons. Porter quickly organized his command and wrote Welles that he could cover an army landing by the end of the month.[53]

The War Department chose Major General Godfrey Weitzel to command the army portion of the expedition, instead of Major General Benjamin F. Butler. The War Department had tried since the summer to replace Butler because of his "total unfitness to command in the field, and his general quarrelsome character." But his superiors feared his political connections and his "facilities for newspaper abuse."[54] Butler, who commanded the Army of the James and was Weitzel's superior, decided to lead the attack, since his men were to take part in the operation. This surprised Grant, who was not even aware of this fact until after the expedition had left. Butler and Porter had become enemies during the New Orleans campaign. Butler claimed that Porter hated him "as the devil hates holy water." Thus they never met in council during the planning of the attack on Fort Fisher.[55] Furthermore, both had large egos, which complicated the relationship and broadened the gap between them.

All the forts in the Cape Fear area had changed a great deal since the Navy Department first planned to capture Wilmington. Over 100 guns protected the two entrances and the approaches to the river. Fort Fisher, in particular, had grown immensely. By 1864, the fort incorporated some of the earlier outlying works and had become a fortification of tremendous size and strength. Federal engineers styled it the "Malakoff of the South." The fort appeared as an inverted L, with the base facing north. The land face, which commenced about 100 yards from the river and stretched about 500 yards, mounted twenty of the heaviest type seacoast guns. The sea face, approximately 1,300 yards long, mounted twenty-four equally heavy guns, including a 150-pound Armstrong rifle and a 170-pound Blakely, both imported from England. Both faces together stretched about a mile and a half, including rifle pits and palisades. The Confederates built the parapets twenty feet high at an angle of forty-five degrees, and they were sodded with marsh grass. To protect the gun crews, the parapets were not less than twenty-five feet thick. They mounted the guns in barbette and placed heavy traverses extending twelve feet high between the guns, to protect the guns and crews from enfilading fire. On the land face, the Confederates had placed a palisade fence of sharpened logs pierced for musketry and a system of subterranean torpedoes to check oncoming infantry. At the extreme end of the sea face stood the sixty-foot-high mound battery. The battery mounted two heavy guns and could produce a plunging fire onto vessels in the channel. Battery Buchanan lay behind the works on the river. This work could cover the landing of troops or act as a citadel to which an overpowered garrison might retreat and, with proper transportation, be carried out of danger.[56]

While Porter assembled his fleet, Butler developed the idea of capturing either Fort Caswell or Fort Fisher with a huge explosive weapon of great destructive power. Butler had studied several accidental explosions of large quantities of powder and concluded that it could be done intentionally with great effect against an enemy fortification. Porter quickly supported the idea in order to move the project swiftly along and believed it would work.[57]

To explode a large quantity of powder near Fort Fisher, Butler wanted to float a vessel as close to shore as possible. Butler secured the worthless 295-ton steamer *Louisiana* and loaded her with 215 tons of powder. She was to have carried 300 tons but had to leave the rest ashore; the weight of the powder increased her draft to such a depth that those planning the expedition feared she might not be able to get close to the fort. A Gomez fuse woven through the powder would simultaneously explode the cargo in the steamer. Two other devices acted as a backup of the first. Finally, they planned to light a small fire, in case all three failed to ignite the powder.[58]

The powder ship became the key element of the combined assault. The warships and Butler's transports were to rendezvous off the coast for the attack. *Louisiana* was to be exploded, with hopes that it would level the works and stun all the inhabitants. Porter believed that the explosion would kill everything within three miles and that "not a place containing a gun will be tenable—casements will go down . . . guns will be capsized, houses will fall . . . " as far as Wilmington and Smithville. A successful explosion would allow the gunboats to move into the river without interference, while the infantrymen would take the fort uncontested. The effort, though, was completely unorganized and uncoordinated as a result of the rift between Butler and Porter, which would ultimately lead to the failure of the attack. In letters to Fox, Porter claimed to have struck up a "great intimacy" with Butler, but privately Porter wrote of his dislike of the general in his journal, "There was an air about him as much to say—'I am going to blow Fort Fisher to the devil, and then blow my own horn!'"[59]

At the beginning of December, Grant began feeling "great anxiety" about the delays in the expedition. As the powder received its final preparations, Butler embarked 6,500 troops, two batteries of artillery, and some cavalry for the attack. On 13 December, General Butler ordered the transports to sail up the Chesapeake Bay and into the Potomac River as far as Mathias Point. That night, they steamed back to Cape Henry and anchored—an effort to deceive enemy spies. This ruse may have deceived the spies, but it also deceived Porter, whose warships steamed to Beaufort to wait for Butler's transports. The transports did not rendezvous at Beaufort; instead they arrived off New Inlet on the evening of 15 December and remained for several days waiting for Porter's warships. Porter's fleet arrived two days later on the 17th. The next day, the sea was too rough to land the troops, and Butler's transports, short of water and coal, returned to Beaufort to be resupplied.[60]

Rough weather delayed the return of the army transports for several days, and Porter decided to go ahead with the explosion of *Louisiana*. Believing that the result of the explosion would be severe, the warships withdrew twelve miles from the fort, drew their fires, and allowed the steam pressure in their boilers to fall. At 1:40 A.M. on the 24th, *Louisiana* exploded over 500 yards from the fort, but at least four distinct reports were heard. The explosion had no effect on the fort, and it seems only to have awakened the fort's inhabitants. One of the sentinels at the fort reportedly said he "reckoned one of them Yankee gunboats off thar had done busted her biler."[61]

From the beginning of the operation, both Porter and Butler had competed to see who could grab the laurels. Porter showed that he had had enough confidence in the powder vessel to explode her, hoping that the fort could be taken without Butler—making it a naval affair. But after it was discovered to be a complete failure, Porter immediately denied having any faith in it. At least one of the participating officers told the truth. Lieutenant Commander James Parker, the executive officer of *Minnesota*, wrote, "We all believed in it [the explosion], . . . from the Admiral down; but when it proved so laughable a failure we of the navy lied its paternity upon General Butler."[62]

The day before Christmas, only hours after the explosion of the powder vessel, Porter's fleet, over fifty warships in all, steamed toward the fort. As the wooden ships slowed, the ironclads *New Ironsides*, *Canonicus*, *Monadnock*, and *Mahopac* steamed to within a mile of the fort. The other ships took positions to the right and left forming an arc of more than a mile. A second line of gunboats lay seaward of the attacking vessels. *New Ironsides* took her position at about 11:30 and fired an eleven-inch shell over the fort. This signaled the start of the battle to the rest of the fleet, which maintained a heavy bombardment until about 5:00 that evening.[63]

As the battle raged, the Confederates, low on ammunition, replied at thirty-minute intervals, saving enough shot in case the Union gunboats attempted to pass the bar. Fort Fisher fired only 672 shots during the first day. The Union vessels kept up an intense bombardment at a rate estimated between 115 to 180 shells a minute. The gunboats directed most of their guns at the flagstaff of the parade ground, and much of it passed over the fort and into the river. Colonel William Lamb, the fort's commander, commented, "Never, since the invention on gunpowder, was there so much harmlessly expended, as in the first day's attack on Fort Fisher."[64] Butler's transports arrived during the battle, but too late in the day to disembark the troops.

At about 10:30 A.M. on Christmas Day, the fleet renewed the bombardment. The gunboats kept the fort's garrison within its bombproofs and aided the landing of Butler's troops, which did not begin until 2:00 P.M. Captain Oliver S. Glisson in the side-wheel steamer *Santiago de Cuba* covered the landing of the troops, while Captain James Alden brought the large steam sloop *Brooklyn* as close to shore as possible. Shelling the woods, *Brooklyn* drove out any rebels that might contest the debarkation of Butler's troops. While Butler's men landed, Porter sent boats in charge of William Cushing to sound the New Inlet bar. Porter contemplated that his gunboats might attack the fort in reverse if a channel could be found. When a shell from Battery Buchanan smashed one of the launches, the Union seamen withdrew.[65]

As the afternoon progressed, Butler managed to land about 2,300 men. His troops moved down the beach and formed a skirmish line about 150 yards from the fort. Butler claimed that heavy surf rendered "further landing nearly impractical." General Weitzel and Colonel Cyrus B. Comstock of Grant's staff also went ashore. Weitzel and Butler had been ordered by Grant to entrench across the peninsula even if they could not assault the fort, the major object being to close the port of Wilmington and to cooperate with the navy to capture the fort. On board the army vessel *Chamberlain*, Butler reconnoitered to within several hundred yards of the fort and found the works uninjured by the naval bombardment, whereupon he concluded that an attack would be suicidal. Comstock and Weitzel concurred, and they ordered a withdrawal. The heavy surf that prevented the reinforcement of the beachhead did not keep Butler from reembarking his men. The navy helped with the withdrawal in a fierce rain, during which the surf became so heavy that every boat that went inside the breakers swamped. The navy managed to get all the infantry off, with the exception of 700 who remained there during the night.[66]

Butler's decision to withdraw was wise. The fort had at least 1,300 men inside and seventeen unharmed guns on the land face. Butler, like Porter, had relied on the powder vessel to destroy the fort, and when it failed, he was left without another plan. The fleet had not been able to tell the effect of the bombardment because of the absence of a breeze, which had caused the smoke to hang over the fort and had masked the bombardment. The lack of fire from the fort had deceived Porter, who believed that the Confederates were unable to return the fire of the warships. In fact, during the battle, only five guns had been disabled—three by fire from the fleet and two by bursting. Shortly after this fiasco, Grant, having "contemplated no withdrawal, or no failure after a landing was made, removed Butler from command."[67]

Burst shells littered the fort, causing Lieutenant Aeneas Armstrong to remark that one could "walk on nothing but iron." The fleet fired about 21,000 projectiles weighing over 1,000,000 pounds and had succeeded in killing only three and wounding sixty-one. In contrast, the fort had fired only 1,272 projectiles. Butler's losses for the attack were extremely light—only two killed. The gunboats, meanwhile, had suffered a larger number of casualties, at least 18 killed and 51 wounded—in part the result of the bursting of several guns and the scalding of seamen when enemy shells struck the boilers.[68]

Both Butler and Porter blamed each other for the debacle. Porter, who did not want to take any responsibility for this attack, quickly blamed Butler for the failure. The rear admiral did not assume any responsibility for the squadron's failure to make the fort's guns inoperable. He likewise claimed that Butler had put Weitzel in charge so that he, Butler, could claim credit if the expedition succeeded and blame Weitzel if it failed. Porter also asserted that the powder "created a perfect panic, stunned and disabled" the fort's garrison and that 200 men could have taken the fort. He further told Welles that the naval gunfire had "completely silenced" the fort. Porter made sure that his views were amply known and wrote to Welles after the attack, "I intend to write my share of the history of this rebellion and place it on record where future historians can have access to it."[69]

Meanwhile, General William Tecumseh Sherman's movement

northward through South Carolina increased the significance of the capture of the port of Wilmington. The port became increasingly important as a depot and as insurance to the success and safety of the Carolinas campaign. The War Department remained committed to Wilmington's capture but made several changes before another expedition got under way. It relieved Weitzel of command and replaced him with Major General Alfred E. Terry, who received the same instructions as his predecessor, except that the department ordered him to return only if a beachhead could not be established.[70]

In the first week of the new year, the vessels again began to rendezvous in Beaufort. On the night of the 12th, Colonel Lamb, walking on the ramparts, spotted the "lights of the great armada, as one after another appeared above the horizon." The new fleet that assembled off the fort had the greatest firepower to that time in United States naval history, 627 guns in over sixty vessels.[71]

At dawn on the 13th, *New Ironsides* repeated her previous role and once again opened the battle by firing an eleven-inch shell. Porter had arranged his vessels into five groups. Four monitors lay approximately one-half mile off the northeast salient of the fort. A second line of gunboats lay seaward of them, with *New Ironsides* in the van; both of these lines attacked the land face of the fort. Two other lines of warships lay off the sea face about a mile from the beach and fired at this portion of the fort. A fifth group of vessels, divided into four divisions, lay outside the attacking warships and acted as reserves, landed troops, and carried dispatches.[72]

Two things differed in the naval gunnery in the second attack. Porter had ordered the vessels not to waste their fire on the flagstaffs and to concentrate on the guns of the fort. The gunboats also maintained their fire during the night of the 14th to prevent the enemy from repairing the damage to the works and remounting their guns. As in the first fight, the fort only responded with "slow and deliberate firing" because of a shortage of ammunition.[73]

Terry's troops steamed from Beaufort in nineteen transports on the 12th. At 8:00 A.M. on the following day, 200 boats began landing troops, and by 2:00 that afternoon, Terry had approximately 8,000 men ashore. The infantrymen passed through marshes and thick underbrush, but by that afternoon, they had dug in, thereby preventing reinforcements to the fort by land. When the fleet arrived, Colonel Lamb had 800 men in the fort, and he received only 700 reinforcements before the battle began. Along with the reinforcements came Major General William H. C. Whiting and his staff. Whiting had been succeeded in command of the Cape Fear region by Major General Braxton Bragg. Whiting approached Colonel Lamb and said to him above the roar of the bombardment, "Lamb my boy, I have come to share your fate. You and your garrison are to be sacrificed." Lamb replied, "Don't say so, General; we shall certainly whip the enemy again."[74] But Bragg, instead of making every preparation possible to relieve the fort, was hastily removing stores and making preparations to withdraw from Wilmington.

At 8:00 A.M. on 15 January, after two days of bombardment, the fleet increased its fire on the land face to ensure that the guns there were inoperable. Sharply at 10:00, a naval column of 400 marines and 1,600 sailors landed. The seamen went ashore with cutlasses, pistols, and rifles, carrying spades to entrench. Shortly after noon, Braxton Bragg countered this Union move by sending about 1,000 men in a steamer to reinforce Lamb, but only about 350 managed to get into the fort about thirty minutes before the Union soldiers stormed the works. The reinforcements merely replaced those killed and wounded during the bombardment, bringing the total effective in the fort to about 1,500.[75]

The Union forces planned a two-pronged attack, with both army and navy forces advancing simultaneously. Porter, who wanted his men to be a part of the assault, instructed the seamen to attack the northeast salient of the fort, while the soldiers attacked the land face near the river. The naval column of 400 marines and 1,600 sailors, led by Lieutenant Commander K. Randolph Breese, marched to within a mile of the fort with the marines in the van. Lieutenant Samuel W. Preston led an entrenching detail forward to dig rifle pits to protect the naval column's assault.[76]

At approximately 3:30, the bombardment stopped, and the shrill steam whistles of the fleet signaled the start of the assault. Breese, observing the movement by the infantry, prepared his seamen to "board the fort in a seaman like manner." Breese, though, had mistaken a feint as the infantry's main attack and sent the seamen ahead. The tars rushed gallantly but unsupported toward the fort, and the Confederates cut them down with two Napoleon guns and one ten-inch Columbiad.

Grapeshot and canister poured into the column, cutting large gaps in the ranks. The marines who occupied the rifle pits, and whose duty was to provide covering fire for the advancing seamen, had been halted too far from the fort to provide effective cover. The rebels thus fired from the parapets without interference. The seamen were "cut down like sheep" by the murderous fire, and the column became disorganized. By the time the seamen had reached the palisades, they resembled a mob. Those who could found cover; others, observing that their support had faltered and that many of their officers lay dead and wounded, began to retreat in disorder.[77]

The naval assault, at the expense of hundreds of casualties, distracted the fort's defenders, and the attacking Union infantry managed to make a lodgment at Shepherd's Battery on the left. The battle that ensued may have been one of the most vicious that occurred during the war. The Confederates contested each traverse, which had to be taken from them by hand-to-hand fighting. Men fired into each others' faces and clubbed one another with their guns. The Union warships supported the infantry by well-directed fire from their guns and helped drive the Confederates from the traverses one by one. The remnants of the naval column, after being reorganized, later supported the infantry in the fight. During the battle, both Whiting and Lamb were wounded, and the command of the fort fell to Major James Reilly. Reilly continued the resistance and eventually retreated to Battery Buchanan. Here he found spiked guns and no transportation. With no other options remaining, Reilly surrendered at 10:00 that night.[78]

The blame for this Confederate defeat can be put squarely on the shoulders of Braxton Bragg, who believed from the beginning that the fort would be captured. Bragg had 6,000 of Lee's best troops within three miles of the fort. He claimed to have made a heavy demonstration at the Union rear, but the Union line was "maintained without the loss or injury of a single Union soldier."[79] Lamb and his men held off their attackers for nearly six hours, and reinforcements within the fort, or pressure on the Union rear, would certainly have influenced the outcome of the battle. Bragg's greatest fear may have been a direct approach by the federals on Wilmington, had he committed to a defense of the fort. But Union troops, doing so, would have had to break away from their naval support, putting them in a precarious position. Bragg could have placed half of his force in the fort, and if the situation had called for an evacuation, the garrison could have crossed the river and reached Wilmington ahead of the Union forces. Had the Union troops marched on Wilmington, the rest of the Confederate troops, strong defenses, and a lack of knowledge of the area would had impeded their progress.

Bragg's failure to make a stand allowed the Union to gain possession of the river, which was a crucial blow to the Confederacy. The loss of Wilmington, the last major port open to the South, forced the Confederate armies to fight the remaining months of the war with the materials on hand or with those that could be produced. General Robert E. Lee now had to rely on impressment for things that once had been brought through the blockade.[80] Likewise, the navy yard at Wilmington was burned, along with the ironclad *Wilmington*, which perhaps could have helped to contest the control of the river. Furthermore, Bragg failed to interfere with Grant's plans to support Sherman's march through North Carolina.

This well-executed and well-coordinated amphibious assault was a great stroke for the Union. The loss of Fort Fisher, the key to the works in the area, forced the abandonment of Forts Caswell, Campbell, Holmes, and Johnston. However, the cost of this Union victory was high. The army suffered about 1,000 casualties, while the navy incurred nearly 400. This nearly equaled the number of effectives that Lamb had in the fort. Terry claimed to have captured more than 2,000 officers and men, but Lamb only had 1,900 all told within the fort, including sick, wounded, and killed. These losses seemed extremely light considering that during the two attacks, the vessels had thrown in over 50,000 shells, equaling over 1,000 pounds of metal per linear yard of the fort.[81]

The victory celebration that filled the sky with pyrotechnics during the night ended quickly the next day when a powder magazine in the fort exploded. The celebration of the surrender became uncontrollable, and intoxicated soldiers and seaman alike wandered around the fort looking for plunder. A board of inquiry concluded that one of these men entered an unguarded bombproof and caused an explosion, which killed twenty-five, wounded sixty-six, and left thirteen missing.[82]

Porter, impressed by the strength of Fort Fisher, wrote to Gideon Welles that the fortifications on the lower Cape Fear River were "not exceeded by anything of the kind in the world." The Union forces learned the real value of the inlet to Sherman's campaign over the next month at New Inlet, as nearly 150 vessels arrived carrying coal, stores, cattle, horses, lumber, troops, mules, forage, ammunition, and sutler and commissary stores.[83]

The battle was over, but Wilmington still remained in Confederate hands. Wilmington's railroad connections could pose a threat or could benefit Sherman's move through North Carolina, and thus the Union forces forged ahead to capture the city. When Bragg might have rallied his forces for a stubborn defense, he chose to retreat, and therefore the evacuation of the forts was haphazard and inefficient. Bragg's greatest blunder during the evacuation was to leave behind the heavy ordnance of the coastal forts, leaving little available to defend the town. The Union gunboats would still have to pass twenty miles up a narrow river, past numerous forts and obstacles, and then face the defenses of the town, which were extensive. The defenses consisted of earthworks, which made valuable use of ponds, dams, rivers, and creeks around the eastern side of the city. The Confederates had protected the city itself with large guns mounted in four forts on the eastern side of the river.[84] Bragg never planned to defend the city, failing to consider Wilmington's value as a Union depot and as means of open communication with Sherman.

Porter consolidated his captures with one of his first moves. On the 18th, he sent Cushing in *Monticello* to Smithville. The town's inhabitants surrendered without a struggle, and by the 20th, the Confederates evacuated all the forts south of New Inlet. Porter forwarded orders that none of the town's inhabitants were to leave. He ordered his officers to "allow no outrages to be committed on the property of the inhabitants . . . [and to] punish anyone severely who resists these orders." Porter also ordered that the lights at the bars be trimmed in a normal manner at the inlets, so that blockade runners that had not heard of the fall of the forts would come into the river. The blockade runners *Owl* and *Rattlesnake* both steamed among the gunboats after the fall of Fort Fisher. But their captains sensed something was wrong and escaped before the Union ships could detect them. Porter's ruse worked on three less lucky ships, the valuable steamers *Stag*, *Charlotte*, and *Blenheim*.[85]

A week was spent getting many of the gunboats and supplies over the bar in preparation for a move up the river. On 22 January, the little wooden vessel *Pequot* steamed up Cape Fear to draw the fire of Fort Anderson, the largest defensive work on the river. *Pequot* fired only seven shells, and the garrison of the fort returned only two shots. After staying in range for two hours, *Pequot* returned to her anchorage downriver. The navy lay in the river for several weeks, while additional troops arrived for a move toward Wilmington. Even though the gunboats lay idle, the crews remained on the defensive and made preparations for a move on Wilmington. The vessels experienced problems similar to those in the James River: the threat of field artillery, torpedoes, and a small number of poorly armed enemy gunboats, including the torpedo boat *Squib*. The crews thus busied themselves rigging torpedo catchers and mounting eleven-inch guns in place of the 100-pound rifles in order to attack Fort Anderson.[86]

Porter set up an elaborate picket system for the vessels as a precaution against torpedoes and torpedo vessels. Six of his gunboats kept a double-banked boat at the gangway ready to shove off if a lookout sighted a torpedo boat. At night, four vessels took station just out of gunshot of Fort Anderson and sent picket boats ahead equipped with pikes, Sharpes rifles, revolvers, and cutlasses to protect the rest of the fleet.[87]

On the evening of 28 January, General Grant, Major General Terry, and their staffs, along with Assistant Secretary of the Navy Fox, all met on board *Malvern*. Pouring over maps and charts, they discussed future operations to capture Wilmington and later movements to support General Sherman's 60,000-man army when it marched north from Georgia. Under the leadership of Terry, the soldiers had entrenched two miles above Fort Fisher, and gunboats lay close ashore protecting their flanks.[88]

Grant placed General John M. Schofield in charge of capturing Wilmington and opening communication with Sherman, while keeping General Bragg from interfering with the campaign. It was decided that Major General Jacob D. Cox would land a corps at Smithville and then march toward Fort Anderson on the west bank of the Cape Fear River to make a coordinated attack with the gunboats. Schofield changed those plans after arriving at Cape Fear on 9 February. Instead of advancing on the west side of the river as agreed, he decided to attack the Confederate positions on the east side of the river. After calling for a council of war and consulting Porter, Cox, and Terry, Schofield decided not to wait for the rest of his troops and attacked with the nearly 13,000 on hand. On 11 February, Schofield pushed Terry's troops up the east bank toward the Confederate earthwork Sugar Loaf, about six miles north of Fort Fisher. Porter sent his gunboats up the river to engage the Confederate batteries at Fort Anderson and Sugar Loaf for four hours on 11 February. Fort Anderson answered only occasionally. The Union forces drove in the enemy pickets and entrenched. Schofield planned to use the gunboats to land his men by sea in the rear of the rebel troops. That night, Porter sent Cushing to examine the river, and the latter managed to get within a mile of Wilmington. On his trip he discovered that the Confederates had obstructed the river with heavy pilings opposite Fort Anderson. A northeast wind caused rough weather, which canceled this movement on the 14th. Schofield then decided to switch his operations back to the west bank. Protected by Porter's gunboats, the army moved back across the river, where it had more room to maneuver.[89]

Thus far, Porter's gunboats had merely annoyed the Confederates whenever possible, while keeping the enemy from strengthening its works. On 17 February, the gunboats began working their way up the river to attack Fort Anderson. Schofield and 8,000 men meanwhile advanced from Smithville, nine miles away. The monitor *Montauk* took an advanced position to fire on the fort, and the wooden steamer *Pawtuxet*, *Lenapee*, *Unadilla*, and *Pequot* fired from a safer distance. Fort Anderson "answered pretty briskly, but quieted down by sunset."[90]

On the 18th, the vessels engaged the fort again, while Schofield moved to flank or isolate Confederate positions. *Montauk* and fourteen other gunboats maintained a "heavy fire through the day" and into the night. During the two days of bombardment, the Confederates struck the gunboats many times but did no major damage and inflicted only a few casualties.[91]

That night, Porter had a "bogus monitor" built out of an old scow and some canvas and barrel staves. Released during a flood tide, it floated past Fort Anderson as if steaming up the river. The primary motive for this trick was to have the enemy expend torpedoes on her, which had the right effect but did not harm the scow. William Cushing took credit for the fake monitor and claimed that the Confederates had retreated without spiking their guns. This sham monitor had hardly elicited any fear from the garrison. It was the Union forces moving up the west bank and gradually flanking the Confederate positions on the river that had forced a withdrawal.[92]

The rebels abandoned Fort Anderson on the 19th and fell back to Town Creek. After the abandonment of the fort, Porter employed about fifty boats to drag for torpedoes in the river, removing the infernal machines. The squadron likewise ferried General Cox's division over the creeks where the bridges had been burned by the enemy.[93]

Porter did not let Schofield's slow manner deter him, and after the abandonment of Fort Anderson, he sent his gunboats to clear the river of obstructions and torpedoes. Confederate engineers had placed obstructions in the river consisting of chains, pilings, and three sunken vessels, *Arctic*, *Yadkin*, and the blockade runner *North Heath*. Late on the 19th, Porter's men, in over a dozen launches, advanced within sight of the Confederate river batteries on a bluff three miles below Wilmington. Fort Campbell fired a few rounds at the launches, and they withdrew.[94]

On 20 February, the Union gunboats slowly advanced up the Cape Fear River, while the army pushed up both the right and left banks. At 3:00 in the afternoon, the gunboats opened a terrific fire at 1,300 yards on Forts Lee, Meares, and Campbell (called Fort Strong by the Union forces). The Union gunboats did a great deal of damage, but the batteries' high elevation protected them from destruction. Porter had lost patience with Schofield's manner of handling the campaign and commented the day before that Wilmington would have been captured "long ago had Grant sent Terry men and kept Schofield away."[95]

The Confederates worked all night making preparations for the next day's fight. The army had meanwhile advanced close to the city. The rebels now could only hope to retard the advance further by sinking a few Union vessels. On the night of the 20th, they sent down 200 torpedoes, each armed with 100 pounds of powder. The Union crews acted swiftly and sent boats ahead to snag the torpedoes and to spread seines across the river to stop them. Men with rifles took stations to fire into the torpedoes to set them off or to let water into them. The effort to neutralize the torpedoes did not completely succeed. One struck the wheel of *Osceola* and "blew her wheelhouse to pieces, and knocked down her bulkheads inboard." A boat from *Shawmut* also came in contact with one, destroying the launch and killing two and wounding two.[96]

The next day, the gunboats continued firing on the forts, while the Confederate soldiers in Wilmington marched, countermarched, and rode trains back and forth in an attempt to make the federal troops believe reinforcements were arriving. In reality, Bragg was removing all the stores and supplies he could. The Union forces were never fooled, because the billowing smoke pouring forth from the city gave away the real purpose. The Confederate forces, not being able to hold the federal troops in check, withdrew up the north side of the North East Cape Fear River before daylight on the 22nd. The Union forces entered the town under no opposition early the next morning, followed by Porter's fully dressed gunboats. The gunboats fired salutes not only to signal victory but also to celebrate Washington's birthday, a combination that they considered a good omen.[97]

Even though the fighting had ceased for the North Atlantic Blockading Squadron in Cape Fear, the vessels performed reconnaissance missions up the river and in the North East Cape Fear River. The double-ender *Lenapee* went as far as Robinson, twenty miles from Fayetteville, only ten days after the fall of Wilmington. On 12 March, the little side-wheel steamer *Eolus* opened communication with General Sherman in Fayetteville and remained in the city until the troops crossed the river there.[98]

The Navy Department's proposal to capture Wilmington during the first months of the war did not bear fruit until early 1865. Thus, for four years, this port helped to sustain Confederate military forces, eventually making it the most important port in the South. Interservice cooperation had been crucial to the capture of the forts and the city. Delays can be attributed to the rivalries between the army and navy during most of the war, which not only interfered with the overall planning and strategy in the eastern theater but also had postponed the capture of Wilmington until the war was nearly over. The first attack on Fort Fisher is a perfect example of the failure that occurred as a result of a lack of unity of command. The expedition may have been destined to fail from the start because of the bad rapport between Butler and Porter. The second attack and the capture of Wilmington, however, was a model operation. It reflected a close coordination and efficiency and proved to be one of

the better interservice expeditions of the war. The capture of the forts
guarding Cape Fear dealt a severe blow to the Confederacy and greatly
contributed to the South's surrender three months later.

FOURTEEN

Weary of the war

Conclusion

In 1865, the Confederacy lay in its death throes. It was surrounded and virtually cut off from the outside, while the Union armies systematically cut wide swaths across the South and destroyed its means to wage war. The Union navy played a decisive role in this defeat, yet scholars have generally failed to credit the navy with the praise it deserves.

The navy's great impact on the war was made possible by the foresight of a few Union leaders and hinged on some of the decisions made during the first months of the war. Gideon Welles inherited a fleet composed mainly of sailing warships, but he quickly grasped the need for steam vessels. His administration built and purchased a huge steam-powered navy capable of blockading the southern coast and supporting the invasion of the South. The United States ended the war with a large and powerful navy, second in the world only to Great Britain.

Steam-propelled warships were largely untried when the war began. Gideon Welles, with great vision, built only steam vessels, thereby creating a modern navy. The use of steam would prove to be decisive. While compromising range and endurance, it allowed the vessels the greater speed that they needed to catch

blockade runners. Unforeseen were the contributions that steam gunboats would make in the rivers. The navy's presence made it possible for
the army to advance and be resupplied or withdrawn virtually at will.

The most often recognized role of the navy during the war was its
maintenance of the blockade. More significant was the Union navy's
control of the ocean and inland waters. The Confederate navy generally
maintained a defensive posture, made only a few attempts to raise the
blockade, and partially succeeded in driving Union flagged shipping
from the seas with commerce raiders. This strategy, however, never
challenged the Union's ability to wage war or its ability to keep its
warships at sea. By early 1862, most of the Confederate ports in the
operational area of the North Atlantic Blockading Squadron were in
Union hands—the most effective way of stopping trade. The closure of
these eastern ports elongated General Lee's supply line and made his
army more vulnerable to the successes or failures of the ships running
the blockade. For the next three years, the squadron watched the coast,
stopping only a small percentage of vessels trying to run the blockade.
The blockade, though not airtight, kept all but a small number of
specialized ships from even attempting to risk capture.

The Confederacy never seriously contested the Union navy's domi-
nation of the seas. It did use its ironclads as mobile forts to control some
rivers and to protect troop positions ashore. This strategy was successful
until the Union forces concentrated overwhelming forces against these
warships or captured their bases, which forced their destruction.

Even without control of the water, the South managed to import
large amounts of arms and munitions to sustain its troops. Yet, late in
the war, Lee's army went hungry, while the Southern states enjoyed a
surplus crop and had brought nearly 1,000,000 rations through the
blockade. In March 1865, there were about 27,000,000 rations of bread
and over 26,000,000 rations of meat in the Confederacy.[1]

The breakdown in transportation was a major reason that these
rations and other supplies were not available to the Southern armies.
The rivers and inland waters of the South had always been important
transportation arteries. The Union navy, early in the war, crippled
inland waterway transportation in both North Carolina and Virginia.
The Union gunboats immediately controlled the Chesapeake Bay and,
by early 1862, controlled most of the navigable rivers and the sounds of

North Carolina. This situation forced the Confederacy to find less practical routes to maintain its logistical connections. The squadron went a step further by embarking on a campaign to destroy small local trading vessels and to interdict the movement of local supplies.

The railroad system also suffered during the war. The railroads of the South were poorly constructed, understocked (partly through attrition), and lacked a standard gauge.[2] This weakness of the Confederacy was aggravated by naval activity. The squadron had closed or successfully constricted trade into a few ports by the middle of 1862. This situation caused all the cargoes to be funneled through a small number of transportation lines, straining the poor and limited rail system, which the war effort depended upon.

The South benefited by keeping Wilmington open to trade and importing the most crucial materials to carry on the war. Food and supplies brought into Wilmington traveled northward over the Wilmington and Weldon Railroad, which was limited to only 200 tons of cargo a day. The South fought much of the war by maintaining its large armies at the front without sufficient logistical support. The inadequate rail system could not maintain the huge amount of supplies needed in the field. Most of the ports in the South that had rail connections were captured or closed by mid-1862. This situation crippled and overloaded the other rail lines. Movement of supplies during the war was further hampered by lines that did not connect, which caused an abundance of congestion, confusion, delays, and great loss.[3]

The South might have solved some of its most crucial transportation problems had the blockade never been implemented. The South would have enjoyed the luxury of importing rails, locomotives, iron, manufacturing equipment, and marine engines. The South instead had to choose between the manufacture of naval ironclads or an expansion of its railroads. In many cases, the iron used on the ships was desperately needed for rail transportation. By the end of the war, the Confederacy was deficient in both railroads and ironclads.

The Confederacy benefited by the Union's inability to stop completely all of its foreign trade. But this was negated by a poorly run interior logistical system. The Union army in the eastern theater failed to exploit this great weakness of the South. Federal forces controlled eastern North Carolina for three years and continued to allow the rebels the use of the Wilmington-Weldon line. With so many other ports closed, had the Union leaders chosen to interrupt or destroy this line, it would have virtually closed down all north–south traffic. This may have starved Lee's army into surrender or forced him to move closer to his lines of supply.

To assess the total impact of the blockade, one would have to look at the entire war economy and the military logistical system of the South, which goes beyond the scope of this study. Suffice it to say that the Union blockade was an important factor in the destruction of the South's ability to wage war.

The squadron's support of infantry positions and the participation in combined operations was often innovative and highly effective and was essential to victory. In both the eastern and the western theaters, the navy permitted the projection of power by the army forces. In the eastern theater, the navy allowed the Union generals to change strategically the center of gravity, by using the rivers as bases to push farther into Confederate territory. The western army leaders tended to understand that naval cooperation was indispensable. In contrast, those in the East, failed to plan many joint projects and acted singularly in almost every campaign. This was a crucial mistake in the East, because the Confederates had less room to maneuver, and the navy could have brought the Union advantages to bear with decisive victories.

The conspicuous difference between the eastern and western theaters was the lack of interservice cooperation. The navy seemed hamstrung during the war because of separate service traditions, organization, doctrine, and lack of unified command. Given a greater understanding and a more cooperative spirit for planning and strategy, Union army and navy coordination would have shortened the war.

This lack of vision and cooperation was evident in North Carolina. Combined Union forces began the conflict with sweeping successes in the coastal areas of the state. The occupation of the eastern counties, along with the southeastern corner of Virginia, was done evidently with no apparent continuing strategy, except to deprive the Confederacy of territory. The Union efforts seemed to have lost direction and purpose. More detrimental to the Union war effort was the services' failure to cooperate in an effort to destroy the ironclads as they were being built in

North Carolina. Once completed, they allowed the Confederacy to project its limited power exponentially.

Strategically the Union armies depended upon the navy to maintain control of the interior waterways. This allowed a greater freedom of movement because their communications and logistics were secure. In the East, the major campaigns succeeded when supported by the navy. In North Carolina, more so than in Virginia, the Union army critically relied on the naval forces. With control of the major cities, the physical isolation subjected each to capture by a superior Confederate force. The Union navy usually prevented this by its presence. Only when the Union navy lost control of the water did the army fail to hold the towns. The army relied so heavily on the gunboats for protection in North Carolina that until late in the war it rarely managed to advance beyond their fire support except for minor raids.

In the East, once the army and navy began to move in unison, the combined operations allowed the Union forces to bring superior power to bear. Only Grant and McClellan used the navy to any extent and found that they could easily move their armies deep into Confederate territory. With naval support, they successfully pressed the rebels to the outskirts of Richmond.

So important was naval power that the final campaign of General Grant would have been difficult or impossible in its execution without the support of the navy. The warships' services were invaluable in protecting logistical bases, helping with the transportation of troops, and providing fire support for Union positions. The Union used advanced bases; protected by gunboats, they were less vulnerable to attack. The bases shortened the Union forces' lines of supply and communication and facilitated the campaigns. In fact, the strategic advantage that the gunboats gave the federal armies was essential to Union victory and may be compared in some ways to modern air strikes and air cover. Furthermore, the mere presence of the Union navy along the coast made it mandatory for the Confederates to disperse their forces to protect vulnerable targets and maintain a defensive perimeter. One might note that in both the eastern and western theaters the naval forces virtually defined the reach of the federal forces.

The mobility that the Union naval forces furnished the United States

Army provided an extreme advantage over the South's forces. In North Carolina and Virginia, the rebels enjoyed the advantage of interior lines of communication. They used rivers and roads and a rail network that allowed an important but limited movement of troops and supplies. Combined Union army and naval raids constantly threatened and sometimes destroyed these interior lines. More importantly, interior lines lost their effect when the Union forces pushed up the rivers and periodically penetrated across them. Thus the Union naval force immobilized a great number of Confederate forces, restricted the South's strategy, and caused a great deal of material attrition.

As has been pointed out, the projection of power in campaigns and logistical support for the army was crucial. But the damage to rebel logistics has never been clearly annunciated. Union naval raids into the interior destroyed Confederate communications and supplies and hampered the Southern war effort. The squadron destroyed and captured hundreds of vessels with Confederate cargoes. Singularly none of these cargoes critically affected the struggle, but added together, their importance is immense and the losses crippling. The presence of a powerful navy had a tremendous cumulative effect on Confederate logistics.

The Southern states failed to exploit situations that they might have turned to their advantage. With the exception of Secretary of the Navy Mallory, the leaders of the Confederacy showed little appreciation of the benefits that the United States enjoyed with a powerful navy. Jefferson Davis's complete lack of understanding toward naval power hindered Mallory's plans of building a larger service. The Confederates, moreover, usually failed to coordinate their efforts with the small naval forces at their disposal. The Union army increasingly became dependent on its navy. So dependent was the army that, had the Confederacy developed a successful naval building program, the war may have ended in a stalemate. The problems of the Confederacy were numerous and more far-reaching than can be concluded here. Certainly its lack of a navy contributed to its problems and denied the South the similar advantages that the Union warships provided the Union armies.

The Union blockade succeeded in isolating the South. It also prevented the Confederates from establishing a full-scale war economy, and by early 1865, the South had expended a great deal of its resources to win the war. The Confederate economy lay in shambles, and inflation had skyrocketed out of control. Raw materials, manpower, and industrial facilities were all in short supply, were inaccessible, or had been consumed or destroyed. The states' rights doctrine of the Confederacy failed to unite the states into coordinated action for the benefit of all. The troops in the field were demoralized, and the last ports of the Confederacy had been closed. Confederate Secretary of the Navy Mallory wrote in April 1865 that the people of the South were "weary of the war and desire peace."[4] The United States Navy was a key factor in making this happen.

Notes

1. The Navy's Response to War

1. The first proclamation included all the southern states except North Carolina and Virginia. The proclamation on 27 April placed those two under blockade. Abraham Lincoln to William Seward, 19, 27 April 1861, Richard Rush et al., eds., *Official Records of the Union and Confederate Navies in the War of the Rebellion,* 31 vols. (Washington, D.C.: Government Printing Office, 1894–1927), ser. 1, 5:620–21 (hereafter cited as *ORN*).

2. U.S. Congress, House, *Number of Vessels in the Navy,* H. Ex. Doc. 159, 40th Cong., 2d sess., 1868, 1; James Russell Soley, *The Navy in the Civil War: The Blockade and the Cruisers* (New York: Charles Scribner's Sons, 1883), 12. The ninety ships included ten ships of the line, ten frigates, twenty sloops of war, three brigs, three store vessels, six receiving ships, seven screw steam sloops, nine third-class steam sloops, two steam tenders, and the *Naugatuck.* "Statement of the Number and Names of Vessels Belonging to or Connected with the Navy on the First of April 1861." Copy of Statement No. 1 called for by House Resolution 6, January 1868. Mobilization and Demobilization, Subject File OL, Naval Records Collections of the Office of Naval Records and Library, Record Group 45, National Archives, Washington, D.C. Hereafter all references to Record Groups will be simply RG and to the National

Archives NA. Soley, *Navy in the Civil War,* 13–14; James M. Merrill, *The Rebel Shore: The Story of Union Sea Power in the Civil War* (Boston: Little, Brown, 1957), 5–6; James Mason Hoppin, *The Life of Andrew H. Foote, Rear-Admiral United States Navy* (New York: Harper and Brothers, 1874), 146; Vessels Ordered Home from Foreign Stations (n.d.), Subject File OL, RG 45, NA.

    3. Pritchard to D. G. Duncan, 15 April 1861, R. N. Scott and et al., eds., *The War of the Rebellion: A Compilation of the Official Records of the Union and Confederate Armies,* 128 vols. (Washington, D.C.: Government Printing Office, 1880–1901), ser. 1, 51 (pt. 2): 11 (hereafter cited as *ORA*).

    4. Welles to Hiram Paulding, 18 April 1861, *ORN*, ser. 1, 4:282; Journal of Commander Stephen C. Rowan, December 1859–April 1861, Stephen C. Rowan Papers, Entry 395, Subseries 28, RG 45, NA; Letter of Edwin McCauley Dropped Off at the Navy Department, 1 March 1890, Area File, Area 7, Entry 463, RG 45, NA; Paulding to Welles, 23 April 1861, *ORN*, ser. 1, 4:290; John G. Nicolay and John Hay, *Abraham Lincoln: A History,* 10 vols. (New York: Century, 1890), 4:96, 144–47; Winfield Scott to Horatio G. Wright, 19 April 1861, *ORA*, ser. 1, 2:23; Thomas J. Wertenbaker, *Norfolk: Historic Southern Port* (Durham, N.C.: Duke University Press, 1931), 227; U.S. Congress, Senate, *Surrender and Destruction of Navy Yards,* S. Rept. 37, 37th Cong., 2d sess., 1861, 70.

    5. Nelson Morehouse Blake, *William Mahone of Virginia: Soldier and Political Insurgent* (Richmond: Garrett and Massie, 1935), 40; John D. Hayes, "Loss of the Norfolk Yard," *Ordnance* 46 (September–October 1961): 223; Horatio Wright to E. D. Townsend, 26 April 1861, *ORA*, ser. 1, 2:21.

    6. Carroll Storrs Alden and Allan Westcott, *The United States Navy: A History* (Chicago: J. B. Lippincott, 1943), 149–51; John Lenthall to Welles, 8 November 1861, Letters Sent to the Secretary of the Navy from the Bureau of Construction and Repair, Entry 49, RG 19, NA; *ORN*, ser. 2, vol. 1, passim; Charles Brandon Boynton, *The History of the Navy during the Rebellion* (New York: D. Appleton, 1867), 24; David D. Porter, *The Naval History of the Civil War* (New York: Sherman, 1886), 32.

    7. *Diary of Gideon Welles*, ed. Howard K. Beale, 3 vols. (New York: W. W. Norton, 1960), 1:53–54 (hereafter cited as *Welles Diary*); Entry 395, Subseries 28, RG 45, NA; Kenneth M. Stampp, "Lincoln and the Strategy of Defense in the Crisis of 1861," *Journal of Southern History* 11 (August 1945): 309, passim.

    8. Glyndon G. Van Deusen, *William Henry Seward* (New York: Oxford University Press, 1967), 300. The nations of Europe adhered to the rules and regulations set down in the Declaration of Paris in 1856. Most of the European and South American nations, forty–six in all, had signed the declaration, which

included four major points dealing with maritime law: (1) privateering is and remains abolished; (2) the neutral flag covers the enemy's goods, with the exception of contraband of war; (3) neutral goods, with the exception of contraband of war, are not liable to capture under the enemy's flag; and (4) for a blockade to be binding, it must be maintained by a force sufficient to prevent access to the coast of the enemy. The United States had not signed the declaration because of the abolition of privateering. It reversed itself on 24 April 1861, when Seward instructed his agents abroad that the United States would now be bound by the declaration. The advantages to the Union would be twofold: Seward hoped that he could stop Southern privateering and deny the Confederate government recognition as a belligerent, but he failed in both. Henry Wheaton, *Elements of International Law* (New York: Oceana, 1964), 381; Seward to Charles Francis Adams, 7 September 1861, quoted in Carlton Savage, *Policy of the United States toward Maritime Commerce in War,* 2 vols. (Washington, D.C.: Government Printing Office, 1934; rpt., New York: Kraus Reprint, 1969), 1:434; Law, International (n.d.), Subject File VL, RG 45, NA; D. P. Crook, *The North, the South, and the Powers 1861–1865* (New York: John Wiley and Sons, 1974), 67; J. Thomas Scharf, *History of the Confederate States Navy from Its Organization to the Surrender of Its Last Vessel* (New York: Rogers and Sherwood, 1887; rpt., New York: Fairfax, 1977), 431; Justin McCarthy, *A History of Our Own Times,* 5 vols. (New York: Harper and Brothers, 1903), 2:193; Stuart Anderson, "1861: Blockade vs. Closing the Confederate Ports," *Military Affairs* 41 (December 1977): 190.

9. S. C. Hills to Welles, 2 May 1861, *ORN,* ser. 1, 4:361.

10. Francis Deak and Philip C. Jessup, *A Collection of Neutrality Laws, Regulations and Treaties of Various Countries,* 2 vols. (Washington, D.C.: Carnegie Endowment for International Peace, 1939), 1:161–62; J. P. Baxter "The British Government and Neutral Rights, 1861–1865," *American Historical Review* 33 (October 1928): 18, 29; *The Times* (London), 10 February 1862; Anderson, "Blockade vs. Closing," 191.

11. Richard S. West, Jr., *Gideon Welles: Lincoln's Navy Department* (New York: Bobbs–Merrill, 1943), 118–19; Norman B. Ferris, *Desperate Diplomacy: William H. Seward's Foreign Policy,* 1861 (Knoxville: University of Tennessee Press, 1976), 88–89; U.S. Congress, Senate, *Congressional Record,* 37th Cong., 1st sess., 12 July 1861.

12. Lord John Russell to Lord Richard Lyons, 19 July 1861, quoted in Henry Glass, "Marine International Law," *U.S. Naval Institute Proceedings* 11, no. 3 (1885): 460.

13. Anderson, "Blockade vs. Closing," 192.

14. G. J. Pendergrast to All Whom It May Concern, 30 April 1861, *ORN,*

ser. 1, 4:356; Pendergrast to J. R. Goldsborough, 15 July 1861, ibid., 5:795; Welles to Stringham, 5 July 1861, ibid., 702; Stringham to Welles, 30 May 1861, ibid., 682; John P. Gillis to Welles, 27 April 1861, ibid., 4:432, and 21 May 1861, ibid., 472; Stephen D. Trenchard to Welles, 31 May 1861, ibid., 5:684.

15. Welles to Stringham, 1 May 1861, *ORN,* ser. 1, 5:621; J. T. Headley, *Farragut and Our Naval Commanders* (New York: E. B. Treat, 1867), 112–17; *Dictionary of American Biography* (New York: Charles Scribner's Sons, 1933), s.v. "Silas Horton Stringham" by Lewis H. Bolander; Lewis R. Hamersly, *The Records of Living Officers of the U.S. Navy and Marine Corps* (Philadelphia: J. B. Lippincott, 1876), 20–21.

16. Welles to Stringham, 17 May 1861, *ORN,* ser. 1, 5:635–36; Stringham to Paulding, 24 May 1861, ibid., 666; Welles to Stringham, 5 June 1861, ibid., 702.

17. William A. Guyer to Treasury Department (n.d.), ibid., 746–47; Hiram Barney to Samuel P. Chase, 12 July 1861, ibid., 6:78; Stoddard and Clark to Seward, 12 July 1861, ibid., 7.

18. Robert Bunch to Lord John Russell, 4 September 1861, Great Britain, Parliament (Commons), *Sessional Papers,* Papers by Command, "Papers Relating to the Blockade of the Ports of the Confederate States," North American Papers 8, 62:784; Consul Archibald to Russell, 27 August 1861, ibid., 759–60; H. D. Hickley to Stringham, 15 August 1861, *ORN,* ser. 1, 6:85; "Statement of Vessels Arrived at and Cleared from the Port of Wilmington N.C. from 1st May to 25 July 1861," North American Papers 8, 62:755; Robert Bunch to Russell, 4 September 1861, ibid., 784; "List of Vessels Arrived at and Cleared from Wilmington N.C. May 1–August 10, 1861," ibid., 797; Welles to Stringham, 10 August 1861, *ORN,* ser. 1, 6:71.

19. Thomas O. Selfridge to Welles, 10 August 1861, *ORN,* ser. 1, 6:72–73; Daniel Drake Smith, Leopold Bierwirth, and William C. Thompson to Welles, 12 August 1861, ibid., 77–78; Thomas Sparrow to Annie, 26 July 1861, Thomas Sparrow Papers, Southern Historical Collection, the University of North Carolina (hereafter cited as SHC); Daniel H. Hill, *Bethel to Sharpsburg,* 2 vols. (Raleigh: Edwards and Broughton, 1926), 1:160; Reed Werden to Goldsborough, 2 November 1861, Area 7, Entry 463, RG 45, NA.

20. William M. Robinson, *The Confederate Privateers* (New Haven, Conn.: Yale University Press, 1928), 102–10; William Harwar Parker, *Recollections of a Naval Officer 1841–1865* (New York: Charles Scribner's Sons, 1883), 211; Hill, *Bethel to Sharpsburg,* 1:158–60; Adam Tredwell, "North Carolina Navy," in *History of the Several Regiments and Battalions from North Carolina in the Great War 1861–65,"* ed. Walter Clark, 5 vols. (Raleigh: Nash Brothers, 1901), 5:299.

21. *Welles Diary* (n.d.), 1:69.

22. Samuel Francis Du Pont to Sophie Du Pont, 28 June 1861, *Samuel*

Francis Du Pont: A Selection from His Civil War Letters, ed. John D. Hayes, 3 vols. (Ithaca, N.Y.: Cornell University Press, 1969), 1:85–86, (hereafter cited as *Du Pont Letters).*

23. James M. Merrill "Strategy Makers in the Union Navy Department, 1861–1865," *Mid-America: An Historical Review* 44 (January 1962): 23; *Du Pont Letters,* 1:viii–ix; Charles Oscar Paullin, *Paullin's History of Naval Administration 1775–1911* (Annapolis, Md.: U.S. Naval Institute, 1968), 263–64.

24. *Du Pont Letters,* 1:lxvii–ix; Paullin, 263–64.

25. Paullin, 263–64; Charles Henry Davis, *Life of Charles Henry Davis, Rear Admiral, 1807–1877* (Boston: Houghton, Mifflin, 1899), 134.

26. Blockade Strategy Board Minutes (n.d.), Subject File ON, RG 45, NA.

27. Ibid., 16 July 1861.

28. William H. Aspinwall to Welles, 25 April 1861, *ORN,* ser. 1, 4:336; note of British Foreign Office, as quoted in Glass, 462.

29. Quoted in Lynn M. Case and Warren F. Spencer, *The United States and France: Civil War Diplomacy* (Philadelphia: University of Pennsylvania Press, 1970), 251–52; Glass, 462.

30. Stringham to Welles, 22 July 1861, *ORN,* ser. 1, 6:24.

31. Blockade Strategy Board Minutes, 10 July, 12 September 1861, RG 45, NA.

32. Figures from the Coast Survey Office, May 1862, James D. Richardson, *A Compilation of the Messages and Papers of the Confederacy, Including the Diplomatic Correspondence 1861–1865,* 2 vols. (Nashville: United States Publishing, 1905), 2:548. Forty-five of these inlets were under 6 feet at high water, 70 between 6 and 12 feet, 42 between 12 and 18 feet, and 32 over 18 feet deep. Edwin B. Coddington, "The Civil War Blockade Reconsidered," in *Essays in History and International Relations in Honor of George Hubbard Blakeslee,* ed. Dwight E. Lee and George E. McReynolds (Worcester, Mass.: Clark University Press, 1949), 286.

33. United States Survey Charts 29 (1875), 37 (1878), Records of the Coast and Geodetic Survey, RG 23, NA.

34. Alexander Crosby Brown, "The Dismal Swamp Canal," *American Neptune* 5 (July–October 1945): 203–22, 297–310; 6 (January 1946): 51–70. The Chesapeake and Albemarle Canal was also an outlet to Norfolk. Reigart B. Lowry to Welles, 1 June 1861, *ORN,* ser. 1, 5:688.

35. Joseph Warner Sanderson, "The James River during the War," in *War Papers Read before the Commandry of the State of Wisconsin Military Order of the Loyal Legion of the United States,* 4 vols. (Milwaukee: Bardick and Allen, 1903), 3:36.

36. Simon Bernard, Jesse D. Elliot, and Joseph G. Totten to John C.

Calhoun, 7 February 1821, W. Edwin Hemphill, ed. *The Papers of John C. Calhoun,* 14 vols. (Columbia: University of South Carolina Press, 1959–1981), 5:594–616; Samuel R. Bright, Jr., "Confederate Coast Defense" (Ph.D. dissertation, Duke University, 1961), 2–3; U.S. Congress, House, *Forts, Arsenals, Arms, &c,* H. Rept. 85, 36th Cong., 2d sess., 18 February 1861, 4.

37. Gilbert Sumter Guinn, "Coastal Defense of the Confederate Atlantic Seaboard States, 1861–1862: A Study in Political and Military Mobilization" (Ph.D. dissertation, University of South Carolina, 1973), 48.

38. Hill, *Bethel to Sharpsburg,* 1:152; Guinn, 75.

39. John G. Barrett, *The Civil War in North Carolina* (Chapel Hill: University of North Carolina Press, 1963), 33; Hill, *Bethel to Sharpsburg,* 1:165; Schenck Journal, 1 July 1861, David Schenck Books, SHC.

40. Guinn, 330; Hill, *Bethel to Sharpsburg,* 1:153.

41. Hill, *Bethel to Sharpsburg,* 1:164; John E. Wool to Winfield Scott, 24 August 1861, *ORA,* ser. 1, 4:603; Special Orders 13 by C. C. Churchill, 25 August 1861, *ORN,* ser. 1, 6:112; Rush C. Hawkins, "Early Coast Operations in North Carolina," in *Battles and Leaders of the Civil War,* ed. Robert Underwood Johnson and Clarence Clough Buel, 4 vols. (New York: Thomas Yoseloff, 1956), 1:633n (Johnson and Buel cited hereafter as *Battles and Leaders*). Army forces were made up of the 9th and 20th New York Volunteers, members of the Union Coast Guard, and a company of the 2nd United States Artillery.

42. The *Susquehanna* arrived on the morning of the 28th in time to take part in the bombardment. John S. Chauncey to Welles, 27 August 1861, *ORN,* ser. 1, 6:116–17; James M. Merrill, "The Hatteras Expedition, August, 1861," *North Carolina Historical Review* 29 (April 1952): 211–13; Stringham to Welles, 2 September 1861, *ORN,* ser. 1, 6:120–23; Butler to Wool, 30 August 1861, *ORA,* ser. 1, 4:582.

43. Abstract Log of the *Monticello,* 28 August 1861, *ORN,* ser. 1, 6:135.

44. Samuel Barron to Stephen R. Mallory, 31 August 1861, ibid., 121; Stringham to Welles, 21 September 1861, ibid., 121; Merrill, "Hatteras Expedition," 214; Barrett, 42.

45. Stringham to Welles, 2 September 1861, *ORN,* ser. 1, 6:122; Barron to Mallory, 31 August 1861, ibid., 139; Thomas O. Selfridge, Jr., *Memoirs of Thomas O. Selfridge, Jr., Rear Admiral, U.S.N.* (New York: G. P. Putnam's Sons, 1924), 40; Barrett, 43.

46. John P. Gillis to Welles, 31 August 1861, *ORN,* ser. 1, 6:126; Henry S. Stellwagen to Welles, 31 August 1861, ibid., 127; Stringham to Welles, 4 September 1861, ibid., 133; entry for 1 September 1861, John D. Hayes and Lillian O'Brien, eds., "The Early Blockade and the Capture of the Hatteras Forts from the Journal of John Sanford Barnes, July 19 to September 1, 1861," *New-York Historical Society Quarterly* 46 (January 1962): 84.

47. Robert S. Browning III, *Two If by Sea: The Development of American Coastal Defense Policy* (Westport, Conn.: Greenwood, 1983), 117.

48. Schenck Journal, 29 August 1861, SHC.

49. W. H. Parker, *Recollections*, 214–15; Merrill, "Strategy Makers," 23; as quoted in Hayes and O'Brien, 85.

50. Stephen C. Rowan to Stringham, 1 September 1861, *ORN,* ser. 1, 6:154; Blockade Strategy Board Minutes, 2 September 1861, RG 45, NA; Welles to Stringham, 3 September 1861, *ORN,* ser. 1, 6:162–63; Stringham to Fox, 11 September 1861, ibid., 199–200; Stringham to Welles, 22 September 1861, ibid., 221; Rowan to Stringham, 18 September 1861, ibid., 222.

51. Rowan to Stringham, 12 September 1861, Entry 395, Subseries 28, RG 45, NA.

52. John P. Bankhead to Fox, 29 September 1861, *Confidential Correspondence of Gustavus Vasa Fox, Assistant Secretary of the Navy 1861–1865,* ed. Robert Means Thompson and Richard Wainwright, 2 vols. (New York: Devine, 1918), 1:385 (hereafter cited as *Fox Correspondence*).

53. Headley, 122; Merrill, "Hatteras Expedition," 219; Gideon Welles, "Admiral Farragut and New Orleans, with an Account of the Origin and Command of the First Three Naval Expeditions of the War," *Galaxy* 12 (July 1871): 671–72; Samuel Du Pont to Sophie Du Pont, 17 September 1861, *Du Pont Letters,* 1:149. Stringham became the first naval victim of the press during the war. Naval officers often took much undeserved criticism because the army had a greater influence over the press. The small number of officers in the navy as compared to the large number in the army, along with the press's greater access to army headquarters, caused the navy to receive less attention. Some army officers curried favor with the press because they were looking for postwar political careers. Richard S. West, Jr., "The Navy and the Press during the Civil War," *U.S. Naval Institute Proceedings* 63 (January 1937): 36–38.

54. Stringham to Welles, 16 September 1861, *ORN,* ser. 1, 6:217; Welles to Stringham, 18 September 1861, ibid., 231–32; Rowena Reed, *Combined Operations in the Civil War* (Annapolis, Md.: U.S. Naval Institute Press, 1978), 19; Richard S. West, Jr., *Mr. Lincoln's Navy* (New York: Longmans Green, 1957), 82.

2. The Capture of Eastern North Carolina

1. Goldsborough to Welles, 23 September 1861, Louis M. Goldsborough Papers, Manuscript Department, William R. Perkins Library, Duke University (hereafter all references to the Manuscript Department at Duke University will be referred to as Duke); Stringham to Goldsborough, 22 September 1861, Silas

Horton Stringham Collection, ZB Collection, Operational Archives, Naval Historical Center, Washington, D.C. (the Naval Historical Center will hereafter be referred to as NHC). The navy had used the designation of flag officer to denote that the commanding officer of a naval squadron could display his broad pennant from the mast of the flagship. On 16 July 1862, Congress established the title of commodore (one star) for up to eighteen individuals. Congress created nine positions for rear admirals (two stars), who ranked above commodores. Clark G. Reynolds, *Famous American Admirals* (New York: Van Nostrand Reinehold, 1978), v–vi.

2. Goldsborough was not the officer next in line for this promotion according to the system of seniority. For Goldsborough to assume command of the squadron, four officers of higher rank were removed from active command. Welles to Goldsborough, 12 October 1861, *ORN,* ser. 1, 6:313–14; *Du Pont Letters,* 1:150n; *Dictionary of American Biography,* 1933 ed., s.v. "Louis Malesherbes Goldsborough" by W. C. Mallalieu; Hamersly, *Records of Living Officers,* 11–12.

3. Welles to Goldsborough, 12 October 1861, *ORN,* ser. 1, 6:313–14; Goldsborough to Welles, 29 October 1861, ibid., 375; Goldsborough to Elizabeth Wirt Goldsborough, 29 September 1861, Louis Goldsborough Collection, Manuscript Division, Library of Congress (hereafter all references to the Manuscript Division of the Library of Congress will be referred to as LCM).

4. William Keeler to Anna Keeler, 14 June 1862, *Aboard the USS Monitor: 1862, The Letters of Acting Paymaster William Frederick Keeler, U.S. Navy, to His Wife, Anna*, ed. Robert W. Daly (Annapolis, Md.: U.S. Naval Institute, 1964), 155 (hereafter cited as *Monitor*).

5. Welles to Goldsborough, 25 September 1861, *ORN,* ser. 1, 6:252–53; Stellwagen to Fox, 29 September 1861, ibid., 268; Stellwagen to Goldsborough, 2 October 1861, ibid., 279–80, and 11 October 1861, ibid., 309; Goldsborough to Reed Werden, 12 October 1861, ibid., 315.

6. Werden to Goldsborough, 13 October 1861, ibid., 316; Lowery to Werden, 24 October 1861, ibid., 378.

7. Daniel L. Braine to J. L. Lardner, 5 October 1861, ibid., 292; Werden to Goldsborough, 2 November 1861, ibid., 377–78; Statement of J. H. Morrison, 1 October 1861, ibid., 276; Statement of George H. Ridgely, 2 October 1861, ibid., 276–77.

8. Goldsborough to Werden, 6 November 1861, ibid., 410; Werden to Goldsborough, 17 November 1861, ibid., 428.

9. Blockade Strategy Board Minutes Memorandum (n.d.), Subject File ON, RG 45, NA; Ambrose E. Burnside, "The Burnside Expedition," in *Battles and Leaders,* 1:660; Ambrose E. Burnside, "The Burnside Expedition," in

Personal Narratives of Events in the War of the Rebellion, Being Papers Read before the Rhode Island Soldiers and Sailors Historical Society, 2d ser., no. 6 (Providence: N. Bangs Williams, 1882), 6–7; Robert W. Daly, "Burnside's Amphibious Division," *Marine Corps Gazette* 35 (December 1951): 30–34.

10. U.S. Congress, Senate, *Report of the Joint Committee on the Conduct of War—Army of the Potomac,* S. Doc. 108, 37th Cong., 3d sess., 1863, 333; *Daily Journal* (Wilmington), 3 September 1861.

11. Norman C. Delaney, "Charles Henry Foster and the Unionists of Eastern North Carolina," *North Carolina Historical Review* 37, no. 3 (July 1960): 353; S. C. Rowan to Welles, 3 September 1861, *ORN,* ser. 1, 6:161; Rush C. Hawkins to John E. Wool, 7 September 1861, *ORA,* ser. 1, 4:608; Francis U. Farquher to J. E. Wool, 7 September 1861, ibid., 592; Rowan to Stringham, 5 September 1861, *ORN,* ser. 1, 6:173.

12. McClellan to Burnside, 7 January 1862, *ORN,* ser. 1, 6:508; Goldsborough to Fox, 4 December 1861, *Fox Correspondence,* 1:208; entry for 12 January 1862, D. L. Day, *My Diary of Rambles with the 25th Mass. Volunteer Infantry, with Burnside's Coast Division; 18th Army Corps, and Army of the James* (Milford, Mass.: King and Billings, 1884), 20.

13. Goldsborough to Fox, 30 January 1862, *Fox Correspondence,* 1:234–35; Burnside, "Burnside Expedition," *Personal Narratives,* 21; Henry Van Brunt, Rough Notes of the Naval Expedition to Roanoke Island, etc., 18, 20 January 1862, Operations of Fleets, Squadrons, Flotillas, and Divisions, Subject File OO, RG 45, NA; William H. Chenery, "Reminiscences of the Burnside Expedition," *Personal Narratives of Events in the War of the Rebellion, Being Papers Read before the Rhode Island Soldiers and Sailors Historical Society,* 7th ser., no. 1 (Providence: The Society, 1905), 16; Goldsborough to Fox, 23 January 1862, *Fox Correspondence,* 1:232; Henry C. Pardee to father, 15 January 1862, Henry Clay Pardee Papers, Duke.

14. A. B. R. Sprague, "The Burnside Expedition," in *Civil War Papers Read before the Commandry of the State of Massachusetts Military Order of the Loyal Legion of the United States,* 2 vols. (Boston: The Commandry, 1900), 1:429–32; H. C. Pardee to mother, 25 January 1862, Pardee Papers, Duke.

15. John S. C. Abbott, "A Military Adventure," *Harpers New Monthly Magazine* 30 (December 1864): 3; Day, entry for 17 January 1862, 23; Burnside, "Burnside Expedition," *Personal Narratives,* 18–19.

16. Goldsborough to Welles, 29 January 1862, *ORN,* ser. 1, 6:536; Goldsborough to Welles, 31 January 1862, ibid., 538; Reno General Order 7, 31 January 1862, Records of United States Army Continental Commands, Record Group 393, Entry 4936, 2d Brigade, Coast Division Orders; Goldsborough to Fox, 30 January 1862, *Fox Correspondence,* 1:234–35.

17. Henry T. Clark to Judah P. Benjamin, 27 September 1861, *ORA*, ser. 1, 4:659–60.

18. R. E. Lee to Anderson, 28 January 1862, ibid., 9:423–24; Benjamin to Huger, 21 January 1862, ibid., 420; Benjamin to Huger, 31 January 1862, *ORN*, ser. 1, 6:760.

19. Hill to Samuel Cooper, 18 October 1861, *ORA*, ser. 1, 4:682; Barrett, 74; Report of the Investigating Committee, Confederate House of Representatives, *ORA*, ser. 1, 9:184; Daly, "Burnside's Amphibious Division," 35.

20. Daniel H. Hill, *Confederate Military History*, vol. 4: *North Carolina*, ed. Clement A. Evans (New York: Thomas Yoseloff, 1962), 30.

21. Walter Gwynn to John W. Ellis, 9 June 1861, *ORA*, ser. 1, 51 (pt. 2): 136–37; *ORN*, ser. 1, 6:554; Sprague, 434; Boynton, 382; Report of the Investigating Committee, *ORA*, ser. 1, 9:184; Lorenzo Traver, "Burnside Expedition in North Carolina: Battles of Roanoke Island and Elizabeth City," in *Personal Narratives of Events in the War of the Rebellion, Being Papers Read before the Rhode Island Soldiers and Sailors Historical Society*, 2d ser., no. 5 (Providence: N. Bangs William, 1880), 14.

22. Hawkins, 640; Day, entry for 6 February 1862, 65; George H. Allen, *Forty-six Months with the Fourth Rhode Island Volunteers in the War of 1861 to 1865, Comprising a History of Its Marches, Battles, and Camp Life* (Providence: J. A. and R. A. Reid, 1887), 64.

23. Abstract Log of the *Hunchback*, 7 February 1862, *ORN*, ser. 1, 6:569; Day, entry for 7 February 1862, 32.

24. W. H. Parker, *Recollections*, 226, 228; Henry Clay Pardee to father, 11 February 1862, Pardee Papers, Duke. The Confederates had two more gunboats. The *Appomattox* had been dispatched to Edenton, and the schooner *Black Warrior* did not take part in the action. Report of the Investigating Committee, *ORA*, ser. 1, 9:185; Goldsborough to Welles, 10 February 1862, *ORN*, ser. 1, 6:551–52.

25. Lynch to Mallory, 15 February 1862, ibid., 594; Report of the Investigating Committee, *ORA*, ser. 1, 9:185.

26. Allen, 68–69; Rowan to Goldsborough, 11 February 1862, Entry 395, Subseries 28, RG 45, NA.

27. Lynch to Mallory, 15 February 1862, *ORN*, ser. 1, 6:594–95; Davenport to Rowan, 9 February 1862, ibid., 558, passim; Report of the Investigating Committee, *ORA*, ser. 1, 9:185.

28. Benjamin H. Porter to Goldsborough, 10 February 1862, *ORN*, ser. 1, 6:578–79.

29. Report of the Investigating Committee, *ORA*, ser. 1, 9:185.

30. Porter to Goldsborough, 10 February 1862, *ORN*, ser. 1, 6:578–79.

31. Lynch to Mallory, 18 February 1862, ibid., 595; Goldsborough to Welles, ibid., 554; Jeffers to Goldsborough, 9 February, ibid., 562.

32. Goldsborough to Welles, ibid., 554; Chenery, 33; Return of Casualties in the Department of North Carolina, 8 February 1862, *ORA,* ser. 1, 9:85; Barrett, 74; Sprague, 437.

33. Fox to Goldsborough, 15 February 1862 [projected date], Louis M. Goldsborough Papers, File ZB, Operational Archives, NHC; Fox to Goldsborough, 24 February 1862, *ORN,* ser. 1, 6:664.

34. See Richard Allen Sauers, "General Ambrose E. Burnside's 1862 North Carolina Campaign" (Ph.D. dissertation, Pennsylvania State University, 1987).

35. "Report of the Investigating Committee," *ORA,* ser. 1, 9:188.

36. The Dismal Swamp Canal was very important to the economy of both states before the war. See A. C. Brown, "Dismal Swamp Canal," 203–21; Lynch to Mallory, 18 February 1862, *ORN,* ser. 1, 6:595.

37. Goldsborough to Welles, 10 February 1862, *ORN,* ser. 1, 6:607. Rowan was a native of Ireland and was the highest-ranking foreign-born officer in the Union navy. Headley, 401–3; *Dictionary of American Biography,* s.v. "Rowan, Stephen Clegg," by Charles Lee Lewis, 16:196–97. Rowan to Goldsborough, 11 February 1862, *ORN,* ser. 1, 6:607.

38. W. H. Parker, *Recollections,* 253. The *Raleigh* was still in Norfolk, the *Forrest* was on the ways at Elizabeth City, and the *Curlew* had been abandoned at Roanoke. Lynch to Mallory, *ORN,* ser. 1, 6:595–96.

39. Rowan to Goldsborough, ibid., 607.

40. James M. Merrill, "The Battle for Elizabeth City, 1862," *U.S. Naval Institute Proceedings* 83 (March 1957): 322; Lynch to Mallory, 11 February 1862, *ORN,* ser. 1, 6:595–96; Allen, 79; Flusser to mother, 14 February 1862, Charles Flusser Papers, ZB Collection, Operational Archives, NHC.

41. Rowan to Du Pont, 14 April 1862, *Du Pont Letters,* 2:3–5; Lynch to Mallory, 18 February 1862, *ORN,* ser. 1, 6:595–96; Rowan to Goldsborough, 11 February 1862, ibid., 608–9; Tredwell, 308.

42. Goldsborough to Welles, 14 February 1862, *ORN,* ser. 1, 6:632; A. Murray to Rowan, 12 February 1862, ibid., 637; Jeffers to Murray, 14 February 1862, ibid., 638–39.

43. Rowan to Goldsborough, 22 February 1862, ibid., 654; Hawkins, 646.

44. Rush C. Hawkins to J. G. Parke, *ORA,* ser. 1, 9:196–97; Thomas C. Parramore, "The Burning of Winton in 1862," *North Carolina Historical Review* 39 (Winter 1962): 19; Allen, 86.

45. David Lucius Craft to sister, 25 February 1862, David Lucius Craft Papers, Duke; Edmund J. Cleveland, "The Early Campaigns in North Carolina

as Seen through the Eyes of a New Jersey Soldier," part 2, *Proceedings of the New Jersey Historical Society* 68 (July 1950): 252; Hawkins to Parke, 21 February 1862, *ORA,* ser. 1, 9:196.

46. *North Carolina Standard* (Raleigh), 12 March 1862; Proclamation Issued by L. M. Goldsborough and A. E. Burnside, 18 February 1862, ORN, ser. 1, 6:639. Columbia, a small town in Tyrell County, was plundered several weeks later by Union soldiers, alienating the populace further. J. M. Hough to W. Pettigrew, 18 March 1862, Pettigrew Family Papers, SHC.

47. Fox to Goldsborough, 9 March 1862, *ORN,* ser. 1, 7:73.

48. During the war, New Bern was spelled New Berne. Rowan to Goldsborough, 20 March 1862, *ORN,* ser. 1, 7:110; Burnside to Lorenzo Thomas, 16 March 1862, *ORA,* ser. 1, 9:197.

49. Rowan to Goldsborough, 20 March 1862, Entry 30, RG 45, NA; John S. Barnes, *Submarine Warfare, Offensive and Defensive, Including a Discussion of the Offensive Torpedo System* (New York: D. Van Nostrand, 1869), 64; Branch to Theophilis H. Holmes, 26 March 1862, *ORA,* ser. 1, 9:241–42.

50. Rowan to Goldsborough, 16 March 1862, *ORN,* ser. 1, 7:108–9; Hill, *Bethel to Sharpsburg,* 1:259; H. C. Pardee to father, 19 March 1862, Pardee Papers, Duke; Lewis Richard General Order 16, 12 March 1862, RG 393, Entry 4936; Day, entries for 12, 13 March 1862, 41, 44.

51. Branch to Holmes, 26 March 1862, ORA, ser. 1, 9:243; W. S. Clark to Edward McNeill, 16 March 1862, ibid., 225; Roderick Sheldon McCook to Rowan, 19 March 1862, *ORN,* ser. 1, 7:113–14.

52. Branch to Holmes, *ORA,* ser. 1, 9:243; Rowan to Goldsborough, 15, 20 March 1862, ibid., 111, 117.

53. Branch to Holmes, 26 March 1862, ibid., 243–44; Burnside to Stanton, 10 April 1862, ibid., 205.

54. Rowan to Goldsborough, 20 March 1862, *ORN,* ser. 1, 7:111–12; David Lucius Craft to sister, 18 March 1862, David Lucius Craft Papers, Duke; Flusser to mother, 15 March 1862, ZB Collection, Flusser Papers, Operational Archives, NHC. The army blamed the Negroes for the looting of New Bern. Burnside to Stanton, 21 March 1862, *ORA,* ser. 1, 9:199; Day, entry for 13 March 1862, 45.

55. Rowan to Du Pont, 14 April 1862, *Du Pont Letters,* 2:5; William Henry Church to Burnside, 9 April 1862, *ORA,* ser. 1, 9:210; Branch to Holmes, 26 March 1862, ibid., 242; Rowan to F. H. Upton, 8 July 1862, Entry 395, Subseries 28, RG 45, NA; Rowan to Samuel Betts, 2 April 1862, Entry 395, Subseries 28, RG 45, NA; *The Federal Cases, Comprising Cases Argued and Determined in the Circuit and District Courts of the United States,* 30 vols. (St. Paul, Minn., 1894–1897), case 4318, 8:388–89.

56. Alexander Murray to Rowan, 26 March 1862, *ORN*, ser. 1, 7:151–52. One of the more important tasks of the navy was to reestablish aids to navigation in the sounds. They recovered a number of lighthouse lenses and worked at raising the lightships sunk by the rebels. Rowan to Governor Stanley, 3, 4 June 1862, passim, Entry 395, Subseries 28, RG 45, NA; Rowan to Goldsborough, 17 June 1862, ibid.

57. Robert E. Lee to Davis, 21 March 1862, *ORA*, ser. 1, 51 (pt. 2): 512; Abstract from Report of the Troops of the Department of North Carolina, *ORN*, ser. 1, 9:455.

58. J. S. Pender to Governor Francis Pickens, 15 April 1861, *ORA*, ser. 1, 51 (pt. 2): 11; Richard Schriver Barry, "Fort Macon: Its History," *North Carolina Historical Review* 27 (April 1950): 164–68; Schenck Journal, 28 June 1861, David Schenck Books, SHC. According to General Daniel Harvey Hill, the fort mounted forty-three guns, while eleven lay in the fort unmounted. Hill, *North Carolina*, 43; Hill, *Bethel to Sharpsburg*, 1:247.

59. John G. Parke to the Commander of the Garrison of Fort Macon, 23 March 1862, *ORA*, ser. 1, 9:277; Moses J. White to Parke, 23 March 1862, ibid., 278; John Parke to Lewis Richmond, 9 May 1862, ibid., 282–84; Burnside to Stanton, 17 April 1862, ibid., 270–71; Burnside to McClellan, 17 April 1862, ibid., 377.

60. Samuel Lockwood to Goldsborough, 27 April 1862, *ORN*, ser. 1, 7:278–79.

61. D. W. Flagler to Charles T. Gardner, 29 April 1862, *ORA*, ser. 1, 9:287–88.

62. Parke to Richmond, 9 May 1862, *ORA*, ser. 1, 9:285; Lockwood to Goldsborough, 26 April 1862, *ORN*, ser. 1, 7:278.

63. Rowan to Goldsborough, 16 April 1862, ibid., 241; Jesse L. Reno to Lewis Richmond, 22 April 1862, *ORA*, ser. 1, 9:305–7; Rowan to Du Pont, 14 April 1862, *Du Pont Letters*, 2:6–7.

64. Rowan to Flusser, 31 March 1862, *ORN*, ser. 1, 7:181; Rowan to Goldsborough, 29 March 1862, ibid., 177–78; Flusser to Rowan, 25 April 1862, ibid., 260–61.

65. Flusser to Rowan, 18 May 1862, ibid., 383–84; Edward R. Colhoun to Rowan, 17, 27 May 1862, ibid., 374–76; Flusser to Rowan, 11 July 1862, ibid., 556; Flusser to Davenport, 4 August 1862, ibid., 622; Hill, *Bethel to Sharpsburg*, 1:259.

66. McClellan to Burnside, 2 April 1862, *ORA*, ser. 1, 9:374; Augustus Woodbury, "Ambrose Everett Burnside," in *Personal Narratives of Events in the War of the Rebellion, Being Papers Read before the Rhode Island Soldiers and Sailors Historical Society,* 2d ser., no. 17 (Providence: N. Bangs Williams, 1882),

26–28; Burnside to Stanton, 7 July 1862, *ORA,* ser. 1, 9:409; Foster to Stanton, 8 July 1862, ibid., 410.

67. Flusser to mother, 28 April 1862, Flusser Papers, ZB Collection, Operational Archives, NHC.

3. The Peninsular Campaign

1. Irwin Silber, ed., *Songs of the Civil War,* arrangements by Jerry Silverman (New York: Columbia University Press, 1960), 331–33.

2. Pendergrast to Daniel Braine, 2 May 1861, *ORN,* ser. 1, 4:355–56; Braine to Pendergrast, 30 April 1861, ibid., 355; Selfridge, 37; Stringham to Welles, 19 May 1861, *ORN,* ser. 1, 5:644; Henry Eagle to Stringham, ibid., 644–45.

3. Braine to Pendergrast, 30 April 1861, *ORN,* ser. 1, 4:355–56; A. B. Fairfax to Pendergrast, 14 June 1861, ibid., 405, John Faunce to Pendergrast, 4 June 1861, ibid., 492–93; Samuel Barrow to John Letcher, 10 June 1861, ibid., 5:803–6.

4. Fort Monroe was often referred to as a fortress. A fortress, however, is a fortified city, one completely enclosed by walls. Robert Arthur, *History of Fort Monroe* (Fort Monroe, Va.: Coast Artillery School, 1930), 48, 50, 102; Israel Everett Vail, *Three Years on the Blockade: A Naval Experience* (New York: Abbey, 1902), 145.

5. William N. Still, Jr., *Confederate Shipbuilding,* (Athens: University of Georgia Press, 1969), 6; William N. Still, Jr., "Facilities for the Construction of War Vessels in the Confederacy," *Journal of Southern History* 31 (August 1965): 285–87.

6. The Confederate ironclad was interchangeably called *Virginia* and *Merrimack* during the war. The Confederate officials, after her conversion from a frigate, rechristened her *Virginia,* and thus the vessel will be referred to by her actual name. The frigate *Merrimack* was sometimes erroneously spelled without the letter *k*. John M. Brooke and John L. Porter, "The Plan and Construction of the Merrimac," in *Battles and Leaders,* 1:715–16; William C. Davis, *Duel between the First Ironclads* (New York: Doubleday, 1975), 9–12. William N. Still, Jr., *Iron Afloat: The Story of Confederate Armorclads* (Nashville: Vanderbilt University Press, 1971), 24–25.

7. W. C. Davis, *Duel,* 14–15; *ORN,* ser. 2, 1:148; John Ericsson, "The Building of the 'Monitor,'" in *Battles and Leaders,* 1:731.

8. Francis W. Smith to Mrs. Smith (n.d.), Francis W. Smith File, ZO Collection, Operational Archives, NHC; John Taylor Wood, "The First Fight of Ironclads," in *Battles and Leaders,* 1:696.

9. Ibid., 698; Austin Pendergrast to John Marston, 9 March 1862, *ORN,* ser. 1, 7:23; Still, *Iron Afloat,* 29–31.

10. Pendergrast to Marston, 9 March 1862, *ORN,* ser. 1, 7:23–24; J. T. Wood, "First Fight," 1:698–700; Still, *Iron Afloat,* 29–31.

11. Francis W. Smith to Mrs. Smith (n.d.), Francis W. Smith File, ZO Collection, Operational Archives, NHC; J. T. Wood, "First Fight," 1:698.

12. W. C. Davis, Duel, 97–98; James Henry Rochelle, *Life of Rear Admiral John Randolph Tucker* (Washington: Neale, 1903), 35–36; G. J. Van Brunt to Welles, 10 March 1862, *ORN,* ser. 1. 7:11; J. T. Wood, "First Fight," 1:700.

13. Still, *Iron Afloat,* 32.

14. Samuel Dana Greene to parents, 14 March 1862, Area 7, Entry 463, RG 45, NA; Ship's Log *Minnesota,* 9 March 1862, Special List 44, RG 24, NA.

15. S. D. Greene to Welles, 12 March 1862, *ORN,* ser. 1, 7:25; G. J. Van Brunt to Welles, 10 March 1862, ibid., 11; The *Virginia* had shown that she could operate as a ram, but her victims had been stationary. The *Monitor* was more maneuverable; the clumsy *Virginia* took forty minutes to make a 180-degree turn. Still, *Iron Afloat,* 25. J. T. Wood, "First Fight," 1:701–7.

16. G. J. Van Brunt to Welles, 10 March 1862, *ORN,* ser. 1, 7:11; William Watson to Goldsborough, 9 March 1862, ibid., 30.

17. William Keeler to Anna Keeler, 11 March 1862, *Monitor,* 43; Van Brunt to Welles, 10 March 1862, *ORN,* ser. 1, 7:12.

18. Pendergrast to Welles, 17 March 1862, Entry 343, Letters Sent by the Commandant of the Philadelphia Navy Yard to the Secretary of Navy, RG 45, NA; E. E. Morgan, Russel Sturgis, C. A. Marshall, and G. N. Blunt to Abraham Lincoln, 11 March 1862, Area 7, Entry 463, RG 45, NA; Edwin Stanton to Governors of New York, Massachusetts, and Maine, 9 March 1862, *ORN,* ser. 1, 7:80; D. H. Rucker to John Dahlgren, 9 March 1862, ibid., 77; Welles to Goldsborough, 15 March 1862, Area 7, Entry 463, RG 45, NA; Goldsborough to Welles, 17 March 1862, *ORN,* ser. 1, 7:134–35. Mallory suggested that the *Virginia* attack New York City the day before she attacked the squadron. Mallory to Buchanan, 7 March 1862, ibid., 780–81.

19. Robert W. Daly, *How the Merrimac Won: The Strategic Story of the CSS Virginia* (New York: Thomas Y. Crowell, 1957), 187. The Navy Department was convinced of the value of ironclads and within six months authorized the construction of thirty-three more coastal monitors. This number included ten of the Passaic class, four Miantonomahs, four Winnebagoes, two Dictators, nine Canonicus, and four of the Onondaga class. Walter Millis, "The Iron Sea Elephants," *American Neptune* 10 (January 1950): 19. Because of the success of the *Virginia,* the North immediately modified its naval building program. John Lenthall, the chief of the Bureau of Construction and Repairs, and Benjamin

Isherwood believed that the United States should emulate England and France and plate its larger wooden vessels with iron, suggesting the department first alter the *Roanoke*. The *Roanoke*, however, was a failure. She rolled so badly that her guns could not be used while at sea, was very clumsy, and was barely buoyant enough to go from harbor to harbor. Lenthall and Benjamin Isherwood to Welles, 19 March 1862, Lenthall to Welles, 17 March 1862, Letters Sent to the Secretary of the Navy from the Bureau of Construction and Repair, Entry 50, RG 19, NA; Hiram Paulding to B. F. Delano, 22 March 1862, Entry 332, Letters Sent by Commandant of the New York Navy Yard, RG 45, NA; U.S. Congress, House, *Report of the Secretary of the Navy,* H. Ex. Doc. 1, 38th Cong., 2d sess., 5 December 1864, 186 (hereafter cited as *RSN*); B. F. Sands to Welles, 11 July 1863, as cited in U.S. Congress, House, *Armored Vessels in the Attack On Charleston,* H. Ex. Doc. 69, 38th Cong., 1st sess., 1864, 49–50, passim.

20. Goldsborough to Welles, 17 October 1861, *ORN,* ser. 1, 6:333–34; Goldsborough to Welles, 16 November 1861, ibid., 437; Goldsborough to William Smith, 4, 18 November 1861, ibid., 393, 439–40; Goldsborough to Welles, 10 January 1862, ibid., 512; Goldsborough Memorandum, 12 January 1862, ibid., 516; Goldsborough to Welles, 1 February 1862, ibid., 540–41.

21. Goldsborough to Welles, 14 March 1862, Letters Received by the Secretary of the Navy from Officers Commanding Squadrons, Entry 30, RG 45, NA.

22. Entry for 20 September 1862, *Welles Diary,* 1:142.

23. Welles to Goldsborough, 14 March 1862, *ORN,* ser. 1, 7:125; A. Ludlow Case to Commanding Officer USS *Currituck,* 16 March 1862, ibid., 130; Welles to Fox, 10 March 1862, *Fox Correspondence,* 2:436; William Keeler to Anna, 30 March 1862, *Monitor,* 63.

24. The Union commanders believed that a vessel weighing 500 tons and steaming at a speed of ten knots had a momentum eighty times greater than a 200-pound projectile with a velocity of 1,000 feet a second. Goldsborough to Stephen C. Rowan, 26 March 1862, *ORN,* ser. 1, 7:170–71; Goldsborough to Welles, 17 March 1862, ibid., 138; P. H. Watson to Stanton, 28 March 1862, ibid., p. 176. Vanderbilt had only intended to lend the *Vanderbilt* to the government. Lincoln and Stanton, however, both thought it was a gift, and the commodore let the government have her. Cedric Ridgely-Nevitt, *American Steamships on the Atlantic* (Newark: University of Delaware Press, 1981), 244; Stanton to Cornelius Vanderbilt, 20 March 1862, *ORN,* ser. 1, 7:148–49; D. B. Barton to Goldsborough, 20 March 1862, ibid., 145; Goldsborough to Welles, 22 March 1862, ibid., 157.

25. Montgomery Meigs to Col. Ingalls, 9 March 1862, *ORN,* ser. 1, 7:79; Dahlgren to Fox, 12 March 1862, ibid., H. K. Lawrence to Welles, 18 April 1862, ibid., 248–49.

26. Francis W. Dawson, *Reminiscences of Confederate Service 1861–1865,* ed. Bell I. Wiley (Baton Rouge: Louisiana State University Press, 1980), 39–40; General Order of Josiah Tattnall, 8 April 1862, *ORN,* ser. 1, 7:759–60; Mallory to Tattnall, 1 April 1862, ibid., 754; W. H. Parker, *Recollections,* 273; Ashley Halsey, Jr., "Seal the Turtle in Its Shell," *Civil War Times Illustrated* 5 (June 1966): 29.

27. William Keeler to Anna, 11 April 1862, *Monitor,* 75; Tattnall to Mallory, 12 April 1862, *ORN,* ser. 1, 7:223–24.

28. William Keeler to Anna, 11 April 1862, *Monitor,* 74–75.

29. George B. McClellan, "The Peninsular Campaign," in *Battles and Leaders,* 2:170; Hill, *North Carolina,* 46; John Bankhead Magruder to Samuel Cooper, 25 February 1862, *ORA,* ser. 1, 51 (pt. 2): 479–80; McClellan to John F. Wool, 9 March 1862, *ORN,* ser. 1, 7:74–75.

30. Welles to Stanton, 14 March 1862, ibid., 125; Goldsborough to Fox, 1 March 1862, *Fox Correspondence,* 1:245. As early as December 1861, John G. Barnard suggested a move on Norfolk by landing 30,000 men between the Elizabeth and Nansemond rivers to cut off the rebel army at Norfolk. Barnard to McClellan, 6 December 1861, as cited in John G. Barnard, *The Peninsular Campaign and Its Antecedents, as Developed by the Report of Maj. Gen. Geo. B. McClellan* (New York: D. Van Nostrand, 1864), 54–55; McClellan to Stanton, 13 March 1862, *ORN,* ser. 1, 7:103; Barnard, *Peninsular Campaign,* 67; U.S. Congress, Senate, *Conduct of the War—Army of the Potomac,* 630.

31. J. G. Barnard to Fox, 12 March 1862; U.S. Congress, Senate, *Conduct of the War—Army of the Potomac,* 629; Goldsborough to Mrs. and Miss E. W. Goldsborough, 13 April 1862, Goldsborough Papers, Duke.

32. Goldsborough to John S. Missroon, 4 April 1862, *ORN,* ser. 1, 7:199; John D. Hayes, "Studies in Naval Failure," *Shipmate* 25 (September–October 1962): 32; U. S. Congress, Senate, *Conduct of the War—Army of the Potomac,* 632; McClellan to Goldsborough, 3 April 1862, *ORN,* ser. 1, 7:196, and 4 April 1862, ibid., 200; Edward Carey Gardiner, "Narrative of Rear Admiral Goldsborough, U.S. Navy," ed. Henry C. Baird, *U.S. Naval Institute Proceedings* 59 (July 1933): 1027; Missroon to McClellan, 6 April 1862, *ORA,* ser. 1, 11 (pt. 3): 79; Daniel P. Woodbury to McClellan, 19 March 1862, ibid., 23; E. D. Keyes to Ira Harris, 7 April 1862, cited in George B. McClellan, *Report on the Organization and Campaigns of the Army of the Potomac* (New York: Sheldon, 1864), 166–67; Missroon to Fox, 12 April 1862, Gustavus Vasa Fox Papers, New-York Historical Society (hereafter cited as Fox Papers, NYHS).

33. Goldsborough to McClellan, 6 April 1862, *ORN,* ser. 1, 7:206; Goldsborough to Missroon, 4 April 1862, ibid., 199; Missroon to McClellan, 6 April 1862, ibid., 207.

34. Missroon to Goldsborough, 8 April 1862, ibid., 210; McClellan to Goldsborough, 8 April 1862, ibid., 211; C. H. Davis, *Life*, 288–89.

35. Goldsborough to McClellan, 6 April 1862, *ORA*, ser. 1, 11, (pt. 3): 80; Missroon to Goldsborough, 17 April 1862, *ORN*, ser. 1, 7:243; Missroon to Goldsborough, 23 April 1862, ibid., 259; Goldsborough to Fox, 21 April 1862, *Fox Correspondence*, 1:268; Goldsborough to McClellan, 3 May 1862, *ORN*, ser. 1, 7:305; Missroon to Fox, 15 April 1862, *Fox Correspondence*, 2:289–90; Missroon to McClellan, 17 April 1862, as cited in George B. McClellan, *McClellan's Own Story: The War for the Union* (New York: Charles L. Webster, 1887), 293–94.

36. Missroon to Goldsborough, 30 April 1862, *ORN*, ser. 1, 7:288–91.

37. Fox to Goldsborough, 7 May 1862, ibid., 327; *Atlas to Accompany the Official Records of the Union and Confederate Armies* (Washington, D.C.: Government Printing Office, 1891), plate 15, no. 1.

38. Goldsborough to Fox, 21 April 1862, Fox Papers, NYHS; U.S. Congress, Senate, *Conduct of War—Army of the Potomac*, 630.

39. McClellan to Stanton, 30 April 1862, *ORA*, ser. 1, 11 (pt. 3): 129; J. G. Barnard Memorandum (n.d.), ibid., 337; *Atlas to Accompany the Official Records*, plate 15, no. 1.

40. W. Smith to Goldsborough, 12 May 1862, *ORN*, ser. 1, 7:312, 315–16.

41. William Keeler to Anna, 4 May 1862, *Monitor*, 101.

42. Abraham Lincoln to Goldsborough, 7 May 1862, *ORN*, ser. 1, 7:326; Goldsborough to Salmon Chase, 7 May 1862, ibid., 327; Rodgers to Ann, 6, 8 May 1862, John Rodgers Collection, LCM; Keeler to Anna, 9 May 1862, *Monitor*, 115; Rodgers to Goldsborough, 9 May 1862, *ORN*, ser. 1, 7:328–29; Rodgers to Goldsborough, 11 May 1862, ibid., 329.

43. William Keeler to Anna, 8 May 1862, *Monitor*, 110–13; W. H. Parker, *Recollections*, 276–77; D. C. Constable to S. P. Chase, 9 May 1862, *ORN*, ser. 1, 7:332–33.

44. Goldsborough to Fox, 1 March 1862, Fox Papers, NYHS; Wool to Lincoln, 12 May 1862, *ORA*, ser. 1, 11:634–35.

45. In abandoning the yard, the Confederates were forced to leave behind one side-wheel steamboat, one screw steamer, and fifteen schooners. William Smith to Goldsborough, 18 May 1862, Entry 30, RG 45, NA; Josiah Tattnall to Mallory, 14 May 1862, ORN, ser. 1, 7:335–38.

46. Goldsborough to Welles, 12 May 1862, ibid., 342–43; Rodgers to Goldsborough, 12 May 1862, ibid., 346; Goldsborough to Welles, 14 May 1862, ibid., 353.

47. Rodgers to Goldsborough, 16 May 1862, ibid., 357; William Faxon to Fox, 17 May 1862, ibid., 366; W. H. Parker, *Recollections*, 286.

48. Rodgers to Goldsborough, *ORN,* ser. 1, 7:357; J. Wall Wilson to Chase, 18 June 1862, Letters from Officers of Cutters, Entry 151, RG 26 Records of the United States Coast Guard.

49. Rodgers to Goldsborough, 16 May 1862, *ORN,* ser. 1, 7:357–58; Robert Erwin Johnson, *Rear Admiral John Rodgers 1812–1882* (Annapolis, Md.: U.S. Naval Institute, 1967), 202–3; Goldsborough to Welles, 18 May 1862, *ORN,* ser. 1, 7:357–58; William Jeffers to Rodgers, 16 May 1862, ibid., 362; William M. Robinson, Jr., "Drewry's Bluff: Naval Defense of Richmond 1862," *Civil War History* 7 (June 1961): 172–74. The *Naugatuck,* a revenue steamer (also known as the *E. A. Stevens*), was a unique vessel having four compartments. The compartments at the bow and stern could be flooded to increase the draft and protect its sides from enemy fire. Another feature that made it adaptable to river service was that the crew could load the ship's gun and not be exposed to enemy fire. See R. A. Redmond, "The Revenue Steamer *E. A. Stevens* in the Civil War," *American Neptune* 20 (July 1960): 156–57.

50. A. H. Drewry, "Drewry's Bluff Fight," *Southern Historical Society Papers* 29 (1901): 284–85; William I. Clopton, "New Light on the Great Drewry's Bluff Fight," ibid., 34 (1906): 82–85; R. E. Johnson, *Rodgers,* 203–4; D. C. Constable to Rodgers, 16 May 1862, *ORN,* ser. 1, 7:363–64; George U. Morris to Rodgers, 16 May 1862, ibid., 363.

51. William Keeler to Anna, 16 May 1862, *Monitor,* 130.

52. L. H. Newman to Rodgers, 16 May 1862, *ORN,* ser. 1, 7:359; Ransford E. Van Gieson to Rodgers, 16 May 1862, ibid., 358–59; William S. Fort to Rodgers, 16 May 1862, ibid., 363; Constable to Rodgers, 16 May 1862, ibid., 364; Ebenezer Farrand to Mallory, 15 May 1862, ibid., 370; Rodgers to Goldsborough, 16 May 1862, ibid., 357; quoted in Charles E. Clark, *My Fifty Years in the Navy* (Boston: Little, Brown, 1917), 88.

53. Goldsborough to Welles, 18 May 1862, *ORN,* ser. 1, 7:386; John Watters to A. L. Case, 19 May 1862, ibid., 387–90; Welles to Goldsborough, 20 May 1862, ibid., 403; W. Smith to Goldsborough, 20 May 1862, ibid., 404; Goldsborough to Fox, 21 May 1862, *Fox Correspondence,* 1:271. On 10 May, McClellan wrote that, if Norfolk was captured and the *Virginia* destroyed, he could change his base to the James River. Had he done so shortly after Norfolk was abandoned, he might have captured Richmond with the help of the navy. McClellan to Stanton, 10 May 1862, *ORA,* ser. 1, 11 (pt. 3): 160.

54. Goldsborough to William Smith, 22 May 1862, *ORN,* ser. 1, 7:397; McClellan to Goldsborough, 2 June 1862, ibid., 444; Jeffers to Goldsborough, 4 June 1862, ibid., 452.

55. W. Smith to Goldsborough, 29 May 1862, ibid., 435; W. Smith to Goldsborough, 27 May 1862, Area 7, Entry 463, RG 45, NA.

56. Goldsborough to Elizabeth, 13 June 1862, Goldsborough Papers, Duke.

57. The Confederates later built a similar vessel called the *Hunley.* Goldsborough to J. P. Gillis, 21 June 1862, *ORN,* ser. 1, 7:495; Welles to Goldsborough, 13, 21 June 1862, ibid., 477, 494; Endorsement by Goldsborough, 4 June 1862, ibid., 497; Rodgers to Goldsborough, 29 June 1862, ibid., 523; Selfridge, 68–71; Thomas O. Selfridge to Welles, 8 August 1862, Design and General Characteristics, Subject File AD, RG 45, NA.

58. Abstract Log of the *Port Royal,* 26, 28 June 1862, *ORN,* ser. 1, 7:724; Goldsborough to Welles, 1 July 1862, ibid., 536; Abstract Log of the *Satellite,* 26–28 June 1862, ibid., 725; Abstract Log of the *Galena,* 26–27 June 1862, ibid., 708–9.

59. John A. Dix to Goldsborough, 30 June 1862, ibid., 530; Rodgers to Goldsborough, 1 July 1862, ibid., 534; McClellan to Goldsborough, 27 June 1862, Area 7, Entry 463, RG 45, NA. The great numbers of vessels used by McClellan as transports required a great number of river pilots. The competition to hire these men was intense, but the army paid a higher salary, leaving the navy with less knowledgeable pilots and making the navy's job more difficult. Goldsborough to Welles, 30 June 1862, *ORN,* ser. 1, 7:530.

60. Daniel H. Hill, "McClellan's Change of Base and Malvern Hill," in *Battles and Leaders,* 2:394.

61. McClellan to Goldsborough, 1 July 1862, *ORN,* ser. 1, 7:532; Goldsborough to Rodgers, 1 July 1862, John Rodgers Collection, LCM.

62. Rodgers to Goldsborough, 1 July 1862, *ORN,* ser. 1, 7:533–34; R. E. Lee to Jefferson Davis, as cited in U.S. Navy, Naval History Division, *Civil War Naval Chronology 1861–1865,* 6 vols. (Washington, D.C.: Government Printing Office, 1971), 2:77, 80.

63. R. E. Johnson, *Rodgers,* 211; Rodgers to Goldsborough, 4 July 1862, *ORN,* ser. 1, 7:541–42; David Herbert Donald, ed., *Gone for a Soldier: The Civil War Memoirs of Private Alfred Bellard* (Boston: Little, Brown, 1975), 122.

64. T. H. Stevens to Rodgers, 4 July 1862, *ORN,* ser. 1, 7:543.

65. William W. Jeffries, "The Civil War Career of Charles Wilkes," *Journal of Southern History* 11 (August 1945): 325; entry for 10 August 1862, *Welles Diary,* 1:73.

66. Welles to Charles Wilkes, 6 July 1862, *ORN,* ser. 1, 7:548; Rodgers to Ann, 16 July 1862, Rodgers Collection, LCM.

67. Goldsborough to Welles, 11 July 1862, *ORN,* ser. 1, 7:565–66.

68. Goldsborough to Wilkes, 10 July 1862, ibid., 563; Wilkes to Rodgers, 15 August 1862, ibid., 653; Wilkes to A. P. Foster, 15 August 1862, ibid., 652; Wilkes to Rodgers, 15 August 1862, ibid., 653; Wilkes to Welles, 28 August

1862, ibid., 686. Wilkes did not take his job very seriously and stayed a great deal with his family in a hotel near Fort Monroe. Gardiner, 1031. During the withdrawal, the Sanitary Commission used the *Vanderbilt* as a hospital ship to evacuate the wounded. Katherine Prescott Wormeley, *The Other Side of War with the Army of the Potomac* (Boston: Ticknor, 1889), 103; Wilkes to Goldsborough, 31 August 1862, *ORN,* ser. 1, 7:692.

69. Goldsborough to Welles, 15 July 1862, Entry 30, RG 45, NA.

70. Goldsborough to Fox, 12 December 1861, Fox Correspondence, 1:217.

71. Goldsborough to Elizabeth, 29 May 1861, Goldsborough Papers, LCM; Christopher Raymond Perry Rodgers to Samuel F. Du Pont, 18 July 1862, Du Pont Letters, 2:163–64; entry for 10 August 1862, *Welles Diary,* 1:73.

4. The Navy in the Eastern Theater

1. Welles to Lee, 2 September 1862, *ORN,* ser. 1, 7:695; Welles to Hannibal Hamlin, 23 December 1862, Gideon Welles Papers, LCM; Headley, 416–17; *Dictionary of American Biography,* vol. 6, s.v. "Lee, Samuel P.," by Walter B. Norris.

2. John Rodgers to Ann, 11 September 1862, Rodgers Collection, LCM.

3. John Sanford Barnes, "My Egotistigraphy," unpublished manuscript, NYHS, 225.

4. Abstract Log Book of the *Minnesota,* 4 September 1862, *ORN,* ser. 1, 8:3. All flag officers who commanded squadrons were given the rank of rear admiral while on this duty. Rodgers to Lee, 9 September 1862, ibid., 15.

5. Rodgers to Lee, 9 September 1862, ibid., 14–15.

6. Lee to Fox, 8 September 1862, Fox Papers, NYHS; Lee to Welles, 12 September 1862, *ORN,* ser. 1, 8:16–17. Lee's fears stemmed in part from communication with John Bankhead of the *Monitor,* who claimed his vessel's machinery could not be relied on. His vessel had been under steam almost continually for seven months and was subject to breakdown at any time. Albert B. Campbell and Charles Loring to John P. Bankhead, 23 September 1862, Bankhead to Lee, 24 September 1862, Samuel Phillips Lee Collection, LCM; Lee to Fox, 17 September 1862, *Fox Correspondence,* 2:214.

7. Welles to Lee, 15 September 1862, *ORN,* ser. 1., 8:67; Order of Acting Rear Admiral S. P. Lee, 16 October 1862, ibid., 46.

8. Foxhall Parker to Lee, 9 January 1863, ibid., 409–10; Lee to Parker, 3 November 1863, ibid., 191; Douglas Southall Freeman, *Lee's Lieutenants: A Study in Command,* 3 vols. (New York: Charles Scribner's Sons, 1949), 2:247–48;

Longstreet to W. H. C. Whiting, 12 March 1863, *ORA,* ser. 1, 18:905; August V. Kautz, "Operations South of the James River," in *Battles and Leaders,* 4:533n.

9.   Lee to Welles, 16 April 1863, *ORN,* ser. 1, 8:729.

10.   The vessels that participated had to be withdrawn from other points, and some therefore did not take part in the first actions. Four of the vessels that took part in these actions were from the Potomac Flotilla. Longstreet had no more than 20,000 troops during the investment. Peck began with 15,000 on 31 March and by 30 April had 25,000 men. Kautz, 4:533n; James Russell Soley, "Closing Operations in the James River," in *Battles and Leaders,* 4:706; Francis P. B. Sands, "A Volunteer's Reminiscences of Life in the North Atlantic Blockading Squadron, 1861–5," in *Military Order of the Loyal Legion of the United States Commandry of the District of Columbia*, War Papers no. 20 (Washington: The Commandry, 1894), 21–22; Lee to Welles, 12 April 1863, *ORN,* ser. 1, 8:714–15; 25 April 1863, ibid., 774–75; E. Keyes to Lee, 14 April 1862 [1863], Lee Collection, LCM.

11.   Lee to William Cushing and R. H. Lamson, 13 April 1863, *ORN,* ser. 1, 8:717; Welles to Lee, 16 April 1863, Lee Collection, LCM.

12.   Lamson to Lee, 13 April 1863, *ORN,* ser. 1, 8:718–19; Lee to Cushing, ibid., 719–20.

13.   John J. Peck to Lee, 13 April 1863, ibid., 720; Lamson to Lee, 22 April 1863, ibid., 722–25; Sands, 21–22; Samuel J. Jones to William Maxwell Wood, 15 April 1863, *ORN,* ser. 1, 8:725; George W. Getty to B. B. Foster, 12 May 1863, *ORA,* ser. 1, 18:302.

14.   Cushing to Lee, 14 April 1863, *ORN,* ser. 1, 8:721.

15.   Lamson to Lee, 17 April 1863, ibid., 732.

16.   Lee to John A. Dix, 18 April 1863, ibid., 740; Peck to Lee, 19 April 1863, ibid., 742.

17.   Lamson to Lee, 19 April 1863, ibid., 741.

18.   Lamson to B. B. Foster, 12 May 1863, *ORN,* 8:746–47; William T. Street to Lee, 1 May 1863, ibid., 744–46; Getty to B. B. Foster, 12 May 1863, *ORA,* ser. 1, 18:304.

19.   Lee to Welles, 22 April 1863, Lee Collection, LCM; Samuel G. French, *Two Wars: An Autobiography of Gen. Samuel G. French* (Nashville: Confederate Veteran, 1901), 160–66; Cushing to Lee, 20 April 1863, Lee Collection, LCM.

20.   Peck to Lee, 21 April 1863, Lee to Peck, 6 May 1863, Dix to Lee, 25 April 1863, Lee to Dix, 4 May 1863, Entry 30, RG 45, NA; Getty to B. B. Foster, 12 May 1863, *ORA,* ser. 1, 18:304; Charles H. Brown to J. Gordon Bennett, 27 April 1863, Lee Collection, LCM.

21.   Cushing to Lee, 23 April 1863, *ORN,* ser. 1, 8:771–72; Lee to Welles, 23 April 1863, ibid., 770–71.

22. T. A. Harris to Lee, 11 April 1863, Lee Collection, LCM; Frank B. Butts, "Reminiscences of Gunboat Service on the Nansemond," in *Personal Narratives of Events in the War of the Rebellion, Being Papers Read before the Rhode Island Soldiers and Sailors Historical Society,* 3d ser., NO. 8 (Providence: The Society, 1884), 65–66.

23. Lee to Dix, 10 May 1863, Area 7, Entry 463, RG 45, NA; Harris to Lee, 10 May 1863, *ORN,* ser. 1, 9:12.

24. Lee to Welles, 24 October 1862, Lee Collection, LCM.

25. Halleck to Welles, 10 September 1862, Welles to Lee, 11 September 1862, ibid.

26. J. H. Gillis to Lee, 6 June 1863, *ORN,* ser. 1, 9:60–61; Lee to Welles, 7 June 1863, ibid., 59–60.

27. Foxhall A. Parker to Lee, 9 January 1863, Entry 30, RG 45, NA; Charles Babcock to Lee, 18 May 1863, *ORN,* ser. 1, 9:28; Lee to John Lenthall, 9 June 1863, Letters Received from Officers, Entry 62, RG 19, NA; J. H. Ellis to Lee, 25 June 1863, Lee Collection, LCM.

28. Peirce Crosby to Lee, 27 June 1863, *ORN,* ser. 1, 9:84–85; Crosby to Lee, 1 July 1863, ibid., 85–86; Ezra J. Warner, *Generals in Gray: Lives of the Confederate Commanders* (Baton Rouge: Louisiana State University Press, 1959), 184; *Dictionary of American Biography,* s.v. "Lee William Henry Fitzhugh" by Richard Douthat Meade, 11:134–35; Samuel P. Spear to D. T. Van Buren, 28 June 1863, *ORA,* ser. 1, 27 (pt. 2): 795–96.

29. Crosby to Lee, 25 June 1863, *ORN,* ser. 1, 9:60–61; Crosby to Lee, 1 July 1863, Lee Collection, LCM; Lee to Welles, 20 July 1863, *ORN,* ser. 1, 9:116; Charles P. Stone to Adjutant-General of the Army, 27 November 1863, ibid., 411; Charles Babcock to Lee, 20 May 1864, Lee Collection, LCM.

30. Lee to Dix, 14 May 1863, Dix to Lee, 5 [15] May 1863, Entry 30, RG 45, NA.

31. Dix to Lee, 5 May 1863, *ORN,* ser. 1, 9:3–4; J. H. Gillis to Lee, 7 May 1863, ibid., 7–8; Gillis to Lee, 2 June 1863, ibid., 52–53.

32. Lee to Welles, 18 October 1863, ibid., 245–46; Endorsement by Fox, ibid., 246.

33. *Virginia II* and *Fredericksburg* were both commissioned in 1864, having been delayed for want of armor. Still, *Iron Afloat,* 168–70; Raphael Semmes, *Memoirs of Service Afloat during the War between the States* (Baltimore: Kelly, Piet, 1869), 803; Lee to Isaac Miller, 6 July 1863, *ORN,* ser. 1, 9:111; Order of Acting Rear Admiral Lee, 18 December 1863, ibid., 360.

34. J. H. Upshur to Lee, 9 April 1864, ibid., 593; R. O. Crowley, "The Confederate Torpedo Service," *Century Magazine* 56 (June 1898): 297; Guert Gansevoort to Lee, 12 April 1864, *ORN,* ser. 1, 9:599–600; Hunter Davidson to

Mallory, 11 April 1864, ibid., 603; John S. Barnes to Lee, 13 April 1864, ibid., 597–98; Lee to Welles, 16 April 1864, ibid., 15–16, passim; Hunter Davidson, "Mines and Torpedoes during the Rebellion," *Magazine of History* 8 (November 1908): 259.

35. Lee to Welles, 21 March 1864, *ORN,* ser. 1, 9:558; Lee to Butler, 27 April 1864, Entry 30, RG 45, NA.

36. Butler to Lee, 27 January 1864, Benjamin Franklin Butler Papers, LCM; Lee to Lizzie Lee, 31 July 1864, Blair-Lee Papers, Princeton.

37. Butler took command of the Department of Virginia and North Carolina in November 1863. On paper, he had over 40,000 officers and men. Benjamin F. Butler, *Butler's Book* (Boston: A. M. Thayer, 1892), 627; Richard S. West, Jr., *Lincoln's Scapegoat General: A Life of Benjamin F. Butler 1818–1893* (Boston: Houghton Mifflin, 1965), 219, 229–30; Lee to Welles, 25 April 1864, *ORN,* ser. 1, 9:90–91.

38. Lee to J. C. Beaumont, 4 May 1864, Area 7, Entry 463, RG 45; William Farrar Smith, "Butler's Attack on Drewry's Bluff," in *Battles and Leaders,* 4:207; Pierre G. T. Beauregard, "The Defense of Drewry's Bluff," in *Battles and Leaders,* 4:196n.

39. Samuel Huse to Gansevoort, 7 August 1863, *ORN,* ser. 1, 9:147; Thomas F. Wade to Welles, 13 May 1864, ibid., 10:14–15; Jefferson Young to J. C. Beaumont, 1 May 1864, ibid., Abstract Log of the *Commodore Morris,* 6 May 1864, ibid., 15; Barnes, 99.

40. W. M. Elliott to C. F. Linthicum, 7 May 1864, *ORN,* ser. 1, 10:30–31; William Rushmore to Welles, 19 November 1864, ibid., 29.

41. Lee to Parrott, 14 May 1862, ibid., 56; Lee to Smith, 3 July 1864, ibid., 236.

42. Lee to John M. B. Clitz, 14 May 1864, J. M. B. Clitz Collection, Entry 395, Subseries 61, RG 45, NA; Lee to Lamson, 12 May 1864, *ORN,* ser. 1, 10:49; Lee to Clitz, 17 May 1864, ibid.; Lee to Welles, 17 May 1864, ibid., 64; Lamson to Lee, 25 May 1864, Lee Collection, LCM.

43. Mallory to Seddon, 19 May 1864, *ORA,* ser. 1, 51 (pt. 2): 946–47; J. B. Jones, *A Rebel War Clerk's Diary at the Confederate States Capital,* 2 vols., 11 May 1864 (Philadelphia: J. B. Lippincot, 1866), 2:205.

44. John K. Mitchell to Mallory, 23, 24 May 1864, *ORN,* ser. 1, 10:649, 650, 653.

45. Still, *Iron Afloat,* 175.

46. Benjamin F. Butler, *Private and Official Correspondence of Gen. Benjamin F. Butler during the Period of the Civil War,* 5 vols. (Norwood, Mass.: Plimpton, 1917), 4:298, 373 (cited hereafter as *Butler Correspondence*); Lee to Welles, 24 May 1864, Entry 30, RG 45, NA.

47. W. F. Smith, 4:211.

48. Thomas P. Bell to Mitchell, 25 June 1864, *ORN,* ser. 1, 10:709.

49. Herman Hattaway and Archer Jones, *How the North Won: A Military History of the Civil War* (Urbana: University of Illinois Press, 1983), 588–89; Henry to Josie, 15 June 1864, Henry A. Phelon Papers, SHC.

50. Lee to Welles, 4 June 1864, *ORN,* ser. 1, 10:117; Lee to Butler, 2 June 1864, Butler to Lee, 2 June 1864, ibid., 131; Lee to Welles, 7 June 1864, ibid., 129.

51. *Herald* (New York), 23 June 1864.

52. Welles to Lee, 4 June 1864, *ORN,* ser. 1, 10:116–17; Lee to Melancton Smith, 3 July 1864, ibid., 233; Lenthall to Stribling, 2 June 1864, Letters Sent to the Commandant, Philadelphia Navy Yard, Entry 54, RG 19, NA; "Letter of Rear Admiral Samuel Phillips Lee to Senator James Rood Doolittle," 20 February 1865, *Publications of the Southern History Association* 9 (March 1905): 114; Lee to Welles, 17 August 1864, *ORN,* ser. 1, 10: 371–72; Grant to Lee, 9 August 1864, ibid., 373.

53. Mitchell to Mallory, 20 June 1864, ibid., 704–5; Lee to Welles, 19 June 1864, ibid., 161; W. H. Parker, *Recollections,* 359.

54. W. H. Parker, *Recollections,* 337.

55. T. A. M. Craven to Lee, 23 June 1864, *ORN,* ser. 1, 10:178–79; Edmund R. Calhoun to Lee, 23 June 1864, ibid., 179; David B. Macomb to E. G. Parrott, 23 June 1864, ibid., 182–83; Lee to Butler, 21 June 1864, ibid., 177.

56. Butler to Lee, telegraph, 18 June 1864, Lee Collection, LCM; Lee to Grant, 23 June 1864, ibid., 184. Three of the seven canal boats sank on the way from Baltimore, two sank while in Hampton Roads, one remained in Hampton Roads, and the remaining vessel was towed back to Baltimore. Lenthall to Stribling, 2 July 1864, Entry 54, RG 19, NA; Lee to M. Smith, 20 July 1864, *ORN,* ser. 1, 10:290; M. Smith to Lee, 16 September 1864, ibid., 464–65; Lee to Farragut, 28 September 1864, Lee Collection, LCM; David D. Porter to Edward T. Nichols, 5 November 1864, Area 7, Entry 463, RG 45, NA; M. Smith to S. P. Quakenbush, 11 July 1864, *ORN,* ser. 1, 10:255; M. Smith to Lee, 13 July 1864, ibid., 266; Quakenbush to M. Smith, 12 July 1864, ibid.; Lee to M. Smith, 9 July 1864, ibid., 242–43; Edward T. Nichols to M. Smith, 12 July 1864, ibid., 262.

57. Hattaway and Jones, 600–601; Lee to Welles, 14 July 1864, *ORN,* ser. 1, 10:272; Downs to Welles, 11 July 1864, ibid.; Welles to Lee, 11 July 1864, ibid.

58. Welles to Lee, 19 July 1864, ibid., 284.

59. M. Smith to Lee, 9 August 1864, ibid., 345; M. Smith to Welles, 13 August 1864, ibid., 350; Porter to Fox, 10 October 1864, Fox Papers, NYHS; Butler, *Butler's Book,* 751.

60. William Read, Jr., to father and mother, 30 October 1864, William Read, Jr., Papers, Duke; Porter to Fox, 19 November 1864, *ORN*, ser. 1, 11:77; Fox to Porter, ibid., 78; Porter to Fox, 20 November 1865, ibid., 78; Porter to Fox, 11 October 1864, Fox Papers, NYHS.

61. In July 1864, Welles had established four divisions in the squadron and given Smith the command of the James River Division. Welles to Lee, 26 July 1864, *ORN*, ser. 1, 10:307. D. D. Porter Papers, Journal 1, 1860–65, 894–95, LCM.

62. Porter to Edward T. Nichols, 30 October 1864, *ORN*, ser. 1, 11:28; Porter to William A. Parker, 2 December 1864, Entry 30, RG 45, NA.

63. Mallory to Mitchell, 16 January 1865, *ORN*, ser. 1, 11:797–98; W. H. Parker, *Recollections*, 343; Scharf, 740; Thomas J. Woodward to Lee, 29 March 1864, Lee Collection, LCM.

64. Parker to Porter, 31 January 1865, *ORN*, ser. 1, 11:656. Parker may have been influenced by Foxhall A. Parker's book on tactics, which was profusely illustrated with tactical maneuvers. Although Parker's tactics were useless in the confinement of the James River, his book was read by the officers of the squadron. Foxhall A. Parker, *Squadron Tactics under Steam* (New York: D. Van Nostrand, 1864), passim.

65. Grant to Fox, 24 January 1865, *ORN*, ser. 1, 11:635; Special Orders to Gunboat Commanders Issued by Lieutenant General U. S. Grant, 24 January 1864, ibid.

66. Mitchell to Mallory, 3 February 1865, ibid., 670.

67. Ibid.

68. C. W. Read to Mitchell, 25 January 1865, ibid., 684; Still, *Iron Afloat*, 185; W. H. Parker, *Recollections*, 343.

69. Mitchell to Mallory, 3 February 1865, *ORN*, ser. 1, 11:671.

70. Welles to Parker, 24 January 1865, ibid., 637; Parker to Porter, 31 January 1865, ibid., 656.

71. Porter to Fox, 5 February 1865, Fox Papers, NYHS; Porter to Parker, 14 February 1865, *ORN*, ser. 1, 11:658. Parker was tried by court-martial for failing to do his utmost to destroy vessels of the enemy. The court dismissed Parker from the navy but recommended clemency because of his thirty-three years of service. Welles did not approve the sentence and dismissed it, though Captain Parker was placed on the retired list. Finding of a Court Martial in the Case of Commander William A. Parker, U.S. Navy (n.d.), ibid., 662–63.

72. Raphael Semmes Diary (n.d.), 1865, Raphael Semmes Papers, Duke; Semmes, 803.

73. Radford to Porter, 28 January 1865, *ORN*, ser. 1, 11:649–50; Circular, 28 January 1865, Area 7, Entry 463, RG 45, NA; Special Order for the James River

Squadron, 25 February 1865, Entry 395, RG 45, NA; General Order of William Radford, 28 February 1865, Area 7, Entry 463, RG 45, NA.

74. Raphael Semmes Diary, 2 April 1865, Raphael Semmes Papers, Duke.

5. Stalemate in North Carolina

1. The army had posts at Morehead City, Beaufort, Fort Macon, New Bern, Washington, Plymouth, and Roanoke Island and on the Outer Banks.

2. Burnside to Stanton, 30 May 1862, *ORN*, ser. 1, 7:462; Burnside to Stanton, 29 May 1862, *ORA*, ser. 1, 9:394–95; Welles to Stanton, 4 June 1862, *ORN*, ser. 1, 7:462; Goldsborough to Welles, 9 June 1862, ibid., 469.

3. Fox to Goldsborough, 23 May 1862, ibid., 419.

4. Foster to Stanton, 8 July 1862, *ORA*, ser. 1, 9:410; Day, 61.

5. Flusser to Rowan, 11 July 1862, *ORN*, ser. 1, 7:556; Thomas J. Woodward to Flusser, 11 July 1862, ibid., 557.

6. Barrett, 134n; John Nix to Southard Hoffman (n.d.), *ORA*, ser. 1, 18:8.

7. Ibid., 8–9; Foster to Halleck, 13 September 1862, *ORN*, ser. 1, 8:7–8; Foster to Halleck, 7 September 1862, *ORA*, ser. 1, 18:4–5.

8. R. T. Renshaw to H. K. Davenport, 8 September 1862, *ORN*, ser. 1, 8:6–7; Edward E. Potter to Hoffman, 5 [6] September 1862, *ORA*, ser. 1, 18:7.

9. Flusser to Davenport, 6 October 1862, *ORN*, ser. 1, 8:108; William B. Cushing, "Outline Story of the War Experiences of William B. Cushing as Told by Himself," *U.S. Naval Institute Proceedings* 38 (September 1912): 947–48.

10. Flusser to Davenport, 6 October 1862, *ORN*, ser. 1, 8:108.

11. J. K. Rawson, Statement of the Principle Engagements and Expeditions in Which Commander Cushing Took Part during the War of the Rebellion 1861–1865, Cushing Papers, ZB Collection, Operational Archives, NHC; Flusser to Davenport, 6 October 1862, *ORA*, ser. 1, 18:19.

12. Dix to Lee, 5 October 1862, *ORN*, ser. 1, 8:106; J. K. Marshall to Samuel G. French, 4 October 1862, *ORA*, ser. 1, 18:19; Cushing, "War Experiences," 948; George R. Mann to Edmund R. Colhoun, 6 October 1862, *ORN*, ser. 1, 8:111; Charles French to Flusser, 4 October 1862, ibid., 112, George W. Gale to Flusser, 3 October 1862, ibid., 109; Peck to D. T. Van Buren, *ORA*, ser. 1, 18:19.

13. Lee to Welles, 14 November 1862, *ORN*, ser. 1, 8:180.

14. John L. Lay to Richard T. Renshaw, 11 November 1862, *ORN*, ser. 1, 8:205; Stephen F. Blanding, *Recollections of a Sailor Boy, or, The Cruise of the Gunboat Louisiana* (Providence: E. A. Johnson, 1886), 202.

15. Cushing to Davenport, 26 November 1862, *ORN*, ser. 1, 8:230–31.

16. Ibid., 231–32.

17. Goldsborough to Welles, 23 May 1862, ibid., 7:416.

18. Davenport to R. T. Renshaw, 14 July 1863, Correspondence of Henry K. Davenport, Letter Books of Officers of the United States Navy at Sea, Subseries 56, Entry 395, RG 45, NA; Lee to Davenport, 16 November 1862, *ORN,* ser. 1, 8:212; Lee to Lenthall, 30 November 1862, Letters Received from Officers, Entry 62, RG 19, NA. Porter's tinclads were covered with more iron than any of Lee's. Porter to Welles, 12 January 1863, *ORN,* ser. 1, 8:484.

19. Flusser to Lee, 17 January 1863, ibid., 475; Lee to Davenport, 20 March 1863, Administration and Organization (Internal) of Ships and Fleet Units 1860–1870, Subject File OA, RG 45, NA.

20. Lee to Lenthall, 30 November 1862, Entry 62, RG 19, NA; Y. F. Furniss to Lee, 21 February 1863, Lee Collection, LCM; Joshua Tollansbee to Thomas A. Dornin, 24 March 1863, Entry 62, RG 19, NA; Lee to Lenthall, 30 March 1863, ibid.; Dornin to Lenthall, 3 April 1863, ibid.; Lee to Isherwood, 30 March 1863, ibid.

21. P. G. Peltz to Lee, 14 April 1863, Lee Collection, LCM; Davenport to James S. Chambers, 18 November 1862, *ORN,* ser. 1, 8:220; A. Murray to Lee, 29 January 1863, Lee Collection, LCM; Lee to Murray, 3 February 1863, *ORN,* ser. 1, 8:500; Lee to Lenthall, 21 February 1863, Lee Collection, LCM; Lee to Lenthall, 18 March 1863, Entry 62, RG 19, NA; W. W. Dungan to Lee, 4 February 1863, Lee Collection, LCM; Lee to Lenthall, 6 February 1863, Entry 62, RG 19, NA; Lenthall to Stribling, 14 February 1863, Letters Sent to the Commandant, Philadelphia Navy Yard, Entry 54, RG 19, NA; Lenthall to Stribling, 19 February 1863, Letters Sent to Officers, Entry 51, RG 19, NA.

22. Lee to Fox, 27, 29 October 1862, *Fox Correspondence,* 1:226–27.

23. Davenport to Lee, 29 October 1862, Lee Collection, LCM; Lee to Welles, 25 October 1862, ibid.

24. Lee to Welles, 14 November 1862, *ORN,* ser. 1, 8:180.

25. C. W. Flusser to Lee, 10 December 1862, *ORN,* ser. 1, 8:275; Charles F. W. Behm to Flusser, 10 December 1862, ibid., 276; Flusser to Lee, 10 December 1862, ibid., 275; Barnabas Ewer to General Foster, 10 December 1862, *ORA,* ser. 1, 18:45–46; J. T. Mizell to E. E. Potter, 16 December 1862, ibid., 48–49.

26. Foster to Halleck, 27 December 1862, *ORA,* ser. 1, 18:54; Alexander Murray to Lee, 30 December 1862, *ORN,* ser. 1, 8:290.

27. Lee to Welles, 24 December 1862, ibid., 289; Murray to Lee, 16 December 1862, ibid., 288; Murray to Lee, 30 December 1862, ibid., 290; David A. Taylor to Albert J. Myer, 22 December 1862, *ORA,* ser. 1, 18:61–62; Beverly H. Robertson to A. L. Evans, 19 December 1862, ibid., 121; Taylor to Myer, 22 December 1862,, ibid., 61–62; *Daily Journal* (Wilmington), 7 January 1863.

28. A. Murray to Lee, 10 February 1863, Lee Collection, LCM.

29. John Withers Special Order 32, 7 February 1863, *ORA,* ser. 1, 18:872, 2; S. Cooper to James Longstreet, 25 February 1863, ibid., 895; Longstreet to Hill, 1 March 1863, ibid., 903.

30. Abstract from Return of the Department of North Carolina, February 1863, ibid., 547; Willis C. Humphrey, *The Great Contest: A History of Military and Naval Operations during the Civil War in the United States of America, 1861–1865* (Detroit: C. H. Smith, 1886), 478.

31. Longstreet to Lee, 19 March 1863, *ORA,* ser. 1, 18:926; Longstreet to Lee, 3 April 1863, ibid., 958; Longstreet to Seddon, 7 April 1863, ibid., 970; Hill, *North Carolina,* 151–152; James Longstreet, *From Manassas to Appomattox: Memoirs of the Civil War in America* (Philadelphia: J. B. Lippincott, 1896), 324; Longstreet to Lee, 30 March 1863, *ORA,* ser. 1, 18:950–51.

32. Murray to Lee, 14 March 1863, *ORN,* ser. 1, 8:604; John J. Pettigrew to D. H. Hill, 17 March 1863, *ORA,* ser. 1, 18:193; Murray to Lee, 20 March 1863, *ORN,* ser. 1, 8:608.

33. Johnathan S. Belknap to Davenport, 15 March 1863, ibid., 609.

34. Murray to Lee, 20 March 1863, ibid.; Foster to Flusser, 16 March 1863, Area 7, Entry 463, RG 45, NA; Murray to Flusser, 19 March 1863, ibid.; Davenport to Flusser (endorsement), ibid.

35. Longstreet to Lee, 22 March 1863, *ORA,* ser. 1, 18:937; Longstreet to Lee, 30 March 1863, ibid., 950; Lee to Longstreet, 30 March 1863, ibid., 907.

36. Foster to Halleck, 30 April 1863, ibid., 212–13; Hal Bridges, *Lee's Maverick General: Daniel Harvey Hill* (New York: McGraw-Hill, 1961), 175; Foster to Halleck, 5 April 1863, *ORA,* ser. 1, 18:211; Richard T. Renshaw to Davenport, 18 April 1863, *ORN,* ser. 1, 8:680; Davenport to Lee (n.d.), ibid., 674; William Gurdon Saltonstall, *Reminiscences of the Civil War and Autobiography of William Gurdon Saltonstall* (by the author, 1913), 41–42; William W. Douglas, "Relief Of Washington, North Carolina, by the Fifth Rhode Island Volunteers," in *Personal Narratives of Events in the War of the Rebellion, Being Papers Read before the Rhode Island Soldiers and Sailors Historical Society,* 3d ser., no. 17 (Providence: The Society, 1886), 12.

37. Davenport to Lee, 6 April 1863, *ORN,* ser. 1, 8:657; R. T. Renshaw to Murray, 1 April 1863, ibid., 650; Edwin McKeever to Murray, ibid.; Blanding, 235; Henry K. Burgwyn to father, 21 April 1863, Burgwyn Family Papers, SHC.

38. Renshaw to Davenport, 18 April 1863, *ORN,* ser. 1, 8:681; entry for 3 April 1863, John M. Taylor, ed., "Francis Josselyn: A Gunboat Captain's Diary," *Manuscripts* 33 (Spring 1981): 118.

39. John MacDarmid to Renshaw, 18 April 1863, *ORN,* ser. 1, 8:686; John

Cheves Haskell, *The Haskell Memoirs,* ed. Gilbert E. Govan and James W. Livingood (New York: G. P. Putnam's Sons, 1960), 43.

40. Henry Prince to Southard Hoffman, 13 April 1863, *ORA,* ser. 1, 18:223; Spinola to Hoffman, 15 May 1863, ibid., 250; entry for 5 April 1863, John Jasper Wyeth, *Leaves from a Diary Written While Serving in Co. E, 44 Mass., Dept. of No. Carolina from September, 1862, to June, 1863* (Boston: L. F. Lawrence, 1878), 46.

41. Pettigrew to Hill, 13 April 1863, *ORA,* ser. 1, 18:985; Renshaw to Davenport, 18 April 1863, *ORN,* ser. 1, 8:683. There is some confusion about the second trip. Foster states it occurred on the 15th, while Renshaw states it was the 14th. Foster to Halleck, 30 April 1863, *ORA,* ser. 1, 18:215; Renshaw to Davenport, 18 April 1863, *ORN,* ser. 1, 8:683; Davenport to Lee, 17 April 1863, ibid., 671; A. P. [D. H.] Hill to W. F. Lynch, 21 April 1863, ibid., 698; Lee to Foster, 17 April 1863, *ORA,* ser. 1, 18:630. The two naval vessels above the blockade had withstood a scathing fire from the Confederate batteries; the *Commodore Hull* was struck 108 times. W. G. Saltonstall to Renshaw, 20 April 1863, *ORN,* ser. 1, 8:695.

42. George P. Erwin to father, 3 April 1863, George P. Erwin Papers, SHC; R. B. Garrett to Hill, 15 April 1863, *ORA,* ser. 1, 18:988; Barrett, 157n; Davenport to Flusser, 17 April 1863, *ORN,* ser. 1, 8:672; Davenport to Fox, 1 May 1863, Fox Papers, NYHS.

43. For a more detailed analysis of this problem see chapter 7.

44. Murray to Lee, 21 January 1863, *ORN,* ser. 1, 8:459–60; Davenport to Lee, 21 April 1863, Subseries 56, Entry 395, RG 45, NA; Lee to Davenport, 5 June 1863, Area 7, Entry 463, RG 45, NA; Robert Townsend to Lee, 3 January 1863, Lee Collection, LCM.

45. Lee to Foster, 17 April 1863, *ORA,* ser. 1, 18:630; Lee to Foster, 1 May 1863, Entry 30, RG 45, NA. An example of the problem, is the distance between New Bern and Washington. While only thirty miles apart by land, they are over 100 miles distant by water. Eastern Portion of the Military Department of North Carolina, May 1862, Civil Works Map File, RG 77, NA.

46. Foster to Lee, 22 April 1863, Area 7, Entry 463, RG 45, NA.

47. Bridges, 181–83; Foster to Halleck, 7 July 1863, *ORA,* ser. 1, 27 (pt. 2): 859–60; Flusser to Lee, 21 August 1863, *ORN,* ser. 1, 9:136.

48. Lee to Welles, 17 August 1863, ibid., 162; Lee to Davenport, 20 August 1863, ibid., 174–75.

49. Robert E. Lee to Davis, 2 January 1864, Robert Edward Lee Papers, Duke. Butler had withdrawn over 1,000 men from New Bern in April. William M. Smith, "The Siege and Capture of Plymouth," in *Personal Recollections of the War of the Rebellion: Addresses Delivered before the New York Commandry of the Loyal Legion of the United States, 1883–1891,* ed. James Grant Wilson and Titus

Munson Coan (New York: The Commandry, 1891), 325; Davis to Lee, 4 January 1864, *ORA*, ser. 1, 33:1064; Lee to Davis, 20 January 1864, ibid., 1101.

50. H. D. Smith, "Cutting Out the 'Underwriter': A Brilliant Exploit in a Southern Harbor," in *Under Both Flags: A Panorama of the Great Civil War as Represented in Story, Anecdote, Adventure, and the Romance of Reality, Written by the Celebrities of Both Sides,* ed. George M. Vickers (Chicago: National Book Concern, 1896), 153–56.

51. Abstract from Return of the Department of North Carolina, February 1864, *ORA*, ser. 1, 33:1201; Pickett to Samuel Cooper, 15 February 1864, ibid., 92–94; Wood to Mallory, 11 February 1864, *ORN*, ser. 1, 9:451–52; George W. Gift to Catesby ap R. Jones, 13 February 1864, ibid., 453; Daniel B. Conrad, "Capture and Burning of the Federal Gunboat 'Underwriter,' in the Neuse, off Newbern, N.C., in February, 1864," *Southern Historical Society Papers* 19 (January–December 1891): 95.

52. Conrad, 95; B. P. Loyall, "Capture of the Underwriter," *Southern Historical Society Papers* 27 (1899): 137–39; *ORN*, ser. 2, 1:228.

53. John Sanford Barnes to Lee, 4 February 1864, *ORN*, ser. 1, 9:458; G. E. Allen to G. W. Graves, 2 February 1864, Lee Collection, LCM; A Confederate, "Capture of the Underwriter," *The Gray Jackets and How They Lived, Fought, and Died for Dixie* (Richmond: Jones Brothers, 1867), 469; Loyall, 140–42; Graves to Davenport, 2 February 1864, *ORN*, ser. 1, 9:442.

54. Scharf, 398; Loyall, 140–42; Wood to Mallory, 11 February 1864, *ORN*, ser. 1, 9:452; Allen to Graves, 2 February 1864, Lee Collection, LCM; Davenport to Lee, 1 March 1864, ibid., 446–47.

55. Davenport to Flusser, 2 February 1864, ibid., 455; Davenport to Lee, 7 February 1864, ibid., 468; Pickett to Cooper, 15 February 1864, *ORA*, ser. 1, 33:94; Flusser to Lee, 5 February 1864, *ORN*, ser. 1, 9:464.

56. Letters of Howard and Ellis, 6 December 1862, Construction, Confederate Subject File AC, NA; Letters of Martin and Elliott, 28 December 1862, ibid.; Lee to Davis, 20 January 1864, *ORA*, ser. 1, 33:101.

57. Still, *Iron Afloat,* 91; Virgil Carrington Jones, "Construction, Fighting Career and Destruction of the Albemarle," *Civil War Times Illustrated* 1 (June 1962): 8. The machinery capable of making marine engines was transferred to Charlotte, North Carolina, along with other machinery from Norfolk, before its recapture by the federal troops. Ralph W. Donnally, "The Charlotte, North Carolina, Navy Yard, C.S.N.," *Civil War History* 5 (March 1959): 72–74; Gilbert Elliott and Edgar Holden, "The Career of the Confederate Ram 'Albemarle,'" *Century Illustrated Monthly Magazine* 36 (July 1888): 420–21; William N. Still, Jr., "The Career of the Confederate Ironclad *Neuse,*" *North Carolina Historical Review* 43 (January 1966): 1–2.

58. U.S. Congress, Senate, *Light-Draught Monitors,* S. Rept. 142, pt. 3, 38th Cong., 2d sess., 1865, 3, 78; RSN 1864, 117; Lee to Fox, 27 October 1862, *Fox Correspondence,* 2:226.

59. Statement of James Willis sworn before H. K. Davenport, 11 November 1863, Lee Collection, LCM; C. W. Flusser to Lee, 27 March 1864, ibid.

60. Lee to Fox, 26 October 1862, *Fox Correspondence,* 2:225.

61. Butler to Fox, 28 November 1863, *ORN,* ser. 1, 9:332; Butler to Lee, 30 December 1863, ibid., 384; Butler to Peck, 20 February 1864, *Butler Correspondence,* 3:441; Lee to Flusser, 12 February 1864, *ORN,* ser. 1, 8:523–24; Davenport to Renshaw, 17 February 1864, ibid., 9:491; Flusser to Lee, 8 June, 5 September 1863, Lee Collection, LCM. The Union torpedoes were cylindrical and were set off by contact or by hand using a line. John L. Lay to Lee, 25 December 1862, Flusser to Lee, 31 October 1863, Lee Collection, LCM; Flusser to Lee, 18 March 1864, *ORN,* ser. 1, 9:556; Flusser to Lee, 27 March 1864, Lee Collection, LCM; Davenport to Lee, 1 July 1863, Entry 30, RG 45, NA; E. A. McDonald to Davenport, 17 June 1863, ibid.; Samuel D. Hines to Davenport, 8 June 1863, ibid.; William H. Stanford to Davenport, 30 June 1863, ibid.; John Peck to Butler, 17 February 1864, Butler Papers, LCM.

62. Flusser to Lee, 21 August 1863, *ORN,* ser. 1, 9:175; R. S. Davis General Orders 29, 11 November 1863, *ORA,* 29 (pt. 2): 447; Lee to Welles, 22 January 1863, *ORN,* ser. 1, 8:468; Lee to Welles, 24 November 1863, Entry 30, RG 45, NA; Welles to Stanton, 17 September 1863, Area 7, Entry 463, RG 45, NA; Butler to Lee, 17 February 1864, *ORN,* ser. 1, 9:491; Pickett to Whiting, 12 April 1864, *ORA,* ser. 1, 33:1278.

63. Bragg to Hoke, 12 April 1864, ibid., 51 (pt. 2): 857–58; Wessels to Flusser, 27 March 1864, Lee Collection, LCM; Peck to Butler, 13 February 1864, Butler Papers, LCM; Butler to Peck, 21 March 1864, *Butler Correspondence,* 3:563. After the capture of Plymouth, the *Neuse* steamed down the Neuse River and ran aground and remained there for a month.

64. Elliott and Holden, 422.

65. Wessels to Peck, addenda, 15 August 1864, *ORA,* ser. 1, 33:301.

66. Cooke to Mallory, 23 April 1864, *ORN,* ser. 1, 9:656–57; Gilbert Elliott, "The First Battle of the Confederate Ram 'Albemarle,'" in *Battles and Leaders,* 4:626–27.

67. "Flusser and the Albemarle," manuscript by Frank W. Hackett, ZO Collection, Operational Archives, NHC.

68. Allen, 59; Flusser to mother, 3 December 1863, Flusser Papers, ZB Collection, Operational Archives, NHC.

69. Flusser quoted in Lee to Butler, 19 April 1864, Butler Papers, LCM; G. W. Barrett to Davenport, 21 April 1864, *ORN,* ser. 1, 9:643; Flusser to

Davenport, 18 April 1864, ibid., 637; "Flusser and the Albemarle," Hackett Manuscripts, ZO Collection, NHC; Elliott and Holden, 423; Elliott, 4:627; Flusser to Lee, 27 March 1864, Lee Collection, LCM; Flusser to Lee, 18 April 1864, Joint Military Naval Engagements, Subject File HJ, RG 45, NA; French to Lee, 19 April 1864, *ORN,* ser. 1, 9:638; French to Lee, 21 April 1864, ibid., 642; Sayres Ogden Nichols to father, 4 May 1864, Roy F. Nichols, ed., "Fighting in North Carolina Waters," *North Carolina Historical Review* 40 (Winter 1963): 81.

70. Sayres Ogden Nichols to father, 4 May 1864, Nichols, 81; P. H. Pursell to Lee, 21 April 1864, *ORN,* ser. 1, 9:645.

71. As quoted in Charles W. Stewart, "Lion-Hearted Flusser: A Naval Hero of the Civil War," *U.S. Naval Institute Proceedings* 31, no. 2 (June 1905): 296; Frank W. Hackett to Davenport, 18 April 1864, *ORN,* ser. 1, 9:638–39; French to Lee, 21 April 1864, ibid., 641.

72. W. M. Smith, 336.

73. Wessels to J. J. Peck, 18 August 1864, *ORN,* ser. 1, 9:654–55. Before learning of Plymouth's capture, General Ulysses Grant suggested to Butler that both Washington and Plymouth be evacuated and that the garrisons be added to Butler's proposed landing at Bermuda Hundred in Virginia. He thought that this would win the Union forces "not only the coast, but probably most of the state." Grant to Butler, 22 April 1864, *ORA,* ser. 1, 33:946; Grant to Halleck, 22 April, ibid., 947; W. M. Smith, 336.

74. 20 April 1864, Flusser Papers, ZB Collection, Operational Archives, NHC.

75. Fox to John Ericson, 21 April 1864, *ORN,* ser. 1, 9:667; Fox to Ericson, 22 April 1864, ibid., 683.

76. Butler to Halleck, 21 April 1864, *ORA,* ser. 1, 33:278–80; Lee to Welles, 24 April 1864, *ORN,* ser. 1, 9:688–89.

77. Grant to Butler, telegram, 24 April 1864, Butler Papers, LCM; Davenport to Lee, 26 April 1864, *ORN,* ser. 1, 9:700; Abstract from Record on Events on Return of the Sub-District of the Pamlico for April, 1864, *ORA,* ser. 1, 33:312; I. N. Palmer to Davenport, 27 April 1864, *ORN,* ser. 1, 9:704; Davenport to Lee, 26 April 1864, ibid., 700.

78. Charles F. Warren, "Washington during the Civil War," in *The Confederate Reveille,* United Daughters of the Confederacy, North Carolina Division, Pamlico Chapter 43 (Raleigh: Edwards and Broughton, 1898), 17–19; John A. Judson, General Orders 5, 3 May 1864, *ORA,* ser. 1, 33:310; John A. Judson Circular Orders, 30 May 1864, ibid., 311.

79. Davenport to Lee, 28 April 1864, ibid., 703; Leslie S. Bright, William H. Rowland, and James C. Bardon, *CSS Neuse: A Question of Iron and Time* (Raleigh: North Carolina Department of Cultural Resources, Division of Ar-

chives and History, 1981), 15; Beauregard to Robert F. Hoke, 1 May 1864, as cited in Alfred Roman, *The Military Operations of General Beauregard in the War between the States 1861 to 1865*, 2 vols. (New York: Harper and Brothers, 1884), 2:544; Beauregard to Hoke, ibid., 2:545.

80. Davenport to Senior Naval Officers in Albemarle Sound, 21 April 1864, *ORN*, ser. 1, 9:670–71; Barnes, "My Egotistigraphy," NYHS, 212. The Navy Department preferred ramming tactics combined with close gunfire, but other tactics, such as torpedoes, fouling the ram's propeller with nets, and throwing shells and water down her stacks, were also considered. Welles to Lee, 23 April 1864, *ORN*, ser. 1, 9:683; Lee to Smith, 23 April 1864, Area 7, Entry 463, RG 45, NA; Henry Phelon to Josephine, 1 May 1864, Henry Phelon Papers, SHC. Smith doubted ramming tactics would work because of the enclosed rudders on both ends of the double-enders. Frank M. Bennett, *The Steam Navy of the United States* (Pittsburg: Warren, 1896), 455; Lee to Smith, 21 April 1864, *ORN*, ser. 1, 9:684, 669; Welles to Lee, 22 April 1864, ibid., 682; Lee to Davenport, ibid., 682–83; Butler to Fox, 22 April 1864, ibid., 650–51.

81. D. W. Wardrop to J. A. Judson, 30 April 1864, Area 7, Entry 463, RG 45, NA; Lee to Smith, 3 May 1864, *ORN*, ser. 1, 9:723.

82. Davis to Beauregard, 4 May 1864, as cited in Roman, 2:547.

83. Nichols to father, 6 May 1864, Nichols, 83–84; Melancton Smith to Lee, 5 May 1864, *ORN*, ser. 1, 9:734–35.

84. Both the *Sassacus* and the *Mattabasett* claimed to have captured the *Bombshell*. Smith to Lee, 5 May 1864, ibid.; F. A. Roe to Smith, 6 May 1864, ibid., 738; John C. Febiger to Smith, May 1864, ibid., 747.

85. Smith to Lee, 5 May 1864, ibid., 734; Edgar Holden, "The 'Sassacus' and the 'Albemarle,'" *Magazine of History with Notes and Queries* 5 (May 1907): 270; Francis Josselyn to Smith, 6 May 1864, *ORN*, ser. 1, 9:756.

86. Roe to John S. Barnes, 11 May 1864, Barnes Collection, NYHS; F. A. Roe to Smith, 5 May 1864, *ORN*, ser. 1, 9:737; C. A. Boutelle to Roe, 6 May 1864, ibid., 741; Edgar Holden, "The 'Albemarle' and 'Sassacus,'" in *Battles and Leaders*, 4:629–30; Roe to Smith, 7 May 1864, Area 7, Entry 463, NA. Roe's actions of 5 May earned him an advancement of five numbers in his grade. Welles to Roe, 22 July 1864, *ORN*, ser. 1, 9:761.

87. Smith to Lee, 5 May 1864, ibid., 734.

88. Sayres Ogden Nichols to father, 6 May 1864, Nichols, 84; Still, *Iron Afloat*, 165.

89. Edgar Holden to Roe, 6 May 1864, *ORN*, ser. 1, 9:742–43; Samuel P. Boyer to John C. Febiger, 5 May 1864, ibid., 735; Roe to Smith, 8 May 1864, ibid., 757; Walter W. Queen to Smith, 6 May 1864, ibid., 751.

90. Smith to Lee, 5 May 1864, ibid., 736; Smith to R. T. Renshaw, 13 May

1864, Area 7, Entry 463, RG 45, NA; William H. Macon to Lee, 7 July 1864, *ORN,* ser. 1, 9:239; Smith to Lee, 13 May 1864, Correspondence of Melancton Smith, Subseries 85, Entry 395, RG 45, NA; note by William H. Macomb, 3 July 1864, Correspondence of William Macomb, Subseries 67, ibid.; Smith to Lee, 24 May 1864, Entry 30, RG 45, NA.

91. Instructions, Macomb, 10 September 1864, Correspondence of William Macomb, Subseries 67, Entry 395, RG 45, NA; Smith to Lee, 6 June 1864, *ORN,* ser. 1, 10:145; James M. Williams to Smith, 8 June 1864, ibid., 135–36; Welles to Lee, 6 June 1864, ibid., 127; Lee to Macomb, 30 June 1864, ibid., 220; Lee to Macomb, 20 July 1864, ibid., 294; Lee to Welles, 9 July 1864, ibid., 244; Lee to Macomb, 9 August 1864, ibid., 345–46.

92. Smith to Lee, 7 May 1864, ibid., 31–32; Smith to Palmer, 23 May 1864, Subseries 85, Entry 395, RG 45, NA.

93. Davenport to Smith, 5 June 1864, *ORN,* ser. 1, 10:121; Welles to Lee, 26 July 1864, ibid., 307; Macomb to Lee, 7 July 1984, ibid., 239; Welles to Lee, 1 September 1864, ibid., 415; Welles to Rowan, ibid.; Lee to Macomb, 9 September 1864, ibid., 449; Welles to Rowan, 22 September 1864, ibid., 474.

94. Sidney Smith Lee to John N. Maffitt, 9 June 1864, ibid., 687. Baker's name became "Lawrence" after the War Department misspelled his name by error. Warner, *Generals in Gray,* 14; Endorsement, Stephen R. Mallory, 30 July 1864, *ORN,* ser. 1, 10:720; William T. Truxtun to Macon, 7–9 August 1864, ibid., 341–42; Mallory to Maffitt, 9 September 1864, Maffitt Papers, SHC. There was also a change of authority in the sounds. Welles, dissatisfied with Lee and wishing for his resignation, had removed Lee from any responsibility in the sounds. On 1 September, he gave Commodore S. C. Rowan command of the naval forces there—a separate and distinct command. Rowan's orders were revoked after three weeks, and the naval forces in the sounds were placed back under Lee. Welles to Lee, 1 September 1864, Area 7, Entry 463, RG 45, NA; Welles to Rowan, 22 September 1864, *ORN,* ser. 1, 10:474.

95. Lee to Cushing, 14 May 1864, Lee Collection, LCM; Smith to Lee, 12 May 1864, Area 7, Entry 463, RG 45, NA; V. C. Jones, "Construction," 43; Smith to Lee, 30 May 1864, *ORN,* ser. 1, 10:95.

96. Lee to Welles, 9 July 1864, ibid., 247–48; William B. Cushing, "The Destruction of the 'Albemarle,'" in *Battles and Leaders,* 4:634–35.

97. Cushing to Porter, 30 October 1864, *ORN,* ser. 1, 10:611–12; Cushing, "Destruction" 4:636–37; A. F. Warley, "Note on the Destruction of the 'Albemarle,'" in *Battles and Leaders,* 4:642.

98. Porter to Macomb, 22 October 1864, *ORN,* ser. 1, 10:594; Samuel Phillips Lee, "Letter of Rear Admiral Samuel Phillips Lee to Senator James

Rood Doolittle," *Publications of the Southern History Association* 9 (March 1905): 115–16.

99. David Dixon Porter, "A Famous Naval Exploit," *North American Review* 153 (September 1891): 296.

100. Macomb to Porter, 1 November 1864, *ORN,* ser. 1, 11:12–14.

101. Ibid., 14; Lincoln to Senate of the United States, 5 December 1864, ibid., 27.

102. Macomb to Porter, 6 November 1864, ibid., 64–65; Porter to Macomb, 8 November 1864, ibid., 26.

103. Jones Frankle to Macomb, 24 November 1864, ibid., 93–94; Porter to Butler, 28 November 1864, Area 7, Entry 463, RG 45, NA; Porter to Macomb, 1 December 1864, *ORN,* ser. 1, 11:115; Macomb to Porter, 13 December 1864, Entry 30, RG 45, NA.

104. U.S. Congress, Senate, *Fort Fisher Expedition: Report of the Joint Committee on the Conduct of War,* S. Rept. 142, pt. 2, 38th Cong., 2d sess., 1865, 6; Macomb to Porter, 11 December 1864, *ORN,* ser. 1, 11:160–61; John M. Batten, *Reminiscences of Two Years in the United States Navy* (Lancaster, Penn.: Inquirer, 1881), 65–67.

105. Macomb to Porter, 11 December 1864, *ORN,* ser. 1, 11:161.

106. Abram D. Harrell to Macomb, 30 December 1864, ibid., 172–73; Macomb to Porter, ibid., 181; Batten, 67. The navy used six boat crews in pairs, rowing twenty feet apart with a chain suspended between them, to drag the bottom in order to snag torpedoes. G. J. Rains, "Torpedoes," *Southern Historical Society Papers* 3 (May–June 1877): 256.

107. John A. J. Brooks to Macomb, 21 December 1864, *ORN,* ser. 1, 11:168–69; John A. J. Brooks to Porter, 27 December, ibid., 169.

108. Earl English to Macomb, 31 January 1864, ibid., 175; Macomb to Porter, 30 December 1864, ibid., 177–80; Macomb to Porter, 15 February 1865, ibid., 12:22; Porter to Grant, 11 February 1865, ibid., 15; Porter to Macomb, ibid., 16; Porter to Macomb, 6 February 1865, ibid., 8–9; Porter to William Radford, 6 February 1865, ibid., 7.

109. Goldsborough to Fox, 1 March 1862, Fox Papers, NYHS.

110. William N. Still, Jr., "Confederate Naval Strategy: The Ironclad," *Journal of Southern History* 27 (August 1961): 338, 340–42.

6. Operations in the Interior Waters

1. Abraham Lincoln to James C. Conkling, 26 August 1863, as cited in Roy P. Basler, ed., *The Collected Works of Abraham Lincoln,* 9 vols. (New Brunswick, N.J.: Rutgers University Press, 1953–1955), 6:409–10.

2. The northern limits of the North Atlantic Blockading Squadron changed several times during the war. The Rappahannock River was the early northern boundary, but in April 1862, the Rappahannock was placed under control of the Potomac Flotilla. In September, the squadron's limits were reduced to include north to the mouth of the Piankatank River. The squadron eventually watched only as far north as Mobjack Bay. In February 1865, this was reduced further when the Potomac Flotilla's limits were extended to the Back River just above Fort Monroe. Welles to Goldsborough, 17 April 1862, *ORN,* ser. 1, 7:245; Welles to Goldsborough, 2 September 1862, ibid., 695; Lee to Farragut, 28 September 1864, Lee Collection, LCM; Welles to Porter, 6 February 1865, *ORN,* ser. 1, 12:6.

3. Foxhall Parker to Thomas Turner, 19 November 1862, Lee Collection, LCM; Lee to Welles, 24 January 1863, *ORN,* ser. 1, 8:473; Lee to Welles, 14 March 1864, ibid., 9:550; Guert Gansevoort to Lee, 7 June 1864, Lee Collection, LCM; Butts, "Reminiscences," 9; Rachel Minick, "New York Ferryboats in the Union Navy," *New-York Historical Society Quarterly* 46 (October 1962): 425–26.

4. Butts, "Reminiscences," 9. Often the vessels used in the interior waters were the worst vessels of the squadron, vessels in bad repair, unseaworthy, or just floating batteries, and were sent to the sounds and bays because they could not function on the outside blockade. Welles to Lee, 24 September 1862, *ORN,* ser. 1, 8:85.

5. Butts, "Reminiscences," 9; H. K. Davenport to Lee, 10 November 1862, Entry 30, RG 45, NA.

6. Flusser to Mrs. Flusser, 21 April 1862, Flusser Papers, ZB Collection, Operational Archives, NHC; Batten, 20 December 1864, 74; A. D. Harrell to W. H. Macomb, 30 December 1864, *ORN,* ser. 1, 11:172–73; Parker to Lee, 6 November 1862, 6 July 1864, Lee Collection, LCM; Blanding, 117, 147; Order of S. P. Lee, 30 June 1864, Subseries 61, Entry 395, RG 45, NA; Lee to C. A. Babcock, 23 June 1864, *ORN,* ser. 1, 10:198; John A. J. Brooks to H. N. T. Arnold, 30 September 1864, ibid., 502; Batten, 29 September 1864, 34–35; Lee to J. C. Chaplin, 10 October 1862, *ORN,* ser. 1, 8:126.

7. Lee to Parker, 6 November 1862, ibid., 202; Melancton Smith to Quakenbush, 4 August 1864, Subseries 85, Entry 395, RG 45, NA. Lee issued precautionary orders just three days after the attack on the *Minnesota* by the torpedo boat *Squib.* Porter issued precisely the same orders upon taking command of the squadron. Order for the Part of the North Atlantic Blockading Squadron Inside of Cape Henry, Order of S. P. Lee, 12 April 1864, Subseries 61, Entry 395, RG 45, NA; Order by Porter, 12 April 1864 [*sic*], ibid.; General Order 49 by D. D. Porter, 16 November 1864, ibid.

8. Butts, "Reminiscences," 8; Thomas T. Craven to Welles, 5 September 1861, *ORN,* ser. 1, 4:658–59.

9. Abstract Log of the *Port Royal*, 22 May 1862, ibid., 723; Abstract Log of the *Hunchback*, 13 May 1862, ibid., 710; R. T. Renshaw to W. R. McCann, 10 April 1863, Area 7, Entry 463, RG 45, NA.

10. Beaumont to Lee, 21 May 1864, *ORN*, ser. 1, 10:80; Cushing to Lee, 23 April 1863, ibid., 8:771–72; Amos P. Foster to F. H. Patterson, 16 October 1862, Lee Collection, LCM; Renshaw to McCann, 10 April 1863, Area 7, Entry 463, RG 45, NA; W. T. Adams, "Guns for the Navy," *Ordnance* 45 (January–February 1961): 508–9; William B. Avery, "Gun-Boat Service on the James River," in *Personal Narratives of Events in the War of the Rebellion, Being Papers Read before the Rhode Island Soldiers and Sailors Historical Society*, 3d ser., no. 3 (Providence: The Society, 1884), 11.

11. Augustus C. Savage to Melancton Smith, 20 August 1864, Subject File OA, RG 45, NA; R. G. Lee to S. P. Lee, 4 July 1864, Lee Collection, LCM; Edward Nichols to Lee, 17 May 1864, ibid.; Lee to Lamson, 17 May 1864, *ORN*, ser. 1, 10:66; Parker General Order, 30 November 1864, Area 7, Entry 463, RG 45, NA; William Parker to Homer C. Blake, 30 November 1864, Subject File OA, RG 45, NA.

12. Endorsement by John M. Stone, 22 May 1863, *ORN*, ser. 1, 8:763; Flusser to Murray, 21 March 1863, ibid., 622.

13. Milton F. Perry, *Infernal Machines: The Story of Confederate Submarines and Mine Warfare* (Baton Rouge: Louisiana State University Press, 1965), 5–6, 13–16; Crowley, 290–91. In October 1862, the Confederacy set an important precedent by establishing a Naval Submarine Battery Service under Davidson's direction, indicating that the Confederacy put a great emphasis on this project. Alex Roland, *Underwater Warfare in the Age of Sail* (Bloomington: Illinois University Press, 1978), 156; *U.S. Navy, Chronology*, 2:105; Crowley, 291; R. H. Lamson to Lee, 25 May 1864, *ORN*, ser. 1, 10:92.

14. Gillis to Lee, 13 October 1863, Lee Collection, LCM; R. H. Lamson to Lee, 25 May 1864, *ORN*, ser. 1, 10:93; Horatio G. Robinson to mother, 18 May 1864, Horatio G. Robinson Collection, Duke; Lee to Welles, 15 May 1864, ibid., 58; Avery, "Gun-Boat Service," 26–27; General Order 6 of David D. Porter, 13 October 1864, Subject File OA, RG 45, NA; William Smith to Goldsborough, 4 November 1861, *ORN*, ser. 1, 6:392–93.

15. The *Shawmut* also lost a launch in the Cape Fear River as a result of a torpedo, making a total of eight sunk and three damaged. M. F. Perry, appendix, 199–201.

16. Thomas J. Woodward to Charles W. Flusser, 10 May 1862, *ORN*, ser. 1, 7:385; Benjamin Porter to Davenport, 26 August 1862, ibid., 663; Earl English to William H. Macomb, 13 July 1864, ibid., 10:265; Flusser to Lee, 25 February 1864, ibid., 9:500; J. H. Gillis to Lee, 2 April 1862, 10 April 1863, ibid., 8:643–46,

707–8; A. Murray to Lee, 5 March 1863, Subseries 56, Entry 395, RG 45, NA; Fred Sherman to father, Fredric Sherman Letters, SHC; Charles Flusser to mother, 13 May 1862, Flusser Papers, ZB Collection, Operational Archives, NHC.

17. James Norcum, "The Eastern Shore of North Carolina, in 1861 and 1862," *Historical Magazine and Notes and Queries* 8 (November 1870): 302–3; Owen Huggins and A. J. Johnston to Zebulon B. Vance, 29 September 1862, *ORA,* ser. 1, 51 (pt. 2): 629–30. A boat could carry a great deal of merchandise. A boat captured in the Chowan River area was carrying two men, four barrels of fish, two barrels of tallow, and 2,000 pounds of salted meat. H. H. Foster to Macomb, 9 January 1865, Area 7, Entry 463, RG 45, NA. Canoes were likewise large by modern standards. The Paquoson and other canoes built in the Chesapeake Bay area were used by oystermen. They had sails and all varied in their hull shapes and rigs, but they measured from twenty-five feet to over forty feet in length. M. V. Brewington, *Chesapeake Bay: A Pictorial Maritime History* (Cambridge, Md.: Cornell Maritime Press, 1953), 63–73; Edwin A. Wild to George H. Johnston, 28 December 1863, *ORA,* ser. 1, 29 (pt. 1): 915; W. H. Macomb to Lee, 22 July 1864, Entry 30, RG 45, NA; F. M. Green to Macomb, 23 August 1864, Area 7, Entry 463, RG 45, NA.

18. O. S. Glisson to Goldsborough, 5 October 1861, Entry 30, RG 45, NA; Goldsborough to Welles, 9 August 1862, ibid.; Lee to Butler, 9 April 1864, ibid.; Goldsborough to Acting Master North, 30 September 1861, *ORN,* ser. 1, 6:272; J. H. Gillis to Lee, 2 May, 24 September 1863, Lee Collection, LCM; Welles to Goldsborough, 2 October 1861, Area 7, Entry 463, RG 45, NA; Frederic B. M. Hollyday, ed., "Running the Blockade: Henry Hollyday Joins the Confederacy," *Maryland Historical Magazine* 41 (March 1946): 7–10; Chase to McGowan, 5 August 1862, Letter Sent, Entry 143, RG 26.

19. The rebels considered the blockade so lax in the York River area in the first year of the war that, following the fight between the *Virginia* and *Monitor,* the Confederates considered trying to run the steamer *Bahama* loaded with munitions into the York River—a pretty bold idea. Caleb Huse to J. Gorgas, 15 March 1862, *ORA,* ser. 4, 3:1003–4; Butts, "Reminiscences," 10–11; David Cambell to Porter, 10 November 1864, *ORN,* ser. 1, 11:59; Edwin McKeever to R. T. Renshaw, 21 December 1862, Lee Collection, LCM. For a thorough list of captured and destroyed vessels, see Robert M. Browning, Jr., appendix E in "From Cape Charles to Cape Fear: The North Atlantic Blockading Squadron During the Civil War" (Ph.D. diss., University of Alabama, 1988).

20. Lee to Welles, 3 October 1863, *ORN,* ser. 1, 9:225.

21. William B. Avery, "The Marine Artillery with the Burnside Expedition and the Battle of Camden, N.C.," in *Personal Narratives of Events in the War*

of the Rebellion, Being Papers Read before the Rhode Island Soldiers and Sailors Historical Society, 2d ser., no. 5 (Providence: N. Banks Williams, 1880), 10; W. A. Howard to R. Aulick, 4 February 1864, Butler Papers, LCM; Charles Graham to E. O. C. Ord, 21 January 1865, *ORA,* ser. 1, 46 (pt. 2): 196; John Caulk to Samuel Chase, 16 December 1861, Letters from Collections of Customs, Entry 150, Record Group 26, Records of the U.S. Coast Guard, Logs of *Reliance, Agassiz, Antietam, Phillip Allen, A. N. Brown,* passim; Logs of Revenue Cutters and Coast Guard Vessels, Entry 159, RG 26, NA; Ottinger to Chase, 15 December 1862, Entry 151, RG 26, NA.

22. Rowan to Quakenbush, 29 April 1862, Subseries 28, Entry 395, RG 45, NA.

23. Memorandum to Gen. Hitchcock, 23 December 1862, Butler Papers, LCM.

24. James Parker to Leonard Paulding, 3 March 1863, Lee Collection, LCM; Lee to Gillis, 21 February 1863, Area 7, Entry 463, RG 45, NA; A. A. Lewis, Phillip G. Low, and H. M. Pierce to Gillis, 21 February 1863, Gillis to Lee, 22 February 1864, Lee Collection, LCM. Gillis's men were again charged with molesting property, which suggests that his men were probably involved in these excessive practices. Gillis to Lee, 26 April 1863, *ORN,* ser. 1, 8:827; Peirce Crosby to Welles, 21 May 1863, Entry 30, RG 45, NA; Lee to Gillis, 5 May 1863, *ORN,* ser. 1, 9:4.

25. Roland F. Coffin to Lee, 26 June 1863, Lee Collection, LCM; William Jennings to Lee, 18 August 1863, *ORN,* ser. 1, 9:161; Charles Babcock to Lee, 24 May 1863, ibid., 40–41; Lee to Welles, 4 June 1863, ibid., 39; Day, entry for 18 April 1864, 134; Lee to Butler, 9 April 1864, *Butler Correspondence,* 4:53.

26. Lee to J. G. Foster, 3 October 1863, *ORN,* ser. 1, 9:226; General Order 24 of Gideon Welles, 21 November 1863, Directives, Entry 43, RG 45, NA; Peter Hayes to Lee, 8 March 1864, Lee Collection, LCM.

27. John Yates Beall, *Memoir of John Yates Beall: His Life; Trial; Correspondence; Diary and Private Manuscript, Found among His Papers, Including His Own Account of the Raid on Lake Erie,* ed. Daniel Bedinger Lucas (Montreal: John Lovell, 1865), 24–27; Lee to Welles, 30 September 1863, *ORN,* ser. 1, 9:206; J. H. Gillis to Lee, 8 October 1863, ibid., 207–9; J. G. Foster to H. W. Halleck, 10 October 1863, ibid., 209–10; Gansevoort to Welles, 28 September 1863, ibid., 204, and Entry 30, RG 45, NA. On 5 March 1864, guerrillas again struck, capturing the army tug *Titan* and boarding and disabling the steamer *Aeolus.* On 25 October 1864, one of the picket boats for Lieutenant William Cushing's attack on *Albemarle* was likewise captured. Lee to Welles, 7 March 1864, *ORN,* ser. 1, 9:527, passim; Edward T. Beardsley to Andrew Stockholm, 25 October 1864, Area 7, Entry 463, RG 45, NA.

28. Governor Zebulon Vance did not make the job of the Union navy any easier; he allowed the mustering of companies for state defense, called the North Carolina Defenders. Each captain became his own mustering officer, which made it easier to create a band of men to operate as guerrillas. Edwin A. Wild to George H. Johnston, 28 December 1863, *ORA*, ser. 1, 29 (pt. 1): 915; H. K. Davenport to Lee, 22 May 1863, 26 July 1863, *ORN*, ser. 1, 9:38, 39; Henry Phelon to Josie, 21 June 1863, Phelon Papers, SHC.

29. Davenport to Lee, 12 December 1863, Lee Collection, LCM; Evidence in Matter of Sch. *Sample* Owned by Isaiah Respies and Her Cargo 1864 (n.d.), *Butler Correspondence*, 3:391–92; J. Bishop to Peirce Crosby, 16 May 1863, *ORN*, ser. 1, 9:23, passim; Alexander Crosby Brown, *Juniper Waterway: A History of the Albemarle and Chesapeake Canal* (Charlottesville: University Press of Virginia, 1981), 76–79.

30. Edward A. Wild to George H. Johnston, 28 December 1863, Butler to Stanton, 31 December 1863, Butler Papers, LCM.

31. Day, entry for 18 April 1864, 143. The navy held the people of Elizabeth City responsible for protecting vessels passing through the canals. In return for this protection, the citizens were allowed to communicate with Roanoke Island, New Bern, and Norfolk. Lee to Welles, 15 September 1864, *ORN*, ser. 1, 10:457; Macomb to Lee, 13 September 1864, ibid., 457–58; Macomb to Wardrop, 11 September 1864, Subseries 67, Entry 395, RG 45, NA.

32. John A. Dix to Stanton, 4 September 1862, *ORN*, ser. 1, 8:23–24.

33. Dix to Halleck, 27 September 1862, *ORA*, ser. 1, 18:407; Lee to Dix, 24 September 1862, ibid., 402; Lee to Dix, 5 October 1862, ibid., 416–17; Lee to Dix, 11 September 1862, ibid., 393. The secretary of the treasury granted permits for items, including coal, to go to Norfolk, allowing the inhabitants to pay with shingles, tobacco, and sweet potatoes. Dix to Lee, 1 October 1862, ibid., 412; Lee to Welles, 14 September 1862, 16 September 1862, *ORN*, ser. 1, 8:19–20; Welles to Lee, 18 September 1862, Lee Collection, LCM.

34. Lee to Dix, 18 September 1862, 23 September 1862, *ORA*, ser. 1, 18:394, 400; A. Ludlow Case to George A. Stevens, 22 September 1862, *ORN*, ser. 1, 8:82. In 1861, when the squadron was still small and Norfolk was still in rebel hands, vessels coming and going reported to the flag officers or senior officer present. Subject File OA, RG 45, NA; Lee to Dix, 27 September 1862, *ORA*, ser. 1, 18:408. On October 1862, thirty-two vessels were employed by the War Department in the Department of Virginia. Less than five months later, this number had increased to forty-nine. List of Steamers in the Employ of the War Department, 22 October 1862, *ORN*, ser. 1, 8:54; List of Vessels Employed by the War Department, 11 March 1863, ibid., 597.

35. Dix to Chase, 21 September 1862, *ORA*, ser. 1, 18:398.

36. The major products of the city were shingles, staves, tobacco, cotton, and some agricultural products. Entries for 10, 18 October 1862, *Welles Diary,* 1:165–66, 177.

37. The major complaint of Dix was that the vessels coming and going from Fort Monroe were examined by the treasury revenue cutter, the captain of the port, and the navy guard vessel. He believed that the navy's examination was not required and caused undue delays. Dix to Lee, 18 October 1862, *ORA,* ser. 1, 18:431.

38. Stanton to Dix, 18 October 1862, Lee Collection, LCM; Dix to Lee, 22 October 1862, ibid.; Lee to Dix, 25 October 1862, *ORA,* ser. 1, 18:440; Welles to Stanton, 9 November 1862, *ORA,* ser. 1, 18:452; John Tucker to Dix, 12 November 1862, ibid.

39. Executive Order, 11 November 1862, *ORN,* ser. 1, 8:66.

40. Schaffer to Butler, 8 July 1864, Welles to Stanton, 22 July 1864, C. A. Dana to Grant, 16 January 1865, *Butler Correspondence,* 4:474, 527, and 5:502; entry for 23 January 1863, *Welles Diary,* 1:226–27.

41. Lee to Dix, 19 January 1863, *ORA,* ser. 1, 18:522; Dix to Lee, 20 January 1863, ibid., 523; Dix to Lee, 31 January 1863, ibid., 531.

42. Ludwell H. Johnson III, "Blockade or Trade Monopoly? John A. Dix and the Union Occupation of Norfolk." *Virginia Magazine of History and Biography* 93 (January 1985): 59, 76.

43. Lee to Dix, 21 February 1863, *ORN,* ser. 1, 8:542–43; Lee to Welles, 4 November 1862, Lee Collection, LCM; Porter to R. B. Lowry, 27 October 1864, *ORN,* ser. 1, 10:608; Welles to Lee, 27 January 1863, ibid., 8:480; Lee to Welles, 4 November 1862, Lee Collection, LCM; Lee to Dix, 19 February 1863, *ORA,* ser. 1, 18:541–42; Dix to Lee, 20 February 1863, ibid., 543; Lee to Dix, 23 December 1862, ibid., 490; Dix to Lincoln, 7 March 1863, Area 7, Entry 463, RG 45, NA.

44. F. H. Peirpoint to Stanton, 20 January 1864, Butler Papers, LCM; Henry Lockwood to Butler, 24 December 1863, ibid.; C. W. Singleton to Butler, 1 January 1864, ibid.; William James to Butler, 12 January 1864, ibid.; William Hennelly to Butler, 15 January 1864, ibid.; Butler to Lincoln, 23 February 1864, *Butler Correspondence,* 3:451–52; Butler to Peck, ibid., 297; H. A. Risley to H. H. Morse, 18 December 1863, ibid., 226; Lee to Farragut, 28 September 1864, Lee Collection, LCM; Abstract of Permits by E. W. Carpenter, 31 October 1863, RG 366, NA, passim; Barnes, "My Egotistigraphy," NYHS, 218.

45. Lee to Butler, 28 May 1864, Butler Papers, LCM; Foxhall Parker to Thomas Turner, 27 November 1862, Lee Collection, LCM; J. H. Gillis to Lee, 30 March 1863, ibid.

46. Gillis to Lee, 15 November 1863, Area 7, Entry 463, RG 45, NA; Gillis to Lee, 15 November 1863, Lee Collection, LCM.

47. Porter to Reigart B. Lowry, 27 October 1864, *ORN,* ser. 1, 10:607; Abraham Lincoln to William H. Seward, 19 November 1864, ibid., 11:109.

48. U. S. Government, *The Statutes at Large: Treaties and Proclamations of the United States of America,* ed. George P. Sanger, vol. 12 (Boston: Little, Brown, 1863), 1263; Edwin M. Stanton to Edward Stanly, 19 May 1862, *ORA,* ser. 1, 9:396–97; U.S. Congress, House, *Impeachment of the President,* Order of Edwin Stanton, 29 September 1862, H. Rept. 7, 40th Cong., 1st sess., 1867, 729.

49. Some congressional leaders were displeased with Stanly's appointment because Lincoln had placed him as military governor of the state without their consent, as prescribed by the Constitution. Norman D. Brown, *Edward Stanly: Whiggery's Tarheel "Conqueror,"* Southern Historical Publications 18 (University: University of Alabama Press, 1974), 3, 214–15, 234, 236; R. D. W. Conner et al., *History of North Carolina,* 6 vols. (Chicago: Lewis, 1919), 2:42; Stanton to Stanly, 20 May 1862, *ORA,* ser. 1, 9:397.

50. N. D. Brown, ibid., 235–36.

51. Lee to Welles, 17 November 1862, Lee Collection, LCM; Murray to Lee, 9 December 1862, Subseries 56, Entry 395, RG 45, NA. The navy was also aided by two Treasury Department revenue cutters, the *Forward* stationed at Beaufort and the *Agassiz* at New Bern, which were to stop illicit trade and had the authority to search vessels, their cargoes, and all private baggage. S. P. Chase to Douglas Ottinger, 23 September 1862, Lee Collection, LCM.

52. Rowan to Viele, 5 July 1862, Subseries 28, Entry 395, RG 45, NA.

53. Lee to Davenport, 2 December 1862, *ORN,* ser. 1, 8:247–49; Lee to Welles, 15 January 1862, ibid., 438; Ottinger to Chase, 15 December 1862, Entry 151, RG 26, NA; N. D. Brown, 238.

54. Permit by Edward Stanly, 4 December 1862, *ORN,* ser. 1, 8:306–7; Davenport to Stanly, 6 December 1862, ibid., 307; Stanly to Davenport, ibid., 307–8; Davenport to Stanly, 7 December 1862, ibid., 308.

55. Davenport to Lee, 8 December 1862, ibid., 305–6.

56. Lee to Murray, 16 December 1862, ibid., 308–9; Murray to Lee, 9 December 1862, ibid., 305.

57. U.S. Congress, House, *Impeachment of the President,* C. P. Wolcott to Stanly, 15 December 1863, 731. Stanly submitted his resignation to Lincoln on 15 January 1863, after the Emancipation Proclamation of 1 January, because he believed that any reconciliation with the state was now hopeless. His resignation was acknowledged on 4 March 1863. Stanly to Lincoln, 15 January 1862, ibid.; N. D. Brown, 239–40, 249–50.

58. Murray to Renshaw, 9 February 1863, *ORN,* ser. 1, 8:516–17; Lee to Murray, 25 March 1863, ibid., 627–28; Lee to Welles, 22 February 1863, ibid., 550; Endorsement by Welles, ibid.; Circular by A. Murray, 9 March 1863, Lee Collection, LCM; Murray to Davenport, 30 March 1863, *ORN,* ser. 1, 8:637–38.

59. Davenport to Lee, 11 May 1863, Subseries 67, Entry 395, RG 45, NA; Charles Eames to A. A. Harwood, 28 April 1863, Lee Collection, LCM. To administer the areas of Union occupation after Stanly left the state, General Foster, the commander of the Department of North Carolina, set up three districts. The District of Neuse, comprising New Bern and its vicinity (the railroad, Morehead City, Carolina City, Beaufort, and Fort Macon), was administered by Brigadier General Henry M. Naglee. Brigadier General Henry Wessels oversaw the District of Albemarle, which included Plymouth and Roanoke Island. Brigadier General Henry Prince commanded the District of the Pamlico, which included Washington and Hatteras Inlet. J. G. Foster General Order 62, 22 April 1863, Lee Collection, LCM.

60. Wild to George H. Johnston, 28 December 1863, Butler Papers, LCM; Ottinger to Chase, 27 February 1863, 15 May 1863, Entry 151, RG 26, NA.

61. Logs of *Agassiz,* January 1863, *Anteitam,* July 1864, *Phillip Allen,* March 1864, *A. N. Brown,* January 1864, *Forward,* February and May 1863, Cutter Logs, Entry 159, RG 26; Davis to Fessenden, 5 January 1865, Ottinger to Chase, 15 December 1862, 11 March 1863, G. R. Slicer to Chase, 15 June 1864, Entry 151, RG 26, NA.

62. U.S. Customs Service, *A History of Enforcement in the United States Customs Service 1789–1875* (San Francisco: Department of Treasury, U.S. Customs Service, 1988), 94–95; Heaton to Chase, 30 May 1863, Records of the Sixth Special Treasury Agency, Records of the Civil War Special Agencies, RG 366, NA.

63. D. Heaton, List of Local Special Agents and Agency Aids, . . . September 1, 1863 to June 30, 1865, Local Rules for the Sixth Special Treasury Agency North Carolina, 11 November 1864, D. Heaton, RG 366, NA.

64. These trade districts were situated in Washington, Tyrell, Hyde, Craven, Carterett, Currituck, and Camden counties, Core Banks, Hatteras Banks, Chicamicomico, Roanoke Island, Collington's Island, Bodie's Island, Kill Devil Hills, and most of Beaufort County, including Washington, and were to be enlarged to include Chowan, Perquimans, Pasquotank, and Gates counties. Notice to Traders, Shippers, and Carriers—D. Heaton, 13 July 1863, Lee Collection, LCM; To Parties Interested—D. Heaton, 27 August 1863, ibid.

65. Heaton to Butler, 23 November 1863, *Butler Correspondence,* 3:152; Evidence in Matter Of Sch. *Sample* Owned by Isaiah Respies, 1864 [n.d.], ibid., 391–92.

66. Butler to Heaton, 20 August 1864, ibid., 5:56–57.

67. Macomb to W. T. Truxton, 6 July 1864, Subseries 67, Entry 395, RG 45, NA; Macomb to Lee, 7 July 1864, ibid.; Benjamin Butler to Stanton, 7 August 1864, Lee Collection, LCM; Enclosure, Welles to Lee, 15 August 1864, ibid.; M.

Smith to Lee, 15 June 1864, *ORN,* ser. 1, 10:163; entry for 23 June 1864, *Welles Diary,* 2:56.

68. Macomb to Welles, 4 January 1865, *ORN,* ser. 1, 11:410; H. H. Foster to Macomb, 9 January 1865, ibid., 418–19.

69. Heaton to Chase, 11 November 1863, RG 366, NA; Abstract Return of the Business Transacted, 6 February 1864, by E. W. Carpenter, Abstract of Fees, Abstract of Permits, ibid.; U.S. Congress, House, *Captured and Abandoned Property in Insurrectionary States,* H. Ex. Doc. 78, 38th Cong., 1st sess., 1864, 2.

70. Percival Perry, "The Naval Stores Industry in the Old South, 1790–1860," *Journal of Southern History* 34 (November 1968): 525; Welles to Lee, 14 July 1863, *ORN,* ser. 1, 9:124–25; Ludwell H. Johnson III, "Northern Profit and Profiteers: The Cotton Rings of 1864–1865," *Civil War History* 12 (June 1966): 101–2.

71. Notice to Purchasers and Shippers of Naval Stores, 18 August 1863, *ORN,* ser. 1, 27:530; Charles C. Upham to Lee, 13 October 1863, Lee Collection, LCM; D. Heaton to Lee, 11 December 1863, Entry 62, RG 19, NA; Davenport to Francis Josselyn, 24 October 1863, Subseries 56, Entry 395, RG 45, NA.

72. Upham to Lee, 14 October 1863, Entry 62, RG 19, NA; Lee to Welles, 25 October 1863, Entry 30, RG 45, NA.

73. Lee to Lenthall, 17 October 1863, Entry 62, RG 19, NA; Upham to Lee, 20 December 1863, 15 February, 2 April, 14 May 1864, ibid.

74. Upham to Lenthall, 1 September 1864, Entry 62, RG 19, NA. At the end of October 1864, the navy had expended $370,000 for naval stores in North Carolina. Upham to Lenthall, 29 October 1864, ibid.

75. Lenthall to Lee, 25 January 1864, Lee Collection, LCM; Lee to Butler, 1 February 1864, Entry 62, RG 19, NA; Lee to Butler, 11 February 1864, *Butler Correspondence,* 3:400.

76. Welles to Lee, 23 October 1862, Lee Collection, LCM.

77. Lee to Welles, 26 October 1862, ibid.; Instructions of S. P. Lee to Blockading Officers, 30 November 1862, *ORN,* ser. 1, 8:244.

78. Lee to Welles, 1 April 1863, ibid., 701.

79. Ibid.; G. H. Ellis to Lee, 27 January 1863, Lee Collection, LCM; Lee to Welles, 21 January 1863, ibid.; Peirce Crosby to T. R. Bacon, 28 April 1863, ibid.

80. Peter Hayes to Lee, 5 March 1864, *ORN,* ser. 1, 9:526–27; Babcock Hayes to Lee, 20 March 1864, Lee Collection, LCM; Peirce Crosby to T. R. Bacon, 28 April 1863, ibid.; Lee to S. P. Chase, 4 November 1863, Entry 30, RG 45, NA; Lee to Gillis, 30 September 1863, *ORN,* ser. 1, 9:223; Charles A. Babcock to Lee, 4 November 1863, Lee Collection, LCM; Lee to Welles, 12 April 1864, Entry 30, RG 45, NA; Gillis to Lee, 15 November 1863, Lee Collection, LCM; Babcock to Gansevoort, 21 November 1863, ibid. When the

Minnesota was attacked by a torpedo boat, the limits were cut back even further in the Hampton Roads area, because Lee feared that a torpedo boat might hide among them. Order of S. P. Lee, 12 April 1864, *ORN,* ser. 1, 9: 608–9; Lee to Dix, 13 January 1863, *ORA,* ser. 1, 18:515; T. A. Harris to Lee, 16 February 1863, Lee Collection, LCM; Chase to Welles, 15 April 1863, Letters Sent to Cabinet Officers, Entry 6, RG 56; J. E. Alexander to Gansevoort, 22 November 1863, ibid.; Babcock to Gansevoort, 24 November 1863, ibid.; Babcock to B. F. Onderdonk, 29 January 1864, Butler Papers, LCM.

81.   Lee to Butler, 11 December 1863, ORN, ser. 1, 9:347; Lee to Babcock, 11 December 1863, Entry 30, RG 45, NA; Lee to Butler, 21, 28 January 1864, Butler Papers, LCM, passim; General Order 102 by David Dixon Porter, 31 March 1865, Area 7, Entry 463, RG 45, NA.

82.   Woodworth to Butler, 12 January 1864, Butler Papers, LCM; Norcum, 306; Porter to Macomb, 4 January 1865, *ORN,* ser. 1, 11:410; Butler to William Bond, J. J. Cannon, and Joseph E. Naff, 10 February 1864, Area 7, Entry 463, RG 45, NA.

7. Acquiring and Maintaining the Fleet

1.   U.S. Congress, House, *Report of the Secretary of the Navy,* H. Ex. Doc. 1, 38th Cong., 1st sess., 7 December 1863, 4:iii.

2.   Some historians have criticized Secretary of the Navy Isaac Touncey for leaving the navy unprepared for war. In fact, Touncey had attempted to strengthen materially the navy by converting the older warships into efficient vessels of war. The blame can be placed squarely on the Congress, which did not give Touncey the appropriations that he had asked for. *RSN,* 2 December 1858; U.S. Congress, Senate, *Surrender and Destruction of Navy Yards,* S. Rept. 37, 37th Cong., 2d sess., 1861, 59; U.S. Congress, House, *Letter of the Secretary of the Navy in Answer to a Resolution in the House to the Number of Vessels in the Navy,* H. Ex. Doc. 159, 40th Cong., 2d sess., 1868, 2; *RSN,* 1858, 6; Lenthall to J. B. Houston, 1 May 1862, Entry 51, RG 19, NA.

3.   Boynton, 1:89; U.S. Congress, Senate, *Letter of the Secretary of War in Answer to . . . Vessels Purchased or Chartered,* S. Doc. 37, 37th Cong., 2d sess., 1862, passim; Contract between the Baltimore Steam Packets Co. and H. S. Stellwagen for the *Adelaide,* 14 August 1861 (Vessels Chartered by the Navy Department to Carry Coal), Subject File OX, RG 45, NA; Paulding to Welles, 3 March 1862, *ORN,* ser. 1, 1:337; Thomas to Wilson to Pendergrast, 7 June 1861, ibid., 713.

4.   Samuel Breese to Barston and Pope, 16 May 1861, Breese to H. B.

Cromwell & Co., 2 May 1861, Entry 332, RG 45, NA; Welles to Du Pont, 9 May 1861, Letters Received from the Secretary of the Navy by Commandant of the Philadelphia Navy Yard, Entry 346, RG 45, NA.

5. Lenthall to Welles, 10 August 1861, Letters Received from Chiefs of Bureau, Entry 32, RG 45, NA; Stringham to Welles, 16 July, 31 July 1861, *ORN,* ser. 1, 6:3, 45–46. *Dawn* was in particularly bad repair and her engines completely exposed to enemy gunfire. Her commander, William Chandler, considered her "helpless for blockading service" and a "poor speculation for the Government." William Chandler to Pendergrast, 15 June 1861, *ORN,* ser. 1, 5:723; Chandler to Stringham, 5 July 1861, ibid., 770; Chandler to Goldsborough, 26 September 1861, ibid., 6:256; Chandler to Messrs. Barstow and Pope, 5 July 1861, Subject File AD, RG 45, NA; Henry Eagle to Pendergrast, 27 May 1861, *ORN,* ser. 1, 5:676; G. M. Went to Stringham, 25 May 1861, ibid.; Daniel Braine to John P. Gillis, 10 July 1861, ibid., 789–90; Joseph Smith to Lenthall, 11 May 1861, Entry 32, RG 45, NA; Smith to Welles, Letters Sent to Secretary of Navy, Commandants, Bureau of Yards and Docks, Entry 1, RG 71, NA.

6. U.S. Congress *Congressional Globe,* 30 July 1861, 37th Cong., 1st sess., 350–51; Pendergrast to Welles, 7 May 1861, *ORN,* ser. 1, 4:379; Breese to Welles, 5 June 1861, Entry 332, RG 45, NA; *ORN,* ser. 2, 1:72, 150, 152. During the war, the government spent a fortune by chartering nearly 2,700 different vessels for all purposes. U.S. Congress, House, *Vessels Bought, Sold and Chartered by the United States,* H. Ex. Doc. 337, 40th Cong., 2d sess., 1868, passim.

7. George D. Morgan to Welles, 29 November 1861, Purchases of Merchant Vessels, Subject File AY, RG 45, NA; Welles to Du Pont, 22 May 1861, Entry 346, RG 45, NA; Welles to Du Pont, W. L. Hudson, Samuel L. Breese, 21 April 1861, Area 7, Entry 463, RG 45, NA.

8. RSN, 1861, 14–15.

9. *Herald* (New York), 12 August 1861; William Jennings, "On the North Atlantic Blockade," *Magazine of History with Notes and Queries* 4 (July 1906): 26; John Niven, *Gideon Welles: Lincoln's Secretary of the Navy* (New York: Oxford University Press, 1973), 361; Fox to Du Pont, 9 September 1861, Entry 346, RG 45, NA.

10. Richard S. West, Jr., "The Morgan Purchases," *U.S. Naval Institute Proceedings* 66 (January 1940): 74–75; U.S. Congress, Senate, *Letter of the Secretary of the Navy in Answer to a Resolution of the Senate of the 9th Instant, Relative to the Employment of George D. Morgan, of New York, to Purchase Vessels for the Government,* S. Ex. Doc. 15, 37th Cong., 2d sess., 1862, 5–6; Morgan to Welles, 29 November 1861, 12 March 1862, Subject File AY, RG 45, NA; U.S. Congress, Senate, *Employment of Morgan,* 405; Boynton, 112–13; Bennett, 217.

During the war, squadron commanders were also permitted to buy vessels they believed were necessary for their squadrons. Subordinate officers were often sent to ports to look at them and arrange for the sale. Lee to Calvin C. Jackson, 25 November 1864, *ORN,* ser. 1, 26:741.

11. John P. Hale to Welles, 24 April 1861, Welles Collection, LCM; Niven, 348; Gardiner, 1024; Charles B. Sedgwick, *Speech of Hon. C. B. Sedgwick of New York on Government Contracts* (L. Towsers, 1862), 4–6; entry for 26 December 1863, *Welles Diary,* 1:496.

12. Stringham to Welles, 30 May 1861, *ORN,* ser. 1, 5:682. The Navy Department during the first months of the war received propositions to purchase "several hundred" foreign vessels but declined these offers. Welles to W. P. Fessenden, 18 July 1861, Misc. Letters Sent by Secretary of Navy, Entry 3, RG 45, NA.

13. *RSN* 1861, 14–15; West, *Mr. Lincoln's Navy,* 47; Soley, *Navy in the Civil War,* 17–18; Bennett, 217; *RSN,* 1865, xiii. The department purchased 214 in 1861, 30 in 1862, 90 in 1863, 79 in 1864, and 5 in 1865. Aubrey Henry Polser, Jr., "The Administration of the United States Navy 1861–1865," (Ph.D. dissertation, University of Nebraska, 1975), 197. By fall 1864, the department realized the war was coming to an end. With the ongoing construction, Welles knew he would not need many more vessels, so the department stopped buying them. Lenthall to A. M. DeCosta, 23 September 1864, Letters Sent by the Bureau of Construction and Repair, Entry 58, RG 19, NA.

14. Vail, 8; O. S. Glisson to Stringham, 30 July 1861, Subject File AD, RG 45, NA; Breese to Charles Green, 21 September 1861, Breese to Welles, 1 May 1861, Entry 332, RG 45, NA. When buying vessels, the government often found it hard to get clear titles to the vessels. Lenthall suggested using the opinion of the U.S. district attorney who was of "the highest legal standing." Lenthall to Stribling, 22 July 1864, Entry 54, RG 19, NA.

15. Lee, 116; Benjamin Garvin, Thomas C. Dunn, and C. B. Dahlgren to Lee, 25 August 1864, Area 8, Entry 463, RG 45, NA.

16. Welles to Stringham, 15 September 1864, Letters from the Secretary of the Navy to the Commandant of the Boston Navy Yard, Entry 319, RG 45, NA.

17. Welles to Lenthall, 6 May, 6 June 1861, Letters to Bureaus of the Navy Department, Entry 13, RG 45, NA; Paullin, 280.

18. Regis De Trobriand, *Four Years with the Army of the Potomac,* trans. George K. Dauchy (Boston: Ticknor, 1889), 135.

19. Construction, Subject File AC, RG 45, NA; *Daily National Intelligencer,* 9 August 1861, passim (Washington, D.C.), August 1861, passim; Welles to William B. Shubrick, 27 December 1861, 28 February 1862, Letters Sent by the Secretary of the Navy to Officers, Entry 1, RG 45, NA.

20. Lenthall to Sir, 30 August 1863, Letters Sent, Entry 59, RG 19, NA; Isherwood to John Sparrow, 23 June 1863, Letters Sent to Contractors, Entry 968, RG 19, NA; Polser, 288.

21. Paullin, 305; Lenthall to Edward Lupton, Letters Sent, Entry 59, RG 19, NA; entry for 18 January 1864, *Welles Diary,* 1:511, passim; Circulars by Secretary of Navy Gideon Welles, January 1864, Entry 61, RG 19, NA; U.S. Congress, Senate, *Certain War Vessels Built in 1862–1865,* S. Rept. 1942, 57th Cong., 1st sess., 1902; John P. Hale, *Speech of Hon. John P. Hale of New Hampshire on Frauds in Naval Contracts* (Washington: H. Polkhorn, 1864), 1, passim; Percival Drayton, *Naval Letters from Captain Percival Drayton 1861–1865,* ed. Gertrude L. Hoyt (New York: New York Public Library, 1906), 16 December 1862, 22; John Mitchell to Lee, 20 July 1863, Lee Collection, LCM; Lenthall to Welles, 27 September 1864, Entry 50, RG 19, NA; Maxwell Woodhull to Welles, 9 July 1862, *ORN,* ser. 1, 7:558–59; Isherwood to Welles, 25 November 1862, Circular by Welles, January 1864, Entry 32, RG 45, NA; Asa Beetham to Emily Beetham, 23 February 1864 [1865], Beetham Papers, LCM.

22. U.S. Congress, *Congressional Globe,* 37th Cong., 1st sess., 6 August 1861, appendix, 41–42; Soley, *Navy in the Civil War,* 19; Bennett, 357; U.S. Congress, Senate, *Certain War Vessels,* 2–3; Lenthall to Welles, 27 August 1861, Entry 32, RG 45, NA.

23. U.S. Congress, Senate, *Certain War Vessels,* 4–9; U.S. Congress, Senate, *Report on Additional Allowance on Contracts,* S. Rept. 61, 38th Cong., 1st sess., 1864, passim; U.S. Congress, Senate, *Report of the Secretary of the Navy on Contracts for Vessels of War.* S. Ex. Doc. 18, 39th Cong., 1st sess., 1866, passim.

24. Welles to G. F. Pearson, 22 July 1862, Entry 1, RG 45, NA.

25. *RSN,* 1863, xv–xvii; Fox to A. D. Bache, 9 June 1862, *Fox Correspondence,* 7:307–8; John D. Hayes, "Captain Fox: He Is the Navy Department," *U.S. Naval Institute Proceedings* 91 (November 1965): 68; F. F. Roland to Wm. E. Everett, 13 May 1862, Letters Received, Entry 71, RG 19, NA.

26. Welles to Lenthall, 23 November 1864, Entry 13, RG 45, NA; Lenthall to Welles, 6 December 1864, Entry 32, ibid.

27. Bennett, 217; West, *Gideon Welles,* 149; Isherwood to Welles, 7 July 1863, Letters Sent from the Bureau of Engineering to the Secretary of the Navy, Entry 963, RG 19, NA; Isherwood to Welles, 27 February 1864, Entry 32, RG 45, NA.

28. Smith to Welles, 16 November 1863, Entry 1, RG 71, NA; Welles to Stringham, 14 December 1863, Entry 319, RG 45, NA; Montgomery to Welles, 18 November 1863, Entry 34 (Boston), RG 45, NA; Isherwood to Welles, 11 January, 13 July 1864, Entry 32, RG 45, NA; Isherwood to Welles, 25 November 1862, Entry 963, RG 19, NA; Lenthall to Freeman H. Morse, 21 May 1864, 4

October 1864, Entry 58, RG 19, NA; Lenthall to Welles, 21 May 1864, Entry 50, RG 19, NA; Isherwood to Boardman, Holbrook & Co., 12 September 1862, Isherwood to Tetlow James, 2 October 1862, Letters Sent to Contractors, Entry 968, RG 19, NA.

29. Goldsborough to Fox, 17 November 1861, *ORN,* ser. 1, 6:438; Goldsborough to Andrew Bryson, 14 February 1862, ibid., 644–45; Lee to Commanding Officers, 16 December 1863, ibid., 9:356–57.

30. William Musgrave to Bryson, 14 February 1861, ibid., 644–45; John B. Lowell to William Wright, 28 May 1863, Lee Collection, LCM; Wright to Lee, ibid.; John Weidman to Guert Gansevoort, 3 September 1863, ibid.

31. Lee to Fox, 20 February 1864, Fox Papers, NYHS; Bennett, 205, 209; Gideon Welles (n.d.), "Regulations for Admission and Promotion In the Engineer Corps," enclosure to letter, Lee to Asaph Dunbar, 29 October 1862, Lee Collection, LCM; Edward William Sloan, *Benjamin Franklin Isherwood, Naval Engineer: The Years as Engineer in Chief 1861–1869,* (Annapolis, Md.: U.S. Naval Institute Press, 1966), 33; J. W. King to Welles, 24 April 1861, Letters from Officers of Rank below That of Commander, Entry 22, RG 45, NA; *RSN,* 1863, xix; *RSN,* 1864, xxix; Fox to George J. Blake, 22 May 1862, *Fox Correspondence,* 2:303.

32. Daniel Ammen, *The Navy in the Civil War: The Atlantic Coast* (New York: Charles Scribner's Sons, 1898), 9; Soley, *Navy in the Civil War,* 13.

33. Case to Lee, 22 February 1863, *ORN,* ser. 1, 8:549; John Humphrey to Welles, 21 September 1861, ibid., 6:244–45; Flusser to Lee, 17 January 1863, ibid., 8:475; Reigart B. Lowery to Goldsborough, 9 October 1861, ibid., 6:301; William A. Porter to Peirce Crosby, 14 October 1863, Lee Collection, LCM; William Keeler to Anna Keeler, 6 November 1863, William Frederick Keeler, *Aboard the USS Florida: 1863–1865,* ed. Robert W. Daly (Annapolis, Md.: U.S. Naval Institute Press, 1968), 111 (hereafter cited as *Florida*).

34. Entry for 13 January 1863, Ship's Log *Cambridge,* Special List 44, RG 24, NA; Welles to Isherwood, 21 November 1862, Entry 13, RG 45, NA; Maxwell Woodhull to Charles Wilkes, 19 August 1862, *ORN,* ser. 1, 7:658; John A. Suer to T. A. Craven, 26 April 1861, Entry 22, RG 45, NA; Ira B. Studley to Goldsborough, 22 December 1861, *ORN,* ser. 1, 6:485.

35. Babcock to Lee, 6 July 1864, Lee Collection, LCM; Davenport to Lee, 8 January, 30 April 1863, ibid.; Hiram Paulding to Welles, 20 December 1861, Letters from Commandants of Navy Yards and Shore Stations (New York Navy Yard), Entry 34, RG 45, NA; Benjamin Garvin to Hiram Paulding, 28 December 1861, Reports of Boards of Survey and Their Equipment, Entry 233, RG 19, NA.

36. Maxwell Woodhull to Goldsborough, 3 September 1862, *ORN,* ser. 1,

7:696; Gillis to Lee, 21 March 1863, Lee Collection, LCM; I. B. Studley to Goldsborough, 10 December 1861, *ORN,* ser. 1, 6:470; Benjamin Garvin to Isherwood, 19 February 1864, Letters from the Secretary of the Navy, Entry 319, RG 45, NA; Gillis to Lee, 21 March 1863, Lee Collection, LCM; Circular, S. P. Lee, 16 February 1864, ibid.

37. William Keeler to Anna Keeler, 6 November 1863, as cited in Keeler, *Florida,* 111; C. E. Stromeyer, *Marine Boiler Management and Construction* (London: Longmans, Green, 1893), 1. Raising steam rapidly is called forcing boilers and is always undesirable, but it became so severe that David Porter issued a general order to prevent the stress on the boilers. Commanding officers were to allow engineers three hours to raise steam in the boilers when filled with cold water.

38. H. Anscom to John W. Livingston, 9 October 1863, Entry 233, RG 19, NA; General Order 19 of Gideon Welles, 16 September 1863, Subseries 61, Entry 395, RG 45, NA; Fox to Goldsborough, 1 March 1862, *ORN,* ser. 1, 6:624; Lee to Welles, 30 September 1863, Lee Collection, LCM; Fred Stuart to Lee, 26 October 1863, ibid.; Welles to William Roberts, 10 October 1863, Entry 30, RG 45, NA.

39. Welles to Lee, 12 December 1862, Lee Collection, LCM; Lee to Garvin, 8 July 1863, *ORN,* ser. 1, 9:118.

40. Charles H. Loring to John Marston, 27 January 1862, Entry 30, RG 45, NA; Benjamin Garvin to Samuel L. Breese, 16 September 1861, Entry 233, RG 19, NA; Daniel L. Braine to Lenthall, 3 February 1862, Entry 62, RG 19, NA; McDonnell to Lenthall, 4 February 1862, ibid.; Benjamin F. Garvin to Isherwood, 11 December 1861, Letters Received, Entry 970, RG 19, NA; Entry 34, RG 45, NA, passim.

41. Isherwood to Lee, 12 January 1863, Lee Collection, LCM; Isherwood to Lee, 9 March 1863, 25 February 1864, Letters Sent to Naval Officers, Entry 966, RG 19, NA; F. W. Behm to Goldsborough, September 1862, Lee Collection, LCM. In 1862, boilers were built for eighteen cents a pound. By 1864, the price had risen to forty cents a pound. Isherwood to James Murphy and Co., 19 August 1862, Entry 968, RG 19, NA; Isherwood to Hazlehurst and Co., 12 November 1862, 3 December 1864, ibid.

42. Charles Wilkes to Fox, 22 July 1862, Area 7, Entry 963, RG 19, NA; Garvin to Lee, 19 June 1863, Lee Collection, LCM; E. A. Dornin to Lee, 15 January 1863, ibid.

43. J. C. Chaplin to Goldsborough, 25 October 1861, *ORN,* ser. 1, 6:357; Thomas Sheer to Gansevoort, 12 January 1864, Lee Collection, LCM; S. C. Hayes to Davenport, 15 November 1863, ibid., W. T. Truxton to Lenthall, 26 August 1864, Entry 62, RG 19, NA; W. T. Truxton to Lenthall, 8 February

1865, Subject File AD, RG 45, NA; Alexander Murray to Lee, 21 January 1863, *ORN*, ser. 1, 8:459–60; Ira B. Studley to William McKean, 14 May 1862, Subject File AD, RG 45, NA; Welles to Stringham, 16 August 1861, *ORN*, ser. 1, 6:87; Lee to Davenport, 4 October 1862, ibid., 115; William Parker to Breese, 21 December 1864, Area 7, Entry 463, RG 45, NA; Henry D. Heiser to Welles, 7 May 1864, ibid.; Flusser to Davenport, 16 September 1863, *ORN*, ser. 1, 9:201; Isherwood to Merrick and Sons, 19 September 1864, Entry 968, RG 19, NA; Renshaw to Macomb, 6 July 1864, Lee Collection, LCM; Ship's Log *Miami*, 29 December 1863, Special List 44, RG 24. In August 1864, nearly half of the gunboats in the sounds of North Carolina needed extensive repairs. Lee to Welles, 15 August 1864, *ORN*, ser. 1, 10:370.

44. Case to Lee, 3 August 1863, Area 7, Entry 463, RG 45, NA.

45. John W. Livingston to Stringham, 16 August 1861, *ORN*, ser. 1, 6:86–87; Gustavus Scott to John Dahlgren, 31 October 1862, Lee Collection, LCM; Goldsborough to Fox, 23 February 1862, *Fox Correspondence*, 1:244; Goldsborough to Welles, 20 February 1862, *ORN*, ser. 1, 6:636.

46. Lee to Henry Wise, 5 August 1864, Lee Collection, LCM; John S. Missroon to Welles, 16 March 1862, *ORN*, ser. 1, 7:130; James F. Armstrong to Goldsborough, 17 March 1862, ibid., 132; Saltonstall to Lee, 4 January 1864, Entry 62, RG 19, NA; P. G. Watmough to Stringham, 9 August 1861, *ORN*, ser. 1, 6:81–82; Goldsborough to Welles, 6 November 1861, ibid., 409; R. S. McCook to Goldsborough, 10 June 1862, ibid., 7:471; O. S. Glisson to Goldsborough, ibid., 673; Foxhall Parker to Lee, 16 October 1862, Lee Collection, LCM.

47. William McCann to Davenport, 25 May 1863, ibid.; R. S. McCook to Goldsborough, Area 7, Entry 463, RG 45, NA; William Flye to Flusser, 25 February 1863, Lee Collection, LCM; Robert Henry Thurston, *A History of the Growth of the Steam Engine* (Ithaca, N.Y.: Cornell University Press, 1939), 379.

48. Boggs to Lee, 29 April 1863, Lee Collection, LCM; Braine to Boggs, 25 April 1863, ibid.; Case to Lee, 12 March 1863, *ORN*, ser. 1, 8:599; Benjamin Sands to Lee, 23 December 1862, ibid., 313; Charles Boggs to Lee, 3 July 1863, ibid., 9:101–2; Lee to Welles, 3 March 1863, Lee Collection, LCM.

49. Sam Huse to Lee, 1 February 1864, ibid.; Lee to Welles, 8 October 1862, *ORN*, ser. 1, 8:123–24; Glisson to Stringham, 22 September 1862, ibid., 6:247; Gillis to Lee, 11, 19 October 1863, Lee Collection, LCM. One of the major tasks of the navy yards in the first months of the war was to sheath with copper the bottoms of vessels being converted for naval service. Benjamin F. Delano to Samuel L. Breese, 16 May 1861, Entry 34 (New York), RG 45, NA.

50. R. S. McCook to Goldsborough, 19 August 1862, Area 7, Entry 463, RG 45, NA; Charles A. Babcock to Lee, 23 July 1863, Lee Collection, LCM; Entry

233, RG 19, passim; Gansevoort to Lee, 19 August 1863, Lee Collection, LCM; Melancton Smith to Lee, 21 June 1864, Subseries 85, Entry 395, RG 45, NA; Lee to Foote, 27 March 1863, Letters Received from Officers, Entry 334, RG 24, NA. The Norfolk Navy Yard had two diving bells for such work. John M. Livingston to Joseph Smith, 9 August 1862, Letters Received from Commandants (Norfolk), Entry 5, RG 71, NA; Rowan to Goldsborough, 22 May 1862, *ORN,* ser. 1, 7:415; Flusser to Lee, 17 January 1862, Lee Collection, LCM.

51. General Order of the Secretary of the Navy Gideon Welles, 29 January 1862, Subseries 61, Entry 345, RG 45, NA.

52. Lee to Welles, 3 March 1863, *ORN,* ser. 1, 8:583–84; Lee to Commanding Officers, 1 September 1863, ibid., 9:188; Porter to Fox, 19, 27 October 1864, "List of Lame Ducks," Porter 1864 [n.d.], Fox Papers, NYHS.

53. *RSN,* 1863, xiv–xvi; *RSN,* 1865, xvii.

54. Soley, *Navy in the Civil War,* 17; Henry Hoover to Du Pont, 18 July 1861, Entry 5, RG 71, NA, passim.

55. *RSN,* 1862, 38–39; Joseph Smith to Welles, 20 February 1863, Entry 1, RG 71, NA. The navy yards had been given small appropriations by Congress before the war. See Robert Carey Johnston, "Navy Yards and Dry Docks: A Study of the Bureau of Yards and Docks 1842–1871" (M.A. thesis, Stanford University, 1953), 61–62; *RSN,* 1862, 38–39; Jamison to Lee, 1 November 1862, Lee Collection, LCM.

56. Welles to Joseph Smith, 30 August 1863, Entry 13, RG 45, NA; Lee to Lenthall, 24 December 1862, Entry 62, RG 19, NA.

57. A. A. Harwood to Commandant of the Navy Yard, New York, 23 April 1862, Subject File AD, RG 45, NA; W. A. Dornin to Dahlgren, 25 April 1863, Orders Issued by the Commandant (Baltimore Naval Station), Entry 315, RG 45, NA; Fox to Lee, 19 December 1862, *Fox Correspondence,* 2:236; U.S. Congress, House, *Sites for Navy Yards,* H. Rept. 100, 38th Cong., 1st sess., 1864, 2; Welles to Joseph Smith, 30 August 1863, Entry 13, RG 45, NA.

58. Stringham to Welles, 18 September 1861, *ORN,* ser. 1, 6:227; F. H. Patterson to Lee, 8 September 1862, Lee Collection, LCM; Livingston to Lee, 30 December 1862, Entry 62, RG 19, NA; John L. Lay to Davenport, 24 March 1863, Lee Collection, LCM; Flusser to Davenport, 29 November 1863, Area 7, Entry 463, RG 45, NA; Butler to Lee, 11 February 1864, Lee Collection, LCM; entry for 12 February 1864, *Welles Diary,* 1:522.

59. Lenthall to Welles, 17 October 1864, Entry 50, RG 19, NA; W. J. Keeler to John B. Montgomery, 7 January 1864, Entry 5, RG 71, NA; Lenthall to Welles, 17 October 1864, Entry 50, RG 19, NA. Green wood also weighed twenty-one pounds more per cubic foot than seasoned timber. West, *Gideon Welles,* 241–42.

60. Entry for December 1863, *Welles Diary,* 1:483; *RSN,* December 1865, xvii, xxvi.

61. U.S. Congress, House, *Evidence Taken by the Board of Navy Officers for Investigating the Condition of the Navy Yards,* H. Ex. Doc. 71, 36th Cong., 1st sess., 1860, 26, passim; Paulding to E. Delafield Smith, 9 August 1864, Entry 332, RG 45, NA; C. K. Stribling to Joseph Smith, 23 June 1864, Entry 5 (Philadelphia), RG 71, NA; Circular by Gideon Welles, 28 January 1864, Lee Collection, LCM; Circular by Gideon Welles to Commandant, New York Navy Yard, 11 November 1863, Mangus S. Thompson, ed., *General Orders and Circulars Issued by the Navy Department from 1863 to 1887* (Washington, D.C.: Government Printing Office, 1887), 12; *RSN,* 1865, xii. When a vessel arrived at one of the yards, between ten and forty men normally worked on her to prepare her again for sea. Entry for 17 April 1863, Ship's Log *Cambridge,* Special Group 44, RG 24, NA; John Mitchell to Welles, 27 June 1863, Lee Collection, LCM; Joseph Delhaven to Lee, 10, 13, 31 August, 7, 14, 28 September 1863, ibid.; Macomb to Welles, 11 April 1864, Subseries 67, Entry 395, RG 45, NA.

62. Work from 20 September until 20 March was to begin one hour after sunrise. One hour was allowed for lunch, and work continued until sunset. Men worked less in the winter but were paid the same weekly wage. Usually from 20 March until 20 September, they worked ten hours a day. Joseph Smith to William Hudson, 3 January 1862, Entry 1, RG 71, NA; Circular, U.S. Navy Yard, Washington, D.C., 16 January 1862, Letters Received by the Commandant of Washington Navy Yard from Secretary of Navy, Entry 356, RG 45, NA; Welles to Harwood, Circular Letter, 10 June 1863, ibid.; J. Hanson to Livingston, 16 November 1863, Entry 34 (Norfolk), RG 45, NA; Welles to Stanton, 7 January 1864, Entry 319, RG 45, NA; Thomas Davidson, Jr., to Henry Hoover, 17 March 1862, Entry 5 (Philadelphia), RG 71, NA; S. R. Wilson to John B. Montgomery, 20 July 1864, ibid. (Washington); T. H. Smith to John B. Montgomery, 29 February 1864, ibid. (Washington); Lenthall to H. Berrien, 15 May 1862, Entry 59, RG 19, NA; John H. Long to John M. Berrien, 23 November 1864, ibid. (Norfolk).

63. Dornin to Welles, 11 August 1862, Entry 34 (Baltimore), RG 45, NA; Welles to Pendergrast, 20 August 1862, Entry 346, ibid.; Stribling to Welles, 29 December 1863, Entry 34 (Philadelphia), ibid.; Montgomery to Welles, 23 August 1862, Entry 34 (Boston), ibid.; Smith to Welles, 20 July 1864, Entry 32, ibid. The navy yards were further crippled by a regulation that allowed only citizens of the United States to work in the yards. Paulding to Welles, 2 January 1862, Entry 332, ibid.; Welles to Montgomery, 17 February 1864, Entry 356, ibid.; Paulding to Welles, 19 December 1862, Entry 34 (New York), ibid.; New York *Tribune,* 4 January 1862; *New York Times,* 13, 16 April, 7 May 1865; Welles

to Harwood, 9 November 1863, Entry 1, RG 45, NA; Paulding to Welles, 19 December 1862, Entry 34 (New York), ibid.; Delano to Paulding, 20 December 1862, ibid.; J. B. Montgomery to Smith, 7 December 1864, Entry 5 (Washington), RG 71, NA; J. B. Montgomery to Welles, 18 November 1862, Entry 5 (Boston), ibid.; Montgomery to Welles, 19 January 1863, Entry 34 (Boston), RG 45, NA; Livingston to Welles, 24 August 1864, ibid. (Norfolk); Welles to Pendergrast, 18 January 1862, Entry 1, ibid.

64. Lee to Welles, 9 April 1864, Entry 30, ibid.

65. Welles to Goldsborough, 12 November 1861, *ORN*, ser. 1, 6:424; Goldsborough to Smith, 23 November 1861, ibid., 452; Foxhall Parker to Thomas Turner, 19 November 1862, Lee Collection, LCM; Lenthall to Du Pont, 7 September 1861, Entry 54, RG 19; Lenthall to Pendergrast, 10 December 1861, ibid.; S. B. Davis to Lee, 20 January 1863, Inventory of Fort Monroe Navy Machine Shop, Entry 62, RG 19, NA.

66. Case to H. Newell, T. N. Bishop to Lee, 10 December 1862, Entry 30, RG 45, NA; Lenthall to Lee, 7 January 1862, Lee Collection, LCM; Lee to Lenthall, 5 January 1863, Entry 62, RG 19, NA; Lee to Lenthall, 7 February 1863, ibid.; Lee to Lenthall, 15 June 1863, Lee Collection, LCM; Goldsborough to Fox, 9 November 1861, *Fox Correspondence,* 1:205.

67. Edward P. Lull, *History of the United States Navy-Yard at Gosport, Virginia (Near Norfolk)* (Washington, D.C.: Government Printing Office, 1874), 64; Livingston to Welles, 18 June 1862, Entry 37, RG 45, NA; U.S. Navy Yard at Gosport, Virginia, RG 77, NA.

68. Lee to Dix, 11 October 1862, Lee Collection, LCM; Lee to Lenthall, 9 November 1862, Entry 62, RG 19, NA; *RSN,* 1864, 763; J. Hanson to John Livingston, 8 October 1863, Entry 5 (Norfolk), RG 71, NA; Lee to Fox, 20 October 1863, *Fox Correspondence,* 2:266; J. Smith to Welles, 28 December 1863, Entry 1, RG 71, NA.

69. Lee to Welles, 9 April 1864, *ORN,* ser. 1, 9:591; Livingston to Smith, 18 June 1864, Entry 5, RG 71, NA; Livingston to Welles, 24 August 1864, Lee Collection, LCM; Repairs, Norfolk, 23 July–3 September 1864, Lee Collection, LCM; Report of U.S. Vessels at the Naval Station–Norfolk, Entry 34, RG 45, NA.

70. Porter Papers, journal (n.d.), 814–16, LCM.

71. Isherwood to Goldsborough, 2 September 1862, Entry 966, RG 19, NA; Lee to Fox, 14 October 1862, *Fox Correspondence,* 2:224; Fox to Goldsborough, 23 May 1862, *ORN,* ser. 1, 7:419; E. W. Roe, "Brief Historical Sketch of the Navy Yard at Washington, D.C.," in *Society of Naval Architects and Marine Engineers Historical Transactions 1893–1943* (New York: The society, 1945), 34–35.

72. Lenthall to Du Pont, 11 June 1861, Entry 54, RG 19, NA; Lenthall to

C. K. Stribling, 22 August 1863, ibid.; Stribling to Joseph Smith, 24 June 1864, Entry 5, RG 71, NA; Arthur Menzies Johnson, "The Genesis of a Navy Yard," *U.S. Naval Institute Proceedings* 81 (September 1955): 993; Stribling to Welles, 12 September 1863, Entry 34, RG 45, NA; Welles to Stribling, 18 September 1863, Entry 1, ibid. Pendergrast to Smith, 8 January 1861, Entry 5, RG 71, NA.

73. Welles to Paulding, 10 November 1863, Entry 1, RG 45, NA.

74. Fox to Goldsborough, 22 September 1861, *ORN,* ser. 1, 6:247; Welles to Marston, 30 January 1862, ibid., 538; Isherwood to Lee, 12 January 1863, Entry 966, RG 19, NA; Isherwood to Welles, 22 August 1862, Entry 32, RG 45, NA; *RSN* 1865, xx; Lee to Fox, 14 October 1862, *Fox Correspondence,* 2:223; Goldsborough to Lenthall, 24 April 1862, Entry 62, RG 19, NA; Goldsborough to Dornin, 10 May 1862, ibid.; Sloan, 34-35.

75. Isherwood to P. G. Pelty, 1 August 1863, Entry 965, RG 19, NA; Welles to Lenthall, 14 November 1863, Entry 13, RG 45, NA; Lee to Fox, 14 October 1862, *Fox Correspondence,* 2:223; Wilkes to Welles, 5 August 1862, *ORN,* ser. 1, 7:631; John Marston to Welles, 22 February 1862, ibid., 6:660; Goldsborough to T. A. Dornin, 10 May 1862, Entry 62, RG 19, NA; Goldsborough to Lenthall, 24 April 1862, ibid.; Goldsborough to Fox, 28 April 1862, *Fox Correspondence,* 1:265.

76. Dornin to Fox, 1 August 1862, Entry 34, RG 45, NA; Dornin to Fox, 13 May 1863, Entry 62, RG 19, NA; Isaac Hallock to father, 7 January 1863, Hallock Papers, LCM; Dornin to Welles, 26 September 1863, Entry 34, RG 45, NA; Dornin to Welles, 26 September 1863, Orders Issued by the Commandant, Entry 315, ibid.

77. Melancton Smith to Lee, 20 May 1864, *ORN,* ser. 1, 10:73.

78. G. H. Scott to Lee, 4 December 1863, Entry 30, RG 45, NA; Davenport to Herman Biggs, 29 July 1863, Subseries 56, Entry 395, ibid., Stuart to Lee, 26 October 1863, Lee Collection, LCM; Stuart to James W. Farrell, 16 October 1863, ibid.; Melancton Smith to W. H. Macomb, 27 June 1864, *ORN,* ser. 1, 10:214; I. N. Palmer to Smith, 24 June 1864, Area 7, Entry 463, RG 45, NA; Saltonstall, 45; R. T. Renshaw to A. Murray, 3 February 1863, Lee Collection, LCM; Murray to Lee, 4 March 1863, ibid.; John L. Lay to Renshaw, 2 February 1863, *ORN,* ser. 1, 8:501; Lay to Davenport, 24 March 1863, Lee Collection, LCM; Murray to Lee, 4 March 1863, *ORN,* ser. 1, 8:587; Lee to Lay, 12 March 1863, Lee Collection, LCM; Lee to Davenport, 20 March 1863, Subject File OA, RG 45, NA; Lee to Davenport, 12 May 1863, Lee Collection, LCM; Isherwood to Lee, 14 May 1863, Entry 966, RG 19, NA; Lay to Davenport, 16 May 1863, Lee Collection, LCM; Davenport to Lee, 3 March 1864, Subseries 56, Entry 395, RG 45, NA.

79. Davenport to Lee, 26 December 1863, Lee Collection, LCM; Daven-

port to M. Smith, 5 June 1864, *ORN,* ser. 1, 10:121–22; Davenport to Lee, 31 May 1863, ibid., 9:54; Davenport to Lee, 23 May 1863, Lee Collection, LCM; Lee to Welles, 2 October 1862, Entry 30, RG 45, NA; G. H. Scott to Lee, 4 December 1863, ibid.; Macomb to Lenthall, 29 August 1864, Subseries 67, Entry 395, RG 45, NA; Macomb to Lenthall, 13 September 1864, Entry 62, RG 19, NA.

80. The log books examined were from *Albatross, Britannia, Cambridge, Chippewa, Commodore Morris, Crusader, Connecticut, Dacotah, Daylight, Dawn, Florida, Henry Brinker, Mahaska, Miami, Morse, Mount Vernon, Mystic, Samuel Rotan, State of Georgia, Valley City, Whitehead,* and *Young Rover.* These vessels were not chosen at random, but because their logs were complete for long periods of time, which gave a better view of their repair records.

81. Lee to Welles, 24 November 1862, Entry 30, RG 45, NA.

82. Murray to Admiral, 21 January 1863, Lee Collection, LCM; Lee to Senior and Each Commanding Officer Present, 16 December 1863, *ORN,* ser. 1, 9:356.

8. Supplying the Squadron

1. Paullin, 260. The eight bureaus were Bureau of Yards and Docks, Bureau of Equipment and Recruiting, Bureau of Navigation, Bureau of Ordnance, Bureau of Construction and Repair, Bureau of Steam Engineering, Bureau of Provisions and Clothing, and Bureau of Medicine and Surgery.

2. Congress kept a watchful eye on Welles and the contracts that the department made. Welles to E. G. Allen, 15 May 1861, Entry 3, RG 45, NA; Welles to Lenthall, 30 July 1861, Circular by Secretary of Navy Gideon Welles, Entry 61, RG 19, NA.

3. John Lenthall to the *Commercial Advertiser* (New York), 2 July 1864, Entry 58, passim, RG 19, NA; Lenthall to S. J. Robinson, 4 September 1862, ibid.; Lenthall to Welles, 6 March 1862, Entry 32, RG 45, NA; Smith to Welles, 28 June 1862, Entry 1, RG 71, NA; Smith to Welles, 8 April 1861, Letters Sent to the Secretary of the Navy, Entry 49, RG 19, NA; Lenthall to Stribling, 17 December 1862, Entry 54, ibid.; J. Smith to Paulding, 8 September 1864, Entry 1, RG 71, NA; Welles to Lenthall, Circular Letter, 23 March 1865, Entry 61, RG 19, NA.

4. Welles to Pendergrast, 28 January 1862, Entry 346, RG 45, NA; J. Smith to Harwood, 18 October 1862, Entry 1, RG 71, NA; James Trow to Welles, 25 March 1862, Letters from Navy Agents and Navy Store Keepers, Entry 33, RG 45, NA; Lenthall to Stribling, 3 January 1863, Entry 54, RG 19, NA; W. H. Allyn to George Sewell, 31 December 1864, Letters Sent to Engi-

neers, Entry 965, RG 19, NA; Lenthall to Welles, 10 February 1864, ibid.; Lenthall to Du Pont, 17 August, 12 September 1861, Entry 54, ibid.

5. J. Henderson to Welles, 7 April 1862, Entry 33, RG 45, NA; *RSN,* 1864, 42; Lenthall to Welles, 21 August 1862, Entry 32, RG 45, NA; *RSN,* 1864, xli; George B. Walter, 3 July 1862, Entry 71, RG 19, NA.

6. Lenthall to Welles, 8 April 1861, 10 February 1864, Entry 49, RG 19, NA.

7. *Instructions for the Government of Inspectors-in-Charge of Stores, Naval Store Keepers, Paymasters, and Assistant Paymasters* (Washington, D.C.: Government Printing Office, 1862), 3–4; Lee to B. J. Totten, 24 April 1863, Lee Collection, LCM; U.S. Congress, House, *Report of the Secretary of the Navy,* H. Doc. No. 1, 39th Cong., 1st sess., 4 December 1865, xxvii; entry for 11 March 1864, *Welles Diary,* 1:541; Stribling to Welles, 8 June 1864, Entry 34, RG 45, NA.

8. Entry for 11 March, 20 June 1864, *Welles Diary,* 1:541, 2:54; Polser, 357–61; William Radford to J. Smith, 11 March 1864, Letters Received from Commandants, Entry 5, RG 71, NA.

9. Lenthall to Welles, 26 March 1862, Entry 50, RG 19, NA; Lenthall to Welles, 11 September 1861, Entry 32, RG 45, NA; Foote to Welles, 30 March 1863, ibid.

10. Lenthall to F. H. Morse, 27 January 1864, Entry 50, RG 19, NA; Lenthall to Welles, 13 June 1864, ibid.; Lenthall to Welles, 19 December 1862, ibid.; Lenthall to Welles, 21 April 1865, ibid.; Dahlgren to Welles, 4 June 1863, Entry 32, RG 45, NA; Blockade Strategy Board Minutes, 12 September 1861, Subject File ON, RG 45, NA.

11. Welles to Goldsborough, 28 October 1861, *ORN,* ser. 1, 6:367; Welles to Goldsborough, 4 November 1861, ibid., 394; Lee to Bridge, 5 February 1863, Entry 62, RG 19, NA.

12. Goldsborough to Samuel Lockwood, 2 May 1862, *ORN,* ser. 1, 7:281; Lee to Rufus C. Spaulding, 15 March 1863, ibid., 8:611–12; Thomas A. Dornin to Welles, 2 May 1862, Entry 34, RG 45, NA.

13. Goldsborough to Elizabeth Goldsborough, 9 April 1862, Goldsborough Papers, LCM; Goldsborough General Instructions, 10 November 1861, ibid., 6:419.

14. Entry for 12 May 1866, *Welles Diary,* 2:504; Lee to William M. Wittemore, 27 September 1862, Lee Collection, LCM; Lee to Bridge, 5 February 1863, Entry 62, RG 19, NA; Lee to R. C. Spaulding, 15 March 1862, Subject File OA, RG 45, NA; Lee to G. H. Scott, 27 September 1862, Lee to Dominick Lynch, 20 June 1863, Welles to Lee, 12 December 1862, Lee Collection, LCM.

15. Lee to Bridge, 5 February 1863, Entry 62, RG 19, NA; Circular, S. P. Lee, 25 January 1864, Subseries 61, Entry 395, RG 45, NA.

16. Lee to Davenport, 28 April 1863, 27 October 1863, Subject File OA, RG 45, NA; Davenport to Vessels under His Command, 7 November 1863, Subseries 56, Entry 395, RG 45, NA; Bridge to Lee, 29 June 1863, Lee Collection, LCM; Lee to Lenthall, 13 June 1863, Entry 62, RG 19, NA; E. L. Norton to Welles, 26 November 1862, Entry 33, RG 45, NA; J. Henderson to Welles, 27 January 1862, 17 February 1864, 20 April 1864, ibid.; Porter to Welles, 6 November 1864, *ORN,* ser. 1, 27:634–35; Davenport to Lee, 22 May 1863, ibid., 9:38.

17. Barnes, "My Egotistigraphy," NYHS, 196–99, 206.

18. David D. Porter General Order 42, 10 November 1864, Subseries 61, Entry 395, RG 45, NA. Porter allowed the James River Flotilla to fill its requisitions at the Norfolk Navy Yard without his approval. When a store vessel was stationed in Hampton Roads, Porter later allowed gunboats stationed there to submit requisitions directly to the paymaster or commanding officer of the store vessel. David D. Porter General Order 11, 20 October 1864, ibid.; Porter to E. T. Nichols, 1 November 1864, Area 7, Entry 463, ibid.

19. Paullin, 291; Bridge to Welles, 25 April 1861, 14 June 1861, Entry 32, RG 45, NA; *Daily National Intelligencer,* 2 July 1861.

20. Ledger of Supplies for the North Atlantic Squadron, 1864–65, Entry 323, RG 19, NA; Lee to Lenthall, 2 March 1863, Entry 62, ibid.; Bridge to Lee, 23 February 1863, Lee to Dominick Lynch, 20 June 1863, Lee Collection, LCM.

21. Davenport to Vessels under His Command (General Order) 18 August 1862, F. A. Roe to Lee, 25 June 1864, Lee Collection, LCM; Homer C. Blake to Lee, 11 February 1864, *ORN,* ser. 1, 9:478; Davenport to Lee, 28 February 1864, Subseries 56, Entry 395, RG 45, NA; Davenport to Lee, 6 July 1863, ibid.; Macomb to Lee, 6 July 1864, Subseries 67, ibid.

22. Lee to Bridge, 5 February 1863, Entry 62, RG 19, NA; A. Murray to Lee, 18 March 1863, Lee Collection, LCM; Totten to Goldsborough, 18 March 1862, *ORN,* ser. 1, 7:141; Flusser to Murray, 1 March 1863, ibid., 8:580; Goldsborough to Totten, 24 May 1862, ibid., 27:441; Henry S. Stellwagen to Goldsborough, 2 October 1861, ibid., 6:279–80; R. B. Lowry to Stellwagen, 10 October 1861, ibid., 303.

23. Flusser to Alexander Murray, 7 March 1863, ibid., 8:591.

24. F. Berlin to Lee, 1 April 1863, Lee Collection, LCM; Lee to Lenthall, 13, 14 June 1863, Entry 62, RG 19, NA.

25. Davenport to Lee, 18 October 1862, 21 November 1863, Subseries 56, Entry 395, RG 45, NA.

26. F. W. Behm to Lee, 10 September 1862, Lee Collection, LCM; Entry for 5 August 1862, Ship's Log *Chippewa,* Special List 44, RG 24, NA; Amos P.

Foster to Clitz, 25 June 1864, Subseries 61, Entry 395, RG 45, NA; G. W. Graves to Edward T. Nichols, 14 November 1864, Subject File OX, ibid.

27. Bridge to Welles, 15 July 1863, Entry 32, ibid.; Welles to Lee, 27 November 1863, Lee Collection, LCM; Frank J. Hastings to Lee, 25 March 1863, ibid.; T. Turner to H. P. Carr, 20 November 1862, ibid.; H. A. Wise to Lee, 30 August 1864, *ORN,* ser. 1, 10:408.

28. R. C. Spalding to Lee, 7 April 1863, Lee Collection, LCM; W. L. Crowell, William Ferrett, and W. W. Paul to Davenport, 23 November 1863, ibid.; Davenport to Lee, 2 December 1863, Subseries 56, Entry 395, RG 45, NA; M. Smith to Lee, 21 June 1864, Subseries 85, ibid.; M. Smith to Macomb, 27 June 1864, *ORN,* ser. 1, 10:214.

29. Davenport to M. Smith, 11 May 1864, Area 7, Entry 463, RG 45, NA.

30. J. A. Hartley to H. W. Hoffman, 20 May 1865, Subject File OX, RG 45, Entry 464, NA; Smith to Lee, 6 June 1864, Subseries 85, Entry 395, RG 45, NA; Smith to Stuart Barnes, 16 May 1864, ibid.; Burnside to Lorezo Thomas, 20 February 1862, *ORA,* ser. 1, 9:365.

31. Lockwood to Goldsborough, 5 May 1862, Area 8, Entry 463, RG 45, NA; Eastern Portion of the Military Department of North Carolina, May 1862, RG 77, NA; John J. Bowen to Lee, 25 February 1864, Lee Collection, LCM; Lockwood to Goldsborough, 4 May 1862, *ORN,* ser. 1, 7:308; Frank F. Hastings to Davenport, 15 June 1863, Lee Collection, LCM; William W. Whitmore to Hastings, 6 June 1863, ibid.

32. Charles Folsom, T. Hathaway Haskill, and James Wilkinson, to James Armstrong, 19 September 1862, ibid.; Spaulding to Lee, 7 April 1863, ibid.

33. Some vessels collected as much as thirty-five dollars of demurrage a day and lay for months before being discharged. Whittemore to Goldsborough, 6 September 1862, Lee Collection, LCM; Welles to Bridge, 3 July 1863, Entry 13, RG 45, NA; Lynch to Lee, 16 September 1863, Lee Collection, LCM; Johnathan Baker to Lynch, 8 October 1863, ibid.; Lee to Bridge, 22 July 1863, ibid.; Welles to William Flye, 3 August 1863, ibid.; D. Lynch to Lee, 16 October 1863, ibid.

34. Goldsborough to Totten, 24 May 1862, *ORN,* ser. 1, 27:441; Edward Bellows to Clitz, 1 July 1864, passim, 6 August 1864, Subseries 61, Entry 395, RG 45, NA; entry for 7 February 1863, Ship's Log *Commodore Morris,* entry for 12 July 1864, Ship's Log *Crusader,* Special List 44, RG 24, NA; T. Blakely Creighton to Lee, 14 March 1863, Lee Collection, LCM; J. H. Gillis to Lee, 20 July 1863, ibid.; Robert Hunter, William L. Lawyer, Charles Brown, George Smith, and Robert Coy to Lee, 16 July 1864, ibid.

35. Bridge to Lee, 17 August 1863, Lee Collection LCM; Welles to Lee, 18, 26 January 1864, Livingston to Welles, 3 September 1864, Entry 34 (Norfolk),

RG 45, NA; Alex Worrall to Livingston, 4 October 1864, Entry 5, RG 71, NA; Porter to Welles, 6 November 1864, *ORN,* ser. 1, 27: 634–35.

36. J. Smith and C. H. Davis to Welles, 1 June 1861, Entry 32, RG 45, NA; Minutes of the Board of Bureau Chiefs, Subject File OL, ibid.; Boynton, 82.

37. Paullin, 291–92.

38. Welles to Stringham, 16 July 1861, *ORN,* ser. 1, 27:357; Maxwell Woodhull to Gideon Welles, 4 October 1861, ibid., 367–68.

39. The abandonment of the Norfolk Navy Yard made it necessary to use the navy yard in Philadelphia as a depot for supplies. The Philadelphia yard was extremely small, and this extra function only created further problems. Bridge to Welles, 29 July 1861, Entry 32, RG 45, NA; Woodhull to Welles, 19 February 1862, *ORN,* ser. 1, 27:417.

40. Woodhull to Welles, 21 June 1862, ibid., 446.

41. List of Cargo of the *USS New Berne,* passim, Lee Collection, LCM; Welles to J. B. Montgomery, 9 May 1863, Entry 319, RG 45, NA.

42. Welles to Samuel Breese, 11 July 1861, Subject File OX, RG 45, NA.

43. Welles to Breese, 2 August 1861, Entry 1, RG 45, NA. The *Arkansas* and the *Blackstone* had made irregular stops off Wilmington with supplies. Ship's Log *Cambridge,* Special List 44, RG 24, NA; Welles to William H. West, 18 July 1863, *ORN,* ser. 1, 27:518; Thomas H. Lookes to Lee, 15 September 1862, ibid., 462–63; Welles to Goldsborough, 18 April 1862, ibid., 428.

44. Lee to Welles, 23 June 1863, ibid., 512–13.

45. Welles to West, 4 March 1863, ibid., 486; Fox to Lee, 14 March 1863, Lee Collection, LCM; Lee to Welles, 16 March 1863, ibid.; Case to Lee, 17 March 1863, ibid.; Lee to Welles, 23 June 1863, Entry 30, RG 45, NA.

46. Bridge to Lee, 30 January 1863, Lee Collection, LCM; Lee to Welles, 23 June 1863, *ORN,* ser. 1, 27:512–13; Welles to T. A. Harris, 3 August 1863, ibid., 523; A. N. Smith to Lee, 20 June 1863, Fair Copies of Letters Sent to Officers, Entry 322, RG 24, NA; William Keeler to Anna Keeler, 9 August 1863, *Florida,* 77.

47. General Order of Samuel P. Lee to the Commanders of the North Atlantic Blockading Squadron, 17 November 1863, Subseries 61, Entry 395, RG 45, NA; Time Table of the U.S. Supply Steamer *New Berne* (n.d.), ibid.; Abstract Log of the *New Berne, ORN,* ser. 1, 27:696–701.

48. William Keeler to Anna Keeler, 12 June, 1 August, 29 September 1863, *Florida,* 49, 75, 98; M. Smith to Lee, 20 July 1864, Subseries 85, Entry 395, RG 45, NA.

49. *RSN,* 1864, 971–72.

50. Breese to Welles, 10 June 1861, Entry 332, RG 45, NA; W. W. Queen to Lee, 6 July 1863, Lee Collection, LCM; Graves to Lee, 4 November 1863, ibid.;

D. L. Braine to W. H. Aspinwall, 2 May 1861, *ORN,* ser. 1, 4:357; James S. Palmer to Welles, 4 September 1861, ibid., 6:168.

51. Lee to Bridge, 5 February 1863, Entry 62, RG 19, NA; R. Aulick to Lee, 3 May 1864, Lee Collection, LCM; Wise to Lee, 16 May 1864, Entry 30, RG 45, NA; C. E Mitchell to R. Aulick, 19 August 1863, Letters Sent by the Commandant of the Washington Navy Yard, Entry 354, RG 45, NA; Dawson Phenix to Lee, 11 December 1862, ibid.; Lee to W. B. Cushing, 14 April 1863, ibid., Lee to J. A. Dahlgren, 21 February 1863, *ORN,* ser. 1, 8:543–44; J. S. Missroon to Goldsborough, 23 April 1862, ibid., 7:259.

52. Lee to D. Lynch, 12 April 1864, ibid., 9:609; Lee to Charles S. Boggs, 7 April 1863, Lee Collection, LCM; Lee to Flusser, 16 April 1863, Area 7, Entry 463, RG 45, NA. At one time, Lee sent double this amount. Lee to Davenport, 7 April 1863, Lee Collection, LCM; Porter to S. B. Comstock, 8 February 1865, Area 8, Entry 463, RG 45, NA; A. Harwood to Welles, 24 June 1862, Entry 32, ibid.; Davenport to Foster, 27 September 1862, *ORN,* ser. 1, 8:94.

53. Schooners cost the government an average of $700 to $800 a month to rent. Subject File OX, RG 45, NA; Lee to Welles, 25 January 1864, Entry 30, RG 45, NA; Goldsborough to Fox, 23 May 1862, *Fox Correspondence,* 1:276–77; Lee to Butler, 1 February 1864, *ORN,* ser. 1, 9:435–36.

54. Dawson Phenix and W. W. Queen to Lee, 24 March 1863, Lee Collection, LCM; Butler to Stanton, 17 December 1863, *Butler Correspondence,* 3:217–18; Wise to Lee, 12 October 1863, 1 March 1864, Lee Collection, LCM; Welles to Lee, 26 January 1864, ibid.; R. Aulick to Lee, 4 February 1864, ibid.; Lynch to Lee, 26 February, 7 March 1864, ibid.; Lee to Wise, 6 January 1864, Entry 30, RG 45, NA; Lee to Butler, 14 April 1864, Butler Papers, LCM.

55. Rats and dampness also took their toll on board the vessels, causing some loss and damage. F. M. Green to Macomb, 6 October 1864, Subject File OX, RG 45, NA; W. T. Truxton to H. A. Wise, 25 October 1864, *ORN,* ser. 1, 10:603; H. H. Foster to Lee, October 1863, Entry 233, RG 19, NA; Queen to Lee, 6 June 1863, ibid.; Jacob Westervelt to Davenport, 14 October 1863, Subject File OX, RG 45, NA; Davenport to Lee, 24 April 1863, *ORN,* ser. 1, 8:675–76.

56. By February 1863, over 11,000 rounds of ammunition were required by the vessels in the sounds. Rowan to Luke B. Chase, 4 April 1862, *ORN,* ser. 1, 9:200; Lee to Davenport, 6 November 1862, ibid., 8:203; E. A. McDonald to Davenport, 23 February 1863, Lee Collection, LCM; Queen to Lee, 6 July 1863, ibid.; Davenport to Lee, 5 May 1863, ibid. [endorsement by Lee same letter].

57. Some of the naval ordnance was stored at Roanoke Island. Lee to Welles, 24 November 1863, Area 8, Entry 463, RG 45, NA; Davenport to Lee, 28 November, 12 December, 24 December 1863, Lee Collection, LCM; Lee to

W. W. Queen, 6 June 1863, ibid.; Macomb to Rowan, 16 September 1864, Area 7, Entry 463, RG 45, NA.

9. Coaling the Gunboats

1. Quoted in West, *Gideon Welles,* 185.

2. Soley, *Navy in the Civil War,* 2; Joseph Smith and C. H. Davis to Welles, 6 June 1861, Entry 32, RG 45, NA; Welles to Smith, 30 May 1861, ibid.; Minutes of the Chiefs of Bureaus of the Navy Department, Subject File OL, RG 45, NA; Memorandum of Commodore Paulding (n.d.), ibid.

3. *RSN,* 5 July 1861, 91.

4. Lenthall to Pendergrast, 13 May 1861, *ORN,* ser. 1, 4:390–91; Pendergrast to Stringham, 14 May 1862, ibid., 393–94; William H. Aspinwall to Welles, 24 April 1861, ibid., 328.

5. Entry for 6 December 1861, Ship's Log *Mystic,* Special List 44, RG 24, NA; Cornelius Carr to Fred K. D. Stuart, 7 January 1864, Lee Collection, LCM; Clitz to Lee, 17 April 1863, ibid.; Lenthall to Freeman H. Morse, 5 July 1864, Entry 58, RG 19, NA; William Chandler to Welles, 4 July 1861, *ORN,* ser. 1, 5:765; Lenthall to Pendergrast, 24 March 1862, Entry 54, RG 19, NA; Entry for 30 December 1861, Ship's Log *Young Rover,* entry for 23 March 1865, Ship's Log *Whitehead,* Special List 44, RG 24, NA.

6. At Port Royal, a steam engine was used to hoist the coal into the steamships. About ten tons an hour could be placed on board a vessel using wheelbarrows. Lenthall to Pendergrast, 13 May 1861, *ORN,* ser. 1, 4:391; entry for 21 March 1865, Ship's Log *Whitehead,* Special List 44, RG 24, NA; note of E. Mellach, 11 March 1865, Subject File OA, RG 45, NA; James M. Frailey to Lee, 6 January 1864, Lee Collection, LCM; John G. Mitchell to Lee, 14 June 1863, ibid.; Case to Lee, 24 February 1863, ibid.; Lee to H. A. Adams, 7 March 1863, ibid.; General Order of S. P. Lee, 16 January 1863, Subseries 61, Entry 395, RG 45, NA; J. Smith to Paulding, 26 October 1864, Entry 1, RG 71, NA.

7. Goldsborough to Davenport, 13 July 1862, *ORN,* ser. 1, 7:572; Chambers Letter of Appointment, 4 May 1861, Entry 33, RG 45, NA; Chambers to Welles, 4, 8 April 1862, ibid.; Abstract of Bills Paid by James S. Chambers, Accounting Officers of the Treasury Department, Office of the Fourth Auditor, RG 217, NA; U.S. Congress, House, *Receipts and Expenditures,* H. Ex. Doc. 8, 38th Cong., 1st sess., 1863; ibid., H. Ex. Doc. 12, 39th Cong., 2d sess., 1866.

8. Adams, a resident of Louisiana, had remained loyal to the Union but was suspected by some of not being loyal. The Department retired him in July

1861 but later placed him on special duty in Philadelphia. *Du Pont Letters,* 1:99N; Lee to Scott, 1 December 1862, Lee Collection, LCM; U.S. Navy, *Chronology,* 2:111.

9. Lee to Hastings, 27 February 1863, *ORN,* ser. 1, 27:485; Davenport to H. A. Adams, 28 May 1864, ibid., 586; Lee to Lynch, 20 June 1863, Lee Collection, LCM; Adams to Davenport, 21 May 1864, *ORN,* ser. 1, 10:77; Davenport to Adams, 28 May 1864, Subseries 56, Entry 395, RG 45, NA; E. Mellach to Davenport, 6 November 1863, Lee Collection, LCM.

10. Lenthall to Welles, 15 July 1861, Entry 49, RG 19, NA; A. N. Smith to Lee, 25 June 1863, Lee Collection, LCM; Fox to Lee, 18 November 1862, ibid.; A. N. Smith to Lee, 3 December 1864, Subject File OX, RG 45, NA; Report of Coal Vessels at Beaufort, 31 March 1863, Lee Collection, LCM.

11. Lee to Welles, 29 October 1862, Lee Collection, LCM; Chambers to Davenport, 8 September 1862, Subject File OX, RG 45, NA; Thomas Townsend and others to Welles, 20 July 1861, Entry 34, RG 45, NA.

12. As quoted in General Order of S. P. Lee, 2 December 1862, Subject File OX, RG 45, NA; Lee to Ottiwell, 9 August 1864, Lee Collection, LCM.

13. Lee to J. H. Fillis, 31 March 1863, ibid.; Circular, S. P. Lee, 14 June 1863, Orders and Circulars Received and Issued by the North Atlantic Blockading Squadron, Subseries 68, Entry 395, RG 45, NA; Livingston to Smith, 4 October 1864, Entry 5 (Norfolk), RG 71, NA. In September, there were thirty-seven colliers at Norfolk with 12,000 tons of coal. William Ottiwell to M. Smith, 1 September 1864, Subject File OX, RG 45, NA.

14. A. N. Smith to Welles, 17 June 1864, Entry 32, RG 45, NA; Foote to Welles, 31 January 1863, ibid.; Charles Moore to Lenthall, 31 January 1862, Entry 71, RG 19, NA; Chambers to Welles, 2 April 1862, Entry 33, RG 45, NA.

15. Welles to Lenthall, 8 July 1861, Entry 61, RG 19, NA; Isherwood to Welles, 3 July 1861, Entry 32, RG 45, NA; Edward T. Nichols to Porter, 10 January 1865, *ORN,* ser. 1, 11:420; Marion V. Brewington, "Maritime Philadelphia 1609–1837," *Pennsylvania Magazine of History and Biography* 63 (April 1939): 99.

16. Lehigh Valley Railroad Company, *Annual Report of the Lehigh Valley Railroad Company,* 1859–1861, rpt. from letter circular; Philadelphia and Reading Railroad Company, *Report of the President and Managers of the Philadelphia and Reading Railroad Company* (Philadelphia: Moss Brothers, 1861–1864); Lehigh Coal and Navigation Company *Report of the Board of Managers of the Lehigh Coal and Navigation Company* (Philadelphia: John C. Clark and Son, 1861–1865).

17. Chester Lloyd Jones, *The Economic History of the Anthracite–Tidewater Canals,* Publications of the University of Pennsylvania Series in Political

Economy and Public Law 22 (Philadelphia: University of Pennsylvania, 1908), 37, 42, 87, 88, 117, 142–44.

18. Welles to James S. Chambers, 27 June 1862, Letters to Commandants and Navy Agents, Entry 6, RG 45, NA.

19. Tyler Stone & Co. to General Montgomery C. Meigs, 30 March 1863, Records of the Quartermaster Generals Department, Record Group 92, Consolidated Correspondence File, Entry 225, NA; F. Charles Petrillo, *Anthracite and Slackwater: The North Branch Canal 1828–1901* (Easton, Penn.: Center For Canal History and Technology 1986), 203; Manville B. Wakefield, *Coal Boats to Tidewater: The Story of the Delaware and Hudson Canal* (South Fallsburg, N.Y.: Steingart, 1965), 59; A. N. Smith to Lee, 27 April 1864, Lee Collection, LCM; Circular of S. P. Lee, 15 July 1864, Subseries 68, Entry 395, RG 45, NA.

20. C. L. Jones, *Anthracite–Tidewater,* 142; S. F. Du Pont to Sophie Du Pont, 29 June 1863, *Du Pont Letters,* 3:188–89.

21. The board of the chiefs of the bureaus thought that the *Charles Phelps* was unsuitable as a coal hulk in June 1861, yet she served the entire war in this capacity. J. Smith and C. H. Davis to Welles, 26 June 1861, Entry 32, RG 45, NA; Goldsborough to Welles, 18 May 1862, *ORN,* ser. 1, 7:396; William Jeffers to Goldsborough, 4 June 1862, ibid., 452; John P. Gillis to Goldsborough, 10 June 1862, ibid., 473; Welles to John Dahlgren, 18 July 1862, Subject File OX, RG 45, NA.

22. Benjamin Totten to Lee, 15 October 1862, Lee Collection, LCM; Totten to Turner, 14 November 1862, ibid.; Totten to Lee, 1 December 1862, 14 March 1863, ibid.; Lee to A. H. Foote, 14 May 1863, ibid.; Lee to Melancton Smith, 3 July 1864, *ORN,* ser. 1, 10:233; Guert Gansevoort to H. A. Adams, 22 May 1864, Letters Sent by Captain Guert Gansevoort, Commanding the *Roanoke,* North Atlantic Blockading Squadron, Subseries 83, Entry 395, RG 45, NA; Clitz to Smith, 10 August 1864, *ORN,* ser. 1, 10:346. Adams to Clitz, 12 June 1864, Subseries 61, Entry 395, RG 45, NA; Lee to Clitz, 17 May 1864, ibid.; Lee to Adams, 2 July 1864, Lee Collection, LCM; Lee to Welles, 7 May 1864, *ORN,* ser. 1, 10:26.

23. Lee to A. N. Smith, 30 June, 27 November 1863, Livingston to Lee, 23 February 1864, Lee to Adams, 2 July 1864, Lee Collection, LCM.

24. Welles to Livingston, 20 August 1864, ibid.; Lee to Welles, 1 August 1864, Entry 30, RG 45, NA; Welles to Livingston, 20 August 1864, Lee Collection, LCM; Livingston to Welles, 24 August 1864, Entry 34 (Norfolk), RG 45, NA.

25. Stringham to Fox, 10 September 1861, *ORN,* ser. 1, 6:192.

26. Goldsborough to Welles, 27 September 1861, *ORN,* ser. 1, 6:258; Rowan to Stringham, 21 September 1861, ibid., 245–46; Rowan to Reed

Werden, 15 March 1862, ibid., 7:128; Rowan to Thomas J. Woodward, 3 April 1862, ibid., 195; James S. Chambers to Goldsborough, 5 May 1862, Subject File OX, RG 45, NA.

27. Davenport to M. Smith, 17 May 1864, Subseries 56, Entry 395, RG 45, NA; E. Boomer to E. Mellach, 11 June 1864, Subject File OX, RG 45, NA; Boomer to M. Smith, 6 May 1864, ibid.

28. Boomer to Mellach, 15 May 1864, ibid.; Davenport to Adams, 28 May 1864, ibid.; Boomer to Smith, 26 May 1864, ibid.; Davenport to Lee, 15 December 1863, *ORN,* ser. 1, 9:351; Boomer to Macomb, 27 July 1864, Subject File OX, RG 45, NA; Macomb to David W. Wardrop, 24 July 1864, Subseries 67, Entry 395, RG 45, NA; M. Smith to Lee, 2 May 1864, Subseries 85, ibid.; Davenport to Adams, 17 June 1863, Subseries 56, ibid.

29. Lee to Macomb, 25 August 1864, Subject File OX, RG 45, NA; Smith to Lee, 11 June 1864, Subseries 85, Entry 395, RG 45, NA; Davenport to M. Smith, 10 May 1864, Subject File OX, RG 45, NA.

30. Davenport to Adams, 28 May 1864, ibid.; Smith to Davenport, 14 May 1864, Subseries 85, Entry 395, RG 45, NA; Lee to Adams, 5 August 1864, Lee Collection, LCM.

31. H. A. Adams to Davenport, 2 June 1864, Subject File OX, RG 45, NA.

32. Edmund R. Colhoun to Rowan, 17 May 1862, *ORN,* ser. 1, 7:375; Flusser to Davenport, 27 March 1864, Subject File OX, RG 45, NA; Alexander Murray to Lee, 1 January 1863, Lee Collection, LCM; Goldsborough to James S. Chambers, 5 March 1862, *ORN,* ser. 1, 6:681; Rowan to Reed Werden, 22 March 1862, ibid., 7:157; Davenport to Flusser, 4 October 1862, Subseries 56, Entry 395, RG 45, NA; Davenport to Herman Biggs, 28 May 1863, ibid.

33. Report of Coal Received and Discharged at New Bern, N.C., for the Half Month Ending 15 December 1864, Subject File OX, RG 45, NA; Lee to Davenport, 3 December 1863, Area 7, Entry 463, RG 45, NA; Davenport to Flusser, 8 December 1863, Subseries 56, Entry 395, RG 45, NA; A. N. Smith to Lee, 5 December 1863, Lee Collection, LCM.

34. Another item that the vessels ran short of and that was crucial to the running of the machinery was oil. The navy kept large quantities of oil at Newport News and Beaufort. In May 1863, the shortage was so severe in the sounds that Davenport wrote Lee that, if oil was not sent soon, "few, if any of the . . . boats will be movable." Davenport to Lee, 29 May 1863, Lee Collection, LCM; Whittemore to Totten, 28 February 1863, ibid.; Benjamin Garvin to Lee, 5 November 1863, ibid.; J. S. Wood, Jr., and W. F. Binge to Sir [Isherwood], 10 November 1863, Letters Received from Officers, Entry 972, RG 19, NA; Flusser to Davenport, 2 December 1862, *ORN,* ser. 1, 8:249; Murray to Lee, 15

December 1862, Subseries 56, Entry 395, RG 45, NA; Davenport to James C. Slaght, 28 November 1862, ibid.; Davenport to Foster, ibid.

35. Goldsborough to Samuel Lockwood, 2 May 1862, *ORN,* ser. 1, 7:281; A. S. Clary to Lee, 28 February 1864, Lee Collection, LCM.

36. Entries for 18, 22 August 1862, Ship's Log *Mystic,* entries for 9, 10 December 1861 and 12, 13 May 1862, Ship's Log *State of Georgia,* Special List 44, RG 24, NA.

37. Lockwood to Goldsborough, 23 May 1862, 12 June 1862, Area 8, Entry 463, RG 45, NA; Edmund R. Colhoun to Benjamin H. Porter, 12 August 1862, *ORN,* ser. 1, 7:643; William M. Whittemore to Lee, 12 December 1862, Lee Collection, LCM; Lee to A. L. Case, 19 June 1863, ibid.; D. Lynch to Lee, 5 November 1863, ibid.; Lee to Butler, 24 December 1863, Entry 334, RG 24, NA.

38. Isaac Hallock to Fuller, 26 June 1862, Hallock Papers, LCM; Lee to A. H. Foote, 18 March 1863, Lee Collection, LCM; O. S. Glisson to Lee, 18 June 1864, Entry 30, RG 45, NA; Glisson to Goldsborough, 8 June 1862, Area 8, Entry 463, RG 45, NA; S. Nicholson to Lee, 6 March 1864, *ORN,* ser. 1, 9:535. A contributing factor to the problem was that the local pilots refused to guide vessels which drew over 13 ¼ feet. David Dixon Porter General Order 72, Orders and Circulars Received and Issued by the North Atlantic Blockading Squadron, Subseries 68, Entry 395, RG 45, NA.

39. Case to Lee, 20 August 1863, *ORN,* ser. 1, 9:159; Lee to Adams, 5 June 1864, Lee Collection, LCM; Benjamin Dove to A. N. Smith, 16 December 1864, Entry 30, RG 45, NA; D. Lynch to Lee, 24 August 1863, Lee Collection, LCM; Note of E. Mellach, 11 March 1865, Subject File OA, RG 45, NA; Lee to H. L. Carr, 13 February 1863, Lee Collection, LCM.

40. G. H. Scott to Lee, 3 November 1862, ibid.; Lee to A. N. Smith, 23 October 1863, ibid.; H. A. Adams to Lee, 11 April 1864, Lee Collection, LCM; Porter to Fox, 10 December 1864, U.S. Congress, Senate, *Fort Fisher Expedition: Report of the Joint Committee on the Conduct of War,* S. Rept. 142, pt.2, 38th Cong., 2d sess., 1865, 217; R. H. Lamson to Porter, 13 November 1864, *ORN,* ser. 1, 11:54; Lee to Henry Adams, 5, 25 August 1864, Lee Collection, LCM; David Dixon Porter General Order 76, General Orders and Circulars Received by the *Juniata,* North Atlantic Blockading Squadron, Commanded by Capt. William R. Taylor, Subseries 90, Entry 395, RG 45, NA.

41. Report Coal Vessels at Beaufort, 31 March 1863, Lee Collection, LCM; Foote to Lee, 24 December 1862, ibid.; Lee to D. Lynch, 20 June 1863, ibid.; Lee to A. N. Smith, 23 October 1863, ibid.

42. Lee to Henry Adams, 26 May 1864, ibid.

43. James M. Frailey to Lee, 21 May 1864, ibid. Borrowing and lending

coal was also practiced with frequency in the Chesapeake Bay. Henry Avery to Porter, 25 March 1865, Area 7, Entry 463, RG 45, NA; Macomb to Mellach, 16 July 1864, Subseries 67, Entry 395, RG 45, NA; Davenport to Lee, 23 November 1862, *ORN,* ser. 1, 8:230; Lee to Foote, 6 February 1863, Lee Collection, LCM; Babcock to Lee, 29 July 1864, ibid.; Murray to Lee, 3 March 1863, ibid.

44. Ship's Logs for *Mount Vernon, Mystic, Brittania, Cambridge, Daylight, Florida, Monticello,* and *Mercida,* Special List 44, RG 24, NA; R. M. Browning, Jr., "From Cape Charles to Cape Fear"; A. S. Clary to Lee, 28 February 1864, Lee Collection, LCM; James Armstrong to Goldsborough, 17 March 1862, *ORN,* ser. 1, 7:132; Lee to Case, 4 September 1863, ibid., 9:191.

45. Case to Lee, 16 May 1863, Lee-Blair Papers, Princeton; James Armstrong to Goldsborough, 23 August 1862, *ORN,* ser. 1, 7:669; William A. Parker to G. H. Scott, 5 November 1862, ibid., 8:196; Sands to Lee, 10 February 1863, ibid., 519; J. D. Warren to Case, 30 March 1863, Lee Collection, LCM; Case to Lee, 28 July 1863, ibid.; William A. Parker to Peirce Crosby, 14 October 1863, ibid.; Lee to Sands, 29 December 1862, *ORN,* ser. 1, 8:331.

46. Supplying the small vessels off Wilmington with coal was a difficult task with the small complement of men assigned to *Fahkee.* The captain had to keep a regular station at night, which required a watch for both night and day. The coaling duties required such a large force that he could not perform the coaling duties as required. Sands to Lee, 26 December 1862, Lee Collection, LCM; Henry Arnold to G. H. Scott, 2 October 1862, ibid.; Sands to Lee, 21 October 1863, *ORN,* ser. 1, 9:249; Case to Lee, 16 May 1863, ibid., 26; Lee to Fox, 6 December 1863, *Fox Correspondence,* 2:271; Francis R. Webb to Lee, 29 September 1864, Lee Collection, LCM; Webb to A. N. Smith, 4 March 1864, Entry 334, RG 24, NA; James Armstrong to Goldsborough, 17 March 1862, *ORN,* ser. 1, 7:132; James B. Collins to father and mother, 3 November 1862, Collins Miscellaneous Manuscripts, NYHS.

47. D. Lynch to Lee, 5 November 1863, Lee Collection, LCM; J. C. Howell to Lee, 30 June 1864, ibid.; Case to Lee, 6 May 1863, ibid.; Benjamin Dove to Lee, 25 April 1864, ibid.

48. Lee to Foote, 18 March, 1 April 1863, Lee-Blair Papers, Princeton; Adams to Lee, 27 March 1863, *ORN,* ser. 1, 8:631. Even in calm water, discharging coal could cause damage to the vessels. Entry for 23 August 1864, Ship's Log *State of Georgia,* Special List 44, RG 24, NA; Lee to Adams, March 1863, Lee Collection, LCM.

49. Foote to Lee, 3 April 1863, Lee-Blair Papers, Princeton; Boggs to Lee, 15 April 1863, Lee Collection, LCM; Case to Lee, 11 April 1863, ibid.

50. Lee to Welles, 9 September 1863, ibid.; Benjamin Dove to A. N. Smith, Entry 30, RG 45, NA; entries for 1 September, 9 November 1864, Ship's Log

Britannia, Special List 44, RG 24, NA; Braine to S. N. Gordon, 18 October 1864, Area 8, Entry 463, RG 45, NA; Emanuel Mellach to Porter, 31 December 1864, *ORN,* ser. 1, 11:398; George W. Young to Porter, 9 January 1865, ibid., 416–17.

10. Men and the Navy

1. Welles to Bridge, 3 June 1861, Entry 13, RG 45, NA; Polser, 26; Paullin, 250; *RSN,* 1865, xxxiii.

2. Lee to A. N. Smith, 7 November 1863, Lee endorsement, 16 November 1863, Francis Josselyn to Lee, 29 January 1864, Davenport to Lee, 29 January 1864, Thomas Sheer to Lee, 23 January 1864, Flusser to Lee, 5 February 1864, W. Wright to Lee, 12 December 1863, D. Lynch to Lee, 22 October 1863, Lee Collection, LCM; Paulding to Saltonstall, 3 August 1864, Entry 332, passim, RG 45, NA; William L. Hudson to Welles, 27 September 1861, Entry 318, ibid.

3. Blanding, 49, 71–72; Lenthall to Du Pont, 7 June 1861, Entry 54, RG 19, NA; Lenthall to Pendergrast, 13 August 1862, RG 19, NA; Breese to Samuel Swartwout, 30 May 1861, Entry 332, RG 45, NA; Welles to Pendergrast, 24 July 1862, Entry 1, RG 45, NA.

4. *RSN,* 1863, xxvi.

5. Francis P. B. Sands, "'Lest We Forget': Memories of Service Afloat from 1862 to 1866," *Military Order of the Loyal Legion of the United States Commandry of the District of Columbia,* War Papers 73 (Washington, D.C.: Companion, 1908), 5; Paulding to Welles, 2 November 1861, Entry 34 (New York), RG 45, NA; Paulding to Fox, 29 November 1861, RG 45, NA.

6. Welles to Paulding, 24 March 1864, Entry 1, RG 45, NA; A. N. Smith to Lee, 30 October 1863, Lee Collection, LCM; Dornin to A. N. Smith, 30 December 1863, Entry 315, RG 45, NA.

7. U.S. Congress, House, *Annals of Congress,* 12th Cong., 2d sess., 3 March 1813, appendix, 1339–40; U.S. Congress, House, *Report to the Secretary of the Navy Transmitting the Instructions Issued to Officers of the Several Depots for the Enlistment of Seamen,* H. Ex. Doc. 7, 37th Cong., 1st sess., 1861, 1; Welles to Breese, 22 May 1861, Entry 1, RG 45, NA.

8. Montgomery to Welles, 12 August 1862, Entry 34 (Boston), RG 45, NA; Saltonstall, 69–70; Vail, 156.

9. Welles to Lardner, 23 September 1861, Entry 346 (Philadelphia), RG 45, NA; Welles to Lee, 21 March 1863, Lee Collection, LCM; A. Ludlow Case to Lee, 11 March 1863, Entry 334, RG 24, NA.

10. Welles to T. F. Craven, 20 April 1861, Entry 1, RG 45, NA; Regulations for the Enlistment and Government of Apprentice Boys for the Navy, 27 May

1864, Subseries 68, Entry 395, RG 45, NA; Joseph Smith to Welles, 14 November 1863, Entry 1, RG 71, NA.

11. William Hudson to Welles, 1 May 1861, Entry 34 (Boston), RG 45, NA; Breese to Welles, 25 April 1861, Entry 322 (New York), RG 45, NA; Rowan to Goldsborough, 21 June 1862, Area 7, Entry 463, RG 45, NA; Goldsborough to William Smith, 1 January 1862, *ORN,* ser. 1, 6:495.

12. Stringham to Welles, 18 July 1861, ibid., 8; Welles to Stringham, 22 July 1861, ibid., 10.

13. Welles to Dahlgren, 25 September 1861, Entry 346 (Philadelphia), RG 45, NA; Circular, Gideon Welles, 18 December 1862, Lee Collection, LCM.

14. Lee to A. N. Smith, 1 October, 1 November 1863, Entry 334, RG 24, NA.

15. Michael Harris Goodman, "The Black Tar: Negro Seamen in the Union Navy, 1861–1865" (Ph.D. dissertation, University of Nottingham, 1975), 202, 244, 249, 395–405, graph 5; David Lawrence Valuska, *The Negro in the Union Navy: 1861–1865* (Ph.D. dissertation, Lehigh University, 1973), 4; Herbert Apetheker, "The Negro in the Union Navy," *Journal of Negro History* 32 (April 1947): 177–87; Dornin to A. N. Smith, 13 February 1864, Entry 315, RG 45, NA; Goldsborough to Gillis, 11 June 1862, *ORN,* ser. 1, 7:474–75; Lee to Dix, 21 December 1862, ibid., 8:311; Welles to Lee, 13 December 1862, Lee Collection, LCM.

16. Sands, "'Lest We Forget,'" 4; *RSN,* 4 December 1865, xiii; Soley, *Navy in the Civil War,* 4–5, 7–9.

17. Breese to Welles, 11 May 1861, Entry 332, RG 45, NA; Welles to Goldsborough, 25 March 1862, Lee Collection, LCM; Welles to Stringham, 31 July 1861, *ORN,* ser. 1, 6:45; Paulding to Welles, 22 December 1861, Entry 34 (New York), RG 45, NA; Circular, Gideon Welles, 9 August 1864, enclosure to Lee to Welles, 20 August 1864, Lee Collection, LCM; Saltonstall, 18; Davenport to Goldsborough, 15 June 1862, Subseries 56, Entry 395, RG 45, NA.

18. Armstrong to Peirce Crosby, 14 February 1863, Lee Collection, LCM; Reuben Elmore Stivers, *Privateers and Volunteers: The Men and Women of Our Reserve Naval Forces, 1766 to 1866* (Annapolis, Md.: U.S. Naval Institute, 1975), 203; Lee to Fox, 20 February 1864, *Fox Correspondence,* 2:276–77.

19. Stringham to Welles, 15 August 1861, *ORN,* ser. 1, 6:83; Welles to Stringham, 3 September 1861, ibid., 163; John Marston to Welles, 31 January 1862, Entry 37, RG 45, NA; Davis to Du Pont, 15 June 1861, Area 7, Entry 463, RG 45, NA.

20. Polser, 55–63; Ship's Log *Mahaska* [at the back of the log, n.d.], RG 24, NA; F. M. Green to Porter, 4 January 1865, Entry 30, RG 45, NA; Ship's Log *Britannia,* entry for 1 June 1864, RG 24, NA.

21. O. S. Glisson to Goldsborough, 29 July 1862, *ORN,* ser. 1, 7:602; Porter General Order 6, 13 October 1864, ibid., 10:561; Lee to Welles, 2 July 1864, ibid., 222–23.

22. Fox to Lincoln, 26 March 1864, Fox Papers, NYHS; A. N. Smith to Lee, 6, 9 February 1864, Lee Collection, LCM; Butler to Lee, 22 March 1864, ibid. By 1 April, the rebel prisoners were on board the *Minnesota.* John H. Upshur to Lee, Entry 30, RG 45, NA.

23. General Order 91, Adjutant Generals Office, War Department, 4 March 1864, Lee Collection, LCM; Butler to Stanton, *Butler Correspondence,* 3:570; Butler to Lee, 28 March 1864, Butler to Marston, 22 March 1864, Lee to Butler, 22 March 1864, Butler Papers, LCM; A. N. Smith to Lee, 26 January 1864, Lee to A. N. Smith, 3 March 1864, Entry 322, RG 24, NA.

24. Babcock to Lee, 20 March 1864, ibid.; entry for 25 March 1864, *Welles Diary,* 1:546–47; Welles to Lincoln, 25 March 1864, *ORN,* ser. 1, 15:382–83; Welles to Bridge, 1 April 1864, Entry 13, RG 45, NA. On 2 April, *The New York Times* reported thirty-five vessels waiting for crews.

25. Special Order 134 from Adjutant General's Office, War Department, 1 April 1864, Lee Collection, LCM; Fox to Lee, 8 April 1864, *ORN,* ser. 1, 9:589.

26. Lee to Welles, 19 July 1864, ibid., 10:285; Stivers, *Privateers and Volunteers,* 215–16; entry for 26 August 1864, *Welles Diary,* 2:121.

27. John P. Bankhead to Lee, 26 June 1864, *ORN,* ser. 1, 10:211; Sands to Lee, 19 October 1863, ibid., 9:247; Lists of Invalids Sent Home from the Blockading Squadron by the U.S. Str. *Rhode Island* for Hospital Treatment, 18, 20 January 1862, Entry 34, RG 45, NA; Kent Packard, ed., "Jottings by the Way: A Sailors Log 1861–1864," *Pennsylvania Magazine of History and Biography* 71 (April 1947): 127; Samuel Pellman Boyer, *Naval Surgeon Blockading the South 1862–1866: The Diary of Dr. Samuel Pellman Boyer,* ed. Elinor Barnes and James A. Barnes (Bloomington: Indiana University Press, 1963), passim; Ship's Log *Daylight,* September 1864, Special List 44, RG 45, NA. In October 1862, only five medical officers served the gunboats in the sounds. Davenport to Lee, 15 October 1862, Subseries 56, Entry 395, RG 45, NA.

28. Flusser to Davenport, 19 September 1862, Flusser Papers, ZB Collection, Operational Archives, NHC; Circular of William Maxwell Wood, 27 January 1864, Subseries 61, Entry 395, RG 45, NA; Paulding to Pierson, 5 September 1863, Entry 332, RG 45, NA.

29. John Marston to Welles, 17 March 1862, *ORN,* ser. 1, 7:82; Wheelan to Lee, 3 November 1863, Lee Collection, LCM; Flusser to Lee, 6 April 1864, ibid. Eventually hospital facilities were built ashore to accommodate smallpox cases. Wheelan to Lee, 21 March 1864, ibid.

30. General Order of Gideon Welles, 28 October 1862, Entry 356, RG 45,

NA; Lee to Murray, 12 February 1863, *ORN,* ser. 1, 8:522; D. Lynch to Lee, 16 September 1863, Lee Collection, LCM.

31. Welles to Woodhull, 27 June 1862, Entry 1, RG 45, NA; G. H. Scott to Lee, 25 September 1862, *ORN,* ser. 1, 8:87; J. W. Smith to Welles, 19 December 1862, ibid., 27:470–71.

32. Journal of Thomas Wilson Hall, 31 May 1863, 5 June 1863, Thomas William Hall Collection, Duke; Goldsborough to Wilkes, 27 July 1862, ibid., 596; Wood to Welles, 2 August 1862, ibid., 616–18; J. C. Spear enclosure, in Wood to Welles, 2 August 1862, ibid., 618; Wood to Lee, 13 September 1863, enclosure, no author, no date, Lee Collection, LCM.

33. Bridge Report, 1 April 1863, Entry 32, RG 45, NA; Lee to Murray, 12 February 1863, *ORN,* ser. 1, 8:522; Welles to Wheelan, 7 March 1862, Entry 13, RG 45, NA; Memorandum, Bureau of Medicine and Surgery, 1 February 1862, Wheelan, Entry 32, RG 45, NA; Paullin, 292; William Wheelan to Welles, 20 March 1862, Entry 32, RG 45, NA; Lee to Welles, 30 October 1863, Lee Collection, LCM.

34. Fox to Goldsborough, 23 May 1862, *ORN,* ser. 1, 7:419; William Keeler to Anna, 20 September 1863, *Florida,* 92; Goldsborough to Welles, 4 July 1862, Entry 30, RG 45, NA; Goldsborough to Fox, 6 June 1862, *ORN,* ser. 1, 7:455.

35. F. S. Ainsworth to Wheelan, 8 November 1863, Lee Collection, LCM; Circular, William Maxwell Wood, 27 January 1864, Subseries 61, Entry 395, RG 45, NA; William Keeler to Anna Keeler, 9 May 1863, *Florida,* 32; Instructions for the Government, 10 September 1864, Subseries 67, Entry 395, RG 45, NA; Thomas Wilson Hall, Journal, 8 June 1863, Hall Collection, Duke; Flusser to Rowan, 22 August 1862, *ORN,* ser. 1, 7:667.

36. Entry for 1 April 1863, Charles A. Post, "A Diary on the Blockade in 1863," *U.S. Naval Institute Proceedings* 44 (October–November 1918): 2346.

37. William Keeler to Anna, 8 [16] March 1863, *Florida,* 8; Sands, "'Lest We Forget,'" 16; W. Paul and G. B. Thompson to Davenport, 3 July 1863, Subject File AD, RG 45, NA.

38. W. T. Truxton to Henry A. Wise, 25 October 1864, Subject File AD, RG 45, NA; Joseph T. Collins to father and mother, 25 January 1863, Collins Miscellaneous Manuscripts, NYHS; Frank B. Butts, "My First Cruise at Sea and the Loss of the Iron-Clad Monitor," in *Personal Narratives of the Battles of the Rebellion, Being Papers Read before the Rhode Island Soldiers and Sailors Historical Society,* 1st ser., no. 4 (Providence: The Society, 1878), 7; W. J. Hotchkiss to Lee, 3 January 1863, Lee Collection, LCM; Joseph E. De Haven to Sands, 27 January 1863, *ORN,* ser. 1, 8:481–83.

39. Truxton to Wise, 25 October 1864, Subject File AD, RG 45, NA; T. Andrews to Lee, 26 April 1863, Lee Collection, LCM.

40. F. W. Behm to Lee, 20 April 1863, Lee Collection, LCM; Flusser to Davenport, 3 June 1863, *ORN,* ser. 1, 9:59; entry for 15 May 1864, Arthur M. Schlesinger, ed., "A Blue Jacket's Letters Home, 1863–1864," *New England Quarterly* 1 (October 1928): 565.

41. Batten, 91; Allen, 61–62.

42. Friend to Mrs. Kate, 2 February 1862, Buie Papers, Duke; Post, entry for 28 April 1863, 2571, J. F. Trow, "Life on a Blockader," *Continental Monthly* 6 (July 1864); Keeler, *Florida,* 28 March 1863, 22 December 1863, 13–14, 128.

43. Keeler, *Florida,* 11 April 1863, 9 May 1863, 12 June 1863, 18, 39, 44; Blanding, 57; Jennings, 27; Collins to parents, 16 January 1863, Collins Miscellaneous Manuscripts, NYHS; William Read, Jr., to father and mother, November 1864, Read Papers, Duke.

44. Batten, 22 April 1865, 107; *Sailor's Magazine* 33 (July 1861): 327, passim; *Seaman's Friend* 35 (April 1863): 247, passim; *Life Boat* 4 (January 1862): 158.

45. William Keeler to Anna, 12 June 1863, *Florida,* 44.

46. Livingston to Welles, 24 August 1864, Entry 34 (Norfolk), RG 45, NA; Welles to Livingston, 20 August 1864, Lee Collection, LCM; Welles to Lee, 26 September 1863, ibid.; Welles to J. B. Montgomery, 4 December 1862, Entry 319 (Boston), RG 45, NA; Batten, 8 May 1864, 19; Douglass, 8; Cleveland, 261; Boyer, entry for 16 December 1864, 343–44.

47. Post, 3 May 1863, 2572; newspaper clipping [n.d.], Subseries 61, Entry 395, RG 45, NA.

48. Livingston to Shepley, 29 September 1864, Entry 34 (Norfolk), RG 45, NA; Lee to Welles, 7 December 1863, Entry 30, RG 45, NA; letter with signature cut out, 11 October 1863, Lee Collection, LCM.

49. U.S. Government, *Statutes at Large,* 1862, 565; Welles to Charles Wilkes and others, 21 July 1862, *ORN,* ser. 1, 7:583–84; Saltonstall, 22; Ottinger to Chase, 5 November 1863, Entry 151, RG 26, NA; Welles to Lee, 22 April 1864, Lee Collection, LCM; letter with signature cut out, 11 October 1863, ibid.

50. Trow, 50; William Keeler to Anna, 9 February, 29 April 1862, *Monitor,* 7, 92–93; An Act to Alter and Regulate the Navy Ration, Subseries 67, Entry 395, RG 45, NA.

51. Vail, 11–12.

52. William Keeler to Anna, 28 February, 29 April 1862, *Monitor,* 20, 93.

53. "An Act to Alter and Regulate the Navy Ration," Subseries 67, Entry 395, RG 45, NA; *Instructions for the Government,* 72–73; Horatio Bridge to Welles, 16 June 1862, Entry 32, RG 45, NA.

54. William Keeler to Anna, 4 March, 3 April 1862, *Monitor,* 23, 70; M.

Smith to Macomb, 27 June 1864, *ORN,* ser. 1, 10:214; Blanding, 66–67; Schlesinger, 10 April 1864, 563.

55. Ship's Log *Mystic,* entry for 2 August 1862, RG 24, NA; Batten, 20 April 1865, 107; Vail, 145; William Keeler to Anna, 14 September 1862, *Monitor,* 219; Avery, *Gun Boat Service,* 12–13.

56. Batten, 4, 16 June 1864, 20–21; Blanding, 138–39, 166; William Keeler to Anna, 14 June 1862, *Monitor,* 156; Post, 6 May 1863, 2572; Isaac Hallock to father, 11 April, 29 July 1862, Hallock Papers, LCM; Henry to Josie, 28 May 1863, Henry A. Phelon Papers, SHC; Keeler, 12 June 1863, *Florida,* 49.

57. Fred to mother, 19 August 1862, Fredric Sherman Letters, SHC; Welles to J. B. Montgomery, 9 May 1863, Entry 319, RG 45, NA.

58. Henry to Josephine, 25 December 1862, Henry A. Phelon Papers, SHC; William Keeler to Anna, 25 December 1863, *Florida,* 129–30.

59. U.S. Government *Statutes at Large,* "An Act for the Better Government of the Navy of the United States," 17 July 1862, 12:600–610. Article 10 of the act stated that no punishment other than those specified in the acts would be permitted on board navy vessels except when a sentence was handed down by a general or summary court-martial. Lee to Welles, 13 March, 29 September 1863, Lee Collection, LCM.

60. William Keeler to Anna, 29 September 1863, *Florida,* 98; Welles to R. W. Mead, 10 June 1861, Entry 1, RG 45, NA.

61. Blanding, 61–62.

62. Schlesinger, 6 July 1864, 566.

63. Post, 27 April 1863, 2569–70.

11. The Coastal Blockade

1. The description of the capture was taken from J. P. Bankhead to Gideon Welles 14 June 1863, *ORN,* ser. 1, 9:73–74. William Keeler to Anna Keeler, 12 June 1863, *Florida,* 44–45.

2. Hill, *Bethel to Sharpsburg,* 1:260.

3. Stringham to Welles, 24 May 1861, *ORN,* ser. 1, 5:664–65; Welles to Stringham, 5 July 1861, ibid., 702.

4. *Daily Journal* (Wilmington), 4 April 1861; Henry Judson Beeker, *Wilmington during the Civil War* (M.A. thesis, Duke University, 1941), 1–3; Richard Everett Wood, "Port Town at War: Wilmington, North Carolina 1860–1865" (Ph.D. dissertation, Florida State University, 1976), 1–2; *Daily Herald* (Wilmington), 2, 9 March 1861, passim.

5. John Johns, "Wilmington during the Blockade," *Harpers New Monthly*

Magazine 33 (September 1866): 497–503; James Sprunt, *Chronicles of the Cape Fear River* (Spartanburg, N.C.: Reprint Company, 1974), 5; Preliminary Chart of Frying Pan Shoals and Entrances to Cape Fear River, North Carolina, 1863, RG 23, NA.

6. Robert C. Black III, *The Railroads of the Confederacy* (Chapel Hill: University of North Carolina Press, 1952), 6; Barrett, 124–400; George Edgar Turner, *Victory Rode the Rails: The Strategic Place of the Railroads in the Civil War* (New York: Bobbs-Merrill, 1953).

7. Welles to Stringham, 14 June 1861, Area 8, Entry 463, RG 45, NA.

8. Law, International (n.d.), Subject File VL, Entry 464, RG 45, NA.

9. Stuart L. Bernath, *Squall across the Atlantic: American Civil War Prize Cases and Diplomacy* (Los Angeles: University of California Press, 1970), 8.

10. Pendergrast to Stringham, 19 August 1861, *ORN,* ser. 1, 6:89; Samuel Lockwood to Stringham, 16 July 1861, ibid., 5:11–12; Abstract Log of the *Daylight,* 21 July [1861], ibid., 691–92; Lockwood to Stringham, 28 July 1861, Area 7, Entry 463, RG 45, NA.

11. John W. Livingston to Stringham, 15 August 1861, *ORN,* ser. 1, 6:85–86; Goldsborough to Welles, 3 October 1861, ibid., 282.

12. Algernon Lyons to Sir A. Milne, 21 November 1861, Great Britain, Parliament, *Sessional Papers,* 881.

13. *RSN,* 2 December 1861, 4.

14. Blockade Strategy Board Minutes, 13, 16 July 1861, Subject File ON, RG 45, NA.

15. Ibid., 2 September 1861; J. G. Foster to Joseph Totten, 18 May 1861, *ORA,* ser. 1, 1:477; Gideon Welles to Silas Stringham, 3 September 1861, *ORN,* ser. 1, 6:162.

16. Daniel L. Braine to Oliver S. Glisson, 5 January 1862, ibid., 499.

17. Blockade Strategy Board Minutes, 16 July 1861, Subject File ON, RG 45, NA.

18. Goldsborough to Welles, 3 October 1861, *ORN,* ser. 1, 6:281; Goldsborough to Welles, 10 November 1861, ibid., 418.

19. Goldsborough to George A. Prentiss, 17 October 1861, ibid., 335; Goldsborough to Lockwood, 13 April 1862, ibid., 7:231; Goldsborough to J. D. Warren, 17 April 1862, ibid., 245; Log of the *Albatross,* 31 December 1861, Log of *Cambridge,* 28 June, 17 July 1862, Special List 44, RG 24, NA; Henry L. Sturges to friend, 20 February 1862, Federal Soldiers Letters, SHC.

20. Benjamin to James M. Mason, 8 April 1862, *ORN,* ser. 1, 3:381.

21. Earl Russell to Lord Lyons, 5 February 1862, Great Britain, Parliament, *Sessional Papers,* 1862, 62:119–20.

22. Goldsborough to Welles, 4 October 1861, *ORN,* ser. 1, 6:286.

23. Statement of Vessels Attached to the North Atlantic Blockading Squadron, 24 July 1862, *ORN,* ser. 1, 7:597.

24. John L. Cantwell to Adjutant General, 17 April 1861, *ORA,* ser. 1, 51 (pt. 1): 1–2; John G. Foster to Joseph G. Totten, 18 May 1861, ibid., 1:477; Louis T. Moore, "The Capture of Fort Caswell," *The State* 12 (23 September 1944): 6–7.

25. Sprunt, *Chronicles,* 381; William Lamb, *Colonel Lamb's Story of Fort Fisher* (Carolina Beach, N.C.: Blockade Runner Museum, 1966), 1–2.

26. Augustus Charles Hobart-Hampden (Roberts), *Never Caught: Personal Adventures Connected with Twelve Successful Trips in Blockade-Running during the American Civil War, 1863–1864* (London: John Camden Hotten, 1867; rpt., Carolina Beach, N.C.: Blockade Runner Museum, 1967), 52.

27. James Collins to father and mother, 11 September 1862, Collins Miscellaneous Manuscripts, NYHS.

28. David to Miss Kate, 18 October 1862, Catherine Buie Papers, Duke; Gustavus H. Scott to Samuel P. Lee, 11 October 1862, Lee Collection, LCM; Friend to Miss Kate, 18 September 1862, Catherine Buie Papers, Duke.

29. Lee to Welles, 8 September 1862, Lee Collection, LCM; Welles to Lee, 10 September 1862, *ORN,* ser. 1, 8:11; Welles to Lee, 25 September 1862, Lee Collection, LCM.

30. Lee to Scott, 21 September 1862, ibid.

31. Lee to Scott, 5 October 1862, Scott to Lee, 12 November 1862, ibid.

32. Lee to Scott, 10 October 1862, ibid.; William H. Macomb to Benjamin Sands, 19 December 1862, ibid.; Scott to Lee, 11 December 1862, ibid. The need for repairs and logistical problems were beginning to take their toll.

33. Sands to Lee, 23 December 1862, ibid.

34. Lee to Welles, 12 January 1863, *ORN,* ser. 1, 8:418–19; Post, 2565; Isaac Hallock to father, 24 April 1863, Hallock Papers, LCM.

35. Ship's Log *Mount Vernon,* February–April 1863, Special List 44, RG 45, NA; Sands to Lee, 23 December 1862, Lee Collection, LCM; Armstrong to Lee, 24 March 1863, ibid.; R. C. Spalding to Lee, 7 April 1863, ibid.; Lee to Sands, 29 December 1862, ibid. Lee did warn the officers not to waste their fuel by running about unnecessarily.

36. Lee to Sands, 2 February 1863, *ORN,* ser. 1, 8:496; Sands to Lee, 17 February 1863, ibid., 532–33; Case to Lee, 21 February 1863, ibid., 547.

37. Case to Cushing, 11 August 1863, Lee Collection, LCM; Scott to Lee, 14 October 1862, ibid.; Lee to Sands, 2 February 1863, *ORN,* ser. 1, 8:496; Lee to Welles, 4 February 1863, ibid., 502.

38. Lee to Case, 10 March 1863, ibid., 594–95; Lee to Sands, 7 March 1863, ibid., 589–90.

39. Case to Lee, 10 March 1863, ibid., 595–96; Lee to John W. Bennett, 27 March 1863, ibid., 631; Charles S. Boggs to Lee, 29 March 1863, ibid., 635; Sands to Lee, 19 October 1863, ibid., 9:246–47; Cushing Journal of Vessels, Entry 37, Letters from Rear Admirals, Commodores, and Captains, RG 45, NA; Case to Cushing, 11 August 1863, Lee Collection, LCM; Cushing to Lee, 28 August 1863, *ORN,* ser. 1, 9:184.

40. Lee to Bennett, 18 April 1863, ibid., 8:801–2. Blockade runners had muffled their escape of steam by leading their pipes carrying escaping steam overboard and underwater. Welles suggested to Lee that the blockaders should have a similar system, but Isherwood believed it would not decrease the noise. Welles to Lee, 29 April 1863, Lee Collection, LCM; endorsement by Isherwood, ibid.

41. Isaac Hallock to father, 9 February 1862, Hallock Papers, LCM; Braine to Goldsborough, 15 April 1862, Area 8, Entry 463, RG 45, NA; Saltonstall, 67; *Army-Navy Journal,* 14 January 1865; case quoted in Lee to Welles, 5 May 1863, Lee Collection, LCM.

42. *Scientific American* 8 (9 May 1863): 310.

43. Thomas E. Taylor, *Running the Blockade: A Personal Narrative of Adventures, Risks, and Escapes during the American Civil War* (New York: Charles Scribner's Sons, 1896), 49–50; Johns, 501; Hobart-Hampden (Roberts), 5–6; Porter Papers, Journal 1, 821, LCM.

44. Post, 6 June 1863, 2578; Lee to Case, 26 May 1863, Lee to Robert B. Forbes, 26 May 1863, *Fox Correspondence,* 2:255, 257–58; Daniel B. Ridgely to Lee, 5 November 1863, *ORN,* ser. 1, 9:262–63; Lee to Commanding Officers, 1 September 1863, ibid., 188.

45. *Scientific American* 8 (9 May 1863): 310.

46. Lee to Welles, 7 August 1863, *ORN,* ser. 1, 9:150; Lee to Welles, 28 August 1863, ibid., 183; Lee to Welles, 10 October 1863, ibid., 230.

47. Ship's Log *Connecticut,* September 1863 passim Special List 44, RG 24, NA; William Keeler to Anna Keeler, 12 June 1863, *Florida,* 44; Lee to Commanding Officers, 1 September 1863, *ORN,* ser. 1, 9:188–89; Lee to W. F. Spicer, 4 September 1863, Lee Collection, LCM.

48. Sands to Lee, 13 October 1863, *ORN,* ser. 1, 9:235; Daniel B. Ridgely to Lee, 29 October 1863, Lee Collection, LCM; Lee to Case, 11 September 1863, *ORN,* ser. 1, 9:197.

49. Peirce Crosby to Lee, 9 December 1863, Lee Collection, LCM; Lee to James M. Frailey, 16 December 1863, *ORN,* ser. 1, 9:358. Before establishing this third line, Lee had had the schooner *Matthew Vassar* cruising between Cape Fear and Cape Hatteras. H. H. Savage to Charles S. Boggs, 3 August 1863, Area

8, Entry 463, RG 45, NA; Lee to Senior and Each Commanding Officer Present, 16 December 1863, *ORN,* ser. 1, 9:355–56.

50. Ibid., 355–58.

51. Lee to Commanding Officers of *Sassacus* and *Pequot,* 29 January 1864, ibid., 418–19; Lee to Welles, 15 February 1864, ibid., 481–82.

52. James F. Armstrong to Goldsborough, 17 March 1862, ibid., 7:131; William A. Parker to Goldsborough, 25 March 1862, ibid., 135–36; Isaac Hallock to father, 28 February 1862, Hallock Papers, LCM; Welles to Charles Green, 20 May 1862, Letters Sent by the Secretary of the Navy to Officers, Entry 1, RG 45, NA; Hill, *Bethel to Sharpsburg,* 1:256, 311; Goldsborough to Fox, 27 March 1862, *Fox Correspondence,* 1:255.

53. Lee to Lenthall, 5 November 1862, Entry 62, RG 19, NA; Lee to John Dahlgren, 5 November 1862, Lee Collection, LCM; Lee to Lenthall, ibid.

54. Sands, "Volunteer's Reminiscences," 11–12; Sands to Lee, 10 February 1863, *ORN,* ser. 1, 8:518–19.

55. S. P. Quakenbush to Lee, 29 March 1864, Lee Collection, LCM; Boggs to Lee, 9 June 1863, Entry 30, RG 45, NA.

56. Sands to Lee, 10 February 1863, *ORN,* ser. 1, 9:518–19; Lee to Welles, 2 February 1863, ibid., 494.

57. West, *Gideon Welles,* 253–54; Isherwood to Welles, 6 April 1864, Letters Sent from the Bureau of Engineering to the Secretary of the Navy, Entry 963, RG 19, NA.

58. Charles Green to Welles, 24 May 1862, *ORN,* ser. 1, 7:265–66; *Wilmington Journal,* 20, 24 September 1864; Robert E. Lee to James A. Seddon, 22 September 1863, *ORN,* ser. 1, 10:747; William H. C. Whiting to Zebulon B. Vance, 26 September 1864, ibid., 750.

59. Scharf, 806–7.

60. DeRossett and Brown to L. H. DeRossett, 2 November 1864, DeRossett Family Papers, SHC; Clarence Cary Diary, 7, 28 October 1864, Records of Boundary and Claims Commission and Arbitrations, RG 76, NA; J. C. Harris to Porter, 6 November 1864, Entry 30, RG 45, NA; Porter to J. C. Beaumont, 3 November 1864, Area 7, Entry 463, RG 45, NA; Porter to J. L. Davis, 4 November 1864, *ORN,* ser. 1, 11:46. After returning to Wilmington, both vessels ceased to be commerce raiders. *Chickamauga* was used as an armed transport, and *Olustee* became a blockade runner again, under a name that suited her, *Chameleon.* Scharf, 807–8.

61. Stephen R. Mallory, Report of the Secretary of the Navy, 30 November 1863, *ORN,* ser. 1, 9:809; Still, *Iron Afloat,* 150, 166; Confederate Subject File AC, 10 February 1864, RG 45, NA.

62. R. E. Wood, "Port Town at War," 110–12; Jimmy to Katie, 21 May

1864, James R. Randall Collection, SHC; extract from Report of the Secretary of the Navy, 5 November 1864, *ORN,* ser. 1, 11:754; William Calder to mother, 5 May 1864, William Calder Papers, SHC.

63. Charles Boggs to Lee, 3 July 1863, Entry 30, RG 45, NA; James Trathen to Case, 21 February 1863, ibid.; William Keeler to Anna Keeler, 13 July 1863, *Florida,* 66.

64. J. W. Balch to W. A. Parker, 7 May 1864, *ORN,* ser. 1, 10:20, passim.

65. Letter dated 15 May 1864, no author, Schlesinger, 564; J. W. Balch to W. A. Parker, 7 May 1864, *ORN,* ser. 1, 10:20, passim.

66. Sands to Lee, 8 May 1864, Lee Collection, LCM; William Keeler to Anna Keeler, 15 May 1864, *Florida,* 171; Lee to Sands, 19 July 1864, *ORN,* ser. 1, 10:288; Sands to Lee, 28 July 1864, ibid., 318; Lamson to Porter, 15 October 1864, Subject File AD, RG 45, NA.

67. William H. Anderson, "Blockade Life," in *Military Order of the Loyal Legion of the United States Maine Commandry* (Portland, Me.: Lefabor-Tower, 1902), 3; Ship's Log *Connecticut,* September 1863, passim, Special List 44, RG 24, NA; Lee to W. F. Spicer, 4 September 1863, Lee Collection, LCM; Sands to Lee, 5 May 1864, *ORN,* ser. 1, 9:731; Instructions for Inshore Blockaders off Wilmington, 16 December 1863, Blair-Lee Papers, Princeton.

68. Lee to Benjamin Sands, 1 September 1864, *ORN,* ser. 1, 10:414–15; Lee to Frederick D. Stuart, 22 September 1864, ibid., 475.

69. Instructions, S. P. Lee, 29 January 1864, ibid., 9:418–19; Lee to Glisson, 3 September 1864, ibid., 420; Lee to Sands, 18 September 1864, ibid., 10:467; Lee to David G. Farragut, 23 September 1864, ibid., 555; Instructions for Inshore Blockaders off Wilmington, 16 December 1863, Blair-Lee Papers, Princeton.

70. Lee to Welles, 13 August 1864, *ORN,* ser. 1, 9:358; Welles to Lee, 6 September 1864, Lee Collection, LCM; Lee to Welles, 28 August 1864, *ORN,* ser. 1, 10:404–5; Case to Lee, 10 March 1863, ibid., 8:595; Boggs to Lee, 29 March 1863, ibid., 635; Lee to Welles, 22 August 1864, Entry 30, RG 45, NA. *Peterhoff* was rammed and sunk by *Monticello* when she was mistaken for a blockade runner. Sands to Lee, 6 March 1864, *ORN,* ser. 1, 9:535–36; Lee to Welles, 19 September 1864, ibid., 10:455–56.

71. Lee to Welles, 6 July 1864, ibid., 232; Lee to Glisson, 18 July 1864, ibid., 286–87; Lee to Sands, 11 August 1864, ibid., 347. For over a year, Welles had tried to get Lee to spend some time at Wilmington and had suggested that Lee take *Minnesota* there. Lee was convinced that *Minnesota* was needed in Hampton Roads to contend with the Confederate ironclads. He believed that if he took a vessel other than *Minnesota* to Wilmington, she would not be practical. He could not take his staff or the records of the squadron, and no other vessel had the accommodations for such a move. Lee complained that both Farragut

and Du Pont had more men of war and that the North Atlantic Blockading Squadron was "the only squadron where the flag ship is assigned to the duty of blockading a special port within the general limits of the blockade." Lee did eventually make a trip to the Wilmington blockade on board *Minnesota* but hurried back to Hampton Roads after a short visit. Welles to Lee, 25 June 1863, Lee to Welles, 27 June, 10 July 1863, Lee Collection, LCM; Lee to Lenthall, 6 July 1863, Entry 62, RG 19, NA.

72. *RSN,* 1864, xi–xii; Welles to Lee, 26 July 1864, *ORN,* ser. 1, 10:307; William Keeler to Anna Keeler, 7 August 1864, *Florida,* 188.

73. Entry for 15 September 1864, *Welles Diary,* 2:146. Rowan, born in Ireland, was the highest-ranking foreign-born officer in the Union navy. Welles to Rowan, 1 September 1864, *ORN,* ser. 1, 10:415. Fox was unfriendly to Lee and worked behind the scenes to remove him. Dudley Taylor Cornish and Virginia Jean Laas, *Lincoln's Lee: The Life of Samuel Phillips Lee, United States Navy,* 1812–1897, (Lawrence: University of Kansas Press, 1986), 134–35, 151; Welles to Porter, 22 September 1864, ibid., 473–74.

74. General Order 6, David Dixon Porter, 13 October 1864, Subseries 68, Entry 395, RG 45, NA; General Order 63, David D. Porter, 1 December 1864, ibid.

75. Penrod G. Watmough to Porter, 30 October 1864, Letters Sent by Lt. Commander Penrod G. Watmough, Subseries 81, Entry 395, RG 45, NA, and 17 November 1864, *ORN,* ser. 1, 11:70–71; List of Vessels in the North Atlantic Squadron and Their Disposition, 1 November 1864, ibid., 11:39–40.

76. D. D. Porter Papers, Journal 1 (n.d.), 824–26, LCM; Porter, *Naval History,* 685–86. Although Porter claims he had ten vessels stationed at the bars, it seems that usually only half that number remained there. This indicated that the vessels were either coaling or repairing or that the faster bar blockaders, who by Porter's orders could chase, were cruising farther out in hopes of securing prizes. Diary of William Lamb, 24 October 1864, passim, William Lamb Papers, Manuscript Collection, College of William and Mary; Orders for Blockaders off the Eastern and Western Bars, 22 October 1864, General Order 18, David D. Porter, Area 8, Entry 463, RG 45, NA.

77. Porter to Sands, 26 October 1864, *ORN,* ser. 1, 10:604–5; Clarence Cary Diary, 5 October 1864, passim, RG 76, NA; William Lamb Diary, 24 October 1864, passim, William and Mary.

78. Lee, 116–17. Porter captured three steamers after the fall of Fort Fisher. If you compute the figures by omitting these vessels, since their capture was not at sea, he would have captured and destroyed forty-two percent inward bound, fifty percent on their way out, and eight percent unknown.

79. D. D. Porter Papers, Journal 1, 819, LCM.

12. The Blockade Runners

1. Marcus W. Price, "Ships That Tested the Blockade of the Carolina Ports, 1861–1865," *American Neptune* 8 (July 1948): 199. A ton was equal to about forty cubic feet. John Lyman, "Register Tonnage and Its Measurement," *American Neptune* 5 (July 1945): 227.

2. Taylor, 17, 29, 33–34, 40–41, 48, 50; Hobart-Hampden (Roberts), 2–3; John Jay Almy, "Incidents of the Blockade," *Military Order of the Loyal Legion of the United States Commandry of the District of Columbia,* War Papers 9 (Washington, D.C.: Companion, 1892), 4; Reston Stevenson, "Wilmington and the Blockade-Runners of the Civil War," *North Carolina University Magazine* 32 (March 1902): 154; Emma Martin Maffitt, *The Life and Services of John Newland Maffitt* (New York: Neale, 1906), 230.

3. Extract from letter from Charles Post to father, 12 April 1863, Post, 2348; Sands to Lee, 26 February 1863, *ORN,* ser. 1, 8:571–72; Macomb to Sands, 19 December 1862, ibid., 314–15; Whiting to George W. Randolph, 14 November 1862, ibid., 846.

4. Lee to Welles, 6 August 1864, ibid., 10:338; John Wilkinson, *The Narrative of a Blockade-Runner* (New York: Sheldon, 1877), 171.

5. Richard Cecil Todd, *Confederate Finance* (Athens: University of Georgia Press, 1954), 175; John C. Schwab, *The Confederate States of America, 1861–1865; A Financial and Industrial History of the South during the Civil War* (New York: Scribner's Sons, 1901), 30.

6. Thomas Stirling Begbie Collection, Duke; Davis to House of Representatives, 20 December 1864, *ORA,* ser. 4, 3:952; A. Sellew Roberts, "High Prices and the Blockade in the Confederacy," *South Atlantic Quarterly* 24 (April 1925): 158–61; S. C. Hawley to Seward, 1 June 1863, *ORN,* ser. 1, 9:80–81; J. B. Jones, 12 November 1863, *Diary,* 2:95; James R. Randall to Katie, 16 December 1863, James R. Randall Collection, SHC.

7. Paul Hendren, "The Confederate Blockade Runners," *U.S. Naval Institute Proceedings* 59 (April 1933): 508; L. Heyliger to Seddon, 10 January 1863, *ORA,* ser. 4, 2:335–36; Scharf, 473; Frank E. Vandiver, *Confederate Blockade Running through Bermuda, 1861–1865* (Austin: University of Texas Press, 1947), 59; William T. Truxton to Lee, 24 November 1862, Entry 30, RG 45, NA; C. G. Memminger, James A. Seddon, "Official Regulations to Carry into Effect the Act to Impose Regulations upon the Foreign Commerce of the Confederate States to Provide for the Public Defense," 5 March 1864, *ORA,* ser. 4, 3:187–89.

8. Sometimes the vessels carried just enough coal to ensure a quick return trip. Affidavits of Men on the *Lillian* Arrived—George Gowanlock, Lee to

Welles, 4 January 1864, *ORN,* ser. 1, 9:385; E. H. Faucon to Welles, 10 October 1864, ibid., 10:549.

9. James Sprunt, "Tales of the Cape Fear Blockade," *North Carolina Booklet* 1, no. 10 (February 1902): 19; Wilkinson, *Narrative,* 132.

10. Charles J. Ost to S. R. Mallory, 27 October 1862, and enclosure, Welles to Lee, 15 January 1863, Lee Collection, LCM; Case to Lee, 4 June 1863, ibid.; Charles Boggs to Lee, 2 May 1863, Lee Collection, LCM, and Entry 37, RG 45, NA; J. D. Warren to Lee, 9 December 1862, *ORN,* ser. 1, 8:273.

11. Wilkinson, *Narrative,* 132.

12. John N. Maffitt, "Blockade-Running," *United Service* 6 (June 1882): 629.

13. Wilkinson, *Narrative,* 132; Lee to Welles, 17 April 1863, *ORN,* ser. 1, 8:812–13; Lee to Welles, 6 August 1864, ibid., 10:338; S. R. Mallory to John Wilkinson, 11 March 1864, ibid., 9:804–5; Tom Henderson Wells, *The Confederate Navy: A Study in Organization* (University: University of Alabama Press, 1971), 66; Stephen R. Mallory to John Wilkinson, 11 March 1864, *ORN,* ser. 1, 8:804–5.

14. Taylor, 72; Wilkinson, *Narrative,* 152–53; Mark DeWolf Stevenson to William DeWolf Stevenson, 17 April 1907, Mark DeWolf Stevenson Papers, SHC.

15. J. C. Howell to Lee, 30 June 1864, Lee Collection, LCM; Charles Boggs to Welles, 14 June 1863, Entry 37, RG 45, NA; Isaac Hallock to father, 6 May 1862, Hallock Papers, LCM; A. Ludlow Case to Lee, 23 March 1863, Lee Collection, LCM; Lee to Lenthall, 20 April 1863, Entry 62, RG 19, NA; Welles to Lee, 30 August 1864, *ORN,* ser. 1, 10:407–8; Hobart-Hampden (Roberts), 7; Post, 24 March 1863, 2343; Case to Lee, 20 April 1863, Lee Collection, LCM.

16. James Ryder Randall to Katie, 17 November 1863, Randall Collection, SHC; Stansbury Smith to Caleb Huse, 23 July 1863, as cited in Vandiver, *Blockade Running,* 75; John Wilkinson, "Blockade Running," *The State* 22 (May 1955): 11–12; Lee to Welles, 10 December 1863, *ORN,* ser. 1, 9:345; Lee to Welles, 3 November 1863, ibid., 258–59.

17. E. M. Maffitt, *Life and Services,* 235; Crosby to Lee, 11 February 1864, *ORN,* ser. 1, 9:475; [no author] "Running the Blockade," *Southern Historical Society Papers* 9 (1881): 375; Lee to Fox, 20 February 1864, *ORN,* ser. 1, 9:496; Daniel L. Braine to John M. B. Clitz, 6 July 1862, ibid., 8:547.

18. Wilkinson, *Narrative,* 131.

19. D. D. Porter Papers, Journal 1, 820, LCM; Catherine Buie to Kate, 8 July 1862, James David McGeachy Papers, Duke; L. Warlick to Cornelia McGinsey, 5 July 1862, Cornelia McGinsey Papers, SHC.

20. George M. Ransom to Lee, 9 May 1864, *ORN,* ser. 1, 10:6–7; enclosure,

Sands to Lee, 10 May 1864, ibid., 7–8; friend to Miss Kate, 5 October 1862, Catherine Buie Papers, Duke; James Sprunt, *James Sprunt's Tales of the Cape Fear Blockade*, ed. Cornelius M. D. Thomas (Wilmington, N.C.: J. E. Hicks, 1960), 122; Wilkinson, *Narrative*, 127.

21. Hobart-Hampden (Roberts), 9; William Keeler to Anna Keeler, 9 September 1863, 3 March 1864, *Florida,* 87, 154; William H. C. Whiting to James A. Seddon, 24 August 1863, *ORN,* ser. 1, 9:173–74; Whiting to Hill, 6 March 1863, ibid., 8:860–61; Thomas A. E. Tuten to Clarisa, 25 August 1863, Arthur Whitford Collection, East Carolina Manuscript Collection, hereafter cited as ECMC; Michael H. Turrentine to sister, 14 July 1863, Michael H. Turrentine Papers, Duke; Whiting to James A. Seddon, 24 August 1863, *ORN,* ser. 1, 9:174.

22. John to cousin Mollie, 13 May 1863, J. A. McMillian to cousin Mary, 14 May 1863, Mary Margaret McNeill Papers, Duke.

23. Taylor, 72; Clarence Cary Diary, 6 October 1864, RG 76, NA; General Order 48, D. D. Porter, 16 November 1864, Subseries 61, Entry 395, RG 45, NA.

24. Case to Lee, 13 February 1863, *ORN,* ser. 1, 8:325–26; Taylor, 54.

25. Scharf, 466; Taylor, 64–65; Records of Confederate Vessels of Bermuda and Nassau, Confederate States of America Papers, LCM; Glisson to Lee, 20 September 1864, *ORN,* ser. 1, 10:456.

26. Hobart-Hampden (Roberts), 13; Begbie Collection, Duke; James Randall to K. Hammond, 17 October 1863, Randall Collection, SHC.

27. D. D. Porter Papers, Journal 1, 820–21, LCM.

28. Sands to Lee, 14 August 1864, *ORN,* ser. 1, 10:361–62; [signature cut out] 11 October 1863, Lee Collection, LCM; Case to Lee, 19 February 1863, ibid.; Case to Lee, 23 March 1863, Entry 30, RG 45, NA; Lee to Welles, 30 June 1863, ibid.

29. Fred Stuart to Lee, 14 December 1863, Lee Collection, LCM; John J. Almy to Lee, 2 February 1864, ibid.; William Keeler to Anna Keeler, 11 April 1863, *Florida,* 20–21.

30. John W. Balch to Lee, 26 September 1864, *ORN,* ser. 1, 10:479; William Keeler to Anna Keeler, 7 August 1864, *Florida,* 189; Abstract Log *Fort Jackson* and *Aries,* 29 October 1864, *ORN,* ser. 1, 11:10–11; Niles Larson to Joseph B. Breck, 9 November 1863, Lee Collection, LCM; Gustavus Scott to Lee, 7 October 1862, ibid.; D. D. Porter Papers, Journal 1, 821, LCM.

31. General Order 41, David D. Porter, Commander of the North Atlantic Blockading Squadron, 9 November 1864, Subseries 61, RG 45, NA; Board of Investigation to David D. Porter, 18 November 1864, *ORN,* ser. 1, 11:38; Francis S. Welles to Lee, 9 December 1863, Area 8, Entry 463, RG 45, NA; Porter to Fox, 8 November 1864, Fox Papers, NYHS.

32. William Keeler to Anna Keeler, 1 April 1863, *Florida,* 21.

33. Wilkinson, "Blockade Running," 12; Wilkinson, *Narrative,* 156; Porter to O. S. Glisson, 13 November 1864, *ORN,* ser. 1, 11:62; Taylor, 68.

34. Sands, "'Lest We Forget,'" 18–19; Jennings, 27; William Keeler to Anna Keeler, 6 November 1863, *Florida,* 111.

35. Lee to J. M. Frailey, 16 December 1863, *ORN,* ser. 1, 9:358; Lee to Welles, 5 February 1864, Entry 30, RG 45, NA; Lee to Oliver S. Glisson, 18 July 1864, *ORN,* ser. 1, 10:287; Lee to Welles, 1 July 1864, ibid., 410–12; *ORN,* ser. 2, 1:30, passim.

36. Lee to Welles, 1 July 1864, ibid., 221–22; Sands, "'Lest We Forget,'" 19; W. H. Anderson, "Blockade Life," 4; Circular, S. P. Lee, 3 September 1863, Lee Collection, LCM.

37. Mark DeWolf Stevenson to William, 19 April 1907, Mark DeWolf Stevenson Papers, SHC; William Keeler to Anna Keeler, 12 June 1863, *Florida,* 46; Welles to Porter, 18 November 1864, *ORN,* ser. 1, 11:75; William A. Parker to Gustavus H. Scott, 5 November 1862, ibid., 8:196; General Order 48, Porter, 16 November 1864, Subseries 61, Entry 395, RG 45, NA.

38. Sands, "'Lest We Forget,'" 20.

39. *Congressional Globe,* 37th Cong., 2d sess., 17 July 1862, appendix, 418; William Keeler to Anna Keeler, 2 March 1864, *Florida,* 148; Lee to Welles, 25 February 1864, *ORN,* ser. 1, 9:503; Lee to Stewart, 22 September 1864, ibid., 10:474; Flusser to Davenport, 8 May 1863, ibid., 9:11.

40. Lee to Welles, 7 December 1862, ibid., ser. 1, 8:263; Lee to Andrew H. Foote, 11 February 1863, ibid., 520; Lee to Welles, 7 March 1863, ibid., 589.

41. Fox to Stringham, 14 September 1861, *ORN,* ser. 1, 6:211–12; *Congressional Globe,* 37th Cong., 3d sess., 3 March 1863, appendix, 218; Polser, 276.

42. Bernath, 8; W. R. Hooper, "Blockade Running," *Harpers New Monthly Magazine* 42 (December 1870): 107.

43. When a vessel of equal or superior force was captured, the prize money went solely to the captors, as in the case of an enemy vessel of war. When a gunboat caught a blockade runner, half the money went to the government and the other half went into the navy pension fund. *The Federal Cases, Comprising Cases Argued and Determined in the Circuit and District Courts of the United States,* 30 vols. (St. Paul, Minn., 1894–97), Federal Case 4368, 8:48; Federal Case 11691, 20:521; W. H. Anderson, "Blockade Life," 4.

44. Hooper, 108; Robert W. Daly, "Pay and Prize Money in the Old Navy, 1770–1899," *U.S. Naval Institute Proceedings* 74 (August 1948): 970; Cornish and Laas, 123.

45. W. H. Anderson, "Blockade Life," 4–5.

46. Hansard's Parliamentary Debates, Lords, 10 February 1862, 165:114–

15; *New York Herald,* 20 November 1863; Stephen R. Wise, *Lifeline of the Confederacy: Blockade Running during the Civil War* (Columbia: University of South Carolina Press, 1988), 221.

47. *The Index* (London), 30 June 1864; S. C. Hawley to Seward, 2 May 1863, Thompson to Seward, 6 July 1863, Kirkpatrick to Seward, 24 September 1864, U.S. Consular Dispatches, Nassau, Entry 78, RG 59, NA; Records of Confederate Vessels at Bermuda and Nassau, Confederate States of America Papers, LCM; Frank Lawrence Owsley, *King Cotton Diplomacy: Foreign Relations of the Confederate States of America* (Chicago: University of Chicago Press, 1931), 243, passim; Judah P. Benjamin to John Slidell, 2 September 1863, Richardson, 550; Milledge L. Bonham, "The British Consuls in the Confederacy," in *Studies in History, Economics and Public Law* 43 (New York: Columbia University, 1911), passim; Warren W. Hassler, "How the Confederates Controlled Blockade Running," *Civil War Times Illustrated* 2 (October 1963): 45.

48. J. T. James, "Historical and Commercial Sketch of Wilmington, N.C.," in Frank D. Smaw, Jr., *Smaw's Wilmington Directory Comprising a General and City Business Directory* (Wilmington, N.C.: Frank D. Smaw, Jr., 1867), 31; Wise, appendix 5, 234–41, and appendix 6; Lamb, *Colonel Lamb's Story,* 7; Jimmy to Katie, 10 June 1864, Randall Collection, SHC.

49. Price, 237; Owsley, 285; *The Index* (London), 30 June 1864; Wise, 221.

50. Benjamin to Slidell, 2 September 1863, *ORN,* ser. 2, 3:885; Bonham, 205.

51. Frank E. Vandiver, *Ploughshares into Swords: Josiah Gorgas and Confederate Ordnance* (Austin: University of Texas Press, 1952), 100–101; Josiah Gorgas, "Notes on the Ordnance Department of the Confederate Government," *Southern Historical Society Papers* 12 (January–December 1884): 80.

52. Wise, 211. A bale of cotton weighed an average of 460 pounds. George McHenry, *A Paper Containing a Statement of Facts Relating to the Approaching Cotton Crisis* (Richmond: Confederate House of Representatives, 1865), 23; *Daily Journal* (Wilmington), 27 November 1863; Bayne to Alexander Lawton, 27 October 1863, as cited in Vandiver, *Ploughshares,* 100–101; Benjamin to Slidell, 2 September 1863, *ORN,* ser. 2, 3:885.

53. Edward Atkinson to A. H. Rice, 18 March 1864, Lee Collection, LCM. Frank Owsley estimated that approximately 450,000 bales of cotton went to the northern states from the South through Nassau, Bermuda, Tampico, and other points of reshipment (289).

54. Seixas is quoted in J. B. Jones, *Diary* 16 June 1863, 1:350; Davis to House of Representatives, 20 December 1864, *ORA,* ser. 4, 3:952; Seddon to Davis, 10 December 1864, ibid., 930.

55. As quoted in the *New York Times,* 19 March 1865; Gorgas, "Notes," 87;

entry for 2 August 1863, Josiah Gorgas, *The Civil War Diary of General Josiah Gorgas,* ed. Frank E. Vandiver (Tuscaloosa: University of Alabama Press, 1947), 57; New York *Herald,* 21 January 1865.

56. For some idea of the amounts brought through, see: J. Gorgas, Abstract Summery of Supplies Purchased and Shipped by Maj. C. Huse, 13 February 1863, *ORA,* ser. 4, 2:382–84; Gorgas to Seddon, 15 November 1863, ibid., 955–56; G. A. Trenholm to Davis, 12 December 1864, ibid., 3:954–55; Gorgas to Seddon, 31 December 1864, ibid., 986; Wise, 226; Richard I. Lester, *Confederate Finance and Purchasing in Great Britain* (Charlottesville: University Press of Virginia, 1975), 150; Owsley, 266, passim; William Diamond, "Imports of the Confederate Government from Europe and Mexico," *Journal of Southern History* 6 (November 1940): 470, passim; Hassler, 48–49; Harry Wandrus and Tom Stich, "Brief Notes on the Arms Brought into the Confederacy by Blockade Runners," *Hobbies* 55 (August 1950): 129; Virgil Carrington Jones, "'We Are Useless': Mr. Lincoln's Blockade," *Civil War Times Illustrated* 10 (December 1971): 18; Vandiver, *Blockade Running,* passim; Vandiver, *Ploughshares,* 93–94.

57. Entry for 11 October 1863, Gorgas, *Diary,* 65; Trenholm to Davis, 12 December 1864, *ORA,* ser. 4, 3:954–55.

58. James Sprunt, "Running of the Blockade," *Southern Historical Society Papers* 24 (1896): 158–59.

59. Wise, 196; entry for 3 January 1865, J. B. Jones, *Diary,* 2:373, 375; Gorgas to Seddon, 31 December 1864, *ORA,* ser. 4, 3:986.

60. Judah Benjamin to H. Holtz, 24 February 1864, Pickett Papers, LCM; entry for 3 January 1865, J. B. Jones, *Diary,* 2:374; Official Regulations . . . to Impose Regulations upon the Foreign Commerce of the Confederates States, *ORA,* ser. 4, 3:187–89; Frank G. Ruffin to Seddon, 14 December 1864, *ORA,* ibid., 941.

61. Price, 215–37; Stansbury Smith to Josiah Gorgas, 1 September 1863, as cited in Vandiver, *Blockade Running,* 91; Lee to Welles, 1 July 1864, *ORN,* ser. 1, 10:222.

62. *The Times* (London), 25 September 1863; Seward to Lyons, 8 August 1864, U.S. Congress, House, *Papers Relating to Foreign Affairs,* H. Ex. Doc. 1, pt. 2, 38th Cong., 2d sess., 1865, 673.

63. Henry B. Rommell to Mr. and Mrs. Rommell, April 1863, Henry B. Rommell Papers, Duke.

13. The Capture of Wilmington

1. Blockade Strategy Board Minutes, 2 September 1861, passim, Subject File ON, RG 45, NA.

2. Armand J. DeRosset to Kate Meares, 29 October 1861, DeRosset Family Papers, SHC.

3. David Buie to Kate McGeachy, 14 January 1862, Catherine Buie Papers, Duke.

4. Friend to Kate McGeachy, 18 January 1862, ibid.

5. D. S. Pemberton to F. Martin, 27 March 1862, Kendall Cox and Company Collection, Duke.

6. Oliver Glisson to Goldsborough, 31 December 1861, *ORN,* ser. 1, 6:493; James Trathen to Lee, 3 August 1863, ibid., 9:143–44; Lee to Welles, 6 August 1863, ibid., 142; Glisson to Daniel Braine, 25 June 1862, ibid., 7:506; Braine to Glisson, 26 June 1862, ibid., 506–7; Glisson to Goldsborough, ibid., 506; Braine to Lee, 24 November 1862, Lee Collection, LCM; Braine to Boggs, 27 April 1863, *ORN,* ser. 1, 8:828–29; Gustavus Scott to Charles Boggs, 3 May 1863, ibid., 838; Lee to Welles, 14 January 1864, ibid., 9:374–75; F. S. Welles to Lee, 4 January 1864, ibid., 375–76; Cushing to Porter, 7 February 1865, ibid., 12:5–6; Peirce Crosby to Lee, 8 September 1863, Entry 30, RG 45, NA.

7. Cushing to Lee, 25 August 1863, *ORN,* ser. 1, 9:177–78.

8. Cushing to Lee, 5 March 1864, ibid., 511; Fox to Lee, 8 April 1864, ibid., 589.

9. Lee to Welles, 26 April 1864, ibid., 672; Sands to Lee, 22 April 1864, ibid., 674–75; Sands to Lee, 30 April 1864, enclosure, Lee to Butler, 30 April 1864, Butler Papers, LCM; William Calder to mother, 25 April 1864, William Calder Papers, SHC; *Wilmington Journal,* 28 April 1864.

10. Elmanson Semon to Edmund Kemble, 19 September 1864, *ORN,* ser. 1, 10:508; Joseph Breck to Lee, 26 May 1864, ibid., 94; Lee to Glisson, 27 September 1864, ibid., 511; Lee to W. A. Parker, 21 November 1862, Lee Collection, LCM.

11. Lee to Welles, 22 December 1863, *ORN,* ser. 1, 9:370–71.

12. Welles to Goldsborough, 11 May 1862, ibid., 8:341; Goldsborough to Welles, 12 May 1862, ibid., 7:342; Goldsborough to Elizabeth Wirt Goldsborough, 12 May 1862, Goldsborough Collection, LCM.

13. Welles to Goldsborough, 13 May 1862, *ORN,* ser. 1, 7:348–49; Fox to Goldsborough, 17 May 1862, *Fox Correspondence,* 1:269; Goldsborough to Fox, 21 May 1862, ibid., 272–73; Fox to Goldsborough, 23 May 1862, *ORN,* ser. 1, 7:419; Goldsborough to Fox, 21 May 1862, *Fox Correspondence,* 1:272–73. The garrisons in the area were undermanned as a result of the Peninsular campaign, which would have aided in a naval attack on the fort. Robert E. Lee to Joseph R. Anderson, 28 January 1862, *ORA,* ser. 1, 9:423–24; Welles to Goldsborough, 2 June 1862, *ORN,* ser. 1, 7:445.

14. Welles to Goldsborough, 4 June 1862, ibid., 453–54; Goldsborough to Fox, 3, 16 June 1862, *Fox Correspondence,* 1:279–80.

15. Fox to Du Pont, 3 June 1862, *Du Pont Letters*, 2:97.

16. Friend to Kate McGeachy, 17 April 1863, Buie Papers, Duke.

17. William Lamb, "Defense of Fort Fisher, North Carolina," *The Military Historical Society of Massachusetts*, 14 vols. (Boston: The Society, 1912), 9:350; William H. C. Whiting to George W. Randolph, 14 November 1862, *ORN*, ser. 1, 8:846-47.

18. Braine to C. P. Patterson or Alexander Bache, 20 August 1862, ibid., 665; Braine to Lee, 29 September 1862, Lee Collection, LCM.

19. Goldsborough to Hiram Paulding, 13 May 1862, *ORN*, ser. 1, 7:348; Welles to Martin Burke, 26 November 1862, *ORN*, ser. 1, 8:235; Fox to George W. Blunt, 28 November 1862, ibid., 237; Lee to Fox, 11 December 1862, *Fox Correspondence*, 2:238-39.

20. Hattaway and Jones, 300-308; A. A. Hoehling, *Thunder at Hampton Roads* (Englewood Cliffs, N.J.: Prentice-Hall, 1976), 188; Samuel F. Du Pont to Sophie Du Pont, 25 January 1863, *Du Pont Letters*, 2:379.

21. Fox to Lee, 7 November 1862, *ORN*, ser. 1, 8:203; Lee to Fox, 2 December 1862, ibid., 245-46.

22. Lee to Fox, 14 December 1862, ibid., 298-99; Fox to Lee, 15 December 1862, *Fox Correspondence*, 2:244.

23. Ibid.

24. Ibid., 244-45.

25. Lee to Fox, 14 December 1862, *ORN*, ser. 1, 8:298-99; Welles to Lee, 15 December 1862, ibid., 301.

26. A. D. to Eliza J. McEwen, 30 November 1862, Eliza J. McEwen Collection, Duke; David to Catherine Buie, 4 December 1862, Buie Papers, Duke.

27. Charles Green to Welles, 24 May 1862, *ORN*, ser. 1, 7:266; Welles to Lee, 30 December 1862, Lee Collection, LCM. Fox's comments were related by Samuel F. Du Pont to Sophie Du Pont, 25 January 1863, *Du Pont Letters*, 2:379; John Bankhead to Lee, 27 December 1862, *ORN*, ser. 1, 8:327-28; 27 December 1862, Lee Collection, LCM.

28. Francis M. Bunce to Glisson, 20 June 1862, *ORN*, ser. 1, 7:493; John Taylor Wood to Jefferson Davis, 14 February 1863, *ORN*, ser. 1, 7:859; Whiting to Seddon, 28 January 1863, ibid., 857.

29. Bankhead to Lee, 27 December 1862, *ORN*, ser. 1, 8:327-28; Percival Drayton to Lee, ibid., 326-27; Fox to Julius H. Kroehl, 1 December 1862, Fox Papers, NYHS; Note of Julius H. Kroehl, 21 December [1862], Lee Collection, LCM; Kroehl to Lee, 23 December 1862, ibid.

30. Lee to Welles, 26 December 1862, *ORN*, ser. 1, 8:320-21; Foster to Halleck, 23 December 1862, *ORA*, ser. 1, 18:489.

31. Lee to Fox, 11, 14 December 1862, Fox to Du Pont, 13 December 1862, Fox to Lee, 15 December 1862, Fox Papers, NYHS.

32. Lee to Welles, 24 December 1862, Welles to Lee, 26 December 1862, Welles Papers, Letter Book, LCM.

33. Bankhead to Lee, 27 December 1862, Area 7, Entry 463, RG 45, NA; Sands to Lee, 30 December 1862, ibid.; Sands to Lee, 29 December 1862, Lee Collection, LCM; George F. Bowden to Braine, 28 December 1862, ibid.; Lee to Welles, 28 December 1862, ibid.; Lee to Foster, 28 December 1862, Area 7, Entry 463, RG 45, NA.

34. Ibid.; Sands to Lee, 2 January 1863, *ORN,* ser. 1, 8:401.

35. Lee to Foster, 28 December 1862, Lee Collection, LCM; Lee to Welles, 28 December 1862, Area 7, Entry 463, RG 45, NA.

36. Lee urged Braine to approach the obstructions at night to determine their extent. Lee to Sands, 29 December 1862, Blair-Lee Papers, Princeton; Welles to Lee, 30 December 1862, Lee Collection, LCM.

37. Bankhead to Lee, 1 January 1863, *ORN,* ser. 1, 8:347–49.

38. Hallock to father, 28 December 1862, Hallock Papers, LCM; Joseph Lewis Stackpole, "The Department of North Carolina under General Foster, July, 1862, to July, 1863," *The Military Historical Society of Massachusetts,* 14 vols. (Boston: The Society, 1912), 9:95; Cleveland, 217; Fox to Du Pont, 11 March 1863, *Du Pont Letters,* 2:486; Du Pont to Sophie, 6 January 1863, ibid., 348; entry for 5 January 1863, *Welles Diary,* 1:216. Two days later, David Porter attempted to get his vessels over the Rip after Fort Caswell was abandoned. It took three days to get the gunboats over the Rip. A similar try in January 1863 may have ended in disaster for the navy. Porter to Welles, 22 January 1865, *ORN,* ser. 1, 11:269–70.

39. C. H. Davis, *Life,* 137–38.

40. Lee to Welles, 4 January 1863, Blair-Lee Papers, Princeton; Welles to Du Pont, 6 January 1863, Welles Papers, LCM.

41. Foster to Lee, 4 January 1863, *ORN,* ser. 1, 8:399–400.

42. Cooper to Beauregard, 8 January 1863, *ORA,* ser. 1, 18:826; Beauregard to Whiting, 8 January 1863, ibid.; Whiting to Beauregard, 13 January 1863, ibid., 842.

43. Welles to Lee, 13 January 1863, Lee Collection, LCM; Braine to Lee, 9 January 1863, ibid.; Foster to Lee, 4 January 1863, *ORN,* ser. 1, 8:399–400; Welles to Lee, 13 January 1863, ibid., 420.

44. Fox to Lee, 12 February 1863, Fox Papers, NYHS; Lee to Welles, 26 February 1863, *ORN,* ser. 1, 8:575.

45. Fox to Du Pont, 26 February 1863, *Fox Correspondence,* 1:184; Du Pont

to Fox, 2 March 1863, ibid., 186; Lee to Welles, 10 May 1863, Letter Book 11, Blair-Lee Papers, Princeton.

46. Whiting to Seddon, 28 January 1863, *ORA,* ser. 1, 18:862; Lee to Welles, 30 March 1863, *ORN,* ser. 1, 8:635; Lee to Welles, 12 May 1863, Entry 30, RG 45, NA; John D. McGeachy to Mary Margaret McNeill, 18 January 1862, Mary Margaret McNeill Papers, Duke; Crowley, 294; W. R. King, *Torpedoes: Their Invention and Use from the First Application to the Art of War to the Present Time* (Washington, 1866), 7. Brigadier-General Gabriel Rains, the Confederates' torpedo expert, was sent to Wilmington to lay out a torpedo system in 1862. *ORA,* ser. 1, 28:750; A. Ludlow Case to Lee, 23 May 1863, *ORN,* ser. 1, 9:50.

47. Lee to Fox, 4 April 1864, Fox Papers, NYHS; Welles to Lee, 28 April 1863, *ORN,* ser. 1, 8:830–31; Lee to Welles, 28 May 1863, ibid., 9:49; John Foster to Lee, 25 April 1863, ibid., 826; Welles to Lee, 1 May 1863, ibid., 834; Boggs to Lee, 14 May 1863, Area 8, Entry 463, RG 45, NA; Fox to General Gillmore, 8 November 1863, Fox Papers, NYHS; Lee to Welles, 10 May 1863, Blair-Lee Papers, Princeton.

48. Welles to Stanton, 2 January 1864, *ORN,* ser. 1, 9:14; Sands to Lee, 23 May 1864, *ORN,* ser. 1, 10:81–82; I. N. Palmer to B. Butler, 31 May 1864, J. C. Howell to Lee, 6 June 1864, Lee Collection, LCM.

49. William Cushing, Journals of Vessels of the U.S. Navy, RG 45, NA, 48–56; J. R. Randall to Katie, 29 June 1864, Randall Collection, SHC.

50. Entry for 30 August 1864, *Welles Diary,* 2:127; Porter Papers, Journal 1:881, LCM.

51. Entry for 27 September 1864, *Welles Diary,* 2:161; Lee to Lizzie, 18 March 1864, Blair-Lee Papers, Princeton; entry for 15 September 1864, ibid., 2:145–47; Barnes, "My Egotistigraphy," NYHS, 225.

52. Welles to Farragut, 5 September 1864, *ORN,* ser. 1, 10:430–31; Welles to Porter, 22 September 1864, ibid., 473–74; entry for 15 September 1864, *Welles Diary,* 2:146.

53. Richard S. West, Jr., "(Private and Confidential) My Dear Fox—," *U.S. Naval Institute Proceedings* 63 (May 1937:, 694; Abstract Log *Malvern,* 12 October 1864, *ORN,* ser. 1, 10:557; Porter General Order 2, ibid., 558; Lee to Welles, 1 October 1864, ibid., 514–15; List of Vessels in the North Atlantic Squadron, and Their Disposition, 1 November 1864, ibid., 11:39–40; Porter Papers, Journal 1, 811, LCM; Porter to Welles, 13 October 1864, *ORN,* ser. 1, 10:563.

54. Hallock to Grant, 3 July 1864, *Butler Correspondence,* 4:458–59.

55. Butler, *Butler's Book,* 819; Charles E. Pearce, "The Expeditions against Fort Fisher," in *War Papers and Personal Reminiscences 1861–1865 Read before the Commandry of the State of Missouri Military Order of the Loyal Legion of the United States* (St. Louis: Becktold, 1892), 363; U.S. Congress, Senate, *Fort Fisher*

Expedition, S. Rept. 142, pt. 2; Ulysses S. Grant, *Personal Memoirs of U. S. Grant,* 2 vols. (New York: Charles L. Webster, 1885), 2:604.

56. Comstock to Terry, 27 January 1865, *ORA,* ser. 1, 47 (pt.1): 406–8. Colonel Lamb's measurements of the defenses are somewhat larger, but his account was written sixteen years after the attack. Lamb, *Colonel Lamb's Story,* 1–5; Sprunt, *Chronicles,* 381.

57. Fox to R. F. Wade, 13 March 1865 [within November 1863 correspondence], Fox Papers, NYHS; Butler, *Butler's Book,* 799–800; Richard Delafield to Charles Dana, 18 November 1864, *ORN,* ser. 1, 11:207–14; Thomas Lincoln Casey to Delafield, 29 December 1864, *ORA,* ser. 1, 42 (pt. 1): 991–93; David D. Porter, *Incidents and Antedotes of the Civil War* (New York: D. Appleton, 1886), 269; Porter to Pendleton G. Watmough, 8 December 1864, *ORN,* ser. 1, 11:217; Porter to Alexander C. Rhind, 17 December 1864, ibid., 222–23.

58. Rhind to Porter, 2 February 1865, ibid., 230; Thomas Lincoln Casey to Delafield, 29 December 1864, *ORA,* ser. 1, 42 (pt. 1): 989–90.

59. Porter to Fox, 8 November 1864, Fox Papers, NYHS; Butler to Weitzal, 30 January 1865, *Butler Correspondence,* 5:515; Porter Papers, Journal 1, 843, LCM.

60. Grant to Butler, 4 December 1864, *Butler Correspondence,* 5:379; U.S. Congress, Senate, *Joint Committee on the Conduct of War,* S. Rept. 142, 52, 55, 69–70; Butler to Grant, 20 December 1864, *ORA,* ser. 1, 42 (pt. 1): 964.

61. Porter to Butler, 16 December 1864, *ORN,* ser. 1, 11:196; A. C. Rhind to Porter, 26 December 1864, ibid., 226; Case to Delafield, 29 December 1864, *ORA,* ser. 1, 42 (pt. 1), 990; Porter to P. G. Watmough, 17 December 1864, *ORN,* ser. 1, 11:220; Porter, *Incidents and Antedotes,* 272; James Parker, "The Navy in the Battles and Capture of Fort Fisher," in *Personal Recollections of the War of the Rebellion Addresses Delivered before the Commandry of the State of New York, Military Order of the Loyal Legion of the United States,* ed. A. Noel Blakeman, 4 vols. (New York: G. P. Putnam's Son's, 1897), 2:108.

62. Porter to Butler, 13 December 1864, *Butler Correspondence,* 5:410; H. C. Lockwood, "The Capture of Fort Fisher," *Atlantic Monthly* 27 (May 1871): 627; Porter to Rhind, 17 December 1864, *ORN,* ser. 1, 1:222; Porter to Welles, 24 January 1865, Area 8, Entry 463, RG 45, NA; J. Parker, "The Navy," 107.

63. Some of the vessels arrived later that night, making a total of fifty-six on the 25th. Porter to Welles, 26 December 1864, *ORN,* ser. 1, 11:255–57; Lamb, *Colonel Lamb's Story,* 15. The three frigates, *Minnesota, Colorado,* and *Wabash,* each mounted more guns than were in the fort. The *Minnesota* and *Colorado* not only carried more shot and shell than all the fort's magazines combined but also expended more ammunition between them than was in the fort. Lamb, "Defense of Fort Fisher," 362.

64. Porter to Welles, 26 December 1864, *ORN,* ser. 1, 11:256; Clarence Cary Diary, 24 December 1864, RG 76, NA; Lamb, "Defense of Fort Fisher," 362, 363–65.

65. Butler to Grant, 27 December 1864, *ORA,* ser. 1, 42 (pt. 1): 965; Butler to Grant, 3 January 1865, *Butler Correspondence,* 5:465; Porter to Welles, 26 December 1864, *ORN,* ser. 1, 11:258; Clarence Cary Diary, 25 December 1864, RG 76, NA; Lamb, *Colonel Lamb's Story,* 17; R. T. Chapman to R. F. Pinkney, 29 December 1864, *ORN,* ser. 1, 11:373.

66. Butler, *Butler's Book,* 70, appendix; Butler to Grant, 27 December 1864, *ORA,* ser. 1, 42 (pt. 1): 966; Grant to Butler, 6 December 1864, *Butler Correspondence,* 5:380; U.S. Congress, Senate, *Joint Committee On The Conduct of War,* S. Rept. 142, 53; Butler to Grant, 3 January 1865, *ORA,* ser. 1, 42 (pt. 1): 968; Sidney Brooks to Butler, 31 December 1864, Butler Papers, LCM; Butler to Grant, 27 December 1864, *ORA,* ser. 1, 42 (pt. 1): 966; Porter to Alden, 26 December 1864, *ORN,* ser. 1, 14:318.

67. Jay Luvaas, "The Fall of Fort Fisher," *Civil War Times Illustrated* 3 (August 1964): 7; Edmund R. Colhoun to Porter, 31 December 1864, *ORN,* ser. 1, 11:276; Lamb, "Defense of Fort Fisher," 365–67; Grant's Endorsement upon General Butler's Report, 7 January 1865, *Butler Correspondence,* 5:472.

68. Aeneas Armstrong to Francis L. Galt, 29 December 1864, *ORN,* ser. 1, 11:375. Three hundred Confederates were captured by Butler's men. It required over 20,000 pounds of metal per Confederate casualty. Butler to Grant, 3 January 1865, *ORA,* ser. 1, 42 (pt. 1): 968; S. Singleton to Lamb, 30 December 1864, *ORN,* ser. 1, 11:370; Lamb to James H. Hill, 27 December 1864, ibid., 366–69. The fort also fired an additional 118 rounds of grapeshot and canister at the troops ashore. M. Long to Lamb, Report of Ordnance Department of Fort Fisher, 24, 25 December 1864, *ORA,* ser. 1, 42 (pt. 1): 1007; Butler to Grant, 3 January 1865, ibid., 969. Ten men were wounded by naval projectiles. Daniel C. Burleigh to Francis M. Ramsey, 27 December 1864, *ORN,* ser. 1, 11:280, passim.

69. Porter, *Naval History,* 701; Porter to Welles, 28 December 1864, *ORN,* ser. 1, 11:263; Porter to Welles, 27 December 1864, ibid., 261; Porter to Welles, 31 December 1864, ibid., 266.

70. Joseph E. King, "The Fort Fisher Campaigns 1864–1865," *U.S. Naval Institute Proceedings* 77 (August 1951): 849.

71. Porter General Orders 84, 6 January 1865, *ORN,* ser. 1, 11:428; Lamb, *Colonel Lamb's Story,* 22; "The Opposing Forces at Fort Fisher, N.C.," in *Battles and Leaders,* 4:662.

72. G. T. Gordon to Archer Anderson, 17 January 1865, *ORN,* ser. 1, 11:594; Plan of Attack on Fort Fisher, 13, 14, 15 January 1865, ibid., facing page 425.

73. David D. Porter Special Order 8, 3 January 1865, ibid., 427; G. T. Gordon to Archer Anderson, ibid., 595; Lamb, *Colonel Lamb's Story,* 23.

74. Had just one of the Confederate ironclads been available, she might have stopped the landing of the troops by laying in the river and firing at the transports or the troops ashore. Brevet Major General Terry General Orders 3, 10 January 1865, Subject File oo, Entry 464, RG 45, NA; Edgar Ketchum, "Personal Reminiscences of the Capture of Fort Fisher and Wilmington, North Carolina," *United Service* n.s. 16 (December 1896): 460; Terry to John A. Rawlins, 25 January 1865, *ORN,* ser. 1, 11:587; Lamb, *Colonel Lamb's Story,* 10, 23.

75. Ibid., 25; Terry to Rawlins, 25 January 1865, *ORN,* ser. 1, 11:589; J. R. Bartlett to father, 18 January 1865, Subject File HJ, RG 45, NA; Edson J. Harkness, "The Expeditions against Fort Fisher and Wilmington," in *Military Essays and Recollections: Papers Read before the Commandry of the State of Illinois Military Order of the Loyal Legion of the United States,* 4 vols. (Chicago: McClurg, 1894), 2:172; K. R. Breese to Porter, 11 January 1865, *ORN,* ser. 1, 11:446–47; Lamb, *Colonel Lamb's Story,* 26–27.

76. Porter boasted that he could take the fort with his forces alone. Porter to Fox, 7 January 1865, Fox Papers, NYHS; Parker to Porter, 16 January 1865, *ORN,* ser. 1, 11:498; Pearce, 376; Harkness, 171–72; Breese to Parker, 16 January 1865, U.S. Congress, Senate, *Fort Fisher Expedition,* 193.

77. Harkness, 172–73; Pearce, 376–77; Lamb, *Colonel Lamb's Story,* 27; Barnes, "My Egotistigraphy," NYHS, 242–43; Adelbert Ames, "The Capture of Fort Fisher," in *Civil War Papers Read before the Commandry of the State of Massachusetts Military Order of the Loyal Legion of the United States* (Boston: The Commandry, 1900), 1:289.

78. Whiting to Lee, 19 February 1865, *ORN,* ser. 1, 11:593; Lamb, *Colonel Lamb's Story,* 28, 30–35; William Radford to Porter, 16 January 1865, *ORN,* ser. 1, 11:461–62; Ketchum, 462; Pearce, 379.

79. Bragg to Lee, 15 January 1865, *ORA,* ser. 1, 46 (pt. 2): 1061; Bragg to W. H. Taylor, 20 January 1865, ibid., pt. 1, 431–35; Lamb, *Defense of Fort Fisher,* 383–84; N. Martin Curtis, "The Capture of Fort Fisher," in *Civil War Papers Read before the Commandry of the State of Massachusetts Military Order of the Loyal Legion of the United States* (Boston: The Commandry, 1900), 1:323–24.

80. J. B. Jones, 1 February 1865, *Diary,* 2:405–6; New York *Herald,* 28 February 1865.

81. The figures given by the sources conflict. *ORN,* ser. 1, 11:444; "The Opposing Forces at Fort Fisher, N.C.," in *Battles and Leaders,* 4:661–62; J. Parker, "The Navy," 113; Daniel Ammen, "Our Second Bombardment of Fort Fisher," in *Military Order of the Loyal Legion of the United States Commandry of*

the District of Columbia, War Papers 4 (Washington, D.C.: The Commandry, 1887), 7, 260; Return of Casualties in the U.S. Forces Engaged in the Storming of Fort Fisher, N.C., 15 January 1865, *ORA,* ser. 1, 46 (pt. 1): 405; Porter to Welles, 17 January 1865, *ORN,* ser. 1, 11:441; Alfred G. Terry to J. A. Rawlins, 25 January 1865, *ORA,* ser. 1, 46 (pt. 1): 399; Lamb, "Defense of Fort Fisher," 384.

82. "The Opposing Forces at Fort Fisher, N.C.," in *Battles and Leaders,* 4:661.

83. Porter to Welles, 1 February 1865, *ORN,* ser. 1, 11:734; List of Vessels Arrived and Departed at New Inlet by Guardship *Fort Donelson,* Transportation of Supplies and Passengers, Subject File OX, RG 45, NA.

84. Chris Eugene Fonvielle, Jr., "To Forge a Thunderbolt: The Wilmington Campaign, February 1865" (M.A. thesis, East Carolina University, 1987); Charles S. Powell Papers, "War Tales 1861–1865," Duke, 24.

85. Cushing to Porter, 31 January 1865, *ORN,* ser. 1, 11:624; Porter to Welles, 20 January 1865, ibid., 619; Porter to P. G. Watmough, 21 January 1861, Area 8, Entry 463, RG 45, NA; Wise, 208–9; Porter to Clitz, 17 January 1865, Subseries 61, Entry 395, RG 45, NA; Porter Papers, Journal 1, 891, LCM.

86. Braine to Porter, 22 January 1865, *ORN,* ser. 1, 11:630; Porter to Fox, 20 January 1865, as cited in James M. Merrill, "The Fort Fisher and Wilmington Campaign: Letters from Rear Admiral David D. Porter," *North Carolina Historical Review* 35 (October 1958): 469. A torpedo boat was raised from Cape Fear after the capture of the town. Thomas Phelps to William Radford, 3 August 1865, *ORN,* ser. 1, 12:173; Special Order, D. D. Porter, 13, 28 January 1865, Subseries 61, Entry 395, RG 45, NA; S. C. Bartlett to sister, 3 February 1865, "The Letters of Stephen Chaulker Bartlett aboard USS 'Lenapee,' January to August, 1865," ed. Paul Murray and Stephen Russell Bartlett, Jr., *North Carolina Historical Review* 33 (January 1956): 72; Ship's Log *Britannia,* 30 January 1865, RG 24, NA; D. D. Porter Papers, Journal 1, 882, LCM.

87. Special Order 12, 27 January 1865, *ORN,* ser. 1, 11:704–5; Special Order 13, 28 January 1865, Subseries 61, Entry 395, RG 45, NA; Routine for Picket Duty (n.d.), ibid.; Bartlett to sister, 3 February 1865, "Letters," 72.

88. Abstract Log *Malvern,* entry for 28 January 1865, *ORN,* ser. 1, 11:240; Fox to Welles, 30 January 1865, ibid., 713; J. M. Schofield to William Tecumseh Sherman, 3 April 1865, *ORA,* ser. 1, 47 (pt. 1): 910; Porter to Henry Rolando, 4 February 1865, *ORN,* ser. 1, 12:5.

89. Abstract Log *Malvern,* 28, 29 January 1865, *ORN,* ser. 1, 11:740; Porter, *Naval History,* 727; Porter Papers, Journal 1, 883, LCM; J. M. Schofield to Porter, 9 February 1865, Civil War Papers (Federal Miscellaneous), SHC; Porter to Schofield, 14 February 1865, *ORN,* ser. 1, 12:29–30; Schofield to

Porter, ibid., 30; Schofield to Stern, 13 April 1865, *ORA*, ser. 1, 47 (pt. 1): 910; S. C. Bartlett to sister, 12 February 1865, "Letters," 74; Porter to Welles, 12 February 1865, *ORN*, ser. 1, 12:16–17.

90. John D. Cox to J. A. Campbell, 15 May 1865, *ORA*, ser. 1, 47 (pt. 1): 960; Porter to Welles, 19 February 1865, *ORN*, ser. 1, 12:33.

91. Ibid., 33–34.

92. There is some confusion as to the day the "bogus" monitor was sent up the river. Porter used a similar trick in February 1863, when he sent a dummy gunboat down the Mississippi River near Warrenton, which made the Confederates abandon the captured *Indianola*. William G. Temple to T. Bailey, 21 February 1865, ibid., 34; entry for 21 February 1865, *Welles Diary*, 2:245.

93. John D. Cox to J. A. Campbell, 15 May 1865, *ORA*, ser. 1, 47 (pt. 1): 960–62; Barnes, "My Egotistigraphy," NYHS, 249; Bartlett to sister, 20 February 1865, "Letters," 77–78; Porter, *Naval History*, 728.

94. P. C. Gaillard to Parker, 19 February 1865, *ORA*, ser. 1, 47 (pt. 2): 1228; *ORA* Atlas, lxviii, 7.

95. Porter to Fox, 19 February 1864, *Fox Correspondence*, 2:200; entry for 20 April 1865, Robert Watson, "Yankees Were Landing Below Us: The Civil War Journal of Robert Watson, C.S.N.," ed. William N. Still, Jr., *Civil War Times Illustrated* 15 (April 1976): 18.

96. Porter Papers, Journal 1, 890, LCM; Porter, *Naval History*, 728; copy of the Ship's Log *Osceola*, 20 February 1865, Subseries 61, Entry 395, RG 45, NA; Porter to Welles, 22 February 1865, Area 8, Entry 463, RG 45, NA; Porter to Welles, 21 February 1865, *ORN*, ser. 1, 12:44; S. C. Bartlett to sister, 20 February 1865, "Letters," 79.

97. Powell, "War Tales," Duke, 19; Bragg to W. H. Taylor, 25 February 1865, *ORA*, ser. 1, 47 (pt. 1): 1077–78; Watson, entry for 21 April 1865, 18; R. Chandler to George Young, 3 March 1865, Area 8, Entry 463, RG 45, NA; Barnes, "My Egotistigraphy," NYHS, 251.

98. George W. Young to Porter, 16 March 1865, *ORN*, ser. 1, 12:70–71. Two weeks later, the *Lenapee* went to Magnolia via the North East Cape Fear River. She also had to travel up small creeks and came so close to shore that seamen could pull branches from trees. The men landed several times and helped themselves to sheep, cattle, hogs, and other foodstuffs, while other vessels near Wilmington sent picket boats up Cape Fear to forage for fresh meat. S. C. Bartlett to parents, 17 March 1865, Bartlett to sister, 4 April 1865, "Letters," 81, 84. After the surrender of the Confederate forces, Porter was detached, and Commander William Radford was assigned to command the squadron. In June, the squadron ceased to exist when it was combined with the South Atlantic Blockading Squadron to become the Atlantic Blockading Squadron

under Radford's command. Welles to Porter, 28 April 1865, *ORN,* ser. 1, 12:129; Welles to Radford, ibid.; Porter to Radford, 1 May 1865, ibid., 132; Circular Letter to Chiefs of Bureau, Navy Department, 24 June 1865, M. S. Thompson, *General Orders,* 34.

14. Conclusion

1. S. B. French to General I. M. St. John, 10 March 1865, *ORA,* ser. 1, 46 (pt. 2): 1297.

2. Black, 228–29.

3. Ibid., 119; Charles W. Ramsdell, "The Confederate Government and the Railroads," *American Historical Review* 22 (July 1917): 794–97. The commissary general tried to establish a reserve supply of grain in Richmond during the last eight months of 1863 but failed because of a lack of transportation. Entry for 20 January 1864, J. B. Jones, *Diary,* 132.

4. Mallory to Davis, 24 April 1865, *ORA,* ser. 1, 47 (pt. 3), 833.

Bibliography

PRIMARY SOURCES

Manuscripts

College of William and Mary, Williamsburg, Virginia
 William Lamb Papers
Duke University Library, Durham, North Carolina
 Thomas Stirling Begbie Collection
 Catherine Jane (McGeachy) Buie Papers
 Kendall Cox and Company Collection
 David Lucius Craft Papers
 Louis Malesherbes Goldsborough Papers
 Thomas Wilson Hall Collection
 Robert Edward Lee Papers
 Eliza J. McEwen Collection
 James David McGeachy Papers
 Mary Margaret McNeill Papers
 Henry Clay Pardee Papers
 Charles S. Powell Papers
 William Read, Jr., Papers
 Horatio G. Robinson Collection
 Henry B. Rommel Papers
 Raphael Semmes Papers
 Michael H. Turrentine Papers
East Carolina University Library, Greenville, North Carolina

Arthur Whitford Collection
Library of Congress, Washington, D.C.
   Asa Beetham Papers
   Benjamin Franklin Butler Papers
   Confederate States of America Papers (Pickett Papers)
   Louis M. Goldsborough Collection
   Isaac Hallock Papers
   Samuel Phillips Lee Collection
   David Dixon Porter Papers
   John Rodgers Collection
   Gideon Welles Papers
National Archives, Washington, D.C.
   Record Group 19, Records of the Bureau of Ships
      Entry 49, Letters Sent to the Secretary of the Navy
      Entry 50, Letters Sent to the Secretary of the Navy from the Bureau of
         Construction and Repair
      Entry 51, Letters Sent to Officers
      Entry 54, Letters Sent to the Commandant, Philadelphia Navy Yard
      Entry 58, Letters Sent by the Bureau of Construction and Repair
      Entry 59, Letters Sent
      Entry 61, Circulars by Secretary of Navy Gideon Welles
      Entry 62, Letters Received from Officers
      Entry 71, Letters Received
      Entry 233, Reports of Boards of Survey and Their Equipment
      Entry 323, Ledger of Supplies for the North Atlantic Squadron 1864–65
      Entry 963, Letters Sent from the Bureau of Engineering to the Secretary
         of the Navy
      Entry 965, Letters Sent to Engineers
      Entry 966, Letters Sent to Naval Officers
      Entry 968, Letters Sent to Contractors
      Entry 970, Letters Received
      Entry 972, Letters Received from Officers
   Record Group 23, Records of the Coast and Geodetic Survey
   Record Group 24, Bureau of Naval Personnel Special List 44, Ship's Logs
      Entry 322, Fair Copies of Letters Sent to Officers
      Entry 334, Letters Received from Officers
   Record Group 26, Records of the United States Coast Guard
      Entry 143, Letters Sent
      Entry 150, Letters from Collectors of Customs
      Entry 151, Letters from Officers of Cutters
      Entry 159, Logs of Revenue Cutters and Coast Guard Vessels

Record Group 45, Naval Records Collection of the Office of Naval Records and Library

Confederate Subject File

A. Naval Ships: Design, Construction, etc.

Entry 1, Letters Sent by the Secretary of the Navy to Officers

Entry 3, Miscellaneous Letters Sent

Entry 6, Letters to Commandants and Navy Agents

Entry 13, Letters to Bureaus of the Navy Department

Entry 22, Letters from Officers of the Rank Below That of Commander

Entry 30, Letters from Officers Commanding Squadrons

Entry 32, Letters Received from Chiefs of Navy Bureaus

Entry 33, Letters from Navy Agents and Navy Store Keepers

Entry 34, Letters from Commandants of Navy Yards and Shore Stations

Entry 37, Letters from Rear Admirals, Commodores, and Captains

Entry 43, Directives

Entry 315, Orders Issued by the Commandant (Baltimore Naval Station)

Entry 318, Letters Sent by the Commandant (Boston Navy Yard)

Entry 319, Letters from the Secretary of the Navy

Entry 332, Letters Sent by the Commandant (New York Navy Yard)

Entry 343, Letters Sent by the Commandant (Philadelphia Navy Yard)

Entry 345, Letters Sent by the Commandant (Washington Navy Yard)

Entry 346, Letters Received from Secretary of Navy by Commandant (Philadelphia Navy Yard)

Entry 356, Letters Received by the Commandant of Washington Navy Yard from Secretary of Navy

Entry 395, Letter Books of Officers of the United States Navy at Sea

Subseries 28, Stephen C. Rowan Papers

Subseries 56, Correspondence of Henry K. Davenport

Subseries 61, J. M. B. Clitz Collection

Subseries 67, Correspondence of William Macomb

Subseries 68, Orders and Circulars Received and Issued by the North Atlantic Blockading Squadron

Subseries 81, Letters Sent by Lt. Commander Penrod G. Watmough

Subseries 83, Letters Sent by Capt. Guert Gansevoort, Commanding the *Roanoke,* North Atlantic Blockading Squadron

Subseries 85, Correspondence of Melancton Smith

Subseries 90, General Orders and Circulars Received by the *Juniata,* North Atlantic Blockading Squadron, Commanded by Capt. William R. Taylor

Entry 463, Area Files

Entry 464, Subject File

AC Construction

AD Design and General Characteristics

AY Purchases of Merchant Vessels

HJ Joint Military Naval Engagements

OA General Instructions, Administration, and Organization (Internal) of Ships and Fleet Units 1860–1870

OL Mobilization and Demobilization, Operations of Naval Ships and Fleet Ships

ON Blockade Strategy Board Minutes

OO Operations of Fleets, Squadrons, Flotillas, and Divisions

OX Transportation of Supplies and Passengers, Lines of Supply and Supply Ships

VL Law, International

Record Group 56, Records of the Department of the Treasury

Entry 6, Letters Sent to Cabinet Officers

Record Group 59, General Records of the Department of State

Entry 78, U.S. Consular Dispatches, Nassau

Record Group 71, Bureau of Yards and Docks

Entry 1, Letters Sent to Secretary of Navy, Commandants

Entry 5, Letters Received from Commandants

Record Group 76, Records of Boundary and Claims, Commissions, and Arbitrations

Clarence Cary Diary

Record Group 77, Civil Works Map File

Record Group 92, Quartermasters Generals Department

Entry 225, Consolidated Correspondence File

Record Group 217, Accounting Officers of the Treasury Department, Office of the Fourth Auditor

Record Group 366, Records of the Civil War Special Agencies of the Treasury Department

Records of the 6th Special Treasury Agency

Record Group 393, Records of United States Army Continental Commands 1821–1920

Entry 4936, Second Brigade, Coast Division Orders
Naval Historical Center, Washington, D.C.
  William B. Cushing Papers, ZB Collection
  Charles Flusser Papers, ZB Collection
  Louis M. Goldsborough Papers, ZB Collection
  Frank W. Hackett, "Flusser and the Albemarle," ZO Collection
  Francis W. Smith File, ZO Collection
  Stringham File, ZB Collection
New-York Historical Society
  Naval History Society Collection, John Sanford Barnes, Unpublished
    manuscript, "My Egotistigraphy"
  Naval History Society Collection, Gustavus Vasa Fox Papers
  James B. and Joseph T. Collins, Miscellaneous Manuscripts
Princeton University Library
  Blair-Lee Papers
Southern Historical Collection, University of North Carolina, Chapel Hill,
  North Carolina
  Burgwyn Family Papers
  William Calder Papers
  DeRosset Family Papers
  George P. Erwin Papers
  Federal Miscellaneous
  Federal Soldiers Letters
  Maffitt Papers
  Cornelia McGinsey Papers
  Pettigrew Family Papers
  Henry A. Phelon Papers
  James R. Randall Collection
  Schenck Journal, David Schenck Books
  Fredric Sherman Letters
  Thomas Sparrow Papers
  Mark DeWolf Stevenson Papers

Government Documents

Great Britain. Parliament. *Sessional Papers* (Commons).
Hansard's Parlimentary Debates, Lords.
The Statutes at Large: Treaties and Proclamations of the United States of America,
  Ed. George P. Sanger, Vol. 12. Boston: Little, Brown, 1863.

U.S. Congress. *Congressional Globe.*

U.S. Congress. House. *Annals of Congress.* 12th Cong., 2d sess., 3 March 1813, appendix.

————. *Armored Vessels in the Attack on Charleston.* H. Ex. Doc. 69, 38th Cong., 1st sess., 1864.

————. *Captured and Abandoned Property in Insurrectionary States.* H. Ex. Doc. 78, 38th Cong., 1st sess., 1864.

————. *Evidence Taken by the Board of Navy Officers for Investigating the Condition of the Navy Yards.* H. Ex. Doc. 71, 36th Cong., 1st sess., 1860.

————. *Forts, Arsenals, Arms &c.* H. Rept. 85, 36th Cong., 2d sess., 18 February, 1861.

————. *Impeachment of the President.* H. Rept. 7, 40th Cong., 1st sess., 1867.

————. *Letter of the Secretary of the Navy in Answer to a Resolution in the House to the Number of Vessels in the Navy.* H. Ex. Doc. 159, 40th Cong., 2d sess., 1868.

————. *Number of Vessels in the Navy.* H. Ex. Doc. 159, 40th Cong., 2d sess., 1868.

————. *Papers Relating to Foreign Affairs.* H. Ex. Doc. 1, 38th Cong., 2d sess., 1865.

————. *Receipts and Expenditures.* H. Ex. Doc. 8, 38th Cong., 1st sess., 1863.

————. *Receipts and Expenditures.* H. Ex. Doc. 12, 39th Cong., 2d sess., 1866.

————. *Report of the Secretary of the Navy.* H. Ex. Doc. 1, 38th Cong., 1st sess., 7 December 1863.

————. *Report of the Secretary of the Navy.* H. Ex. Doc. 1, 38th Cong., 1st sess., 5 December 1864.

————. *Report of the Secretary of the Navy.* H. Ex. Doc. 1, 39th Cong., 1st sess., 4 December 1865.

————. *Report to the Secretary of the Navy Transmitting the Instructions Issued to Officers of the Several Depots for the Enlistment of Seamen.* H. Ex. Doc. 7, 37th Cong., 1st sess., 1861.

————. *Sites for Navy Yards.* H. Rept. 100, 38th Cong., 1st sess., 1864.

————. *Vessels Bought, Sold and Chartered by the United States.* H. Ex. Doc 337, 40th Cong., 2d sess., 1868.

U.S. Congress. Senate. *Certain War Vessels Built in 1862–1865.* S. Rept. 1942, 57th Cong., 1st sess., 1902.

————. *The Congressional Record.*

————. *Fort Fisher Expedition: Report of the Joint Committee on the Conduct of War.* S. Rept. 142, pt. 2, 38th Cong., 2d sess., 1865.

————. *Letter of the Secretary of the Navy in Answer to a Resolution of the Senate of the 9th Instant, Relative to the Employment of George D. Morgan, of New*

York, to Purchase Vessels for the Government. S. Ex. Doc. 15, 37th Cong., 2d sess., 1862.

————. *Letter of the Secretary of War in Answer to . . . Vessels Purchased or Chartered.* S. Doc. 37, 37th Cong., 2d sess., 1862.

————. *Light-Draught Monitors.* S. Rept. 142, pt. 3, 38th Cong., 2d sess., 1865.

————. *Report of the Joint Committee on the Conduct of the War—Army of the Potomac.* S. Doc. 108, 37th Cong., 3d sess., 1863.

————. *Report of the Secretary of the Navy.* S. Ex. Doc. 1, 35th Cong., 2d sess., 1858.

————. *Report of the Secretary of the Navy.* 2 December 1858, S. Ex. Doc. 2, 36th Cong. 1st sess., 1859.

————. *Report of the Secretary of the Navy.* S. Doc. 1, 37th Cong., 1st sess., 4 July 1861.

————. *Report of the Secretary of the Navy.* S. Doc. 1, 37th Cong., 2d sess., 2 December 1861.

————. *Report of the Secretary of the Navy on Contracts for Vessels of War.* S. Ex. Doc. 18, 39th Cong., 1st sess., 1866.

————. *Report on Additional Allowance on Contracts.* S. Rept. 61, 38th Cong., 1st sess., 1864.

————. *Surrender and Destruction Of Navy Yards.* S. Rept. 37, 37th Cong., 2d sess., 1861.

Newspapers and Periodicals

Army-Navy Journal
Daily Advertiser (Boston)
Daily Herald (Wilmington, N.C.)
The Daily Journal (Wilmington, N.C.)
Daily National Intelligencer
Herald (New York)
The Index (London)
Journal (Wilmington, N.C.)
The Life Boat
The New York Times
North Carolina Standard (Raleigh, N.C.)
The Sailor's Magazine
The Scientific American
The Seaman's Friend
The Times (London)

Tribune (New York)
The Wilmington Journal

Printed Primary Sources

Abbott, John S. C. "A Military Adventure." *Harpers New Monthly Magazine* 30 (December 1864): 3–20.

Allen, George H. *Forty-six Months with the Fourth Rhode Island Volunteers in the War of 1861 to 1865, Comprising a History of its Marches, Battles, and Camp Life.* Providence: J. A. and R. A. Reid, 1887.

Almy, John Jay. "Incidents of the Blockade." In *Military Order of the Loyal Legion of the United States Commandry of the District of Columbia,* 1–10. War Papers 9. Washington, D.C.: Companion, 1892.

Ames, Adelbert. "The Capture of Fort Fisher." In *Civil War Papers Read before the Commandry of the State of Massachusetts Military Order of the Loyal Legion of the United States,* 1:271–95. Boston: The Commandry, 1900.

Ammen, Daniel. *The Navy in the Civil War: The Atlantic Coast.* New York: Charles Scribner's Sons, 1898.

———. "Our Second Bombardment of Fort Fisher." *Military Order of the Loyal Legion of the United States Commandry of the District of Columbia,* 1–8. War Papers 4. Washington, D.C.: The Commandry, 1887.

Anderson, William H. "Blockade Life." In *Military Order of the Loyal Legion of the United States Maine Commandry,* 2–10. Portland, Me.: Lefabor-Tower, 1902.

Atlas to Accompany the Official Records of the Union and Confederate Armies. Washington, D.C.: Government Printing Office, 1891.

Avery, William B. "Gun-Boat Service on the James River." In *Personal Narratives of Events in the War of the Rebellion, Being Papers Read before the Rhode Island Soldiers and Sailors Historical Society.* 3d ser., no. 8. Providence: The Society, 1884.

———. "The Marine Artillery with the Burnside Expedition and the Battle of Camden, N.C." In *Personal Narratives of Events in the War of the Rebellion, Being Papers Read before the Rhode Island Soldiers and Sailors Historical Society.* 2d ser., no. 5. Providence: N. Bangs Williams, 1880.

Barnard, John G. *The Peninsular Campaign and Its Antecedents, as Developed by the Report of Maj. Gen. Geo. B. McClellan.* New York: D. Van Nostrand, 1864.

Barnes, John S. *Submarine Warfare, Offensive and Defensive, Including a Discussion of the Offensive Torpedo System.* New York: D. Van Nostrand, 1869.

Bartlett, Stephen Chaulker. "The Letters of Stephen Chaulker Bartlett aboard USS 'Lenapee,' January to August, 1865." Ed. Paul Murray and Stephen Russell Bartlett, Jr. *North Carolina Historical Review* 33 (January 1956): 66–92.

Basler, Roy P., ed. *The Collected Works of Abraham Lincoln.* 9 vols. New Brunswick, N.J.: Rutgers University Press, 1953–1955.

Batten, John M. *Reminiscences of Two Years in the United States Navy.* Lancaster, Penn.: Inquirer, 1881.

Beall, John Yates. *Memoir of John Yates Beall: His Life; Trial; Correspondence; Diary and Private Manuscript, Found among His Papers, Including His Own Account of the Raid on Lake Erie.* Ed. Daniel Bedinger Lucas. Montreal: John Lovell, 1865.

Beauregard, G. T. "The Defense of Drewry's Bluff." In *Battles and Leaders of the Civil War,* ed. Robert Underwood Johnson and Clarence Clough Buel, 4:195–205. 4 vols. New York: Thomas Yoseloff, 1956.

Bellard, Alfred. *Gone for a Soldier: The Civil War Memoirs of Private Alfred Bellard.* Ed. David Herbert Donald. Boston: Little, Brown, 1975.

Blanding, Stephen F. *Recollections of a Sailor Boy, or, The Cruise of the Gunboat Louisiana.* Providence: E. A. Johnson, 1886.

Blatchford, Samuel. *Reports of Cases in Prizes, Argued and Determined in the Circuit and District Courts of the United States, for the Southern District Of New York, 1861–65.* New York: Baker, Voorhis, 1866.

Boyer, Samuel Pellman. *Naval Surgeon Blockading the South 1862–1866: The Diary of Dr. Samuel Pellman Boyer.* Ed. Elinor Barnes and James A. Barnes. Bloomington: Illinois University Press, 1963.

Brooke, John M., and John L. Porter. "The Plan and Construction of the Merrimac." In *Battles and Leaders of the Civil War,* ed. Robert Underwood Johnson and Clarence Clough Buel, 1:715–17. 4 vols. New York: Thomas Yoseloff, 1956.

Burnside, Ambrose E. "The Burnside Expedition." In *Personal Narratives of Events in the War of the Rebellion, Being Papers Read before the Rhode Island Soldiers and Sailors Historical Society.* 2d ser., no. 6. Providence: N. Bangs Williams, 1882.

———. "The Burnside Expedition." In *Battles and Leaders of the Civil War,* ed. Robert Underwood Johnson and Clarence Clough Buel, 1:660–69. 4 vols. New York: Thomas Yoseloff, 1956.

Butler, Benjamin F. *Butler's Book.* Boston: A. M. Thayer, 1892.

———. *Private and Official Correspondence of Gen. Benjamin F. Butler during the Period of the Civil War.* 5 vols. Norwood, Mass.: Plimpton, 1917.

Butts, Frank B. "My First Cruise at Sea and the Loss of the Iron-Clad Monitor." In *Personal Narratives of Battles of the Rebellion, Being Papers Read before the Rhode Island Soldiers and Sailors Historical Society.* 1st ser., no. 4. Providence: The Society, 1878.

———. "Reminiscences of Gunboat Service on the Nansemond." In *Personal Narratives of Events in the War of the Rebellion, Being Papers Read before the Rhode Island Soldiers and Sailors Historical Society.* 3d ser., no. 8. Providence: The Society, 1884.

Chenery, William H. "Reminiscences of the Burnside Expedition." In *Personal Narratives of Events in the War of the Rebellion, Being Papers Read before the Rhode Island Soldiers and Sailors Historical Society.* 7th ser., no. 1. Providence: The Society, 1905.

Clark, Charles E. *My Fifty Years in the Navy.* Boston: Little, Brown, 1917.

Cleveland, Edmund J. "The Early Campaigns in North Carolina as Seen through the Eyes of a New Jersey Soldier." Part 2. *Proceedings of the New Jersey Historical Society* 68 (July 1950): 216–66.

Clopton, William I. "New Light on the Great Drewry's Bluff Fight." *Southern Historical Society Papers* 34 (1906): 82–98.

A Confederate. "Capture of the Underwriter." *The Gray Jackets and How They Lived, Fought, and Died for Dixie.* Richmond: Jones Brothers, 1867.

Conrad, Daniel B. "Capture and Burning of the Federal Gunboat 'Underwriter,' in the Neuse, off Newbern, N.C., in February, 1864." *Southern Historical Society Papers* 19 (January–December 1891): 93–101.

Crowley, R. O. "The Confederate Torpedo Service." *Century Magazine* 56 (June 1898): 290–300.

Curtis, N. Martin. "The Capture of Fort Fisher." In *Civil War Papers Read before the Commandry of the State of Massachusetts Military Order of the Loyal Legion of the United States,* 1:299–327. Boston: The Commandry, 1900.

Cushing, William B. "The Destruction of the 'Albemarle.'" In *Battles and Leaders of the Civil War,* ed. Robert Underwood Johnson and Clarence Clough Buel, 4:634–41. 4 vols. New York: Thomas Yoseloff, 1956.

———. "Outline Story of the War Experiences of William B. Cushing as Told by Himself." *U.S. Naval Institute Proceedings* 38 (September 1912): 941–91.

Davidson, Hunter. "Mines and Torpedoes during the Rebellion." *Magazine of History* 8 (November 1908): 255–61.

Davis, Charles Henry. *Life of Charles Henry Davis, Rear Admiral, 1807–1877.* Boston: Houghton, Mifflin, 1899.

Dawson, Francis W. *Reminiscences of Confederate Service 1861–1865.* Ed. Bell I. Wiley. Baton Rouge: Louisiana State University Press, 1980.

Day, D. L. *My Diary of Rambles with the 25th Mass. Volunteer Infantry, with*

Burnside's Coast Division, 18th Army Corps, and Army of the James. Milford, Mass.: King and Billings, 1884.

De Trobriand, Regis. *Four Years with the Army of the Potomac.* Trans. George K. Dauchy. Boston: Ticknor, 1889.

Douglas, William W. "Relief of Washington, North Carolina, by the Fifth Rhode Island Volunteers." In *Personal Narratives of Events in the War of the Rebellion, Being Papers Read before the Rhode Island Soldiers and Sailors Historical Society.* 3d ser., no. 17. Providence: The Society, 1886.

Drayton, Percival. *Naval Letters from Captain Percival Drayton 1861–1865.* Ed. Gertrude L. Hoyt. New York: New York Public Library, 1906.

Drewry, A. H. "Drewry's Bluff Fight." *Southern Historical Society Papers* 29 (1901): 284–85.

Du Pont, Samuel Francis. *Samuel Francis Du Pont: A Selection from His Civil War Letters.* Ed. John D. Hayes. 3 vols. Ithaca, N.Y.: Cornell University Press, 1969.

Elliott, Gilbert. "The First Battle of the Confederate 'Ram Albemarle.'" In *Battles and Leaders of the Civil War,* ed. Robert Underwood Johnson and Clarence Clough Buel, 4:625–27. 4 vols. New York: Thomas Yoseloff, 1956.

Elliott, Gilbert, and Edgar Holden. "The Career of the Confederate Ram 'Albemarle.'" *Century Illustrated Monthly Magazine* 36 (July 1888): 420–40.

Ericsson, John. "The Building of the 'Monitor.'" In *Battles and Leaders of the Civil War,* ed. Robert Underwood Johnson and Clarence Clough Buel, 1:730–44. 4 vols. New York: Thomas Yoseloff, 1956.

The Federal Cases, Comprising Cases Argued and Determined in the Circuit and District Courts of the United States. 30 vols. St. Paul, Minn., 1894–1897.

Fox, Gustavus Vasa. *Confidential Correspondence of Gustavus Vasa Fox, Assistant Secrety of the Navy 1861–1865.* Ed. Robert Means Thompson and Richard Wainwright. 2 vols. New York: Devine, 1918.

French, Samuel G. *Two Wars: An Autobiography of Gen. Samuel G. French.* Nashville: Confederate Veteran, 1901.

Gardiner, Edward Carey. "Narrative of Rear Admiral Goldsborough, U.S. Navy." Ed. Henry C. Baird. *U.S. Naval Institute Proceedings* 59 (July 1933): 1023–31.

Gorgas, Josiah. *The Civil War Diary of General Josiah Gorgas.* Ed. Frank E. Vandiver. Tuscaloosa: University of Alabama Press, 1947.

———. "Notes on the Ordnance Department of the Confederate Government." *Southern Historical Society Papers* 12 (January–December 1884): 67–94.

Grant, Ulysses S. *Personal Memoirs of U.S. Grant.* 2 vols. New York: Charles L. Webster, 1885.Hale, John P. *Speech of Hon. John P. Hale of New Hampshire on Frauds in Naval Contracts.* Washington, D.C.: H. Polkhorn, 1864.

Harkness, Edson J. "The Expeditions against Fort Fisher and Wilmington." In *Military Essays and Recollections: Papers Read before the Commandry of the State of Illinois Military Order of the Loyal Legion of the United States,* 2:145–88. 4 vols. Chicago: McClurg, 1894.

Haskell, John Cheves. *The Haskell Memoirs.* Ed. Gilbert E. Govan and James W. Livingood. New York: G. P. Putnam's Sons, 1960.

Hawkins, Rush C. "Early Coast Operations in North Carolina." In *Battles and Leaders of the Civil War,* ed. Robert Underwood Johnson and Clarence Clough Buel, 1:632–59. 4 vols. New York: Thomas Yoseloff, 1956.

Hemphill, W. Edwin, ed. *The Papers of John C. Calhoun.* 14 vols. Columbia: University of South Carolina Press, 1959–1981.

Hill, Daniel H. *Bethel to Sharpsburg.* 2 vols. Raleigh: Edwards and Broughton, 1926.

———. *Confederate Military History.* Vol. 4: *North Carolina,* ed. Clement A. Evans. New York: Thomas Yoseloff, 1962.

———. "McClellan's Change of Base and Malvern Hill. In *Battles and Leaders of the Civil War,* ed. Robert Underwood Johnson and Clarence Clough Buel, 2:383–95. 4 vols. New York: Thomas Yoseloff, 1956.

Hobart-Hampden (Roberts), Augustus Charles. *Never Caught: Personal Adventures Connected with Twelve Successful Trips in Blockade-Running during the American Civil War, 1863–1864.* London: John Camden Holton, 1867; rpt., Carolina Beach, N.C.: Blockade Runner Museum, 1967.

Holden, Edgar. "The 'Albemarle' and the 'Sassacus.'" In *Battles and Leaders of the Civil War,* ed. Robert Underwood Johnson and Clarence Clough Buel, 4:628–33. 4 vols. New York: Thomas Yoseloff, 1956.

———. "The 'Sassacus' and the 'Albemarle.'" *Magazine of History with Notes and Queries* 5 (May 1907): 267–73.

Hollyday, Frederic B. M., ed. "Running the Blockade: Henry Hollyday Joins the Confederacy." *Maryland Historical Magazine* 41 (March 1946): 1–10.

Hooper, W. R. "Blockade Running." *Harpers New Monthly Magazine* 42 (December 1870): 105–8.

Instructions for the Government of Inspectors-in-Charge of Stores, Naval Storekeepers, Paymasters, and Assistant Paymasters. Washington, D.C.: Government Printing Office, 1862.

James, J. T. "Historical and Commercial Sketch of Wilmington, N.C." In Frank D. Smaw, Jr., *Smaw's Wilmington Director Comprising a General and City Business Directory,* 15–46. Wilmington, N.C.: Frank D. Smaw, Jr., 1867.

Jennings, William. "On the North Atlantic Blockade." *Magazine of History with Notes and Queries* 4 (July 1906): 26–29.

Johns, John. "Wilmington during the Blockade." *Harpers New Monthly Magazine* 33 (September 1866): 497–503.

Jones, J. B. *A Rebel War Clerk's Diary at the Confederate States Capital.* 2 vols. Philadelphia: J. B. Lippincott, 1866.

Josselyn, Francis. "Francis Josselyn: A Gunboat Captain's Diary." Ed. John M. Taylor. *Manuscripts* 33 (Spring 1981): 113–22.

Kautz, August V. "Operations South of the James River." In *Battles and Leaders of the Civil War,* ed. Robert Underwood Johnson and Clarence Clough Buel, 4:533–37. 4 vols. New York: Thomas Yoseloff, 1956.

Keeler, William Frederick. *Aboard the USS Florida: 1863–1865, The Letters of Acting Paymaster William Frederiick Keeler, U. S. Navy, to his Wife , Anna.* Ed. Robert W. Daly. Annapolis, Md.: U.S. Naval Institute Press, 1968.

———. *Aboard the USS Monitor: 1862, The Letters of Acting Paymaster William Frederick Keeler, U.S. Navy, to his Wife, Anna.* Ed. Robert W. Daly. Annapolis, Md.: U.S. Naval Institute Press, 1964.

Ketchum, Edgar. "Personal Reminiscences of the Capture of Fort Fisher and Wilmington, North Carolina." *United Service* (n.s.) 16 (December 1896): 457–69.

King, W. R. *Torpedoes: Their Invention and Use from the First Application to the Art of War to the Present Time.* Washington, 1866.

Lamb, William. "Defense of Fort Fisher, North Carolina." *The Military Historical Society of Massachusetts,* 9:347–88. 14 vols. Boston: The Society, 1912.

———. *Colonel Lamb's Story of Fort Fisher.* Carolina Beach, N.C.: Blockader Runner Museum, 1966.

Lehigh Coal and Navigation Company. *Report of the Board of Managers of the Lehigh Coal and Navigation Company.* Philadelphia: John C. Clark and Son, 1861–1864.

Lehigh Valley Railroad Company. *Annual Report of the Lehigh Valley Railroad Company.* 1859–1861. Reprinted from Letter Circular.

Lehigh Valley Railroad Company. *Ninth Annual Report of the Board of Managers of the Lehigh Valley Railroad Company.* Philadelphia: Alexander, 1865.

Lehigh Valley Railroad Company. *Seventh Annual Report of the Board of Managers of the Lehigh Valley Railroad Company.* Mauch Chunk, Penn.: Tolan & Hobbs, 1863.

Lockwood, H. C. "The Capture of Fort Fisher." *Atlantic Monthly* 27 (May 1871): 622–636.

Longstreet, James. *From Manassas to Appomattox: Memoirs of the Civil War in America.* Philadelphia: J. B. Lippincott, 1896.

Loyall, B. P. "Capture of the Underwriter." *Southern Historical Society Papers* 27 (1899): 136–44.

McClellan, George B. *McClellan's Own Story: The War for the Union.* New York: Charles L. Webster, 1887.

———. "The Peninsular Campaign." In *Battles and Leaders of the Civil War,* ed. Robert Underwood Johnson and Clarence Clough Buel, 2:160–87. 4 vols. New York: Thomas Yoseloff, 1956.

———. *Report on the Organization and Campaigns of the Army of the Potomac.* New York: Sheldon, 1864.

McHenry, George. *A Paper Containing a Statement of Facts Relating to the Approaching Cotton Crisis.* Richmond: Confederate House of Representatives, 1865.

Maffitt, John N. "Blockade-Running." *United Service* 6 (June 1882): 626–33.

Nichols, Roy F., ed. "Fighting in North Carolina Waters." *North Carolina Historical Review* 40 (Winter 1963): 75–84.

Norcum, James. "The Eastern Shore of North Carolina, in 1861 and 1862." *Historical Magazine and Notes and Queries* 8 (November 1870): 301–6.

Packard, Kent, ed. "Jottings by the Way: A Sailor's Log 1861–1864." *Pennsylvania Magazine of History and Biography* 71 (April and July 1947): 121–51, 242–82.

Parker, Foxhall A. *Squadron Tactics under Steam.* New York: D. Van Nostrand, 1864.

Parker, James. "The Navy in the Battles and Capture of Fort Fisher." In *Personal Recollections of the War of the Rebellion Addresses Delivered before the Commandry of the State of New York, Military Order of the Loyal Legion of the United States,* ed. A. Noel Blakeman, 2:104–17. 4 vols. New York: G. P. Putnam's Sons, 1897.

Parker, William Harwar. *Recollections of a Naval Officer 1841–1865.* New York: Charles Scribners' Sons, 1883.

Pearce, Charles E. "The Expeditions against Fort Fisher." In *War Papers and Personal Reminiscences 1861–1865 Read before the Commandry of the State of Missouri Military Order of the Loyal Legion of the United States,* 354–81. St. Louis: Becktold, 1892.

Philadelphia and Reading Railroad Company. *Report of the President and Managers of the Philadelphia and Reading Railroad Company.* Philadelphia: Moss Brothers, 1861–1864.

Porter, David Dixon. "A Famous Naval Exploit." *North American Review* 153 (September 1891): 296–303.

———. "The Fort Fisher and Wilmington Campaign: Letters from Rear Admiral David D. Porter." Ed. James M. Merrill. *North Carolina Historical Review* 35 (October 1958): 461–75.

———. *Incidents and Anecdotes of the Civil War.* New York: D. Appleton, 1886.

———. *The Naval History of the Civil War.* New York: Sherman, 1886.

Post, Charles A. "A Diary on the Blockade in 1863." *U.S. Naval Institute Proceedings* 44 (October–November 1918): 2333–50, 2567–94.

Rains, G. J. "Torpedoes." *Southern Historical Society Papers* 3 (May–June 1877): 255–60.

Richardson, James D. *A Compilation of the Messages and Papers of the Confederacy, Including the Diplomatic Correspondence 1861–1865.* Nashville: United States Publishing, 1905.

Roman, Alfred. *The Military Operations of General Beauregard in the War between the States 1861 to 1865.* 2 vols. New York: Harper and Brothers, 1884.

"Running the Blockade." *Southern Historical Society Papers* 9 (1881): 369–78.

Rush, Richard et al., eds. *Official Records of the Union and Confederate Navies in the War of the Rebellion.* 31 vols. Washington, D.C.: Government Printing Office, 1894–1927.

Saltonstall, William Gurdon. *Reminiscences of the Civil War and Autobiography of William Gurdon Saltonstall.* By the author, 1913.

Sanderson, Joseph Warner. "The James River during the War." *In War Papers Read before the Commandry of the State of Wisconsin Military Order of the Loyal Legion of the United States,* 3:33–40. 4 vols. Milwaukee: Burdock and Allen, 1903.

Sands, Francis P. B. "'Lest We Forget': Memories of Service Afloat from 1862 to 1866." *Military Order of the Loyal Legion of the United States Commandry of the District of Columbia.* War Papers 73. Washington, D.C.: Companion, 1908.

———. "A Volunteer's Reminiscences of Life in the North Atlantic Blockading Squadron, 1861–5." *Military Order of the Loyal Legion of the United States Commandry of the District of Columbia.* War Papers 20. Washington, D.C.: The Commandry, 1894.

Schlesinger, Arthur M., ed. "A Blue Jacket's Letters Home, 1863–1864." *New England Quarterly* 1 (October 1928): 554–67.

Scott, R. N., et al., *The War of the Rebellion: A Compilation of the Official Records of the Union and Confederate Armies.* 128 vols. Washington, D.C.: Government Printing Office, 1880–1901.

Sedgwick, Charles B. *Speech of Hon. C. B. Sedgwick of New York on Government Contracts.* L. Towers, 1862.

Selfridge, Thomas O., Jr. *Memoirs of Thomas O. Selfridge, Jr., Rear Admiral, U.S.N.* New York: G. P. Putnam's Sons, 1924.

Semmes, Ralphael. *Memoirs of Service Afloat during the War between the States.* Baltimore: Kelly, Piet, 1869.

Smith, H. D. "Cutting Out the 'Underwriter': A Brilliant Exploit in a Southern

Harbor." In *Under Both Flags: A Panarama of the Great Civil War as Repre-sented in Story, Anecdote, Adventure, and the Romance of Reality,* ed. George M. Vickers, 153–56. Chicago: National Book Concern, 1896.

Smith, William Farrar. "Butler's Attack on Drewry's Bluff." In *Battles and Leaders of the Civil War,* ed. Robert Underwood Johnson and Clarence Clough Buel, 4:206–12. 4 vols. New York: Thomas Yoseloff, 1956.

Smith, William M. "The Seige and Capture of Plymouth." In *Personal Recollec-tions of the War of the Rebellion: Addresses Delivered before the New York Commandry of the Loyal Legion of the United States, 1883–1891,* ed. James Grant Wilson and Titus Munson Coan, 322–43. New York: The Commandry, 1891.

Soley, James Russell. "Closing Operations in the James River." In *Battles and Leaders of the Civil War,* ed. Robert Underwood Johnson and Clarence Clough Buel, 4:705–7. 4 vols. New York: Thomas Yoseloff, 1956.

———. *The Navy in the Civil War: The Blockade and the Cruisers.* New York: Charles Scribner's Sons, 1883.

———. "The Union and Confederate Navies." In *Battles and Leaders of the Civil War,* ed. Robert Underwood Johnson and Clarence Clough Buel, 1:611–31. 4 vols. New York: Thomas Yoseloff, 1956.

Sprague, A. B. R. "The Burnside Expedition." In *Civil War Papers Read before the Commandry of the State of Massachusetts Military Order of the Loyal Legion of the United States,* 1:427–46. 2 vols. Boston: The Commandry, 1900.

Sprunt, James. *Chronicles of the Cape Fear River.* Spartanburg, N.C.: Reprint Company, 1974.

———. *James Sprunt's Tales of the Cape Fear Blockade.* Ed. Cornelius M. D. Thomas. Wilmington, N.C.: J. E. Hicks, 1960.

———. "Running of the Blockade." *Southern Historical Society Papers* 24 (1896): 157–65.

———. "Tales of the Cape Fear Blockade." *The North Carolina Booklet* 1 (February, 1902): 1–112.

Stackpole, Joseph Lewis. "The Department of North Carolina under General Foster, July, 1862, to July, 1863." *Military Historical Society of Massachusetts,* 9:85–110. 14 vols. Boston: The Society, 1912.

Stevenson, Reston. "Wilmington and the Blockade-Runners of the Civil War." *North Carolina University Magazine* 32 (March 1902): 152–57.

Taylor, Thomas E. *Running The Blockade: A Personal Narrative of Adventures, Risks, and Escapes during the American Civil War.* New York: Charles Scribner's Sons, 1896.

Thompson, Mangus S., ed. *General Orders and Circulars Issued by the Navy Department from 1863 to 1887.* Washington, D.C.: Government Printing Office, 1887.

Traver, Lorenzo. "Burnside Expedition in North Carolina: Battles of Roanoke Island and Elizabeth City." In *Personal Narratives of Events in the War of the Rebellion, Being Papers Read before the Rhode Island Soldiers and Sailors Historical Society.* 2d ser., no. 5. Providence: N. Bangs Williams, 1880.

Trow, J. F. "Life on a Blockader." *Continental Monthly* 6 (July 1864): 46–55.

Vail, Israel Everett. *Three Years on the Blockade: A Naval Experience.* New York: Abbey, 1902.

Warley, A. F. "Note on the Destruction of the 'Albemarle.'" In *Battles and Leaders of the Civil War,* ed. Robert Underwood Johnson and Clarence Clough Buel, 4:641–42. 4 vols. New York: Thomas Yoseloff, 1956.

Warren, Charles F. "Washington during the Civil War." In *The Confederate Reveille,* 7–20. United Daughters of the Confederacy, Raleigh: Edwards and Broughton, 1898. North Carolina Division, Pamlico Chapter 43.

Watson, Robert. "Yankees Were Landing below Us: The Civil War Journal of Robert Watson, C.S.N." Ed. William N. Still, Jr. *Civil War Times Illustrated* 15 (April 1976): 12–21.

Welles, Gideon. "Admiral Farragut and New Orleans, with an Account of the Origin and Command of the First Three Naval Expeditions of the War." *The Galaxy* 12 (July 1871): 699–83.

———. *Diary of Gideon Welles.* Ed. Howard K. Beale. 3 vols. New York: W. W. Norton, 1960.

Wilkinson, John. "Blockade Running." *The State* (7 May 1955): 11–12.

———. *The Narrative of a Blockade-Runner.* New York: Sheldon, 1877.

Wood, John Taylor. "The First Fight Of Ironclads." In *Battles and Leaders of the Civil War,* ed. Robert Underwood Johnson and Clarence Clough Buel, 1:692–711. 4 vols. New York: Joseph Yoseloff, 1956.

Woodbury, Augustus. "Ambrose Everett Burnside." In *Personal Narratives of Events in the War of the Rebellion, Being Papers Read before the Rhode Island Soldiers and Sailors Historical Society.* 2d ser., no. 17. Providence: N. Bangs Williams, 1882.

Wormeley, Katherine Prescott. *The Other Side of War with the Army of the Potomac.* Boston: Ticknor, 1889.

Wyeth, John Jasper. *Leaves from a Diary Written While Serving in Co. E, 44 Mass., Dept. of No. Carolina from September, 1862, to June, 1863.* Boston: L. F. Lawrence, 1878.

Secondary Sources

Adams, W. T. "Guns for the Navy." *Ordnance* 45 (January–February 1961): 508–9.

Alden, Carroll Storrs, and Allan Westcott. *The United States Navy: A History.*
    Chicago: J. B. Lippincott, 1943.

Anderson, Stuart. "1861: Blockade vs. Closing the Confederate Ports." *Military
    Affairs* 41 (December 1977): 190–93.

Apetheker, Herbert. "The Negro in the Union Navy." *Journal of Negro History*
    32 (April 1947): 169–200.

Arthur, Robert. *History of Fort Monroe.* Fort Monroe, Va.: Coast Artillery
    School, 1930.

Barrett, John G. *The Civil War in North Carolina.* Chapel Hill: University of
    North Carolina Press, 1963.

Barry, Richard Schriver. "Fort Macon: Its History." *North Carolina Historical
    Review* 27 (April 1950): 163–77.

Baxter, J. P. "The British Government and Neutral Rights, 1861–1865." *American Historical Review* 33 (October 1928): 9–29.

Beeker, Henry Judson. "Wilmington during the Civil War." M.A. thesis, Duke
    University, 1941.

Bennett, Frank M. *The Steam Navy of the United States.* Pittsburgh: Warren,
    1896.

Bernath, Stuart L. *Squall across the Atlantic: American Civil War Prize Cases and
    Diplomacy.* Los Angeles: University of California Press, 1970.

Black, Robert C., III. *The Railroads of the Confederacy.* Chapel Hill: University
    of North Carolina Press, 1952.

Blake, Nelson Morehouse. *William Mahone of Virginia: Soldier and Political
    Insurgent.* Richmond: Garrett and Massie, 1935.

Bonham, Milledge L. "The British Consuls in the Confederacy." In *Studies in
    History, Economics and Public Law.* New York: Columbia University, 1911.

Boynton, Charles Brandon. *The History of the Navy during the Rebellion.* New
    York: D. Appleton, 1867.

Brewington, M. V. *Chesapeake Bay: A Pictorial Maritime History.* Cambridge,
    Md.: Cornell Maritime Press, 1953.

Brewington, Marion V. "Maritime Philadelphia 1609–1837." *Pennsylvania
    Magazine of History and Biography* 63 (April 1939): 93–117.

Bridges, Hal. *Lee's Maverick General: Daniel Harvey Hill.* New York: McGraw-
    Hill, 1961.

Bright, Leslie S., William H. Rowland, and James C. Bardon. *CSS Neuse: A
    Question of Iron and Time.* Raleigh: North Carolina Department of Cultural
    Resources, Division of Archives and History, 1981.

Bright, Samuel R., Jr. "Confederate Coast Defense." Ph.D. dissertation, Duke
    University, 1961.

Brown, Alexander Crosby. "The Dismal Swamp Canal." *American Neptune* 5 (July–October 1945): 203–22, 297–310; 6 (January 1946): 51–70.

———. *Juniper Waterway: A History of the Albemarle and Chesapeake Canal.* Charlottesville: University Press of Virginia, 1981.

Brown, Norman D. *Edward Stanly: Whiggery's Tarheel "Conqueror."* Southern Historical Publications 18. University: University of Alabama Press, 1974.

Browning, Robert M. Jr. "From Cape Charles to Cape Fear: The North Atlantic Blockading Squadron during the Civil War." Ph.D. dissertation, University of Alabama, 1988.

Browning, Robert S., III. *Two If by Sea: The Development of American Coastal Defense Policy.* Westport, Conn.: Greenwood, 1983.

Case, Lynn M., and Warren F. Spencer. *The United States and France: Civil War Diplomacy.* Philadelphia: University of Pennsylvania Press, 1970.

Chesneau, Roger, and Eugene M. Kolesnik. *Conway's All the World's Fighting Ships 1860–1905.* New York: Mayflower, 1979.

Coddington, Edwin B. "The Civil War Blockade Reconsidered." In *Essays in History and International Relations in Honor of George Hubbard Blakeslee,* ed. Dwight E. Lee and George E. McReynolds, 284–305. Worchester, Mass.: Clark University Press, 1949.

Conner, R. D. W., et al., *History of North Carolina.* 6 vols. Chicago: Lewis, 1919.

Cornish, Dudley Taylor, and Virginia Jean Laas. *Lincoln's Lee: The Life of Samuel Phillips Lee, United States Navy, 1812–1897.* Lawrence: University of Kansas Press, 1986.

Crook, D. P. *The North, the South, and the Powers 1861–1865.* New York: John Wiley and Sons, 1974.

Daly, Robert W. "Burnside's Amphibious Division." *Marine Corps Gazette* 35 (December 1951): 30–37.

———. *How the Merrimac Won: The Strategic Story of the CSS Virginia.* New York: Thomas Y. Crowell, 1957.

———. "Pay and Prize Money in the Old Navy, 1770–1899." *U.S. Naval Institute Proceedings* 74 (August 1948): 967–71.

Davis, William C. *Duel between the First Ironclads.* New York: Doubleday, 1975.

Deak, Francis, and Philip C. Jessup. *A Collection of Neutrality Laws, Regulations and Treaties of Various Countries.* Washington, D.C.: Carnegie Endowment for International Peace, 1939.

Delaney, Norman C. "Charles Henry Foster and the Unionist of Eastern North Carolina." *North Carolina Historical Review* 37, no. 3 (July 1960): 348–66.

Diamond, William. "Imports of the Confederate Government from Europe and Mexico." *Journal of Southern History* 6 (November 1940): 470–503.

Dictionary of American Biography. 16 vols. New York: Charles Scribner's Sons, 1933.

Dictionary of American Naval Fighting Ships. 8 vols. Washington, D.C.: Navy Department, Naval History Division, 1959–1981.

Donnelly, Ralph W. "The Charlotte, North Carolina, Navy Yard, C.S.N." *Civil War History* 5 (March 1959): 72–79.

Ferris, Norman B. *Desperate Diplomacy: William H. Seward's Foreign Policy, 1861.* Knoxville: University of Tennessee Press, 1976.

Fonvielle, Chris Eugene, Jr. "To Forge a Thunderbolt: The Wilmington Campaign, February 1865." M.A. thesis, East Carolina University, 1987.

Freeman, Douglas Southall. *Lee's Lieutenants: A Study in Command.* 3 vols. New York: Charles Scribner's Sons, 1949.

Glass, Henry. "Marine International Law." *U.S. Naval Institute Proceedings* 11, no. 3 (1885): 355–609.

Goodman, Michael Harris. *The Black Tar: Negro Seamen in the Union Navy, 1861–1865.* Unpublished Ph.D. dissertation, University of Nottingham, 1975.

Guinn, Gilbert Sumter. "Coastal Defense of the Confederate Atlantic Seaboard States, 1861–1862: A Study in Political and Military Mobilization." Ph.D. dissertation, University of South Carolina, 1973.

Halsey, Ashley, Jr. "Seal the Turtle in Its Shell." *Civil War Times Illustrated* 5 (June 1966): 28–31.

Hamersly, Lewis R. *General Register of the United States Navy and Marine Corps.* Baltimore: William K. Boyle, 1882.

———. *The Records of Living Officers of the U.S. Navy and Marine Corps.* Philadelphia: J. B. Lippincott, 1876.

Hamersly, Thomas H. S., ed. *Complete General Navy Register of the United States of America from 1776 to 1877.* New York: T. H. S. Hamersly, 1888.

Hassler, Warren W. "How the Confederates Controlled Blockade Running." *Civil War Times Illustrated* 2 (October 1963): 43–49.

Hattaway, Herman, and Archer Jones. *How the North Won: A Military History of the Civil War.* Urbana: University of Illinois Press, 1983.

Hayes, John D. "Captain Fox: He Is the Navy Department." *U.S. Naval Institute Proceedings* 91 (November 1965): 64–71.

———. "Loss of the Norfolk Yard." *Ordnance* 46 (September–October 1961): 220–23.

———. "Studies in Naval Failure." *Shipmate* 25 (September–October 1962): 32–33.

Hayes, John D., and Lillian O'Brien, eds. "The Early Blockade and the Capture of the Hatteras Forts from the Journal of John Sanford Barnes, July 19 to September 1, 1861." *New-York Historical Society Quarterly* 46 (January 1962): 60–85.

Headley, J. T. *Farragut and Our Naval Commanders*. New York: E. B. Treat, 1867.

Hendren, Paul. "The Confederate Blockade Runners." *U.S. Naval Institute Proceedings* 59 (April 1933): 506–12.

Hoehling, A. A. *Thunder at Hampton Roads*. Englewood Cliffs, N.J.: Prentice-Hall, 1976.

Hoppin, James Mason. *The Life of Andrew W. Foote, Rear-Admiral United States Navy*. New York: Harper and Brothers, 1874.

Humphrey, Willis C. *The Great Contest: A History of Military and Naval Operations during the Civil War in the United States of America, 1861–1865*. Detroit: C. H. Smith, 1886.

Jeffries, William W. "The Civil War Career of Charles Wilkes." *Journal of Southern History* 11 (August 1945): 324–48.

Johnson, Arthur Menzies. "The Genesis of a Navy Yard." *U.S. Naval Institute Proceedings* 81 (September 1955): 992–1003.

Johnson, Ludwell H., III. "Blockade or Trade Monopoly? John A. Dix and the Union Occupation of Norfolk." *Virginia Magazine of History and Biography* 93 (January 1985): 54–78.

———. "Northern Profit and Profiteers: The Cotton Rings of 1864–1865." *Civil War History* 12 (June 1966): 101–15.

Johnson, Robert Erwin. *Rear Admiral John Rodgers 1812–1882*. Annapolis, Md.: U.S. Naval Institute, 1967.

Johnston, Robert Carey. "Navy Yards and Dry Docks: A Study of the Bureau of Yards and Docks 1842–1871." M.A. thesis, Stanford University, 1953.

Jones, Chester Lloyd. *The Economic History of the Anthracite–Tidewater Canals*. Publications of the University of Pennsylvania Series In Political Economy and Public Law 22. Philadelphia: University of Pennsylvania, 1908.

Jones, Virgil Carrington. "Construction, Fighting Career and Destruction of the Albemarle." *Civil War Times Illustrated* 1 (June 1962): 6–11, 43–46.

———. "'We Are Useless': Mr. Lincoln's Blockade." *Civil War Times Illustrated* 10 (December 1971): 10–24.

King, Joseph E. "The Fort Fisher Campaigns 1864–1865." *U.S. Naval Institute Proceedings* 77 (August 1951): 843–55.

Lee, Samuel Phillips. "Letter of Rear Admiral Samuel Phillips Lee to Senator James Rood Doolittle." *Publications of the Southern History Association* 9 (March 1905): 111–22.

Lester, Richard I. *Confederate Finance and Purchasing in Great Britain.* Charlottesville: University Press of Virginia, 1975.

Long, E. B., and Barbara Long. *The Civil War Day by Day: An Almanac 1861–1865.* New York: Doubleday, 1971.

Lull, Edward P. *History of the United States Navy-Yard at Gosport, Virginia (Near Norfolk).* Washington, D.C.: Government Printing Office, 1874.

Luvaas, Jay. "The Fall of Fort Fisher." *Civil War Times Illustrated* 3 (August 1964): 4–9, 31–35.

Lyman, John. "Register Tonnage and Its Measurement." *American Neptune* 5 (July 1945): 223–34.

McCarthy, Justin. *A History of Our Own Times.* 5 vols. New York: Harper and Brothers, 1903.

Maffitt, Emma Martin. *The Life and Services of John Newland Maffitt.* New York: Neale, 1906.

Merrill, James M. "The Battle for Elizabeth City, 1862." *U.S. Naval Institute Proceedings* 83 (March 1957): 321–23.

———. "The Hatteras Expedition, August, 1861." *North Carolina Historical Review* 29 (April 1952): 204–19.

———. *The Rebel Shore: The Story of Union Sea Power in the Civil War.* Boston: Little, Brown, 1957.

———. "Strategy Makers in the Union Navy Department, 1861–1865." *Mid-America: An Historical Review* 44 (January 1962): 19–32.

Millis, Walter. "The Iron Sea Elephants." *American Neptune* 10 (January 1950): 15–32.

Minick, Rachel. "New York Ferryboats in the Union Navy." *New-York Historical Society Quarterly* 46 (October 1962): 422–36.

Moore, Louis T. "The Capture of Fort Caswell." *The State* 12 (23 September 1944): 6–7.

Nicolay, John G., and John Hay. *Abraham Lincoln: A History.* 10 vols. New York, Century, 1890.

Niven, John. *Gideon Welles: Lincoln's Secretary of the Navy.* New York: Oxford University Press, 1973.

Owsley, Frank Lawrence. *King Cotton Diplomacy: Foreign Relations of the Confederate States of America.* Chicago: University of Chicago Press, 1931.

Parramore, Thomas C. "The Burning of Winton in 1862." *North Carolina Historical Review* 39 (Winter 1962): 18–31.

Paullin, Charles Oscar. *Paullin's History of Naval Administration 1775–1911.* Annapolis, Md.: U.S. Naval Institute, 1968.

Perry, Milton F. *Infernal Machines: The Story of Confederate Submarine and Mine Warfare.* Baton Rouge: Louisiana State University Press, 1965.

Perry, Percival. "The Naval Stores Industry in the Old South, 1790–1860." *Journal of Southern History* 34 (November 1968): 509–26.

Petrillo, F. Charles. *Anthracite and Slackwater: The North Branch Canal 1828–1901.* Easton, Penn.: Center for Canal History and Technology, 1986.

Polser, Aubrey Henry, Jr. "The Administration of the United States Navy, 1861–1865." Ph.D. dissertation, University of Nebraska, 1975.

Powell, William H. comp. *List of Officers of the Army of the United States from 1779 to 1900.* New York: L. R. Hammersly, 1900.

Price, Marcus W. "Ships That Tested the Blockade of the Carolina Ports, 1861–1865." *American Neptune* 8 (July 1948): 24–39.

Ramsdell, Charles W. "The Confederate Government and the Railroads." *American Historical Review* 22 (July 1917): 794–810.

Redmond, R. A. "The Revenue Steamer *E. A. Stevens* in the Civil War." *American Neptune* 20(July 1960): 155–66.

Reed, Rowena. *Combined Operations in the Civil War.* Annapolis, Md.: U.S. Naval Institute Press, 1978.

Reynolds, Clark G. *Famous American Admirals.* New York: Van Nostrand Reinhold, 1978.

Ridgely-Nevitt, Cedric. *American Steamships on the Atlantic.* Newark: University of Delaware Press, 1981.

Roberts, A. Sellew. "High Prices and the Blockade in the Confederacy." *South Atlantic Quarterly* 24 (April 1925): 154–63.

Robinson, William M., Jr. "Drewry's Bluff: Naval Defense of Richmond 1862." *Civil War History* 7 (June 1961): 167–75.

Robinson, William M. *The Confederate Privateers.* New Haven, Conn.: Yale University Press, 1928.

Rochelle, James Henry. *Life of Rear Admiral John Randolph Tucker.* Washington, D.C.: The Neale, 1903.

Roe, E. W. "Brief Historical Sketch of the Navy Yard at Washington, D.C." In *Society of Naval Architects and Marine Engineers Historical Transactions 1893–1943* (1945): 34–35.

Roland, Alex. *Underwater Warfare in the Age of Sail.* Bloomington: Illinois University Press, 1978.

Sauers, Richard Allen. "General Ambrose E. Burnside's 1862 North Carolina Campaign." Ph.D. dissertation, Pennsylvania State University, 1987.

Savage, Carlton. *Policy of the United States toward Maritime Commerce in War.* 2 vols. Washington, D.C.: Government Printing Office, 1934; rpt., New York: Kraus, 1969.

Scharf, J. Thomas. *History of the Confederate States Navy from Its Organization to the Surrender of Its Last Vessel.* New York: Rogers and Sherwood, 1887; rpt., New York: Fairfax, 1977.

Schwab, John C. *The Confederate States of America, 1861–1865: A Financial and Industrial History of the South during the Civil War.* New York: Scribner's Sons, 1901.

Silber, Irwin, ed. *Songs of the Civil War.* Arrangements by Jerry Silverman. New York: Columbia University Press, 1960.

Sloan, Edward William. *Benjamin Franklin Isherwood, Naval Engineer: The Years as Engineer in Chief 1861–1869.* Annapolis, Md.: U.S. Naval Institute Press, 1966.

Stampp, Kenneth M. "Lincoln and the Strategy of Defense in the Crisis of 1861." *Journal of Southern History* 11 (August 1945): 297–323.

Stewart, Charles W. "Lion-Hearted Flusser: A Naval Hero of the Civil War." *U.S. Naval Institute Proceedings* 31 (June 1905): 274–313.

Still, William N., Jr. "The Career of the Confederate Ironclad *Neuse.*" *North Carolina Historical Review* 43 (January 1966): 1–13.

———. "Confederate Naval Strategy: The Ironclad." *Journal of Southern History* 27 (August 1961): 330–43.

———. *Confederate Shipbuilding.* Athens: University of Georgia Press, 1969.

———. "Facilities for the Construction of War Vessels in the Confederacy." *Journal of Southern History* 31 (August 1965): 285–304.

———. *Iron Afloat: The Story of Confederate Armorclads.* Nashville: Vanderbilt University Press, 1971.

Stivers, Reuben Elmore. *Privateers and Volunteers: The Men and Women of Our Reserve Naval Forces, 1766–1866.* Annapolis, Md.: U.S. Naval Institute, 1975.

Stromeyer, C. E. *Marine Boiler Management and Construction.* London: Longmans, Green, 1893.

Thurston, Robert Henry. *A History of the Growth of the Steam Engine.* Ithaca, N.Y.: Cornell University Press, 1939.

Todd, Richard Cecil. *Confederate Finance.* Athens: University of Georgia Press, 1954.

Tredwell, Adam. "North Carolina Navy." In *History of the Several Regiments and Battalions from North Carolina in the Great War 1861–65,* ed. Walter Clark, 5:299–313. 5 vols. Raleigh: Nash Brothers, 1901.

Turner, George Edgar. *Victory Road the Rails: The Strategic Place of the Railroads in the Civil War.* New York: Bobbs-Merrill, 1953.

U.S. Customs Service. *A History of Enforcement in the United States Customs Service 1789–1875.* San Francisco: Department of Treasury, U.S. Customs Service, 1988.

U.S. Navy. Naval History Division. *Civil War Naval Chronology 1861–1865*. 6 vols. Washington, D.C.: Government Printing Office, 1971.

Valuska, David Lawrence. "The Negro in the Union Navy: 1861–1865." Ph.D. dissertation, Lehigh University, 1973.

Van Deusen, Glyndon G. *William Henry Seward*. New York: Oxford University Press, 1967.

Vandiver, Frank E. *Confederate Blockade Running through Bermuda, 1861–1865*. Austin: University of Texas Press, 1947.

———. *Ploughshares into Swords: Josiah Gorgas and Confederate Ordnance*. Austin: University of Texas Press, 1952.

Wakefield, Manville B. *Coal Boats to Tidewater: The Story of the Delaware and Hudson Canal*. South Fallsburg, N.Y.: Steingart, 1965.

Wandrus, Harry, and Tom Stich. "Brief Notes on the Arms Brought into the Confederacy by Blockade Runners." *Hobbies* 55 (August 1950): 129–31.

Warner, Ezra J. *Generals in Gray: Lives of the Confederate Commanders*. Baton Rouge: Louisiana State University Press, 1959.

———. *Generals in Blue: Lives of the Union Commanders*. Baton Rouge: Louisiana State University Press, 1964.

Wells, Tom Henderson. *The Confederate Navy: A Study in Organization*. University: University of Alabama Press, 1971.

Wertenbaker, Thomas J. *Norfolk: Historic Southern Port*. Durham, N.C.: Duke University Press, 1931.

West, Richard S., Jr. *Gideon Welles: Lincoln's Navy Department*. New York: Bobbs-Merrill, 1943.

———. *Lincoln's Scapegoat General: A Life of Benjamin F. Butler 1818–1893*. Boston: Houghton Mifflin, 1965.

———. *Mr. Lincoln's Navy*. New York: Longmans Green, 1957.

———. "The Navy and the Press during the Civil War." *U.S. Naval Institute Proceedings* 63 (January 1937): 33–41.

———. "The Morgan Purchases." *U.S. Naval Institute Proceedings* 66 (January 1940): 73–77.

———. "(Private and Confidential) My Dear Fox—." *U.S. Naval Institute Proceedings* 63 (May 1937): 694–706.

Wheaton, Henry. *Elements of International Law*. New York: Oceana, 1964.

Wise, Stephen R. *Lifeline of the Confederacy: Blockade Running during the Civil War*. Columbia: University of South Carolina Press, 1988.

Wood, Richard Everett. "Port Town at War: Wilmington, North Carolina 1860–1865." Ph.D. dissertation, Florida State University, 1976.

Index

INDEX

Wilmington, 298
France: accepts blockade, 5; reacts to
possible obstruction of inlets, 10
Franklin, Virginia, 97; attack on, 86–87
Franklin, William B., USA, 51
Fredericksburg (CS ironclad), 73; passes
obstructions, 74; moves down James,
79
Fredericksburg, Virginia, 91, 278
French, Charles A., USN: at Plymouth,
105; takes command of *Southfield*, 105
Frying Pan Shoals, North Carolina, 220,
230, 236, 247, 254

Galena (ironclad), 42; runs aground, 51;
and attack on Drewry's Bluff, 53–54;
shells City Point, 56; on James River,
62; and proposed use against
Wilmington, 274
Gatlin, Richard C., CSA, 32
Gemsbok (bark), engages Fort Macon,
35–36
General Putnam (armed tug), 36
Genesee (gunboat), 275
Geography: shallow waters hinder naval
operations, 6, 10, 223, 277, 280–81; of
Virginia, 10; of North Carolina, 11;
aids Confederate attacks in North
Carolina, 83; complicates blockade,
220, 234–35
Getty, George, USA, 65
Gettysburg campaign, 97
Gillis, John P., USN, 126
Glisson, Oliver S., USN, 275, 291
Gloucester Point Battery, 50
Goldsboro, North Carolina, attack on, 91
Goldsborough, Louis Malesherbes, USN,
80, 287; assumes command of North
Atlantic Blockading Squadron, 17,
318 (n. 2); orders obstruction of inlets,
18–19; and fear of *Virginia*, 45–46;
during Peninsular campaign, 48–55,

57–59; discredited for actions, 58–59;
resigns, 59; transfers vessels from
North Carolina, 84; protects naval
vessels with iron, 88; allows trade to
proceed to Norfolk, 129; comments
on repair work, 163; orders supplies
to Hatteras, 170; problems with
ordnance, 181; orders coal to New
Bern, 192; on personnel, 203;
blockade of Wilmington, 224–25, 228;
on escape of *Nashville*, 237; plans
attack on Wilmington, 274–77, 278
Gorgas, Josiah, CSA (chief of the
Ordnance Bureau), 265, 266
Grand Gulf (gunboat), 255
Granite (sloop), expedites coal movement,
192
Grant, Ulysses S., USA, 74–75, 289, 291,
307; appointed to command of Union
armies, 71; siege of Petersburg, 77–78;
advises Butler, 106; asks that S. P. Lee
be replaced, 287; removes Butler from
command, 292; meets to discuss
capture of Wilmington, 298; use of
navy, 307
Great Britain: reacts to blockade, 5, 7;
reacts to Ports Act, 6; reacts to
possible obstruction of inlets, 9; and
laxity of blockade, 225, 303
Greene, Samuel D., USN, in command
of *Monitor*, 45
Greenville, North Carolina, Union
reconnaissance of, 87
Gregory, Francis, USN, supervises work
outside navy yards, 162
Guerrilla activity, in coastal areas, 125–28
Gulf Coast Blockading Squadron, 178

Hale, John P. (senator), critical of Welles,
145
Halleck, Henry, USA, 285
Hamilton, North Carolina, naval activity
at, 85

About the Author

Robert M. Browning Jr. earned his Ph.D. at the University of Alabama and is currently the chief historian for the U.S. Coast Guard. He is the author of *U.S. Merchant Vessel War Casualties of World War II* and *Success Is All That Was Expected: The South Atlantic Blockading Squadron during the Civil War.*